Third Edition

CRIME SCENE INVESTIGATION AND RECONSTRUCTION

Robert R. Ogle, Jr.

Prentice Hall

Boston   Columbus   Indianapolis   New York   San Francisco   Upper Saddle River
Amsterdam   Cape Town   Dubai   London   Madrid   Milan   Munich   Paris   Montreal   Toronto
Delhi   Mexico City   Sao Paulo   Sydney   Hong Kong   Seoul   Singapore   Taipei   Tokyo

Editorial Director: Vernon Anthony
Acquisition Editor: Eric Krassow
Editorial Assistant: Lynda Cramer
Director of Marketing: David Gesell
Marketing Manager: Adam Kloza
Senior Marketing Coordinator: Alicia Wozniak
Marketing Assistant: Les Roberts
Production Manager: Holly Shufeldt
Creative Director: Jayne Conte
Cover Design: Suzanne Duda
Cover Illustration/Photo: Fotolia
Full-Service Project Management/Composition: Integra Software Services, Pvt. Ltd.
Printer/Binder: Courier
Cover Printer: Courier

Library of Congress Cataloging-in-Publication Data

Ogle, Robert R.
    Crime scene investigation and reconstruction / Robert R. Ogle, Jr.—3rd ed.
        p. cm.
    Includes bibliographical references and index.
    ISBN-13: 978-0-13-609360-2
    ISBN-10: 0-13-609360-4
    1. Criminal investigation—Handbooks, manuals, etc.   2. Crime scene searches—Handbooks, manuals, etc.
3. Evidence, Criminal—Handbooks, manuals, etc.   I. Title.
HV8073.O382 2012
363.25'2—dc22

                                                                                2010024357

10 9 8 7 6 5 4 3

Prentice Hall
is an imprint of

www.pearsonhighered.com

ISBN-13: 978-0-13-609360-2
ISBN-10:   0-13-609360-4

CONTENTS

FOREWORD

The issuance of the third edition of Robert Ogle's *Crime Scene Investigation and Reconstruction* is testimony to the high regard with which this textbook is held by both active crime scene investigators (CSIs) and academic instructors who are tasked with the responsibility of educating a new generation of criminal investigators. This new edition builds on the features of its predecessors. Most of the chapters have been updated and the text is replete with new photographs to illustrate key points regarding crime scene investigation. The author has added extensive information to the book regarding legal requirements for the collection of physical evidence.

Interest in the role of the modern CSI has been sparked not only by a spate of popular TV shows, but grows out of the realization that new technology has increased the effectiveness of the crime scene investigator. Recent studies have shown dramatic increases in success rates associated with the solving of burglaries and other property crimes as a result of recovering DNA evidence that a perpetrator may have simply touched. This news is already reinvigorating police to pursue investigations of scenes that in the past were assigned a low priority.

The role of the CSI is demanding. He/she must be capable of comprehending the scope of the crime scene and skilled at rapidly planning a strategy to extract all useful information from the crime site. At the same time, the CSI must be thoroughly familiar with the science underlying the laboratory examination of physical evidence. For, in truth, no matter how sophisticated a forensic laboratory may be equipped, or how well trained its scientists are, the failure of the CSI to recognize objects possessing evidential value at the crime scene and not knowing how these objects must be packaged and preserved for subsequent laboratory examination will prove fatal to the overall conduct of the investigation. Many horror stories can be cited to exemplify how botched efforts at the scene resulted in an unsolvable crime.

Merely reading Robert Ogle's work will not in itself produce a competent CSI. This must come with proper education, appropriate training, and mentored experience. But documentation protocols, fundamental collection and preservation techniques, and laboratory analytical strategies are appropriately discussed in this text. The book concludes with insights into how best to pull together all data and observations collected from the crime scene investigation into a coherent view of the events that occurred during the commission of a crime. To these ends, *Crime Scene Investigation and Reconstruction* will prove to be a valuable resource and essential instructional tool for practitioners, instructors, and students of crime scene investigation.

Richard Saferstein, Ph.D.

PREFACE

NEW TO THIS EDITION

- A chapter introduction and/or a chapter summary has been added to each chapter which lacks either (Chapters 1–3, 5–12, and 15).
- A total of thirty-nine new or re-drawn figures and photographs have been added to the chapters (Chapters 1 (1), 2 (2), 3 (8), 4 (5), 5 (9), 6 (6), 7 (4), 8 (2), and 13 (2)).

Chapter 1   Introduction to Physical Evidence

- History of forensic science and physical evidence.
- Introduction of the "Linkage Profile" concept.
- Section on search and seizure laws.
- Section on admissibility requirements for expert testimony.
- New appendix on search and seizure laws, including *Brady* evidence and exclusionary rule.

Chapter 3   Crime Scene Photography

- New section on digital cameras.
- Glossary of photography terminology, especially for digital cameras.

Chapter 5   Latent Fingerprint Evidence

- New section on the history of the use of fingerprints for individual identification.

Chapter 6   Trace Evidence

- New figure for using Post-its™ to attach trace evidence to bindles.

Chapter 7   Biological Fluid Stain Evidence

- Figures for documentation of bloodstain patterns moved to Chapter 7 from Chapter 15.
- Sections on DNA evidence deleted and replaced with less technical explanations.
- Section on saliva evidence added.

Chapter 8   Firearms Evidence

- New figures to illustrate nomenclature of revolver and semi-auto pistol added.

Chapter 11   Document Evidence

- New table of sources for request exemplars added.

INTENT OF REVISIONS

The intent of the revisions for the third edition is to bring the materials up to date, to add an introduction and/or summary to each chapter lacking either in order to make the chapters uniform, and to make the text materials more easily understood by readers.

- New materials are added to reflect new information in the field of crime scene investigation.
- Nearly all chapters will now have both an introduction and summary for that chapter, providing uniformity for chapter structure.
- Revisions throughout the chapters were designed to make the materials more readily understood by students of crime scene investigation.

The third edition presents a great deal of new material in the first seven chapters of the text. New materials and illustrations are added to the remaining chapters in order to further clarify the essential aspects of those chapters. Key additions are explained here in the Preface.

A brief history of the development of criminalistics and forensic science has been added to Chapter 1. The concept of the linkage profile is introduced with an illustration to show the linkage between victim, suspect, primary and secondary scenes, suspect profiling, and suspect identification. In addition, extensive information regarding the legal requirements for the collection of physical evidence and its introduction into evidence at the courtroom level has been added to Chapter 1, including an appendix of search and seizure case law.

A brief history of the use of latent fingerprint impressions for the identification of the individual who left the impression has been added to Chapter 5 in order to acquaint the student with the long and convoluted development of this important class of physical evidence.

ABOUT THE AUTHOR

Robert Ogle attended the University of California in Berkeley, California, earning a Bachelor's degree in Letters and Science, with a major in Zoology. He attended several California State Universities as a graduate student in Biology and in Criminology. Mr. Ogle is the author of *O. J. Simpson: Not Guilty by Reason of Inanity;* and (with coauthor Michelle J. Fox) *Atlas of Human Hair Microscopic Characteristics.* He was a Criminalist with the Contra Costa County, California, Sheriff-Coroner and was a Criminalist and Managing Criminalist with the California Department of Justice before entering private practice as a forensic consultant. Also, he has served as a forensic consultant for defense counsel in a number of homicide cases, including *People v. Randy Kraft* (the largest serial murder case tried in the United States). He was a guest instructor in crime scene investigation courses in California Community Colleges and Law Enforcement Training Centers. Mr. Ogle has given many papers to forensic meetings and has published many articles in forensic journals and law enforcement publications. Currently retired from active teaching and consulting, he restricts his professional activities to writing in the field of forensic science.

ACKNOWLEDGMENTS

The author thanks the many individuals, both within and without the field of criminalistics, who have provided materials and support for this effort. The author thanks in particular Criminalist IV Bruce Moran, Sacramento County District Attorney's Forensic Laboratory; Criminalist Lucien (Luke) Haag, Forensic Science Services, Carefree, Arizona; Crime Scene Reconstructionist Alexander Jason, ANITE Productions Pinole, California; Deputy Inspector

General Bruce Beckler, JD (dec.), State of California, Office of Inspector General; Criminalist Steve Ojena; Dr. Richard Saferstein; Forensic Consultant [Director (ret.) of the New Jersey State Police Laboratory]; and Sheriff-Coroner Warren Rupf and the staff of the Criminalistics Laboratory, Contra Costa County, California, for their many contributions to this work.

The author would like to acknowledge his reviewers Dana C. DeWitt, Mount Mary College; Steven Gilbert, SUNY at Canton; Caoimhin O Fearghail, Southwestern Oregon Community College; and Sandra K. Robertson, Tri County Technical College, whose many insightful suggestions provided immense assistance to him in his development of the third edition. Their suggestions demonstrated not only their commitment to excellence in the fields of crime scene investigation and forensic science, but also their acumen in these fields.

Last, but certainly not least, the author thanks Dr. Duayne Dillon, Chief (ret.), Contra Costa County Sheriff-Coroner Criminalistics Laboratory; John Murdock (former Chief, Contra Costa County Criminalistics Laboratory), Firearms Examiner, ATF laboratory, Walnut Creek, California; and Professor of Criminalistics (ret.) Dr. John Thornton, each of whose influence on this author can be seen in every page of this textbook, with the exception of any errors present, which are the sole responsibility of the author.

Robert Ogle
Forensic Scientist

1 INTRODUCTION TO PHYSICAL EVIDENCE

*Some circumstantial evidence is very strong, as when you find
a trout in the milk.*

Henry Thoreau. Unpublished Manuscripts, in Miscellanies,
Biographical Sketch (1918), Vol. X, p. 30.

Key Words: Locard exchange principle, criminalistics, comparative analysis, recognized, collected, preserved, linkage profile, reconstruction, linkage, linkage triangle, investigative leads, physical nature, types of examinations, branch of examiners, class characteristics, class only, individual characteristics, identification, individualization, comparative analysis process, questioned, unknown source, known source, comparison standard, reference standard, exemplar, controls, objective, curtilage, probable cause plus, chain of possession, contamination.

INTRODUCTION

BRIEF HISTORY OF FORENSIC SCIENCE AND THE EXAMINATION OF PHYSICAL EVIDENCE

The inception of modern forensic scientific examination of physical evidence occurred in the field of toxicology (the scientific examination of poisons) in France, Sweden, Germany, and Spain, beginning in the 1770s through the early 1800s with the works of the Frenchman Fodere, the Swede Scheele, the German Ross, and the Spaniard Mathieu Orfila. Orfila's treatise on toxicology established forensic toxicology as a legitimate scientific endeavor.[1] In the mid-Nineteenth century, microscopic procedures for identifying sperm, a presumptive test for blood, and a microcrystalline test for hemoglobin were developed.[2] In the late nineteenth century, Alphonse Bertillon in France developed what he termed *anthropometry*, a system of bodily measurements used for personal identification, which was later replaced by the simpler and more accurate method of fingerprinting.[3]

The scientific examination of physical evidence and its application to criminal investigation was first described in the publication in 1893 of *Handbuch fur*

Untersuchungsrichter als System der Kriminalistik by Hans Gross, a prosecutor and judge in Austria (later published in English under the title *Criminal Investigation*).[4] The publication of this work by Gross marked the beginning of "Criminalistics" and the various forensic sciences as *professions*.

In the twentieth century, the pace of the development of scientific methods for examination of physical evidence increased considerably.[5] A method for the identification of ABO blood types in bloodstains was developed by Dr. Leone Lattes in Italy. In France, Edmond Locard, director of the Institute of Criminalistics in Lyons, described the theory that when two objects came into contact, there would be a cross-transfer of traces of materials. His theory became known as the **Locard exchange principle**, a central theme in the forensic sciences, especially those dealing with trace evidence (hairs, fibers, soil, etc.). In America, U.S. Army Colonel Calvin Goddard advanced firearms identification extensively by developing the use of the comparison microscope to compare bullets from a crime to bullets fired through a suspect's firearm. The comparison microscope was later used to compare hairs, fibers, and other types of trace evidence.

One of the major influences on crime scene investigation and physical evidence examination was the publication of *Techniques of Crime Scene Investigation* in the 1930s by the Swedish workers Svensson and Wendel (edited for several editions and now authored by Barry Fisher,[6] currently in its seventh edition). Another textbook of importance to crime scene investigation and criminalistics, *An Introduction to Criminalistics: An Application of the Physical Sciences to the Detection of Crime*,[7] was authored by Charles E. O'Hara and James W. Osterburg in 1952. The textbook *Homicide Investigations* by Dr. Lemoyne Snyder (third edition in 1977[8]) offered considerable useful information to those crime scene investigators and other investigators whose duties included the investigation of homicides.

In the middle of the twentieth century, the forensic science specialty known as **Criminalistics** achieved a watershed moment with the publication in 1953 of *Crime Investigation*[9] by Dr. Paul L. Kirk, a professor of Biochemistry and Criminalistics at the University of California at Berkeley, California. Dr. Kirk, called the "father of criminalistics," created the first generation of professional criminalists from his students at Berkeley. The professional field of criminalistics owes a debt of gratitude to Dr. Kirk (and his students) for the formation of the California Association of Criminalists (the first professional organization of criminalists), which has cultivated the ethical, moral, and scientific standards found in most professional criminalists and allied professionals today.

Subsequent to the publication of Kirk's textbook, many techniques were developed by forensic scientists for the determination of genetic markers in blood and semen stains, making a landmark leap with the development of DNA testing by Sir Alec Jeffreys in England. A further landmark in DNA testing was the development of the PCR technique to analyze forensic samples by Dr. Erlich, Dr. Higuchi of the Cetus corporation, and Dr. Edward T. Blake of the Forensic Science Associates laboratory.[10] These leaps in the identification and individualization of blood and other body fluids were followed in the last part of the twentieth century by the development of computer techniques to compare latent fingerprints to a fingerprint database (AFIS) and DNA from bloodstains and other tissue stains from crime scenes to a database (CODIS) with blinding speed, two accomplishments thought entirely impossible at the midpoint of the twentieth century.

TYPES, VALUE, AND ADVANTAGES OF PHYSICAL EVIDENCE

Thoreau's quote in the beginning of this chapter embodies two types of evidence: (1) physical evidence (the trout) and (2) circumstantial evidence (the presence of the trout in the milk, which raises the presumption that the milk was diluted with creek water). Evidence is typically classified into (1) *direct evidence*, (2) *circumstantial evidence*, (3) *testimonial evidence*, and (4) *physical evidence*. These categories of evidence can overlap, as in the Thoreau quote mentioned earlier. The value of physical evidence comes from the data it provides for crime scene reconstruction, determining whether or not a crime occurred, linking an individual with another or with a crime scene, and investigative leads, and to link serial rapes, homicides, or burglaries. The advantages of physical evidence over other types of evidence include the factor that it is tangible, which means that a jury can view and touch the physical objects and can take the object(s) into the jury room and that some cases cannot be solved without the physical evidence. Further, physical evidence cannot be distorted by the defendant, it is not subject to memory loss, and the defendant can have the evidence examined by an expert of his/her choosing. Taken together, these advantages demonstrate that physical evidence is an important component of modern criminal and civil investigations. The types, value, and advantages of physical evidence are detailed and explained in the appropriate sections to follow.

CATEGORIES OF PHYSICAL EVIDENCE

Physical evidence is classified into divisions based on either the types of examinations performed (chemical, physical, microscopical, etc.) or on the type of material comprising the evidence (firearms, toolmarks, biological materials, etc.). In most jurisdictions, the forensic science laboratory is divided into sections based on the type of material examined, as described in the section on the major categories of physical evidence.

LABORATORY ANALYSIS OF PHYSICAL EVIDENCE

The laboratory analysis of physical evidence involves a wide variety of scientific methodologies, borrowed and adapted from the basic sciences, such as chemistry, physics, and biology. Laboratory examinations include the identification of the class and individual characteristics of the evidence from the victim, the suspect, and the crime scene. Typically, these methodologies are adapted to the **comparative analysis** (detailed later and in Figure 1-1) of the physical evidence; for example, comparison of the chemical analysis of the automotive paint found on a victim's clothing to the paint on a suspect's vehicle in a hit-and-run case, and the comparison of DNA from a suspect to DNA extracted from a vaginal swab from a rape victim. The laboratory analysis techniques for the various types of physical evidence are explained later and in the chapters for each of the physical evidence categories.

TYPES OF EVIDENCE

Evidence can be direct evidence, circumstantial evidence, testimonial evidence, or non-testimonial, as in the case of physical evidence.

Direct evidence

Direct evidence is evidence that proves a fact without the necessity of an inference or a presumption, that, when true, conclusively establishes that fact. An example is testimony by a completely credible witness that proves the fact stated in the testimony.

Circumstantial evidence

Circumstantial evidence involves a series of facts that, although not the fact at issue, tends, through inference, to prove a fact at issue. This type of evidence is usually a chain of circumstances from which a fair assumption can be made as to the validity of the fact at issue.

Testimonial evidence

Testimonial evidence is evidence given by lay or expert witnesses. The principal test for this type of evidence is the *credibility* of the witness. The trier of fact (judge or jury) in a court proceeding determines the credibility of the witness and thus the believability of the testimony given by the witness. This point cannot be overstated, since the testimony of a witness who is not credible can be (and often is) ignored by the trier of fact. This reality of testimony is the principal reason that law enforcement officers and expert witnesses must be diligent in establishing their credibility (see Appendix II, "Courtroom Testimony" at the rear of the book).

Physical evidence

Physical evidence consists of physical objects that are linked to the commission of a crime or tort. Virtually any type of physical object can become physical evidence in a criminal investigation. In this chapter, the major types of physical evidence encountered in criminal investigations are listed, but the investigator needs to remain alert to the possibility that physical objects not mentioned in this text or other texts relating to physical evidence may become valuable evidence in an investigation.

VALUE OF PHYSICAL EVIDENCE

Physical evidence can be defined as *physical objects associated with a crime or a tort*. Analysis and interpretation of the physical evidence may assist in the investigation of a crime or tort in a number of ways. However, in order to be of any value, it is critical that the physical evidence be **recognized** as potential evidence, **collected** in an *appropriate manner*, and **preserved** *properly* for transmittal to the laboratory. Failure to recognize, collect, or preserve the physical evidence may compromise or destroy the evidence, thereby impeding the investigation. In the worst case scenario, the failure to preserve crucial evidence may lead to the erroneous conviction of an innocent party or the inability to convict a guilty party. The failure to collect the evidence may also hinder a subsequent civil action on behalf of an injured party.

Physical evidence may play a crucial role in many criminal investigations. The primary roles of physical evidence in the investigation of crimes include those that follow.

Reconstruction of the crime scene

Reconstruction of the crime scene is one of the *major purposes* for the collection of physical evidence. This procedure may involve the reconstruction of a single event, such as the determination of muzzle-to-target distance in a shooting, or it may involve the determination of the sequence of a series of events, such as the interpretation of blood-stain patterns at a crime scene. Reconstruction of the crime scene frequently allows the investigator to determine the accuracy of statements from witnesses: The statement of a witness may be corroborated by a reconstruction of the crime scene, or the statements of the witness may be shown to be false.

EXAMPLE

In a prison homicide case, several "witnesses" to the crime came forward and offered to testify in exchange for reduced sentences. The statements of each of the "witnesses" were proven to be false by reconstruction of the crime by using bloodstain pattern interpretation coupled with the laboratory typing results from the bloodstains. Each "witness" placed the two stabbing victims in areas where they could not have been during the assault. One "witness" indicated that the assaults took place at one end of the tier where no bloodstains were located (the bloodstain patterns proved that the assault occurred at the opposite end of the tier).

Determines whether or not a crime occurred

The physical evidence may also establish whether or not a crime occurred. For example, reconstruction of a shooting event can help establish whether the shooting was an accident, suicide, or homicide.

EXAMPLE

In a suspected homicide, a wife stated that while sitting downstairs reading, she heard a gunshot upstairs, ran upstairs to the bedroom, and found her husband in bed with a gunshot wound to the head. She indicated that with one hand she picked up the revolver next to her husband's head, transferred it to the other hand, placed it on the nightstand, and then called the police. Tests for gunshot residue (GSR) on her husband's hands revealed a high level of GSR on the back of the husband's right hand but no residues on either palm or the back of the left hand. GSR tests on the wife's hands revealed medium levels of gunshot residue on each palm but no residues on the back of either hand. Experimental testing that duplicated the conditions as stated by the wife revealed GSR levels that were virtually the same as those found on the wife's hands and the hands of the deceased husband, confirming the statement of the wife and thus verifying that the death was a suicide.

Links an individual with another individual, a crime scene, or other crimes

Many types of evidence may be used to associate a suspect with the victim of a crime, with the crime scene where the crime occurred, or with other crimes committed by the suspect. These types of evidence are commonly referred to as "linkage," "associative," or "transfer" evidence. That is, the evidence may tend to show a contact between individuals, or between the suspect and the crime scene, that resulted in a transfer of evidence between the individuals involved or a transfer from an individual to a crime scene or vice versa. This process of the transfer of trace evidence follows the Locard principle described earlier. This transfer of evidence, which creates a linkage between a suspect, the victim, the crime scene, and other crime scenes is illustrated in Figure 1-1, which shows the **linkage profile** of the potential exchange of physical evidence between the suspect, the victim, the crime scene(s), and other crimes committed by the same suspect.

Provides investigative leads to investigators

An important function of the crime scene investigator is to provide **investigative leads** to the detectives and other investigators charged with the responsibility of investigating the crime. For example, the finding of a specific hair type in a homicide may provide information about the hair color and racial group[11] of the assailant. In one case known to the author, the racial characteristics of a single hair led to the rapid arrest of a suspect in a robbery homicide (see the following case example below). Without this crucial investigative information, none of the additional critical evidence (currency bearing bloodstains from the victim in the possession of the perpetrator) would have been retrieved. Often, the initial examinations of physical evidence from the crime scene, although not conclusive evidence, may provide sufficient leads to the investigators such that the follow-up investigation will uncover conclusive evidence as to the identity of the perpetrator(s).

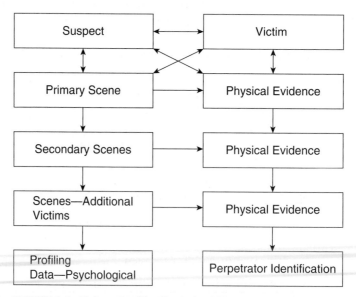

FIGURE 1-1   Linkage Profile: Physical Evidence

CASE EXAMPLE

"Caught by a Hair"

Criminalist John E. Murdock of the Contra Costa Sheriff's Criminalistics Laboratory was summoned to the scene of a robbery/homicide at a liquor store in Concord, California, later joined by Criminalist Mitosinka from the same laboratory. A thorough and systematic processing of the crime scene was conducted by Criminalists Murdock and Mitosinka and evidence technicians from the Concord Police Department. In order to avoid potential loss of trace evidence from the deceased during transport to the mortuary, Criminalist Murdock removed visibly adherent trace evidence from the body and clothing of the deceased. One item of special interest had the physical characteristics of a hair that had the typical appearance of a hair from an individual of African heritage.

The only person of African heritage associated with the liquor store's owner was a close acquaintance of his family. Concord detectives proceeded to this subject's residence for an interview. On their arrival, they were informed that the subject had left for Long Beach, California, in the early hours of the morning. This subject then became the prime suspect and preparations were made to prepare a search warrant for the suspect's vehicle. At the conclusion of the scene processing and attendance at the autopsy of the victim, Criminalists Murdock and Mitosinka returned to the criminalistics laboratory. A telephone conversation was had with the district attorney's office, where the search warrant for the suspect's vehicle was being prepared. The search warrant was obtained, and Concord detectives and Criminalist Mitosinka traveled to Long Beach to execute the search warrant. During the execution of the search warrant, currency from the robbery was recovered from the subject's vehicle that had fresh bloodstains with the same blood type as that of the victim. The suspect was arrested and subsequently convicted of the robbery/homicide at trial. Although the evidence hair could not be *individualized*, the determination of its racial type provided the *investigative lead* that led to the successful conclusion of this case. ◼

Provides facts to a jury to assist in determination of guilt or innocence

Frequently in homicide, sexual assault cases, and other crimes, the analysis of physical evidence provides evidence of the guilt or innocence of an accused person. In one of the author's cases, the analysis of hair, semen typing, and latent fingerprint identifications led to the exoneration of an accused and the identification of the true rapist in a "serial rapist" case. The analysis of semen eliminated the accused person in three victims' cases, while hair analysis could have eliminated the accused in two of the cases. It was the identification of the latent fingerprint evidence in one of the victim's cases through an automated fingerprint system that ultimately identified the true rapist.

Provides evidence to link serial homicide or rape cases

In serial homicide or serial rape investigations, the physical evidence is often the strongest link between the series of crimes and the perpetrator. In homicides, firearms evidence and trace evidence often provide the link between the crimes and the perpetrator, as in the Wayne Williams case, in which fibers provided the link between the victims and the suspect. In serial rape cases, both trace evidence and semen typing (particularly DNA typing) may link the perpetrator to each of the crimes.

SOME ADVANTAGES OF PHYSICAL EVIDENCE

Physical evidence has a number of advantages over testimonial evidence because of the tangible nature of this type of evidence. These advantages include those that follow.

Provides a tangible object for the jury to see

Unlike testimonial evidence, the physical evidence can be seen by the jury and thus provides the added impact of the visual senses on the jury.

The physical evidence can be taken into the jury room

The impact of the physical evidence is carried into the jury room with the evidence and therefore continues its argument in the jury deliberations.

The defendant cannot distort the physical evidence

The physical evidence speaks for itself and cannot be misrepresented by the defendant. Often, the physical evidence will effectively rebut statements by the defendant and in some cases will prove that the defendant's statements are false.

Some cases cannot be solved without the physical evidence

In many crimes, the case is solved by the physical evidence that has been collected and analyzed in the case. Some cases may be solved by a single latent print collected at the scene. This outcome has been especially true since the introduction of the Automated Latent Fingerprint Identification systems, which allow the latent fingerprint examiner to search a very large database for a match to the latent print.

Physical evidence is not subject to memory loss

One of the shortcomings of witnesses' testimony is the inevitable memory loss that occurs over time. The sometimes lengthy delays experienced before a case comes to trial may have a deleterious effect on the witnesses' memory and thus weaken the impact of their testimony. The proper collection and analysis of the physical evidence results in a permanent record that is immune to memory loss.

The evidence can be tested by an independent expert

One of the factors that adds to the credibility of physical evidence is the defendant's ability to have the evidence examined by an outside expert. It is rare for the defendant's expert to contradict the opinions of the prosecution's experts.

MAJOR CATEGORIES OF PHYSICAL EVIDENCE

Physical evidence can be categorized in several different ways. The evidence can be classified according to the **physical nature** of the evidence (e.g., blood, latent prints, firearms evidence, etc.), by the **types of examinations** performed on the evidence (e.g., microscopic, macroscopic, or instrumental), or by the **branch of examiners** who perform the examinations on the evidence (e.g., forensic chemist, document examiner, firearms examiner, etc.). The classification of evidence varies from one geographical area to another, but the majority of jurisdictions classify physical evidence according to the following outline:

- Fingerprints (friction ridge evidence)
- Firearms evidence (firearms, discharge residues, fired components)
- Biological evidence (blood, semen, other types)
- Trace (microscopic, transfer) evidence
- Document evidence (questioned handwriting, typewriting, papers, inks, etc.)
- Physical matching evidence (matching of items that have been broken apart)
- Toxicology evidence (drugs, poisons in body fluids and tissues)
- Drug evidence
- Other types (various evidence types not included in the preceding listing)

It is not unusual for the investigator to utilize many different types of evidence in order to investigate successfully a major criminal case. It may be necessary to use witness testimony, criminal profiling and victimology, physical evidence and suspect interrogation, and polygraph testing to solve a given case. It is the blending of these investigative approaches that provides both a challenge to the modern investigator and the ability to solve crimes that might otherwise go unsolved.

CLASS AND INDIVIDUAL CHARACTERISTICS OF PHYSICAL EVIDENCE

The concepts of "class" and "individual" characteristics must be understood by the crime scene investigator in order to interpret reports from the crime laboratory. **Class characteristics** are those characteristics shared by *all members* of a class. Since class characteristics are shared by all members of a class, those types of physical evidence having only class characteristics cannot be identified to a single source. These types of evidence are referred to as **class only** types of evidence. For example, the fibers from a garment would have only "class characteristics," since the fibers used to produce the garment are produced in very large quantities, as are the dyes used to dye the fibers. Human hair is another example of an evidence type with "class" characteristics only.[12] The characteristics in human hair that are used for comparison are under genetic control and thus are shared by large segments in some populations (hairs from Asian populations, for example), whereas in other populations, the hair characteristics are shared by much smaller populations (reddish-blond hair in European populations, for example). When the hair from a crime scene "matches" the hair from an individual, the examiner may state that the evidence hair "may have come from that individual," since other individuals in the population under consideration may also have hair that matches the evidence hair. Class-only types of evidence may, however, be used conclusively to eliminate a suspected source. Reddish-blond hair, for example, could not have come from a specific Asian individual having only black hair.

Identity is defined as "the collective aspect of the *set of characteristics* [emphasis added] by which a thing is definitively recognizable or known."[13] This set of characteristics ("pattern") includes all the class characteristics of the class to which the object belongs and, additionally, those individual characteristics that serve to set the object apart from all other objects in its class. Thus, the pattern of class and **individual characteristics** establish the individuality of a specific object. This pattern of class and individual characteristics of an object, when unique to only one member of a class, allows for the **identification** of the individual source of the evidence item, a process called "**individualization**." The questioned item is individualized when the examiner is able to "match" the set of class and individual characteristics found in the questioned item to the same set of characteristics in the *known sample* or its *exemplar* (see the section, "Comparison Standards and Controls"). In many cases, the set of class and individual characteristics of an object is transferred to an evidence item, for example, the class and individual characteristics of a firearm's barrel interior are transferred to the surface of bullets fired in the weapon. The characteristics on the bullet are used to identify the weapon through comparison of these characteristics with those on a bullet known to have been fired in the suspect weapon, rather than attempting to compare the characteristics within the barrel directly with the characteristics on a bullet suspected of being fired in that weapon.

TABLE 1-1 Types of Evidence with Class and/or Individual Characteristics	
Class Only Characteristics	**Class and Individual Characteristics**
Drugs	Fingerprints
Fibers	Fired bullets/Cartridge cases
Hair	Toolmarks
Bloodstains (blood types)	Bloodstains (DNA)
Glass	Footwear impressions
Soil	Handwriting

Those types of evidence that have individual characteristics can be identified to a single source, that is, can be "individualized." Latent fingerprints are an example of a physical evidence type that can be individualized. Although each characteristic (minutia) used to identify the source of the latent print is a class characteristic, the combination of the *occurrence* and the *spatial relationships* of the minutiae is considered to establish a unique pattern for a given area of friction ridge skin, thus allowing for the individualization of the latent print. *Note:* The terms "identification" and "individualization" are sometimes used interchangeably for certain types of evidence, such as fingerprints and firearms.

See Table 1-1 for examples of those types of evidence considered to have class only characteristics or those with individual characteristics that allow the examiner to identify the individual source of the evidence item.

Another type of evidence with individual characteristics consists of "physical matching" evidence. When an object is torn or broken apart, the fracture edges can often be matched by placing the parts together "jigsaw puzzle" style to illustrate the matching of the fractured or torn edges. Examples of these types of evidence include paint or glass fragments, adhesive tapes used as bindings, and broken pry bars.

Note: Some of the evidence types with class only characteristics may still be individualized through other means. Hair that has been pulled from a scalp may have the fleshy portion of the hair root adhering (the root "sheath") and may be analyzed for DNA type, and thus that hair may be individualized (although the DNA is technically a product of the scalp tissue rather than the hair itself). If there is no scalp tissue adhering to the root, the hair may still be analyzed for mitochondrial DNA. Other types, such as soil, may have a particular set of class characteristics in which the set of characteristics is so rare as to verge on being unique and thus be thought of as individual. In some drug seizures, the particular combination of the diluents used and the by-products of manufacture may constitute a "pattern" that allows the analyst to link the drug seizure to the larger source with varying degrees of confidence. Also, the class characteristics of a given item of evidence allow the examiner rapidly to screen suspected sources for the evidence item. If the class characteristics of the suspected source do not match those of the questioned item, then that suspected source is eliminated from further consideration by the analyst.

In some cases, a specific item of physical evidence in the "Individual Characteristics" column may have an insufficient number of the individual characteristics present to allow for a positive identification (smudged latent fingerprints or damaged bullets, for example). The analyst will usually note the lack of sufficient detail in the evidence item in the laboratory report. For example, the fingerprint examiner may state

TABLE 1-2	Class and Individual Characteristics for Firearms
Division:	Firearms
Class:	38 caliber revolvers, 6 lands and grooves, right-hand twist
Family:	38 caliber revolvers, 6 lands and grooves, right-hand twist, having land and groove widths with the same measurements
Individual:	Striated markings imparted to the bullet by the barrel interior (the "signature" of the firearm)

that the latent print recovered from a crime scene "lacks sufficient individual detail to allow for a positive identification." In this case, the examiner is indicating that there are insufficient individual details (points of comparison) in the latent print to allow for an unqualified opinion as to the source of the latent print.

The classification of the various evidence types into class only and individual characteristics types is a simplification of the classification schemes for the different classes of evidence. The universe of physical evidence can be classified in a hierarchical scheme for all the evidence types, but at the present time, little work has been done to provide a comprehensive classification scheme for all physical evidence. Classification efforts heretofore have been limited to attempts by specialists in certain types of evidence, such as firearms evidence. Table 1-2 gives examples of some of the classification levels of firearms evidence. These classification levels and sublevels are generally of interest only to researchers in their respective specialties and have little effect on the investigator's understanding of class and individual characteristics. They are presented here only to acquaint the investigator with the terms that may be encountered in the literature of forensic science.

Table 1-3 lists some class and individual characteristics for some of the other types of physical evidence commonly encountered in crime scene investigations that have individual characteristics in addition to their class characteristics. *Note:* "Individual" characteristics for DNA patterns are based on statistical analysis of the patterns found in the evidence sample rather than on the aggregate experience of forensic serologists.

LABORATORY ANALYSIS OF PHYSICAL EVIDENCE

The usual purpose of the laboratory analysis is to individualize the physical evidence. Individualization is defined as the identification of the individual source of the evidence item. This process usually involves the *comparison* of the questioned (*unknown source*)

TABLE 1-3	Class and Individual Characteristics of Physical Evidence Types	
Evidence Type	**Class Characteristics**	**Individual Characteristics**
Fingerprints	Basic patterns	Minutiae patterns
Toolmarks	Size of toolmark	Striations in marks
Bloodstains	ABO, enzyme types	DNA patterns
Footwear	Size, sole patterns	Wear damage to sole
Handwriting	Handwriting system	Variations from system

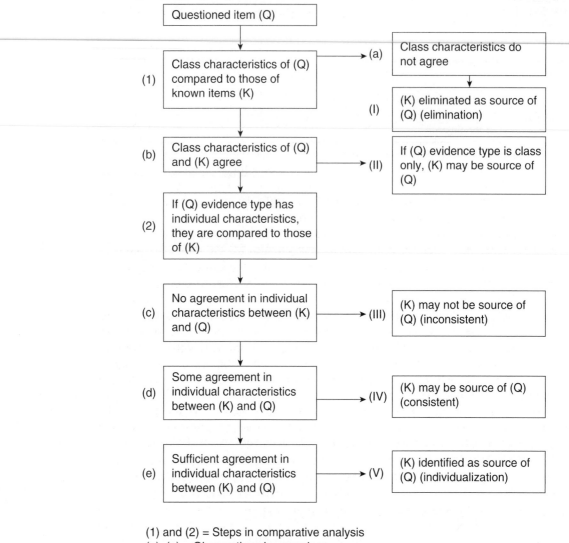

Questioned item (Q)

(1) Class characteristics of (Q) compared to those of known items (K)

(a) Class characteristics do not agree

(I) (K) eliminated as source of (Q) (elimination)

(b) Class characteristics of (Q) and (K) agree

(II) If (Q) evidence type is class only, (K) may be source of (Q)

(2) If (Q) evidence type has individual characteristics, they are compared to those of (K)

(c) No agreement in individual characteristics between (K) and (Q)

(III) (K) may not be source of (Q) (inconsistent)

(d) Some agreement in individual characteristics between (K) and (Q)

(IV) (K) may be source of (Q) (consistent)

(e) Sufficient agreement in individual characteristics between (K) and (Q)

(V) (K) identified as source of (Q) (individualization)

(1) and (2) = Steps in comparative analysis
(a)–(e) = Observations by examiner
(I)–(V) = Conclusions (opinions) of examiner

FIGURE 1-2   Comparative Analysis Process for Physical Evidence

item to a known item (an item from a *known source*). Figure 1-2 illustrates the comparison process, known as the comparative analysis process, utilized by all examiners of physical evidence, regardless of the evidence type.

Comparative analysis process

Prior to the comparison of the questioned item to the known item, a thorough examination of the questioned item is accomplished using one or more of the following techniques: the unaided eye, a magnifier, a stereoscopic microscope, and, often, examination with an alternate light source. The choice of techniques for this examination depends on the particular evidence type of the questioned item. This preliminary examination is performed first in order to locate the presence of any trace evidence which may be present. Any trace evidence present is removed and preserved for further examination. The second purpose for the preliminary examination is to appreciate the full nature of the questioned item and make a preliminary evaluation of the class and individual characteristics of that item. After the preliminary survey of the questioned item, it is ready for comparison to any known items suspected as a potential source of the questioned item.

The first step in the **comparative analysis process** (see Figure 1-2) involves the comparison of the class characteristics of the questioned item to those of the known item [Figure 1-2, Step (1)]. If the class characteristics do not agree [Figure 1-2, (a)], the known item can be eliminated as the source for the questioned item [Figure 1-2, (I)]. If the class characteristics are found to agree [Figure 1-2, (b)], and the questioned evidence item type has only class characteristics, the examiner may conclude that the known item may be the source for the questioned item [Figure 1-2, (II)].

If the class characteristics of the questioned and known items agree, and the questioned item is an evidence type that has individual characteristics, the examiner compares the individual characteristics of the questioned item to those of the known item [Figure 1-2, Step (2)]. If the examiner finds no agreement between the individual characteristics of the questioned and known items [Figure 1-2, (c)], the examiner may conclude that the known item may not be the source (inconsistent) of the questioned item [Figure 1-2, (III)]. If the examiner finds some agreement between the individual characteristics of the known item and the questioned item [Figure 1-2, (d)], the examiner may conclude that the known item may be consistent with being the source of the questioned item, but the degree of agreement noted between the two is insufficient to establish that the known item is the source of the questioned item [Figure 1-2, (IV)].

If the examiner finds sufficient agreement between the individual characteristics of the known item and the questioned item [Figure 1-2, (e)], the examiner identifies the known item as the individual source of the questioned item [Figure 1-2, (V)]. This identification of the known item as the individual source of the questioned item is the process termed individualization in forensic science, especially in the forensic discipline known as criminalistics.

The questioned item in the comparison is usually an item collected at a crime scene, from the victim or from the suspect. The known item is an item of known source or an "exemplar" prepared from the known item (see Table 1-4 for examples of questioned and known items).

TABLE 1-4 Comparison Components of Physical Evidence		
Questioned Item (Q)	**Exemplar (K)**	**Known Source (K)**
Latent fingerprint	Inked fingerprint	Suspect's fingers
Hair from scene	Hair from person	Hair from suspect
Shoe impression	Test impressions	Shoe from suspect
Bullet from victim	Test fired bullet	Firearm from suspect
Fiber on victim	Fibers from shirt	Shirt of suspect
Bloodstain	Liquid blood	Blood sample from suspect

Results of the comparison process

The comparison between the questioned item **(Q)** and the known item **(K)** (*see Figure 1-2*) may reveal one of the following observations (and its typical conclusion):

1. The *class characteristics* of the questioned item (Q) ***do not*** *agree* with those of the known item (K).

   Conclusion: (K) **eliminated** as the source of (Q).

2. The *class characteristics* of (Q) ***agree*** with those of (K).

   Conclusion: If (Q) has only class characteristics, (K) **may be the source** of (Q) (**identification of the class** of (Q)).

3. The *class* characteristics of (K) and (Q) ***agree***, but there is **no agreement** in individual characteristics.

   Conclusion: (K) ***may not be*** the source of (Q) (*inconsistent*).

4. The *class* characteristics of (K) and (Q) ***agree***, and there is *some agreement* in individual characteristics between (Q) and (K).

   Conclusion: (K) may be the source of (Q) (*consistent*).

5. There is **sufficient agreement** in *class* and *individual* characteristics between (Q) and (K) to establish that (K) is the source of (Q).

   Conclusion: (K) is identified as the source of (Q) (*individualization*).

COMPARISON STANDARDS AND CONTROLS

Since most laboratory analyses involve a comparison of the questioned item with known items, the quality of the laboratory analysis depends heavily on the collection and submission of the proper *standards* and *controls* for each item submitted. The term "**questioned** item" refers to an item with an unknown source. Other terms used to characterize the questioned item include "unknown," "evidence," "crime sample," "latent" (fingerprints), and additional terms from various specialists. All of these terms refer to an item with an **unknown source** that is to be compared with an item from a **known source** in order to establish whether or not the questioned and known samples share the same source. "Knowns" (both the original sample and the derived exemplar samples) are frequently referred to by the capital letter "K," and the questioned or evidence item is referred to as the "Q" sample.

Knowns consist of two categories: (1) *standards* and (2) *exemplars*. Standards consist of materials from a *known source* and can be either a *comparison standard* or a *reference standard*. **Comparison standards** are those materials collected from a known source for comparison with a questioned sample, in order to determine whether the questioned sample came from the same source as the comparison standard. An example of a comparison standard is a blood sample from a known individual that is used to compare its blood types against an evidence bloodstain's types. The blood standards are usually obtained from the principals in a particular case, such as the victim(s) and the suspect(s). Other examples of comparison standards are the inked fingerprints from a known individual to compare with latent fingerprints from a crime scene, a hair sample from a suspect to compare with hairs found at a crime scene, fiber samples from a carpet at a crime scene to compare with fibers found on a suspect's shoes, and a firearm seized from a suspect to compare with bullets retrieved from a victim in a shooting. Items derived from these standards for use in the laboratory comparison with the questioned items are referred to as "exemplar" items.

Reference standards are specimens kept in a reference collection by the various laboratories. These standards consist of specimens that have been collected from different sources and that have been authenticated as to source and composition. These reference standards are used to verify the type and composition of known samples obtained in casework. Examples of reference standards are paint collections obtained from manufacturers, hair collections obtained from specific body sites from individuals of known racial composition, drug standards from manufacturers, and blood samples obtained from individuals of known blood types.

Exemplar is the term used to describe either a sample of the comparison standard (known) that is collected or prepared from the comparison standard for the purposes of comparison with the questioned item (see Table 1-3) or the entire comparison standard used for the comparison with the questioned item. The exemplar item must be a true representation of the known sample in order to be useful in the comparison process. The exemplar utilized should contain both the class and the individual characteristics (if the evidence type is one with individual characteristics) of the known. It is important for the crime scene investigator to consider the variations present in any standards collected for the laboratory analysis, making sure that the standards collected represent the variations present in the "known" (e.g., a carpet fiber sample should contain all the colors in the carpet being sampled). *Note:* Different specialties may refer to exemplar items by other terms ("inked print" by the fingerprint examiner, "test fired bullet" by the firearms examiner, and so forth).

Controls are those items tested simultaneously with the questioned item to reveal any problems associated with the integrity of the evidence item or the testing procedure. Controls consist of the *standards* mentioned before and those items that will show the effects of "background" on the questioned item (*background controls*). Background effects may be the result of an interaction between the questioned item and the material on which the questioned item is found. For example, a bloodstain on a garment may be damaged by a chemical agent already on the garment. A control (unstained) portion of the garment near the site of the bloodstain is tested simultaneously with the stained area. Any problem associated with a chemical on the garment would then be apparent in the analysis results for the control. The known standard specimen and the background controls are subjected to the same tests as the evidence bloodstain in order to determine that the blood typing technique being employed gives the correct answer for the blood types being tested for by the analysis. If the standards or controls tested give the wrong result in the testing procedure, the analyst knows that there is some error in the testing system and so must troubleshoot the system before repeating the analysis. Control specimens must be collected for most biological stains, such as bloodstains, semen stains, and saliva stains, as interference from the background is always a consideration for the testing of these types of evidence. Blood or semen stains collected from a surface must always be accompanied by a control sample collected from the same surface as near to the stain as feasible yet sufficiently far away to assure that the control specimen is not contaminated with the stain. Specific information for each type of physical evidence with regard to its proper collection procedures, storage requirements, and the types of standards and controls needed for the laboratory analysis will be presented in the chapter for that type of evidence. If any question exists about the collection of standards or controls needed, the crime scene investigator should contact the laboratory that will analyze that particular evidence for detailed instructions on the preferred method of collection and on the standards and controls needed for that laboratory.

ETHICAL, LEGAL, AND SCIENTIFIC REQUIREMENTS FOR EVIDENCE COLLECTION

Ethical requirements

The first consideration in the scientific processing of a crime scene is that the crime scene investigator must be **objective** with regard to the recognition, documentation, and collection of physical evidence at any scene. The purpose of the crime scene investigation is always to *determine the facts* with regard to what events took place at the crime scene. It is not the role of the crime scene investigator to gather data that support a theory, incriminate a suspect, or exonerate a suspect. Rather, it is the duty of the crime scene investigator to gather all relevant data, regardless of the impact the facts may have on any theory of a case. This ethical requirement applies equally to crime scene investigators, laboratory forensic scientists, and any individual attempting a crime scene reconstruction. Any other approach is an unscientific method and will not bear scientific or legal scrutiny.

In order to be utilized effectively and to be admissible in a court of law, evidence collected must meet both the legal requirements and the scientific requirements for evidence collection. If an item of evidence is collected legally but is not collected in a manner that satisfies a scientific requirement necessary for preserving the integrity of the evidence for examination purposes, the laboratory may not be able to perform meaningful examinations on the evidence. Conversely, if the evidence collection meets all the scientific requirements for its collection but cannot pass a legal test for its admissibility, the evidence may be excluded in court.

Legal requirements

SEARCH AND SEIZURE LAWS*

Relevant Constitutional Amendments   The two amendments to the U.S. Constitution most applicable to search and seizure laws are the Fourth and the Fourteenth Amendments, which state:

> **FOURTH AMENDMENT:**
>
> The right of the people to be secure in their persons, houses, papers, and effects, against unreasonable searches and seizures, shall not be violated, and no Warrants shall issue, but upon probable cause, supported by Oath or affirmation, and particularly describing the place to be searched, and the persons or things to be seized.

> **FOURTEENTH AMENDMENT:**
>
> Section 1. All persons born or naturalized in the United States, and subject to the jurisdiction thereof, are citizens of the United States and of the State wherein they reside. No State shall make or enforce any law which shall abridge the privileges or immunities of citizens of the United States; nor shall any State deprive any person of life, liberty, or property, without due process of law; nor deny to any person within its jurisdiction the equal protection of the laws.

---

* Bruce Beckler, JD. *Personal communication*, April 7, 2003 (Appendix 1-A). [Extracted from Appendix 1-A, with editing by the author for this section.]

The Fourth and Fourteenth Amendments are the foundation for virtually all the *search and seizure* case law generated by the courts, as described below and in Appendix 1-A.

Warrantless Searches   *Definitions*: A search occurs when an expectation of privacy in an area that society is prepared to consider is reasonable and hence due protection by the Fourth Amendment may be infringed by a warrantless search of that area. The seizure of property occurs when there is some meaningful interference with an individual's possessory interest in that property by confiscating that property (*Horton v. California* (1990) 496 U.S. 128) by agents of the government. The Fourth Amendment does not proscribe all state-initiated searches and seizures; it merely proscribes those which are *unreasonable* (*Florida v. Jimeno* (1991) 500 U.S. 248, 250). Governmental intrusions that have been determined by the Supreme Court to be reasonable do not violate the Fourth Amendment. An individual's "capacity to claim the protection of the Fourth Amendment depends . . . upon whether the person who claims the protection of the Amendment has a legitimate expectation of privacy in the invaded place" (*Minnesota v. Carter* (1988) 525 U.S. 83, 88). In other words, an individual must have a sufficient connection to the place the government searched in order to assert the protection of the Fourth Amendment.

If a crime occurs on *public property*, a search warrant is not needed, and law enforcement can search the scene for as long and as often as they desire. However, if a crime occurs on *private property*, law enforcement officers have a right to enter that property pursuant to a court-recognized emergency (termed "exigent circumstances"—see below and in Appendix 1-A) such as to look for suspects or victims of the crime. Once the circumstances that produced the exigency (emergency entry into private premises) no longer exist, or the search for suspects and victims has been completed, law enforcement officers must desist from searching the scene for evidence of the crime until *either*:

1. The officers have received consent to search the property from a person who has the authority to give such consent, OR
2. A magistrate has issued a search warrant for the premises.

Search of Places Without a Search Warrant   The Supreme Court has carved out several exceptions to the Fourth Amendment warrant requirement justifying warrantless intrusions into areas protected by the Fourth Amendment to promote the public safety as well as officer safety. You may not search a crime scene without consent or a search warrant *unless* a court-recognized exception to the warrant requirement exists, termed an **exigent circumstance**. The following are the major court-recognized exigencies that impact crime scene searches:

1. To Preserve the Life or Health of a Person.
2. To Prevent the Destruction of Evidence.
3. To Stop a Crime in Progress.
4. Hot Pursuit.
5. Protective Sweep.

Exclusionary Rule   Any evidence that is discovered after the exigency has ceased, but prior to obtaining consent to search or a search warrant for the premises has been approved by a magistrate, will be suppressed at a trial pursuant to the Exclusionary Rule. The exclusionary rule is a *judicially created* legal procedure, requiring that *evidence obtained during a search in violation of the Fourth Amendment* must be excluded from a criminal trial as evidence against the defendant. The only time such evidence can be presented is as impeachment evidence to prove that a defendant who has taken the witness stand has testified falsely. The exclusionary rule, which does not appear anywhere in the U.S. Constitution, was created to dissuade law enforcement from conduct that violates provisions of the Constitution by making any evidence seized in violation of the Constitution inadmissible at trial (see Appendix 1-A for case history of this rule). The exclusionary rule applies to both federal and state law enforcement officers, as well as to both state and federal courts (*Mapp v. Ohio* (1961) 367 U.S. 643). Because of the potential for exclusion of evidence due to failure to obtain a search warrant when required, it is essential that lead investigators be well versed in search and seizure laws. Moreover, in the investigation of major crimes such as homicide, it is advisable to have a prosecuting attorney as a member of the response team.

The Fruit of the Poisonous Tree   It is obvious that evidence procured by a direct violation of constitutional rights or privileges is subject to the exclusionary rule. But, what about evidence that is discovered as a result of evidence which was obtained in violation of a person's constitutional rights? Should this evidence also be inadmissible pursuant to the exclusionary rule? The U.S. Supreme Court has held in numerous case decisions that if the government makes an illegal search or arrest and uses the knowledge it gains to obtain other evidence, then this new evidence must also be excluded. Refer to Appendix 1-A for a discussion of the development of the fruit of the poisonous tree by court decision.

Consent Searches   The U.S. Supreme Court has determined that "a search conducted pursuant to a valid consent is constitutionally permissible" *Schneckloth v. Bustamonte* (1973) 412 U.S. 218, 222. For this reason alone, each time you are interested in searching private property, even if you have already secured a search warrant, it is always best to ask for consent to search the premises first. If given, it may eliminate any arguments that the defense may raise later about the validity of the search warrant or the accuracy of its supporting affidavit. While a person's constitutional rights are to be zealously guarded by law enforcement at all times, every person has the right to waive his or her constitutional rights, including their Fourth Amendment rights. But, in order for a person to validly waive their Fourth Amendment rights, their consent to the search must first and foremost have been given *voluntarily*. In addition, the person giving the consent must be shown to have had the authority (or "apparent authority") to give such consent. Further, law enforcement cannot exceed the *consensual scope* of the search, both in *what items* they were given permission to search for and the *area where* they were given permission to search. It is almost imperative that a "Consent to Search form be filled out and signed by the person giving consent in order to avoid any question about the person giving the consent voluntarily. Another form that complements the above Consent to Search form is the "*Completed Search Form*." It states that nothing was taken by law enforcement during the search. This form provides substantial presumptive proof that nothing was removed by police during the search, protecting the officers who conducted the search from a later civil action alleging that something valuable was taken and never returned. (See Appendix 1-B for sample forms for Consent to Search and Completed Search.)

Consent Must be Voluntary   In order for a consent to search to be considered voluntary, it *must* be the result of freewill without any fear for declining to give such consent. Consent cannot be the product of any form of coercion, duress, tricks, promises, or other misrepresentation, no matter how slight. The prosecution bears the burden of proving that the consent was freely and voluntarily given. (See Appendix 1-A for further explanation of the determination that a consent to search was free and voluntary.)

Authority to Consent   Any person who has *custody and control* of certain premises or items has the *authority to consent* to a search of the area or item. However, where more than one person has custody over or control over the area to be searched, or items requested to be seized, then consent to a search of that item or area is permitted only to the extent that the person giving the consent has a right to its access and control.

Apparent Authority to Consent   Courts will generally uphold a consent search if the consenting party did not have the authority to give consent to search where the officers had reasonable, good faith belief that the consenting party had the authority to consent. This is termed *"apparent authority."* If there is any question concerning the consenter's authority, officers should ask more questions to determine authority to give consent, making notes on the exact wording of the questions and the responses to them. All questions and responses to them should be exact quotes if possible. This will serve as substantial evidence of apparent authority if this becomes an issue later. If, during this questioning, the officer develops any doubts about the authority of the consenting party, the officer should opt for getting a search warrant to ensure the admissibility of the evidence.

Scope of the Consent   The *places* that you may search and the *items* for which you may search are *limited by the consent given*. When consent is requested, officers need to *be specific about what they are searching for and where they want to search for these items*. Appendix 1-A gives further details on how the scope of the consent allows for additional evidence under the *"plain view"* doctrine.

Consent to Search Given by Third Parties   In some circumstances, the police officer will encounter a situation where a third party is the only person present who may be able to give consent to the search because they have been given *shared authority*, sometimes called common authority. Shared or common authority means that the person has an unrestricted right to use or access the area or item in question. The fact that the person giving the consent does not use or access the area is not the controlling factor. It is their unrestricted *right to access and use of* the items or area that is controlling for authority purposes. (See Appendix 1-A for further delineation of the conditions for shared authority.)

Implied Consent to Search   There also exists a form of consent known as *implied consent*. This situation occurs when the owner or person in possession of an item or place reports that a crime has been committed and summons help. For example, when the owner of a car reports that his vehicle has been stolen, the owner grants an implied consent for the police to search the vehicle when it is located. This search is limited to the extent necessary for positively identifying it as the vehicle stolen, its safe recovery by the police, and protection of any evidence that may identify the person or persons responsible for stealing the vehicle. If during such search contraband is located, it may be seized under the plain view doctrine, explained below.

Consent to Search from a Person in Custody   The situation for a consent to search is dramatically different when a request to search personal belongings, vehicles, or premises has been requested from a *person who has been placed under arrest, or is already in custody*. This is especially true if the requested search is meant to find incriminating evidence to be used against the defendant. Where a suspect has been placed under arrest and a consent to search is requested by law enforcement, courts have held that the *advice of rights is required prior to making such a request*, and, the courts have insinuated, although not specifically held, that the defendant be provided a warning that he/she has *the right to refuse the consent* without any adverse consequences.

Whether a custodial consent to search requires a separate advice of rights and an admonishment that the defendant has the right to refuse to give his consent and force the officers to attempt to obtain a search warrant is still an open question. There has been no definitive ruling by the Supreme Court. Thus, to be certain that your case is not lost on a suppression motion, if the suspect is in custody, it is best to preface any post-arrest request for consent to search with at least a cautionary warning that the defendant has the right to refuse such consent. And, such a request should only be made if the defendant has been read his constitutional rights and has waived them.

The Plain View Doctrine   The *plain view doctrine* alone cannot justify the warrantless seizure of evidence because no amount of probable cause can justify a warrantless search or seizure *absent exigent circumstances*. Any evidence observed in plain view can be legally seized and used in a criminal prosecution. The law enforcement officer who seized it only has to be able to articulate what facts led him/her to believe that an **exigent circumstance** existed, justifying their presence. The plain view doctrine has *two limitations* on the seizure of evidence pursuant to the doctrine:

First, the *incriminating nature* of the object (evidence) must be *immediately apparent*.

Second, the officer must have a *lawful right of access* to the object itself.

As the plain view doctrine applies to protective sweeps, any evidence discovered in plain view during a protective sweep will be admissible in court providing that it was located in a place where a person might reasonably be hiding. This would eliminate drawers and small cabinets, but not closets or under beds, etc. Similarly the courts have upheld the discovery of evidence in plain view when officers accompany an arrestee into another room to dress before being taken to jail. For further material on the plain view doctrine, refer to Appendix 1-A.

The Open Fields Doctrine   The words "open fields" do not adequately portray how the courts have interpreted their meaning in this judicially created exception to the warrant requirement. The term *open fields* means any unoccupied or undeveloped area that is *outside* the **curtilage** of a home. *Curtilage* is defined as a relatively small, well-defined area immediately adjacent to a residence. The courts have extended the private activities of the home to this area. *In order for an area to qualify under the open fields doctrine, it does not have to be open or a field.* Since there is no expectation of privacy in these areas, the Fourth Amendment has no application to these areas. Hence, entry into any area determined to be an "open field" is accepted as an entry onto public land, and therefore requires no warrant. Open fields are *not protected* by the Fourth Amendment. Therefore, if any person, citizen, or law enforcement officer passing by could view the area unhindered, even if the area is surrounded by "no trespassing" signs, fencing, or trees, that area qualifies as "open field." Entry into open fields, while technically a trespass, would not constitute a search regardless of who does the entering. *The basis of the open fields* *doctrine* is that certain areas of land are so open to public view that the person who owns the land has given up his right to privacy in these areas and has even implicitly invited the public to view the land. The open fields doctrine was established by the U.S. Supreme Court in the case *Hester v. United States* (1924) 265 U.S. 57. In that case the Supreme Court stated, "The special protection accorded by the Fourth Amendment . . . is not extended to the open fields."

Defining a residence is relatively easy. It is generally a structure designed for human habitation. Immediately adjacent to that residence is usually an area where the occupant can establish a legitimate expectation of privacy, although it is less than that expected within the residence, but more than that expected in an open field. This expectation of privacy is established by putting up a fence, trees, or bushes to surround the yard adjacent to the home, where the occupant can plant a garden, have a swimming pool, or have a place for children to play away from the prying eyes of the public. This area is called the *curtilage* of the home. This area and the activities occurring in this area are subject to the same Fourth Amendment protections as the actual residence. The test to determine what is curtilage for search and seizure purposes considers the proximity of the area to the home; whether it is surrounded by a fence or steps have been taken to place other obstructions to protect it from public view; and the uses of the area (*United States v. Dunn* (1987) 480 U.S. 294). If the area searched is in close proximity to the dwelling and is an area where "normal" family activities occur, there is a *reasonable expectation of privacy* (i.e., "curtilage") and the area is protected.

Search Warrants   *Definition*: A *search warrant* is a written order, signed by a magistrate after the magistrate has determined that there is probable cause to believe that certain persons or items are located in a specific location, directing law enforcement to search for a person(s), physical item(s), or documentary evidence of a crime in that particular location.

The U.S. Supreme Court has held that searches conducted pursuant to search warrants are by definition reasonable searches under the Fourth Amendment. The Court has also identified certain exceptions to the warrant requirement as being reasonable searches and permissible under the Fourth Amendment, such as searches incident to arrest, consent to search, and a variety of emergency situations (see exigent circumstances). Unless one of these exceptions exists, any search of private property can only be conducted by the government if the government's agents have the authority of a search warrant. Any time a search is conducted pursuant to a search warrant, the search is presumed lawful and the burden shifts to the defendant to prove otherwise.

A separate document, called an *affidavit*, is *attached to the request for the search warrant*. It is made under oath and provides the basis for the "probable cause" to believe that the specific evidence or person being sought is located at a particular place. An affidavit can be either oral or written, but the search warrant must be written. (See Appendix 1-A for detailed information regarding the preparation of search warrants and the affidavit attached to the search warrant.)

Searches and Seizures of Evidence from a Suspect's Body   A suspect may try to hide evidence by swallowing it, or placing it inside a body cavity; the evidence may be stored there naturally for some period of time (e.g., alcohol, drugs), or permanently (e.g., DNA); or the evidence may be stored there unnaturally (e.g., a bullet). In these situations, recovering the evidence constitutes a "search" of, if not also a "seizure from," the suspect's body

(*Schmerber v. California* (1966) 384 U.S. 757, 767). And, because such searches may be highly invasive, embarrassing, and sometimes risky, the courts have imposed some special requirements that must be met before officers may conduct a bodily intrusion search, or authorize a medical professional or technician to do so. Some bodily intrusion searches must be authorized by a warrant or court order, while others, such as ones incident to a lawful arrest, do not require a warrant. In either case, however, there must always be probable cause to conduct the search; the need for the search must outweigh its intrusiveness; and police must employ reasonable procedures in conducting the search (*Schmerber v. California* (1966) 384 U.S. 757, 768). The Supreme Court ruled that such mandatory tests, if limited to blood, breath, or urine, while they are "searches" governed by the Fourth Amendment, are "reasonable" if "compelling governmental interests" outweigh privacy concerns.

Bodily Intrusion Warrants   A warrant can authorize a bodily intrusion search, but must say so expressly. Thus, a bodily intrusion search would not be covered or included by a warrant that simply authorized the search of the suspect's home, vehicle, and person. Like every warrant, a bodily intrusion search warrant must be supported by facts contained in an affidavit. However, unlike a standard warrant, *a bodily intrusion warrant requires more than the usual probable cause to search*. This extra showing is known as **probable cause plus**.

Probable cause plus means that in addition to demonstrating a fair probability that the search will result in the discovery of evidence of a crime, the affidavit must also show that the need for the evidence outweighs the reasonably foreseeable damage and intrusiveness of the procedure (*Winston v. Lee* (1985) 470 U.S. 753). To demonstrate a strong need for a body search, and to show that the search is neither dangerous nor unduly intrusive, *the affidavit should address the following*:

1. *Probable cause*, i.e., the likelihood the search will result in the discovery of relevant evidence;
2. The *seriousness* of the crime;
3. The *importance* of the evidence, i.e., the extent to which it is necessary to establish guilt;
4. The *practicality* of using other, less intrusive means, if any exist, to establish guilt;
5. The extent to which the search may *threaten the suspect's health and safety*, or result in psychological harm; And,
6. The *extent* to which the search may intrude on the suspect's *dignity and privacy* interests (*Ibid.*, 761–766).

Blood Test Warrants   Police commonly seek a warrant to authorize testing of a suspect's blood for alcohol or drugs. Testing for DNA typing is also common. An affidavit for a blood test warrant will usually be sufficient if it establishes that there is probable cause to believe the test results will constitute evidence of a crime, and that the blood removal will be performed by trained medical personnel and in accordance with accepted medical practices. No more is required because the "evanescent" quality of the evidence automatically provides exigent circumstances.

The "Brady" Material Requirement   *Brady v. Maryland* (1963) 373 U.S. 83.   In 1963, the U.S. Supreme Court ruled in *Brady* that a prosecutor has a *duty to disclose* evidence discovered during a criminal investigation against him/her to the criminal defendant that impacts upon issues of their *culpability* and/or the *severity of the penalty* that is to be assessed against them for their conduct. This relates to criminal prosecutions only. The favorable information has to be material to the crime and not the defendant's character, etc. The bottom line for this is that any prosecutor in the land has a duty to disclose evidence to a criminal defendant that impacts the defendant's culpability and/or penalty for the offense. The prosecution's disclosure obligation is determined by the cumulative effect of all of the undisclosed evidence favorable to the defense, without having to evaluate the evidence item by item. Such evaluation is the responsibility of the prosecutor who is required to assess the net effect of all such evidence and to make disclosure of favorable evidence if there is a "reasonable probability" that the results of the proceedings would possibly be affected by its disclosure. Moreover, the Court held that this responsibility remains with the prosecution regardless of any failure of law enforcement to bring the evidence favorable to the defendant to the prosecutor's attention. Thus, the law requires that prosecutors have a duty to proactively seek out *Brady* material that might exist. This would include anything discovered at the crime scene, or any reasonable interpretation of the evidence found at the crime scene.

DOCUMENTATION OF THE SCENE

The second legal requirement for any crime scene investigation is to provide proper documentation of the crime scene and the collection of evidence. Although each crime scene has a number of unique features that sets it apart from all others, there are a number of requirements for each scene that must be met in order to document properly the condition of the scene and the actions taken to process the scene. Proper documentation of the scene involves adequate notes, photographs, and sketches necessary to re-create the crime scene in the mind's eye of investigators, attorneys, and the judge and jury in any judicial proceeding. Notes may be handwritten or dictated into a handheld tape recorder, or a combination of both. Photography may be accomplished with still cameras, digital cameras, videotape recorders, or a combination of these (see the chapter on photography for a discussion of the advantages and disadvantages of still and video photography). It is important that the scene be documented in the condition in which it was found rather than attempt to replace any items that have been moved prior to arrival at the scene. The documentation should be an ongoing process, involving taking notes, preparing sketches, and taking photographs as the investigation proceeds. This approach gives coherence to the crime scene search and avoids having to go back and fill in gaps.

IDENTIFICATION OF PHYSICAL EVIDENCE COLLECTED

The third legal requirement for evidence collection is that each item of evidence collected must be properly identified with sufficient information to ensure that the item can be identified by the collector at any time in the future. The item or its sealed package should have the following minimum information affixed to the item or its package (referred to throughout this text as *Standard Identification Data*):[14]

- Case number for investigator's agency.
- Day/date/time of collection (e.g., Thursday, December 24, 2006).
- Item number (this may be augmented with the collector's badge/ID#) (e.g., 187/1 = Badge #187, item #1).
- Initials of collector (or personalized logo). *Note:* It is best to print the collector's last name, then to add the initials or logo.

When these conditions for collection and identification of the item are met, the collector will be able to identify unambiguously the item as that same item collected by the investigator. These precautions will help immeasurably to establish the credibility of the collector's report or testimony and will effectively avoid any suggestion that the item has been misidentified. Oftentimes, judicial proceedings are had long after the processing at a scene, during which time the crime scene investigator will have processed many additional scenes having similar evidence. The proper documentation of the evidence at the time it is collected will prevent confusion of the evidence item with any other collected by the crime scene investigator during the time span between collection and testimony regarding the specific item.

CHAIN OF POSSESSION (CHAIN OF CUSTODY)

Another essential legal requirement for the introduction of physical evidence in the courtroom is that the item must be identified as the same item collected at the scene and further that the item has not been altered in any significant fashion. Usually, the handling and analysis of the evidence will produce some alteration of the evidence or its packaging. For this reason, it is essential that the **chain of possession** be established and maintained so that any apparent or real alteration of the evidence can be explained by the person who effected the change. This person can testify as to how the alterations were necessitated (by the laboratory analysis, for example). The collector's notes and report should reflect to whom and when the evidence was relinquished, as well as the general nature and condition of the evidence relinquished (e.g., "expended cartridge case in sealed manila envelope"). It is also important to establish that the evidence remains in a secure environment, so that any personnel with potential access to the evidence can be identified in order to eliminate any suggestion of tampering or of any other artifice that may be used in an attempt to exclude the evidence on legal grounds. Properly maintained evidence rooms meet this requirement, whereas storage in personal lockers or desks may be suspect as to the integrity of the chain of possession.

Admissibility Requirements For Expert Testimony   The admissibility of scientific expert testimony is governed by case law (see Appendix 1-A for complete case cites) that establishes the criteria used by courts to determine the admissibility of that testimony. For many years, the determination of the admissibility of scientific evidence was based on the decision in *Frye v. United States* by the District of Columbia Circuit Court in 1923. This decision, commonly referred to as the *Frye* decision, required that the scientific techniques and principles involved in the testing of the evidence had to be "generally accepted" by the relevant scientific community from which the principles and techniques underlying the tests were established. The new Federal Rules of Evidence, especially Rule 702, adopted in 1975, were also used as a basis for determining the admissibility of expert testimony by listing three criteria expert testimony must meet for the admissibility of that testimony:

1. "The testimony must be based on sufficient facts or data";
2. "The testimony is the product of reliable principles and methods"; and,
3. "The witness has applied the principles and methods reliably to the facts of the case."

In 1993, the U.S. Supreme Court, in the case of *Daubert v. Merrell Dow Pharmaceutical*, Inc., ruled that "general acceptance" was not an absolute requirement for the admissibility of scientific testimony, since the Trial Judge acts as a "gatekeeper" by determining the relevance and the reliability of scientific testimony. *Daubert* added four criteria* by which scientific testimony must be evaluated:

1. Testability of the scientific principle,
2. Known or potential error rate,
3. Peer review and publication, and,
4. General acceptance in a *particular* scientific community.

In 1999, the decision in the case of *Kumho Tire Co., Ltd. v. Carmichael* extended *Daubert* by ruling that the gatekeeping role of the trial judge applied not only to scientific evidence, but also to *all expert testimony*. *Kumho* held that *Daubert* applied to testimony of a technical nature or from other specialized fields of knowledge and that *Daubert*'s list of specific factors (see above) did not necessarily apply to all experts in every case, thus leaving the determination of admissibility to the trial judge's gatekeeping function.

Scientific requirements

Of equal importance to the legal requirements are the scientific requirements for evidence collection, which also must be satisfied in order for the evidence to be admissible in the courts. The scientific requirements for evidence collection are essential parameters that insure the scientific integrity of the physical evidence collected and include those that follow.

PREVENTING CONTAMINATION OF THE EVIDENCE
Prevention of **contamination** of the evidence requires proper protection of the evidence at the scene prior to its collection. Prevention measures include limiting access to the scene to only those individuals of the investigative team with a legitimate need to enter the scene, preventing casual inspection of evidence at the scene, protection from inclement weather, and the proper packaging of the evidence. The observance of these measures will help to insure the scientific integrity of the physical evidence recovered from the scene.

PRESERVING THE CONDITION OF THE EVIDENCE AS FOUND
Preserving the condition of the evidence as found is accomplished by using proper collection and packaging techniques for that particular type of evidence and, further, insuring that the evidence is properly stored until its transmittal to the laboratory. Items requiring refrigeration or freezing during storage should be clearly marked on the outside of the package to indicate the type of storage required, so that the property officer can take the appropriate actions for preserving the evidence.

COLLECTION OF ADEQUATE COMPARISON STANDARDS
The comparison standards collected should be adequate and appropriate for the anticipated laboratory examinations (see collection of standards and the sections on standards needed in the appropriate chapter for a specific evidence type). The quality and integrity of the laboratory examinations depend heavily on the quality of the comparison standards collected by the investigator. The standards must be of adequate size and quantity and must be an accurate representation of the source of the standards.

---

*From Haag, Lucien C. (2006). *Shooting Incident Reconstruction*, Academic Press (imprint of Elsevier), Burlington, MA.

Summary

HISTORY OF FORENSIC SCIENCE

Orfila's treatise on toxicology
Bertillon's anthropometry
Gross' *Criminal Investigation*
Locard's exchange principle
Svensson and Wendel's *Techniques of Crime Scene Investigation*

HISTORY OF CRIMINALISTICS

Osterburg and O'Hara's *An Introduction to Criminalistics*
Paul L. Kirk's *Crime Investigation*
Formation of California Association of Criminalists
Jeffrey's development of DNA testing
Erlich, Higuchi, and Blake: application of PCR technique to forensic science DNA testing
AFIS and CODIS computer databases for fingerprints and DNA

PHYSICAL EVIDENCE: TYPES, VALUE, AND ADVANTAGES

Types of evidence:
  Direct
  Circumstantial
  Testimonial
  Physical
Value of physical evidence:
  Crime scene reconstruction
  Provide investigative leads
  Provide facts to a jury
  Linkage Profile (Figure 1-1)
    Suspect to Victim
    Victim to Suspect
    Suspect to crime scene(s)
    Serial homicides, rapes
Advantages of physical evidence.
  Tangible objects for jury to see
  Jury can take into jury room
  Some cases unsolvable without physical evidence
  Not subject to memory loss
  Can be tested by independent expert

MAJOR CATEGORIES OF PHYSICAL EVIDENCE

Fingerprints
Firearms and toolmarks
Biological (blood, semen, etc.)
Trace (hairs, fibers, soil, etc.)
Documents
Physical matching
Toxicology
Drugs
Other types

CLASS AND INDIVIDUAL CHARACTERISTICS

Class: Shared by all members of class; allow *identification of the class* of an item
Individual: Set of characteristics which allow for *individualization* of an evidence item

LABORATORY ANALYSIS OF PHYSICAL EVIDENCE

Comparative analysis process (Figure 1-2)
Comparison Standards (Known source)
Evidence items (Questioned source)
Controls
  Blanks
  Positive
  Background

COMPARISON OBSERVATIONS AND CONCLUSIONS (FIGURE 1-2)

Class characteristics of (Q) and (K) do not agree
  Elimination of (K) as the source of (Q)
Class characteristics of (Q) and (K) agree
  (K) may be the source of (Q)
Individual characteristics do not agree
  (K) may not be the source of (Q)
Some agreement in individual characteristics
  (K) may be the source of (Q)
Sufficient agreement in both class and individual characteristics:
  (K) *identified as the source* of (Q) (individualization)

REQUIREMENTS FOR EVIDENCE COLLECTION

Ethical
    investigator must be objective
    determine facts, not support theory
Legal
    Fourth and Fourteenth Amendments
    Search and seizure laws
    Scene documentation
    Identification of each item
    Chain of possession
    Warrantless searches
    Search warrants
Scientific
    Prevent contamination
    Preserve condition as found
    Collection of adequate comparison standards
    Package in appropriate containers
    Store in appropriate conditions

ADMISSIBILITY REQUIREMENTS FOR EXPERT TESTIMONY

Frye decision
Federal Rules of Evidence, Rule 702 (three criteria)
Daubert decision (four criteria)
Kumho decision (attenuated *Daubert*, added technical and specialized fields to judges' gatekeeping function)

Review Questions

1. Physical evidence can be defined as _____ associated with a crime or tort.
2. In order to be of value, physical evidence must be _____, _____, and _____ properly.
3. One of the major purposes for the collection of physical evidence is _____.
4. Physical evidence may help determine whether or not a _____ occurred.
5. Physical evidence may _____ an individual with another person or with a crime scene.
6. The Locard exchange principle states that a _____ of physical evidence may occur when there is contact between two individuals.
7. Physical evidence may provide _____ to a jury that may assist in the determination of guilt or innocence of an accused.
8. The linkage triangle illustrates the possible transfer of physical evidence between the _____, the _____, and the _____.
9. "Class" characteristics are those characteristics shared by _____.
10. _____ is the identification of the individual source of an evidence item.
11. Glass, soil, and fibers have only _____ characteristics.
12. The term "known" refers to the known _____ of an item.
13. The term "exemplar" refers to an item prepared from a _____.
14. In order for physical evidence to be effective and admissible, the collection of the evidence must meet both _____ and _____ requirements.
15. Standard identification data includes _____, _____, _____, and _____.

Further References

Jackson, A.R.W., and J.M. Jackson. 2004. *Forensic Science*.* Pearson Education Limited, Essex, England.

Kirk, P.L., and John, I. Thornton (ed.) 1974. *Crime Investigation* (2nd ed.). New York, NY: John Wiley & Sons.

Osterburg, J.W., and R.H. Ward. 2000. *Criminal Investigation: A Method for Reconstructing the Past* 3rd ed. Cincinnati, OH: Anderson Publishing Co.

Richard, S. 2009. *Forensic Science: From the Crime Scene to the Crime Lab*, Upper Saddle River, NJ: Pearson Education Inc.

White, Peter (ed.) 1998. *Crime Scene to Court*.* (The Essentials of Forensic Science.) Cambridge, U.K: The Royal Society of Chemistry.

* Written primarily for audiences in the United Kingdom, but highly relevant for U.S. audiences.

APPENDIX 1–A

Crime Scene Search and Seizure Law*

INTRODUCTION

Law enforcement officers may erroneously believe that they have the right to search for evidence at any public or private premises where a crime has occurred. Such is not the case. Occasionally, a victim may become the suspect, such as at a reported burglary. Perhaps the victim sold items to collect on the insurance and then staged a burglary scene. In other cases, the premises of the perpetrator may still have Fourth Amendment protection, requiring a search warrant or consent to search the premises. For example, it is not always legal to conduct a warrantless search of a homicide crime scene. If the victim was the only occupant of a private dwelling, then there is no one to complain about a violation of rights or to give consent to search the premises (the victim being deceased). However, if the victim shared the premises with another person, such as a spouse or roommate, then the other person still has a privacy right in the premises. After determining that there are no more victims at the crime site, and that the perpetrators have left the premises, law enforcement officers must first either obtain consent to search from the other occupant or obtain a search warrant in order to search the scene for evidence of the crime.

The best example of this situation occurred in the U.S. Supreme Court case of *Mincey v. Arizona* (1978) 437 U.S. 385. Mincey shot and killed a narcotics officer at Mincey's apartment during an undercover buy of narcotics. After Mincey was taken into custody, detectives performed a warrantless search of the apartment over a four-day period. The officers believed that since Mincey had allowed the undercover officer into his apartment, this permitted them to lawfully be present after the shooting. The U.S. Supreme Court suppressed all of the evidence seized after Mincey had been arrested. The Court held: "The 'murder scene exception' created by the Arizona Supreme Court to the warrant requirement is inconsistent with the Fourth and Fourteenth Amendments, and the warrantless search of petitioner's apartment was not constitutionally permissible simply because a homicide had occurred there" (*Mincey*, 437 U.S. 386, 386). "Nor can the search be justified on the ground that a possible homicide inevitably presents an emergency situation, especially since there was no emergency threatening life or limb, all persons in the apartment having been located before the search began" (*Ibid.*, 391–392).

Arson crime scenes present another type of situation with a result similar to the above. After a fire on private premises has been extinguished, fire officials may then enter the structure without a search warrant or any probable cause to believe that evidence of a crime is present for a reasonable period of time to investigate the cause of the blaze. The courts have ruled that this may even include a re-entry after leaving the premises *if* the reason for leaving the premises was reasonable (such as darkness or the presence of smoke) *and* the re-entry took place within a short period of time (only for a few hours, not days). It should be noted that this is *only* to determine the cause of the fire. If the

---

* Court case decisions are cited using California style; citation of federal and other state decisions may differ as to style/format.

purpose of the re-entry or any entry after the fire has been extinguished is to gather criminal evidence, then the officials must first secure a search warrant or obtain valid consent to enter the structure, even if it has been completely burned to the ground.

WARRANTLESS SEARCHES

Generally, the Fourth Amendment to the U.S. Constitution prohibits the government from making a warrantless entry into private premises either to search for evidence of a crime or to seize a criminal. The Fourth Amendment to the U.S. Constitution states, "The right of the people to be secure in their persons, houses, papers, and effects, against unreasonable searches and seizures, shall not be violated, and no warrants shall issue, but upon probable cause, supported by oath or affirmation, and particularly describing the place to be searched, and the persons or things to be seized." This is the supreme law of the land in the area of search and seizure: the yardstick by which all search and seizure statutory as well as procedural law is to be measured. Any statute or procedure that violates any of the provisions of the Fourth Amendment as the U.S. Supreme Court has interpreted them is unconstitutional, and therefore cannot be enforced. However, nothing in the Constitution precludes a state from requiring more stringent protections for individual rights than is required by the Fourth Amendment, which merely establishes the minimum acceptable standards for search and seizure law. Most state constitutions have language that essentially mirrors the language found in the Fourth Amendment.

Definitions of the words "search" and "seizure" should first be made before their application to crime scene searches can continue. A *search* occurs when an expectation of privacy that society is prepared to consider is reasonable and hence due protection may be infringed (*United States v. Jacobsen* (1984) 466 U.S. 109). But a search does not infringe upon the Fourth Amendment if it is "reasonable." The reasonableness of a search is measured by a totality of the circumstances surrounding the search (*Ohio v. Robinette* (1996) 519 U.S. 33). The *seizure* of property occurs when there is some meaningful interference with an individual's possessory interest in that property (*Horton v. California* (1990) 496 U.S. 128). "The touchstone of the Fourth Amendment is reasonableness. The Fourth Amendment does not proscribe all state-initiated searches and seizures; it merely proscribes those which are unreasonable" (*Florida v. Jimeno* (1991) 500 U.S. 248, 250). Thus, the message is that the Fourth Amendment protects an individual's reasonable expectation of privacy against unreasonable governmental intrusion. Governmental intrusions that have been determined by the Supreme Court to be reasonable do not violate the Fourth Amendment. An individual's "capacity to claim the protection of the Fourth Amendment depends . . . upon whether the person who claims the protection of the Amendment has a legitimate expectation of privacy in the invaded place" (*Minnesota v. Carter* (1988) 525 U.S. 83, 88). In other words, an individual must have a sufficient connection to the place the government searched in order to assert the protection of the Fourth Amendment.

If a crime occurs on *public property*, a search warrant is not needed, and law enforcement can search the scene for as long and as often as they desire. However, if a crime occurs on private property, law enforcement officers have a right to enter that property pursuant to a court-recognized emergency (termed "exigent circumstances") such as to look for suspects or victims of the crime. Once the circumstances that produced the exigency (emergency entry into private premises) no longer exist, or the search for suspects and victims has been completed, law enforcement officers must desist from searching the scene for evidence of the crime until *either*:

1. The officers have received consent to search the property from a person who has the authority to give such consent, *or*
2. A magistrate has issued a search warrant for the premises.

EXCLUSIONARY RULE

Any evidence that is discovered after the exigency has ceased, but prior to obtaining consent to search or a search warrant for the premises has been approved by a magistrate, will be suppressed at a trial pursuant to the exclusionary rule. The exclusionary rule is a *judicially created legal procedure* requiring that evidence obtained during a search in violation of the Fourth Amendment must be excluded from a criminal trial as evidence against the defendant. The only time such evidence can be presented is as impeachment evidence to prove that a defendant who has taken the witness stand has testified falsely. The exclusionary rule, which does not appear anywhere in the U.S. Constitution, was created to dissuade law enforcement from conduct that violates provisions of the Constitution by making any evidence seized in violation of the Constitution inadmissible at trial. The exclusionary rule applies to both federal and state law enforcement officers, as well as to both state and federal courts (*Mapp v. Ohio* (1961) 367 U.S. 643).

CONSENT SEARCHES

The U.S. Supreme Court has determined that "a search conducted pursuant to a valid consent is constitutionally permissible" *Schneckloth v. Bustamonte* (1973) 412 U.S. 218, 222. For this reason alone, each time you are interested in searching private property, even if you have already secured a search warrant, it is always best to ask for consent to search the premises first. If given, it may eliminate any arguments that the defense may raise later about the validity of the search warrant or the accuracy of its supporting affidavit. While a person's constitutional rights are to be zealously guarded by law enforcement at all times, every person has the right to waive his or her constitutional rights, including their Fourth Amendment rights. But, in order for a person to validly waive their Fourth Amendment rights, their consent to the search must first and foremost have been given voluntarily. In addition, the person giving the consent must be shown to have had the authority (or "apparent authority") to give such consent. Further, law enforcement cannot exceed the consensual scope of the search, both in what they were given permission to search for and where they were given permission to search.

CONSENT MUST BE VOLUNTARY

In order for a consent to search to be considered voluntary, it *must* be the result of freewill without any fear for declining to give such consent. Consent cannot be the product of any form of coercion, duress, tricks, promises, or other misrepresentation, no matter how slight. The prosecution bears the burden of proving that the consent was freely and voluntarily given. The determination that a consent to search was free and voluntary depends greatly upon the conduct and demeanor of the officer(s) while requesting the consent. In evaluating the voluntary nature of a consent to search, the courts will evaluate the totality of the circumstances surrounding the consent. This includes the defendant's knowledge and understanding of his constitutional rights, his age, physical and mental condition, background, and education. But even then there are some circumstances that indicate that the consent was coerced. For example, if more than two officers in uniform request consent to search a residence or other area where a person has a reasonable expectation of privacy, this has been ruled as coercive, making the person's consent involuntary and hence all evidence seized during the search inadmissible. However, if the officers' conduct is polite and the person giving the consent has legal background, then this probably would not be seen as coercive. Then again, if the officers requesting the consent to search have their guns drawn and are in "raid jackets," then the consent will probably be seen as given under duress, vitiating the consent and making any evidence seized inadmissible at trial. Of course any threat of force on the part of the police is considered to give rise to an involuntary consent. However, there is no constitutional requirement that the police advise the person that he/she has the right to refuse to give consent to the search without any adverse consequences. Even if a person has been placed under arrest prior to the request to search, failing to advise a suspect of his/her right to refuse does not automatically render his/her consent involuntary, as long as he/she had been advised of his/her other constitutional rights before the request was made (*U.S. v. Watson* (1976) 423 U.S. 411). If an officer makes the statement that he will obtain a search warrant for the premises if the consent to search is not given, such consent is considered involuntary if there was not sufficient probable cause to obtain a warrant at the time the statement was made. The courts have consistently ruled that such consent is submitting to the authority of the search warrant rather than freely given (*U.S. v. Matlock* (1974) 415 U.S. 164). However, consent searches have been held to be valid if an officer states that he will attempt to get a search warrant if consent is refused (*People v. Montoya* (1981) 114 Cal.App.3d 556). The difference between the two statements is that in the latter the officers are only advising the suspect what they plan to do and are not stating that they have enough probable cause to obtain a search warrant. And it must be remembered that the consent to search is not permanent. It may be revoked at any time and takes effect instantaneously. If this occurs, the police must cease their search immediately and exit the premises if so requested. However, any contraband, instrumentalities of a crime, or other evidence of a crime which were found before the consent was withdrawn are still admissible and may be used as a basis for an arrest. In addition, if the officers developed enough probable cause to obtain a search warrant based on the evidence found before the consent to search was withdrawn, the officers may legally remain on the premises to prevent the destruction of other evidence while a search warrant is being obtained. However, no further search is permitted until the search warrant arrives.

AUTHORITY TO CONSENT

The authority to consent to a search is another issue entirely. Any person who has custody and control of certain premises or items has the authority to consent to a search of the area or item. However, where more than one person has custody over or control over an area or item requested to be searched, then consent to a search of that item or area is permitted only to the extent that the person giving the consent has a right to its access and control. The U.S. Supreme Court held that: "The consent of one who possesses common authority over premises or effects is valid as against the absent, non-consenting person with whom that authority is shared" (*U.S. v. Matlock* (1974) 415 U.S. 164, 170). In other words, if two people share an apartment, one of the roommates has the authority to give valid consent to search only those common areas where he/she has an equal, unrestricted access with the other roommate, such as the kitchen, living room, or bathroom, and those portions of the apartment where he/she has exclusive use, such as his/her own bedroom (*Stoner v. California* (1964) 376 U.S. 483). If the other roommate is present when the request to search is made, and that the roommate objects to the search and refuses to give consent, then the only places that the police may search are those areas over which the consenting party has exclusive control, such as his own bedroom. None of the common areas may be searched as long as one of the persons who has a privacy right in those areas is present and objects, absent a search warrant. It is this same lack of authority that precludes a landlord from giving his consent to search a tenant's premises; nor can a hotel manager, owner, or clerk give valid consent to a search of the room of any guest.

APPARENT AUTHORITY TO CONSENT

Courts will generally uphold a consent search if the consenting party did not have the authority to give consent to search where the officers had reasonable, good faith belief that the consenting party had the authority to consent. This is termed "apparent authority." If there is any question concerning the consenter's authority, officers should ask more questions to determine authority to give consent, making notes on the exact wording of the questions and the responses to them. All questions and responses to them should be exact quotes if possible. This will serve as substantial evidence of apparent authority if this becomes an issue later. If, during this questioning, the officer develops any doubts about the authority of the consenting party, the officer should opt for getting a search warrant to ensure the admissibility of the evidence.

SCOPE OF THE CONSENT

The places that you may search and the items for which you may search are limited by the consent given. When consent is requested, officers need to be specific about what they are searching for and where they want to search for these items. If during this search the searching officers come across other contraband or instrumentalities of a crime in places where they have consent to search, then they may seize these items and use them as evidence pursuant to the plain view doctrine. For example, if the officers request permission to search for stolen handguns and want to search the entire house, and consent is given, almost anywhere in the house handguns can be hidden: drawers, closets, luggage, etc. If, during this search, the searching officers come across a plastic baggie containing a white powdery substance that they suspect to be cocaine, they can legally seize it and test it. If presumptive tests show it to be cocaine, then an arrest for its possession can be made. However, if the officers request permission to search the entire house for stolen shotguns, and consent is given, and a plastic baggie containing a white powdery substance that turns out to be cocaine is found in a small bathroom drawer, it cannot be used as evidence against the residents of the house because it exceeded the scope of the search: the drawer could not conceal a shotgun. However, since cocaine is contraband and the residents of the house are not entitled to possess it, the cocaine can still be seized and later destroyed pursuant to departmental policy. It just cannot be used as criminal evidence against the persons who reside in the house.

CONSENT TO SEARCH GIVEN BY THIRD PARTIES

In some circumstances, the police officer will come across a situation where a third party is the only person present who may be able to give consent to the search because they have been given shared authority, sometimes called common authority. Shared or common authority means that the person has an unrestricted right to use or access the area or item in question. The fact that the person giving the consent does not use or access the area is not the controlling factor. It is their unrestricted right to access and use the item or area that is controlling for authority purposes. This would be different if roommate 1 had access to the office area of a home, but roommate 2 keeps his desk in the office locked. Roommate 1 does not have the authority to give consent to search the desk since he does not have access to the contents of the desk. Roommate 1 can give a valid consent to search the office in general, except for the desk, since roommate 1 has access to the general area of the office as a room. In such a situation, unlocked containers, desks, or cabinets can be searched pursuant to roommate 1's consent. It is reasonable to assume that if roommate 1 has complete access to the room, he would also have access to any unlocked containers in the room. The law enforcement officers are not required to ask roommate 1 about each container that they find and whether or not he has authority to consent to its search if they are not locked. Thus, the police officer must determine whether or not this person has the authority to validly consent to a search of the desired areas. If not, then the police may not search them or any evidence that they find will be inadmissible. For example, a landlord or owner of a building has no authority to consent to a search of his tenant's property, even though he may own the building. The tenant has a reasonable expectation of privacy in those premises, and that privacy expectation cannot be waived by anyone but the tenant. Even if the tenants seem to have abandoned the premises, the police cannot rely upon the landlord's consent to enter those premises until the tenants' lease expires, or the landlord takes possession through due process of law.

Similarly, a maid cannot validly consent to a search of the residence of her employer for she is given authority only to enter the house for cleaning purposes. An attorney or an accountant, who is a confidential agent for his client, may not validly consent to a search of his client's files, even if they are in his exclusive possession, because he does not have the authority to grant such consent. The client retains the privacy interest in those files and it is the client's consent that law enforcement must obtain to search them. Even if the client consents to a search of his files, the attorney may still refuse to give his consent to the search because the files are in his office, and he may claim his privacy interest in that area, or in some of the papers in the client's file himself. Therefore, if documents that law enforcement desires to search are in the possession of an attorney, law enforcement cannot rely on the client's consent to search alone, but must also get the attorney's or accountant's consent. That is why it is usually easier to get a search warrant for these items. But in these particular cases, this often requires the appointment of a "special master" by the court. A special master is a person with specialized training who is appointed to represent the court in a particular action. For example, special masters appointed to supervise the search of an attorney's files pursuant to a search warrant will usually also be attorneys. They understand the attorney–client privilege and the legal ramifications of the search. Usually they will review the files first to determine if they contain evidence of the sort covered by the search warrant, excluding documents that are not covered from the viewing of the law enforcement officers present.

IMPLIED CONSENT TO SEARCH

There also exists a form of consent known as implied consent. This situation occurs when the owner or person in possession of an item or place reports that a crime has been committed and summons help. For example, when the owner of a car reports that his vehicle has been stolen, the owner grants an implied consent for the police to search the vehicle when it is located. This search is limited to the extent necessary for positively identifying it as the vehicle stolen, its safe recovery by the police, and protection of any evidence that may identify the person or persons responsible for stealing the vehicle. If during such search contraband is located, it may be seized under the plain view doctrine, explained below.

CONSENT TO SEARCH FROM A PERSON IN CUSTODY

The situation for a consent to search changes dramatically when a request to search personal belongings, vehicles, or premises has been requested from a person who has been placed under arrest, or is already in custody. This is especially true if the requested search is meant to find incriminating evidence to be used against the defendant. Where a suspect has been placed under arrest and a consent to search is requested by law enforcement, courts have held that the advice of rights is required prior to making such a request. And, the courts have insinuated, although not specifically held, that the defendant be provided a warning that he/she has the right to refuse the consent without any adverse consequences.

In noncustodial situations, reliance on a consent to search does not require the law enforcement officer to advise the person consenting to the search of his/her constitutional rights, nor his/her right to refuse without any jeopardy attaching to that refusal. While these warnings are not essential to obtaining a valid consent to search, they do provide strong support for the inference that the person consenting to the search has done so knowingly and voluntarily. A written waiver containing these warnings and requiring the consenting party's signature in front of witnesses is even more convincing that the suspect acted knowingly, intelligently, and voluntarily; but again, it is not required by law.

Whether a custodial consent to search requires a separate advice of rights and an admonishment that the defendant has the right to refuse to give his consent and force the officers to attempt to obtain a search warrant is still an open question. There has been no definitive ruling by the Supreme Court. Thus, to be certain that your case is not lost on a suppression motion, if the suspect is in custody, it is best to preface any post-arrest request for consent to search with at least a cautionary warning that the defendant has the right to refuse such consent. And, such a request should only be made if the defendant has been read his constitutional rights and has waived them.

Another form that complements the Consent to Search form is the Completed Search form. It states that nothing was taken by law enforcement during the search. This form provides substantial presumptive proof that nothing was removed by police during the search, protecting the officers who conducted the search from a later civil action alleging that something valuable was taken and never returned.

SEARCH OF PLACES WITHOUT A SEARCH WARRANT

The Supreme Court has carved out several exceptions to the Fourth Amendment warrant requirement justifying warrantless intrusions into areas protected by the Fourth Amendment to promote the public safety as well as officer safety. You may not search a crime scene without consent or a search warrant *unless* a court-recognized exception to the warrant requirement exists, termed an exigent circumstance. The following are the major court-recognized exigencies that impact crime scene searches.

1. To Preserve the Life or Health of a Person. For example, a police officer arrives at a burning building before the fire department does. The fire has just started in one portion of the house, permitting entry into another portion. The police officer is permitted to run inside and check for victims. If he then sees narcotics in plain view, he may seize them and use them as a basis for obtaining an arrest warrant.

2. To Prevent the Destruction of Evidence. For example, an undercover police officer purchases narcotics from the defendant. Later, pursuant to an arrest warrant, the defendant is arrested outside of his house. Another person comes to the residence to see what is going on, then turns and runs inside. If the police believe that there are narcotics on the premises and that the other man is going to destroy that evidence, they are justified in entering the house and preventing the destruction of the evidence. Evidence seen in plain view is subject to seizure. The police may remain on the premises until a search warrant is obtained.

3. To Stop a Crime in Progress. The police may enter any structure to prevent the perpetration of a crime they have reason to believe is taking place. Police who receive a report from a reliable citizen that a man is being beaten up in an apartment and who arrive to hear loud noises and groaning coming from the apartment may enter without a search warrant to thwart the battery to the victim.

4. Hot Pursuit. The police may enter any structure to search for the perpetrator of a recent crime when they have reason to believe that he has just entered that structure. The justification for this warrantless entry is to prevent a suspect from escaping while a search warrant is prepared. The amount of time permitted for such entry during hot pursuit depends upon the type of crime that was committed. A longer period of time is generally allowed for the more heinous crimes, while hot pursuit of a less serious offense may require a warrant before entry is permitted after the elapsed time of only 15 or 20 minutes. Other considerations that enter into the courts' decision on how long is reasonable for hot pursuit is the potential danger the perpetrator presents to the public, the area in which the crime took place, and the propensities of the perpetrator if he is known.

5. Protective Sweep. Officers may be lawfully present to execute an arrest warrant, respond to a call for help, secure a crime scene, or to make a proper warrantless arrest. In such cases, the officers are permitted to immediately conduct a protective sweep of the premises for unknown persons who may be hiding on the premises to do harm to the officers, or for victims of a crime or who are in need of medical attention. A protective sweep may be conducted even if the officers have no suspicion that anyone or other victims exist.

THE IN PLAIN VIEW DOCTRINE

Any evidence observed in plain view can be legally seized and used in a criminal prosecution. The law enforcement officer who seized it only has to be able to articulate what facts led him/her to believe that an exigent circumstance existed, justifying their presence. The "Plain View Doctrine" was first approved by the U.S. Supreme Court as an exception to the warrant requirement in the case of *Harris v. U.S.* (1968) 390 U.S. 234, and later ratified in 1971 in the case of *Coolidge v. New Hampshire* (1971) 403 U.S. 433 which established *two limitations* on the seizure of evidence pursuant to the plain view doctrine.

The plain view doctrine alone cannot justify the warrantless seizure of evidence because no amount of probable cause can justify a warrantless search or seizure *absent exigent circumstances*. Then came the case of *Horton v. California* (1990) 496 U.S. 128, in which the U.S. Supreme Court held that the "inadvertence" requirement was not a necessary part of the plain view doctrine. "The Fourth Amendment does not prohibit the warrantless seizure of evidence in plain view even though the discovery of the evidence was not inadvertent." Although inadvertence is a characteristic of most legitimate plain view seizures, it is not a necessary one. The Court continued, "In order for a warrantless seizure of an object in plain view to be valid, two conditions must be satisfied in addition to the essential predicate that the officer did not violate the Fourth Amendment in arriving at the place from which the object could be plainly viewed."

"**First** [emphasis added], the object's incriminating character must be 'immediately apparent' [quoting Coolidge at page 466] . . ., **Second** [emphasis added], the officer must have a lawful right of access to the object itself" (*Horton*, 129–130). This requirement permits a seizure under the plain view doctrine only if the officer is lawfully present within the premises of any area protected by the Fourth Amendment *and* can lawfully access the evidence. For example, police officers may be present on the premises to execute a search warrant for stolen property. If during their search for stolen property they inadvertently discover narcotics in plain view in a place where the stolen property could have been found, they may seize the narcotics and charge those persons in possession of the premises. The key to this type of plain view seizure is that the evidence found in plain view must have been in a place where it is possible that the items named in the search warrant could be located. If the search warrant was issued for stolen 19-inch television sets and the searching officers found narcotics in the drawer of a jewelry chest, then the seizure would be illegal and excluded from court because a 19-inch television set could not be hidden in a jewelry box drawer.

As the plain view doctrine applies to protective sweeps, any evidence discovered in plain view during a protective sweep will be admissible in court providing that it was located in a place where a person might reasonably be hiding. This would eliminate drawers and small cabinets, but not closets or under beds, etc. Similarly, the courts have upheld the discovery of evidence in plain view when officers accompany an arrestee into another room to dress before being taken to jail.

THE OPEN FIELDS DOCTRINE

The words "open fields" do not adequately portray how the courts have interpreted their meaning in this judicially created exception to the warrant requirement. The term open fields means any unoccupied or undeveloped area that is *outside* the curtilage of a home. *Curtilage* is defined as a relatively small, well-defined area immediately adjacent to a residence. The courts have extended the private activities of the home to this area. *In order for an area to qualify under the open fields doctrine, it does not have to be open or a field.* Since there is no expectation of privacy in these areas, the Fourth Amendment has no application to these areas. Hence, entry into any area determined to be an "open field" is accepted as an entry onto public land, and therefore requires no warrant. Open fields are *not* protected by the Fourth Amendment. Therefore, if any person, citizen, or law enforcement officer passing by could view the area unhindered, even if the area is surrounded by "no trespassing" signs, fencing, or trees, that area qualifies as "open field." Entry into open fields, while technically a trespass, would not constitute a search regardless of who does the entering. *The basis of the open fields doctrine* is that certain areas of land are so open to public view that the person who owns the land has given up his right to privacy in these areas and has even implicitly invited the public to view the land. The open fields doctrine was established by the U.S. Supreme Court in the case *Hester v. United States* (1924) 265 U.S. 57. In that case the Supreme Court stated, "The special protection accorded by the Fourth Amendment . . . is not extended to the open fields."

Defining a residence is relatively easy. It is generally a structure designed for human habitation. Immediately adjacent to that residence is usually an area where the occupant can establish a legitimate expectation of privacy, although it is less than that expected within the residence, but more than that expected in an open field. This expectation of privacy is established by putting up a fence, trees, or bushes to surround the yard adjacent to the home, where the occupant can plant a garden, have a swimming pool, or have place for children to play away from the prying eyes of the public. This area is called the curtilage of the home. This area and the activities occurring in this area are subject to the same Fourth Amendment protections as the actual residence. The test to determine what is curtilage for search and seizure purposes considers the proximity of the area to the home; whether it is surrounded by a fence or steps have been taken to place other obstructions to protect it from public view; and the uses of the area (*United States v. Dunn* (1987) 480 U.S. 294). If the area searched is in close proximity to the dwelling and is an area where "normal" family activities occur, there is a *reasonable expectation of privacy* (i.e., "curtilage") and the area is protected.

SEARCHES AND SEIZURES OF EVIDENCE FROM A SUSPECT'S BODY

A suspect may try to hide evidence by swallowing it, or placing it inside a body cavity; the evidence may be stored there naturally for some period of time (e.g., alcohol, drugs), or permanently (e.g., DNA); or the evidence may be stored there unnaturally (e.g., a bullet). In these situations, recovering the evidence constitutes a "search" of, if not also a "seizure from," the suspect's body (*Schmerber v. California* (1966) 384 U.S. 757, 767). And, because such searches may be highly invasive, embarrassing, and sometimes risky, the courts have imposed some special requirements that must be met before officers may conduct a bodily intrusion search, or authorize a medical professional or technician to do so. Some bodily intrusion searches must be authorized by a warrant or court order, while others, such as ones incident to a lawful arrest, do not require a warrant. In either case, however, there must always be probable cause to conduct the search; the need for the search must outweigh its intrusiveness; and police must employ reasonable procedures in conducting the search (*Schmerber v. California* (1966) 384 U.S. 757, 768). The Supreme Court ruled that such mandatory tests, if limited to blood, breath, or urine, while they are "searches" governed by the Fourth Amendment, are "reasonable" if "compelling governmental interests" outweigh privacy concerns.

THE EXCLUSIONARY RULE

As can be seen by reading the California and U.S. Constitutions, neither document contains any language respecting a penalty that could be imposed for its violation, to protect the integrity of its search and seizure provisions from governmental abuse. Similarly, neither document specifically authorizes civil suits as a penalty for violations of their provisions. It is this very precarious situation that prompted the establishment of the *judicially created* exclusionary rule; at first, only a concern for federal officers, but now a constant concern for all law enforcement, the exclusionary rule bars judges and juries from considering evidence that has been seized in violation of a person's constitutional rights. But when the exclusionary rule was established by the U.S. Supreme Court in 1914 in the case of *Weeks v. U.S.* (1914) 232 U.S. 383, the Court held that it only applied to violations of the Fourth Amendment by federal officers, but not state law enforcement officers.

In *Weeks*, the Court stated, "The efforts of the courts and their officials to bring the guilty to punishment, praiseworthy as they are, are not to be aided by the sacrifice of those great principles established by years of endeavor and suffering which have resulted in their embodiment in the fundamental law of the land" (*Weeks v. U.S.* (1914) 232 U.S. 383, 394). The Court was saying that the only effective way to compel respect for the Fourth Amendment, which has no punishment of its own for a failure to comply with its terms, was to remove the incentive for disregarding it. However, the Court was very specific in only applying the exclusionary rule to the conduct of federal officers. State officers were exempt from the exclusionary rule. This situation created the so-called "*silver platter doctrine.*" The silver platter doctrine referred to the practice of federal agents using evidence provided to them by state and local law enforcement officers who violated the individual's constitutional rights in gathering the evidence. The theory advanced by the federal law enforcement agents was that they had no part in the collection of the evidence, and the exclusionary rule as espoused in the *Weeks* case only applied to federal agents, not state officers. Therefore the evidence, while obtained illegally under federal guidelines, was still admissible because no federal action was involved in its collection, and the evidence was handed to the federal agents "on a silver platter." In the case of *Elkins v. U.S.* (1960) 364 U.S. 206, the Supreme Court struck down as unconstitutional the so-called "silver platter doctrine." The case law also indicates that the actions of private individuals may result in the exclusion of the evidence if the evidence was obtained for the purpose of assisting the government in a pending proceeding. This development in the law is beginning to gain popularity to prevent a situation where a police officer has made an arrest, but does not have enough probable cause to secure a search warrant. Instead, he mentions this to a victim of the accused or an informant whose sympathies obviously lie with the law enforcement officer. The victim or the informant then takes it upon himself to obtain the evidence in a way that the law enforcement officer legally could not. An acceptance of this evidence by the courts is tantamount to an indirect request or an indirect sanction of the private activity by the law enforcement agent. As such the action of the law enforcement officer is as poor and illegal as if he had performed the activity himself.

THE EXCLUSIONARY RULE IS EXTENDED TO THE STATES

From 1914 until 1961, the exclusionary rule was not applied to the states as a constitutional requirement. Instead, a few states adopted their own version of the exclusionary rule and applied it to their own state officers. California was one of these states. In 1955, the California Supreme Court decided the case of *People v. Cahan* (1955) 44 Cal.2d 434, making California the first state to voluntarily institute the exclusionary rule as a matter of state law. In that case, the California Supreme Court declared that the exclusionary rule now applied to violations of the California Constitution and laws. The justices supported their decision with the following cogent reasoning, "Thus without fear of criminal punishment or other discipline, law enforcement officers, sworn to support the Constitution of the United States and the Constitution of California, frankly admit their deliberate, flagrant acts in violation of both constitutions and the laws enacted thereunder. It is clearly apparent from their testimony that they casually regard such acts as nothing more than the performance of their ordinary duties for which the city employs and pays them" (*People v. Cahan* (1955) 44 Cal.2d 434, 438).

Thus, California had long been following the terms of the exclusionary rule when the U.S. Supreme Court declared that the exclusionary rule is constitutionally required by the Fourth Amendment, that it must be applied to the states through the Fourteenth Amendment, and that it cannot be abolished by Congress since it is an integral part of the Fourth Amendment. This startling development took place in 1961 in the U.S. Supreme Court case of *Mapp v. Ohio* (1961) 367 U.S. 643. But the real importance of the *Mapp* decision was that it declared that the Fourth Amendment is incorporated by the Fourteenth Amendment's due process clause, thereby requiring that all states exclude evidence obtained by governmental searches and seizures which are unlawful within the meaning of the Fourth Amendment. It is interesting to note that the Court was very specific in stating that the exclusionary rule applied only to governmental intrusions upon one's constitutional rights. This statement permits the inference that the prosecution may use evidence obtained by private parties not acting as agents for the government, even if those private parties obtained the evidence in violation of the Fourth Amendment.

THE FRUIT OF THE POISONOUS TREE

It is obvious that evidence procured by a direct violation of constitutional rights or privileges is subject to the exclusionary rule. But, what about evidence that is discovered as a result of evidence which was obtained in violation of a person's constitutional rights? Should this evidence also be inadmissible pursuant to the exclusionary rule? The U.S. Supreme Court has held in numerous case decisions that if the government makes an illegal search or arrest and uses the knowledge it gains to obtain other evidence, then this new evidence must also be excluded.

Beginning with the case of *Silverthorne Lumber Company v. U.S.* (1920) 251 U.S. 385, the Supreme Court held, "The essence of a provision of forbidding the acquisition of evidence in a certain way is that not merely evidence so acquired shall not be used before the Court but that it shall not be used at all. Of course this does not mean that the facts thus obtained become sacred and inaccessible. If knowledge of them is gained from an independent source they may be proved like any others, but the knowledge gained by the Government's own wrong cannot be used by it in the way proposed." Then in the 1939 case of *Nardone v. U.S.* (1939) 308 U.S. 338, the Supreme Court affirmed the ruling in *Silverthorne Lumber Co.* by holding that courts were to exclude not only that evidence which was directly seized illegally, but also that evidence which is indirectly related to an illegal arrest or search. The Court first applied the term "fruit of the poisonous tree" to refer to evidence that also must be excluded from criminal consideration because it was seized in violation of a person's constitutional rights. The Court did reserve the possibility that certain evidence may have been so attenuated from the original taint as to dissipate the taint and become admissible. This point was expanded in the Supreme Court case of *Wrong Sun v. U.S.* (1963) 371 U.S. 471. In that case, the Supreme Court explained what degree of attenuation would be sufficient to dissipate the taint of illegality and render the evidence admissible. "We do not hold that all evidence is 'fruit of the poisonous tree' simply because it would not have come to light but for the illegal actions of the police. Rather, the more apt question in such a case is 'whether, granting establishment of the primary illegality, the evidence to which instant objection is made has been come at by exploitation of that illegality or instead by means sufficiently distinguishable to be purged of the primary taint'" Maguire, *Evidence of Guilt* (1959) 221) (*Wrong Sun*, 371 U.S. 471, 488).

SEARCH WARRANTS

Definition: A search warrant is a written order, signed by a magistrate after the magistrate has determined that there is probable cause to believe that certain persons or items are located in a specific location, directing law enforcement to search for a person(s), physical item(s), or documentary evidence of a crime in a particular location.

The U.S. Supreme Court has held that searches conducted pursuant to search warrants are by definition reasonable searches under the Fourth Amendment. The Court has also identified certain exceptions to the warrant requirement as being reasonable searches and permissible under the Fourth Amendment, such as searches incident to arrest, consent to search, and a variety of emergency situations. Unless one of these exceptions exists, any search of private property can only be conducted by the government if the government's agents have the authority of a search warrant. Any time a search is conducted pursuant to a search warrant, the search is presumed lawful and the burden shifts to the defendant to prove otherwise.

A separate document, called an affidavit, is *attached to the request for the search warrant*. It is made under oath and provides the basis for the "probable cause" to believe that the specific evidence or person being sought is located at a particular place. An affidavit can be either oral or written, but the search warrant must be written. The search warrant itself should contain descriptions of every place to be searched and items or persons being sought with such specificity that any law enforcement officer who is tasked with executing the search warrant, even if not involved in the case prior to that time, would know with reasonable certainty what or who is being sought and specifically where the search for them is authorized to take place. If the descriptions of these items or persons to be seized, or the place to be searched, do not have enough information to confidently distinguish them from other items, persons, or places similarly situated, then the court may rule the descriptions "overbroad" and invalidate the search warrant, even if it had been signed by a magistrate, because the descriptions did not meet the Fourth Amendment's requirement for "particularity." The basis for this is to prevent "exploratory" searches based upon hunches rather than probable cause to believe that the items exist. This is further enforced by the fact that only those items described in the search warrant may be seized, unless they are in plain view and their criminal evidentiary nature is readily apparent.

If the search warrant is being sought to search a large parcel of land that has several buildings on it, the affidavit should include the address of the land, the parcel identification if possible, the size of the land, a brief description of the buildings on this land, and a photograph of the land and the buildings if at all possible. It should be noted at this point that a search warrant for a private residence authorizes a search of the curtilage of that residence as well. However, if any vehicles are expected to be searched for the evidence being sought, their specific descriptions should be included in the application for the search warrant with probable cause for their search. Then they must also be listed on the search warrant as a particular location to be searched. This should include the vehicle's license number, color, year, make, and model, and include a photograph of the vehicle if that is at all possible.

When a search warrant is requested, it is expected that the search warrant lists any and all items expected to be seized and the location at which they are expected to be seized, along with the probable cause to believe that they will be present. The very fact that a crime scene exists is enough probable cause to justify searching that particular location, but it still needs to be described with particularity as required by the Fourth Amendment. The following is a sample of such a description.

> . . . you are therefore COMMANDED TO SEARCH:
> (1) The premises at 1000 Any Street, Napa, further described as a single-story dwelling with white stucco exterior, red wood trim, and a tile roof; and all rooms, attics, basements, and all other parts therein, the surrounding grounds, and any garages, storage rooms, and outbuildings of any kind located thereon; (2) The vehicle described as a black, 1994 Chrysler New Yorker, four door sedan, bearing California license 555-121, believed to be located in the garage at the above residence.

The next problem is to list the items that you believe will be discovered at the crime scene. Standard items are usually found at any crime scene in relation to any specific crime, like homicide, drug storage and dealing, or rape.

BODILY INTRUSION WARRANTS

A warrant can authorize a bodily intrusion search, but must say so expressly. Thus, a bodily intrusion search would not be covered or included by a warrant that simply authorized the search of the suspect's home, vehicle, and person. Like every warrant, a bodily intrusion search warrant must be supported by facts contained in an affidavit. However, unlike a standard warrant, a bodily intrusion warrant requires more than the usual probable cause to search. This extra showing is known as "probable cause plus."

Probable cause plus means that in addition to demonstrating a fair probability that the search will result in the discovery of evidence of a crime, the affidavit must also show that the need for the evidence outweighs the reasonably foreseeable damage and intrusiveness of the procedure (*Winston v. Lee* (1985) 470 U.S. 753). To demonstrate a strong need for a body search, and to show that the search is neither dangerous nor unduly intrusive, the affidavit should address the following:

1. Probable cause, that is, the likelihood the search will result in the discovery of relevant evidence;
2. The seriousness of the crime;
3. The importance of the evidence, that is, the extent to which it is necessary to establish guilt;
4. The practicality of using other, less intrusive means, if any exist, to establish guilt;
5. The extent to which the search may threaten the suspect's health and safety, or result in psychological harm; And,
6. The extent to which the search may intrude on the suspect's dignity and privacy interests (*Ibid.*, 761–766).

BLOOD TEST WARRANTS

Police commonly seek a warrant to authorize testing of a suspect's blood for alcohol or drugs. Testing for DNA typing is also becoming more common. An affidavit for a blood test warrant will usually be sufficient if it establishes that there is probable cause to believe the test results will constitute evidence of a crime, and that the blood removal will be performed by trained medical personnel and in accordance with accepted medical practices. No more is required because the "evanescent" quality of the evidence automatically provides exigent circumstances, i.e., the level of alcohol or drugs in the blood becomes less simply due to the passage of time. Also, blood testing has become so common it has been determined to be safe, reliable, and relatively nonintrusive (*Schmerber v. California* (1966) 384 U.S. 757, 770–772). Officers may use reasonable force, that is, the amount necessary to overcome a suspect's resistance, to obtain a blood sample from a person suspected of DUI or other offense. If police have a legal right to conduct a bodily intrusion search, either with or without a search warrant or court order, reasonable force may be used to carry out the search. Reasonable force is that degree of force necessary to overcome the suspect's resistance. In determining what degree of force is reasonable, courts will consider the seriousness of the crime; the extent of resistance or use of force by the suspect; the degree of force used by the officers, and whether it threatened the health of the suspect; and bodily integrity.

STOMACH PUMPING/VOMITING WARRANTS

Often suspects, especially drug dealers or users, will hide evidence in their mouths so they can, if necessary, dispose of it by swallowing. If officers have probable cause to believe there is evidence in a suspect's mouth, they may use reasonable force to remove it, on grounds of preventing the destruction of evidence. The use of reasonable force may also be justified on grounds it is necessary for the suspect's safety, if the size of the object was such that there was a very real danger it would become lodged in the suspect's throat if he attempted to swallow it, or if officers reasonably believed the suspect was about to swallow drugs that were not in a container, or drugs in a container that was not secure.

If the suspect swallowed the evidence, such as heroin-filled balloons, it may be possible to recover the evidence simply by waiting for it to pass through the person's digestive tract. On the other hand, if the suspect has swallowed an object that could result in serious injury or death, it may be necessary to recover the object immediately by having a physician pump the suspect's stomach, or by having a physician administer a solution (emetic) to induce vomiting. Because such procedures are so highly intrusive, stomach pumping and forced vomiting are generally permitted only if the suspect voluntary consents, or a treating physician determines independently that the suspect's life is in danger. If the physician pumps the stomach of a suspect upon the urging of a law enforcement officer, even if the suspect's life is in danger, the evidence will be ruled inadmissible in court because it was the product of illegal law enforcement conduct, the physician acting as an agent of law enforcement.

Fingernail scrapings may also be taken from a suspect against his will and without a warrant since the intrusion is so minimal that it is greatly outweighed by the exigency of the evidence being lost.

CHECKLIST FOR SEARCH WARRANTS

1. Be certain all appropriate statutory grounds for issuance have been checked and are identical on both the search warrant and the affidavit.
2. Be certain that the affiant's name(s) appears on both the affidavit and the search warrant exactly the same.
3. Be certain that all places to be searched and things to be seized are described with sufficient particularity and are identically described in both the search warrant and the affidavit.
4. Be certain that the "Statement of Probable Cause" that supports the issuance of the search warrant contains no statements that are conclusive in nature.
5. Be certain that all addresses and names are correct.
6. Be certain when using preprinted forms that all blanks are properly filled in and all inapplicable words are lined out.
7. Make certain that the time and date the warrant is signed by the magistrate is correct and that the magistrate has signed the search warrant in the correct place.
8. If any errors are discovered *prior* to serving the search warrant, have them corrected before the warrant is served.
9. If errors are discovered *after* the search warrant is served, bring this to the attention of the district attorney and solicit his/her advice. This will not necessarily invalidate the search warrant, but bringing it to the attention of the district attorney may preclude further problems.
10. Attempt to have the return to the search warrant filed with the court within 10 days after the date the search warrant was issued.

THE "BRADY" MATERIAL REQUIREMENT
BRADY v. MARYLAND (1963) 373 U.S. 83

In 1963, the U.S. Supreme Court ruled that a prosecutor has a duty to disclose evidence discovered during a criminal investigation against him/her to the criminal defendant that impacts upon issues of their culpability and/or the severity of the penalty that is to be assessed against them for their conduct. This relates to criminal prosecutions only. The favorable information has to be material to the crime and not the defendant's character, etc. The bottom line for this is that any prosecutor in the land has a duty to disclose evidence to a criminal defendant that impacts the defendant's culpability and/or penalty for the offense. Evidence favorable to the defendant that is withheld by the prosecution violates the defendant's Fourteenth Amendment rights, provided that the evidence is relevant either to the defendant's guilt or the penalty for the offense, regardless of the good or bad faith on the part of the prosecution. Even if the prosecutor withholds evidence that could be exculpatory inadvertently, this can justify the overturning of a defendant's conviction by an appellate court. Thus, the term "Brady Discovery" evolved to mean information that must be turned over to the defense prior to trial simply because it is favorable to the defendant and material either to the defendant's guilt or severity of punishment. Sometimes this information is not what most persons would associate with "exculpatory evidence." For example, any evidence that the investigating officer(s) was untruthful in any proceeding where he/she was administered an oath or made an affirmation under penalty of perjury would have to be turned over to the defense.

The U.S. Supreme Court ruled in the case of *United States v. Agurs* (1976) 427 U.S. 97 that the failure of the defense to request favorable evidence did not relieve the government of its duty to disclose such evidence pursuant to *Brady v. Maryland*. In 1985 the Supreme Court adjusted its position and held that exculpatory evidence withheld by the government must first be considered "material" (and therefore relevant) in order to violate the Brady decision. The Court further held that evidence is "material" only if there was a reasonable possibility that the result of the proceeding would have been different if that evidence had been provided to the defense (*United States v. Bagley* (1985) 473 U.S. 667).

Then in 1995 the Supreme Court decided the case of *Kyles v. Whitley* (1995) 514 U.S. 419, further refining the definition of "material exculpatory evidence." In that case the Court held that *all favorable evidence is material*, and that constitutional error results when the government fails to disclose it to the defense when there is a reasonable possibility that had the evidence been disclosed the results of the proceeding would have been different. The Court went on to explain that the prosecution's disclosure obligation is determined by the cumulative effect of all of the undisclosed evidence favorable to the defense, without having to evaluate the evidence item by item. Such evaluation is the responsibility of the prosecutor who is required to assess the net effect of all such evidence and to make disclosure of favorable evidence if there is a "reasonable probability" that the results of the proceedings would possibly be affected by its disclosure. Moreover, the Court held that this responsibility remains with the prosecution regardless of any failure of law enforcement to bring the evidence favorable to the defendant to the prosecutor's attention. Thus, the law requires that prosecutors have a duty to proactively seek out *Brady* material that might exist. This would include anything discovered at the crime scene, or any reasonable interpretation of the evidence found at the crime scene.

Source: Beckler, Bruce, JD. *Personal Communication 4/7/2003*, with minor edits by this author.

APPENDIX 1–B

Consent to Search and Completed Search Forms

CONSENT TO SEARCH FORM

DATE: _____ TIME: _____

LOCATION: _____

I, _____ having been informed of my constitutional right not to consent to a search of the premises hereinafter mentioned without a search warrant being produced, do hereby authorize officers of the City/County/State of

_____, to conduct a complete and unlimited search of my premises located at:

_____

These officers are authorized by me, the lawful occupant, to take from these premises any letters, documents, materials, physical items, or any other property which they may desire and which may be used against me as criminal evidence.

I give this written permission to officers of the above named department voluntarily and without any threats, inducements, or promises of any kind.

Signed,

_____
SIGNATURE

_____
PRINT NAME

WITNESSED:

_____
SIGNATURE

_____
PRINT NAME

COMPLETED SEARCH FORM

DATE: _____

TIME: _____

LOCATION _____

_____

I hereby state that on the above date and at the above location police officers/sheriff's deputies/State investigators of

_____ conducted a

search of my premises, specifically located at:

_____

I certify that nothing was removed from my custody by said police officers/sheriff's deputies/State investigators representing

Signed,

_____
SIGNATURE

_____
PRINT NAME

WITNESSED:

_____
SIGNATURE

_____
PRINT NAME

2 | CRIME SCENE SEARCH PRINCIPLES

"It is of the first importance," he cried, "not to allow your judgement to be biased by personal qualities."

"Sherlock Holmes," in The Sign of Four.
Sir Arthur Conan Doyle.

Key words: Safety first responder, hypothesis, pathway, perimeter, initial survey, fragile evidence, scene data, notes, photographs, layout sketches, detailed sketches, blowup sketches, separate areas, strip method, grid (double strip) method, zone method, spiral method, debriefing.

INTRODUCTION

The quote in the beginning of the chapter by the fictional character Sherlock Holmes embodies a central attribute of the integrity of the crime scene investigator: the lack of bias in the investigator's judgment. The lack of bias is also a crucial aspect of critical thinking, which is essential to the task of crime scene investigation.

Those factors influencing the quality of a crime scene search include the department's general orders defining who has the authority and responsibility to direct a crime scene search. In addition, the department needs to ensure that the planning and organization for crime scene equipment, personnel, and all training needs is accomplished in order to provide the framework for adequate and appropriate response by crime scene units to all crime scenes.

At the crime scene, it is the responsibility of the first responder(s) to ascertain first any medical needs of any subject(s) and to arrange for a medical response team(s) to care for that subject(s). Concurrently, the first responder(s) must ensure the safety of the personnel responding to the scene. This responsibility extends to the individual who assumes authority for the search, and remains a priority throughout the search.

Once the safety needs at the scene have been addressed, the crime scene search must be conducted in an orderly and systematic manner, in order to optimize the efficiency and effectiveness of the search. In the sections to follow, the systematic approach to processing a crime scene is presented in the approximate order that each task is accomplished at the scene. These tasks include (but certainly not limited to) appropriate field notes, suitable photography and sketches of the scene, and continual communication between members of the response team and any specialized personnel summoned to the scene by the team leader.

DEPARTMENT ORDERS REGARDING CRIME SCENES

One of the most important factors determining the quality of crime scene investigations is the existence of departmental policies that define the conduct of crime scene investigations.[1] Central to these policies is the delineation of authority and responsibility at the crime scene.

Authority

It is essential that each law enforcement department have a clear and comprehensive policy with regard to the individual or rank assigned the authority for conducting a crime scene investigation. Without the proper authority, the crime scene investigator may not be able to conduct the crime scene search in the systematic manner required for a superior investigation. The policy should delineate the manner in which this authority is respected by ranking officers, as well as other officers who may have ancillary duties at the scene. In the event that it is necessary for a ranking officer to assess the crime scene, the ranking officer should be accompanied by the individual charged with authority for the crime scene, making certain that the pathway established by the crime scene investigator is used for any such assessment. As with all other individuals who enter the crime scene, the ranking officer should be entered into the crime scene entry log.

Responsibility

The investigator charged with the responsibility for conducting the crime scene investigation *must have the necessary authority to carry out that responsibility*. For example, if the scene has several sites requiring additional personnel and equipment, the investigator must have the authority to assign the additional sites to other personnel in order to accomplish the processing of those sites. If this authority is not delegated in concert with the responsibility for processing the crime scene, it is likely that the scene cannot be processed without compromising the quality of the work effort. It is axiomatic in management science that necessary authority must be delegated in conjunction with each responsibility assigned.

FIRST RESPONDERS AT THE SCENE

Safety

The **safety** and physical well-being of officers and other individuals, in and around the crime scene, are the first responder(s) first priority.[2] The first responder(s) should scan the area for sights, sounds, and smells that may present danger to personnel (e.g., hazardous materials such as gasoline, natural gas). If the scene involves a clandestine drug laboratory, biological weapons, or radiological or chemical threats, the appropriate agency should be contacted prior to entering the scene. The first responder should approach the scene in a manner designed to reduce risk of harm to first responder while maximizing the safety of victims, witnesses, and others in the area. The first responder should survey the scene for dangerous persons and should control the situation, notify supervisory person-nel, and call for backup when needed.[3]

Emergency care

After controlling any dangerous situations or persons, the first responder(s)' next respon-sibility is to ensure that medical attention is provided to injured persons while minimizing contamination to the scene. Initial responding officer should take the following actions:[4]

- Assess the victim(s) for signs of life and medical needs and provide immediate medical attention.
- Call for medical personnel.
- Guide medical personnel to the victim to minimize contamination/alteration of the crime scene.
- Point out potential physical evidence to medical personnel, instruct them to minimize contact with such evidence (e.g., ensure that medical personnel preserve all clothing and personal effects without cutting through bullet holes, knife cuts), and document movement of persons or items by medical personnel.
- Instruct medical personnel not to "clean up" the scene and to avoid removal or alteration of items originating from the scene.
- If medical personnel arrived first, obtain the names, unit, and telephone number of attending personnel, and the name and location of the medical facility where the victim is to be taken.
- If there is a chance that the victim may die, attempt to obtain a "dying declaration."
- Document any statements/comments made by victims, suspects, or witnesses at the scene.

Approaching the scene

The actions taken by the **first responder(s)** at the scene may have a profound impact on the quality of the crime scene investigation. The first responder(s) should promptly but cautiously approach and enter the scene, remaining observant of any persons, vehicles, events, potential evidence, and environmental conditions.[5] After taking any emergency actions necessary, such as securing medical attention for any injured parties or the arrest or detention of any suspect(s), the first responder(s) should secure the scene as soon as feasible. The limits of the scene should be determined and a perimeter established with crime scene control tape. Once the perimeter is secured, it must remain secured until completion of the crime scene search and documentation. A permanent record of all individuals present at the scene and those who enter the scene should be started and maintained until completion of the crime scene search (see Appendix 2-A for sample form). The crime scene log is important to establish the integrity of the scene and to provide follow-up investigators with the names of those individuals who may be respon-sible for certain items at the scene, such as latent fingerprints or footwear impressions. The log should be signed or initialed by each person who enters the scene.

It is important that any suspects be kept out of the scene in order to avoid contam-ination of the scene by any transfer evidence from the suspect, such as latent fingerprints, footwear impressions, hairs and fibers, and so forth, which may be used to link the suspect to the scene. If any suspect is allowed into the scene, any evidence linking the suspect to the scene then has an "innocent placement" explanation by the suspect.

Once the scene is secured, the first responder should tour the crime scene, making notes as to the conditions of the scene. Particular attention should be made of any suspected points of entry or exit by the suspect, conditions of doorways and windows, and the presence of any evidence that needs to be brought to the attention of the investigators. An attempt should be made to determine the circumstances of the crime, keeping in mind that this attempt is a *working theory* (**hypothesis**) only, which can be revised as new facts come to light. The first responder officer needs to establish a **pathway** for those individuals entering and leaving the scene, such as emergency medical personnel, other officers, detectives, and the crime scene investigators. The pathway will help minimize the possibility of evidence destruction and will also establish an orderly crime scene search. The pathway should be documented in the officer's notes and sketches in order to provide a permanent record for follow-up investigators. The officer should continue to keep notes as to the progress of the investigation until relieved by other personnel in order to minimize any loss of details.

The first responder should be prepared to answer the following questions when the investigators arrive: (1) What happened? (2) What physical area does the crime scene cover? (3) Who was involved? (4) What time did the incident take place? (5) Who has entered the scene? (6) What items in the scene have been disturbed? (7) If anything has been removed, where is it now and who has custody? (8) If the victim has been removed, where is the victim? Anticipating these questions will help the investigators in their task of investigating the incident.

The first responder should assume that all actions taken at the scene prior to the arrival of the investigative team will need to be explained in court. For this reason, the documentation of the officer's actions is very important to the outcome of the investigation. Most investigations begin at the crime scene, and the initial actions taken may have a profound effect on the case. There is no substitute for precise documentation, with adequate notes of the crime scene actions; diagrams; and crime scene data forms completed accurately and thoroughly.

Actions to be taken by the first responder

DETERMINE THE NEED FOR LIFESAVING PROCEDURES AND EMERGENCY PERSONNEL

The first priority at any crime scene is the treatment of any injured party and the summoning of emergency medical personnel. It is important to keep in mind the potential loss of evidence through the actions of medical personnel at the scene. Whenever feasible, the first responders should establish an indirect *pathway* for the medical personnel to approach the victim needing emergency treatment and transport to a medical facility. The few moments taken to use this indirect route to reach the victim and remove him/her to the ambulance may save valuable evidence without any danger to the treatment of the victim.

The pathway established for the medical personnel should also be used by the first responders and the follow-up investigators for the initial surveys of the scene. This procedure will avoid any further damage to the evidence present at the scene. It is particularly helpful to avoid common pathways for travel inside a residence or to avoid the

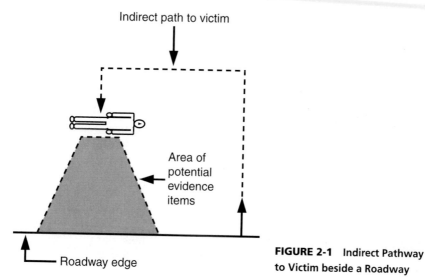

Indirect path to victim

Area of
potential
evidence
items

Roadway edge

**FIGURE 2-1 Indirect Pathway
to Victim beside a Roadway**

direct route from the roadway to the site of the victim in an outdoor setting, as these pathways are the usual routes taken by the perpetrator of the crime (see Figure 2-1).

REMOVE AND DETAIN WITNESSES AND SUSPECTS FROM THE SCENE

Witnesses and potential suspects should be removed from the scene as soon as practical. In no case should a potential suspect be admitted to the crime scene, as this action allows for cross-contamination between the scene and the suspect with respect to impression and trace evidence, thus providing an "innocent" explanation for the presence of these types of evidence at the scene. Appropriate data should be obtained from each witness for follow-up contacts by investigators assigned to the case.

SECURE THE SCENE AND ESTABLISH THE CRIME SCENE PERIMETER

Once the emergency actions have been taken and the witnesses and suspect(s) have been identified and removed, the scene should be secured in order to preserve the evidence present. It is necessary to determine the limits of the crime scene and to establish the **perimeter** with crime scene tape. For indoor crime scenes, the residence or building will ordinarily define the scene limits, but in some cases the property on which the structure is located is also part of the crime scene. In outdoor crime scenes, the first responder(s) need to exercise good judgment as to the extent of the scene, keeping in mind it is better to err on the side of caution and to provide a safety margin in establishing the secure perimeter of the scene. The scene should be secured with crime scene tape or other markers. *It is important to ensure that only those personnel with legitimate business at the crime scene be allowed inside the perimeter established.*

COMPILE SCENE DATA

As soon as the scene is secured, the first responder should begin compiling the necessary data with regard to response to the scene and initiate the crime scene log that lists the entry of all individuals into the crime scene, including those present upon arrival. Most departments will have forms for these tasks. See the list of pertinent data under the heading for the crime scene investigators.

MAKE AN INITIAL SURVEY OF THE CRIME SCENE

The **initial survey** of the scene should be done in a *systematic* manner, taking notes of observations as to possible evidence present, any evidence that has been removed, the person responsible for this evidence, and observations regarding the pertinent data listed in a later section. It is imperative that nothing be disturbed at the scene until the scene has been photographed and sketched in the condition found. Do not attempt to replace evidence that has been moved, disturbed, or collected prior to the crime scene documentation, but rather take notes as to how and why the evidence has been disturbed.

The initial survey of the scene should be issue-oriented and include an assessment of the potential evidence present at the scene based on the working theory for the Ws of any investigation: What happened? Who did it? Why? Where did the events take place? What was the sequence of events? Where were the points of entry and exit? These questions and the working theory should help to provide a basis for determining the presence of potential evidence. It is important to keep an open mind with regard to the working theory, making adjustments as new facts come to light.

TAKE STEPS TO PRESERVE ANY FRAGILE EVIDENCE AT THE SCENE

Fragile evidence includes that evidence that may be destroyed by inclement weather. Items such as footwear impressions that may be exposed to rain should be covered with a cardboard box or other protective covering to avoid loss of the evidence.

Other types of fragile evidence include trace evidence such as hairs and fibers which may be blown away by wind, small objects which may not be seen in time to avoid being stepped on, and items which hinder pathways and thus may be knocked out of place.

CRIME SCENE INVESTIGATOR

The role of the crime scene investigator

The principal function of the crime scene investigator(s) is to *document the scene* with adequate and appropriate methods, to convey the scene findings to other members of the investigative team via oral and written reports, and to testify as to the findings at the scene in the courtroom. These methods include, but are not limited to, (1) taking *ongoing notes* of all observations, (2) preparation of essential *sketches*, (3) *photographing* the scene location and evidence items using appropriate photographic equipment, (4) *recovering all evidence items* using proper collection and packaging methods for each type of evidence, and (5) *preparation of comprehensive reports* concerning all actions taken at the scene. The diligence shown by the crime scene investigator in the discharge of these duties will be of considerable benefit to the management of the overall investigation. The crime scene investigator should keep in mind that all the actions taken at the scene will need to be reported in courtroom testimony, so that the quality of the scene investigation can be communicated effectively to the court. Finally, the crime scene investigator, depending on the investigator's education, training, and mentored experience (see Chapter 15), may be called upon to provide a *reconstruction* of the events of the incident in reports and in court testimony.

Choice of crime scene investigator

The crime scene investigator(s) may be the patrol officer assigned to the detail, a crime scene investigator from the crime scene unit, or the detective assigned to the case. The choice as to the personnel assigned to process the crime scene is usually based on the type of crime committed, department guidelines for the level of response for these crimes, the size of the agency, and the size of the crime scene to be processed. In major crimes, the crime scene(s) will usually be processed by a team of investigators. Regardless of the number or classification of the crime scene personnel, it is essential that the crime scene be processed in an orderly, systematic manner. It is important to have clearly established departmental orders as to who is in charge of the crime scene, what the responsibilities are of the various personnel involved, what procedures are to be implemented, and, of most importance, who is permitted access to the scene.

Record pertinent data immediately

Most departments will have departmental forms for recording **scene data** that must be filled out at the crime scene detailing the information listed in the following sections. The advantages of having forms for the information needed include not having to write in all the necessary headings, having a standardized format for data retrieval, having a convenient memory assist for needed details, and having a format for the orderly accumulation of crime scene information.

TIME CALLED TO SCENE/BY WHOM
The time of the call to the scene should be accurate, since alibis are based on time and place. Although most departments will have a log of call-outs, it is a good practice to document the time in your notes. The individual making the call should also be included for thoroughness in the **notes**.

TIME ARRIVED AT SCENE
It is important to have an accurate time for arrival at the scene for first responders and the crime scene investigative team members as the first step in the accurate documentation of the scene.

ACTIONS TAKEN TO SECURE THE CRIME SCENE
The first responders to the scene should have secured the scene prior to your arrival. If this procedure has not been done, then the scene should be secured immediately and the perimeter delineated with crime scene tape. If the entire crime scene is inside a dwelling, the scene can be secured by keeping the door closed and having an officer maintain security at the door. If the extent of the crime scene at the dwelling is not known, the entire plot for the dwelling should be secured with crime scene tape.

PERSONS AT SCENE
This record should be in addition to the log started by the first responders, so that a complete record of all individuals entering the crime scene is established. The first responders will often need to respond to another detail before the crime scene processing is completed, and the crime scene investigator's entry log will supplement the log started by the first responders, thus providing a complete record from start to finish at the crime scene.

ALL CASE FILE DATA FOR ALL DEPARTMENTS INVOLVED

Record the department(s) involved, the case file number(s), and the contact person from each department involved in this case. It is important to have the telephone numbers and usual working hours for each individual for follow-up investigations.

NAMES OF ALL VICTIMS AND SUSPECTS KNOWN AT THE TIME

Enter the names of the victim(s) and suspect(s) in the department crime scene forms or your notes, if this information is known at the time. If not, make a notation that the names are not known at the time of response to the scene.

CONTACT THE FIRST RESPONDER AT THE SCENE

Obtain overview of circumstances known and observations made by the responding officer

The first responders to the scene will have information about the conditions at the scene prior to any alterations and other information about the incident known at that time.

Determine areas that can be crossed without destroying potential evidence

If a pathway for entering and surveying the scene has not been established, *it should be established at this point.* Obtain information from the first responder as to what areas have been entered and by whom, so that *elimination samples* can be obtained from these individuals should the need arise.

Tour the scene with the first responder

Tour the scene with the first responder, making sure to follow any established pathway. Record all pertinent observations during the tour with the first responder, comparing notes with the officer as to the observations made with regard to the types of physical evidence that may be present. Any alterations to the condition of the scene prior to the arrival of the investigating team should be noted. Note especially any evidence that has been collected by the first responders at the scene. Make notations as to which items were collected and by whom, whether or not the chain of custody was initiated, and who will be responsible for booking the evidence into the evidence room.

ESTABLISH A COMMAND CENTER FOR THE OPERATION

The command center may be as simple as a staging area set aside at the scene for the placement of the equipment necessary to process the scene in the case of a small scene, or it may be a complex command post in the case of a large and complex scene. For most crime scenes, up to and including homicide scenes, the crime scene equipment should include a complete crime scene kit, containing at a minimum the items enumerated in Appendix 2-B, Section C. For complex crime scenes, such as a homicide scene involving multiple victims, the command center may require a completely equipped crime scene van, either one designed and equipped by departmental personnel, or one of the commercially available crime scene vans.

ESTABLISH A PLAN FOR PROCESSING THE SCENE

Confer with all individuals assisting in the search. Advise everyone that all evidence is to be collected only by the team members responsible for evidence collection. Those individuals assisting in the search should not move or disturb any evidence item before it has been documented with notes, sketches, and photographs, and processed for latent fingerprints if applicable. Establish the plan for processing the scene, making sure that each team member is certain of her/his role in the search and the way that the search is to proceed. This step is crucial for those crimes that have a number of areas to be covered by separate teams or individuals.

The crime scene processing plan should also include consideration of the safety of the search team. For those scenes where hazardous materials are encountered, individuals with the proper training, experience, and equipment should be in charge of processing that scene. Take note of the safety precautions at the end of the chapters on latent fingerprints (Chapter 5) and homicide scenes (Chapter 14). *Clandestine laboratory crime scenes present exceptional hazards and should be processed only by specialized personnel with hazardous material training and equipment.*

CASE EXAMPLE

The case of *People v. Stephen Hammack* involved three homicide victims, two males found at one location (the primary crime scene), and one female in the Salinas River, approximately twenty to thirty miles from the primary scene. Additional crime scenes included the suspect's van, the suspect's residence, the autopsies of each victim, and a second autopsy for the female victim. A large amount of evidence was recovered by a number of investigators at each of the scenes, which included blood and tissue stains, clothing from the victims, and a portion of the female victim's skull found in the suspect's van. Many items of evidence, including the portion of the female victim's skull, were found in the suspect's van, packaged in large trash bags.

At the outset of the investigation, an organizational meeting was held with members of each of the agencies participating in the investigation. The complexity of the number of scenes, the number of victims, the number of investigating agencies, and the large volume of physical evidence was addressed by the agencies present. Each scene was given an identifying number, each investigator was given an identifying letter, and each item of evidence was given an identifier that included the identification letter of the investigator who recovered the item, and an item number for each item (e.g., "B-15" for item 15 collected by investigator "B"). A rigorous system was set up to keep a complete record for the chain of possession for each item. At trial, the court, the prosecuting and defense attorneys, and each investigator thus had a complete record of the chain of possession for each item, which began with identifying the individual who collected the item, the scene from where the item was collected, and the custody of each item from scene to court.

This initial organizational meeting prevented any confusion between evidence items and any question with regard to its integrity. Thus, the introduction of each item into evidence was accomplished smoothly and effectively. Had the agencies involved in the investigation not organized the evidence handling system at the outset, the introduction of the evidence would have presented a cumbersome task for the prosecution.

The case of *People v. Stephen Hammack* also acts as a sterling example of the role serendipity sometimes plays in a criminal investigation. One of the witnesses at the primary crime scene (the location of the bodies of the two male victims) called the investigator who had interviewed her shortly after the homicide. She asked the investigator if he recalled her description of a van she had seen at the scene. When the investigator replied in the affirmative, she replied, "Well, I'm parked right behind it now," prompting the investigator to rush to the area where she was parked. The investigator noticed material with the appearance of blood on the back bumper of the van. The investigator then contacted the DOJ crime lab managed by the author. The author responded to the scene and tested the blood-like stains on the bumper and received a positive test for the presence of blood. Upon receiving a search warrant to search the suspect's van, numerous items bearing bloodstains were discovered in the van, including a portion of the female victim's skull. The suspect was then arrested for the homicides, and additional search warrants were obtained that led to the seizure of more evidence that helped convict the suspect of homicide. Thanks to this witness, a potential delay in the identification of Hammack was avoided, and evidence critical to his prosecution was seized before he was able to destroy it. ■

DATA TO BE COMPILED BEFORE COLLECTION PROCESS

The following data may be entered on the appropriate form or, if no departmental forms exist, the data should be entered in the notes of the crime scene investigator.

Presence of unusual odors

The presence of unusual odors may be short-lived. The odor of accelerants should be noted in the case of suspected arson.

Presence and condition of bloodstains

The condition of any bloodstains should be noted, especially if the bloodstains constitute "spatter" patterns. Note also large pools of blood and the signs of blood-clotting.

Signs of struggle

Note any furniture out of place or knocked over. Do not move the displaced items until the scene has been thoroughly documented. Note any smearing of bloodstains that may indicate a struggle after wounds have been inflicted.

Points of entry and exit

The points of entry and/or exit may have evidence that will help identify the perpetrator, including latent fingerprints, trace evidence such as hairs and fibers, footwear impressions, and toolmarks in the case of forced entry.

Condition of windows and doors

Occasionally, it is necessary to open or close doors and windows during the scene investigation. It is important to note the condition of the doors and windows, so that any changes effected at the scene are documented.

Condition of trash containers

The layer sequence of trash containers may help in reconstructing time sequences of events at the scene. The layer sequence and any dated materials should be noted.

Condition and contents of ashtrays

Note the presence and brand(s) of cigarettes in ashtrays. Remember that DNA typing may need to be attempted on the cigarette butts in the ashtrays, so that handling should be done with gloved hands or forceps.

Evidence of drinking and/or drug use

Note the presence of liquor bottles and glassware and the approximate contents of each. The bottles and glassware offer excellent surfaces for latent prints and should be handled accordingly. Drug outfits may also be processed for latent impressions, with precautions taken for infectious agents.

Evidence disturbed or collected prior to arrival

Any evidence disturbed or collected prior to the arrival of the crime scene investigator should be noted. Determine who collected the evidence and that the chain of possession has been documented.

Condition of light switches

In your notes, document the condition of the light switches. It may be necessary to turn the switches on or off during photography, especially for photographs during forensic light examinations or photographs of luminol-treated bloodstains.

CRIME SCENE SEARCH: BE SYSTEMATIC!

A crime scene search is defined as a systematic, methodical search for any physical evidence at a crime scene. A systematic approach to the documentation of the scene and the collection of the physical evidence present is essential in order to ensure that all necessary steps have been taken which will realize the potential of the physical evidence and that the evidence is admissible in a court of law. A systematic approach to crime scene processing also has the advantage of providing the most efficient and effective use of the investigative team's time and resources, while at the same time providing the optimum benefit of the physical evidence present at the scene. The sequence of actions that follows is recommended at the scene.

Adequate notes of actions taken at the scene

Adequate notes should be taken during the entire crime scene search to reflect all actions taken at the scene, and the notes should include notations regarding (a) listing of photographs taken, (b) listing of evidence collected, (c) any sketches prepared, and (d) observations made during the processing of the scene. The notes must be taken concurrent with the ongoing investigation.

Photography of the scene

- Layout (overview) photographs to illustrate the condition of the scene.

    Photographs should be taken to document the condition of the scene as found, before processing and collection of evidence begins. See Chapter 3 for an in-depth discussion of crime scene photography.
- Photographs from the *point of view of all witnesses.*

    Photographs from the point of view of eyewitnesses should be taken in order to document whether or not the witness or witnesses were in a position to see the area and objects recorded in the witness statements. Record both the vertical and the horizontal position of the camera in the notes and the sketches. These photographs will assist the investigators in determining the accuracy of witness statements.
- *Midrange* photographs.

    Midrange photographs should be taken to illustrate spatial relationships of all evidence items and their relationship to the overall scene.
- Photographs of the *evidence items.*

    Specific photographs of each evidence item should be taken to illustrate the location and the condition of all items of evidence (include item number markers and/or rulers as needed). The position and condition of evidence items may be important in reconstructing the crime scene. Photographs of each evidence item, combined with adequate notes and sketches, will allow for accurate re-creation of the scene for reconstruction efforts. The use of measurement rulers is essential for those items for which spatial characteristics are important in a reconstruction (e.g., bloodstain patterns and bullet impacts).

Sketches of the scene

- **Layout sketches**.

  The layout sketches illustrate the relationship of the various crime scene areas to each other and assist in orienting the reader of reports to the nature of the crime scene and its component parts. The layout sketches are not necessarily measured, as the purpose of these sketches is to provide a visual framework for the detailed, measured sketches and the photographs taken. See Chapter 4 for a detailed explanation of crime scene sketches.

- **Detailed sketches** of pertinent areas.

  Detailed sketches with measurements of pertinent areas should be prepared, showing all measurements for the area and the exact location of evidence items. Include large items such as furniture to show spatial relationships.

- **Large-scale ("blowup") sketches** (see Figure 4-4 in Chapter 4).

  Prepare large-scale sketches of those areas needing greater detail:

  - *Bloodstain patterns.*

    Prepare sketches of each area having bloodstain patterns. Complement the sketches with photographs showing each area sketched. It is helpful to use the "grid," "corner label," or "perimeter scale" method (see the section titled "Bloodstain Pattern Documentation" in Chapter 15) for these sketches.

  - *Bullet entry and exit holes.*

    Measure carefully the location of each bullet hole and describe its appearance. Photograph each hole (both entry and exit sites) with a measurement scale next to the hole (see Chapter 15 for documentation of bullet trajectories).

  - *Location and orientation of impression evidence.*

    Sketch the location of footwear impressions and toolmark impressions, showing their orientation and directional characteristics.

  - *Areas having a large number of small evidence items.*

    Prepare a large-scale sketch of each area having a large number of small evidence items, such as expended casings. It is helpful to use the secondary reference points method (see Figure 4-12, Chapter 4) for the measurements.

Crime scene search

- Use systematic search methods.
  - *Strip method* for outdoor scenes (see Figure 2-2).
  - *Grid (double strip) method* for outdoor scenes (see Figure 2-3).
  - *Zone method* for indoor or outdoor scenes (see Figure 2-4).
  - *Spiral method* for large objects in large outdoor scenes (see Figure 2-5).

- *Recording of evidence.*
  - Make sure that each item is photographed and located on the sketch(s) before collection. It is strongly recommended that at least two individuals locate and mark each item, so that either can testify as to the documentation and collection of the evidence in a court proceeding in the event that one of the individuals is unavailable for testimony.

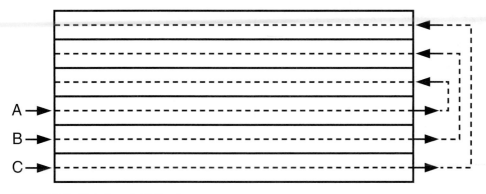

FIGURE 2-2   Strip Search Method

- Process for fingerprints at the time the item is collected whenever possible. (CAUTION! Make certain that fingerprint processing does not destroy trace evidence.) If latent print processing of the item is not done at the scene, package carefully and label "FOR TRACE EVIDENCE/LATENT FINGERPRINT PROCESSING" in large letters.
- Mark and record each item on the evidence list at the time of its collection. This procedure will avoid any mix-up of evidence item numbering. Check item numbering to ensure that the item numbers correspond to the numbering system used on the sketches.
- Package each item of evidence securely, so that any trace evidence present is not disturbed, lost, or contaminated. Make sure that evidence items containing biological stains are dried thoroughly before packaging in paper bags or envelopes (see Chapter 7 for drying and packaging instructions).

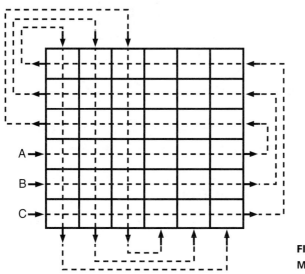

FIGURE 2-3   Grid Search Method

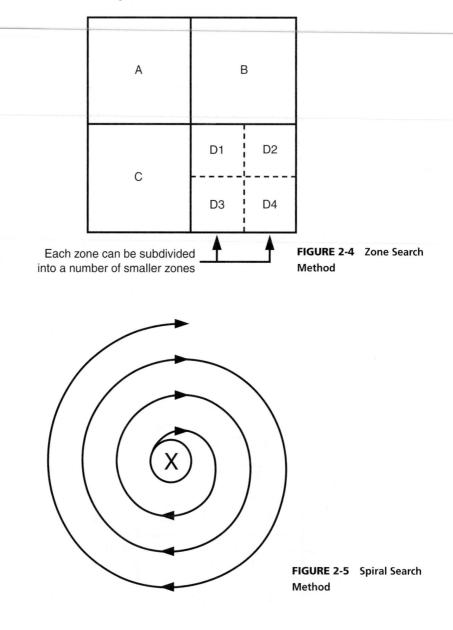

Each zone can be subdivided
into a number of smaller zones

FIGURE 2-4   Zone Search Method

FIGURE 2-5   Spiral Search Method

SEPARATE AREAS/COLLECTORS

Separate areas and/or collectors can be coded with letters or Roman numerals to avoid confusion when the inventory list is completed. This procedure will be exceptionally helpful in large-scale areas or investigations, where there are a number of scenes and individuals involved in the search and collection of physical evidence. The coding system should be developed during the planning of the search, before the actual search and collection begins.

EXAMPLE

A large-scale search involving three separate areas and three search teams can be coded as Areas A, B, and C. Each area should have one individual assigned as the evidence collection officer for each area. Each evidence item would then be coded with the letter prefix corresponding to the particular area (Item A-1, A-2, A-3; B-1, B-2; C-1, C-2; etc.). For very-large-scale searches (multiple burial sites in a serial murder case, for example), it may be necessary to subdivide further the evidence-collection responsibilities. In this case, coding can be done by following an outline form, designating the larger areas with Roman numerals and designating the subsections of each larger area with capital letters. Each evidence item collected would then have a Roman numeral designating the major subdivision, a capital letter for the smaller subdivision, and a number designating the item number from that site (I-A-1, I-A-2; I-B-1, I-B-2; II-A-1, II-A-2; etc.). The preplanned evidence numbering system will give the evidence list compilations coherence for the investigators and prosecutors.

SYSTEMATIC SEARCH METHODS

There are several different methods used to search a crime scene systematically. The advantage of using these methods is the thoroughness with which the crime scene is searched. The choice of method depends on the size and number of scenes, the type of crime scene to be searched, and the number of personnel available for the search. The principal methods used include the *Strip method*, the *Grid method*, the *Zone method*, and the *Spiral method*. Additionally, there is the "wheel," or "radius," method whereby the investigator follows a straight line from the center of the scene to the perimeter, returns to the center, and then follows another line of radius, continuing until the circle is covered. Since this last method is very time-consuming and may lead to missing a portion of the "pie" during the search, it is therefore not recommended (see Chapter 12 for the search of a vehicle where the vehicle is a crime "scene").

Strip method

The **strip method** (see Figure 2-2) involves setting up lanes or strips, each strip to be searched by one searcher. The lanes should be as narrow as feasible, so that each searcher can scan the lane thoroughly from side to side without missing any item of evidence. This technique is especially good for outdoor scenes, particularly when the area to be searched is large and involves a team of searchers. The search lanes should not be wider than the area that can be easily seen by each individual searcher. A lane width of approximately arm's length on either side of each search member should be the maximum width for the lanes. The lanes need to be marked to avoid missing any portion of the scene. This task can be accomplished by driving stakes at each end of the lanes and tying heavy twine to the stakes in order to delineate each lane. When the end of each lane is reached, the stakes and their lines are moved parallel fashion to maintain continuity of the lanes across the area to be searched.

The strip search is particularly suited for outdoor scenes where the search party is looking for items that are relatively small, such as ejected cartridge cases. This method is equally good for those items that are intermediate in size, such as handguns, footwear impressions, or items discarded by a suspect while fleeing the scene. The strip method can also be used for indoor scenes where the areas to be covered have relatively large floor spaces, such as those found in a sizable warehouse. Indoor areas found in residences or small buildings are usually more easily searched by using the zone method.

Grid method

The **grid method**, sometimes called the double-strip method (see Figure 2-3), requires a first search as in the strip method. A second search is completed by orienting the lanes at right angles to the first lanes searched. Use the stakes-and-twine method for establishing the lanes to be searched, using the same guidelines for lane width as in the strip method.

The advantage of the grid method over the other methods is the thoroughness of the search that it provides. Each area of the grid is effectively searched twice, thus reducing considerably the chance that an evidence item will be missed in the search. For evidence items that are very difficult to find, such as expended cartridge cases in tall grass, the search team may have to conduct the search on their hands and knees in order to ensure that no items are missed during the search. Although tedious and time-consuming, this technique will ensure that no items have been missed by the search team.

Zone method

The **zone method** (see Figure 2-4) consists of dividing the scene into "zones" to be searched. This method is sometimes referred to as a "sector" method or a "cupboard" method. Each zone can then be subdivided into smaller and smaller zones as circumstances require. For example, large indoor scenes or outdoor scenes can be divided into large zones for search by separate teams. Each zone can then be subdivided by its search team in order to increase the efficiency of the overall search. This method is also the one of choice for recording the location and shapes of bloodstain patterns, firearm projectile trajectories, or other types of evidence where the interrelationship of each of the components of the area is a paramount concern.

Spiral method

In the **spiral method** (see Figure 2-5), the search team starts at the designated center of the scene and follows a spiral path outward from the center until the perimeter of the scene is reached (not recommended for indoor scenes or smaller outdoor scenes, as the zone method and strip methods are much more efficient for these areas). The spiral method may be used effectively for searching a large outdoor scene where the search team is looking for very large objects that are easy to see (dumped bodies, for example). The size of the lanes should be kept to a minimum.

FINISHING THE CRIME SCENE SEARCH: DEBRIEFING

At the conclusion of a crime scene search, a crime scene debriefing team should be assembled prior to releasing the scene. The debriefing team should include the investigator(s) in charge of the crime scene, other investigators, and evidence collection personnel (e.g., photographers, evidence technicians, latent print personnel, specialized personnel, and initial responding officer(s), if still present). The **debriefing** allows the members to share information regarding particular scene findings and provides an opportunity for input regarding follow-up investigation, special requests for assistance, and the establishment of postscene responsibilities.[6] The debriefing team should address the topics and questions that follow:

- Have all areas been documented and searched?
- Have witness statements developed information that indicates that further searches are necessary—additional areas, other evidence and so on?
- Have all parties completed their assignments?
- Is all evidence collected, properly packaged, and accounted for?
- Has a re-search of the scene(s) been made? Carefully go over the scene again, looking for any evidence items missed. *Note:* A scene searched at night almost always should be re-searched when the sun comes up.
- Should the scene remain preserved/secured? Often, information gained at a homicide autopsy or medical examination in a sexual assault case will indicate additional actions necessary at the crime scene. The scene should ordinarily be secured until completion of an autopsy or medical examination. Remember, if the scene is left unprotected, it will never be the same again, and any additional search may require an additional search warrant.
- Initiate any action(s) identified in the debriefing required to complete the crime scene investigation.
- Discuss potential forensic testing and the sequence of tests to be performed.
- Brief the person(s) in charge upon completion of assigned crime scene tasks.
- Establish postscene responsibilities for law enforcement personnel and other responders.
- Perform final survey of the crime scene.

FINAL SURVEY OF THE CRIME SCENE

After the crime scene debriefing has been held and before the scene is released to the appropriate individual or agency, a final survey of the scene should be conducted. This survey ensures that pertinent evidence has been collected, that evidence, equipment, or materials generated by the investigation are not inadvertently left behind, and that any dangerous materials or conditions have been reported and addressed. The investigator(s) in charge should conduct a walk-through and ensure that each area identified as part of the crime scene is visually inspected. At the conclusion of the debriefing and final walk-through, the investigator releases the scene in accordance with jurisdictional requirements.

Summary

Crime Scene Search

ACTIONS TO BE TAKEN BY THE FIRST RESPONDER(S)

- Determine the need for life-saving procedures and emergency personnel.
- Remove and detain witnesses and suspects from the scene.
- Secure the scene and establish the crime scene perimeter.
- Compile scene data.
- Make initial survey of the crime scene.
  - Establish pathway for subsequent personnel.
  - Prepare notes regarding observations at the scene.

- Take steps to preserve any fragile evidence at the scene.

ACTIONS TO BE TAKEN BY CRIME SCENE INVESTIGATOR(S)

- Record pertinent data immediately.
  - Time called to scene/by whom.
  - Time arrived at scene.
  - Actions taken to secure the crime scene. If this has not been done, secure the scene immediately!
  - Record persons at scene/present on arrival/left scene prior to arrival/arriving after your arrival (persons/times).
  - Record all case file data for all departments involved.
  - Record names of all victim(s) and suspect(s) known at the time.
- Contact the first responder at the scene.
  - Obtain overview of circumstances known and observations made by the responding officer.
  - Determine areas which can be crossed without destroying potential evidence.
- Establish a command center for the operation.
- Establish a plan for processing the scene.
- Compile necessary data before collection process.
  - Presence of Unusual odors.
  - Presence and condition of bloodstains.
  - Signs of struggle.
  - Point(s) of entry and exit.
  - Condition of windows and doors (locked, unlocked, open, closed).
  - Condition of trash containers (especially layer sequence).
  - Condition and contents of ashtrays.
  - Evidence of drinking and/or drug use.
  - Evidence disturbed or collected prior to arrival, person(s) who are responsible for this evidence.
  - Condition of light switches.

CRIME SCENE SEARCH

- Adequate notes of actions taken at the scene.
- Photography of the scene: *before the scene is disturbed*.

- Overview (layout) photographs.
- General photographs to illustrate the condition of the scene.
- Photographs from the point of view of all witnesses.
- Midrange photographs to illustrate location of all pertinent objects and evidence items.
- Photographs of the evidence items.
- Sketches of the scene to document any evidence present.
  - Layout (overview) sketches.
  - Detailed sketches of pertinent areas.
  - Large-scale (blowup) sketches.
    1. Bloodstain patterns.
    2. Bullet entry and exit holes.
    3. Location and orientation of impression evidence.
    4. Areas having a large number of small evidence items.
- Search scene with systematic method.
  - Strip method for outdoor scenes.
  - Grid (double strip) for outdoor scenes.
  - Zone method for indoor or outdoor scenes.
  - Spiral method for large objects in large outdoor scenes.
- Recording of evidence.
  - Make sure each item is photographed and located on the sketch(s) before collection.
  - Process for fingerprints at the time the item is collected whenever feasible.
  - Mark and record each item on the evidence list at the time of its collection.
  - Package each item of evidence securely so that any trace evidence present is not disturbed, lost, or contaminated.
  - Make sure that evidence items containing biological stains are dried thoroughly before packaging in paper bags or envelopes.
- Separate areas/collectors
  - Code each separate area with Roman numeral or letter.
  - Assign a team or individual to process each separate area; ensure that all evidence items collected are coded with scene code and item number.

FINISHING THE CRIME SCENE SEARCH: DEBRIEFING

- Have all areas been documented and searched?
- Have witness statements developed information which indicates further search necessary—additional areas, other evidence, and so on?
- Have all parties completed their assignments?
- Is all evidence collected, properly packaged, and accounted for?

- Re-search of the scene(s).
- Should the scene remain preserved/secured?
- Initiate any action(s) identified in the debriefing required to complete the crime scene investigation.
- Discuss potential forensic testing and the sequence of tests to be performed.
- Brief person(s) in charge upon completion of assigned crime scene tasks.
- Establish postscene responsibilities for law enforcement personnel and other responders.
- Perform final survey of the crime scene.

Review Questions

1. The first responder at the scene should establish a _____ for medical personnel and investigating officers to follow.
2. The first responder should _____ and _____ witnesses and suspects from the scene.
3. The scene should be _____ until the crime scene processing has been completed.
4. The _____ should be conducted to determine possible evidence present at the scene.
5. The first responder should take steps to preserve any _____ evidence at the scene.
6. The first responder should establish an _____ log of which individuals were present at the scene or who left before the officer's arrival.
7. The initial survey of the crime scene should be done in a _____ manner, taking _____ of observations at the scene.
8. The crime scene investigator should contact the first responder at the scene to obtain an _____ of the scene.

9. The investigator should determine which areas can be crossed without _____ _____ _____.
10. The investigator should _____ the scene with the first responder.
11. The investigator should establish a _____ for processing the scene.
12. As a general rule, _____ should be the first step in documenting the crime scene.
13. Three systematic search methods are the _____, _____, and _____ methods.
14. When finishing the crime scene search, the investigator should have a _____ with the participants to determine that all areas have been searched and documented.
15. The strip search method involves setting up _____ to be searched by the participants.

Further References

Osterburg, J. W., and R. H. Ward. 2004. *Criminal Investigation*, 4th ed. Cincinnati, OH: Anderson Publishing.

Rynearson, J. 2002. *Evidence and Crime Scene Reconstruction*, 6th ed. Redding, CA: National Crime Investigation Training (NCIT).

U.S. Department of Justice. Office of Justice Programs. 2004. *Crime Scene Investigation: A Guide for Law Enforcement*. Washington, DC: GPO. http://www.ncjrs.org.

APPENDIX 2-A

Sample Crime Scene Entry Log

☐ SUPPLEMENT
☐ FOLLOW-UP

SONOMA COUNTY SHERIFF'S DEPARTMENT
MAJOR INCIDENT ACCESS LOG

CASE NUMBER

DATE/TIME	INCIDENT/CRIME		
LOCATION			

OFFICER INITIATING LOG	TIME	RELIEF OFFICER	TIME	RELIEF OFFICER	TIME

PERSONS ENTERING SCENE
All persons/teams entering crime scene are required to submit a written report documenting actions taken.

NAME (Print)	RANK	ASSIGNMENT	TIME IN	OUT	REASON FOR ENTRY
SIGNATURE	EMP. #	AGENCY			
NAME (Print)	RANK	ASSIGNMENT	TIME IN	OUT	REASON FOR ENTRY
SIGNATURE	EMP. #	AGENCY			
NAME (Print)	RANK	ASSIGNMENT	TIME IN	OUT	REASON FOR ENTRY
SIGNATURE	EMP. #	AGENCY			
NAME (Print)	RANK	ASSIGNMENT	TIME IN	OUT	REASON FOR ENTRY
SIGNATURE	EMP. #	AGENCY			
NAME (Print)	RANK	ASSIGNMENT	TIME IN	OUT	REASON FOR ENTRY
SIGNATURE	EMP. #	AGENCY			
NAME (Print)	RANK	ASSIGNMENT	TIME IN	OUT	REASON FOR ENTRY
SIGNATURE	EMP. #	AGENCY			
NAME (Print)	RANK	ASSIGNMENT	TIME IN	OUT	REASON FOR ENTRY
SIGNATURE	EMP. #	AGENCY			
NAME (Print)	RANK	ASSIGNMENT	TIME IN	OUT	REASON FOR ENTRY
SIGNATURE	EMP. #	AGENCY			
NAME (Print)	RANK	ASSIGNMENT	TIME IN	OUT	REASON FOR ENTRY
SIGNATURE	EMP. #	AGENCY			
NAME (Print)	RANK	ASSIGNMENT	TIME IN	OUT	REASON FOR ENTRY
SIGNATURE	EMP. #	AGENCY			
NAME (Print)	RANK	ASSIGNMENT	TIME IN	OUT	REASON FOR ENTRY
SIGNATURE	EMP. #	AGENCY			
NAME (Print)	RANK	ASSIGNMENT	TIME IN	OUT	REASON FOR ENTRY
SIGNATURE	EMP. #	AGENCY			
NAME (Print)	RANK	ASSIGNMENT	TIME IN	OUT	REASON FOR ENTRY
SIGNATURE	EMP. #	AGENCY			

REPORTING OFFICER/ID	DATE/TIME OF REPORT	APPROVED BY	FOLLOW UP ☐ INVEST ☐ PATROL	COPIES TO

Courtesy of Sonoma County Sheriff's Office.

APPENDIX 2-B

Customized Crime Scene Search Kits

LEVEL OF CRIME SCENE SEARCH KIT NEEDED

The level of sophistication in the crime scene kit ranges from a simple kit in a tool-box or a fishing tackle box tailored to an individual officer's needs up to a large van containing an extensive array of equipment used as a mobile crime scene process-ing unit and laboratory. In this appendix, four levels of crime scene kits are described: (1) a personal kit for the individual officer;[7] (2) a kit for first responders (usually the patrol officer assigned to the beat), which is kept in the patrol vehicle from shift to shift or in the sergeant's vehicle; (3) a kit for the crime scene investigator or evidence technician; and (4) specialty kits for the collection of specific types of evidence.[8]

A. **Personal Crime Scene Kit for the Patrol Officer (see Figure 2-6)**

1. **Packaging materials**
   a. Manila envelopes $(4 \times 6; 2 \times 3\frac{1}{2})$
   b. Evidence tags
   c. Property forms
   d. Paper towels
   e. Property bags (medium to large)
   f. Small boxes (pillbox type)

2. **Writing supplies**
   a. Extra ink pen, pencil
   b. Indelible ink pens
   c. Lumber crayon (yellow)
   d. Yellow chalk
   e. Straight-edge for sketches
   f. Clipboard for sketches

3. **Fingerprinting supplies**
   a. Fiberglass brushes
   b. Magnetic brush kit
   c. Fingerprint powder containers
   d. Ample supply of latent lift cards (3×5)
   e. Fingerprint tape—several rolls
   f. Surgical gloves
   g. Magnifying glass

4. **Crime scene forms (departmental)**
   a. Crime scene response
   b. Crime scene entry log
   c. Property forms
   d. Scene report cover sheet

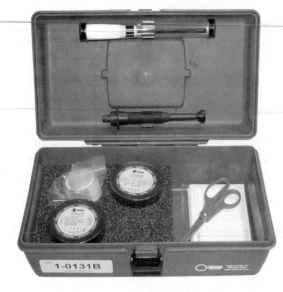

FIGURE 2-6   Standard Latent Print Kit   Courtesy of Lightning Powder Company, an Armor Holdings Product Division

    e. Photo logs

    f. Consent/search forms

5. **Measurement items**

    a. Steel tapes: 25 and 100 feet

    b. Measuring rulers (metric and inches)

    c. ABFO American Board of Forensic Odontologists scale

6. **Tools**

    a. Phillips screwdrivers, two sizes

    b. Blade screwdrivers, two sizes

    c. Pliers with cutting edge

    d. Forceps, hemostats, tweezers

    e. Small scissors

    f. Small metal probe

    g. Small pencil magnet (magna brush [magnetic latent finger print brush] will do)

    h. Small crescent wrench

    i. Small metal scribe

    j. Rubber-tipped metal tongs

7. **Miscellaneous items**

    a. Thermometer (0–250 degrees Fahrenheit, with Celsius scale)

    b. Sterile, individually packaged cotton swabs

    c. Roll of crime scene perimeter tape

    d. Small stapler

    e. Supply of handy wipes

    f. Supply of sterilization wipes

    g. Small container of distilled water

    h. Sterile gauze pads

    i. Gunshot residue kits

    j. Directional compass

B. Crime Scene Kit for Patrol Vehicle (or Sergeant's Vehicle)

  1. Essential

Note: These items should be in police vehicles or readily available to first respond-ing officer(s).

    a. Consent/search forms

    b. Crime scene barricade tape

    c. First-aid kit

    d. Flares

    e. Flashlight and extra batteries

    f. Paper bags

    g. Personal protective equipment (PPE)

  2. Optional

    a. Audiotape recorder

    b. Camera with flash and extra film

    c. Chalk

    d. Directional marker/compass

    e. Disinfectant

    f. Maps

    g. Pocket knife

    h. Reflective vest

    i. Tape measure

    j. Tarps (to protect evidence from weather)

    k. Traffic cones

    l. Waterless hand wash (towelette with germicide)

    m. Wireless phone

C. Crime Scene Investigator/Evidence Technician Kit (see Figure 2-7)

  1. Essential

Note: These items should be in police vehicles or readily available to first respond-ing officer(s).

    a. Bindle paper

    b. Biohazard bags

    c. Body fluid collection kit

    d. Camera (35 mm) with flash/film/tripod

    e. Casting materials

    f. Consent/search forms

    g. Crime scene barricade tape

    h. Cutting instruments (knives, box cutter, scalpel, scissors)

    i. Directional marker/compass

    j. Disinfectant

    k. Evidence collection containers

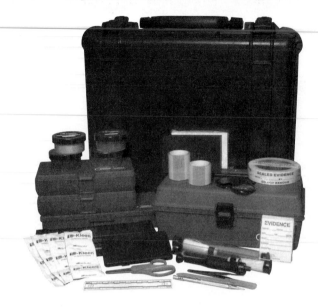

FIGURE 2-7 **Model 300 Crime Scene Kit** Courtesy of Lightning Powder Company, an Armor Holdings Product Division

l. Evidence identifiers
m. Evidence seals/tape
n. First-aid kit
o. Flashlight and extra batteries
p. High-intensity lights
q. Latent print kit
r. Magnifying glass
s. Measuring devices
t. Permanent markers
u. Personal protective equipment (PPE)
v. Photographic scale (ruler)
w. Presumptive blood test supplies
x. Sketch paper
y. Tool kit
z. Tweezers/forceps

2. **Optional**
   a. Audiotape recorder
   b. Bloodstain pattern examination kit
   c. Business cards
   d. Chalk
   e. Chemical enhancement supplies
   f. Entomology collection kit
   g. Extension cords
   h. Flares
   i. Forensic light source (alternate light source, UV lamp, laser, goggles)
   j. Generator
   k. Gunshot residue kit
   l. Laser trajectory kit

    m. Maps

    n. Marking paint/snow wax

    o. Metal detector

    p. Mirror

    q. Phone listing (important numbers)

    r. Privacy screens

    s. Protrusion rod set

    t. Reflective vest

    u. Refrigeration or cooling unit

    v. Respirators with filters

    w. Roll of string

    x. Rubber bands

    y. Sexual assault evidence collection kits (victim and suspect)

    z. Shoe print lifting equipment

    aa. Templates (scene and human)

    ab. Thermometer

    ac. Traffic cones

    ad. Trajectory rods

    ae. Videotape recorder

    af. Cellular phone

D. Specialty Crime Scene Kits

  1. Blood collection

    a. Bindle

    b. Coin envelopes

    c. Disposable scalpels

    d. Distilled water

    e. Ethanol

    f. Evidence identifiers

    g. Latex gloves

    h. Photographic rulers (ABFO scales)

    i. Presumptive testing chemicals

    j. Sterile gauze

    k. Sterile swabs

    l. Test tubes/test tube rack

  2. Bloodstain pattern documentation

    a. ABFO scales

    b. Calculator

    c. Laser pointer

    d. Permanent markers

    e. Protractor

    f. String

    g. Tape

  3. Excavation

    a. Cones/markers

    b. Evidence identifiers

     c. Metal detectors
     d. Paintbrushes
     e. Shovels/trowels
     f. Sifting screens
     g. String
     h. Weights
     i. Wooden/metal stakes

4. **Fingerprints**
     a. Black-and-white film
     b. Brushes
     c. Chemical enhancement supplies
     d. Cyanoacrylate (Superglue) wand/packets
     e. Flashlight, spare batteries
     f. Forensic light source
     g. Lift cards
     h. Lift tape
     i. Measurement scales
     j. One-to-one camera
     k. Powders

5. **Impression**
     a. Bowls/mixing containers
     b. Boxes
     c. Dental stone
     d. Evidence identifiers
     e. Measurement scales
     f. Permanent markers
     g. Snow Print Wax
     h. Water

6. **Pattern print lifter**
     a. Chemical enhancement supplies
     b. Electrostatic dust lifter
     c. Gel lifter
     d. Wide format tape

7. **Toolmarks**
     a. Casting materials

8. **Trace evidence collection**
     a. Acetate sheet protectors
     b. Bindle paper
     c. Clear tape/adhesive lifts
     d. Flashlight (oblique lighting)
     e. Forceps/tweezers
     f. Glass vials
     g. Slides and slide mailers
     h. Trace evidence vacuum with disposable collection filters

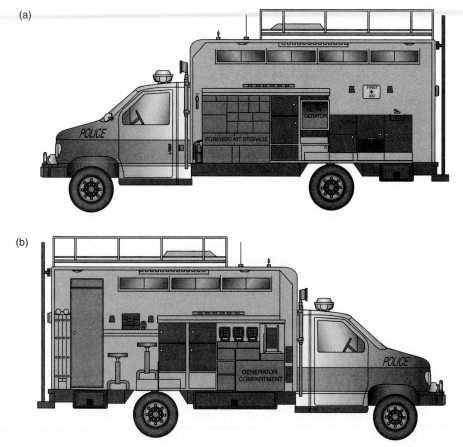

FIGURE 2-8   Crime Scene Van with All Essential and Optional Supplies for Crime Scene Processing
Courtesy of Sirchie Fingerprint Laboratories.

9. **Trajectory**
   a. Calculator
   b. Canned smoke
   c. Dummy
   d. Laser light source
   e. Mirror
   f. Protractor
   g. String
   h. Trajectory rods

E. **Crime Scene Van with Scene Equipment** (see Figure 2-8).

3 | CRIME SCENE PHOTOGRAPHY[1]

Key Words: Digital single lens reflex (DSLR), shot, frame, exposure, memory card, auto-focus, sequence of photographs, photo log, overview, medium range, close-up, point of view, night photographs, latent impressions, wounds, high quality lenses, resolution, correct exposure, image stabilization (IS), digital image, image sensor, image processor, pixels, single photosensitive unit, liquid crystal display (LCD), optical view finder, secure digital (SD), secure digital high capacity (SDHC), image resolution.

INTRODUCTION

Crime scene photography differs significantly from the typical photography of amateur and professional photographers. Amateur hobbyists and professional photographers strive to create artistic photographs, whereas crime scene photography seeks to avoid artistic renderings of the crime scene and to portray accurately the features of the scene and any evidence therein. For example, photographers will typically place the main subject in a photograph to one side of the frame in order to make the resultant photograph more artistic, but crime scene photographers need to place the main subject in the center of each photograph, in order to focus on the main subject of the photograph and maximize the clarity of the subject.

The emergence of digital photography in recent years has had a major impact on crime scene photography, especially because of the development of the **digital single lens reflex (dSLR or DSLR)** cameras. The addition of DSLRs to the familiar point-and-shoot digital cameras has created a line of cameras that rival the best of SLR film cameras in resolution, ease of use, and flexibility. A large increase in the number of pixels in the newer digital cameras and the availability of interchangeable lenses for the DSLRs have led to improvement in their image quality. Coincidental with the major improvement in image quality of the DSLRs, the cost of these cameras has dropped steadily, so that high quality DSLRs are now very affordable. The quality and affordable price of DSLRs, along with the many features that represent much greater flexibility, have allowed many law enforcement agencies to replace film cameras with DSLRs. This pattern will probably continue into the foreseeable future.

A great deal of the terminology pertaining to film photography is carried over into digital photography. The section on Basic Camera and Photography Information is revised to include the terms unique to digital photography. Also, some of the technical information relating to digital imaging is included to familiarize the crime scene investigator with the operation of digital cameras. The term "**shot**" is routinely used instead of the other somewhat synonymous terms "**frame**," "**exposure**," and "photograph" to describe a single exposure on a roll of film, or on a digital camera's digital **memory card**.

OBJECTIVES OF CRIME SCENE PHOTOGRAPHY

The objectives of crime scene photography are to record the *condition* of the scene *before alterations occur*, record the *location and position of evidence items* collected, document the *point of view of principals and potential witnesses*, and document *spatial relationships of pertinent items*. Photography provides visual images of the crime scene and has the distinct advantage of illustrating physical objects in a way that closely approximates the human eye, although photographs lack the depth perception afforded by the eye. Photographs of the scene, particularly when taken in conjunction with videography, capture the visual aspects of the scene that are needed to convey the look of the scene to investigators, attorneys, and jurors, who will not have the opportunity to view the scene firsthand as the crime scene investigator views it.

Photography is *not a substitute for notes or sketches* but rather is an essential *supplement* to these other modes of crime scene documentation. The photographs will be a crucial visual record of the conditions at the scene during the follow-up investigations as well as valuable tools for any reconstruction efforts undertaken. When combined with the notes and sketches of the scene and evidence items, photographs will assist the crime scene investigator in painting an accurate picture of the crime scene during courtroom testimony. The ability to portray accurately the crime scene and the physical evidence therein will go a long way in helping to establish the credibility of the crime scene investigator.

Photography also plays an important role in the efforts to *reconstruct the events of the crime*. In conjunction with sketches, photographs capture the physical aspects of evidence at the crime scene that are amenable to reconstruction by a qualified professional. Photographs of bloodstain patterns are crucial to the reconstruction of those events that produced the patterns and their sequence. These photographs are taken with scales in view in order to reestablish accurately the sizes of the evidence items. Photographs of bullet trajectories are taken with probes in place (see Chapter 8).

NUMBER OF PHOTOGRAPHS AT THE SCENE

The number of photographs that need to be taken at any crime scene cannot be established with certainty at the time the scene is being processed, because additional information and questions will arise as the investigation continues. For this reason, it is a better policy to take *too many* photographs rather than too few, since the opportunity to take the photographs is usually limited to the time at hand. The cost of the film and the crime scene investigator's time will be repaid by the savings in the subsequent investigation.

The position of evidence items can never be reproduced exactly after they are moved, hence the photographs must be taken before any disturbance of the scene whenever possible (emergency medical actions, etc., will often disturb the scene, but this situation is unavoidable). Oftentimes, it is helpful to take both videotapes and still photographs of the scene in order to more fully capture the conditions at the scene (see the discussion under Videotaping of Crime Scenes later in this chapter). In some circumstances, the crime scene investigator may need to use instant photography in addition to the still photographs, particularly if the scene is not videotaped (see the section below on, Digital Imaging Cameras).

CONDITIONS AT THE SCENE

The crime scene may be as small as a bathroom or a closet, or it may cover an area of several square miles. More often it is a dwelling, an automobile, or a portion of a lot or a street. The conditions for photographing the crime scene may vary considerably. Lighting, weather, and security at the scene present the greatest challenges for the crime scene photographer. If it is possible to wait for better weather and lighting, then do so. If not, then one must use either the available lighting or lighting provided by other means. When taking a photograph of an object at the scene, one should ask the following questions: Why am I taking this photograph? Does the object show or have any relationship to the overall scene? Does the object have any relationship to other items of potential value? Will the photograph represent what I saw? Will the object be distorted or out of perspective with other things at the scene? Will the object be properly exposed? Will reflections off windows, mirrors, or glossy wallpaper wash out my photograph? Will I recognize the photograph after it's developed? Will I be able to explain to the jury what the photograph depicts? Considering these questions will help obtain the best photo documentation of the crime scene.

CHOICE OF CAMERA TYPE FOR CRIME SCENE PHOTOGRAPHY

Single lens reflex (SLR) film camera

The type of camera best suited for crime scene photography is the *single lens reflex (SLR)* camera. The SLR is very compact and comes in a wide variety of formats, from the manually focused unit to the fully automatic unit with automatic focusing, automatic flash set, and automatic winding. Lenses come in a wide assortment and are of sufficient quality for both long-range and close-up (macro) photographs. Of particular value at the crime scene are the zoom lenses having macro capabilities. A zoom lens in the range 35–70 mm with macro capability coupled with a long-range zoom lens in the range 80–200 mm should be adequate for virtually all crime scene photography. Some specialized photographs (e.g., aerial photographs needing a large format negative) may require the use of larger format cameras, but the 35-mm SLR will provide excellent photographs in all but these specialized circumstances. The SLRs with autofocusing and exposure will usually provide excellent photographs at a crime scene, but in some circumstances, the camera may be fooled by conditions at the scene. For this reason, the crime scene investigator needs to be familiar with both the camera and those conditions that may affect the quality of the photographs.

Digital Single Lens Reflex (DSLR) Cameras

The first generation of digital cameras (called "point and shoot" cameras) lacked the resolution of the SLR film camera, but the introduction of digital single lens reflex (DSLR) camera (see Figure 3-1) models from major manufacturers has improved the resolution of the images produced by the cameras, due to the higher number of pixels (picture elements) in the image sensor and the many high quality **auto-focus** lenses in many formats (including zoom lenses) available for these cameras. Most manufacturers offer affordable DSLR

FIGURE 3-1 **Digital Evidence Photo System** Courtesy of Sirchie Fingerprint Laboratories.

cameras with resolution exceeding 10 megapixels, which produce images virtually comparable to those of an SLR camera using traditional film. Many lens choices are now available for these cameras, including wide-angle, short zooms (28–70 mm), long zooms (80–200 mm, 80–400 mm, etc.), and macro lenses, including zoom lenses with macro capability. The end result is that DSLRs are superior in many important respects to the film SLRs.

A distinct advantage of the digital camera is the ability to illustrate the image on television monitors. This feature is very beneficial to the investigator when presenting testimony to a jury or to prosecutors or other investigators. When illustrating features of the crime scene or evidence items to others, the portrayal of the images on television monitors seen by the entire audience adds ease and clarity to the presentation. Certain features of the scene can easily be pointed out to the audience using the on-screen arrow, so that the viewers are certain of what is being pointed out by the investigator.

An additional advantage of the digital camera is the ease with which the investigator can prepare copies of the photograph file in the case. The images can easily be transferred to floppy disks, CD writable disks, or thumb drives for storage or transfer to another agency. These media also afford a simple means of transporting the photographs of the scene to court for testimony purposes. In addition, the images may be transported via e-mail to other computers.

One disadvantage of the digital camera is that the images can be manipulated by a skilled computer operator with the proper equipment and computer software. This drawback is not fatal, however, since the introduction of photographs as evidence has historically relied on the testimony of a sworn witness that the photograph being offered accurately depicts the item or scene photographed. However, the ability to manipulate the image places a stronger burden on the crime scene investigator to document each photograph in the photography log and the investigator's notes so that the investigator can easily assure a court or jury that the photograph is an accurate representation of the scene as seen by the investigator.

A good strategy for those departments that have film SLR photo systems for crime scene photography, but lack funding for digital SLRs is to purchase point-and-shoot digital cameras (with 5 or more megapixels) to augment the film camera system. The point and shoot digital cameras are now extremely reasonable in price, so their purchase should not burden the department budget. In this manner, the crime scene investigator has the ability to take digital photos in those instances where it is crucial to verify that the evidence item in question has been successfully photographed before any changes to the scene have been effected.

TYPE OF FILM FOR CRIME SCENE PHOTOGRAPHY

Color print film

Color print film is the film of choice for most crime scene photography for many reasons. Color film has replaced black-and-white film for all forensic applications except special needs, such as photographs of latent impressions, infrared photography, and photographs for research or publications. The cost of color film is comparable to that of black-and-white and is available in many formats and film speeds for the investigator. Color film has an enormous advantage in presenting a "natural" look to the viewer. Moreover, many types of evidence cannot be easily distinguished from the background when black-and-white film is used (bloodstains, for example, look like any other dark stain). In one of the author's cases, a critical aspect in the reconstruction of a homicide was the blood spatter present at the scene. The blood-spatter patterns were on mottled black-and-white tile, thereby preventing the reconstruction of the blood-spatter pattern, since the black patterns on the tile could not be distinguished from the bloodstains.

VIDEOTAPING OF CRIME SCENES

Videotaping of crime scenes is often a rule in many agencies and may be required by some. Videotape has some advantages and some disadvantages when compared with still camera photography. The videotape of a crime scene has the advantage of providing a lifelike view to the viewer, in effect taking the viewer on a "tour" of the crime scene, and also avoiding the frequent changing of film in the camera (it is recommended that the audio be *locked off* at all times for videotaping of crime scenes *unless the investigator is dictating the scene onto the tape*). This precaution will avoid having offhand remarks by the team individuals made a permanent record, a situation that may cause embarrassment to the investigator. The videographer should also avoid having scene equipment or investigators in view while taping. The disadvantages of videotaping include the addition of unnecessary detail in the filming and the lower resolution of the video camera as opposed to that of the still camera (unless *very* expensive studio quality equipment is used). It is very difficult to obtain exhibit quality still photographs from a videotape for presentation in the courtroom. When the video camera is used to document the crime scene, the videotaping should be augmented with still camera photography of all evidence items and especially of those items that may be needed for reconstruction efforts (bloodstain spatter patterns, bullet trajectories, firearm discharge patterns, etc.).

Another distinct advantage of using videotape to photograph the crime scene is the ability of the photographer instantly to review the videotape at the scene. This feature of videotapes is very helpful in those circumstances when it is necessary to be certain that critical features of the crime scene have been adequately photographed before any alterations to the scene have been effected, much as the use of a digital camera allows for a preview of the photographs taken.

SUGGESTED SYSTEMATIC APPROACH

The paramount consideration for crime scene photography is to follow a *systematic procedure* that ensures that all necessary photographs are taken at the scene prior to any actions that may compromise the integrity of the scene. As the crime scene investigator gains experience in the photography of various types of crime scenes, the systematic approach can be refined to optimize the information content of the photographs without sacrificing thoroughness. The **sequence of photographs** should follow closely the *sequence of sketch preparation* by working from the perimeter toward the center, continuing to take additional photographs as required. This approach mirrors the way in which the crime scene is registered in the mind's eye of the investigators and will facilitate the presentation of the photographs in the courtroom by providing an overall view of the scene for the jurors that will establish a framework for the subsequent midrange and close-up photographs. The jurors will thus be able to relate each evidence photograph to the overall picture of the scene. For outdoor scenes, it is usually a good practice to wait until daybreak to shoot the photographs, since many details of the scene cannot be shown without daylight filling the scene. The interrelationships of the areas of the scene are difficult to portray without full daylight.

LOG OF ALL PHOTOGRAPHS TAKEN

A **photo log** should be kept of all photographs taken at each scene as the photographs are taken. The log should include data regarding the camera, film type, and lens used to take the photographs. In addition, the log should contain information regarding the roll number and frame number for each photograph, exposure data, and a description of the content of each frame, so that each photograph can be properly identified after development. The log of photographs should be kept as a permanent record in the case file. It is much better to have a two-member team for the photographs. A two-member team is much more efficient than a single photographer, with one member taking the photographs and the other keeping the log current, while assisting in the placement of evidence marker stands, rulers, and so on.

TYPES OF PHOTOGRAPHS OF A CRIME SCENE

Overview/Layout photographs (long-range)

The first series of photographs taken should convey the nature of the crime scene from pertinent angles and distances. The photographs of the scene from the perimeter (**overview** or **layout** photographs) will furnish a framework for the spatial relationships to the scene for the later photographs. Photographs taken closer in can be referenced to the overview/layout photographs and the layout sketches for orientation to the scene.

(a)   (b)   (c)

FIGURE 3-2 Overview/Layout Photos of the Front of a Residence. Note that the Three Shots (a), (b), and (c) Overlap

Particular attention should be given to point(s) of entry and exit of the perpetrator, carefully documenting any signs of disturbance that may be the site of evidence transfer. In some circumstances, such as illustrating the positions of principals in a shoot-out, it may be necessary to augment the perimeter photographs with aerial photographs.

Figure 3-2 illustrates layout photos of the front of a residence. Note that shots (a), (b), and (c) *overlap*, so that the entire front of the residence can be viewed without any gap between the shots.

Figure 3-3 depicts overview/layout photos of the rear (a, b, c, d) and sides (e, f) of the residence in Figure 3-2. Note that *these photos also overlap*, so that together they depict the entire rear and sides of the residence.

Medium-range photographs

When the overview/layout photographs are completed, photographs should be taken from closer range (**medium-range** photographs) to show the layout of smaller areas at the scene, such as a room or the central location of the crime scene. Because the degree of closeness will vary from scene to scene, the photo team should try to "paint" a picture

(a)   (b)   (c)   (d)

(e)   (f)

FIGURE 3-3   Overview/Layout Photos of the Rear and Sides of the Residence

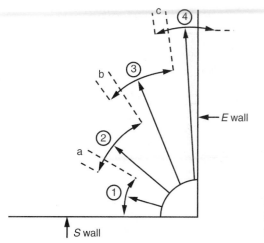

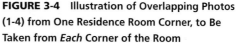

FIGURE 3-4 Illustration of Overlapping Photos (1-4) from One Residence Room Corner, to Be Taken from *Each* Corner of the Room

of the scene with the photographs, so that the photograph viewer can visualize the scene much as the person taking the photographs. Consideration should be given to taking additional photographs with *evidence markers* in place, in order to better show spatial relationships of the evidence items. This procedure is an ongoing process as new items of evidence are discovered during the investigation. These photographs are essential to show the spatial relationships of the individual items of evidence.

When the crime scene is located in a room of a dwelling, the medium-range photographs should include *overlapping photographs* from *each of the four corners* of the room (see Figure 3-4). The investigator should ensure that the overlap of the photographs covers the full 90 degrees of the corner (see Figure 3-5), so that the photos can be arranged

FIGURE 3-5 Overlapping Photos Taken From One Corner of Residence Room

FIGURE 3-6 Overlapping Photos Taken from One Corner Merged to Illustrate One Wall of the Room

to show the full view from that corner (see Figures 3-5 and 3-6). Wide angle (28–35 mm focal length lenses) or zoom lenses with a wide-angle format (35–55 mm zoom lenses) are helpful, due to the wider angle of view of these lenses.

The overlapping photos from each corner can be combined using a cut and paste method or using an electronic photo management program (see Figure 3-6).

Close-up photos showing evidence items require first a medium-range photograph to place the evidence item in its context (see Figure 3-7). Figure 3-7 (a) depicts the location of a toolmark on the patio door of a burglarized residence. Figure 3-7 (b) is a close-up photo of the toolmark on the patio door frame. Figure 3-7 (c) shows the toolmark from the door frame compared to a test mark made with the pair of scissors in Figure 3-7 (d), (e), and (f).

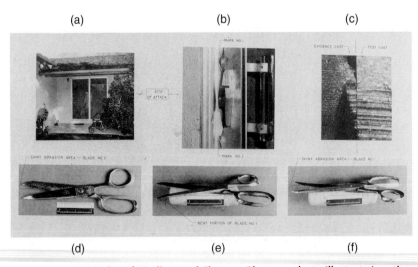

FIGURE 3-7 Courtroom Display of Medium and Close-up Photographs to Illustrate Location of Toolmark at Victim Residence and Comparison of Evidence Toolmark with Test Marks Made with Scissors Courtesy of Dr. Duayne Dillon.

FIGURE 3-8   Photograph of Victim on Porch with Evidence Markers in Place
Courtesy of Sirchie Fingerprint Laboratories.

After the medium-range photos have been taken, the evidence items can be marked with photo evidence numbers, then photographed with the evidence numbers in place (see Figure 3-8).

Close-up photographs

Close-up photographs should be taken of all items where finer detail of the evidence is needed. Those items that require accurate documentation of their size need to be photographed with a measurement scale placed as near to the item as possible without obscuring any detail in the evidence. Each item should be photographed first without the markers in place, then rephotographed with the markers in place. This arrangement is necessary to avoid any claim that important evidence was obscured. Photographs taken with a ruler in place must be shot with the camera centered over the item "normal" to the surface (90 degrees off the surface, with the *film plane parallel to the plane of the surface*), in order to minimize any distortion or parallax (see Figure 3-9). It is essential to use a tripod when photographing footwear or tire impressions (see Chapter 9).

The use of a measurement scale allows for accurate reproduction of the size of the item or enlargement to a known size for detailed study. Close-up photographs require a camera/lens combination capable of sufficient resolution for blowups up to (8×12) inches. A good quality 35-mm SLR or DSLR camera with a zoom/macro lens is sufficient for this purpose and will suffice for almost every application in routine fieldwork. For those situations in which extreme blowups are necessary, a camera with a larger film format, such as $(2\frac{1}{4} \times 2\frac{1}{4})$ or (4×5) inches may need to be used, but these circumstances are rare.

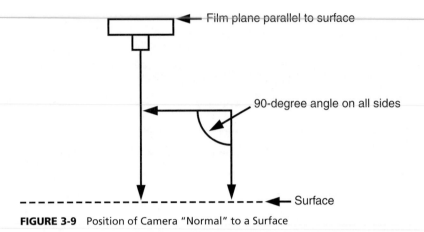

FIGURE 3-9   Position of Camera "Normal" to a Surface

Point of view of witnesses

Photographs should be taken to illustrate the **point of view** of the *principals* or any *witnesses* to the crime. These photographs should be taken prior to the scene being disturbed, so that the statements of principals or witnesses can be supported or disputed by the documentation of the point of view (was the person in a position actually to see what he/she claims to have seen?). Make certain that the crime scene sketches show the exact distances depicted in the point-of-view photographs, so that you can testify as to the exact distances shown in the photographs. The use of slide film is very helpful when taking the point-of-view photographs, owing to the ease with which the investigator can demonstrate to a jury what could be seen from the position of the witness.

Photographs taken during the night

If the crime occurs during the night, it is best to wait until daylight to take the photographs of the scene. The lighting available at night is normally inadequate to provide proper lighting for **night photographs**, especially in outdoor scenes. Moreover, many items of evidence may not be discovered without full daylight. The crime scene investigator should always consider waiting until full daylight to make sure that the lighting is adequate and that all evidence items have been discovered. The ability to "paint" a crime scene with a flash usually requires a specialist in photography. Some situations, however, may need darkness to achieve optimum photo conditions (photographs of florescent dye–enhanced fingerprints or luminol-treated bloodstains, for example, where the light coming from the item has a very low intensity that requires a dark background for timed photography).

If it is not feasible to wait until daylight to accomplish the scene photography, fire departments or public works departments have lighting equipment that will provide adequate lighting for virtually all scenes. The activities of these professionals should be monitored during the set-up period, so that evidence at the scene is not disturbed or destroyed.

Photography of latent impressions

In most cases, it is a good practice to *photograph any developed latents prior to lifting attempts* as a safety measure. In some cases, the surface may be such that the latent may be lost or destroyed during the lifting process. The latents may be photographed with a latent print camera, a 35-mm SLR camera with a macro lens, or with a Digital camera. The best film to use for latent impressions in most circumstances is black-and-white film, because of the better contrast achieved with black-and-white film. However, good quality photographs can be achieved with color film and appropriate filters, especially when colored latent powders are used. Photographs of **latent impressions** should include a measurement scale and item identifier in the field of view on the same plane as the latent. The camera should be oriented perpendicular to the surface of the latent, with the film plane parallel to the plane of the latent and the frame filled with the latent, scale, and identifier. The camera lens should be set at a higher f-stop to increase the depth of field in the photograph. This step is especially important when the latent is located on a curved or an irregular surface. The flash unit should be held to one side to avoid a hotspot in the latent image and to increase the contrast of the latent with the surface. Oblique lighting is essential if the impression is an indented patent impression or if the surface is relatively porous or reflective. The best angle for positioning the flash unit can be previewed by using a flashlight at various angles to illuminate the impression.

Patent impressions in blood should be photographed with color film rather than black-and-white film. If the impression is to be developed with luminol or a blood-testing reagent such as phenolphthalein, it may be necessary to take a series of photographs as the image develops, in order to capture the image with the highest contrast between the impression and the background. The crime scene investigator will need to experiment with the photography of luminol-treated stains, in order to develop expertise in the photography for these techniques.

Photography of wounds

Wounds should be photographed both before and after cleansing of the wound by medical personnel in the case of a living subject or by the forensic pathologist in the case of a deceased subject. The wound site(s) and periphery should be searched thoroughly for any trace evidence before cleansing. In the case of bite marks, the wound site and a control site adjacent to each mark should be sampled for saliva before any cleansing begins. Since the investigator may not be able to rephotograph the wounds in the event the photographs are unsatisfactory, it may be prudent to photograph the wounds with a digital camera in order to make sure that the wound has been documented to the satisfaction of the investigator prior to photography with color film. Medium-range photographs of the wound(s) should be taken first, in order to orient each wound to the location on the body where the wound occurs. The photography of wounds should always be taken with color film, both without and with a measurement scale in place immediately adjacent to the wound. The camera lens must be positioned "normal" to the skin surface (i.e., with the film plane parallel to the plane of the wound) bearing the wound in order to minimize distortion. Since most body surfaces are curved rather than flat, the camera should be centered on the wound, with approximately equal curvature of the body surface in all directions from the wound (see Figure 3-10). The wounds should be rephotographed at one-day intervals, because the bruising of the tissue develops over several days and the detail may be enhanced considerably by the bruise development. For deceased subjects, the wounds should be rephotographed after embalming, since the embalming process may enhance the patterns in the wounds. For wounds in general, and bite marks in particular, the use of an ABFO (American Board of Forensic Odontology) #2 scale is recommended for use as the measurement scale. The wound should be centered between the horizontal and vertical legs of the ABFO scale for the photographs, and the camera lens should be centered on the wound.

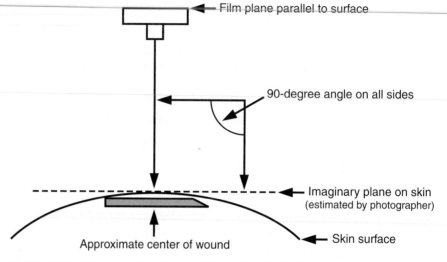

FIGURE 3-10   Photographing Wounds "Normal" to the Surface

The flash unit for the wound photographs should be held to one side to produce oblique lighting for the wound. Oblique lighting will highlight the indented impressions in the wound (see Figure 9-7 in Chapter 9). If the wound is a bite mark, oblique lighting may be crucial to the reproduction of the wound's features.

It is recommended that the photographs of wounds be bracketed for exposure times or f-stop settings, because the wound may need more or less exposure time than the surrounding skin surface, and the measurement scale should be placed in the field of view. This precaution may prevent having to rephotograph the wound(s) after development of the film. Digital cameras are very helpful in this regard by permitting a preview of the appearance of the wound in the photographs.

BASIC CAMERA AND PHOTOGRAPHY INFORMATION

The lens and focusing

Light can be thought of as an infinite number of "rays" emanating or being reflected from every point on an object and traveling from it in straight lines. Because they travel in all directions, rays will not form an image on a screen unless something is used to control them, and in a camera, this task is performed by the lens.

There are two basic types of lenses:

1. Positive (converging) lens: This is the only type of lens that will form an image.
2. Negative (diverging) lens: This forms a virtual image that cannot be projected onto a screen.

In modern lenses, the lens is formed with a series of elements (see Compound lenses). Both positive and negative lenses are cemented together, in order to produce a lens which eliminates most of the aberrations in a single lens. These **high quality lenses** constitute one of the three factors which produce sharp images in the photograph. The second factor in producing sharp images is the **resolution** of the film type in film cameras or the image sensor in digital cameras. The third factor is **correct exposure** by the camera.

Focal length

In general, the thicker and more curved the surface of a lens, the greater its ability to bend light. This ability is usually measured as its "focal length"—the distance from the center of the lens to the point at which parallel rays entering the lens converge, and the more the light is bent, the shorter the focal length of the lens. The depth of field is related to the focal length. Longer focal length lenses have a smaller depth of field than the lenses with shorter focal lengths. The focal length also determines the magnification of the view. The longer the focal length is, the higher the magnification of the field of view and the more narrow the angle of view. A 28-mm lens has a wide angle of view with a small magnification of the view, whereas a 150-mm lens has a very narrow angle of view and considerable magnification of the field of view, hence the term "telephoto" for the long focal length lenses.

Compound lenses

Compound lenses serve to eliminate defects or aberrations caused by the use of just a single lens. In a compound lens, the light passes through a series of "elements" (positive and negative lenses) that are designed so that their individual defects cancel one another when used together. There are wide-angle lenses (fish eye: up to 21 mm; large depth of field; field 70 degrees or more); standard lenses (50–55 mm; field 45–50 degrees; normal depth of field); long-focus lenses (80–135 mm; field 18–28 degrees; shallow depth of field); and zoom lenses that allow the photographer to select the focal length by adjustment (28–80 mm, 35–100 mm, 70–200 mm, etc.). The zoom lens is very practical in the field, since it allows for a wide variety of views without changing lenses (especially good are the zoom lenses with a macro format, allowing for close-up photographs).

The shutter

There are two basic types of shutter mechanisms:

1. The focal plane shutter, which is positioned just in front of the film (hence the name) and is used almost exclusively in SLRs.
2. The leaf shutter, which is positioned either just inside the lens housing close to the diaphragm (in the case of the compound lens) or behind the lens (in the case of a simple lens).

The principal function of the shutter is to keep light from striking the film prior to shooting and upon pressing the shutter to let light strike the film—for a fraction of a second. The speeds marked on most modern cameras follow a sequence that, like the sequence of f numbers, is based on halving the exposure at each step (1 second, 1/2, 1/4, 1/8, 1/15, 1/30, 1/60, 1/125, 1/250, 1/500, 1/1000 second, etc.).

The aperture and exposure

The eye adjusts very rapidly to changes in the intensity of light, and only when the eye is moving from one extreme to another does the wide range of intensities found every day become obvious. The eye, in fact, has an automatic aperture (the iris), which opens and closes to regulate as far as possible the brightness of the image reaching the retina.

A given photographic film similarly requires a fairly exact amount of light to record a good image, and unless there is some device to reduce or increase the brightness, the camera will be restricted to taking pictures only if the light itself remains constant. Several factors affect the amount of light reaching the film, principally the duration of the exposure and the diameter of the aperture. The aperture is calibrated in f-numbers that are found on the barrel of the lens. They can range from 1.2 to 22. The larger the f-stop, the smaller the aperture; the smaller the f-stop, the larger the aperture. *Example:* An exposure of (1/60 sec at f/8) is the same exposure as (1/30 sec at f/11).

Camera Shake

Camera shake (tremor, vibration) is the movement passed to the camera by involuntary hand and body tremors, causing less sharp photographs. This phenomenon can be minimized in several ways. For long-distance photographs with long focal length lenses, it is necessary to mount the camera on a tripod, since the camera shake is considerably magnified by the long focal length lenses. For shorter focal length lenses, many cameras have **image stabilization** (IS) in the lens (lens based) or camera body (body based) which compensates for hand shake. In film cameras, faster film and/or faster shutter speed may compensate fully for hand shake.

Depth of field

When a lens is focused on a point a certain distance away, there will be a zone both in front of and behind this point that also appears acceptably sharp on the film; this zone is called the "depth of field." Depth of field can be controlled because it is affected by changes in the aperture size. With the aperture fully open, a lens has a small depth of field, and the further the lens is stopped down, the more the depth of field. *Example:* With a 50-mm lens focused at 2 meters, an aperture of f/16 will ensure that everything between about 1.5 and 3 meters (5–10 feet) is in focus. An aperture of f/2, however, will reduce the depth of field to a fraction of a meter either side of the original 2 meters. Two general principles are worth noting: First, the greater the distance, the greater the depth of field; thus shallow depth of field becomes an extremely awkward problem at very close distances. Second, depth of field tends to be greater behind the main object of focus than in front of it.

The depth of field is also affected by the focal length of the lens (see previous discussion). A lens with a short focal length has a greater depth of field than a lens with a longer focal length. The choice of focal length for the lens and the aperture size provides the photographer with the ability to ensure a clear focus for the items in a particular photograph.

The light meter and exposure

Two materials traditionally used for measuring accurately the brightness of the available light are selenium and cadmium sulfide (CdS). An increasing number of cameras include their own metering systems, the most sophisticated kind being the "through the lens" (TTL) meters (nearly all use CdS), which monitor the brightness of the actual image formed by the lens. Some are directly linked to the shutter and aperture controls to give fully automatic exposure. Three types of TTL metering are (1) average reading, with two photosensitive cells; (2) center weighted, with two overlapping photosensitive cells for intensity of center readings; and (3) spot meter, with one small spot in the center of view. Although handheld light meters can be very tricky, they are useful in the hands of a professional photographer.

Lighting

Light radiates in all directions from a point, and its illuminating effect diminishes with the square of the distance away from the source. For example, a surface ten feet away will receive one-fourth the light received on a surface five feet away (five squared is twenty-five, ten squared is one hundred). There are several types of artificial lighting (flash cube, electronic flash, strobe). Virtually all modern cameras use the electronic flash. Since light spreads as it travels, it is possible, if one cannot get light nearer to the object, to use slave strobes, screens, reflectors, and in some special cases, mirrors to enhance the lighting. Manual flash units have to be set by the photographer for the camera-to-subject distance for each photograph. Automatic flashes, which compensate for the distance between camera and subject, will automatically adjust the flash for the distance. It is important to remember that the camera shutter speed must be set to the flash synchronization speed when using the flash.

Filters

Filters are used to add contrast to the picture, provide special effects, or (in the case of polarizing filters) eliminate unwanted glare or reflections. There are many specialized uses for filters, such as providing more information in low relief shots. The following are for use only with black-and-white film: red filters allow only reds in; blue filters allow only blues in; and green filters allow only greens in. Different filters are used in color photography to compensate for the lighting available (fluorescent bulbs or incandescent light bulbs, for example). Polarizing filters remove much of the light reflected off surfaces and are essential in some circumstances (photography of fabric impressions on the surfaces of a hit-and-run vehicle, for example). Filters are also used when taking photographs with a laser or a forensic light as the source of the light for the photograph.

The single lens reflex camera

In the single lens reflex camera, one lens serves for both viewing and taking the picture, thus overcoming the problem of parallax. Because the view-finder automatically shows the image exactly as it will be recorded, the SLR is the most popular type of camera today using 35-mm film. Nearly all SLRs are fitted with an automatic diaphragm, which ensures that the image on the screen is bright enough to allow accurate focusing and clear viewing. Instead of closing down as soon as the aperture ring is turned, the aperture remains fully open until the moment the picture is taken. When the shutter release is pressed, the camera performs a complex series of actions. First, the diaphragm closes down to the preselected aperture; the mirror flips up out of the way, temporarily blacking out the viewing screen; the shutter then exposes the film at the selected speed; and finally, the mirror returns to its original position, and the diaphragm reopens.

Digital Cameras

Digital (imaging) cameras capture a **digital image** on a digital **image sensor**, also called an **image processor**. The image sensor is composed of **pixels** on the surface of the sensor. A pixel is a **single photosensitive unit** (cell) which senses the amount of light and the color of the light striking it. The image sensor records the data from all the pixels at the moment of exposure and transfers the data as an image to a storage card. The number of pixels in a sensor totals in the millions. One megapixel equals one million pixels, and the quality of the image produced by the sensor is largely determined by the number of megapixels in the sensor. Modern DSLRs with ten or more megapixels in the sensor produce prints virtually equal to that of film cameras.

Point-and-shoot digital cameras have a **liquid crystal display** (LCD) screen which acts as the view finder. DSLR cameras have an **optical view finder** and an LCD screen for viewing the captured images. The optical view finder has the advantage that it is not affected by strong ambient lighting, whereas the LCD view finder is difficult to see in bright light.

Storage cards are of several types, the most common of which are the **Secure Digital** (SD) card, which stores from one to eight megabytes, or the **Secure Digital High Capacity** (SDHC) card, which stores from one to sixteen megabytes of memory.

Image resolution is determined by the *quality of the camera lens* and the *number of megapixels* of the camera image sensor. In DSLR cameras, the image sensor is about 21.5 mm by 14.4 mm, larger than most point-and-shoot digital cameras. Most lenses are of high quality, so the limiting factor in image resolution is the number of megapixels in the image sensor. Technically, the term **resolution** refers to the ability to distinguish two small dots on a surface at certain distances. However, the term, as applied to the image sensor, refers to the *clarity of the image*. For crime scene cameras, the minimum acceptable number of megapixels is six, but every effort should be made to obtain a camera with ten or more megapixels, now offered by most camera manufacturers at very affordable prices. Cameras with ten megapixel or more image sensors are virtually equal to film cameras with respect to resolution and print quality.

Film types

BLACK-AND-WHITE FILM
There are five basic types of black-and-white film available:

1. Blue sensitive: This is used for extremely high resolving power.
2. Orthochromatic: This includes green but not red and orange.
3. Panchromatic: This is standard film, which includes the entire visible spectrum.
4. Infrared: This is beyond the visible spectrum (heat-sensitive).
5. X-ray: This is used for medical purposes.

COLOR FILM
There are three major types of color film employing the following color principles:

1. Agfa: The Agfacolor principle uses dye couplers immobilized by long chain hydrocarbon residue to prevent diffusion.
2. Ektachrome: The Ektachrome principle is substantive resin-protected dye couplers dispersed in emulsion.
3. Kodachrome: The Kodachrome principle is a nonsubstantive dye couplers in processing solutions.

FILM SPEED

Film speed is a way of measuring sensitivity to light. The "faster" the film, the more sensitive the film is to light. There are two common measuring systems for film speed:

1. ISO (International Organization for Standardization [same as the old ASA, American Standards Association]): This film speed value is based on an arithmetic scale.
2. DIN (German Institute for Standardization): This film speed value is based on a logarithmic scale.

In the ISO system, a film rated at 200 ISO is twice as fast as one rated at 100 ISO (i.e., it requires half as much exposure). In the DIN scale, an increase of 3 DIN is equivalent to doubling the speed. Thus, a 25 DIN is twice as fast as 22 DIN.

Ranges of various film speeds can be categorized as follows:

On the ISO scale:	20–50 ISO:	slow films
	80–200 ISO:	medium films
	400–1250 ISO:	fast films

Many films will have both the ISO speed and the DIN speed on the label (e.g., "ISO 400/27 DIN").

Infrared photography

Infrared photography uses infrared film, which records images formed by infrared light. Infrared photography is used in questioned document photography to locate and document alterations on documents, in aerial photography to assist in locating gravesites, and in the crime laboratory to detect and document gunshot residues on bloody or dark fabrics. The focus for infrared film is different from that for white light and so must be adjusted after focusing with white light to the index mark on the lens for infrared light.

Ultraviolet photography

Ultraviolet photography is used to document materials that glow under ultraviolet light, such as semen, certain fibers, and latent fingerprints dusted with fluorescent powders. The photographs are usually taken with black-and-white film and a filter that allows only ultraviolet light to pass (Kodak Wratten #18A, for example). Ultraviolet photography is also used to photograph body wounds such as bitemarks, sometimes providing enhanced contrast.

Summary

Work systematically
Crime scene photography should be an orderly and a systematic process. This approach will help ensure the efficiency and the effectiveness of the investigation.

Work from the perimeter toward the center
This approach mirrors the way in which the scene is registered in the investigator's mind, notes, and sketches.

Keep a log of all photographs taken

The photo log is essential to ensure the accuracy of testimony regarding the crime scene photographs.

Take notes of pertinent data

Take notes at the time of observations to avoid memory loss. This step is crucial when using a digital camera, in order to authenticate the digital photographs in court.

Use a two-member team whenever possible

A two-member team is much more efficient and effective than a single person. The additional time investment is more than offset by increased efficiency and the enhanced effectiveness of having the experience of two individuals, often manifested when determining the types and numbers of photographs needed in order to adequately document the scene.

Use color film or DSLR camera

Except for special circumstances, color print film is the film of choice for crime scene photography.

Continue to take additional photographs as needed

Additional photographs should be taken at the time they are needed, rather than going back and trying to "fill in" at a later time.

Take photographs for the point of view of each witness or principal at the crime scene

These photographs may be crucial to establish the credibility or lack thereof of a witness.

Too many photographs are better than not enough

It is better to have too many photographs than to miss one essential photograph, because the investigator will not be able to re-create exactly the conditions of the scene at a later date.

Take photographs during daylight hours whenever possible

Whenever feasible, it is best to wait until daylight to take outdoor photographs. The human eye is far more proficient in daylight than in night light.

Review the photograph log before departing the scene

- Have all the overview and medium-range photographs been taken?
- Have all evidence items been photographed with and without evidence markers in place?
- Are any additional photographs necessary? Review the photograph log with other team member(s).

Review Questions

1. One objective of crime scene photography is to record the condition of the scene before _____ occur.

2. An advantage of photography over sketches is that photographs closely approximate the way the _____ views the scene.

3. Photography is not a substitute for _____ or _____, but supplements these modes of documentation.

4. It is a good policy to take _____ _____ photographs rather than _____ _____, because the investigator cannot go back to the scene at a later date to photograph the scene in its original condition.

5. The best choice for crime scene photography is the _____ camera.

6. _____ print film is the film of choice for most crime scene photography.

7. A _____ should be kept of all photographs taken at a crime scene.

8. The first series of photographs to be taken at a crime scene are referred to as _____ or _____ photographs.

9. After completion of the photographs in item 8, _____ photographs should be taken of smaller areas at the crime scene.

10. Close-up photographs that require accurate documentation of their size should be taken both _____ and _____ a measurement scale in place.

11. Photographs should be taken to illustrate the _____ of principals and witnesses when applicable.

12. When feasible, it is better to wait until _____ to photograph the scene of a crime that occurs at night.

13. It is a good practice to _____ latent prints prior to attempting to lift the developed latent with fingerprint tape.

14. Wounds should be photographed with the camera plane _____ to the plane of the wound.

15. Crime scene photography should be an orderly and a _____ process.

16. Before the investigator departs the scene, the photograph _____ should be reviewed for completeness.

Further References

The editors of *Petersen's PHOTOgraphic Magazine*, and M. Stevesvold. 2002. *The Complete Idiot's Guide to Photography Like a Pro*, 2nd ed. New York: Alpha Books.

McDonald, J. A. 1992. *The Police Photographer's Guide*. Arlington Heights, IL: Phototext Books.

Staggs, S. 1997. *Crime Scene and Evidence Photographer's Guide*. Temecula, CA: Stagg Publishing.

APPENDIX 3-A

Basic Equipment List for Crime Scene Photography

1. **Camera(s)**
   1. SLR film camera
   2. Point-and-shoot digital camera
   3. Digital SLR
   4. Video camera
2. **Lenses**
   1. Normal
   2. Wide angle
   3. Zoom (35–70)
   4. Macro (close-up)
   5. Supplemental macro
3. **Filters**
   1. Polarizing
   2. Color selection
4. **External Flash**
   1. External flash
   2. Sync cords
   3. Extra batteries
5. **Measuring Scales**
   1. Standard 6" rulers
   2. Adhesive-backed rulers
   3. ABFO #2 ruler
   4. Folding rulers
   5. Measuring tapes
6. **Color Scales**
   1. Gray scale
   2. Color scale
7. **Item Markers**
   1. Numbered stands
   2. 3 × 5 Cards
   3. Felt pens (regular, indelible)
   4. Outdoor flags
8. **Lighting Accessories**
   1. 5-cell flashlight
   2. Quartz halide lamps
   3. Alternate light source
   4. Long wave UV light
   5. Short wave UV light
   6. Laser lights
9. **Film Selections**
   1. Color print film
   2. Black-and-white film

    3. Color Slide film

    4. Infrared film

10. Tripods

    1. For 35-mm camera

    2. Video Camera for panning

    3. Mini for trace evidence photos

11. Camera Cases

    1. Digital camera and accessories

    2. SLR film camera and accessories

    3. Lenses (11.1 and 11.2)

12. Extra Batteries

    1. Camera(s)

    2. External flash

    3. Battery chargers (flash, cameras)

APPENDIX 3-B

Common Photography Terminology

Angle of view (Angle of coverage). The amount of a scene taken in by a particular lens' focal length, expressed in degrees. The shorter the focal length of the lens, the wider the angle of view.

Aperture, lens. A fixed or adjustable window in the lens diaphragm that allows light through to the film. Auto-exposure cameras automatically adjust this window's size, called the f-stop (see f-stop), to control the exposure.

Aperture, maximum. The largest useful opening of the lens; wide open.

Aperture. Size of the opening of the lens diaphragm, expressed as a fraction of the focal length. The f/number.

Autoexposure. The system with which the camera automatically sets the lens aperture and shutter speed to get the correct amount of light to the film or (in a digital camera) the image sensor.

Autoflash. Flash mode in which the camera automatically decides whether or not flash is needed, turning the flash on in dim light and keeping it off in bright light.

Autofocus. Automatic focusing by the camera; may be turned on or off in most cameras to allow manual focusing.

Backlight compensation. Adjustment of exposure to prevent the subject from turning out too dark when light is coming from behind the subject.

Bounce light. Light directed away from the subject toward some nearby light-toned surface, which reflects and diffuses the light to avoid hot spots in the subject.

Bracket. To make a number of exposures with different exposure times, or f-stops, some at normal exposure times, some higher and some lower times, to ensure a proper exposure.

Burned out. An area of the print image that lacks detail, usually because of severe overexposure of the negative.

Camera shake. The movement passed to your camera by involuntary hand and body tremors, causing less sharp photographs.

Charge-coupled device (CCD). Electronic image sensor that is the equivalent to film in most digital point-and-shoots. The CCD uses rows of microscopic cells to measure and record light energy, storing the pattern they create as digital information. CMOS (complementary metal-oxide semiconductor) is an alternative image sensor technology used increasingly in digital camera.

Close-up lens. A positive supplementary lens that shortens a lens' focal length and permits closer-than-normal (macro) focusing.

Contrast. The difference in darkness and lightness in adjacent objects, or the subject, in the film negative, color slide, or a digital image.

Date print (Quartz-date). Term for cameras with the ability to imprint the date on photographic negatives or digital image, the date image itself.

Default. A mode, or group of modes, that a camera returns to after settings are changed for a particular shot or roll.

Depth of field. Region of acceptably sharp focus around the subject position, extending toward the camera and away from it, from the plane of sharpest focus. The boundaries of the depth of field are referred to as the near limit and the far limit.

Diaphragm. The assembly of thin metal leaves, usually incorporated into the lens barrel or shutter assembly, which can be adjusted to control the size of the lens aperture. Same as iris diaphragm.

Digital. Pertaining to computer language and operation. A digital camera captures and stores pictures without film, for direct use in computer software and printing applications.

Distortion. The inability of a photographic lens to record an accurate image—not to be confused with perspective (so called distortion) when referring to a photograph.

Downloading. The process of transferring picture files from your digital camera to a computer; also, of transferring a digital file from the Internet to your personal computer.

Exposure, correct. The specific amount of light that must strike a given film or image sensor to produce the best possible picture quality; a function of exposure time, f-stop, and light source intensity.

Exposure. The act of subjecting a photosensitive material to the action of light; amount of light striking the material, one shot on a film negative, slide, or image card.

f/stop (f/number). The numerical expression of the aperture diameter of a lens diaphragm as a fraction of the focal length (e.g., f/2.8, f/5.6, f/11, etc.). The f/numbers are inscribed on the lens and represent the f/stops to which the camera lens can be set. Each adjacent f/stop doubles or cuts in half the amount of light coming through the lens (e.g., an f/stop of 2.8 allows twice as much light to strike the film or image sensor as does that of an f/stop setting of f/5.6).

Fill flash. (also known as flash-on). Flash mode in which the camera fires the flash for every shot, used to fill shadows with light in bright outdoor light or directed into the shadow areas of the subject to reduce the lighting contrast.

Film, slow. Film with relatively low sensitivity to light, reflected in its lower ISO rating—usually ISO 200 and below.

Film, slide. Film designed to produce a positive transparent image of the subject on the original film itself. Mainly intended for projection or scanning rather than printing, though prints can be made directly from slides.

Film speed. The measure of a film's sensitivity to light, film speed is indicated with an ISO number—ISO 400, for example. The higher the number, the more sensitive the film.

Film, fast. Film with a high sensitivity to light, reflected in its high ISO rating—usually ISO 400 and above.

Filter. A sheet or disk of plastic, glass, or other material, usually colored, which can be used to absorb selected components of transmitted light.

Flash, electronic. Extremely useful light source for crime scene photography; the flash fires in an action-stopping burst and often has several different modes.

Focal length. Technical term indicating how wide or narrow a section of a scene the lens includes in a picture (angle of view), and/or how big or small it makes the subject (magnification).

Focal length, normal. Focal length setting—usually around 55 mm with 35 mm models and, 40 mm with APS models—that helps reproduce the most natural-looking size relationships in a scene (e.g., similar to what the eye perceives).

Focal length range. Focal lengths offered by a zoom lens. It's specified by the shortest and the longest, in millimeters—for example, 38–90 mm.

Focus point. Small brackets, lines, or a circle in the middle of an auto-focus viewfinder or viewing screen; it indicates where the camera is focusing.

Frame numbers. Numbers printed on the paper backing strip and along the edges of roll film, and outside the perforation of 35-mm film strips, which can be used to identify the individual pictures (or frames).

Frame lines. Light or dark lines or brackets just inside the viewfinder frame that indicate the area of the scene that will be recorded on the film.

Frame counter. The display that tells how many shots have been taken on a roll of film, or on a digital camera.

Frame. (1) The rectangle you see when you look through a camera's viewfinder or at its viewing screen (2) To adjust the position and angle of the camera with respect to the subject for the purpose of composing the image within the boundaries of the view-finder (3) The image (picture) itself and (4) One exposure on a film or digital card.

Hot spot. An undesirable concentration of light on an area of the subject, often due to the flash when it is not oblique to the subject surface.

Image sensor. The electronic equivalent to film in a digital camera, the rectangle of microscopic, light-sensitive cells with which the camera records the picture (see CCD).

Image. The representation of the subject photographed. The visible result of exposing and developing a photographic emulsion; in digital cameras, the visible result captured and/or displayed by the camera's memory; and a print produced from film or a digital memory card.

Inverse square law. Illumination intensity on a surface will vary inversely with the square of the distance from the light source to the illuminated surface, for example, subject twice as far from the flash receives 1/4th the amount of light.

ISO number. Number that indicates a film's specific sensitivity to light; it's also now used to describe the (adjustable) sensitivity of the image sensor in a digital camera.

LCD screen. Liquid crystal display screen at the back of point-and-shoot digital cameras, used for composing the shot and viewing the resultant image; in DSLRs, the viewing screen on the camera back for viewing the image from an exposure; in some DSLRs, it also acts as LCD panel for camera settings.

LCD (liquid crystal display) panel. Usually found on the top of a camera, it indicates camera status and settings. Not to be confused with the color LCD screen (also called an LCD monitor) used for shooting and reviewing pictures in a point-and-shoot digital camera.

Lens mount. Portion of the camera body which holds the lens in position.

Lens, long. A lens of longer-than-normal focal length; telephoto lens.

Lens, interchangeable. A lens which can be removed from the camera body as a complete unit and replaced by another.

Lens, macro. Also occasionally micro-lens. A term used to describe lenses especially corrected for use at short subject distances. The prefixes "macro" or "micro" often appear in the lens name. Zoom lenses may have macro settings.

Lens, zoom. A lens of adjustable focal length. The camera operator can zoom to increase or decrease the lens's magnifying power, making the subject larger or smaller in the frame (see zooming in and zooming out).

Lens, normal. Any lens whose focal length is approximately equal to the diagonal measurement of the film frame, usually about 50–55 millimeters across the film frame diagonal in a 35-mm camera.

Lens hood. A device for shielding the front element of a lens from direct light from outside the subject area, so as to prevent or reduce flare from extraneous light sources.

Lens, telephoto. Also called a long focal length lens. A lens with a focal length 70 mm (with 35-mm cameras) and beyond. The subject is magnified, as with a telescope.

Lens, wide angle. Lens with a short focal length, in which the lens takes in a relatively large section of the total scene (e.g., 28-mm and 35-mm lenses); a lens whose angular coverage is substantially greater than that of a "normal" lens.

Lens. A cylinder of shaped pieces of glass or plastic at the front of a camera; it projects an image of the subject onto the film or image sensor.

Light meter. The built-in device that the camera uses to measure light levels and determine the correct exposure setting for a photograph.

Macrophotography. The photography of objects at moderate degrees of reduction or magnification.

Megabyte. A million bytes of digital information, the unit of measurement generally used to describe the size of a picture file. (A byte is the amount of information needed to create or reproduce one color pixel.)

Megapixel. One million pixels (see pixel), used as a unit of measurement to describe the resolution of a digital camera.

Memory card. The small plastic and silicon wafer on which most digital cameras store their pictures; it comes in a variety of types, physical sizes, and capacities (indicated in megabytes).

Mode. A setting that causes the camera to perform a specific function or operation.

Muddy. Term for prints that are lacking in detail, contrast, and color brilliance.

Neutral density filter. A thin sheet or disk of glass, plastic, or gelatin having plane and parallel faces, toned to some uniform and specific shade of gray and intended to be used over the camera lens during exposure for the purpose of reducing the intensity of the exposing light without changing its color. Sometimes called ND filters, they are available in accurately calibrated densities from 0.1 to 4.0.

Overexposed. Refers to a photographic image which has received too much light.

Parallax error. The difference between what the lens sees and what the camera operator sees through the camera's viewfinder; especially pronounced at longer focal lengths and with closer subjects.

Perspective. To photograph a scene or objects as it would appear to the eye; the different views afforded by lenses of different focal length.

Photomicrography. Photography through a microscope.

Picture file (also called an image file). The photographic equivalent of a text file, it's the digital file with which a photograph is displayed on a computer and/or reproduced as a print. It can be created without film with a digital camera, or by scanning film negatives, slides, or prints.

Pixel. The small color sensitive component of an image sensor. The image sensor consists of millions of pixels (one million pixels = one megapixel) that act together to convert the light image to an electronic file, the digital image. The digital image is visualized on LCD screens and converted to pictures with computer printers.

Positive. An image in which the tones or colors are similar to those of the subject.

Printer. Desktop computer peripheral designed to produce prints from picture files; should be a "photo quality" model for photographic purposes.

Random access memory (RAM). The amount of active digital storage in your computer, RAM must be relatively high to allow work with photographs and digital-imaging software.

Resolution. Technical term for the measurement of photographic sharpness; it applies to lenses, film, and the image sensors in digital cameras. The resolution of digital cameras is often described in megapixels, for example, 4, 6, 10, or 12 megapixels.

Scanning. The process of translating a photograph (negative, slide, or print) into an electronic form that can be used by computers.

Sharpness. The degree to which clear, distinguishable details of the subject are rendered in a photographic negative or print, or digital image.

Shot, photographic. The typical term for the taking of a single photograph with a camera. Other somewhat synonymous terms are "exposure," "frame," "picture," etc., and the photograph or image itself.

Shutter button. The button that you press to take a picture. On auto-focus cameras, the shutter button also activates and locks the focus when pressed halfway.

Shutter speed. (1) The length of time (usually a small fraction of a second) that the shutter in a camera's lens stays open to let light through to the film; (2) the duration of the interval of exposure; (3) the marked settings on a shutter dial. The numbers represent the denominators of fractions of which 1 is the numerator, for example, a setting of $100 = 1/100$th of a second exposure time, a setting of $400 = 1/400$ of a second exposure time.

Side light (oblique light). Light striking the subject from one side; increases dramatically the texture of the subject and used extensively in forensic sciences to show depth features of the subject for comparison purposes.

Single lens reflex (SLR). A reflex camera in which the viewfinder image is formed by the camera lens and reflected to a top-mounted viewing screen by a hinged mirror normally inclined behind the camera lens. During exposure of the film, the mirror flips up to seal the ground-glass opening, allowing the image light to pass through to the film chamber. In most designs, a focal plane shutter is employed.

Slide. A transparency mounted in cardboard, metal, plastic, or glass, for projection onto a screen for viewing.

SLR. Abbreviation for single lens reflex.

Stop down. To reduce the size of the aperture of a lens (e.g., change from f/5.6 to f/22).

Subject. The thing or view photographed.

Supplementary lens. A simple lens or lens system to be used over a camera lens for the purpose of altering effective focal length, for example, a macro supplementary lens for close-up shots (sometimes in the form of a lens in a filter ring for quick attachment).

Thumbnails. Small reference images of the shots on a roll of film or a memory card, appearing in an index print or on a computer screen.

Time exposure. Specifically, a camera exposure made by setting the shutter dial on T, but generally used to refer to any exposure, timed manually, of longer than a second or so.

Time. One of the marked speeds on most shutters. A shutter set on "time" will open when the shutter release is pressed and close when it is released. It is a convenient setting for exposure intervals of more than a second.

Transparency. See Slide.

Tripod. A three-legged stand, usually adjustable in height and provided with a tilting and swivelling head, on which a camera can be fastened for support and stability during use.

Ultraviolet. The common name for the band of short wavelength, high-frequency electromagnetic radiations which border the visible spectrum beyond visible violet light.

USB (Universal Serial Bus). Common system for connecting digital cameras, card readers, and other peripherals to your computer via a USB cord.

Viewfinder. Window on the camera through which you see the rectangular frame used to view and compose your subject.

Viewing screen (also called an LCD screen or LCD monitor). The small, TV-like screen on the back of a digital camera with which you can compose pictures, review pictures you've taken, and adjust the menu.

Zooming out. Setting a shorter focal length on your zoom lens, to include more of the scene in the picture.

Zooming in. Setting a longer focal length on your zoom lens, to make the subject larger in the picture.

4 | CRIME SCENE SKETCHES

It is said that a picture is worth a thousand words, but in crime scene investigation, that picture is worth much more when accompanied with an accurate and detailed sketch.

Robert Ogle

Key Words: Accurate location, systematic, critical areas, equal accuracy, two individuals, layout sketch, rough sketch, detailed sketch, blowup sketch, exploded view sketches, elevation sketches, finished sketches, display sketches, computer-drawn sketches, critical accuracy, rectangular coordinate, triangulation, secondary reference points, transecting baseline.

INTRODUCTION

The value of crime scene sketches derives from their ability to present a great deal of information about the scene without extraneous details, thus providing vital data for reconstruction and re-creation efforts for the events of the crime. The objectives for crime scene sketching include presenting a clear illustration of the scene framework, complementing notes and photographs, and showing the location and relationships of objects at the scene. It is essential that the sketches be prepared in a systematic manner, in order to maximize their value to the investigation.

VALUE OF SKETCHES

Crime scene sketches are an essential *supplement* to the investigator's notes and photographs at the crime scene. Although photographs provide a view of the scene similar to what the eye sees, they are two-dimensional and lack information about precise spatial relationships of the items seen. Sketches provide precision with regard to these spatial relationships and to the geometric characteristics of the scene. These geometric attributes are essential as a foundation for reconstruction efforts and for re-creation of the scene(s) in the mind's eye of a judge or juror. The sketches also furnish a visual model to illustrate the investigator's testimony in court.

OBJECTIVES OF CRIME SCENE SKETCHES

Present a clear "mind's eye" picture of the crime scene

The sketch differs from photographs by eliminating objects at the scene that do not have evidentiary value. Major features, such as furniture, should be included, so as to allow for reconstruction efforts and to provide accurate spatial relationship data for items in the photographs.

Complement the investigator's notes and photographs

The sketch complements the investigator's notes and photographs, but it replaces neither. Whereas photographs give a "normal" view, the notes add details of observation that are not obvious in the photographs or sketches.

Show the accurate location and relationships of the evidence items

The sketches provide a means of documenting the **accurate location** of evidence items and other objects through accurate, recorded measurements. The measurements are placed on the sketch or in a separate legend on the same page or on a clearly labeled attachment.

Refresh the memory of investigators

Many investigations require months or even years to complete. Although the details of a scene may be clear in the investigator's mind initially, the sketch will be needed to re-create the scene at later dates, particularly for judicial proceedings, where crisp and accurate testimony depends on accurate details in the sketches. No matter how robust the investigator's memory, well-drawn sketches at the scene are required to reconstruct the scene at a future date and to add credibility to the investigator's testimony during court proceedings.

Illustrate the testimony of witnesses

The testimony of witnesses will appear vague to a judge or jury unless there is a framework to *illustrate* the area referred to by the witness. Moreover, the sketches will allow for assessment of whether or not the witness could have seen the actions testified to by the witness, on the basis of the dimensions of the scene and the stated position of the witness.

Provide factual data for crime scene reconstructions

Reconstruction of the events and their sequence at the crime scene is one of the primary purposes for the collection and analysis of physical evidence. Any reconstruction effort must rely on accurate spatial relationships of the evidence items at the scene. Well-drawn sketches are the most efficient and effective way to provide the *factual* data needed for reconstruction efforts.

RULES OF THUMB FOR SKETCHES

Plan systematically for sketching the scene

As in the other operations performed at the crime scene, the investigator should have a clear idea as to the types of sketches needed to convey the essential details of the scene to other investigators in the case, to the attorneys who will handle the prosecution, and to the judge and jury who may ultimately hear the case. A **systematic** plan provides the best approach to ensure that the investigator prepares an adequate number and type of sketches of the scene.

First roughly show the overall layout of the scene

These layout/overview sketches provide the framework for showing the relationship of subsequent, detailed sketches. These sketches will also provide a distinct frame of reference for the photographs of the scene and the investigator's report regarding the crime scene processing. The use of graph paper is helpful when preparing these and the other types of sketches.

Prepare detailed sketches of pertinent area with measurements

Detailed sketches with *measurements* for pertinent areas should follow the layout sketches. Each area sketched should be readily referenced to the layout sketches.

Prepare blowup sketches as necessary

Blowup sketches for **critical areas** and measurements can be made as circumstances dictate. Bloodstain patterns, bullet trajectories, and areas containing a *large number of evidence items* are some of the circumstances that are better illustrated with blowup sketches for each area of interest.

Additional sketches

Additional sketches should be prepared as needed during the investigation. It is better to have a number of clear, uncomplicated sketches, rather than have one or two sketches with objects and measurements crammed into the space available. Too much detail in a small area may make the sketch unreadable.

EXAMPLE

In a residence where several rooms contain evidence, each room should be presented on a separate sketch, since each room can be related to the layout sketch of the residence.

ADDITIONAL POINTS TO KEEP IN MIND

Show compass point on sketch

It is traditional to show the north arrow on sketches, although this practice is of little value other than in outdoor rural scenes where there are no streets for orientation. The investigator will need a magnetic compass for rural scenes to determine the direction of (magnetic) north.

Make accurate measurements for all evidence items

Show the accuracy used to make your measurements (e.g., 28', $6\frac{1}{2}$"). The "$\frac{1}{2}$" indicates the measurement was made to the nearest one-half inch. It is difficult to make measurements closer than the nearest half-inch, since it is difficult to achieve exact 90-degree angles when using the rectangular coordinate method of measurement or to achieve an exact zero for the triangulation method of measurement. If extreme accuracy is needed for crime scene measurements, the measurements can be made by a surveying team or with laser-based measurement systems.

Use equal accuracy for measurements for items on the same sketch

It is a good practice to use **equal accuracy** for all the measurements on the same sketch. If higher accuracy is needed for some of the items in the scene, it is both easier for the preparer and more clear to the viewer when a separate blowup sketch is prepared for these items.

Use fundamental methods for measurements

Use only metal tapes of good quality to make the crime scene measurements. "Range finder" measurement devices can be used for many measurements, providing the investigator has personally calibrated the device with a good metal tape. Walker wheels can be used for long distances (these devices should also be calibrated on a periodic basis). Avoid the use of esoteric measuring devices or methods, especially those that are understood only by you. The measurements should be in feet and inches (except in metric measurement countries) and fractions of inches. *One exception to the rule of using English measurement units is the measurement of bloodstains for bloodstain pattern reconstructions, for which measurements, by convention, are taken in metric units.* Metric measurement is necessary for bloodstains because of the small size of the droplet stains, which creates difficulty when trying to measure them with the English system of measurements.

Make sure that the tape is straight and does not sag when the measurement is taken

Sagging of the tape when it is suspended can introduce a significant *error,* especially in measuring long distances. If the tape is not straight, an error in the measurement will occur.

Avoid common errors such as the following

- Reading numbers upside down (6 for 9).
- Reading the wrong foot mark.
- Confusing the zero point of tape.
- Reading tenths of a foot for inches (engineer's tape).

Have two individuals verify all measurements

It is a good practice to have **two individuals** verify all the measurements in each sketch. This precaution allows for either individual to authenticate the sketches and measurements in court proceedings. In the event that either individual is unavailable for testimony at the court proceedings, the other can provide the testimony necessary for admission of the sketches and measurements at the crime scene.

TYPES OF SKETCHES

Rough sketches at the scene

LOCALITY (OVERVIEW OR GENERAL AREA LAYOUT) SKETCHES

The locality **layout sketch** (see Figure 4-1) illustrates the general area in which the crime scene occurs. The locality layout sketch is used for orientation of the other sketches prepared at the scene. The locality layout sketch is a **rough sketch** designed to provide an overview of the crime scene locality in order to "place" the spatial relationships of the various areas in the mind's eye. This sketch is drawn without measurement and only approximates the relative sizes of the various areas. If accurate locality sketches are needed, they can be prepared later by a survey team or by reference to locality maps of the city.

LAYOUT SKETCHES OF SMALLER AREAS

The layout sketches of smaller areas (see Figure 4-2) are used to show the spatial relationships of the detailed sketches of each of the smaller areas sketched. Layout sketches are prepared without accurate measurements, since they are used only to orient readers of the report to the spatial relationships of other sketches and the photographs taken at the scene. This type of sketch is not needed when the crime scene consists only of a small, confined area needing only one or two sketches. The layout sketch of smaller areas is similar in concept to the locality sketch except that the area is smaller and an attempt is made to make the sketch closer to the actual proportions of the scene, without actual measurements being taken of the area.

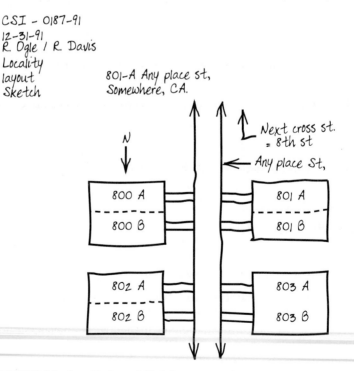

FIGURE 4-1 Locality Layout Sketches

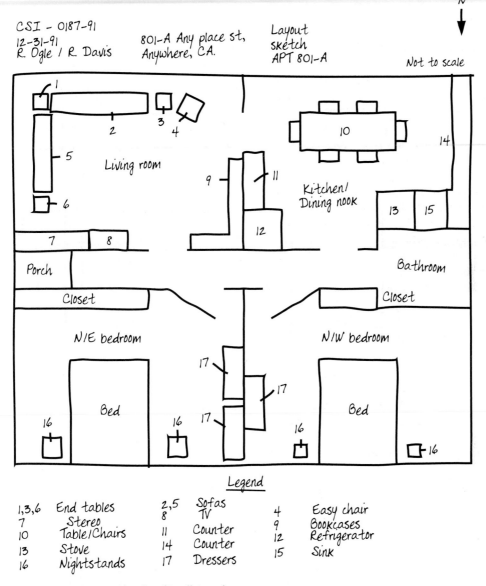

CSI - 0187-91
12-31-91
R. Ogle / R. Davis

801-A Any place st,
Anywhere, CA.

Layout
sketch
APT 801-A

N

Not to scale

1
2
3
4
5
Living room
6
7
8
Porch
Closet
N/E bedroom
Bed
16
16
17
17
17
16

9
11
12
10
14
Kitchen/
Dining nook
13   15
Bathroom
Closet
N/W bedroom
Bed
16

Legend

1,3,6	End tables	2,5	Sofas	4	Easy chair
7	Stereo	8	TV	9	Bookcases
10	Table/Chairs	11	Counter	12	Refrigerator
13	Stove	14	Counter	15	Sink
16	Nightstands	17	Dressers		

FIGURE 4-2 Layout Sketches (Small Areas)

DETAILED SKETCHES (NOT TO SCALE) WITH MEASUREMENTS

The **detailed sketch** (see Figure 4-3) is what the term "sketch" or "diagram" usually refers to when referencing a crime scene sketch. This sketch hand drawn at the scene contains measurements for all evidence item locations and other pertinent objects such as furniture. These sketches are not drawn to scale, but it is helpful to make the proportions similar to those at the scene, so that the sketch will have a "normal" appearance. This rough sketch is prepared by first drawing the area to be sketched in a roughly proportional fashion. The objects and physical evidence in the area are then

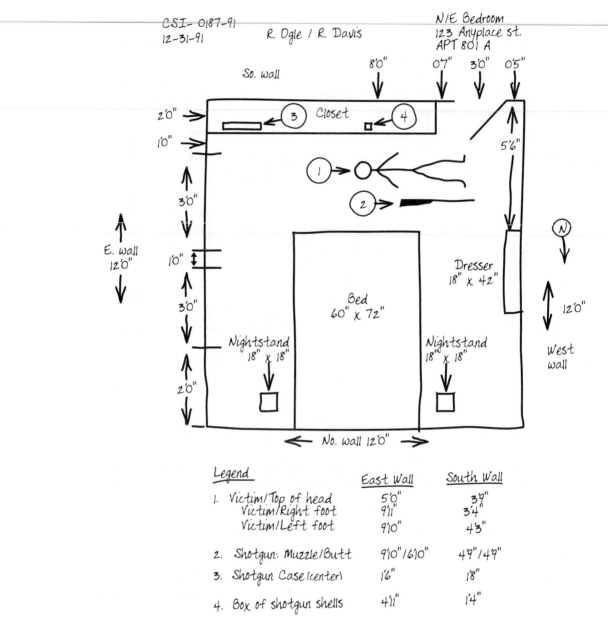

FIGURE 4-3   Detailed Sketch (Bird's-Eye View)

drawn in and measurements to each object and evidence item are made and placed on the sketch.

BLOWUP SKETCHES FOR FINE DETAILS

The **blowup sketch** (see Figure 4-4) allows for higher accuracy of measurements for blood spatters, bullet trajectories, or other pattern evidence that requires measurements that are more accurate than those in the larger format sketches. Blowup sketches are detailed

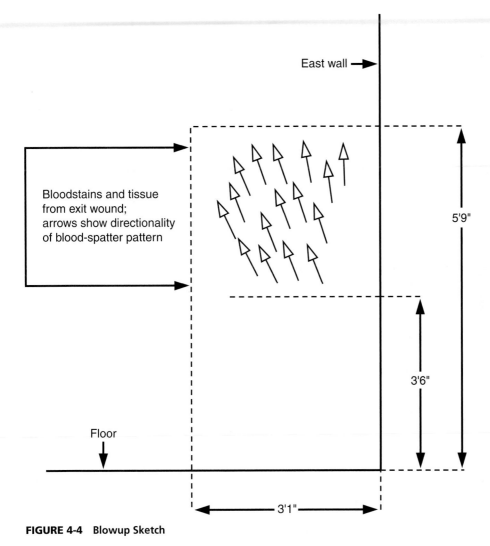

FIGURE 4-4 Blowup Sketch

sketches of small areas inside a larger sketch. The blowup sketch is used where there are a large number of evidence items or where there is a pattern that needs to be documented with very accurate measurements (e.g., multiple bullet holes, bloodstain spatter patterns on a floor or a wall). Use the secondary reference points method to establish secondary points for measurement to each item in the detailed area sketch (see Figure 4-12).

EXPLODED VIEW SKETCH SHOWING THE WALLS LYING FLAT
Exploded view sketches (see Figure 4-5) are used to illustrate the interrelationships of blood spatters, bullet holes, and trajectories or other patterns of significance. This type of sketch shows the walls (and occasionally the ceiling) lying *flat* (folded down) as though there had been an "explosion" that knocked the walls down. This is a finished sketch prepared from the rough sketches made at the scene. Its use is limited to those applications for which it is advantageous to show the spatial relationships of detail on the walls (bullet holes, for example) that need to be seen simultaneously with the layout of the floor plan.

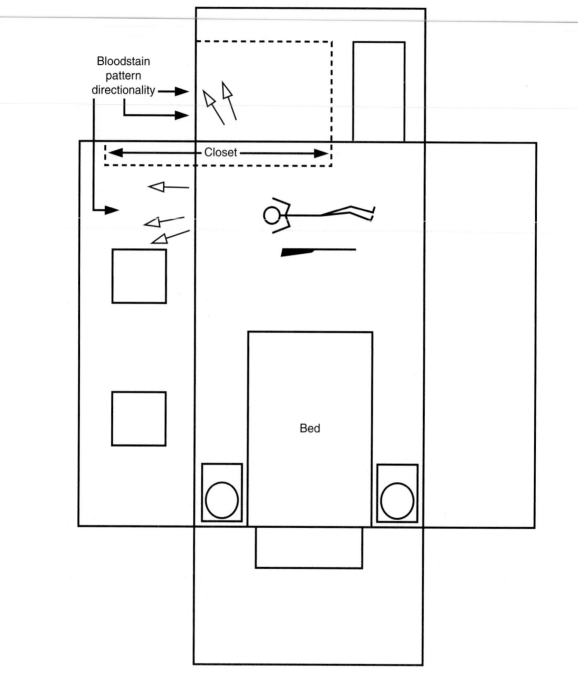

FIGURE 4-5   Exploded View Sketch

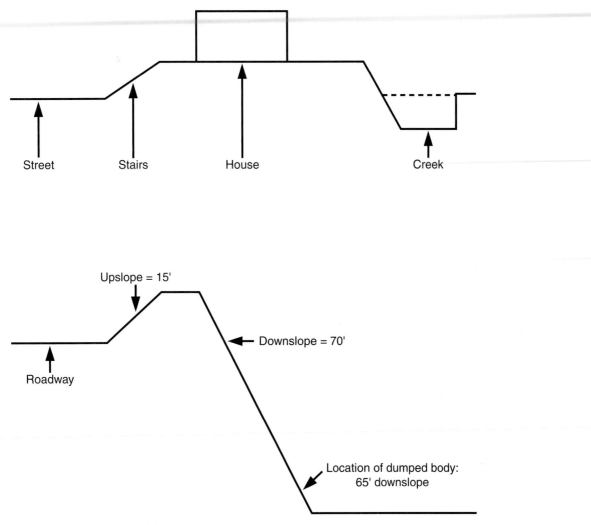

FIGURE 4-6 Elevation Sketches

ELEVATION SKETCHES

Elevation sketches (see Figure 4-6) are used to show the slopes present in the scene. The elevation drawings are rough sketches made in order to show the elevation perspective of a crime scene. An elevation drawing is a rough representation of the terrain without elevation measurements and is a supplement to photographs. If accurate elevation drawings are needed, they can be made by a surveying crew or by other professional crews using surveyor's equipment.

Finished sketches

FINISHED SKETCH (NOT TO SCALE)

Finished sketches (see Figure 4-7) are for report purposes, not for courtroom use. Although these sketches are not to scale, the preparer should try to make proportions

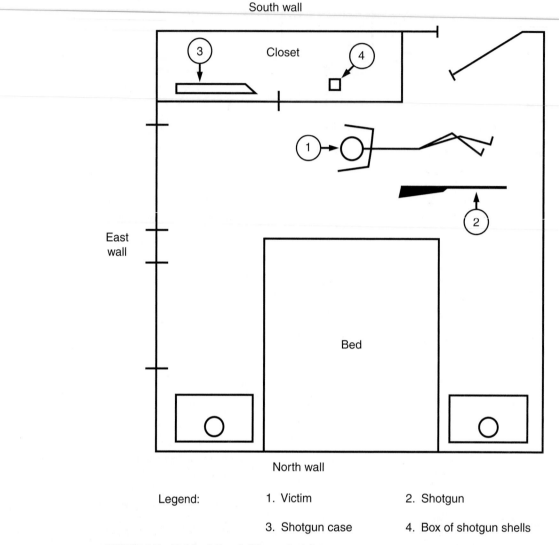

FIGURE 4-7   Finished Sketch (Not to Scale)

approximately to scale to help in visualizing the spatial relationships of the items at the scene. Make sure that all pertinent objects and data appear in the sketch. Label the sketch "NOT TO SCALE" clearly, so that the reader will know that the proportions are only approximate.

FINISHED SKETCH (DRAWN TO SCALE)

Use an architect's scale for accuracy in the drawing. The scale for the drawing should be appropriate for the size of the area drawn and the size of the paper being used. Table 4-1 lists suggested guidelines for appropriate scales to be used in drawing a sketch to scale. The finished sketch drawn to scale should be first drawn with pencil; then when the pencil drawing is finished, the pencil lines can be drawn over using drawing pens designed

TABLE 4-1	Suggested Guidelines for the Scale of Sketches Drawn to Scale
Scale	**Size of Area Drawn**
1/2" = 1'0"	Small rooms
1/4" = 1'0"	Larger rooms
1/8" = 1'0"	Apartment buildings, outdoor areas

for finished sketches, and the excess pencil lines can be erased with a white eraser. Legends and other data should be added using letter guides or transfer lettering in order to give the sketch a finished look.

Courtroom display sketches

Display sketches, which are for courtroom display purposes only, represent a wide variety of sketches, from a simple sketch drawn to scale to a very large drawing in color by an architect or a professional graphics artist; or, in some cases, they may be **computer-drawn sketches** that may be printed out on paper of various sizes or may be projected onto a courtroom video display screen of very large size.

It is expected that video display sketches will gain popularity in the future, as computer technology becomes more and more common in law enforcement agencies. For courtroom displays, use large dimensions of paper or large matte board, so that detail can be seen by the jurors.

Critical accuracy sketches (reconstruction, courtroom displays)

MANUALLY DRAWN SKETCHES
Critical accuracy sketches should be drawn using an architect's scale for measurement and placement of items in the sketch. Bullet trajectory angles, blood-spatter patterns, and other data necessary for reconstruction efforts can then be placed on the scaled drawing in a manner that reflects the facts as determined at the scene.

PROFESSIONALLY DRAWN SKETCHES
Enlist the aid of architects or professional graphic illustrators when necessary. These professionals are invaluable in many cases in which large-scale exhibits need to be prepared. The architects/graphics illustrators have the necessary equipment and experience to produce first-rate exhibits at a reasonable cost.

COMPUTER DRAWN SKETCHES
Sketches can be drawn with the computer using computer aided drafting and design (*CADD*) programs (the acronym CADD is used here to avoid confusion with CAD, computer aided dispatch). There are a number of CADD programs available at reasonable cost. CADD-drawn sketches can be drawn to high accuracy and can be projected onto large screens for courtroom use. There are also CADD programs with symbol libraries (see Figure 4-8) for placement of items into the sketch and symbol libraries available that can be used with many different CADD programs. The advantages of a CADD sketch are the ease of using exact measurements in the sketch. In addition, the CADD sketch can

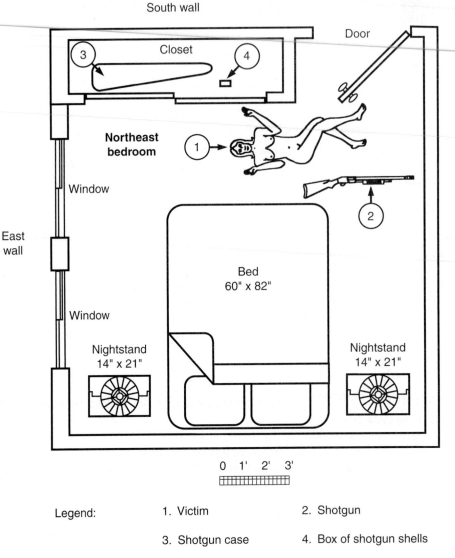

South wall

Door

Closet

③   ④

Northeast
bedroom   ①

Window

East
wall

Window

Bed
60" x 82"

Nightstand
14" x 21"

Nightstand
14" x 21"

②

0 1' 2' 3'

Legend: 1. Victim   2. Shotgun

3. Shotgun case   4. Box of shotgun shells

FIGURE 4-8   Computer-Drawn Sketch
Courtesy of Don Truitt, dataSketch Law Enforcement Software Products, Stockton, CA.
dataSketch™ is a trademark of dataSketch Law Enforcement Software Products, Stockton,
CA. All symbols in this figure are copyrighted by dataSketch Law Enforcement Software
Products. All rights reserved.

easily be edited to add additional data or additional detail to the sketch for reports or
courtroom exhibits.

Figures 4-9 and 4-10 also illustrate sketches prepared with commercially available
computer-based (CAD) drawing programs. The low cost and ease of use make these
types of CAD programs affordable and desirable for the crime scene units tasked with the
preparation of sketches suitable for courtroom displays.

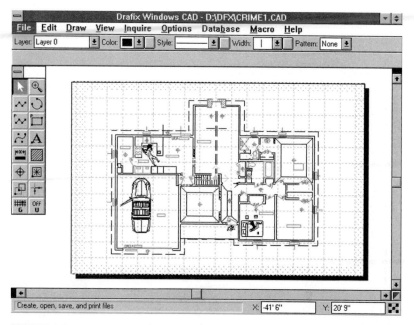

FIGURE 4-9   Screen View of CAD Drawing Program Showing Computer-Drawn Sketch of Residence
Courtesy of Sirchie Fingerprint Laboratories.

Three-dimensional computer drawn sketches

There are also a number of computer drawing programs that provide three-dimensional views of the scene. These programs are especially helpful to the individual preparing a crime scene reconstruction, since the programs permit viewing of the scene from a number of different aspects, from side views at differing angles to overhead viewing. In addition, several of the programs afford the opportunity to present an animated version of the sequence of events that transpired during the commission of the crime. Some of these programs also allow the drawer to insert symbol library figures that permit the drawer to manipulate the figures into their proper position to illustrate a crime scene reconstruction. (See Figure 15-36 in Chapter 15 for an example of a three-dimensional drawing program with figures inserted to depict a crime scene reconstruction.)

PREPARATION OF SKETCHES: SUGGESTED SYSTEMATIC PROCEDURE

Preparation of the crime scene sketches should follow the same sequence followed in the initial survey of the scene, the taking of photographs, and the preparation of the scene notes. The crime scene investigator should first prepare the layout (overview) sketch(es) in order to provide a framework for the detailed sketches to be prepared. Once the layout sketches are prepared, a rough sketch should be prepared for each area containing pertinent objects or evidence. If more than one area is to be sketched, the areas should be sketched sequentially. If a blowup sketch of a smaller area is needed, it can be drawn once the larger area sketch is completed. The following should be kept in mind when preparing the sketches:

- Measure dimensions of each area accurately.
- Two individuals should verify all measurements.

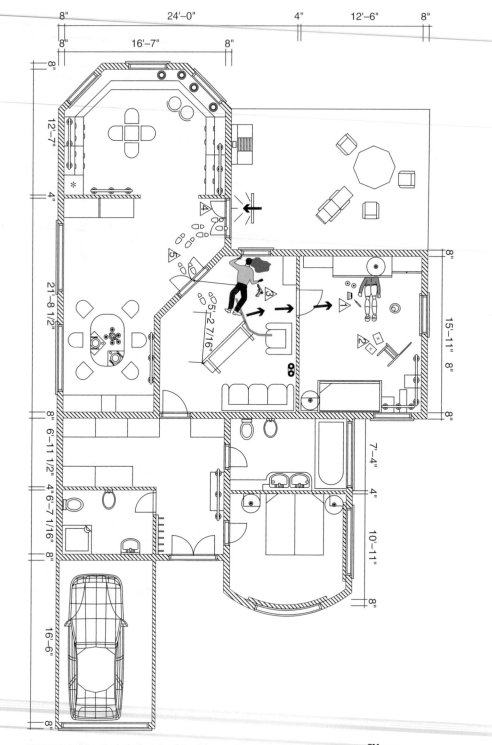

FIGURE 4-10 Scaled Sketch of Residence Created with 3DEyeWitness™ CAD Program by DesignWare
Courtesy of DesignWare [www.designwareinc.com].

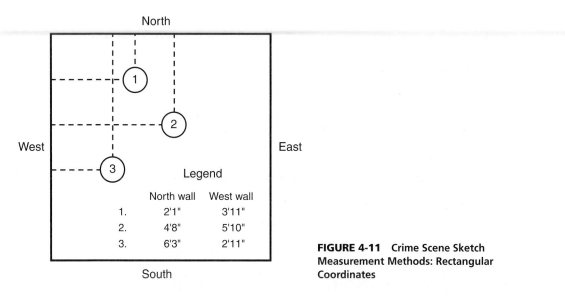

FIGURE 4-11 Crime Scene Sketch Measurement Methods: Rectangular Coordinates

- Each evidence item requires measurements to at least two fixed points (see Figures 4-11 through 4-16, for appropriate measurement methods).
- Measure the dimensions and location of furniture and other objects pertinent to the scene.
- Measure the location of windows and doors; show the direction of the door opening.
- Label furniture and other objects with letters, or label them directly in the sketch; label evidence items with numerals; and place labeled items in the legend with their measurements.
- Check each sketch for accuracy and completeness of the case data, as well as the location of furniture items and each evidence item before collection of evidence.

MEASUREMENT TECHNIQUES

There are a number of measurement techniques that exist, but for the measurements in crime scene sketches, it is best to use those techniques that are in common use and that will be understood by those individuals expected to review the sketches during the subsequent investigation. These techniques include rectangular coordinates, triangulation, secondary reference points, and transecting baseline. An additional measurement method, polar coordinates, is rarely used, but it is illustrated here for completeness.

Rectangular coordinates measurement method

The **rectangular coordinate** measurement method (see Figure 4-11) is the easiest to use for indoor scenes where there are four walls in a rectangular format. Note that each item must have measurements to *two walls that abut each other* (i.e., north and east, north and west, south and east, or south and west). This method can also be used outdoors where there are fixed areas with rectangular formats (i.e., driveways, areas within sidewalks, etc.) where the two measurements can be made at right angles to each other. Note especially that the wall dimensions, sidewalk dimensions, etc. must be measured in order to provide a framework for the measurements made to the physical objects in the area.

Triangulation measurement method

The **triangulation** measurement method (see Figure 4-12) can be used anywhere, indoors or outdoors. Its chief advantage is the ease with which the measurements can be made, whether the scene is a small room or a large outdoor area. This method requires a two-person team (or better, a three-member team) to make the measurements (one at each end of the tape). All measurements from the first reference point can be made at one time, then the team member at the zero end of the tape can move to the second reference point for all the measurements from the second reference point. In order to prepare a sketch to scale from these measurements, the investigator must know how to use a compass and an architect's scale to measure the exact location of each item in the sketch (some computer sketch programs may be capable of using these measurements directly). Remember to use permanent fixtures for the reference points.

Secondary reference points measurement method

The **secondary reference points** method (see Figure 4-13) is an extension of either the rectangular coordinates method or the triangulation method (illustrated here). Where the area to be sketched is distant from the primary reference points, secondary reference points can be established by measurement from the primary reference points (points A and B). These secondary reference points (X and Y in this illustration) can then be used for the two measurements to each physical object or evidence item. There is no limit to the number of secondary reference points that can be established from the primary points (allowing for several areas to be sketched without making many long-distance measurements). This method is very useful for sketching small areas that require measurement of many small items or an area where critical accuracy is necessary (e.g., bloodstain patterns).

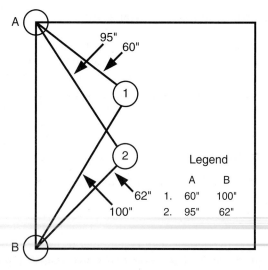

FIGURE 4-12 Crime Scene Sketch
Measurement Methods: Triangulation

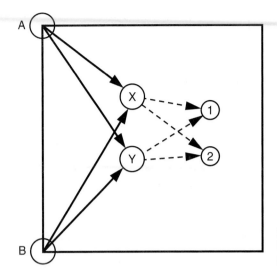

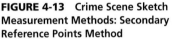

FIGURE 4-13 Crime Scene Sketch Measurement Methods: Secondary Reference Points Method

Transecting baseline measurement

The **transecting baseline** measurement method (see Figure 4-14) requires laying a metal measuring tape in a line between two fixed points (A and B in this illustration). The measurements to each item are made at 90 degrees to the measuring tape (baseline) and the length measurement along the baseline recorded, thus giving the required two measurements for each item for location on the finished sketch (distance from the baseline and the tape zero point A). Although this method is acceptable for a large outdoor area, it is less efficient than the rectangular coordinates or triangulation methods for indoor scenes.

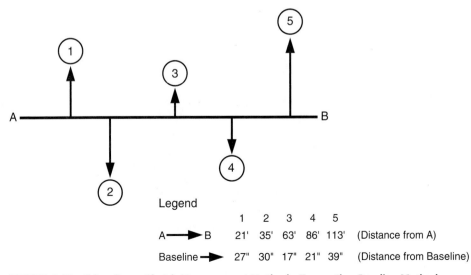

Legend

	1	2	3	4	5	
A ⟶ B	21'	35'	63'	86'	113'	(Distance from A)
Baseline ⟶	27"	30"	17"	21"	39"	(Distance from Baseline)

FIGURE 4-14   Crime Scene Sketch Measurement Methods: Transecting Baseline Method

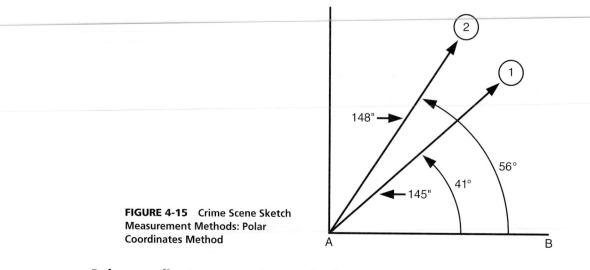

FIGURE 4-15 Crime Scene Sketch Measurement Methods: Polar Coordinates Method

Polar coordinates measuring method

The polar coordinates measuring method (see Figure 4-15) is the method by which laser-based sketching (mapping) methods measure the location of the objects at a scene. The instrument measures the distance from each of the objects to the measuring device (A) and the angle from a fixed line (A to B) to each of the objects. This method provides an exceptionally accurate means for determining the location of the objects at the scene. Figure 4-15 demonstrates the two-dimensional location of evidence items at the scene, that is, each object is located with reference to its position on a flat surface (plane), such as the floor of a residential room. The laser measurement device can also measure the vertical height of each item, so that the scene items can be displayed in a three-dimensional format by the computer program mated with the measuring device (see Figure 4-16).

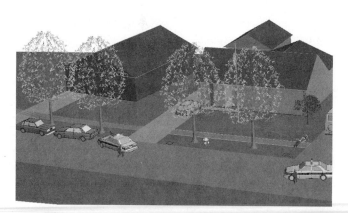

FIGURE 4-16 Crime Scene Sketch Methods: Sketch Prepared Using MapScenes® Mapping Technique

Courtesy of MicroSurvey Software Inc.

Personnel requirements

A three-person team is the most efficient approach for preparation of sketches. In the three-member team, one team member prepares the sketches while the other two members take the measurements with the tape. Each measurement is readily verified by both the individual preparing the sketch and the member having the end of the tape showing the measurement. A two-member team is less efficient than the three-member team because of the necessity of releasing the tape frequently in order to place measurements on the sketches. However, in many instances, the crime scene sketches will be prepared by one or two individuals, depending on the size of the scene and the complexity of the physical evidence present.

Equipment needed

TAPE MEASURES

Metal tape measures are essential, since they have the best accuracy, sag the least, and are the easiest to handle. Only in extreme cases should cloth tapes be used for crime scene measurement. Wheel walkers of good quality can be used for long distances, but these should be calibrated periodically with a good quality metal tape. The crime scene kit should contain both a 25-foot tape and a longer (100- or 150-foot) tape for measuring longer distances. The 25-foot tape should be as wide as feasible (usually 1 or $1\frac{1}{2}$ inch), since the wider tape is easier to handle and the thinner blades tend to wobble and cannot span much distance when suspended.

SKETCHING MATERIALS

Sketching materials consist of writing materials, paper, straight edge, and clipboard or pad holder. These items should be of good quality and kept in good supply in the crime scene vehicle or patrol vehicle. Lined paper or graph paper is helpful in drawing the outlines of the area being sketched, but it is not essential. A straight edge such as a ruler helps in drawing the lines in the sketch and forming boxes for legends. A clipboard, pad holder, or "posse box" is essential as a portable drawing table for preparation of the sketches.

Triangulation: using the compass

When the sketch measurements have been made using the triangulation measurement method, the measurements in the finished sketch will have to be placed using a compass. For those who haven't used a compass, the measurements are placed on the sketch in the manner shown in Figure 4-17.

The outline of the sketched area is placed on the sketch, which is drawn to scale with the aid of an architect's scale. This technique gives the reference points for the subsequent measurements by the triangulation method. The needle side of the compass is placed on the zero point of the scale, and the sharpened point of the pencil is stretched to the point on the scale equal to the exact measurement. The needle of the compass is then placed at the first reference point, and an arc is drawn. The measurement from the second reference point is made in the same manner. This preparation should result in the two arcs crossing at the exact point where the measurements appear on the scaled drawing. Each measurement point is determined in the same manner until all the points measured appear on the sketch. Each item is then placed on the sketch, conforming to these measurements using a pencil. Once the items have been drawn in the sketch, the final drawing can be

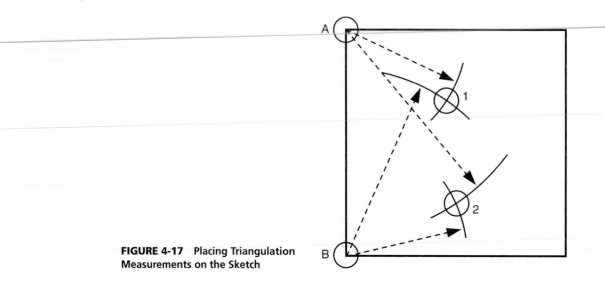

FIGURE 4-17   Placing Triangulation
Measurements on the Sketch

made by drawing over the penciled items with a drawing pen and then erasing the excess
pencil marks with a white rubber eraser, leaving the sketch in final form.

Summary

CRIME SCENE SKETCHES

- Prepare layout (overview) sketches for orientation of the detailed sketches.
- Prepare an area rough sketch for inclusion of measurements.
- Measure dimensions of each area accurately.
- Have two individuals verify each measurement.
- Remember that each evidence item requires measurements to at least two fixed points (see Figures 4-11 through 4-15 for appropriate measurement methods).
- Measure the dimensions and location of furniture and other objects pertinent to the scene.

- Measure the location of windows and doors; show the direction of the door opening.
- Label furniture and other objects with letters, or label them directly in the sketch; label evidence items with numerals, and place labeled items in the legend with their measurements.
- Check each sketch for accuracy and completeness of the case data, the location of furniture items, and each evidence item before collection of evidence.
- Recheck all sketches during debriefing at the conclusion of the scene processing.

Review Questions

1. Sketches do not replace notes and photographs, but they _____ these modes of crime scene documentation.
2. Sketches provide a means of documenting the _____ location of evidence items.

3. The crime scene sketch can be used to _____ the testimony of witnesses.
4. Sketches provide _____ data for crime scene reconstructions.

5. Investigators should plan _____ for sketching the scene.

6. The first sketch(es) should be _____ sketch(es) to show the overall scene.

7. Detailed sketches contain _____ to show accurately the relationships of evidence items and other items at the scene.

8. Blowup sketches are for _____ areas and those areas with a large _____ of evidence items.

9. Measurements on the same sketch should have _____ accuracy.

10. The sketcher should use only _____ measurement methods.

11. If the measurement tape sags, there will be an _____ in the measurement.

12. _____ individuals should verify all measurements.

13. Each evidence item requires measurement to _____ points.

14. The rectangular coordinate measurement method requires measurements to two walls that _____ each other.

15. The exploded view sketch shows the scene with the walls _____.

5 LATENT FINGERPRINT EVIDENCE

Every human being carries . . . his signature, his physiological autograph . . . there is no duplicate of it among the swarming populations of the globe . . . This autograph consists of the delicate lines or corrugations with which Nature marks the insides of the hands and the soles of the feet.

Pudd'nhead Wilson, 1894. Mark Twain.*

Key Words: Inked fingerprint, latent prints, patent prints, positive transfer impression, negative impression, print age, print deposit, sweat glands, eccrine, apocrine, contaminants, nondestructive, laser light, alternate light source, long-wave ultraviolet light, water soluble, fluorescence, water insoluble, systematic approach, latent powders, cyanoacrylate, small particle reagent, ninhydrin, DFO (diazafluorenone), latent development, nonabsorbent surfaces, absorbent surfaces, amido black, TMB (tetramethylbenzidine), elimination prints, personal protective equipment.

INTRODUCTION

The use of fingerprints as a means of identifying an individual in a criminal case has a convoluted history, a history which was distorted considerably by the duplicity of Francis Galton. In 1858, William Herschel, an Englishman, began experimenting with fingerprints while in India.[1] In 1877, while still in India, he instituted the use of fingerprints as signatures on land titles and jailer's warrants.[2] In 1878, Dr. Henry Faulds, a Scottish missionary in Japan, found impressed fingerprints on ancient pottery and began extensive experiments with fingerprints to determine if they would be useful as instruments of personal identification, *based on the prints of all ten fingers.* He was the first person to suggest the use of fingerprints for personal identification in a letter published in 1880 in the scientific journal *Nature*.[3] In 1886, Faulds began his attempts

---

*Extracted from *Fingerprints* (The Origins of Crime Detection and the Murder Case that Launched Forensic Science), 2001. Colin Beavan, Hyperion, New York.

to convince Scotland Yard to adopt fingerprints for identifying criminals. In 1888, Galton began experiments with fingerprints to determine if they could be a means of determining physical and intellectual prowess of an individual. Although Galton could not establish a correlation between these traits, he would later pilfer Faulds' concept of fingerprints as a means of establishing personal identity.[4]

In 1892, in Argentina, the detective Juan Vucetich used a fingerprint at the crime scene to extract a confession from a mother who had murdered her two children.[5] News of this case would not reach Europe for years. In 1893, Edward Henry, a police chief in Bengal, India, began to add thumbprints to the anthropometric system of Bertillon he had been using for a year as a means for identifying criminals. Azizul Haque, Henry's assistant, devised a comprehensive system for classifying fingerprints, a system which made the use of (ten finger) fingerprints without anthropometry a valid system for the identification of criminals. Galton had purloined Faulds' ideas and presented them as his own, Haque borrowed some of them from Galton to develop his system, whereupon Edward Henry (Haque's boss) then presented the classification concept as his own at the 1899 meeting of the British Association for the Advancement of Science; thus the system became known as the "Henry" classification system.[6]

The use of latent/patent fingerprints from crime scenes to identify suspects was first used by Vucetich in Argentina. The first use of latent fingerprints as evidence in the courtroom was in the 1902 Harry Jackson case in Britain. Later in 1905, the Stratton brothers were convicted and hanged for the murder of Thomas and Ann Farrow. In this case, Henry Faulds argued against the use of a single fingerprint as evidence, since no study had been conducted to establish the reliability of a *single finger* print to prove the identity of its source[7]—an argument which is still true as of this writing. It is the worldwide acceptance by fingerprint examiners of the validity of single print identification (without scientific verification) that maintains the acceptance of a single print as being sufficient to establish the identity of its source.

In the United States, the U.S. Bureau of Identification in 1904 established a fingerprint collection. The first person to be convicted on the basis of fingerprint evidence was Thomas Jennings, who was convicted of murder in 1911. The use of fingerprints became widespread in the United States, culminating in the installation of an AFIS computer at the FBI (the first AFIS computer in the United States was installed at the San Francisco Police Department, and that computer played a key role in establishing the innocence of a prison inmate in one of the author's cases cited in this chapter [*p.v. Jackson*]).

In 1938, Scotland Judge George Wilton began a campaign to organize support for the long-overdue recognition of Faulds' pioneering work in establishing fingerprints for the identification of criminals. Wilton's efforts were successful in showing the fundamental contribution of Faulds to the acceptance of fingerprints as a valid means of establishing the identity of the perpetrator of a crime. In addition, the endeavors of Judge Wilton led two U.S. fingerprint experts (James Mock, California, and Michael Carrick, Oregon)[8] to locate Faulds' grave and, with the help of Britain's fingerprint society, to restore the grave and install a headstone appropriate for an individual who made such valuable contributions to the criminal justice system worldwide. In addition, their efforts succeeded in garnering government payments to his two daughters, since Faulds died penniless.

Latent fingerprints are one of the more common types of physical evidence and certainly one of the most valuable. Fingerprints constitute a positive form of personal identification and often provide the identification of a perpetrator in the absence of any other type of evidence. With the advent of computerized fingerprint search systems such as the automated fingerprint identification system (AFIS), the value of latent fingerprints has risen dramatically. One clear impression from a crime scene can be rapidly compared with a very large database and can result in dramatic identifications, such as the identification of the "Night Stalker" Richard Ramirez. In one of the author's cases, the automated fingerprint system identified the true rapist in a "series" of rapes, leading to the release of another suspect previously convicted of the crimes.

Latent fingerprints are somewhat fragile and can be destroyed by a single careless act at the crime scene. Efforts should be undertaken to educate first responders to the necessity of caution at the crime scene in order to avoid loss of this valuable evidence prior to the arrival of the crime scene investigator. The fact that many impressions are "invisible" requires prudence on the part of the officer so that the prints may be recovered by the investigators.

Every individual, with few exceptions, has friction ridges on the fingers, palms, and soles of the feet. Certain features of the friction ridges make them suitable for personal identification. The patterns of the ridges are normally stable from birth to death, barring permanent destruction of the ridge-forming layer of the skin. In the experience of latent print examiners, no two areas of friction ridge skin have been found to be identical to another area of skin on the same individual or another individual. For these reasons, a single finger impression allows for the identification of the person responsible for the impression. The inked impressions of an individual's fingers thus become a permanent record for identification of that individual.

Latent prints constitute such important evidence that the investigator should make every effort to recover the latents at each crime scene. Particular attention needs to be directed to objects that may have been touched by the perpetrator, such as surfaces at the point of entry and exit, areas where washing may have occurred, the toilet, doorknobs, telephones, and any items moved or brought to the scene by the perpetrator. The effort to process tho-roughly the scene for latents will be repaid many times by the solution of an otherwise unsolvable crime.

The rapid development of DNA technologies for bloodstain analysis makes the recovery of bloodstained latent impressions more valuable but also generates the need for the crime scene analyst to work closely with forensic personnel in the recovery of bloody latents. Teamwork between these professionals will enhance the information content of the bloody print.

TYPES OF FINGERPRINTS AND IMPRESSIONS

Inked Fingerprints

An **inked fingerprint** is the direct impression of an individual's fingers and thumbs (the friction ridges beyond the distal joint) taken with fingerprint ink and placed on a standard format fingerprint card. Inked palm impressions are impressions of the friction ridges of the palm area. Major case prints include all the friction ridges of the hand, which include

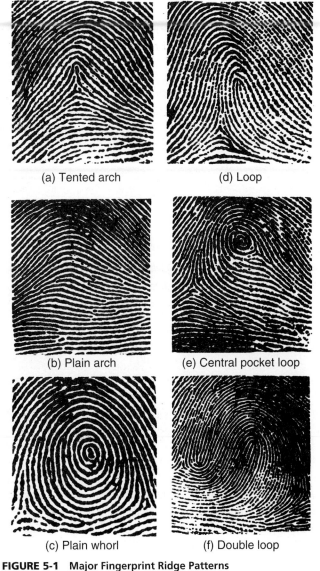

    (a) Tented arch   (d) Loop

    (b) Plain arch   (e) Central pocket loop

    (c) Plain whorl   (f) Double loop

FIGURE 5-1 **Major Fingerprint Ridge Patterns**
Source: U.S. Department of Justice, FBI, *The Science of Fingerprints*
(Washington, DC: GPO, 1973).

the ridges on the sides and tips of the fingers and the sides of the palm. These areas are not found on a standard inked fingerprint card. Other areas, such as the toes and soles of the feet, may also be taken in this manner. The inked card is classified by using standard criteria and may be entered into a computer database for comparison against latent fingerprints taken from a crime scene.

Figure 5-1 illustrates the major patterns of the finger ridges.

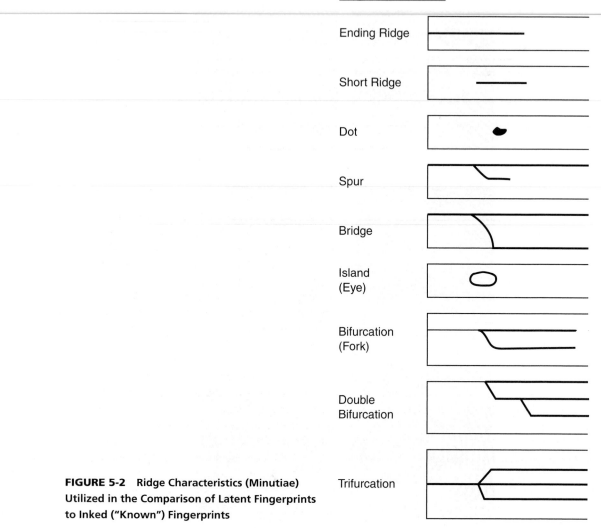

Ridge Characteristic

Ending Ridge

Short Ridge

Dot

Spur

Bridge

Island
(Eye)

Bifurcation
(Fork)

Double
Bifurcation

Trifurcation

**FIGURE 5-2   Ridge Characteristics (Minutiae)
Utilized in the Comparison of Latent Fingerprints
to Inked ("Known") Fingerprints**

Figure 5-2 Illustrates the ridge characteristics (minutiae) of the ridges used in the comparison and identification of latent fingerprints.

Latent Fingerprints

Latent prints are those prints left on a surface by contact with the friction ridges. These types of impressions are "invisible" and require *development* with a suitable medium to allow visualization of the impressions, such as powder for nonabsorbent surfaces or ninhydrin for absorbent surfaces. The latent impressions can also be visualized with the aid of a laser beam or other high-energy light sources with or without the use of chemicals used to enhance the image. Other techniques for visualizing latent fingerprints include cyanoacrylate (superglue) processing, dyes such as crystal violet, DFO reagent, small particle reagent, and many others. The choice of developer depends on the surface on which the fingerprints occur, the chemical nature of the latent deposit, and the environmental history of the impression. In some cases, the latent impressions may need to be developed with a sequence of techniques in order to maximize the likelihood of obtaining usable prints. It is usually a good procedure to photograph any developed latents before attempting to lift the prints with fingerprint tape, because of the possibility of loss of the print during the lifting process.

Patent Prints

Patent prints are those prints that are *visible to the naked eye* without first processing with powder or other means. The print may be of a finger, palm, foot, or other area of the skin. There are several types of patent impressions found at crime scenes. Each type of impression occurs as a result of contact between the skin surface with a material that leaves the visible impression or as a result of contamination on the skin surface that is transferred to the surface touched by the skin surface bearing the contamination.

The first type of patent print to be considered is the print resulting from *transfer* of a contaminant material on the skin surface (such as blood, grease, stains, etc.) to the surface receiving the patent impression. This type of patent impression is referred to as a **positive transfer impression**, similar to the impression made by an inked rubber stamp on a surface. The procedure for collection of these types of impressions is first to photograph the impressions with a close-up lens or a fingerprint camera. When feasible, the object bearing the impression is then collected and transported to the laboratory for additional testing (e.g., blood testing and staining of the blood with dyes that enhance the clarity of the print). If the patent impression is in a material that may be lost during transport, the impression should be protected by fashioning a "tent" of cardboard over the impression with tape or it should be covered with latent lifting tape.

The second type of patent impression results from the *removal* of surface material by contact of the friction ridges with the material, creating a **negative impression**. The visible portion of the impression is the area not touched by the fingerprint ridges, hence the term "negative" for this type of impression. These impressions are collected by first photographing the impression and then collecting the object bearing the impression for transport to the laboratory for processing of the impression according to the type of contaminant present. Patent prints in dust may be collected (after first photographing the print) from nonporous surfaces by lifting with rubber lifters or latent fingerprint tape, or else by the use of an electrostatic dust impression lifter.

The third type of patent impression results from contact of the skin surface with a soft substance such as clay, fresh paint, and the like, where the friction ridges are impressed into the surface, creating a *negative impression of the ridge formations*. This type of impression should be photographed with oblique lighting and a close-up lens before further processing. The object bearing the impression should be collected for transport to the laboratory when feasible. A cast of the impression can be made at the laboratory or in the field by first spraying the impression with a release agent, then casting the impression with silicone casting material such as Mikrosil or Duplicast.

AGE OF THE LATENT FINGERPRINT

At the present time, there are no reliable means for determining the length of time that a latent fingerprint has been on a particular surface. The **print age** can be established only by determining the time that the surface was cleaned in a manner that would remove any previous latent impressions present. Attempts to estimate the age of a latent impression on a surface are only guesswork at best, since many factors can alter the appearance of a latent print other than time. In some cases, the age of the latent impression can be estimated by appropriate experimentation. Such experimentation should be employed only in collaboration with a forensic scientist knowledgeable in the strict requirements for scientific experimentation. It is also not feasible to determine the race, sex, age, or occupation of the individual responsible for the latent impression, since there are many variations that may account for the features seen in the impression. Certain features of a latent print may, however, provide investigative information to the investigator, such as very small impressions that are consistent with a child's fingerprints.

NATURE OF THE LATENT PRINT DEPOSIT

Latent prints are composed of a mixture of materials, which may include secretions from the sweat glands in the friction ridges and various contaminants present on the ridge surface, including transfer of sebum from the sebaceous glands on the hairy surfaces of the skin. The materials that comprise the latent impression are referred to collectively as the latent **print** "**deposit**." The deposit usually contains materials that are either *water soluble* or *water insoluble*. In those instances in which the latent impression has been exposed to water, the water-insoluble components of the latent deposit will usually survive, whereas the water soluble components will be lost. Therefore, the choice of processing methods will depend to a large measure on whether or not the surface bearing the impressions has been exposed to water.

Contributions from the skin glands

There are two types of **sweat glands** in the skin: (1) eccrine and (2) apocrine. The **eccrine** sweat glands in skin (including the friction ridge surfaces) secrete a large amount of water that contains many of the water-soluble components of the deposit (amino acids, urea, sodium chloride, and others). The **apocrine** sweat glands are found in the armpits, groin, and nipples and rarely contribute to the latent deposit. The sebaceous glands, found on skin other than the palms, soles, and certain other areas, secrete sebum, which contains mostly water-insoluble components, including fats. The sebaceous glands are very numerous on the head, face, neck, and upper limbs. Contact with these areas by the hands transfers the sebaceous secretions to the friction ridges. Most latent deposits will contain contributions from both the eccrine sweat glands and the sebaceous glands. It is the contributions from these glands, along with the contributions from contaminants on the friction ridges (from contact of the ridges with the contaminants) that comprise the chemical nature of the latent deposit.

Contributions from contaminants

The **contaminants** on the friction ridges that may contribute to the latent deposit can originate from a wide variety of sources and thus may be composed of materials that will react with those processing methods that detect either the water-soluble components or the water-insoluble components of the deposit. The contaminants may also include substances that have inherent fluorescent properties, which may be detected by the use of ultraviolet, laser, or alternate light sources. This consideration makes the search of suspect surfaces with ultraviolet, laser, or alternate light sources prior to using other detection techniques an essential step in the sequential processing for latent impressions.

DEVELOPMENT OF LATENTS

CAUTION! The use of powders, chemicals, laser lights, and other high-energy light sources constitute a potential safety hazard to the crime scene investigator. A respiratory mask should always be used when working with powders of any kind, including the common latent fingerprint powders. The safety hazards for all chemicals to be used should be identified prior to the use of the chemicals, and all safety precautions should be followed closely. All chemicals should be handled and used under a fume hood or in well-ventilated areas with the aid of a special mask for organic vapors, since the chemicals may be toxic, flammable, or potentially carcinogenic. Lasers and other high-energy lights should be operated only when all nearby personnel, including the user, are wearing *safety glasses* designed specifically for *laser viewing*. Chemical and high-intensity-light development of latents should always be learned under the guidance of a qualified instructor because of the potential hazards involved in these techniques. (See Appendix 5-1 for safety recommendations appropriate for latent fingerprint development techniques.)

GENERAL CONSIDERATIONS FOR LATENT PRINTS

The first consideration at the scene is the safety of the personnel present, including the crime scene investigator. Many of the techniques for detecting latent impressions constitute safety hazards. High-energy lights are potential hazards to eyesight, and the chemicals used may be corrosive, flammable, or potentially carcinogenic. These techniques should be used only by qualified personnel who are fully aware of the safety hazards for each technique and the appropriate precautions that must be taken to ensure the safety of the investigator and any nearby personnel (see Appendix 5-1 for safety guidelines).

The second consideration for the choice of development techniques at the scene is a matter of common sense. The physical and chemical methods for latent development should always be preceded by the **nondestructive** methods for latent detection: (1) a thorough visual search using adequate lighting for the presence of patent impressions and any trace evidence pre-sent, and (2) a search with the **laser light** or an **alternate light source** and a **long-wave ultraviolet light.** These nondestructive procedures may detect latent impressions or trace evidence that may be destroyed or lost by the other recovery methods.

At the crime scene, the chances for detecting and recovering latent impressions are greatly enhanced by following a specific sequence of techniques for recovery of the impressions. The specific sequence followed will depend on several factors: (1) safety considerations for personnel at the scene, (2) the particular surface type to be processed, (3) whether or not the surface has been exposed to water, (4) the availability of the types of equipment to the investigator, and (5) exposure of the surface to extreme heat. Each of these factors needs to be considered prior to the attempt to recover latent impressions.

The detection of the **water-soluble** components is usually accomplished with the following methods, used either singly or in a specified sequence: (1) fingerprint powders and brush for nonabsorbent surfaces, (2) DFO or ninhydrin for absorbent surfaces, (3) cyanoacrylate fuming for nonabsorbent surfaces, (4) silver nitrate for absorbent surfaces, or (5) **fluorescence** examination for either absorbent or nonabsorbent surfaces. The detection of the **water-insoluble** components is usually accomplished with one of the following methods, used either singly or in a specified sequence: (1) brush and powders, (2) small particle reagent, (3) iodine fuming, or (4) fluorescence examination with or without luminescent dye preparation. The water-insoluble components will usually survive exposure to water or moisture, and those techniques that detect the water-insoluble components of the latent deposit may offer the best chance for recovery of the latents present.

For each of these techniques, the *nature of the surface will affect the choice* of the *methodology* to be used. Techniques for smooth, nonporous surfaces may not be suitable for rough, nonporous surfaces (e.g., rough, nonporous surfaces are usually not suitable for powders and should be processed with small particle reagent or cyanoacrylate fuming). In most instances, a sequential application of methods will provide the best chance of detecting the latent deposit. Suggested sequences at the crime scene are given in the sections for the various surface types. The reader interested in exhaustive sequences for latent processing, including advanced methods suitable for use at the scene or only in the laboratory, are referred to Margot and Lennard, *Scene of Crime Handbook of Fingerprint Development Techniques*, or Lee and Gaensslen.[9]

Prior to processing any surface for latent prints, the analyst should carefully examine the surface to be processed for visible prints and the presence of trace evidence such as hairs, fibers, paint, and blood. Processing for latents without regard to the potential presence of other types of evidence present may destroy the other evidence permanently through loss or contamination. If other types of evidence are present, it is usually best to submit the item to the laboratory with specific instructions to process for trace evidence and latent fingerprints, thus allowing for the collection of all the evidence types present.

It is important to use a **systematic approach** to the detection and collection of fingerprint evidence at the crime scene in order to maximize the likelihood of finding and collecting usable impressions. The sequence of actions taken should ensure that each step in the sequence *does not interfere with subsequent steps* in the process by following those sequences that have been tested in the laboratory for the effect that each step has on the following steps in the sequence. Recommended sequences for each type of surface and contaminant are given in the section for that surface type. It is important that the beginning crime scene analyst, under the supervision of a qualified latent print examiner, experiment with the various types of surface/contaminant combinations and the recommended sequences prior to attempting a particular sequence on actual case material.

The analyst should process items for latent impressions at the scene when feasible. This approach has the advantage of processing the scene in a systematic manner and also avoiding the necessity of transporting a number of items to the laboratory for processing. However, many items will require specialized techniques that can be performed only in the laboratory, because of the special equipment needed and the hazardous nature of the methods employed. The analyst should use good judgment at the scene with regard to the selection of the particular methods and sequences to be employed. It is imperative that the analyst experiment with the various surfaces and techniques prior to using those techniques in case situations in order to develop the necessary experience and judgment needed to maximize the recovery of usable latents from the crime scene.

The choice of the methods employed at the crime scene may depend on factors other than the surface type. First, the level of response to a crime scene usually hinges on the degree of the crime committed. For the more serious crimes, a team of investigators that typically includes a forensic crime scene specialist will usually be dispatched to the crime scene. The forensic specialist, of course, will have the equipment and knowledge necessary to perform many advanced techniques of latent development at the crime scene. In contrast, the crime scenes of less serious crimes will ordinarily be investigated by the patrol officer, whose training and equipment will allow for only the basic procedures for latent print collection. Fortunately, the basic procedure of using powder and brush suffices for most situations in the less serious crimes. Indeed, the solving of many crimes is a direct result of the actions of the patrol officer in gathering evidence, particularly latent print evidence.

Second, the size of the responsible agency often limits the resources that are available for crime scene investigation. Smaller agencies may not have forensic crime scene specialists but instead rely on the patrol officers or detectives to process the crime scenes in all but the most serious offenses, for which outside assistance is available. The lack of a specialized crime scene unit does not, however, in itself prevent a superior effort in the crime scene investigation. Indeed, in this author's experience, some of the finest crime scene work observed was accomplished by smaller departments having officers committed to superior crime scene investigation.

TECHNIQUES SUITABLE FOR THE CRIME SCENE

The techniques and sequences outlined in this chapter for the collection of latent impressions at the crime scene are based on the assumption that no unusual circumstances will be encountered. Those circumstances requiring advanced latent print processing techniques will require the presence at the scene of a forensic specialist trained in advanced latent print processing or will require the collection of the object bearing the latent impressions for transmittal to the latent print section, where both the specialized equipment and trained personnel are available to perform the advanced techniques.

As mentioned before, the selection of methods for use at the crime scene depends on a number of factors. Of the techniques available to the crime scene investigator, the following are suitable for routine use at the scene: (1) laser light and alternate light sources; (2) development with brush and the various latent fingerprint powders; (3) cyanoacrylate (superglue) fuming (especially with portable cartridge-based fuming wands); (4) small particle reagent; (5) iodine fuming; and in some instances, (6) ninhydrin or its analogues or substitutes such as DFO. These methods are sufficiently portable and cost-efficient to be considered for routine use in the field. The use of other methods will be restricted by the availability of specialist personnel, budget constraints, and safety factors.

Laser Light, Alternate Lights, and Ultraviolet Light

Laser lights, alternate lights, and ultraviolet light examination may be used to reveal latent fingerprints on nonabsorbent or absorbent surfaces. Chemical powders may be used to enhance the fluorescence of the latents for both visualization and photography. The fluorescence in latent prints is due to certain natural constituents in the sebaceous secretions and any contaminants present that fluoresce under laser light. The advantage of these special light examinations is that they are nondestructive and may be used prior to any other development method as a rapid screening device, in addition to their ability to produce identifiable impressions for photography. *Note:* The use of laser lights, alternate lights, ultraviolet lights, and enhancement stains should always be learned under a qualified instructor because of the potential safety hazards involved in the use of these lights and chemicals.

Alternate lights come in many sizes and formats, from large units with multiple wavelength filters for visualizing inherent luminescence to small handheld flashlight units (see Figure 5-3). When fingerprint powders and chemicals are applied with a fingerprint brush to the latent, these units will cause the latent to luminesce at specific wavelengths. The resultant luminescing print is then photographed to provide a permanent record of the print.

Development with powder and brush

Fingerprints on smooth, nonporous surfaces such as glass, paint, glossy plastics, and other polished surfaces can usually be developed with **latent powders**. The fingerprint brush should be clean and free from oils or other materials that may affect the efficiency of dusting with the brush. The brush should be swirled vigorously to remove excess

FIGURE 5-3   Alternate Light in Flashlight Format with Viewing Screen
Courtesy of Sirchie Fingerprint Laboratories.

powder, then dipped *lightly* into the powder with a swirling action, lifted, and swirled again, then applied lightly to the surface in a circular manner. Once the latent becomes visible, the print should be dusted lightly in the direction of the ridges until clearly visible. It is important to avoid overdusting, since the print may be wiped clean by too much dusting. The print is then lifted with fingerprint tape and placed on a latent fingerprint card designed for this purpose. The card should be labeled immediately and a sketch placed on the card illustrating the location and orientation of the print otherwise, the cards may become mixed up before labeling, resulting in confusion as to which print came from which object. The student should practice dusting many objects with varying surfaces to gain insight into the proper amount of dusting necessary for quality development of the latents before attempting the processing of a crime scene.

The use of a large, widemouthed (about 8 ounces or larger) plastic jar (see Figure 5-4) for the working supply of fingerprint powder is suggested for several reasons. First, an amount of powder approximately one-half-inch deep should be placed in the jar. If the powder becomes contaminated during use, the small amount of powder can be discarded, and the jar rapidly cleaned and refilled with new powder. Second, this size jar allows the fiberglass brush to be stored in the open jar between successive lifts, so that the brush does not have to be set down on a surface. Third, the size of the jar allows the analyst to dip the brush lightly into the powder and to swirl the head to apply powder to the brush. Fourth, the excess powder can be removed by swirling the brush in the jar above the powder layer, thus avoiding contaminating the scene or the analyst's clothing with the powder. These jars, which are very inexpensive, are particularly suitable for the patrol officer's latent print kit.

The analyst may choose to use a magnetic brush with magnetic powder instead of the standard brush. The magnetic brush is superior to the standard brush in some applications and should be a part of the standard equipment for the scene kit.

The fingerprint tape should be applied by releasing an adequate length of tape from the roll, placing the leading edge above the print, then sliding the finger down the tape to cover the entire area of the print while holding the tape roll in the other hand so that

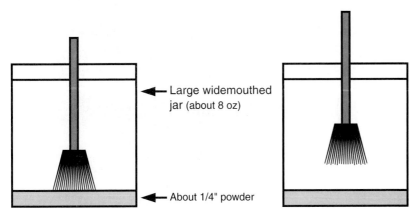

1. Dip brush lightly into powder.
2. Swirl lightly to charge brush.
3. Lift brush above powder.
4. Swirl to remove excess powder.

FIGURE 5-4 **Large Plastic Jar Technique for Charging Fingerprint Brush**

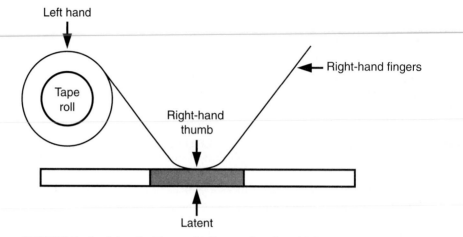

FIGURE 5-5 **Applying the Fingerprint Tape to Developed Print**

it does not fall onto the surface of the print (see Figure 5-5). The tape should be rubbed sufficiently to remove any air bubbles present. If the tape cannot be removed without destroying the print, then the tape is left on the surface and the object collected. If the tape can be removed, the tape should be pulled up from the end away from the tape roll, and the tape should then be transferred to a latent card. Once secured, the tape can be cut with scissors or a sharp blade.

When processing larger areas (automobile exteriors, etc.), a larger size brush (see Figure 5-6) will increase the efficiency of the processing effort. For odd-shaped surfaces, the developed latent may be lifted with a liquid rubber kit (see Figure 5-7).

FIGURE 5-6 **Large (sweeper) Format Brush for Dusting Larger Areas Such As Automobile Surfaces**
Courtesy of Sirchie Fingerprint Laboratories.

FIGURE 5-7 Developed Latent Print Lifted with Liquid Rubber Kit
Courtesy of Sirchie Fingerprint Laboratories.

Development with Cyanoacrylate

There are a number of approaches to the use of **cyanoacrylate** fuming for latent print development. The fuming can be accomplished by placing the items to be processed in a *fuming chamber* and then fuming with any of a number of commercially available kits or with kits prepared by the analyst. Fuming chambers are also available commercially or can be constructed by the analyst. The investigator should refer to the commercial suppliers of crime scene equipment and supplies for availability of equipment and supplies. Of particular interest is the development of the superglue fuming wand for cyanoacrylate fuming. This technique should allow for effortless fuming in the field by investigators. The cyanoacrylate cartridges can also be ordered with dye added to the cyanoacrylate, which can be visualized with fluorescent lighting, thus eliminating the additional step of treating the fumed impressions with a fluorescent dye. Fuming wands are available from most crime scene products distributors (see Figure 5-8).

Processing with iodine fuming

Iodine fuming can be accomplished at the scene with the use of an iodine fuming apparatus. Iodine fuming is the oldest technique for visualizing latent fingerprints, but is still used by crime scene investigators. Iodine consists of solid crystals, but can, when heated, pass from a solid to a gas form without becoming a liquid first, a process termed sublimation by scientists. The fumes thus created can react with the latent print to produce a

FIGURE 5-8   **Cyanoacrylate Portable Fuming Wand**
Courtesy of Sirchie Fingerprint Laboratories.

temporary (begins to fade when the fuming ends) color which must be photographed to preserve the image. The image can be preserved longer by spraying with a 1 percent solution of starch in water, which forms a blue color that lasts for weeks or months. Iodine fuming is typically accomplished at the scene by using a "fuming gun," usually a commercial iodine cartridge (see Figure 5-9). The operator blows through the cartridge, generating iodine fumes due to the heat from the operator's breath. The fumes are directed toward the surface suspected of bearing latent prints. Developed prints are photographed immediately, as the colored complex of iodine/latent (exact nature of complex unknown) lasts a short time. The iodine color complex can be fixed with iodine-fixing reagents such as

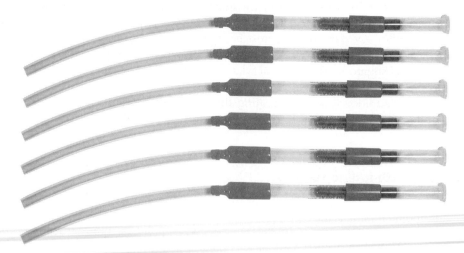

FIGURE 5-9   **Commercial Iodine Cartridges**
Courtesy of Sirchie Fingerprint Laboratories.

starch spray, or a benzoflavone reagent (the most common method) which prolongs the life of the image. The resultant fixed color is then photographed to produce a permanent record.

Processing with Small Particle Reagent

Small particle reagent (SPR) is a suspension of molybdenum sulfide grains in a detergent solution. The grains adhere to the fatty components of a latent print deposit, and therefore the spraying method is useful for *processing wet items at the scene without prior drying* or by inserting the small particle reagent processing into a sequential scheme for a particular surface type (see the sequences under the sections on particular surface types). The reagent is first shaken to disperse the molybdenum sulfide grains in the liquid, and then sprayed onto the surface suspected of bearing latent deposits. The surface is then sprayed with clean distilled water to remove excess reagent. Developed impressions are then photographed or lifted with tape after drying. In most instances, the other methods are more sensitive, and the small particle reagent should preferably be used only in a sequence approach or for items that cannot be dried prior to processing.[10]

Processing with Ninhydrin, Ninhydrin Analogues, or DFO

The use of **ninhydrin**, ninhydrin analogues, or **DFO (1,8-diazafluorenone)** may be necessary in some instances at the scene (raw wood surfaces, for example). *The investigator should use only ninhydrin dissolved in a nonflammable solvent* at the scene, and the ninhydrin should be applied only in well-ventilated areas. Ninhydrin formulations in flammable or toxic chemicals should be used *only in the laboratory under the fume hood* or in the outdoors well away from any flame source and with adequate safety equipment for the investigator. If DFO and ninhydrin are used, the DFO method must be performed before the ninhydrin method.

In this text, the focus is on crime scene investigation; therefore, suggested techniques and their proper sequence for treatment in the field will be outlined for each of the types of surfaces usually encountered at the crime scene. For a more detailed discussion of both the techniques useful at the scene and those that are better employed back at the laboratory, see the further references listed at the end of this chapter.

SEQUENTIAL APPROACHES TO LATENT IMPRESSION DETECTION AND COLLECTION

The methods to be employed at the crime scene described in this text are based on a selection of those techniques that are readily utilized at the crime scene, as opposed to those methods that are better performed in the laboratory or that can be accomplished only in the laboratory because of equipment, personnel, and safety considerations. The following sequences of procedures for each surface type at the scene will help to optimize the recovery of useful latent impressions.

The *best approach* to latent processing for all surface/latent deposit combinations should follow this sequence:

1. **Visual examination followed by laser/alternate light/ultraviolet light search.**
   The search for latent prints should begin with those methods that are nondestructive and that preserve the latent prints, patent prints, and other types of

physical evidence that may be present at the scene (particularly trace evidence) and that may be lost or destroyed by latent processing. The *first step* in the examination for fingerprint impressions is a *visual examination* of the suspect surfaces, using adequate lighting for the presence of visible impressions and other types of physical evidence that may be destroyed by fingerprint processing. This search should be augmented with high-intensity lighting, laser illumination, or alternate light sources, which may reveal impressions or trace evidence not seen without the illumination (many fibers will fluoresce under these lights).

2. **Photographs of all patent prints and other evidence in the impressions prior to removal or tape lifting.**

   Any patent impressions found in this preliminary search *should be photographed* prior to further treatment. Indented prints should be collected for processing in the laboratory when feasible. If it is not feasible to transport the impression-bearing object to the laboratory, then the analyst must process the impressions at the scene. The impressions should be photographed with oblique lighting and a cast prepared from silicone casting material in the case of indented patent impressions. Patent impressions in blood are treated with the methods for bloody prints.

3. **Processing with physical or chemical methods.**

   The choice of methods for latent print processing of the scene is a function of the surfaces to be processed for latents, the chemical nature of the deposit, and the environmental history of the impression. The crime scene analyst should choose the method or the sequence of methods that have the most promise for the detection and collection of latents from each surface processed. In the sections to follow, the appropriate techniques for the various surfaces and composition of the latent deposit will be described. The analyst needs to be familiar with the best choice of method for each type of surface, combined with a consideration of the nature of the latent impression's composition. In addition, the history of the object bearing the impression plays an important role in the determination of which techniques and their sequence are likely the best choice, since wetting or exposure to moisture may destroy the water-soluble portions of the impressions but have little effect on the water-insoluble portions of the impression. The use of the wrong sequence of techniques may destroy any impression present and may prevent further treatment with other techniques.

4. **Photographs of latent prints after development or visualization.**

   It is a good practice to photograph the latent impressions after development at each step as a safety factor, particularly on those surfaces that may partially peel off or fragment, thus obscuring some or all of the impression. In addition, the photograph of the developed latent in situ is helpful during testimony to illustrate the location and condition of the latent prior to lifting with tape.

5. **Sketches of the location and orientation of the latent impression on the lift card or in the investigator's notes.**

   The documentation of the *location* and *orientation* of the latent impressions detected will provide details for any reconstruction efforts for testing statements by a suspect with regard to innocent placement of the latent impressions.

WET SURFACES: DRY AT ROOM TEMP; TREAT AS FOR DRY SURFACES

As a rule, wet items or surfaces should be allowed to air-dry without the use of heat or forced air before processing. Temperatures above 30° C (86° F) may damage latents. Items in freezing weather should be allowed to warm to room temperature before dusting attempts. When drying is not feasible, the item may be processed for latents by using those techniques applicable to wet surfaces, particularly small particle reagent (SPR). Alternate processing for wet surfaces will be addressed under the appropriate section for surface types.

The water-soluble components may have been lost during wetting, so that only those methods that detect the fatty components may be effective in detecting the latent. Common fingerprint powders will detect the fatty components, so that in the majority of cases, dusting with powders should detect the prints. If the analyst decides to proceed with processing the wet surface, small particle reagent may be used without first drying the surface. If the crime scene analyst decides not to process these items at the scene, the items should be dried at room temperature and forwarded to the laboratory for processing with those methods that should be performed only at the laboratory.

SEQUENCING OF METHODS FOR LATENT DEVELOPMENT

Suggestions for the proper sequence of methods on a particular surface type are given under each surface type heading. It is important that the crime scene investigator consider the history of the item to be processed before determining the sequence to be used. The methods for **latent development** generally fall into three categories: (1) methods that detect the water-soluble components in a latent, (2) methods that detect the water-insoluble components, and (3) special conditions, such as bloody prints, prints on adhesive surfaces, and prints on plastic cling films. The particular sequence to be followed should incorporate considerations of the surface type, the environmental history of the item to be processed, and the potential effect of the method on subsequent methods in the sequence to be employed. The sequences suggested under the sections on surface types are adapted from *Scene of Crime Handbook of Fingerprint Development Techniques*. 1993. London, England: Police Scientific Development Branch, Home Office, for use at the crime scene and do not include those methods suitable for use only in the laboratory. For those readers interested in exhaustive sequences for latent development in the laboratory, see the further references listed at the end of this chapter.

For each surface type, a suggested method or sequence of methods will be given for processing the surface after the preliminary steps that follow have been accomplished. Steps one and two are nondestructive (with the possible exception of overuse of laser lights), will not interfere with subsequent methods utilized, and may reveal impressions that may be affected by subsequent steps.

Once steps one and two for each surface type have been completed, the investigator needs to select a method or sequence of methods for developing any latent impressions present on the suspect surface. Selection of the appropriate method for further development of latents should be based on the particular surface type of the target surface, the chemical nature of the impression deposit, and the environmental history of the target surface, such as wetting of the surface or exposure to excessive heat. It is important to perform a sequence of methods in the proper order, so that each step in the sequence does not interfere with any subsequent steps.

All surface/latent deposit combinations

The initial procedures at the crime scene for *all surface/latent deposit combinations* (both **nonabsorbent surfaces** and **absorbent surfaces**) should be the following:

1. Visual examination with adequate lighting, followed by laser/alternate light. The search for latent prints and other types of physical evidence present at the scene, particularly trace evidence that may be lost or destroyed by latent processing, should begin with a visual examination in good light, followed by examination with a laser light, an alternate light source, and an ultraviolet light. These methods are nondestructive, and they are prudent precautions against the loss of latent prints or trace evidence that may be lost by premature processing for latent impressions with physical or chemical techniques.

2. Photographs of all patent prints, developed latent prints, and other evidence in the impressions prior to removal or tape lifting. It is strongly recommended that developed or visualized impressions be photographed prior to collection or lifting attempts, so that in the event the impression is not successfully recovered, a permanent record of the impression is available. The visualized impressions should be photographed at each stage of the sequence as they are developed, since the impressions developed at an early stage may be superior to those developed at a later stage in the sequence.

Steps one and two are assumed to have been completed before proceeding to the next step in the sequence for each surface type in the sections to follow. The suggested techniques for each of the following sections thus begin with step three, with the assumption that steps one and two have been accomplished or given due consideration prior to proceeding to step three in the sequence for each surface/deposit combination to be processed.

3. Selection of the physical and/or chemical process or sequence in the following sections based on surface type, nature of the latent deposit, and its environmental history.

4. Photographs of developed prints as processing proceeds.

5. Documentation of recovered latents in notes and sketches.

Nonabsorbent surfaces

SMOOTH, NONPOROUS SURFACES (GLASS, PAINT, VARNISHES, GLOSSY PLASTICS)

3a. Processing with brush and powder.

   The majority of surfaces to be processed for latents consists of smooth, nonporous surfaces. Most of these surfaces can be dusted with brush and powder, which is usually the most effective method for this type of surface. In some instances (e.g., surfaces that are or have been wet, or latents contaminated with blood or grease), it will be better to use an alternate method to process the surface (see sections on surface types).

3b. (1) Superglue (cyanoacrylate, or CA) processing, (2) photography of developed impressions, and (3) powder development of visualized impressions.

   The use of cyanoacrylate fuming followed by photography and powder development may reveal impressions not revealed by powder alone. For this reason, cyanoacrylate fuming may be done routinely or only in those circumstances in which the analyst determines that powder alone may not be effective.

4. Small particle reagent.

   Small particle reagent can be used after the previous treatments or for wet objects prior to drying.

ROUGH, NONPOROUS SURFACES (PEBBLED OR GRAINY SURFACED PLASTICS)

Rough, nonporous surfaces usually cannot be processed with latent fingerprint powders. Most of these surfaces will require chemical processing to develop latent impressions. The chemical method used depends on the particular surface type of the object suspected of containing latents. For most wet, nonporous surfaces, dry the surface and then treat as for dry surfaces, or use small particle reagent.

3. Cyanoacrylate fuming.

   Cyanoacrylate fuming may be better than powders on these surfaces. The use of dye-impregnated CA in the fuming wand may eliminate the need for postfuming dusting with luminescent powders.

4. Small particle reagent (especially for wet surfaces).

PLASTIC FOAMS (POLYSTYRENE CUPS, CEILING TILES, PACKAGING FOAMS)

3. Small particle reagent (dish development for small items, spray for larger items).

4. Photograph of developed impressions.

PLASTIC PACKAGING MATERIAL (MOST POLYETHYLENE BAGS AND OTHER PACKAGING PLASTICS, POLYETHYLENE, POLYPROPYLENE, CELLULOSE ACETATE, PLASTIC COATED OR LAMINATED PAPER OR CARDBOARD, BUT NOT CLING FILMS)

3. Superglue fuming (especially with fluorescent dye).

   If no impressions are visualized with the laser/alternate light examination, the object should be fumed with cyanoacrylate. Luminescent dye-impregnated CA in the fuming wand is particularly helpful, but it may not be effective on articles that have been exposed to water.

SOFT VINYL (PVC), RUBBER, LEATHER, CLING FILMS (SIMULATED LEATHER UPHOLSTERY, CHECKBOOK HOLDERS, SPORTS BAGS)

3. Superglue fuming, photographs of developed impressions. (Laser/alternate light examination should also be attempted after other processes [fluorescence may be enhanced].[11])

   Cyanoacrylate fuming is usually more effective than powders with these surfaces. The surface itself may retain powder and may obscure any latents developed.

4. Powder development, photographs of developed impressions (poor for cling films, soft vinyl).

   Powders may be ineffective on these surfaces but may be attempted when no other means are available or circumstances do not warrant sending the article to the laboratory.

5. Small particle reagent (wet items).
   Spray method for larger objects, dish method for smaller objects.

UNTREATED METAL (i.e., NOT PAINTED OR LACQUERED)

3. Superglue fuming.

Cyanoacrylate fuming may be more effective than powders. Photograph the developed impressions, dust with powder, and lift with tape.

4. Powders.

5. Small particle reagent (wet items).

Spray method for large objects, dish method for small objects; photograph the developed impressions; developed impressions can be lifted with tape when dry.

WAX AND WAXED SURFACES (CANDLES, WAXED PAPER, AND CARTONS)

3. Sudan Black staining, photograph the developed impressions.

4. Superglue fuming, photograph the developed impressions.

5. Small particle reagent.

Use dish method for small items, spray for larger items; photograph the developed impressions. May be lifted with tape after drying.

ITEMS CONTAMINATED WITH GREASES

3. Sudan Black.

Sudan Black staining of the surface is preferred to Crystal Violet, which is very toxic. Photograph any developed impressions. If the surface is heavily contaminated with grease or oils, then powders and small particle reagent will usually blanket the surface, so that the latent does not stand out from the background.

4. Cyanoacrylate fuming[12] (if Sudan Black is unavailable).

In the alternative, the investigator should transmit the object(s) to the laboratory for Sudan Black staining by laboratory personnel.

5. Small particle reagent (wet items).
Spray for large items, dish for small items.

Absorbent surfaces

Absorbent surfaces that may bear latent prints should be carefully handled with plastic gloves, packaged for transport to the laboratory, and labeled clearly "FOR LATENT FINGERPRINTS." Chemical processing should always be done under a fume hood to avoid fire or exposure of the analyst to the fumes that may be toxic. If chemical processing is to be attempted in the field, it is essential that the investigator know and follow rigorously all safety precautions for these chemicals, many of which may be flammable, explosive, toxic, or potentially carcinogenic.

The most common chemical used to process absorbent materials for latent fingerprints is ninhydrin, sometimes referred to simply as "nin." This compound is usually dissolved in very flammable solvents that should *always be used under the fume hood or outdoors,* well away from any spark or flame source. Ninhydrin in nonflammable solvents is available for use indoors. Newer methods for processing absorbent surfaces include DFO (diazafluorenone, which is used instead of or before ninhydrin), modified ninhydrin, and ninhydrin analogues. Wearing chemical resistant gloves and safety glasses is a must when working with any chemical. Powders may be successful with these surfaces when the prints are fresh but may not detect the latents once the prints have dried. There are many methods for chemical and physical detection of latents in the laboratory that will not be covered in this text, because the focus here is on methods for use at the crime scene. The interested analyst is referred to the references at the end of this chapter for information regarding these advanced laboratory methods.

Note: Chemicals used to dissolve ninhydrin and other chemical detection reagents are often capable of readily dissolving inks, so that any documents that are to be processed should always be photographed with color film prior to processing with chemical development techniques. Make sure that the photographs are of good quality before proceeding with the ninhydrin processing, or use a formulation specifically designed to avoid dissolving inks. These precautions will help to avoid the disaster of finding good latent fingerprints on a document that ceases to exist after the chemical processing.

PAPER AND CARDBOARD ITEMS[13]

3. DFO (diazafluorenone), laser/alternate light examination, and photographs of visualized impressions.

4. Ninhydrin, photograph the developed impressions.

> *Note:* If DFO and ninhydrin are both used, be sure to process with DFO before ninhydrin processing.

RAW WOOD (UNTREATED)

3. DFO treatment, photograph the visualized impressions.

4. Ninhydrin (instead of or following DFO).

FABRICS (FINE, SMOOTH FABRICS ONLY)

There are no proven processes for development of latents on fabrics. If the latent prints are in blood, use the process for prints in blood.[14]

Adhesive tapes

ADHESIVE SIDE

The adhesive sides of tapes are usually treated with Crystal (Gentian) Violet (*Note:* Crystal Violet is very toxic) for latents after processing of the nonadhesive sides according to the type of tape. In the case of paper tapes, the treatment of the nonadhesive side with physical developer will also develop latents on the adhesive side. *Note:* Physical developer treatment should be done only in the laboratory by qualified personnel using appropriate safety equipment. Physical developer will interfere with other development methods.[15]

NONADHESIVE SIDE

Glossy Plastic Tapes[16]

3. Powders.

Soft Vinyl Tapes[17]

3. Superglue (CA) fuming (Only While Stuck Down), photographs of developed impressions.

Fabric Tapes. There are no proven processes for fabric tapes. If prints are in blood, process as for fingerprints in blood.[18]

Paper Tapes (if not wetted)

3. DFO, laser/alternate light examination, photograph the visualized impressions.

4. Ninhydrin, photograph the developed impressions.

Paper Tapes (if wetted)

3. Physical developer (laboratory only); will also develop adhesive side prints. (Interferes with subsequent methods and blood examinations.[19])

4. Photograph the developed prints.

Fingerprints in blood

Latent fingerprints in blood can be developed or enhanced in one of two general ways: (1) staining with a protein dye such as *Amido Black* or (2) treating with bloodstain testing reagents (such as tetramethylbenzidine) that form colored compounds by reaction with the heme portion of hemoglobin. Since the bloodstain testing methods are about ten times as sensitive as the staining methods and may reveal "invisible" blood, it may be preferable to use the bloodstain testing methods for fingerprints in blood rather than one of the protein staining methods.[20] **Amido black** is preferred to Crystal Violet for the protein dye, since Crystal Violet is toxic and should be used only in the laboratory by qualified analysts or chemists with access to proper safety equipment.

POROUS SURFACES

3. **TMB (tetramethylbenzidine)**, photograph the developed impressions.

4. Ninhydrin, heat to develop; photograph the developed impressions.
   Alternate method: Amido Black staining, photograph the developed impressions.

NONPOROUS SURFACES[21]

A. *If the entire print is contaminated with blood*
   3. DFO, laser/alternate light; photograph the developed impressions.
   4. Amido Black, photograph the developed impressions.
   5. Physical developer (laboratory only), photograph the developed impressions.

B. *If the print is partially blood and partially latent*

   3. Powders, photographs (do not lift).

   4. Amido Black, photograph the developed impressions.

   5. Physical developer (laboratory only), photograph the developed impressions.

Latent and patent prints on skin

Latents ordinarily cannot be developed on the skin of live subjects because of absorption by the hydrolipid layer of the skin. In the list that follows are sequential methods (see Table 5-1) described for developing latent impressions on skin in references cited later (see references for details on techniques). *Note*: A search for patent prints/trace evidence and a search with laser or Alternate light should precede all other techiques. Photograph all visualized prints before proceeding to the next step in the sequence.

TABLE 5-1 Development of Latent and Patent Impressions on the Skin			
Storage Condition or Print Type	**Ref [1]**	**Ref [2]**	**Ref [3]****
FRESH/ROOM T	(1) CA, LUM DYE*	(1) Chamber* over body	(1) CA*
	(2) LAS/ALT		(2) LUM DYE
	(3) MAG POW	(2) CA*, with water vapor	(3) LAS (or ALT)
	(4) GRIT		
	(5) IOD, transfer to AG plate UV to 14 Hrs.	(3) Fume 0.5–1.0 hour	
		(4) Rh6G	
	(6) CA, BY40	(5) LAS or ALT	
	(7) RTX		
COLD STORAGE	(1) IOD		(1) IOD
	(2) Transfer to AG plate		(2) Transfer to AG plate
	(3) RTX		(3) RTX
VISIBLE PRINT	(1) PHOT		(1) Transfer to glossy paper
	(2) Transfer to glossy paper		(2) IOD
	(3) IOD, transfer to AG plate		(3) AG plate
	(4) RTX		(4) RTX
INDENTED	(1) PHOT		(1) PHOT
	(2) SIL CAST		(2) SIL CAST

*CA fuming wands may obviate necessity for fuming chamber over body.

**Precede all methods with forensic light source.

ACRONYMS: See glossary of acronyms at the end of this chapter.

For further information on latent and patent impressions on the skin see also (REF[1]) Pierre Margot and Chris Lennard, *Fingerprint Detection Techniques* (Lausanne, Switzerland: University of Lausanne, Institute of Police Science and Criminology, 1994); (REF[2]) *Scene of Crime Handbook of Fingerprint Development Techniques* (London, England: Police Scientific Development Branch, Home Office, 1993); and (REF[3]) Henry C. Lee and R. E. Gaensslen, eds., *Advances in Fingerprint Technology*, 2nd ed. (Boca Raton, FL: CRC Press, 2001).

SUBMISSION OF LATENT PRINT EVIDENCE TO THE LABORATORY[22]

All packages shipped to the laboratory for latent print examinations should be marked "ATTENTION: LATENT PRINT SECTION." In all cases in which a firearm is submitted, it should always be unloaded, and the package should be clearly marked that it contains an unloaded firearm.

Marking of evidence

- Evidence submitted to the laboratory or its sealed package should be marked with standard identification data, just as with any other type of physical evidence.
- Lifted, developed latent prints should also be marked or sealed in marked envelopes with the submitter's name, date, and case number.
- When photographs are taken of developed latent impressions, an identifying label should be placed near the print, and this label should also be photographed so that it will show on the negative. If a 1:1 fingerprint camera is not used, a ruler or some other item should be included in the photograph to show the amount of magnification.

Collection of elimination prints

Elimination prints are inked fingerprints of those individuals who may have contributed latent fingerprints at the scene. Ideally the elimination prints can be taken at the scene with a portable fingerprint elimination kit (see Figure 5-10). These kits have all the supplies necessary for taking high-quality inked prints. If the investigator does not have an elimination kit available, the elimination prints can be prepared using a small "pocket" inking pad and the backs of latent cards as a substitute.

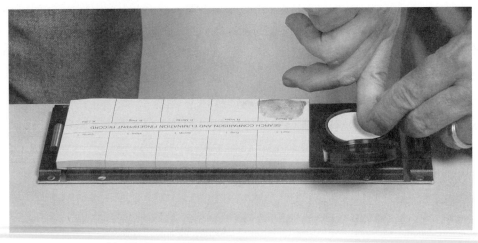

FIGURE 5-10   Portable Elimination Fingerprint Kit
Courtesy of Sirchie Fingerprint Laboratories.

Submission of inked fingerprints for comparisons

The importance of obtaining good quality, clear inked impressions of the fingers and palms cannot be overstressed, whether the prints are obtained with standard ink and fingerprint cards or through a scanner that captures the print image. A current set of inked finger and palm prints of identified subject(s) should be forwarded to the Forensic Laboratory (ATTN: LATENT PRINT SECTION) when requesting a fingerprint comparison. Adherence to this procedure will ensure the following:

- That the submitting agency can provide a witness to establish that the inked finger-prints belong to the specific suspect(s) in question.
- That an admissible court exhibit can be prepared, should this case go to the superior court or grand jury.
- That the suspect(s) in the case is (are) the same individual(s) whose inked finger-prints are on file (quite often, because of the large number of prints on file, different individuals may have the same names, dates of birth [DOBs], and physical descriptions).
- That inked prints submitted for comparisons should be
  - Properly inked and fully rolled.
  - Accompanied by the full name and description of the subject for comparison.
  - Dated and signed by the individual in the submitting agency who rolled the prints and can testify, in court, as to the origin of the fingerprints.
  - Sent to the attention of the latent print analyst currently assigned to the case if previous work on the case has been done.

Preservation of evidence

- In all cases, it is of the utmost importance to prevent contamination of latent print evidence by subsequent handling that can damage those prints already present.
- Most fingerprints submitted will be on paper, glass, metal, or other smooth-surfaced objects. When articles that may contain latent fingerprints must be picked up, they should always be touched as little as possible (gloves will not protect the impressions from smearing, etc.).
- Metal articles and firearms should be placed on wood or heavy cardboard and then fastened down firmly with string or wire to prevent shifting and contact with other objects in transit. When such evidence is to be submitted frequently, a Peg-Board™ should be obtained on which wooden pegs can be moved as desired to surround exhibits and keep them from moving.
- Even though gloves or a handkerchief may be used to pick up items of evidence, any unnecessary contact should be avoided. Although this method of handling exhibits will prevent leaving additional prints on the articles, the gloves or cloth used may destroy prints originally present unless great care is exercised.
- Bottles and glass can be placed vertically on a board and placed in the bottom of a box. The base of the bottle can be surrounded with nails to hold it in position, and the mouth can either be inserted through a hole in a piece of cardboard or be held in place with a wooden board nailed to the lid of the container.

- ~~Paper and documents~~ containing latent prints should be placed individually in manila envelopes or plastic containers. Such containers can be placed between two sheets of stiff cardboard and wrapped or placed in a box for mailing.
- If the object containing the fingerprints cannot be removed or submitted to the latent print section, dust the prints with suitable developing powders and lift with latent lifting tape. Lifted prints can be placed on latent lift cards for preservation.

Elimination prints

Submit fingerprint cards on any other individual who may have handled the objects to be examined, either before or after the crime was committed. Include fingerprint cards of any investigators who may have accidentally touched the exhibits. This step will permit the rapid elimination of any latent impressions found that were made by such individuals.

Courtroom presentation of latent print evidence

The typical courtroom presentation of latent print evidence uses a photographic display consisting of a photo of the latent impression on one side and a photo of the corresponding inked impression of the suspect on the other side. Both the latent impression (Q) and the inked impression (K) have a numbered account of the constellation of minutiae in each which corresponds to the matching minutiae constellation in the other. Figure 5-11 illustrates a courtroom display of a latent fingerprint on a window frame from the scene which matches the right middle finger of the suspect in a burglary case. Figure 5-12 illustrates the match of a latent palmprint with the inked palmprint of the suspect in another case.

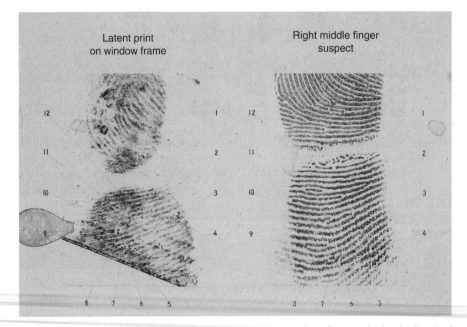

FIGURE 5-11 Courtroom Display of a Latent Fingerprint Identification (individualization)
Courtesy of Dr. Duayne Dillon.

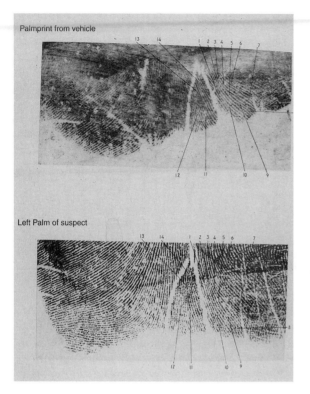

Palmprint from vehicle

Left Palm of suspect

FIGURE 5-12   Courtroom Display of a Latent Palmprint Identification (individualization)
Courtesy of Dr. Duayne Dillon.

Special considerations

For any circumstance in which there is any doubt about how to proceed with latent fingerprint processing, contact your local laboratory's latent fingerprint section for advice prior to proceeding with the processing. One fingerprint saved may be the solution to the crime.

Summary

Note:

For transportable objects, the investigator may transmit the object (s) to the laboratory for latent print development (recommended for chemical processes).

SYSTEMATIC PROCEDURE: ALL SURFACE/LATENT DEPOSIT COMBINATIONS

Steps One and Two Should Be Completed For All Surfaces Prior To Step Three Below!!

1. Visual examination with adequate lighting, followed by laser/alternate light/ultraviolet light.
2. Photographs of all patent impressions and any other evidence in the impressions prior to removal or tape lifting.
3. Selection of the physical and/or chemical process or sequence in the following chapter sections based on *surface type, nature of the latent deposit, and its environmental history.*

4. Photographs of developed prints *as processing proceeds.*
5. Sketch(es) of developed impressions.
6. Documentation of recovered latents in notes.

NONPOROUS SURFACES

Smooth, nonporous surfaces

1. Processing with brush and powder; or,
2. Cyanoacrylate processing.
3. Photography of developed impressions.
4. Powder development of visualized impressions.
5. Photos of cyanoacrylate/powder developed impressions.
6. Small particle reagent for wet (or dry) surfaces.

Rough, nonporous surfaces

1. Cyanoacrylate fuming.
2. Small particle reagent (especially for wet surfaces).

Plastic Foams

1. Small particle reagent (dish development for small items, spray for larger items).
2. Photograph the developed impressions.

Plastic packaging material

1. Laser or alternate light examination.
2. Superglue fuming.

Soft vinyl (PVC), rubber, leather, cling films

1. Superglue fuming, photographs of developed impressions.
2. Powder development, photographs of developed impressions.
3. Small particle reagent (wet items).
4. Spray for larger objects, dish method for smaller objects.

Untreated metal

1. Superglue fuming.
2. Powders.
3. Small particle reagent (wet items).

Wax and waxed surfaces

1. Sudan Black staining; photograph of developed impressions.
2. Superglue fuming; photograph of developed impressions.
3. Small particle reagent.

Items contaminated with greases

1. Sudan Black; photograph of developed impressions.* Preferred to Crystal Violet (very toxic).
2. Cyanoacrylate fuming* (if Sudan Black is unavailable).
3. Small particle reagent (wet items). Spray large items, Dish for small items.

ABSORBENT SURFACES

Paper and cardboard items

1. a. DFO; photograph of developed impressions.
   b. Laser/Alternate light; photograph of developed impressions.
2. Ninhydrin; photograph of developed impressions.

Raw wood (untreated)

1. DFO; photograph of developed impressions.
2. Ninhydrin; photograph of developed impressions.

Fabrics (fine, smooth fabrics only)

No proven processes; If in blood, process for prints in blood.

Adhesive tapes

A. NONADHESIVE SIDE (develop first).

1. Glossy plastic tapes: powders.
2. Soft vinyl tapes: Superglue (CA) fuming (Only While Stuck Down); photograph of developed impressions.
3. Fabric tapes: No proven processes.
4. Paper tapes (if not wetted)
   a. DFO,
   b. Laser/alternate light; photograph of developed impressions.

---

*Fluorescence may be improved after Sudan Black and Superglue Fuming.

c. Ninhydrin; photograph of developed impressions.
5. Paper tapes (if wetted)
   a. Physical developer (laboratory only); (will also develop adhesive side prints (interferes with subsequent methods and blood examinations).
   b. Photograph the developed prints.

B. ADHESIVE SIDE.

1. Crystal Violet (Note: Crystal Violet is very toxic)
2. Paper tapes: Physical developer.
   a. Only in laboratory by qualified personnel.
   b. Interferes with other development methods.

FINGERPRINTS IN BLOOD

General policy

1. Photograph prints *BEFORE treatments*.
2. Can be developed or enhanced:
   a. Staining with a protein dye such as Amido black.
   b. Treating with bloodstain testing reagents.
   c. Photograph the developed print.

Porous surfaces

1. TMB (Tetramethylbenzidine); photograph of developed impressions.

2. Ninhydrin, heat to develop; photograph of developed impressions.
3. Amido Black straining; photograph of developed impressions.

Non-porous surfaces

1. If *entire print* is contaminated with blood:
   a. DFO; photograph of developed impressions.
   b. Laser/alternate light; photograph of developed impressions.
   c. Amido black; photograph of developed impressions.
   d. Physical developer (laboratory only), photograph of developed impressions.
2. If the print is **partially blood and partially latent**.
   a. Powders, photograph (do not lift) of developed impressions.
   b. Amido Black; photograph of developed impressions.
   c. Physical developer (**LABORATORY ONLY**); photograph of developed impressions.

Development of Latent and Patent Impressions on Skin	
Storage Condition	**Print Type**
FRESH/ROOM T	**VISIBLE PRINTS**
(1) CA (Fume 0.5–1.0 hour)	(1) PHOT
(2) LUM DYE	(2) Transfer to glossy paper
(3) ALT	(3) IOD, transfer to Ag plate
(4) IOD, transfer to Ag plate, UV to 14 hrs.	(4) RTX
(5) RTX	
COLD STORAGE	**INDENTED PRINTS**
(1) IOD	(1) PHOT
(2) Transfer to Ag plate, UV to 14 hrs	(2) SIL CAST
(3) RTX	

Review Questions

1. Latent fingerprints are invisible to the naked eye and must be _____ for visualization.
2. Patent prints are those prints that are _____ to the _____.
3. At the present time, the age of a latent print _____ be established accurately.
4. Latent prints are constituted of materials that are either _____ or _____ in water.
5. In addition to secretions from the skin, latent prints may be composed partially or wholly of _____.
6. Laser lights should be operated only when all personnel are wearing _____.
7. The first consideration at the scene is the _____ of all personnel present.
8. The nature of the surface bearing possible latent prints will affect the _____ of methodology used to recover the latents.
9. Prior to processing any surface for latents, the analyst should carefully _____ the surface to be processed.
10. It is important to utilize a _____ approach in order to maximize the likelihood of finding and collecting latent impressions.
11. Each step in processing for latents should not _____ with subsequent steps.
12. When developing latents with fingerprint powder, the brush should be dipped _____ in the powder and swirled.
13. When developing objects with cyanoacrylate, the objects should be developed in a fuming _____.
14. If a wet surface cannot be suitably dried, the surface can be processed with _____ _____ _____.
15. At the scene, the analyst should use ninhydrin dissolved only in a _____ solvent.
16. The first step in processing the scene for latents is a thorough _____ examination, followed by or _____ or _____ light source examination.
17. Patent impressions and any trace evidence present should be _____ prior to processing.
18. A sketch of the latent print _____ and _____ should be placed on the latent lift card prior to lifting.

Further References

Beavan, Colin. 2001. *Fingerprints* (The origins of crime detection and the murder case that launched forensic science) New York, NY: Hyperion.

Cowger, J. F. *Friction Ridge Skin*. 1992. Boca Raton, FL: CRC Press.

Hebrard, J., and A. Donche. 1994. Fingerprint Detection Methods on Skin: Experimental Study on 16 Live Subjects and 23 Cadavers. *Journal of Forensic Identification* 44:623–621.

Lee, H. C., and R. E. Gaensslen, eds. 2001. *Advances in Fingerprint Technology*. Boca Raton, FL: CRC Press.

Margot, P., and C. Lennard. 1994. *Fingerprint Detection Techniques*, 6th rev. ed. Lausanne, Switzerland: University of Lausanne, Institute of Police Science and Criminology.

Menzel, E. R. 1991. An Introduction to *Lasers, Forensic Lights and Fluorescent Fingerprint Detection Techniques*. Salem, OR: Lightning Powder Co.

Report of Special Committee for Safety. 1986. Alameda, CA: The International Association for Identification.

Scene of Crime Handbook of Fingerprint Development Techniques. 1993. London, England: Police Scientific Development Branch, Home Office.

Glossary of Acronyms for Table 5-1

AG Silver or silver nitrate. Silver nitrate reacts with chloride in sweat to form silver chloride (AGCL). May intensify ninhydrin developed prints. Not recommended for paper because of more effective combination of ninhydrin followed by physical developer.

AL Aluminum; aluminum fingerprint powders.

ALT Alternate light sources (alternates to laser lights), including high-intensity lights and specific wavelength filters.

AMBL Amido Black; naphthalene black; protein stain used for bloody prints. Must be used in sequences, as it does not detect fingerprint constituents other than proteins. Interferes with most forensic examinations. Serology samples must be taken before treatment with AMBL.

8-ANIL 8-anilonaphthalene-1-sulfonate, used in greasy surface scheme.

ARD Ardrox 970-P10. Luminescent liquid stain for CA prints (Ardrox Limited, Canada).

BR28 Basic red 28. Luminescent dye for cyanoacrylate developed prints.

BY40 Basic yellow 40. Luminescent dye for cyanoacrylate developed prints.

BZFL Benzoflavone (7,8-alpha-naphthyl-flavone, 7,8-benzoflavone, alpha-naphthyl-flavone). Fixing reagent for iodine developed prints.

CA Cyanoacrylate esters (usually ethyl ester). Also known as Superglue. Overexposure may lose detail, particularly after luminescent stains. Should be left overnight before staining to allow polymer to harden sufficiently so that the print is not lost in the staining process.

CV Crystal Violet (Gentian Violet). Stain for prints on adhesives, cyanoacrylate developed prints (*toxic*).

DAB Diaminobenzidine. Blood-testing reagent and staining reagent for bloody stains.

DFO (1,8-diaza-9-fluorenone). Shows strong *luminescence* at room temperature. Dipped, dried, dipped again, then dried at 100°C for 20 minutes. Can be followed by ninhydrin, ninhydrin analogues, or zinc (Zn) or cadmium (Cd) treatment.

DMAC (4-dimethylaminocinnamaldehyde). Porous, dark red print must be photographed immediately. Reacts with urea in print. Good only for fresh prints. The urea in the deposit diffuses to give blurring of print.

GRIT (Glass recovery investigative technique.) Glass sheet recovery of latents from skin, followed by physical or chemical methods.

IOD Iodine vapor (oil and fatty acid material). Poor on prints older than 3–5 days. Chamber fuming or fuming pipe. Prints fixed with 7,8-benzoflavone (can be mixed fresh at scene).

LAS Laser light used for fingerprint visualization, before and after treatment with fluorescent powders.

LUM DYE "Luminescent" (or fluorescent) stain for cyanoacrylate fumed prints.

MAG POW Magnetic fingerprint dusting powder.

MMD Multimetal deposition (colloidal gold plus physical developer). Immersion in gold chloride (proteins, peptides, amino acids) followed by immersion in modified physical developer.

NBD-CL (7-chloro-4-nitrobenzo-2-oxa-1, 3-diazole). Reacts with amino acids and amines, forms luminescent prints not visible to the eye; special lighting needed because of background luminescence.

NIN Ninhydrin. Reacts with amino acids. Forms dark purple (Ruhemann's purple). Can be followed with metal salts that form complex with Ruhemann's purple (salts = zinc, cadmium, or mercury (Hg), usually zinc or cadmium).

NINLOG Ninhydrin analogues. Sensitivity equal to ninhydrin, but after treatment with metal salts, have stronger luminescence than ninhydrin developed prints. (Benzoninhydrin, 5-methoxyninhydrin; and others in development but not commercially available.)

PD Physical developer (paper and untreated wood). Aqueous solution of silver, ferrous/ferric system, buffer and detergent. Silver deposited preferentially on latents, ridges dark gray against light gray background. (Ninhydrin is sensitive to water-soluble components, and silver is sensitive to non-water-soluble components–sebaceous secretions). Can improve ninhydrin developed prints or develop prints not found with ninhydrin. Should be systematically applied after any sequence on paper.

PHOT Photograph any visualized latent.

POW Fingerprint powders in general, usually referring to standard fingerprint powder.

R6G Rhodamine 6G. Luminescent dye for cyanoacrylate developed prints.

RADACT Radioactive compounds. Sulfur dioxide (S-35); iodine monochloride (I-128); thiourea A (S-35); and sodium sulfide (S-35).

RAM Mixture of rhodamine 6G, ardrox (ardrox 970-P10), MBD [4-(4-methoxybenzylamino) 7-nitrobenzofurazan].

Rh6G Rhodamine 6.

RTX ~~Osmium tetroxide and ruthenium~~ tetroxide. Reacts with unsaturated organics (sebaceous). Exposed to vapors of reagent in chamber 1–12 hours. Particularly good for paper such as banknotes, which react with ninhydrin. (*Osmium is an extreme toxin.*) Cannot be used in most sequences (incompatible).

SIL CAST   Silicone dental casting material (e.g., Mikrosil, etc.).

SPR   Small particle reagent (wet powdering method). Non-water-soluble portion of latents. Suspension of molybdenum disulfide.

SUD BL   Sudan Black. General stain for proteins, peptides, and amino acids.

TEC   Theonyl europium chelate. Luminescent dye for CA (long-wave UV; abs = 350 nm, em = 614 nm).

TMB   Tetramethylbenzidine. Color-forming compound for blood testing and development of bloody latents.

UV   (Ultraviolet), *Long wave* ultraviolet light (Wood's lamp).

VMD   Vacuum metal deposition. Gold evaporated under vacuum to form thin layer (invisible); second layer of zinc or cadmium deposited in same manner. Zinc deposited preferentially on exposed gold but does not penetrate print deposit, leaving ridges transparent. May be successful when all other methods fail.

XRAY   Lead powder followed by XFR (X-ray fluorescence radiography).

APPENDIX 5-A

Safety Precautions for Latent Print Development[23]

The following guidelines for field and laboratory safety are adapted from recommendations by the International Association for Identification's (IAI) *Report of Special Committee for Safety*[24] for chemical and physical methodologies used in the development of latent impressions (see Chapter 7 for safety recommendations on biological hazards). The safety committee report is an excellent resource for the analyst and is available from the IAI at a very reasonable cost and should be obtained by interested individuals.

GENERAL GUIDELINES FOR SAFETY

Handling of chemicals

Many of the chemical techniques for the development of latent prints are exceedingly hazardous and should be performed only in the laboratory by qualified chemists or thoroughly trained technicians. The analyst should never attempt a technique before being adequately trained in the proper manner for use of the technique, in safety requirements for the technique, and in proper emergency procedures if an accidental exposure occurs.

Personal protective equipment

Personal protective equipment (PPE) must be worn in the field or laboratory when working with chemical or physical techniques. Protective equipment should include protective eyewear, outer garments such as jumpsuits or laboratory coats, chemically and biologically impervious gloves at all exposure times, and puncture-proof gloves when handling sharp items.

Eating, drinking, and/or smoking is prohibited

Eating, drinking, and/or smoking is prohibited at or near the crime scene or in the laboratory. Eating, drinking, or smoking should only be done away from these areas and only after removing all PPE and washing the hands and face thoroughly. New PPE items must be put on before re-entering the crime scene or laboratory.

Chemical and biological hazardous materials

Chemical and biological hazardous materials must be disposed of using OSHA required disposal bags. Disposal of hazardous materials should be coordinated through the Fire Department's hazardous material team.

Doubts about proper procedures

When in doubt about any procedure's safety precautions or the proper use of the technique, the analyst should review the safety precautions and techniques for that procedure and material safety data sheets for all chemicals used in the method.

GUIDELINES FOR SAFETY AT THE CRIME SCENE

Personal protective equipment

Personal protective equipment must be worn in the field when working with chemical or physical techniques. Protective equipment should include protective eyewear, outer garments such as jumpsuits or laboratory coats, chemically and biologically impervious gloves at all exposure times, and puncture-proof gloves when handling sharp items. Footwear covers should be worn whenever biological materials are present on the floor area, such as a bloody crime scene. Outerwear should be either disposable or commercially laundered to ensure decontamination.

Spray or fuming of chemicals

Spray or fuming of chemicals at the scene requires wearing of personal protective equipment to include jumpsuit, glasses, full face shields, gloves, and full face breathing apparatus. The use of powders requires the use of dust filter masks to avoid exposure of the analyst to the powder through inhalation.

Chemical cleanup and decontamination procedures

Chemical cleanup procedures and full decontamination procedures should be an integral part of the crime scene processing protocol. Proper disposal equipment and bags should be included in the crime scene equipment list, and an adequate supply of each item should be maintained in the crime scene vehicle and supply containers.

Periodic checking and maintenance of equipment

All equipment used in the field must be periodically checked for safety hazards. This includes electrical equipment, spraying equipment, and any other piece of equipment used in the field that may constitute a safety hazard.

Safety equipment for the crime scene vehicle/kits

Safety equipment such as first aid kits, decontamination kits for chemical or biological exposure, and fire suppression equipment should be an integral component of the crime scene vehicle's contents.

Small tools and implements

Small tools and implements used for evidence collection or handling should be disposable or decontaminated after each use.

SAFETY GUIDELINES IN THE LABORATORY

Clerical and evidence reception areas

Clerical and evidence reception areas must be kept clean and periodically disinfected. The routine inspections for safety in the laboratory should include the reception area.

Handling of chemicals

The use of protective eyewear, gloves, masks, and outerwear is a must when handling chemicals.

Volatile chemicals, finely divided powders

Handling of volatile chemicals or finely divided powders should be done only in the fume hood while wearing personal protective equipment.

Safety and emergency measures for chemicals

The analyst should not use any chemical without first being fully aware of the safety hazards and the proper handling techniques for that chemical. The analyst must be aware of the appropriate emergency measures to take after exposure to that chemical. Safety and emergency measures are contained in the material safety data sheet for that chemical.

Separation of fume hoods for biological materials and fume hoods for chemical agents

Fume hoods for biological materials and chemical agents should be separated. Fume hoods should be cleaned and decontaminated on a regular basis. A permanent record of fume hood safety checks and decontamination should be kept for each hood.

Sealing of chemically treated items

Any items chemically treated in the laboratory should be sealed to prevent exposure to subsequent handlers. Transparent packaging with appropriate hazardous warning labels must be used for evidence that is to be presented in court to prevent exposure to court personnel and juries.

Storage of chemicals

Chemicals must be stored in appropriate cabinets at all times (e.g., flammable liquids in a flammable storage cabinet away from all exits, radioactive chemicals in a cabinet with radioactive labeling, biologicals in a refrigerator with biological hazard labeling, etc.). Small quantities of working solutions may be stored in the laboratory area by using appropriate cabinets or shelving with protection against falling.

GUIDELINES FOR BIOLOGICAL HAZARDS

See Appendix 7-1 in Chapter 7 for safety guidelines for biological hazards.

GUIDELINES FOR SAFETY AT AUTOPSIES

See Chapter 14, Appendix 14-1, for safety guidelines at homicide crime scenes, and Appendix 14-2 for safety guidelines at the postmortem examination.

6 | TRACE EVIDENCE

It has long been an axiom of mine that the little things are infinitely the most important.

Sherlock Holmes in "A Case of Identity," *The Adventures of Sherlock Holmes,* by Sir Arthur Conan Doyle.

Key Words: Trace evidence, transfer evidence, secondary transfer, mitochondrial DNA, anagen, catagen, telogen, hair pigments, cuticle, cortex, medulla, hair standards, natural fibers, synthetic fibers, dyes, fiber classification, tape seal, loss at the seams, fiber lifting tape, refractive index, density, physical matching, transfer paint, mineralogical profile, added flammable, volatile, accelerant, fire triangle, fire tetrahedron, igniter, control standard, background controls.

INTRODUCTION

The concept of trace evidence embodies two definitions of the term "trace." The first definition refers to a "visible mark or sign of the former presence or passage of some person, thing, or event."[1] A second definition (among others) of the term is "a minute quantity."[2] Both of these definitions apply to the term **trace evidence** in forensic science, since the term "transfer evidence" refers to the transfer of material embodied in the Locard Exchange Principle, and the use of the term trace evidence to signify physical evidence that is very small. In the latter definition, the term *trace evidence* implies that the evidence requires examination by either microscopy or electronic instruments, or a combination of the two. The examination of trace evidence is accomplished in the laboratory in various sections, which may be classified by the type of evidence examined, by the professional category of the examiner, or by the type of examinations performed on the evidence (microscopy, spectroscopy, etc.).

The term **transfer evidence** embodied in the Locard exchange principle includes not only the transfer of trace evidence from an individual or object to another individual or object, but also the **secondary transfer** of trace evidence. Secondary transfer of evidence refers to the subsequent transfer of trace evidence from the place to which it was transferred to in its primary transfer to another place or thing.

160

For example, fibers transferred from a victim's sweater to an assailant's shirt can be subsequently transferred from the assailant's shirt to the fabric of a chair that the assailant sits in, thus becoming a secondary transfer of the fibers.

HAIR EVIDENCE

Introduction to hair evidence

The value of hair evidence has been revolutionized as a result of the development of techniques for analyzing **mitochondrial DNA** (deoxyribonucleic acid) in the hair shaft (see Chapter 7 for explanation of DNA types). Previously, DNA analysis was limited to those hairs that had a portion of the hair root adhering to the hair shaft. This was the situation that the forensic scientist was limited to in the analysis for *nuclear DNA* (DNA in the nucleus of each cell, designated "nDNA" or "nuc-DNA") in follicle cells adhering to hair that had been forcibly removed from the scalp. In recent times, techniques for analyzing mitochondrial DNA have been developed. Mitochondrial DNA (designated "mtDNA") is present in the cell outside the nucleus, so that cells that have no nucleus (hair, fingernails, toenails, epidermis) can be analyzed for this type of DNA. This development heightens considerably the value of hair evidence, since the hair can be examined and compared with conventional microscopic techniques and then analyzed for its mitochondrial DNA types. For further discussion of mitochondrial DNA analysis, see Chapter 7, "Biological Fluid Stain Evidence: Blood, Semen and Saliva."

Hair evidence consists of both animal and human hair. Most hair evidence encountered by the crime scene investigator consists of human hair, but the presence of possible animal hairs should not be overlooked, since animal hairs do occur as evidence occasionally. Human hairs that occur most frequently are either scalp or pubic hairs. Occasionally, other body hairs are encountered, usually in conjunction with an assault involving stabbing or a blunt instrument. Hair occurs frequently as evidence because of its abundance on the scalp and in the pubic region. One of the primary features of hair that makes it of interest to the investigator is its ability to withstand severe environmental conditions or decomposition. But the living cells of hair (the portion of the follicle attached to some pulled hairs) are very fragile and require special attention to save the potential for genetic typing of the living cellular material.

Hair is an outgrowth of the epidermis consisting of dead cellular materials. Hair consists of three layers: (1) the outer layer of scales (*cuticle*), (2) the middle layer called the *cortex,* and (3) the inner core called the *medulla* (sometimes fragmentary or absent). The structure of hair has been likened to the structure of a lead pencil: the cuticle (scales) of the hair is analogous to the outer paint layer; the cortex (the thick middle layer of the hair) is analogous to the wood of the pencil; and the medulla of the hair (the central canal of the hair) is analogous to the lead center of the pencil (see Figure 6-1). Each hair grows from a hair follicle in the skin in three phases. In the **anagen** phase, the hair follicle actively produces the hair shaft and extrudes it through the skin. The second phase (**catagen** phase) is a transitional phase leading to the third phase (**telogen** phase), during which the hair stops growing and "rests" until it falls from the skin or is pushed out by its replacement hair shaft.

In cross section, scalp hair shafts vary from round to flattened or ribbonlike shapes, or, in the case of beard hairs, triangular. The cross-sectional shape is related to the curliness

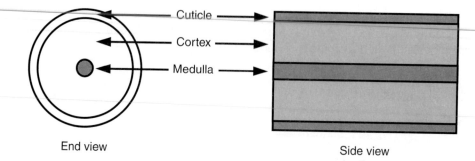

FIGURE 6-1 **Structure of Human Hair**

of the hair. Straight hair has a round cross-section, "wavy" hair has an oval cross section, and tightly curled hair has a flattened cross section. The cross-sectional shapes and degree of waviness are somewhat related to racial characteristics of human scalp hair, although there is a considerable overlap between racial groups.[3] Asian, Native American, and Hispanic racial groups all have straight hair with a rounded cross-section.[4] African racial groups have a ribbonlike cross section associated with tightly curled hair. European racial groups have scalp hair that ranges from straight to very curly and have a considerable overlap with the other two major racial groups with respect to the degree of hair curliness. Some Europeans, for example, have long, straight black scalp hair virtually indistinguishable to that of the Asians, whereas others have tightly curled black hair similar to that of the African hair type.

Pubic hairs from all racial groups are flattened in cross section, with the curliest hairs belonging to the African racial groups and the least curly belonging to the Asian racial groups. The Asian racial groups have pubic hairs that are only slightly curled and have a wavy appearance. African racial groups have tightly curled pubic hairs. European racial groups have pubic hairs that are intermediate between the Asian and the African racial groups, with the curliness ranging between tightly curled and loosely curled. The color of the pubic hair is related in general to the scalp hair color but can vary significantly from that color.

Significant features of hair

The most significant feature of hair, both to the investigator and to the laboratory analyst, is *hair color*. Hair color is due to two **hair pigments**, *melanin* (brown) and *tricosiderin* (red) present in the hair (see Table 6-1). A third pigment (yellow) has been postulated but not confirmed. Black hair, found in the large majority of humans, is actually a very deep brown, which appears as black to the unaided eye.[5] Blond hair is actually very light brown hair, which appears "blond" to the unaided eye. Red-brown hair colors are due to the combination of the red and brown pigments, which can occur in a wide variety of combinations ranging from a very dark red-brown (sometimes called "auburn") to very light red-brown ("strawberry blond"). The various shades of hair colors are obvious to the viewer because of the human eye's exceptional ability to distinguish between color shades. Under the comparison microscope, differences in color are readily distinguished by the laboratory examiner. "White" hairs are hairs that have no pigment in the shaft.

TABLE 6-1 Macroscopic (Seen by the Unaided Eye) Features of Human Hair

Hair Colors and Shades
(Color is also a microscopic characteristic of hair.)

White ("White" hair is actually colorless because of the lack of pigment in the cortex.)

Blonds	*Browns*	
Pale yellow	Very light brown	Dark brown
Medium yellow	Light brown	Very dark brown
Dark yellow	Light to medium brown	Extremely dark brown
	Medium brown	("black")
	Medium to dark brown	

Red/Browns (Darker red/browns are also known as "auburns.")

Blond/Very light red	Medium brown/Very light red
Blond/Light red	Medium brown/Light red
Blond/Medium red	Medium brown/Medium red
Blond/Dark red	Medium brown/Dark red
Blond/Very dark red	Medium brown/Very dark red
Light brown/Very light red	Dark brown/Very light red
Light brown/Light red	Dark brown/Light red
Light brown/Medium red	Dark brown/Medium red
Light brown/Dark red	Dark brown/Dark red
Light brown/ Very dark red	Dark brown/Very dark red

Length (Macroscopic)	*Curl (Macroscopic)*
<2.5 cm	Straight
2.5–7.5 cm	Wavy
7.5–15 cm	Curly
15–30 cm	Very curly
>30 cm	Tightly curled

Other hair features of significance to both the investigator and the hair examiner are the hair length and the degree of curl of the hair. The length of scalp hair is a feature that is readily seen by the viewer and may be included in a list of characteristics of importance to the investigator's description of a possible suspect in a criminal case. In the laboratory, the length of the evidence hairs is an important feature to the hair examiner during the hair comparisons. An evidence hair of short length that has been recently cut, for example, would not match much longer hair from an individual whose hair has not been recently cut. Hair length may be *suggestive of the gender* of the source, but the considerable overlap between male and female hair lengths precludes any assignment of gender based on hair length.

Microscopic features of human hair

Most of the other features of hair are microscopic in nature and can be seen only under the microscope. Features seen only through the microscope include the pigment granules, medulla, cortical fusi (small air sacs), the cuticle scales, root characteristics, hair damage, and diameter of the hair shaft. Each of these features is used by the hair examiner in making a comparison between a questioned hair and the standard hairs from a suspected source. It is the pattern of the combination of these characteristics that enables the hair examiner to distinguish between the hair from different individuals. Table 6-2 lists the microscopic features found in human hair.

THE CUTICLE

The **cuticle** of hairs consists of a number of *scales* that surround the hair shaft. The cuticle is composed of a large number of scales that overlap in a manner similar to that of roofing shingles. As seen under the microscope, only the edges of the scales are visible unless the hair has been damaged. The appearance of the scales (the scale "pattern") is sometimes helpful in the laboratory comparison of hairs and is quite diagnostic for

---

TABLE 6-2 Microscopic Characteristics of Human Hair

Pigment Characteristics

Density	Size	Distribution
Absent	Absent	Absent
Sparse	Fine	Uniform
Light	Medium	About medulla
Medium	Large	Unilateral
Heavy	Very large	Clusters

Medulla Characteristics

Absent		
Continuous/Opaque	Interrupted/Opaque	Fragmentary/Opaque
Continuous/Translucent	Interrupted/Translucent	Fragmentary/Translucent
Continuous/Opaque/ Translucent	Interrupted/Opaque/ Translucent	Fragmentary/Opaque/ Translucent

Hair Shaft Characteristics

Shaft Variation	Maximum Diameter	Tip	Root
Constant	Fine (< 0.04 mm)	Natural taper	Absent
Slight/Smooth variation	Medium (0.04–0.08 mm)	Recent cut	Atrophied
Wide/Smooth variation	Coarse (> 0.08 mm)	Rounded	Bulbous/No sheath present
Slight/Abrupt variation		Rounded/Frayed	Bulbous/Sheath present
Wide/Abrupt variation		Split	
		Crushed	

(continued)

Cortex Features and Inclusions

Cortical Fusi	Ovoid Bodies	Cortex Texture
Absent	None	Smooth
Present-root	Sparse	Streaky
Sparse-shaft	Frequent	Very streaky
Frequent-shaft	Dense	Granular
Dense-shaft		

	Treatment	Cuticular Margin
	None	Smooth
	Dyed	Slightly serrated
	Bleached	Serrated
	Curled/Permed	

human hair, since the pattern of animal hair scales differs markedly from that seen in human hairs. The exposed tips of the scales point toward the tip of the hair and allow for the analyst to orient the hair in its proximal-distal direction in the absence of the root and tip portions of the hair.

THE CORTEX

The **cortex** of the human hair consists of elongated fibers composed of keratinized filaments. The hair is quite strong because of the properties of the keratinized proteins, which are similar to the material found in the fingernails. The cortex contains most of those features used by the analyst to compare hairs: the pigment granules, cortical fusi, ovoid bodies, and other microscopic features. The *pigment granules* are discrete particles within the cortex and contain the *melanin,* which gives the hair its shades of *brown color* (the red pigment appears to be dissolved in the cortex, and granules of red pigment cannot be seen in the light microscope, although they can be seen with the scanning electron microscope). Cortical fusi are small sacs of air, normally having a spherical to ovoid shape. Ovoid bodies are, as the name implies, small bodies with an oval shape, and they have a characteristic light brown color.

THE MEDULLA

The **medulla** of the human hair appears dark or opaque under the microscope when the medulla is filled with air. If the medulla becomes filled with liquid, it may appear a light brown or translucent. The medulla may appear to be absent, it may be continuous throughout the hair shaft, or it may be intermittent, appearing in some portions of the shaft but not in others. The shape of the medulla is referred to as amorphous, meaning "without form," because the shape varies along the shaft and may have a distinct appearance from one individual to the next. The medulla in animal hair, on the other hand, has a well-defined pattern in most species and is used along with other features for species identification of the hair. The medulla in human hair is narrow, usually less than one-third of the hair shaft's diameter, whereas in animal hair, the medulla may be almost as wide as the shaft.

Other comparison characteristics in hair

Other characteristics used in the forensic comparison of hair include the degree of curl of the hair, the maximum diameter of the hair shaft, and the characteristics of the hair tip. These features of the questioned hair shaft are used by the hair analyst to compare against the same features of the known hair standards. The hair diameter and degree of curl are related to the racial group of the individual from whom the hair originated, whereas the hair length and appearance of the tip are the result of grooming. The appearance of the tip is related to the manner in which the hair was cut, the type and frequency of hair grooming, and the length of time since the hair was cut.

Treatment of the hair also lends comparison characteristics for the hair examiner. Bleached and dyed hair has a distinctive appearance, and if the hair root remains on the hair, an estimate of time since the bleaching and dying can be made by the examiner. The cuticle of the hair may be damaged by cosmetic treatment and may offer additional comparison criteria for the examiner.

The types of microscopic hair comparison characteristics used by the hair examiner are found in Table 6-2. The examiner will compare each of the characteristics listed for similarity between the questioned hairs and any standard hair specimens submitted by the investigator. Note that the hair color (see Table 6-1) is also a microscopic feature of hair used by the hair examiner for hair comparisons. The hair color is a result of both optical properties and the size, density, and distribution of the hair pigment granules (melanin) and the degree of red pigment present in the hair.[6]

Laboratory examinations of hair evidence

Laboratory examinations of hair evidence consist of two main approaches: (1) *microscopic examination* and *comparison* of the questioned hairs to the known hairs; and (2) *genetic marker analysis,* including DNA of the follicular material when present and possible DNA analysis of the hair shaft (see discussion of mitochondrial DNA in Chapter 9). The microscopic examinations include the following.

UNAIDED EYE AND STEREOSCOPIC (LOW-POWER) MICROSCOPE EXAMINATIONS
The general examination is for hair type, length, curl, and color. The exterior surfaces of the hair are also examined for any trace evidence present on the hair, such as fibers and louse eggs. These features provide investigative information for the investigators as well as comparison information for the hair examiner.

HIGH-POWER MICROSCOPIC EXAMINATION
The hairs are examined with the high-power microscopic for contaminants, hair treatments, and any unusual features that may be present. Any trace evidence present may be further characterized.

COMPARISON MICROSCOPE EXAMINATIONS
The comparison microscope examinations of the microscopic features of hair (see Table 6-2) consist of comparisons between the evidence hair and submitted standards from suspected sources for the hair. This comparison allows the examiner to make a side-by-side comparison of the questioned and standard hairs in order to note similarities and dissimilarities between the two.

DNA ANALYSIS OF THE HAIR

Hair evidence is now examined for its DNA content in the root sheath using techniques for nuclear DNA analysis. Techniques for determining the mitochondrial DNA in the hair shaft are used to examine the hair for its mitochondrial DNA types.

Collection of hair evidence[7]

Evidence hairs can be collected by the collection of individual hairs, collection of the object bearing the hairs, performing a "tape lift" technique, by combing or brushing (in the case of foreign pubic hairs in the pubic region), or by vacuuming the area suspected of containing evidence hairs. Each method may be used, depending on the particular circumstances at the scene. Collecting individual hairs is the method of choice, since each hair can be identified as to its specific location at the scene or on a specific object. In some cases, however, it may be necessary to use one of the other methods for hair collection.

PRECAUTIONS FOR EVIDENCE HAIRS

Before attempting the specific collection procedures in the following list, note these precautions.

Package Individual Hairs in an Individual Container   Single hairs should be packaged in a bindle or vial and then packaged in a small envelope. Both the bindle or vial and the envelope should be marked with standard identification data.

Do not Package Wet Evidence   Hairs or objects containing hair evidence should be air dried before placing in appropriate containers. Biological materials degrade with time. This process is accelerated when wet items are sealed in airtight containers such as plastic bags.

Place Exhibits only on a Clean Table Surface   Do not place exhibits on a tabletop without first thoroughly cleaning that surface. The best procedure is first to clean the table surface and cover it with new paper before placing the exhibits on the table. Avoid cross contamination between all evidence and control samples by handling the exhibits one at a time.

Label each Evidence Container with Standard Identification Data   Each container should have the following minimum data: *submitter's initials, case number, item number, source,* and *date.* Document the chain of custody.

COLLECTION AT THE SCENE

Hairs Visible and Firmly Attached to an Inanimate Object   Photograph the hairs in place (if feasible). Leave hairs intact on the object. Diagram and note the exact location and the number of hairs adhering to each object. Package the object so that the hairs cannot become dislodged in transit. Label the object and its package, and transport it to the laboratory.

Hairs Visible but not Firmly Attached to an Object   Photograph the hair before collection (if feasible). Sketch and note the location of the hairs and the number of hairs present. Then carefully *remove the hairs* with a clean pair of forceps or gloved hand and package. Place the hairs in small pill boxes, glass vials, or other tightly capped containers. Hairs may also be

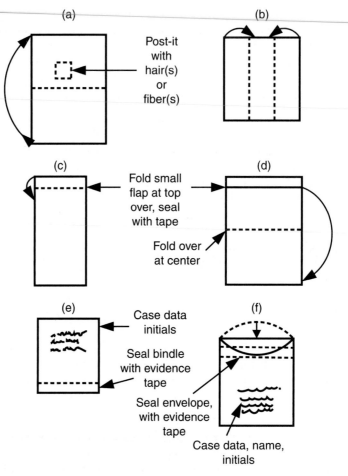

FIGURE 6-2 **Preparation of Bindle and Securing of Hair or Fiber Evidence to Bindle**

placed in folded paper bindles (see Figure 6-2) and then packaged in an envelope. Label the packages with standard identification data, and reference the collection in the field notes.

1. Recover hair or fiber with sticky strip of Post-it^{TM}.
2. Affix Post–it to bindle paper, (a).
3. Fold bottom portion over Post-it^{TM}, (a).
4. Fold sides (1/3 EA) over middle, (b).
5. Fold a strip at top over side folds, (c).
6. Fold top half over bottom half, (d).
7. Seal bindle with evidence tape, (e).
8. Label bindle with case#, item#, and collector's initials.
9. Place bindle in gummed–flap envelope, seal gummed flap with evidence tape, label envelope with case#, item#, collector's (printed) name, and initials or logo, (e), (f).
10. Enter item# and description into evidence log.

Hairs Possibly Transferred to the Clothing of a Victim or Suspect Be sure that the clothing is dry before packaging to preserve any biological materials present. Keep each clothing item separate from the others to avoid cross-contamination of any trace evidence present. Avoid disturbing any soil, dust, blood, seminal stains, or other foreign materials that may be adhering to the clothing. If any of the aforementioned evidence materials are apparent, see the appropriate chapter for special instructions for those evidence types. Place an identification mark on each item in an easily located area that does not damage the clothing, and note the location of the marks in the field notes. After allowing wet apparel to air-dry, carefully fold, wrap, and package each article separately in a paper bag (do not use plastic bags).

Fingernail Scrapings/Clippings   Take scrapings from both the suspect and the victim. Use a clean instrument such as fingernail clippers, a file, or a new toothpick to perform the scraping. Use a separate folded paper bindle for each hand to collect the scrapings. Place the folded, labeled bindle in a separate pill box, glass vial, or other small tightly capped container.

Tape Lifting of Dead Bodies   When there are many hairs or fibers present on a dead body, the analyst may elect to tape lift sections of the body. (See the section on autopsies in Chapter 14 "Homicide Investigations.") If there are discrete, visible clusters of hairs or fibers on the decedent, the investigator should collect these first, using a Post-it™ to collect each clump and secure it to a bindle (see Figure 6-2).

Hairs with Possible Roots Adhering to the Hair Shaft   Blood protein/enzyme types and DNA types may be detectable if the hair has been recently pulled and there is root material adhering to the hair. These hairs should be treated in the same manner as physiological fluids. Refrigerate and transport to the laboratory as soon as possible, or dry the specimens and freeze after drying. Keep the specimens frozen until they can be transported to the laboratory. Standard blood samples of the victim(s) and any suspect(s) should also be submitted to the laboratory (see Chapter 7 for appropriate standard blood specimens).

Vacuuming for Trace Evidence   When an area such as a vehicle's floorboards has a large quantity of hairs and/or fibers present, the area may be vacuumed for trace evidence. It is recommended that all visible hairs and fibers be collected from the surface prior to vacuuming, when feasible. It is also necessary to check the area after vacuuming in order to locate any hairs that are entrapped in the surface area, as a precautionary measure. The materials collected by the vacuum trap should be sealed in a plastic bag or an envelope with taped corners to avoid loss of the materials collected.

Standard/control specimens of hair

SCALP HAIR STANDARDS
The preferred method of sample collection is in this order: (1) *pulled hairs,* (2) *backcombed hairs,* and (3) *cut (near the skin) hairs.* It is not essential to have pulled hairs for standards provided that the hairs collected are cut very close to the skin, but the laboratory prefers hair specimens collected in the order indicated, because the growth phase of the hair may be a consideration in the examinations (the growth phase is determined by examination of the root). The investigator should record the overall color (i.e., gray, red, dark brown, reddish-blond, etc.) of the subject's hair; his/her age; and any signs of hair treatment. Take samples of each color present on the scalp for comparison purposes.

Scalp **hair standards** should also be collected from other individuals related to the case who may have been the source of any evidence hairs collected. Members of the household where hair evidence is recovered or other individuals who frequent the residence should be requested to provide hair standards for elimination purposes. This precaution may save considerable time in the laboratory and also may account for any hairs that do not match either the victim or the suspect. This step may be important in those cases in which mistaken identity is claimed as a defense by eliminating unknown sources for those hairs not matching a suspect or a victim.

Combed Hair Specimens   *New (unused)* plastic combs should be used to collect loose hair from all parts of the scalp. Combs should be used for only one subject and packaged with the hair sample. Back comb the scalp hair briskly. Catch falling hairs in a large sheet of paper, fold into a bindle, and place bindle and comb into an envelope. Seal and label appropriately. The combing of the subject's scalp will help collect any foreign hairs present and will also provide a specimen of the hairs that are ready to fall from the scalp.

Pulled or Cut Scalp Hair Standards   The sample of hair standards should be *representative of the entire scalp* and should include samples from the front, the left side, the right side, the crown area, and the back of the scalp (see Figure 6-3 for sampling sites). At least fifteen to twenty hairs from each area should be submitted for a *total of seventy-five to one hundred hairs.*

PUBIC HAIR STANDARDS

Collect about *fifty hairs total* by collecting approximately ten hairs from the top left, top right, top center, middle left, and middle right of the pubic region (see Figure 6-4). It is preferred to collect pulled hairs, but hairs cut as close to the skin as possible are adequate for the laboratory examinations and comparisons.

OTHER BODY HAIR STANDARDS

Collect body hairs from the area immediately surrounding the appropriate region (at least twenty to thirty hairs from each area are recommended). Use a separate container for each area, labeling each container with the exact location where the specimens were collected. It should be noted that little research has been accomplished on human hairs other than scalp and pubic hairs, so the laboratory analyst may not be able to derive strong conclusions from the examination and comparison of these types of hairs.

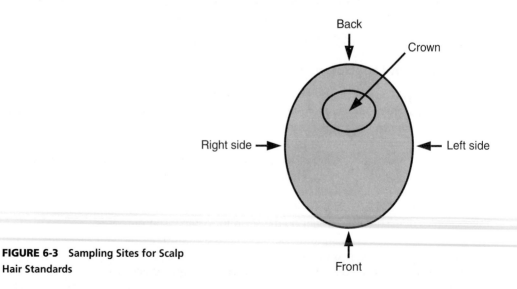

FIGURE 6-3 Sampling Sites for Scalp Hair Standards

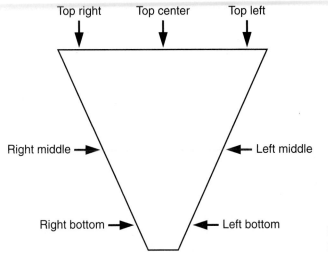

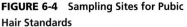

FIGURE 6-4 **Sampling Sites for Pubic Hair Standards**

ANIMAL HAIR STANDARDS

Comb and pull a total of approximately one hundred hairs (pulling is again preferred, because roots are needed for species identification in some animals). Hair samples should be pulled from the head, back, tail, and underbelly of animals. Label each sample as to its location on the animal, and package appropriately. All samples must include the coarse guard hair (the long outer hairs on the animal's coat) and the fine fur hair (the inner layer of hair). If the animal is multicolored in patches or stripes, samples from all the major color areas should be included in the standard specimens.

Laboratory reports concerning hair examinations

WHAT LABORATORY EXAMINATIONS CAN REVEAL

Whether the Hair is Animal or Human   If the hair is an animal hair, the analyst may be able to determine the species of animal from which the hair originated.

The Body Type of the Hair   Virtually all forensic human hair comparisons involve either scalp or pubic hairs. Very few data are available regarding the conclusions that can be drawn from the examination of other body hairs.

Investigative Leads   Investigative leads from hair evidence include the color, length, and form (straight, wavy, curly, highly curled) of the hair(s) present as evidence. These factors may allow the investigator to infer the hair color, length, and form of the suspect's hair. In addition, the hair form may permit the possible inference of the suspect's racial group (African, Asian*, European) and possibly the gender of the suspect (although longer hair is commonly seen in males as well as females). If visible flesh is adhering to the root(s) of the hair(s), the investigator may conclude that the hair was forcibly removed from its source.

---

*Note that all native Americans (North, Central, South) belong to the Asian racial groups, although typically these native Americans are referred to by a language designation (Hispanic, Latino, etc.).

CASE EXAMPLE

"Saved by a Hair"

In the case of *People v. Jackson*, the author served as a consultant to the defendant's lawyer. Jackson was convicted of a "series" of four rapes, each of which cases had physical evidence that, when properly interpreted, should have exonerated the defendant. At Jackson's first trial, he was convicted in each of the four cases and was sentenced to thirty-three years in prison before eligibility for parole. The physical evidence that should have excluded Jackson as the responsible in the four victims' cases included hair, semen typing, and fingerprint evidence. At a hearing for a re-trial, the hair evidence from the first victim's case* convinced the court to order a new trial.

*The victims are arbitrarily assigned numbers one through four for the purpose of this case example.

At the second trial, the defendant was convinced that the compelling testimony from one of the victims would result in another conviction, at which point he plead guilty to all four crimes. After his sentencing, the latent fingerprint evidence from one of the victims' cases was positively identified as having come from another individual who was currently in prison as a result of being convicted of a rape in San Francisco. It was the automated latent fingerprint system at the San Francisco Police Department (one of the first in the country) that identified the latent print from Victim Three's case as that of the true perpetrator of that crime.

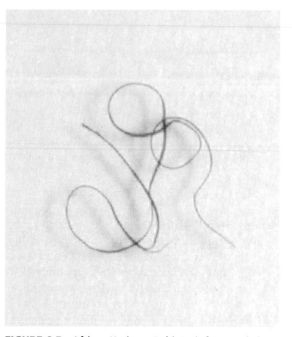

FIGURE 6-5   **African Heritage Pubic Hair from Bed Sheet, Victim One's Residence**

VICTIM ONE

An African heritage pubic hair (see Figure 6-5) was recovered from the sheet of the bed upon which the rape of the victim occurred. The only African heritage individual known to have been in the house of Victim One was the individual who raped her. The African heritage pubic hair from the sheet (see Figure 6-5) was compared to Jackson's pubic hair and the analyst determined that this hair could not have originated from the defendant Jackson. *This conclusion should have eliminated Jackson as the perpetrator in this case.* Instead, this evidence was not introduced at the first trial of Jackson, thus allowing Jackson to be convicted of the rape of Victim One.

VICTIM TWO

Two African heritage pubic hairs were recovered from Victim Two's pubic combings (see Figure 6-6). Note the high degree of similarity between the African heritage pubic hairs from Victim

One's pubic combing. In the opinion of the laboratory analyst who examined these hairs, the defendant Jackson could not be excluded as the source of these two hairs, although the analyst excluded Jackson as the source of the African heritage pubic hair from the bed sheet in Victim One's case. In this author's opinion, *the examination results for these hairs should have excluded Jackson as the source of these two hairs.*

In addition to the hair evidence, the semen typing in Victim Two's case should also have excluded Jackson as the responsible in this victim's case, since the defendant Jackson was an "A" secretor, which meant that his blood type should have been found in the vaginal swabs from the victim. No trace of blood type "A" was found in the vaginal swabs.

VICTIM THREE

The vaginal swabs from Victim Three showed a PGM subtype foreign to that of the victim. This finding indicated that there was sufficient semen present in the swab to obtain a positive result

(continued)

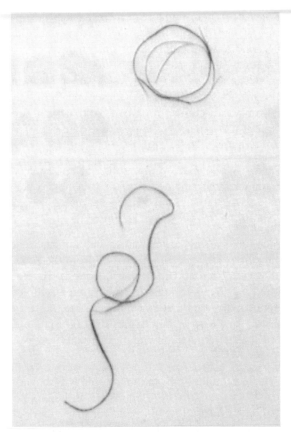

FIGURE 6-6   Two African Heritage Hairs from Pubic Combing of Victim Two

for ABO secretor typing, since the ABO antigen lasts longer than the PGM enzyme in the vagina postcoital. The laboratory analyst did not find "A" secretor semen in the vaginal swab, which is inconsistent with the semen originating from the defendant Jackson. Re-examination by an independent laboratory found that the semen on the vaginal swab originated from a nonsecretor, which eliminated Jackson as the source of the semen.

VICTIM FOUR

In Victim Four's case, the perpetrator entered the victim's residence by climbing upon an air conditioner, removing the window screen, and entering through a window. The perpetrator's identifiable palm prints were placed on a drainage pipe next to the window and his identifiable latent fingerprints were placed on the frame of the

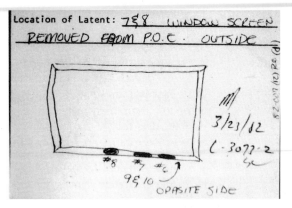

FIGURE 6-7   Latent Fingerprint on Window Screen from Point of Entry of Victim Four's Residence

window screen (see Figure 6-7). The identification of this window as the point of entry (POE) was made by the crime scene investigator as a result of the placement of the palm prints on the drain pipe, the placement of the latent fingerprints on the screen that was pulled off the window, and additional palm impressions on the window sill (an example of reconstruction from latent finger and palm prints).

The source of the latent print from the window screen (see Figure 6-8) was eventually identified by entering the latent into the automated latent fingerprint system of the San Francisco Police Department. As a result of this latent fingerprint identification, Jackson was allowed to leave one guilty plea in place, and the remaining cases were dropped, permitting Jackson to leave prison, since he had already served sufficient time for one victim.

As a result of the hair evidence from Victim One's case, the defendant Jackson received a new trial, and moreover, provided the impetus for this author to continue his investigation, which led to the identification of the latent fingerprint and to the release of Jackson from prison, a case of being *"saved by a hair."* ■

FIGURE 6-8   Latent Fingerprint from Window Screen of Victim Four's Residence, Identified as Being from True Assailant

Whether the Hair "Matches" a Suspected Source   When the hair is said to "match" a submitted standard, the analyst indicates in the report that the hair "could have come from the same source as the standard." This is a conditional identification, since hair types are not unique to any individual except in extremely rare cases. The strength of the opinion is related directly to the rarity of the evidence hair and the hair from the person it matches. If the hair is a rare type, the strength of the match is much stronger than a match of hair involving a common hair type (e.g., hair from Asian ethnic groups). Note that there are no hard data for the frequency of the different hair types, so the examiner must be cautious in interpreting the data from the hair comparison.

If the Hair does not Match a Suspected Source   When the questioned hair has no similarity to the submitted standard hair, the examiner may conclude that the questioned hair did not originate from the same individual as did the submitted hair standard. This is a positive *elimination* of the subject as the source of the questioned hair.

The Hair Comparison is Inconclusive   Occasionally, the hair examiner may indicate that no conclusion can be drawn with regard to the evidence hair originating from the same individual from whom the hair standard was collected. There may be one of several explanations for this opinion: the questioned hair may be fragmentary and therefore not adequate for the comparison; the submitted hair standards may not be adequate in quality or quantity; or the questioned hair may share some similarities with the standard hair specimen but also have some differences that counter the weight that may be given to the similarities.

DNA in Hair   If the evidence hair(s) has flesh adhering from being forcibly removed, the flesh tissue can be analyzed for nuclear DNA using the PCR technique. If there is no fleshy material adhering to the root, the hair shaft can still be analyzed for mitochondrial DNA (mtDNA), sometimes referred to as "mito" DNA. Mitochondrial DNA is inherited only from the subject's mother and is not as definitive for identifying the subject as nuclear DNA, but allows the analyst to state that the evidence blood sample's source is one of the children of that mother.

FIBER EVIDENCE

Introduction to fiber evidence

Fibers that occur as evidence may be textile fibers (fibers used to make cloth), carpet fibers, or fibers used in rope and cordage manufacture. Fibers are classified in a number of different ways, but the most common method of classifying fibers is to divide the types into **natural fibers** or **synthetic fibers** (see Table 6-3). These categories are then subdivided into the various types of fibers within the natural or synthetic categories. In addition to the fiber composition, there are many dyes added to the fibers to give color to the end product. The addition of **dyes** to the fibers contributes further characteristics to the fiber that can be used by the laboratory analyst to distinguish between fibers from different sources. Originally, the dyes used for fibers were of natural origin, but modern dyes are almost exclusively manufactured dyes designed specifically for the fiber class to be dyed.

| **TABLE 6-3** | Fiber Classification by Type and Composition | | |

I. Natural Fibers

Vegetable Fibers	Animal Fibers	Mineral Fibers
Cotton	Sheep wool	Asbestos
Linen	Alpaca	
Flax	Angora	
Hemp	Camel	
Jute	Silk	
Sisal		

II. Synthetic Fibers

Acetates, Triacetates	Acrylics	Nylons
Aramids (e.g., Kevlar)	Teflon	Glass fibers
Modacrylics (e.g., Dynel)	Rayons	Metallic
Olefins (e.g., Polyethylene)	Spandex	
Polyesters (e.g., Dacron)	Vinyons	

Table 6-3 is a partial listing of the various fiber types and does not include some of the rarely seen fibers or the many subtypes of a number of the fiber types. Some of the fiber types may be used in textiles, carpets, and cordage manufacture, whereas some types are limited to only textile, carpet, or cordage use. Hemp, for example, is found typically in cordage, whereas nylons are used in textiles, carpets, and rope manufacture. This division between textile, carpet, and cordage fibers is sometimes used in classification schemes, but **fiber classification** based on the fiber composition is more useful to the forensic examiner.

Occurrence of fiber evidence

Fiber evidence occurs in a variety of crimes, especially those types of crimes in which there is contact between an assailant and a victim. Fibers are frequently *transferred* as a result of *contact* of an individual with another individual or thing. Examples of fiber transfer include the transfer of carpet fibers to the shoes or clothing of individuals coming in contact with the carpet, transfer of clothing fibers between an assailant and a victim, transfer of clothing fibers from an individual's clothing to a point of entry and/or exit, and transfer of fibers from clothing to a weapon during an assault. Fibers are thus referred to as "transfer," "linkage," "associative," or "contact" evidence, since they tend to show contact or association between the objects involved in the transfer of the fibers and establish a link between the two. Although fibers themselves as a rule cannot be positively identified to a particular source, the two-way transfer of a number of different fiber types between two objects offers strong circumstantial evidence that the two objects were in contact at some time. Fibers do not persist for a lengthy period of time on garment fabrics with a hard finish, but fibers may persist for some time on fabrics with coarse finishes, such as wool garments or sweaters of most fiber types. It is therefore essential that the garment be collected as soon as possible after the incident in order to maximize the fiber recovery by the laboratory examiner.

In addition to the primary transfer of fibers from one object to another, the fibers may also be transferred via secondary transfer, as discussed earlier in the introduction to the trace evidence section.

Laboratory examinations of fiber evidence

Laboratory examinations of fiber evidence involve a comparison of the questioned fiber(s) to the submitted fiber standards. The questioned and standard fibers are compared on the basis of fiber type, color, microscopic appearance, cross-sectional shape, and the composition of the dye present. The examinations of the fibers include low-power microscopy with the stereoscopic microscope, high-power microscopic examination, examination by polarized microscopy, and comparisons of questioned and known fibers using the comparison microscope. Dyes in the fibers are examined by chemical analyses and with modern spectroscopic methods.

MICROSCOPIC EXAMINATIONS

The fibers are first examined with low-power stereomicroscopes for general form and color and any adherent materials that may have forensic significance. Any adherent materials are removed for further examinations. The fibers are then separated into single fibers for additional examinations.

After the examinations with the stereomicroscope, the examiner may use a polarizing microscope to identify the fiber type. The polarizing microscope transmits polarized light through the fiber, and the analysis of the interaction between the polarized light and the fiber allows the analyst to distinguish the various fiber types.

The fibers are then compared with the aid of a comparison microscope to judge the degree of similarities between the evidence and standard fibers. The qualities of color, size, and form are compared to see whether the questioned and known fibers are a "match" or a nonmatch. If the fibers "match" in the comparison microscope, the analyst will examine the fibers with an infrared spectrophotometer to determine whether the questioned and standard fibers are chemically identical.

If the questioned and standard fibers are found to be chemically identical with the infrared spectrophotometer the analyst will compare the dyes in both to determine whether the dyes are chemically identical. The dyes may be compared in two ways. They may be compared using a procedure called thin layer chromatography, or TLC, or the analyst may examine the dyes using a spectrometer, which measures the absorption of visible light by the fiber dye. The latter technique is becoming more common and may eventually supplant thin layer chromatography as the method of choice for comparing fiber dyes.

If the questioned fiber and the known fibers match in all the comparison criteria, the analyst will indicate that the questioned and known fibers could have originated from the same source, that is, they both share the same class characteristics. Although only circumstantial as evidence, the opinion is strengthened when more than one type of fiber is transferred. In some cases, a number of different fibers may be transferred in each direction, thus further strengthening the probative value of the circumstantial evidence. For example, fibers may be transferred from an assailant's clothing to the victim's clothing, and from the victim's clothing to the assailant's clothing; or fibers from the scene may be transferred to either the victim or the suspect in addition to the fiber transfer between victim and suspect.

Collection of fiber evidence[8]

The primary obstacle in the collection of fiber evidence is the difficulty encountered in *locating single fibers*. The discovery of single fibers on bodies, for example, requires diligent search methods in order to avoid missing the fibers. The surfaces to be searched should be scanned with strong lighting, with variation of the angle that the light strikes the surface in order to maximize the likelihood of seeing the fibers. In addition, the surface should be searched with an ultraviolet lamp and a laser/alternate light, since many fibers show strong florescence under UV light and other light sources, thus making their visualization easier.

The fibers can be collected in a number of different ways, depending on the location of the evidence fibers. Fibers can be collected with forceps, gloved fingers, or fiber collection tape, or by the use of a vacuum collection system. Where there is a loose fiber or a loose clump of fibers, they may be picked up with a Post-it™ and secured to a bindle with the Post-it™ sheet (see Figure 6-2). The primary consideration for the collection of fibers is to avoid loss or contamination of the fibers during collection or packaging. Special care should be used when collecting the fibers. Forceps (tweezers) are helpful in grasping the fibers tightly to avoid loss. Some fibers can be collected with the gloved fingers but may be lost when trying to place into the packaging material. When packaging fiber evidence in a paper bindle or an envelope, it is essential to **tape seal** the bindle and envelope to avoid **loss at the seams**. The extra effort expended in sealing the seams is critical to ensure that the fibers are not lost or contaminated during storage or transport. Another useful technique is to place the fibers in a bindle and then to place in an airtight vial and to tape the vial cap closed. Each bindle and its package or vial should have all identifying data affixed so that the evidence can be properly identified by the collector at any time in the future.

FIBERS ON IMMOVABLE OBJECTS (WINDOW SILLS, SMOOTH FLOORING)

Collection with Fiber Lifting Tape   One of the ways to collect fibers from a smooth surface is to use **fiber lifting tape** (Scotch brand #355, for example) to lift the fibers and then to place the tape onto a clear plastic surface such as Saran™ wrap. In this way, the fibers are mounted in a fashion that allows for their visualization by the laboratory analyst but are trapped to avoid loss. In addition, the fiber(s) may be secured to a bindle with a Post-it™ sheet (see Figure 6-2).

Visible Fibers   Sketch the location of the fibers, and indicate in the field notes and the evidence list the location of the fibers collected. Package each fiber or clump of fibers in a bindle, seal, and place in a vial, pill box, or coin envelope. Make sure to seal the seams of the pill box or envelope to avoid loss or contamination during storage and handling. The fiber(s) may be collected using a Post-it™ sheet.

FIBERS ON GARMENTS

For fibers on garments, the best procedure is to wrap the garment in butcher paper, collect the entire garment, and package in a paper bag, immediately taking special care to avoid contact with any other garment or surface. Garments that have biological stains such as semen or bloodstains must be air dried if wet and packaged in paper bags, making sure to seal the seams of the bag with tape to avoid loss during handling of the bag. If it is not feasible to air-dry the garment immediately, the garment can be packaged in a plastic bag, refrigerated, then removed and air dried *immediately* upon return to the station or laboratory (this is one of the few exceptions to the rule that plastic bags should never be used to package bloody clothing).

FIBERS IN VEHICLE FLOORBOARD CARPETS

First collect large, visible fibers with the gloved hand or forceps. Secure the fiber(s) to a bindle (see Figure 6-2), then place in an envelope, seal the envelope, and add case data to the envelope. The remaining fibers may be collected by using a vacuum collection device, packaging the debris collected in a bindle, and sealing in a manila envelope, taking care to seal all the seams of the envelope with tape to avoid loss of fibers through openings in the seams.

Fiber comparison standards needed for laboratory analysis

The examination of fiber evidence involves primarily the comparison of the fibers with those fibers removed from a suspected source for the evidence fiber (known fibers). The quality of the laboratory examinations is limited by the quality of the standards submitted for comparison with the evidence fibers. It is therefore crucial that an adequate supply of fiber standards be collected and transmitted to the laboratory along with the evidence fibers to be examined. Whenever possible, submit the entire object suspected as the source of the evidence fibers to the laboratory. The following guidelines are suggested for the indicated type of suspected source for the questioned fibers.

CARPET FIBER STANDARDS

Collect a substantial sample of fibers from each *differing area* of the carpet, so that the *range of fiber types and colors* is adequately represented by the standards. If there are stained areas on the suspect carpet, a standard should be collected from both the stained and the unstained areas to act as controls for the tests performed in the laboratory. A sample that approximates an area of the carpet about the size of a quarter for each will usually suffice (cut a few strands from a number of sites in a larger area, so as not to damage the carpet). Take specimens from each area of the carpets that may show different wear/treatment histories. Cut the fiber strands close to the backing, place in new vials or bindles, label as to origin, and make notes and sketches of the location(s) where the samples were collected.

GARMENT FIBER STANDARDS

Take the entire garment, making sure that the garment is dry if biological stains are suspected. Package in a paper bag, and with sealing tape, seal all seams where fibers might fall through. Handle the garment carefully, so as not to lose any adhering fibers during the packaging. Submit the entire garment to the laboratory for examination.

GLASS EVIDENCE[9]

Introduction to glass evidence

The value of glass as evidence is not always fully recognized. Windows, automobile glass, broken bottles, and other glass objects may be crucial evidence in burglaries, murders, hit-and-run accidents, and many other types of crime. It is known that any person standing in close proximity to glass when it is broken will pick up fragments of the broken glass, particularly on the clothing. Consequently, the clothing of burglary suspects, in cases in which windows have been broken, will often retain microscopic glass fragments. Frequently, as a result of hit-and-run accidents, headlight lenses and other lamps are broken, leaving glass fragments at the scene and in the clothing of vehicle-pedestrian hit-and-runs. Less common, but also possible, is the breaking of windshield glass. The analysis of the glass fragments present at the scene and in the garments of victims may provide evidence to associate the responsible vehicle to the crime. In some instances, broken head-light lenses may be matched "jigsaw puzzle" style to the fragments remaining in the head-lamp, thus providing conclusive evidence of the source of the glass fragments at the scene.

Laboratory examinations of glass evidence

FRACTURE EDGE MATCHES

If the *fracture edge* of a piece of broken glass can be made to fit an edge of a glass stan-dard in the manner of a jigsaw puzzle, a positive conclusion can be drawn that the two pieces were formerly part of the same pane or portion of glass. Even glass fragments as small as the head of a pin can be compared, although in most instances, *fracture matches* are found only with larger pieces, particularly with portions of broken headlamp lenses (see Figure 6-9). In addition to the "jigsaw" match, the edges of the fracture may be com-pared for a match between the *conchoidal striations* and other marks called "hackle" marks to determine whether these marks also correspond to each other. Conchoidal striations occur along the fracture edges of broken glass fragments (see Chapter 15) and are mirror images of the same markings on the edge of the portion that was broken away.

DIRECTION OF FORCE, SEQUENCE OF IMPACTS, AND THERMAL FRACTURES

If a window has been struck with a blunt instrument such as a rock, stick, or fist, the labora-tory analyst may be able to determine the side of impact and the nature of the force involved. If a window has been penetrated by a bullet, it is possible to determine the direction from which it was fired. If two or more bullet holes are in close proximity, it is possible to deter-mine the sequence of firing (see Chapter 15 for details on glass fracture analyses). If a glass object has been exposed to fire, it can often be determined whether the glass fractured as a result of the heat or by mechanical force, a fact that may have significance in an arson fire.

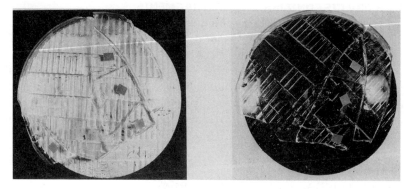

FIGURE 6-9   Fracture Match of Headlight Lens Fragments from Scene of Automobile Accident to Lens Fragments Remaining in Headlight of Suspect Automobile
Courtesy of Dr. Duayne Dillon.

COMPARISON OF PHYSICAL PROPERTIES OF THE GLASS

The laboratory comparison of evidence glass to submitted standards involves the comparison of the *physical properties* of the two specimens. The color of the glass fragments permits the analyst rapidly to screen fragments of different color, since fragments with different color could not have originated from the same source. Other features, such as the curvature of the surface, thickness, and surface texture, allow the analyst rapidly to screen samples that did not originate from the same object. If the questioned and standard glass specimens have the same physical characteristics, the analyst compares the physical properties of the glass specimens. The two physical properties most often compared in glass evidence are the *refractive index* and the *density* of the specimens. The **refractive index** of glass is a measure of how much the glass will bend light rays passing through the glass. **Density** is a measure of the relative mass (weight = mass × gravity) of a substance per unit volume (e.g., one cubic foot of iron weighs more than one cubic foot of glass). These properties can be measured very accurately in the laboratory, even on small fragments of glass.

OPINIONS DERIVED FROM LABORATORY COMPARISONS OF GLASS

In the case of a *fracture match,* the analyst can give a positive opinion that the questioned fragment and the known specimen were once part of the same glass object. When the questioned and standard glass specimens match in *physical properties,* the analyst can only indicate that the two could have a common origin.

Collection of glass evidence

CLOTHING CONTAINING GLASS FRAGMENTS

Microscopic-sized glass fragments are usually found on articles of clothing, including shoes, when the wearer has broken a pane of glass. The clothing of hit-and-run victims may also contain glass fragments from broken headlight lenses. In order to avoid loss of the glass fragments from the clothing, handle the clothing carefully. Wrap each article of clothing in butcher paper, then in a separate paper bag, seal, and label each bag with standard identification data. Wet or bloodstained clothing should first be dried, then packaged in paper bags (see the section on packaging of bloody clothing, Chapter 7).

TOOLS OR OTHER OBJECTS CONTAINING GLASS FRAGMENTS

Carefully place the object bearing the glass fragments in the smallest container into which the object will comfortably fit (e.g., bullets can be placed in small pill boxes, and shoes and tools in shoe boxes). Do not pack with cotton or other protective material directly touching the object. To prevent rattling, the object may be wrapped and sealed in butcher or brown paper and then packed with crumpled paper or packing material. Seal the package completely, leaving no holes or open seams through which the glass may be lost should it become loose from the object. Label the container with standard identification data, and transmit to the laboratory.

LARGE VISIBLE FRAGMENTS

There is a chance that **physical matching** (jigsaw-puzzle type) may be accomplished with large, visible glass fragments. Therefore, collect *all the fragments* present to permit reconstruction of the pane or headlight. If a determination of the nature of the breaking force or its direction is desired, all available fragments must be collected. The glass should be placed in a sealed paper bindle or a folded and sealed paper or plastic bag, depending on the size of the fragments collected; or place the fragments in a pill box or similar box with a tight-fitting lid. To prevent further breakage, wrap the paper or plastic bag with cushioning material such as crumpled paper or "bubble-pak," and place in a larger container, preferably a cardboard box. Do not use glass containers. If the glass fragments are being submitted for the purpose of determining the direction of impact of a bullet or other fracture analysis, record which side of the glass remaining in the window frame was on the outside. This step can be accomplished by placing a small piece of tape on one surface and labeling the tape with the appropriate side.

GLASS COMPARISON STANDARDS

Glass Standards from Windowpanes   Collect as much as possible of the broken glass for the comparison standard. If size limitations preclude collecting all the glass, always attempt to obtain a sample from an area near the point of impact and then collect and mark separate specimens from distant corners of the pane as well. Always keep the comparison samples separate from the questioned fragments. Place in separate containers, and label accurately.

Glass Standards from Bottles   Collect as much as possible of the bottle fragments. Occasionally, it is necessary to reconstruct the bottle or to develop latent fingerprints on the surface. The more fragments collected, the better the chance of obtaining latent prints from the bottle surface.

Glass Standards from Automobile Headlights   Glass from automobile headlights may be needed to compare with glass fragments in an accident victim's clothing or to identify the make of vehicle involved. Collect as many fragments as feasible from the roadway. If the vehicle is located, collect the entire headlight remaining in the lamp housing.

PAINT EVIDENCE[10]

Introduction to paint evidence

Paint is one of the more common types of physical evidence encountered. Paint evidence will be found in the majority of hit-and-run accidents and many burglary cases, where it may prove to have material value. Most paint evidence submitted to the laboratory for identification and comparisons consists of automotive or other vehicle paints, although house paints and other surface coatings may occasionally be encountered as evidence. The paint evidence may be a smear on the surface of a vehicle struck by another, small flakes of paint left at an accident scene, or larger flakes that have been dislocated from the responsible vehicle in a hit-and-run case. Paint from a pry bar used at a burglary scene may be compared with any paint from the pry mark at the scene. In one of the author's cases, paint was found on a pipe that was used to batter the victim in a homicide. The paint from a pipe found in a field was found to match all the layers of paint from an indented mark on the wall of the room where the victim was killed. Although most paint identifications are not conclusive as to the origin of the questioned paint, the finding of paint that matches the paint layers from a suspected source offers evidence that links the object bearing the paint transfer to the suspected source of the paint.

Paints belong to a class of substances referred to as "protective coatings." Protective coatings include many types of materials used to coat a surface in order to provide protection from environmental damage, and more often than not, also provide a decorative appearance to the surface coated. In the case of vehicle coatings, the paints provide protection against rusting and other corrosion in addition to their value as a decorative medium.

Hit-and-run cases: vehicle to pedestrian

Paint transferred to the clothing of pedestrian victims is usually present in microscopic quantities, either as *smears* of paint or as small *flakes* embedded in the fabric DEC. Such paint will at least show the color of part of the responsible car. It must be remembered, however, that many modern cars have more than one color, and the paint transferred represents only the color of the particular area on the car that made contact with the victim. It is sometimes possible to indicate the manufacturer and year of vehicle from a paint transfer. When this type of study is desired, it is of considerable assistance to the laboratory to receive any information available concerning the responsible vehicle. A copy of the officer's report often aids the laboratory examination. Also include any other evidence found at the scene, such as broken plastic lenses or other vehicle parts, which may in themselves indicate the make and year of the vehicle.

Sometimes whole chips of paint will be transferred to the clothing. If these flakes contain several layers and particularly if they came from a repainted car, such evidence may have great value when the responsible car is located. Chips of paint may also be found on the ground near the point of impact. In some cases in which the paint flakes are sufficiently large, it may be possible physically to match chips found at the accident scene with paint remaining on the fender of the suspect's vehicle (see Figure 6-10). This type of physical matching offers conclusive evidence that the suspect vehicle was involved in the hit-and-run incident.

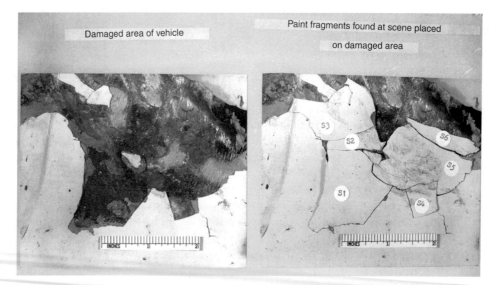

FIGURE 6-10 Paint Fragments at Scene of Accident Fitted to Damaged Area of Suspect Automobile Showing Fracture Edge Match ("Jigsaw" Match)
Courtesy of Criminalist Steve Ojena.

Hit-and-run cases: vehicle to vehicle

The paint smear transferred from one vehicle to another is referred to as "paint transfer." Cross-transfers of paint (paint from the responsible vehicle to the victim vehicle and vice versa) commonly occur in hit-and-run cases involving two or more vehicles. If the responsible vehicle can be located and appropriate paint samples collected, cross-transfers on both the victim vehicle and the responsible vehicle can be documented by the laboratory examinations when present.

Burglary cases

Tools used to gain entry into buildings or safes often contain traces of paint as well as other substances such as plaster or safe insulation. Care must be taken that this type of trace evidence is not lost. If such transfers may be present, wrap the end of the tool containing the material in a paper bag, and seal with plastic tape to prevent loss. Never attempt to fit the tool into marks or impressions found. If this attempt is made, the toolmarks and transfers of paint or other trace evidence materials found on the tool will have no significance as evidence, since the toolmark impression comparison characteristics and the transfer of trace evidence may have occurred during the attempted fitting. The tool itself may contain paint or other coatings, traces of which may be left in the toolmark or at the crime scene. A careful search should be made of each toolmark for any such evidence.

Laboratory examinations of paint evidence

The laboratory examinations of paint evidence include both microscopic and chemical analysis of the submitted specimens. Items suspected of containing paint evidence are first examined with the aid of the stereoscopic (low-power) microscope. Once the traces of paint are located on the submitted object, the traces are removed for optical, chemical, and spectroscopic analysis. Optical methods include stereomicroscopic examination of the colors present; the layers present, if any; the texture of the surface; and the layer edges. These properties can be compared directly with the known standards submitted, either under a comparison microscope or side-by-side under a stereomicroscope after mounting. If these features of the questioned and known paint specimens are determined to match by the analyst, the questioned and known standards are analyzed by chemical and spectroscopic means.

The chemical analysis of the paints may include wet chemistry for the solubility of the paints, which will indicate the basic paint type present in the specimens. The paints can then be examined using spectroscopic methods that will further characterize the type of paint and provide additional criteria for comparison between the questioned and known specimens. If the suspect vehicle is unknown, the data from the chemical analysis can be compared with paint reference standards prepared by the U.S. Bureau of Standards for late model American vehicles. These data may allow the analyst to state the particular make of the vehicle involved, in addition to the color of the vehicle.

Laboratory reports concerning paint evidence

The report from the laboratory may state that the paint from the suspected vehicle does not match the paint on a pedestrian victim's clothing or paint from the transfers found on a victim vehicle. In this situation, the analyst can eliminate the suspect vehicle as the one responsible for the paint transfers. The analyst may be able to provide a list of suspect vehicle makes through comparison of the questioned paint with data derived from analysis of vehicle manufacturers' paint topcoats.

If the analyst finds that the paint from the suspect vehicle matches the paint in the smear from the victim vehicle, the report will state that the paint in the smear matches the suspect vehicle's paint in all the tests performed. This is a conditional identification, because the paint on a vehicle is not unique to that vehicle but could have come from another vehicle with the same paint type(s), since vehicles are mass-produced and mass-painted, including the layers found in the paint specimens. Vehicles or residences that have been repainted many times may provide stronger evidence when a match is found between the layers present in the paint, particularly if there are specimens from several areas having different color/layer sequences.

Collection of Paint Specimens

PAINT SPECIMENS FROM VEHICLES

Obtain generous samples of the **transfer paint** from each area of damage and a *standard paint sample* next to each damaged area for comparison from all areas showing fresh damage on all vehicles involved (see Figure 6-11). This step is very important, since the paint may be different in type or composition in different locations even though the outer color is the same. If the paint can be flaked off by bending the metal slightly, remove it in this manner. If not, scrape paint off using a new razor blade. Make certain that samples of all layers down to the metal are collected. Place each sample collected from different areas in separate containers. Samples should represent an area of at least $\frac{1"}{4}$ by $\frac{1"}{4}$ to provide sufficient material for laboratory examination and identification purposes. It is better to take more samples than not enough, so a generous sample should be taken whenever possible. If loose paint chips are located on the vehicle, document their location with photographs and sketches, and attempt to remove and wrap them in folded paper bindles.

A very useful method for obtaining paint specimens from vehicles, walls, and similar locations is to secure a manila envelope to the surface just below the area to be sampled (see Figure 6-12) with transparent tape or fingerprint tape. Once the paint sample has been scraped into the envelope, it can be removed, the top folded down several times, and sealed with tape.

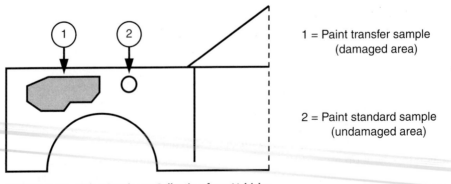

1 = Paint transfer sample
(damaged area)

2 = Paint standard sample
(undamaged area)

FIGURE 6-11 Paint Specimen Collection from Vehicles

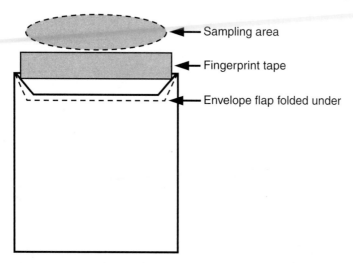

Sampling area

Fingerprint tape

Envelope flap folded under

FIGURE 6-12 Technique for Obtaining Paint Scrapings from Vehicle or Wall Surfaces

PAINT SPECIMENS FROM GARMENTS

Paint specimens on garments should be collected by taking the *entire garment*. If the garment is damp or bloody, dry the garment completely before packaging. (*Note:* Package bloody clothing only in paper bags after drying.) Carefully wrap each garment separately by rolling in paper, and place each garment in a separate paper bag for delivery to the laboratory. Seal the bag seams with *tape* so that small particles of paint cannot be lost through the seams.

PAINT SPECIMENS FROM TOOLMARK IMPRESSIONS

Collect specimens of paint from all areas that the tool may have contacted at the crime scene. These samples should include all paint layers present. If the sample is very small or difficult to remove and the complete exhibit itself can be sent to the laboratory, this is the best procedure, because it will make available to the analyst all of the paint transfer in the toolmark without loss. Always scrape or otherwise remove samples of all the layers of paint or other materials present if the complete exhibit containing the paint is not to be submitted to the laboratory.

PACKAGING OF PAINT SPECIMENS

Small glass vials or cardboard pill boxes are excellent containers for paint. Small plastic bags or vials also may be used, but they will make removal of small chips very difficult for the laboratory analyst. Use wrapped paper bindles instead of plastic bags whenever possible. The paper bindles can then be placed in a sealed plastic bag or vial to prevent loss of the enclosed fragments. Paper envelopes should not be employed for the submission of paint unless the specimen is very large in size. If such envelopes are used, always seal all four corners with plastic (transparent or fingerprint) tape to prevent loss. Markings placed on labels, envelopes, or other containers should include the case file number, item number, officer's name, and date and time of collection, as well as the specific source of the sample (e.g., "L/F fender 1970 Ford, blue in color, license #ABC 123"), which can be referenced to the officer's notes and sketches.

Avoid placing any conclusions or examination requests directly on the envelopes containing the paint samples. Include the police report of the incident whenever possible. The report will help guide the laboratory examinations and will provide data that may suggest additional examinations to the laboratory analyst.

SOIL EVIDENCE[11]

Introduction to soil evidence

Naturally occurring soil is a complex and changing mixture of living organisms, decaying organic matter, air, water, and relatively stable rock and mineral fragments such as clay and sand. Although there are many different types of soils in a given state, specific local areas contain relatively few of these varieties. Each type may exist for a few square yards or for many square miles, with the amount of variation in a single soil being quite limited. Hence, it is not feasible to pinpoint exactly the origin of a particular naturally occurring soil sample, but it may be feasible to relate it to areas of occurrence. Unless a crime is committed that involves the digging of a grave, most samples for soil comparison will be from the *top surface* of the soil. Typically, soil evidence occurs as soil found on the shoe soles of suspects in burglaries, sexual assaults, or homicides.

Soil samples may also contain debris from human habitation or industrial operations. This type of debris found in soils (e.g., paint droplets, cinders, chemicals, or fibers, etc.), if sufficiently varied and unique, can be valuable in individualizing a specimen. Soil samples containing such unusual features can be excellent and unexpected physical evidence. Consequently, all soil samples should be submitted in anticipation that this rare occurrence may actually happen. The character and composition of soils vary not only laterally but also with depth. Fortunately for the investigator, most crimes are committed near human habitations, where the debris of human activities is found in the soil. These inclusions of human activities in the soil enhance its value as evidence significantly, because the soil inclusions from one small area to the next will exhibit considerable variation when compared with soils that are removed geographically from human activities.

Soil may have the potential for determining the likeliest area for the source of the soil in question. Biological inclusions such as plant materials, insects, or their growth stages may be identified by a biologist from the appropriate specialty who may be able to indicate a possible site of origin for the soil. Soil scientists may be able to pinpoint the most likely area for the sample's source by identification of the soil type, which may be found in a limited area in the investigator's jurisdiction.

Although the color and texture of soils visually do not appear to vary along the ground, the chemical composition and the inclusions found in the soil can change considerably in a short distance, so that it may be significant in localizing the source of the soil sample. Therefore, sufficient samples should be submitted in order to establish the normal distribution of soil of a particular type in and about a crime scene.

Laboratory examinations of soil evidence

COLOR OF THE QUESTIONED AND KNOWN SOIL SAMPLES

The laboratory examinations of soil evidence all involve the comparison of the questioned soil with the soil standards submitted to the laboratory. The comparison of the two may include a variety of techniques for comparison, because of the properties of the soil that form the basis of the comparison. One of the more significant features used in a soil comparison is the color of the soil after drying and sieving. The color of the soil specimens affords the analyst a rapid means of sorting those soils that need further examinations for the comparison, or those soils that can be eliminated as possible sources for the questioned soil sample. If the color of the questioned sample and the known sample match, however, the analyst considers this similarity along with the other properties of the questioned and known samples to arrive at a conclusion as to whether or not the soils share the same origin.

DENSITY PROFILE OF THE SOIL PARTICLES

Each of the particles present in a soil sample has a specific density, depending on the particle's chemical composition. By adding a small sample of the dried and sieved soil specimen to a density gradient tube (a tube containing liquid that is very heavy at the bottom and lighter at the top, with a smooth gradient of density from top to bottom), each of the particles will float in the gradient liquid at the level where the density of the particle matches the density of the liquid. Since soils contain a number of particles of varying density, the grains will produce a pattern in the tube, as a result of the different heights at which the mineral fragments float in the tube on the basis of the density of each mineral (see Figure 6-13). The density gradient technique is a powerful method for discriminating between soils from different sites.

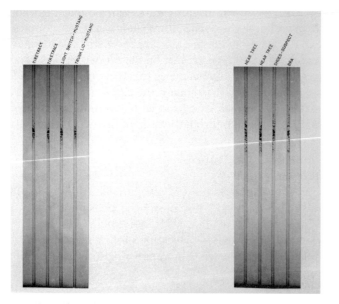

FIGURE 6-13   Soil Sample Comparison Using the Gradient Tube Method

Courtesy of Criminalist Steve Ojena.

Figure 6-13 illustrates a match of soil samples in density gradient tubes between soil from the scene and samples from the suspect's vehicle and between samples from the scene to the suspect's shoes and the victim's brassiere.

MINERALOGICAL PROFILE

The various minerals present in a soil sample can be identified using a polarizing microscope, which exhibits the optical characteristics of each particle under the microscope. The frequency distribution of the minerals present in the soil specimen can be determined by counting methods. The frequency distribution of the various minerals in a soil specimen is referred to as the "**mineralogical profile**." The mineralogical profile in soils varies considerably from one site to another, and this profile is a powerful tool for discriminating between soil samples.

OTHER TECHNIQUES FOR SOIL COMPARISONS

Other techniques for soil comparison include the assay of enzymes in the sample and the identification of biological fragments, such as insect parts, pollens, and plant fragments.[12] Although not used frequently in soil comparisons, the identification of certain insects, pollens, and plant fragments offers investigative clues as to the general area from which the soil originated.

Collection of soil evidence

SOIL FROM IMPRESSIONS

Ensure that impressions in soil such as footprints or tire tread patterns are photographed using oblique lighting with a scale in place and a plaster cast that was made before disturbing the impression in any manner. Impression evidence frequently allows for a much more positive opinion regarding individualization than a soil comparison (see Chapter 9). Do not attempt to clean the soil from the plaster cast, because the soil adhering to the cast may be the best example of the soil type present on the footwear soles of a suspect. Wrap the plaster cast in strong paper (such as butcher paper) and then seal it in a strong paper bag, or, preferably, a cardboard box. The soil on the cast can be removed and the loose soil in its package recovered for analysis by the laboratory analyst at the lab for use as evidence soil. If soil samples are taken from the area of the impression, take the samples *after the cast has been prepared*.

SUSPECT (QUESTIONED) SAMPLES

A tablespoonful is sufficient quantity for a soil comparison. If the soil is firmly attached to some object, do not remove the soil, but air-dry the object and place the object in a paper bag or other appropriate container, seal, and label. Loose soil or sand can be swept onto a clean piece of paper that is then folded into a bindle to enclose the specimen and, when completely dried, sealed in an appropriate container, and labeled as to its source.

COMPARISON (STANDARD) SAMPLES

Obtain samples consisting of at least three (3) tablespoonfuls of soil from each area where the suspect is known or is believed to have been at the scene, including any "alibi" sites provided. Comparison samples must be representative of the soil type in the area of collection. If, for example, suspect shoes have been recovered and soil is present on the shoes, recover a soil sample in the area of the shoe impression in the soil that corresponds to the physical location of the soil on the shoes. If soil on the shoe(s) appears to be from the surface where the footwear impressions are found, collect surface samples (top quarter inch) for the soil standard.

If the soil may be from an excavation of some type, collect specimens at many different depths, and mark the depth at which each was recovered. It is also advisable to collect samples from other locations in the vicinity of the crime scene so that the laboratory can determine how much variation there is in the soil of that area. In a yard, for example, collect standard samples from several areas in the yard and also from the adjoining property.

In open areas, the following systematic method for recovery of soil samples can be used: Start at point number one (footprint, tire impression, area of obvious scuffle), and collect a soil sample from each of the points one through eleven (see Figure 6-14). Make accurate measurements to each sampling site from the sketch reference points, and record the measurements on the sketch.

Seal each dry soil sample in a pill box or vial, and label the container completely as to the location where the sample was recovered, the officer collecting the sample, date, time, and the sample item number that identifies the area on the sample grid where the sample was collected. Always air-dry damp soil samples prior to final packaging, or mold growth will occur (the samples can be temporarily packaged at the scene and dried upon return to the station or laboratory). Record a description of the physical location from where the soil sample was collected (e.g., ditch), and note any unusual conditions in the vicinity (e.g., close to petroleum tank).

Collect soil samples as soon after the event as feasible, before any changes in the site can occur. Submit samples personally or by mail as soon as possible to your nearest forensic laboratory.

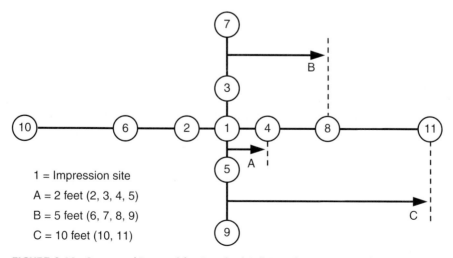

1 = Impression site
A = 2 feet (2, 3, 4, 5)
B = 5 feet (6, 7, 8, 9)
C = 10 feet (10, 11)

FIGURE 6-14 Suggested Protocol for Standard Soil Samples

ARSON ACCELERANT EVIDENCE[13]

Introduction to arson investigations

An arson investigation is a complex endeavor that requires a well-trained and experienced arson investigator to be in charge of the investigation. Arson investigators use several important considerations in determining whether the cause of a fire is accidental or intentional. The arson investigator is trained in the interpretation of the "burn pattern" of a fire, which will indicate whether or not an accelerant (often called "**added flammable**") was used to start and spread the fire. The investigator will also seek to eliminate accidental causes of the fire, such as faulty wiring or materials on a stove that were left unattended. The presence of an identified accelerant in the burn areas is an important factor in the arson investigator's determination that an arson has been committed. Thus, the investigator will make every effort to locate and collect accelerant residues for laboratory analysis in order to assist in establishing that a crime occurred. The specific type of accelerant used can then be compared with standard samples seized from a suspect in order to link the suspect to the arson.

The role of the crime scene investigator in arson scene investigations is typically to assist the arson investigator in the documentation and collection of physical evidence at the scene. In some instances, the crime scene investigator may be a competent, certified arson investigator, in which case, he or she also acts as the arson investigator, analyzing the scene for evidence of arson and also collecting the physical evidence samples necessary to assist in the determination of arson or fire from natural causes. In this instance, additional crime scene investigators will assist the arson investigator in documenting the scene and collection of the physical evidence.

Nature of volatile flammables

The term "**volatile**" refers to that attribute of a liquid that permits the liquid to evaporate rapidly, thus forming a gas above the surface of the liquid. Some liquids are very volatile but not flammable, such as chloroform, whereas others may be both volatile and flammable, such as gasoline. The most common term applied to volatile flammables used in arson fires is "**accelerant**." Volatile flammables used to commit an arson are referred to as "accelerants" because they *accelerate* the fire, resulting in its rapid spread and destruction of the structure involved. Examples of volatile flammables often used as accelerants in arson cases are gasoline, kerosene, lighter fluid, and white gasoline.

The process of combustion requires three elements for its propagation: *heat, oxygen,* and *fuel,* commonly referred to as the "**fire triangle**." Fire will be extinguished when any one of these three elements is absent. Fire does not burn solids or liquids (in general) but instead burns the gasses formed above them. Heat acts to vaporize the liquid or solid, converting it into a gas that then combines with oxygen to "burn" above the liquid pool. Thus, when flammable liquids soak into material or run into "cracks" there will be insufficient oxygen to support combustion. In these cases, residues of the flammable substance can be collected by collecting the material into which the liquid has soaked. The process of the *chemical reaction* that occurs during the fire has been added to the fire triangle in recent times, so the fire triangle is currently referred to as the "**fire tetrahedron**" (four-sided figure, see Figure 6-15).

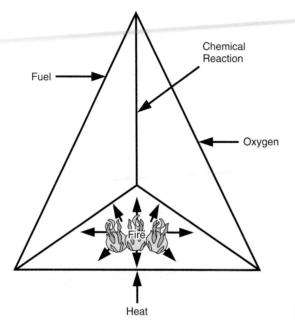

Fuel

Chemical
Reaction

Oxygen

Fire

Heat

FIGURE 6-15 The Fire Tetrahedron

At the scene

PRECAUTIONS AT THE ARSON SCENE

It is important to remember that *many types of physical evidence* may be present at a suspected arson scene. The investigator should always consider the presence of latent fingerprints, toolmarks, footwear impressions, and trace evidence such as hairs and fibers. Bloodstains may be present in those circumstances in which the arsonist sustained an injury during the commission of the crime. Glass fragments at the site of suspected entry should be collected for examination in the laboratory to determine whether the glass was broken by the arsonist or was fractured by the heat of combustion. Arson "sets" or items suspected of being part of an arson set, such as matches or matchbooks, should be collected and submitted along with the accelerant evidence. One common "**igniter**" found at arson scenes is a match used to ignite the fire. Figure 6-16 illustrates a partially burned match collected at an arson scene compared to a matchbook from the suspect. The igniter match is shown fitting into the matchbook (left top), a fracture match, and the comparison of the inclusions in the match to those of the adjacent match (right top) remaining in the matchbook seized from the suspect.

It is also important that the scene remain undisturbed until the arson investigator assigned to the case has had the opportunity to assess the burn patterns present at the scene. Once the arson investigator has assessed the burn patterns present, areas suspected of containing accelerant residues should first be documented with proper photographs, sketches, and notes before collection procedures are undertaken. This precaution is standard practice for good crime scene investigation and will help ensure a professional presentation in the investigator's report and testimony in any judicial proceeding. The investigator should also photograph the crowd observing the fire, because arsonists occasionally remain at the scene or return in order to observe the fire.

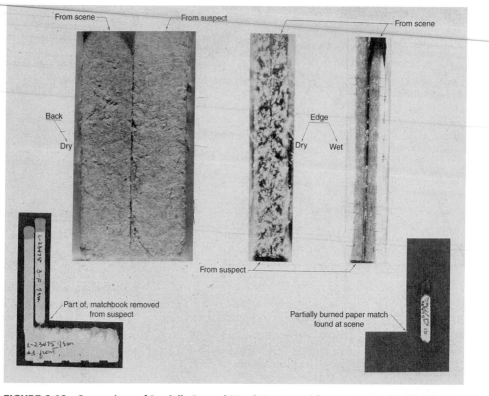

FIGURE 6-16 Comparison of Partially Burned Match Recovered from an Arson Scene with the Matchbook Seized from the Suspect

Courtesy of Dr. Duayne Dillon.

Multiple points of origin are typical in an accelerated fire. An arsonist will often pour the volatile flammable in more than one place to be certain that the fire will spread rapidly and engulf the entire structure. This use of an excessive amount of accelerant means that frequently, enough residues of the accelerant will remain after the fire has been suppressed for collection by the investigator. It is therefore important to collect specimens from each suspected site of origin, along with the appropriate controls, to help establish these multiple points of origin. The amount needed for laboratory analysis is very small, since the laboratory analyst will use methods that concentrate the residues recovered and allow for instrumental analysis of the residues.

LOCATING THE EVIDENCE

The suspected point(s) of origin for a fire should be located by an experienced arson investigator, combining the use of a combustible vapor detector and personal observation based on the investigator's specialized experience and training in arson investigation. In recent years, dogs have been trained to locate arson accelerants at a suspected arson scene and may be available to the investigator. The training and experience of the arson investigator are invaluable tools for determining a correct cause. For example, arsonists have been known to pour a volatile liquid around each electric outlet to make the fire appear as though it was of electrical origin. Without the specialized training of the arson investigator, the simulation of an electrical origin may be incorrectly inter-preted or missed by the crime scene investigator.

Newspapers, furniture, carpet and padding, or piled trash may serve to insulate an accelerant liquid from heat that would otherwise have vaporized and burned away. The investigator, when present at the scene, should consider these sources of evidence. Remember that if a liquid is poured on a dry surface, it will act like water in the sense that it will wet, run, spill, leak, drip, pool, or spread. To some extent it will be absorbed by porous materials. Areas where the liquid may have run or absorbed should be considered as sources for collection of the accelerant. The liquid may flow downward into and along cracks and through holes. It may then be protected by cracks and seams of the flooring, the soil, or the surface below the floor.

A liquid will protect the surface underneath it until the liquid is vaporized away, since the liquid will not burn until it is vaporized, at which point the area where the liquid pooled will char. The unburned areas around and beneath the char may still contain an adequate amount of the suspected liquid for analysis and identification of any accelerant present.

COLLECTING THE EVIDENCE

Within reason, the investigator should collect as much of the suspected material as possible and should place it in a sealed container. A *new, clean* one-gallon widemouthed *paint can* (see Figure 6-17) or airtight *glass jar* is usually sufficient. These items are available from crime scene equipment and supplies vendors. Do not use a container that has been used previously to hold any volatile flammable, solvent, or oil. Do not use plastic bottles or bags; they are porous to volatile flammables or may be dissolved by the accelerant. Always remember to collect a **control standard** of the material bearing the

FIGURE 6-17 Metal Paint Cans for Collection and Storage of Material Suspected of Containing Arson Accelerant

Courtesy of Sirchie Fingerprint Laboratories.

suspected accelerant that does not have any accelerant present. The control standard serves to help evaluate the analytical results for the material bearing the suspected accelerant. Some materials may produce by-products during combustion that may mimic some of the components of an accelerant, so it is imperative that the control standard be collected for the laboratory analyst's evaluation of the analysis results.

LABELING OF SUSPECTED ACCELERANT RESIDUES

Collect specimens from different areas for each suspected arson set, placing each specimen in a separate labeled container. Do not overlook other types of physical evidence that may be present: fingerprints, shoeprints, broken glass, toolmarks, or other types of evidence that may serve to identify the perpetrator or establish the act of arson.

Label each container with the following minimum data:

- Location where the sample was collected. (Provide an exact description of where the sample was found or obtained. Sketches and photographs are of considerable help in this endeavor.)
- Date and time of collection.
- Name of suspect and/or victim (if known).
- Department case numbers (fire and police departments).
- Name (last, first initial) of evidence collector.

COMPARISON ACCELERANT STANDARDS

Always attempt to obtain comparison samples (known standards) of any liquids that could possibly have been used as the volatile flammable accelerant. A *liquid ounce* is adequate for the laboratory analysis and comparison purposes. Also obtain background comparison standards (**background controls**) of other unburned "fuels" at the scene (such as carpets, drapes, upholstery), since they may contribute to the residues detected in the analysis procedures. Collect an amount of the background control materials approximately equal to the amount of the material collected that is suspected of containing the accelerant residue. Collect the background control material as close to the area suspected of containing the accelerant residue as is feasible without danger of contamination by the accelerant. Screening the background control area with the combustible vapor detector will help in this determination.

When gasoline is the suspected accelerant, collect samples from the gasoline stations where the accelerant might have been purchased. If siphoning from a car tank is suspected, include a sample from that vehicle's gas tank. This is an important step, since the gas tank may contain a mixture of gasolines from several different stations and thus may have additional identifying characteristics for comparison with any residues collected.

Place each comparison standard (background controls and known standards of suspected accelerants) in separate airtight glass or metal sealed containers. Always label each comparison standard as carefully and completely as any other evidence material (see earlier). Always transport the evidence samples and control standards in such a way that there can be no question regarding the possible accidental contamination of any of the questioned (evidence) samples.

The narrative reports describing the fire scene, the fire's suppression, and follow-up investigation should be forwarded to the laboratory with the evidence and controls, since these reports will help guide the laboratory analysis and interpretations. The reports will also assist the laboratory examiner in determining which additional standards may be needed in order to make the laboratory analysis and report more complete or precise. Often, additional standards will be needed to clarify an inconsistency in the laboratory data (another brand of an accelerant, for example).

Laboratory analysis of accelerant residues

The laboratory can identify the class of volatile flammables if they are present in sufficient quantity in the residues. In some cases, the laboratory may not be able to identify the specific type of accelerant present because of changes undergone by the liquid during or after the fire. In cases of unusual or extensively burned accelerant, the lack of a comparison standard can make identification difficult. The flammable accelerant may be identified as "consistent in origin" with a submitted known standard specimen. However, unless unusual contaminants are present, absolute identification to a brand origin or batch cannot be established because of the very large production quantities from the manufacturers of petroleum products.

The laboratory will first concentrate the accelerants recovered in order to facilitate the analysis. Some of the methods employed to concentrate the accelerants are (1) distillation, (2) solvent extraction, and (3) vapor concentration by purging the vapors from the container and passing the vapors through a tube filled with a trapping agent, such as charcoal. The concentrated vapors are routinely analyzed with a gas chromatograph, an instrument that can separate the components of the vapor, which can be compared directly with the results obtained from known specimens of accelerants or with the suspected accelerant submitted by the investigator.

The introduction of the gas chromatograph/mass spectrometer (GC/MS, an instrument that couples a gas chromatograph with a mass spectrometer) and the gas chromatograph/infrared spectrophotometer (GC/IR, an infrared spectrophotometer coupled with a gas chromatograph) provided the analyst with an improved ability to identify the specific accelerant present in arson residues. Most larger laboratories will have one or both of these instruments.

Summary

TRACE EVIDENCE

- Hairs.
- Fibers.
- Glass.
- Soil.
- Arson accelerants.

HAIR EVIDENCE

Microscopic features of human hair.

- Cuticle.
- Cortex.

- Medulla.
- Other characteristics.

Collection of hair evidence.

- Package individual hairs in an individual container.
- Do not package wet evidence.
- Place exhibits only on clean table surface.
- Label each evidence container with standard identification data.
- Post-it™ bindle packaging.

Collection at the Scene

- Hairs visible and firmly attached to an inanimate object.
- Hairs visible but not firmly attached to an object.
- Hairs possibly transferred to the clothing of a victim or suspect.
- Fingernail scrapings/clippings.
- Tape lifting of dead bodies.
- Hairs with possible roots adhering to the hair shaft.
- Vacuuming for trace evidence.

STANDARD/CONTROL SPECIMENS OF HAIR

Scalp hair standards.

- Combed hair specimens.
- Pulled or cut scalp hair standards.

Pubic hair standards.

Other body hair standards.

Animal hair standards.

LABORATORY EXAMINATIONS OF HAIR EVIDENCE

- General examination.
- High-power microscope.
- Comparison microscope.
- DNA analysis of the hair.

LABORATORY REPORTS CONCERNING HAIR EXAMINATIONS

- Whether the hair is animal or human.
- The body type of the hair (scalp, pubic, beard, other).
- Investigative leads such as hair length, color, and "racial" characteristics.
- Whether the hair "matches" a suspected source.
- If the hair does not match a suspected source.
- The hair comparison is inconclusive.
- Nuclear DNA (nDNA) analysis of root material.
- Mitochondrial DNA (mtDNA) analysis of hair shaft.

FIBER EVIDENCE

Nature/occurrence of fiber evidence.

Laboratory examinations of fiber evidence

COLLECTION OF FIBER EVIDENCE

Fibers on immovable objects.

- Collection with fiber lifting tape.
- Visible fibers.
- Fibers on garments.
- Fibers in vehicle floorboard carpets.

Fiber standards/controls.

- Carpet fiber standards.
- Garment fiber standards.

GLASS EVIDENCE

Nature/occurrence of glass evidence.

- Laboratory examinations of glass evidence.
- Fracture edge matches.
- Direction of force.
- Sequence of impacts.
- Thermal fractures.
- Comparison of physical properties of the glass.

Opinions derived from laboratory comparisons of glass.

Collection of glass evidence.

- Clothing containing glass fragments.
- Tools or other objects containing glass fragments.
- Large visible fragments.

Glass comparison standards.

- Window Panes.
- Bottles.
- Automobile Headlights.

PAINT EVIDENCE

- Nature/occurrence of paint evidence.
- Hit-and-run cases: vehicle to pedestrian.
- Hit-and-run cases: vehicle to vehicle.
- Burglary cases.

Laboratory examinations of paint evidence.
Laboratory reports concerning paint evidence.
Collection of paint specimens.
- Paint specimens from vehicles.
- Paint specimens from garments.
- Paint specimens from toolmark impressions.

Packaging of paint specimens.
SOIL EVIDENCE
- Nature/occurrence of soil evidence.

Laboratory examinations of soil evidence.
- Color.
- Density profile.
- Mineralogical profile.
- Bacterial profile.

Collection of soil evidence.
- Soil from impressions.
- Suspect (questioned) samples.
- Comparison (standard) samples.

ARSON ACCELERANT EVIDENCE
- Collection of volatile flammables.
- Arson investigations.
- Nature of volatile flammables.

At the scene.
- Precautions at the arson scene.
- Multiple points of origin.
- Locating the evidence.
- Collecting the evidence.

Labeling of suspected accelerant residues.
- Location where the sample was collected.
- Date and time of collection.
- Name of suspect and/or victim (if known).
- Department case numbers (fire and police departments).
- Name (last, first initial) of evidence collector.

Comparison standards.
Laboratory analysis of accelerant residues.

Review Questions

1. Examination of hair evidence has been revolutionized because of the development of analysis for mitochondrial _____.
2. The most significant feature of hair, to both the investigator and the laboratory analyst, is the hair _____.
3. Hair length may be _____ of the gender of the individual from whom the hair originated.
4. The cuticle of the hair consists of a number of overlapping _____.
5. Melanin, the primary content of the pigment granules, gives the hair its _____.
6. Each evidence container should be labeled with _____ _____ _____.
7. It is recommended that all _____ hairs and fibers be removed before vacuuming an area.
8. The preferred scalp hair standard consists of _____ hairs.
9. Combed hair specimens should be collected with a _____ comb.
10. The sample of scalp hair standards should be _____ of the entire scalp.
11. A scalp hair standard should consist of approximately _____ hairs.
12. A pubic hair standard should consist of approximately _____ hairs.
13. Laboratory examinations of hair consist primarily of a _____ of the evidence hair(s) to the known hair specimens.
14. When an evidence hair "matches" a submitted standard, the analyst can say that the hair _____ _____ come from the same individual source as the submitted standard.
15. When the evidence hair has no similarity to the submitted standard hair, the analyst can _____ the individual from whom the standard was collected, as the source of the evidence hair.
16. The most common classification schemes for fibers divide them into classes of natural or _____ fibers.

17. Fiber evidence occurs especially in those crimes in which there is _____ between victim and suspect.

18. The primary difficulty in the collection of fiber evidence is _____ single fibers.

19. It is essential to _____ _____ the corners of bindles or envelopes containing fiber evidence.

20. A fiber standard collected from a carpet should include samples from each _____ area of the carpet.

21. When glass is broken, the edges may be matched _____ style to show that they were once part of the same object.

22. Color, density, and refractive index are _____ properties of glass that may be used for comparison purposes.

23. In a vehicle to pedestrian hit-and-run case, paint may be transferred to the victim's clothing as _____ or _____.

24. In a vehicle to vehicle hit-and-run, a sample of the _____ paint and a paint _____ should be collected.

25. Paint specimens on garments should be collected by taking the _____ _____.

26. If envelopes are used for packaging paint flakes, the seam edges of the envelope should be _____.

27. Most soil evidence comes from the _____ _____ of the soil.

28. Soil samples from impressions should be collected _____ preparation of a cast of the impression.

29. Known soil samples should consist of at least _____ tablespoonfuls from each area.

30. The term "accelerant" refers to a material that _____ a fire.

31. The process of combustion requires _____, _____, and _____.

32. The three elements of combustion are commonly referred to as the _____ _____.

33. It is important to remember that _____ _____ of physical evidence may be present at an arson scene.

34. _____ _____ of origin are typical in an accelerated arson fire.

35. Debris suspected of containing accelerant residues should be packaged in a new, clean _____ _____ or an airtight _____ jar.

36. In addition to collecting the debris suspected of containing accelerant residues, the investigator should also collect _____ _____ for each sample of debris collected.

37. A _____ _____ of a standard liquid is sufficient for laboratory analysis.

Further References

Bisbing, R. 2002. The Forensic Identification and Association of Human Hair. Chap. 5 in vol. 1 of *Forensic Science Handbook*, 2nd ed., ed. R. Saferstein. Upper Saddle River, NJ: Prentice Hall, Inc.

DeHaan, J. D. 2002. *Kirk's Fire Investigation*, 5th ed. Upper Saddle River, NJ: Prentice Hall, Inc.

Gaudette, B. D. 2002. The Forensic Aspects of Textile Fiber Examinations. Chap. 5 in vol. 2 of *Forensic Science Handbook*, 2nd ed., ed. R. Saferstein. Upper Saddle River, NJ: Prentice Hall, Inc.

Koons, R. D., et al. 2002. Forensic Glass Comparisons. Chap. 4 in vol. 1 of *Forensic Science Handbook*, 2nd ed., ed. R. Saferstein. Upper Saddle River, NJ: Prentice Hall, Inc.

Kubic, T. A., and N. Petraco. 2005. Microanalysis and Examination of Trace Evidence. Chap. 16 in *Forensic Science* (An Introduction to Scientific and Investigative Techniques), 2nd. ed., ed. S. H. James., and J. J. Nordby. Boca Raton, FL: CRC Press.

Murray, R. C., and L. Solebell. 2002. Forensic Examination of Soil. Chap. 11 in vol. 1 of *Forensic Science Handbook,* 2nd ed., ed. R. Saferstein. Upper Saddle River, NJ: Prentice Hall, Inc.

Redsicker, D. R. 2005. Chapter 24: Basic Fire and Explosion Investigation, in *Forensic Science* (Practical Aspects of Criminal and Forensic Investigation), James, S. H., and Nordby, J. J. (eds.) Boca Raton, FL: CRC press.

Saferstein, R. 2004. Chap. 8 in *Criminalistics,* 8th ed. Upper Saddle River, NJ: Prentice Hall, Inc.

Saferstein, R. 2009. *Forensic Science* (From the Crime Scene to the Crime Lab), Chap. 12: Trace Evidence I: Hairs and Fibers, Chap. 13: Trace Evidence II: Paint, Glass, and Soil, and Chap. 15: Forensic Aspects of Fire Investigation.

Thornton, J. I. 2002. Forensic Paint Examination. Chap. 8 in vol. 1 of *Forensic Science Handbook*, 2nd ed., ed. R. Saferstein. Upper Saddle River, NJ: Prentice Hall, Inc.

7

BIOLOGICAL FLUID STAIN EVIDENCE: BLOOD, SEMEN, AND SALIVA

I've found it!...I have found a re-agent which is precipitated by haemoglobin, and by nothing else.

Sherlock Holmes in *A Study in Scarlet*,
by Sir Arthur Conan Doyle.

Key Words: Universal precautions, bloodstain pattern interpretation, genetic marker typing, DNA (deoxyribonucleic acid), nuclear DNA (nDNA), mitochondrial DNA (mtDNA), presumptive tests, phosphorescence, cross-contamination, liquid pools, porous surfaces, buccal swabs, swab boxes, postmortem subjects, bloodstained clothing, PCR (polymerase chain reaction), short tandem repeat (STR), CODIS, semen, aspermic, sperm, P-30 protein, sperm acid phosphatase mapping.

PRECAUTIONS FOR BIOLOGICAL EVIDENCE

Biological material must be considered hazardous! Follow universal precautions for handling stains. The term "universal precautions" means that one must assume that any biological material is contaminated with biological pathogens such as HIV, Hepatitis B, or others. Use protective eyewear, respirator masks, latex gloves, and protective clothing when working with materials having biological stains (see Appendix 7-A).

INTRODUCTION

Biological fluid stain evidence consists of stains from blood, semen, saliva, and stains from other miscellaneous body fluids such as vomitus. The majority of biological fluid stains encountered at the crime scene consists of blood, semen, or saliva. Bloodstains are typically found in crimes of violence, where the victim sustains wounds from gunshots, knives, or blunt instruments. Semen and saliva stains typically result from sexual assault crimes. Bloodstains are also frequently encountered in sexual assaults, since these assaults usually stem from violent, rather than sexual, motives.

BLOODSTAIN EVIDENCE

Introduction to bloodstain evidence

Bloodstain evidence may be encountered as physical evidence in a variety of crimes, such as homicide, sexual assault, vehicular hit-and-run, and burglary. The identification and typing of bloodstains can assist in establishing elements of the crime and the identification or elimination of a suspect, and can also be used to corroborate or dispute the statements of principals when the bloodstains play a part in a reconstruction of the crime. The proper collection of bloodstain evidence is essential to the quantity and quality of information derived from the stains.

Bloodstain evidence has two primary categories of examination important to the crime scene investigator: (1) **bloodstain pattern interpretation** and (2) **genetic marker typing**. The first category, bloodstain pattern interpretation, is often overlooked by both the investigator and the laboratory personnel even though the patterns of the bloodstains may often be more significant than the typing of the stains. In many cases, the interpretation of the bloodstain patterns may establish whether or not a crime occurred (murder versus suicide or accident). The interpretation of the patterns also may dispute or corroborate witnesses' statements. Genetic marker typing is an integral part of the interpretation of the bloodstain patterns, since it is important to establish from whom the bloodstain pattern emanated.

The proper documentation of the location and patterns of the bloodstains should always be a primary consideration of the crime scene investigator at the scene. Collection of the bloodstains should not be attempted until the patterns of the stains have been recorded in the investigator's notes, sketches, and photographs, so that later attempts to interpret the patterns are not precluded. The location, size, and appearance of the patterns must be carefully measured, sketched, and photographed with measuring scales in the photographs. Often, it will be essential for the individual performing the bloodstain pattern interpretation to view firsthand the stain patterns before the stains are disturbed. The documentation of bloodstain patterns is illustrated in Chapter 15.

Genetic markers in bloodstains

MODERN AND HISTORICAL GENETIC MARKER TESTING

Modern forensic biology laboratories now rarely perform genetic marker testing in the ABO system, protein and enzyme systems, and the DNA RFLP system. More specifically, forensic laboratories usually limit their genetic marker testing procedures now to *short tandem repeat* (STR) profiling of the blood, semen, and tissue specimens, since the PCR-based STR system is the basis for the electronic database of DNA types (CODIS, described in a later section), which is shared nationally and standardized for the laboratories. Moreover, the STR system provides considerably more information about the source of the questioned material than all the older systems combined. In addition, more laboratories are instituting genetic marker testing for *mitochondrial DNA* (mtDNA), another PCR-based system. The older genetic marker typing systems are profiled here primarily for their historical significance, and for the interpretation of forensic evidence found in older cases, some of which are used in this text as case examples.

NATURE OF DNA

The chromosomes, which carry the genetic material in the cells, are made up of DNA. Genes are situated at specific sites, or loci, on the chromosomes. The chromosomes exist in matching pairs and, therefore, so do the genes. The result is that two copies of a gene, or other DNA segment, are present at a given locus in any one individual. Genes are "polymorphic" (poly = many, morph = form) and therefore may exist in different forms or alleles. In the general population, many forms of a single gene may exist, which in fact accounts for the variation in many traits from one individual to another. The particular pair of alleles at a locus defines a given individual's genotype.

DNA is the material that carries all the genetic information for inheritance from generation to generation. DNA is referred to as a "double helix," meaning that the structure of the DNA molecule is made up of two strands hooked together and twisted into a helical configuration. The complete structure looks like a ladder that has been twisted at the ends to form the helix.

There are two types of cells in the body (somatic cells) with respect to the presence or absence of a cell nucleus (see Figure 7-1 for a cell with a nucleus). Examples of cells with a nucleus include the cells lining the mouth, the cells in the liver, and the cells of the muscles. Cells with a nucleus have two types of DNA. The nucleus has the first type of DNA, **nuclear DNA** (or **nDNA**). Nuclear DNA has a chromosomal component from each parent—called "diploid," since the DNA contains one member of each chromosome pair from each parent—making up the full complement of chromosome pairs found in humans. Nucleate cells also have mitochondrial DNA, because of the presence of mitochondria in the cell (see Figure 7-1).

Cells without a nucleus begin with a nucleus, but during maturation of the cell, the nucleus is removed from the cell, resulting in a cell called "enucleated" or "enucleate." Examples of cells without a nucleus are the red blood cells, the cells of the epidermis (outer skin layer), and cells of the finger and toe nails. The reproductive cells (sperm and ova) are a special case with regard to their status as a "cell." The ova (eggs) in the ovaries have a nucleus after maturation, but the chromosome complement has been split in half to produce a "haploid" cell (one in which only one member of a chromosome pair is

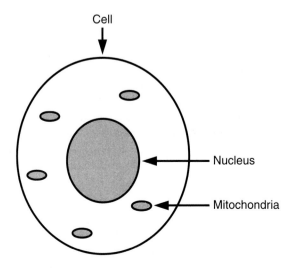

Cell

Nucleus

Mitochondria

FIGURE 7-1 Mitochondria in the Cell

present). The ova have all the other characteristics of a cell, including the presence of mitochondria, which carry the second type of DNA, **mitochondrial DNA (mtDNA)**. Sperm cells, however, do not have mitochondria, and thus lack mitochondrial DNA. Biological evidence originating from enucleated cells cannot be analyzed for nuclear DNA, but can be analyzed for mitochondrial DNA. This innovation in forensic biology represented a quantum leap in the evidentiary value of hair and other biological material or stains from enucleated cells.

Crime scene documentation of bloodstains

The processing of bloodstains at the crime scene must be preceded by a systematic documentation of the crime scene to include adequate note-taking, photographs, and sketches. Bloodstain evidence has some special requirements in addition to those discussed for the other types of evidence. First among these additional requirements is the necessity to follow the safety precautions for handling of biological evidence. Second, the nature of biological evidence requires special handling to avoid decomposition of the biological materials by the action of microorganisms such as mold and bacteria. As a general rule, bloodstained evidence should be dried at room temperature and then kept frozen until it is submitted to the crime laboratory, whereas liquid specimens should be refrigerated, not frozen. *For all types of biological evidence, the sooner they are transmitted to the laboratory, the better the chances of avoiding loss of the information content in the evidence.*

NOTES

Take careful notes regarding the location and the appearance of bloodstains at the crime scene. Information such as the presence of pooling, clotting, mold growth, and other features of the stains should be documented in the notes. The presence of any directional characteristics in the bloodstains should be noted along with documentation with sketches and photography. This information will help to interpret the conditions of the bloodstains and the laboratory results obtained from them during analysis, and may also allow for the reconstruction of the events producing the bloodstain patterns.

PHOTOGRAPHS

Photographs of suspected bloodstains should always be taken with color film. Black-and-white film will not distinguish other dark stains from bloodstains and will hamper, if not preclude, interpretation of the bloodstain patterns. Photographs must be taken in a manner that will allow for accurate re-creation of the spatial relationships of the stains, in order to assist in interpreting the patterns. All photographs need to be taken at 90 degrees from the surface upon which they occur (the "normal" to the surface). Take photographs both with and without a measurement scale in view so that the sizes of the stains can be verified (see Chapter 3). Remember to take overview photographs of the area containing the bloodstains, so that each area can be related to the overall pattern.

SEARCHING FOR BLOODSTAINS

The search for bloodstains is usually routine, since the bloodstains are normally visible and have a characteristic red-brown appearance. Those stains that appear to be blood can be checked with a blood-screening agent by lightly moistening a swab, rubbing the swab

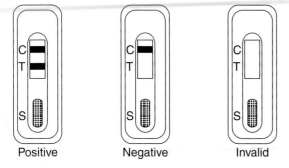

Positive   Negative   Invalid

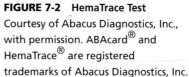

FIGURE 7-2 HemaTrace Test
Courtesy of Abacus Diagnostics, Inc.,
with permission. ABAcard® and
HemaTrace® are registered
trademarks of Abacus Diagnostics, Inc.

tip in the stain lightly (any coloration of the swab is sufficient for the test, since these chemicals are highly sensitive), and then testing the swab for the presence of blood with a blood-testing reagent such as phenolphthalein. If the bloodstains are very small, this testing should not be done in order to preserve as much sample as possible for the laboratory analysis. These blood-testing reagents are available in kit form from commercial crime scene product distributors. Stains that are not blood will not react with the screening chemicals and can be safely regarded as not being bloodstains. Those stains that give a positive reaction with the blood-testing reagents must be confirmed as blood in the laboratory, since the testing reagents are only **presumptive tests** for screening of suspected stains.

The development of the ABAcard HemaTrace testing method by Abacus Diagnostics provides both a rapid screening test for the field and a confirmatory test for human hemoglobin in the laboratory (see Figure 7-2). This test is based on the precipitation of the hemoglobin by an antibody prepared to react specifically with human (and higher ape) hemoglobin. It seems that the fictional character Sherlock Holmes foresaw this innovation (see quote at beginning of this chapter).

Those bloodstains that are "invisible" (i.e., cleaned up or wiped off) can often be visualized by spraying with *luminol* and viewing in the dark. Luminol is a blood-screening reagent that reacts with a portion of the hemoglobin in blood to produce a chemical that glows in the dark (phosphoresces). The **phosphorescence** can then be photographed with the room darkened. Either black-and-white or color film is adequate for this purpose. Photographs of the stains will provide a permanent record of the stains and any patterns present. Footwear impressions and tracks, finger/palm prints, and stains that have been washed or wiped are some of the ways in which "invisible" stains are produced. Samples of the stains should be collected after spraying and photography, and then submitted to the lab for confirmation of human blood and possible genetic marker analysis.

BLOODSTAIN PATTERN DOCUMENTATION

The documentation of bloodstain patterns requires accurate sketches and photographs taken with markers in the field of view which will orient each of the photographs to the sketches drawn to scale. The crime scene investigator should first prepare overall sketches and take overall photographs of the entire area bearing the bloodstain patterns. Then, the analyst should take mid-range photographs and prepare blow-up sketches for each area of bloodstain patterns. The overall and mid-range sketches and photographs will provide the framework for assembling the close-up photographs and sketches for any

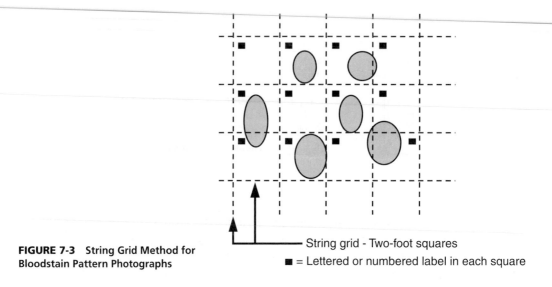

String grid - Two-foot squares

■ = Lettered or numbered label in each square

FIGURE 7-3   String Grid Method for Bloodstain Pattern Photographs

reconstruction efforts undertaken. Next, the analyst will need to take close-up photographs to document the bloodstain patterns. The close-up photographs must have markers in the field of view of each photograph frame in order to provide measurement data for the patterns.

Rynearson[1] advocates the use of grids of two-foot squares constructed from string and thumbtacks to document the bloodstain patterns (see Figure 7-3). *Note*: The strings should not be allowed to touch the stains. The squares are labeled according to their position in the grid, then photographed with the camera normal to the surface and centered in each square photographed in order to minimize distortion. When feasible, the surface(s) bearing the bloodstains should be collected and submitted to the laboratory. Note that dry bloodstains may easily flake off smooth surfaces, so that photography of the stains is necessary even if the surface bearing the stains is collected. The photography of the stains using the grid system allows for the reconstruction of the entire pattern by assembling the photographs "jigsaw puzzle" style.

The string grid method is especially helpful when there are a large number of areas on a wall or floor containing bloodstain patterns. The grid can be constructed for the size of the area containing the patterns, whether it is a small corner of a wall or it covers the entire wall, floor, and ceiling. The analyst may choose to use other methods for documenting the bloodstain patterns if the areas of patterns are less extensive (see Figures 7-4 and 7-5).

The bloodstain patterns may also be documented by placing lettered or numbered markers in the upper left and lower right margins of each area photographed. Each label should be marked with an "x" for the point on the label where the measurements to reference points are taken. The measurements to each marker should be documented in the sketches of each bloodstain pattern area photographed (see Figure 7-4). "Blow-up" sketches (see Chapter 4, Crime Scene Sketches) are especially helpful in this regard, particularly when there are a number of areas bearing bloodstain patterns. The photographs must be taken normal to the surface (i.e., with the film plane parallel to the surface) in order to minimize distortion.

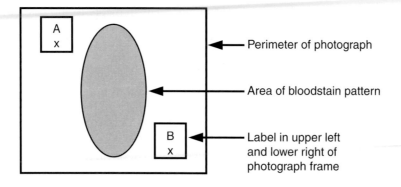

A, B = Letter designations placed on labels for identification

"x" = Point on each label used for measurements to reference points
(rectangular coordinates or triangulation method)

FIGURE 7-4   Corner Label Method for Bloodstain Pattern Photographs

Wolson[2] advocates placing measurement scales around the perimeter of the area photographed in order to provide reference points for the bloodstain patterns and the placement of sequentially numbered, smaller metric scales adjacent to each area of bloodstain patterns (see Figure 7-4). Overall photographs depicting the perimeter scales are taken to show the location of both the perimeter scales and the smaller sequentially numbered metric scales placed in the field of interest. Close-up photographs of each area of interest are then taken, making sure to include at least one of the small metric scales in each photograph. The entire bloodstain pattern can be reconstructed using the blow-up photographs and the overall photographs.

Each of the three methods illustrated for bloodstain pattern photography is adequate for the documentation of patterns for later reconstruction efforts, providing

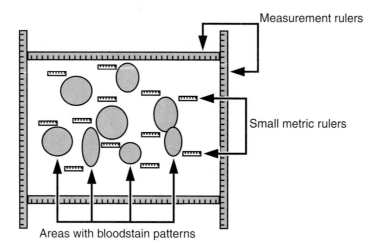

FIGURE 7-5   Perimeter Measurement Ruler Method for Bloodstain Pattern Photographs

that the crime scene investigator makes accurate measurements to the reference points in the photographs. The photographs can be assembled into a one-to-one mural of the bloodstain patterns if necessary for the reconstruction efforts owing to the measurements in each photograph. The choice of method for the bloodstain pattern photographs will depend on several factors, including availability of large scale measurement rulers, assistance available at the scene, geometric considerations at the scene, and the size and number of patterns present. It is essential to use color film for the photographs in order to distinguish the bloodstains from other stains which may be present in the same area.

MacDonell[3] advocates lifting the various bloodstains from the surface using fingerprint lifting tape in the manner used for developed latent fingerprints. *Note: that it is essential to document the bloodstains in the usual manner with sketches and photographs as described earlier before attempting the lift technique.* This technique is usually successful for hard, smooth surfaces and may also yield useful lifts on other surfaces as well. The exact location and orientation of each lift must be documented in the sketches and photographs. This technique allows for the measurement of the shape of each bloodstain in the laboratory.

Once the photographs of the bloodstains have been completed, the analyst may need to treat the bloodstains with luminol or other blood enhancing reagents in order to develop fainter bloodstain patterns. The treatment of the bloodstain patterns with these reagents should always be preceded by photographs of the patterns in order to document the location and the condition of the stains before treatment. This precaution is needed in order to explain to a jury the appearance of the stains both before and after treatment and the need for enhancement of the stains.

Collection of bloodstain evidence

The introduction of DNA typing in bloodstain analysis presents additional challenges for the crime scene investigator. Although contamination and **cross-contamination** of evidence samples have always been of paramount concern to the crime scene investigator, the use of the PCR techniques for DNA tying of bloodstains compels the use of added precautions to prevent cross-contamination of evidence blood samples because of the extreme sensitivity of this technique. Since the PCR technique involves replication of the DNA material present in the bloodstain, even small amounts of contaminants may interfere with the laboratory analysis. This factor requires the crime scene investigator to take additional precautions against cross-contamination. The best approach to prevention of cross-contamination of samples is to use individually packaged, sterile cotton swabs for collection of the bloodstains and to package each swab used for collection in a separate container. *As a general rule, bloodstained evidence should be dried and frozen to preserve the genetic markers in the stains.*

The particular technique used for the collection of bloodstain evidence will depend on the nature of the bloodstain, whether wet or dry, and on the nature of the surface bearing the bloodstain. As a general rule, it is best to collect the object bearing the bloodstains and submit the object to the laboratory for examination. In many circumstances, however, the object bearing the bloodstains cannot be collected, so that the crime scene investigator will need to collect the bloodstains using the technique best suited for the surface bearing the bloodstains. The following guidelines indicate the techniques best suited to the type of surface bearing the bloodstains.

SMALL ITEMS CONTAINING POTENTIAL BLOODSTAINS

As a general rule, collect the *entire* object bearing the stains (even by cutting out the stained section). Allow the stains to air-dry completely, then package each item in a separate paper bag or envelope.

Note: Do not package bloodstained evidence in plastic bags, because plastic bags promote the growth of microorganisms by retaining moisture.

LARGE, IMMOBILE OBJECTS WITH HARD, SMOOTH SURFACES (METAL, GLASS, ETC.)

For bloodstains on large, immobile objects, the stains should be collected by immersing swabs in the stain if moist, or by slightly moistening swabs with distilled water and then swabbing the stains, collecting as much material on the swabs as feasible. Once the swabs have been collected, they should be labeled (see Figure 7-6), air dried, the tip wrapped in bindle paper, and sealed in a manila envelope. Alternatively, the swabs can be packaged in specially prepared "swab boxes" (available from commercial suppliers), which allow the swabs to dry while in the box. Figure 7-7 illustrates a commercially prepared swab box. The swab boxes should be sealed with appropriate seals for storage in the freezer.

A *control swab* from an unstained area using the same type of swab and the same liquid as that used for the stains must also be taken so that the laboratory analyst may test for background contamination. Allow the swabs to air-dry, then package in appropriately marked paper envelopes or folded paper bindles.

LARGE LIQUID POOLS OF BLOOD

Liquid pools should be sampled by absorbing a sample of the pool onto sterile cotton swabs. Allow the swabs to air-dry completely, and then package in paper bindles and seal in paper envelopes or swab boxes. Additionally, samples may be collected with sterile pipets and placed in sterile containers provided for this purpose. The liquid sample needs to be refrigerated as soon as collected, transported as soon as feasible to the laboratory, and frozen.

LARGE OBJECTS WITH A SOFT, POROUS SURFACE (WOOD, CARPETS)

Allow the stains on soft, **porous surfaces** to air-dry completely before collection. Cut out the stained area, and package in a paper bag or an envelope. Collect a portion of the unstained surface as a control and then package separately in the same type of packaging materials.

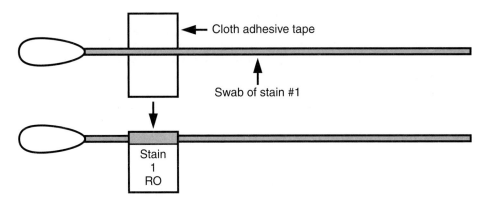

FIGURE 7-6 Swab Containing Collected Bloodstain

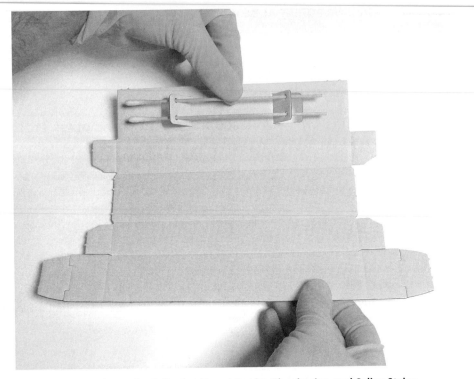

FIGURE 7-7   Swab Box for Collecting Buccal Swabs, Bloodstains, and Saliva Stains
Courtesy of Sirchie Fingerprint Laboratories.

LARGE OBJECTS WITH A HARD, NONPOROUS SURFACE (BRICK WALL, CONCRETE, PAVEMENT, ETC.)

- Collect the stain by using slightly dampened (with distilled water) sterile cotton swabs for hard, nonporous surfaces. Allow to air-dry and package each swab in separate envelopes, or in swab box (see Figure 7-7).
- A background control swab of an unstained area of the surface must be obtained.

CLOTHING

Whenever possible, the *entire garment* bearing the bloodstains *should be collected*. The garments should be hung up or laid out on new, clean butcher paper for drying prior to packaging. Special care should be taken to avoid folding or crumpling of the garment and to arrange it in its normal configuration before drying, in order to avoid alteration of the stain pattern or wiping transfer from one location to another on the garment. Special care should also be taken to avoid loss or contamination of the trace evidence on the garment. Once dried thoroughly, the garment should be wrapped in clean paper by placing clean butcher paper under and over the garment and folding (using the paper upon which the garment was dried as the bottom sheet if the garment was dried in this manner) to further ensure protection of the trace evidence and bloodstain patterns. Package each garment in a separate paper bag, and seal appropriately.

Comparison standard samples for DNA typing

The preferred comparison standard for DNA typing from living subjects consists of **buccal swabs** (swabs of cheeks of mouth interior). These samples are obtained by swabbing the interior cheeks with sterile swabs, packaging the swabs in **swab boxes** (see Figure 7-7), which allows the swabs to dry after packaging. Each swab box should then be packaged in an envelope which allows for air circulation (may be provided with the swab box), labeled with standard identification data, and sealed with tape. Alternatively, the comparison standard can be a blood sample drawn in an appropriate blood tube containing an anticoagulant (see Table 7-1).

Blood samples for blood typing, DNA typing, or toxicology (blood alcohol and other drugs) from living subjects should be collected in new, sterile Vacutainer™ tubes or the equivalent and should be kept refrigerated until submission to the laboratory. Collect at least one tube each (approximately 5 to 7 cc) in the following tube types:

- Sample for DNA typing: purple-stoppered tube (EDTA tube). *Purple-stoppered tubes are adequate for all genetic marker tests.*
- Sample for blood alcohol: gray-stoppered tubes (DUI kit).

Note: Inform the laboratory if the subject received a recent blood transfusion. Each tube of blood drawn should be labeled with the following minimum data:

- Full name of subject from whom the blood is drawn.
- Name and initials of the person drawing the blood sample.

TABLE 7-1	Preservation of Specimens for DNA Analysis
Sample	**Action(s)**
Tissues	Freeze ($-20°C$)
Blood	
Liquid	EDTA (purple cap) or gray-top tube—refrigerate
Dried	Keep dry—freeze
Semen	
Liquid	Add EDTA—refrigerate
Dried	Keep dry—freeze
Saliva	
Wet	Separate buccal cells—dry and freeze
Dry	Keep dry—freeze
Bones	
Fresh	Freeze ($-20°C$)
Dry	Keep dry—freeze
Urine	
Liquid	Isolate cellular material—freeze ($-20°C$)
Dry	Keep dry—freeze

Adapted from an untitled FBI handout on DNA.

- Date and time of the blood draw.
- Name and initials of individual taking possession of the sample.

Package the blood tube in an envelope, seal the envelope, enter chain of possession data, and package the envelope in a container designed to avoid breakage of the tube.

Blood samples from postmortem subjects

Blood samples from **postmortem subjects** should be obtained from nonbody cavity areas such as the *heart* or one of the *major blood vessels*. Blood samples for the crime laboratory should be collected in addition to those samples collected by the autopsy pathologist for postmortem toxicology. The crime laboratory samples should be collected in the same tube types as those used for living subjects.

If decomposition and putrefaction have begun, in addition to the blood sample, have the autopsy pathologist collect a portion of deep muscle tissue for blood-typing purposes. The muscle tissue may show less decomposition than the blood and thus be a better sample for blood typing.

If the subject received a blood transfusion, the crime laboratory should be notified. The transfused blood may interfere with the typing of the standard blood sample. Bloodstains from the subject's **bloodstained clothing** may be used for blood-typing purposes in this instance, since the bloodstains will not be mixed with the transfused blood. For this reason, it is important that the clothing be collected and preserved.

General comments

- Submit all items to the laboratory in your area *as soon as feasible*.
- Avoid exposing biological evidence to *heat*, *humidity*, and *sunlight*.
- If the evidence cannot be immediately submitted to the laboratory, then
  - *Refrigerate* liquid blood samples.
  - *Air-dry* all bloodstained items. Do not subject to heat.
  - *Freeze* the bloodstained items *after drying* until submission to the crime laboratory.
  - *Package* all bloodstained items in paper bags to avoid mold growth.
  - Contact the laboratory in your jurisdiction for any questionable circumstances that may affect the way in which the samples should be collected or for any special controls or standards needed by that laboratory.

Laboratory analysis of bloodstains

The laboratory analysis of bloodstains consists of preliminary procedures designed to determine whether or not the sample is blood, and if so, what species. Following these preliminary steps, the bloodstain may be analyzed for its DNA genetic markers.

DNA ANALYSIS OF BIOLOGICAL STAINS

DNA analysis in the laboratory

PCR techniques are now the method of choice in forensic laboratories for several reasons. First, PCR techniques allow for the analysis of biological stains which are very small and do not require high molecular weight (intact) DNA. Second, PCR techniques allow for the analysis of stains which have become degraded from environmental damage or age (samples from mummies, for example, have been analyzed with PCR techniques). Third, PCR techniques provide data for discrete alleles on the chromosome, an enormous advantage because the explanation of the statistical analyses of these data is easy to convey to a jury. Fourth, and most importantly, the data in **CODIS** (see below) are derived from STR analyses (a PCR technique) of known blood samples, against which the data from an unknown biological stain can be compared via computer search. Finally, PCR techniques allow for the determination of the gender of the source of the biological stain.

PCR analysis

The term "PCR" (**polymerase chain reaction**) refers to the process whereby the DNA (technically a "polymer" of the sugar ribose) in a biological specimen is replicated many times to produce an adequate amount of DNA for the analysis. The structure of DNA molecules, with their ability to reproduce themselves exactly, is exploited in the PCR process. Without the PCR technique, the laboratory would be unable to perform DNA analysis on those samples which have been degraded or which, by virtue of small size, have an insufficient amount of DNA present for traditional DNA analysis methods.

PCR techniques use portions of the DNA which determine genetic traits (e.g., the human leucocyte antigens, or "HLA"). The DNA is not cut up by restriction enzymes, but only specific regions of the DNA molecules (the sites of the HLA antigen genes) are replicated by the PCR process, thereby producing a large quantity of DNA fragments for analysis via capillary electrophoresis. DNA analysis on semen specimens from sexual assaults can be analyzed by PCR techniques when as few as 100 sperm are present. On hair roots, PCR analysis can be performed on a single hair root follicle sheath.

The most useful of the PCR-based techniques is the system which analyzes for **short tandem repeats (STR)** in the DNA molecule, the system which forms the basis for **CODIS** (see below), the DNA computer database used throughout the United States to search for a match with the STR data from an unknown blood or semen stain. This system is the one used in forensic laboratories, and the techniques for analysis of blood-stains in the STR system have been standardized for the laboratories. STR analysis can be performed using plate electrophoresis techniques, but the predominate method for STR analyses involves capillary electrophoresis, because the data are produced in a graphical format, which allows for the direct comparison of the unknown STR graph to the known STR graph, using computer graphics.

CODIS is an acronym for "**Co**mbined **D**NA **I**ndex **S**ystem," a national database system of a number of specified STR alleles, and which is standardized for all laboratories entering data or using the system to search for a match with the data from an unknown blood or semen stain, much like the AFIS system for latent fingerprints. Most states are in the process of implementing a program to obtain the STR profile of all individuals convicted of certain violent crimes. CODIS has been instrumental in exonerating many individuals wrongly convicted of a crime (many of whom were on death row) and solving cold cases by finding a match for the DNA in those cases. The value of this system to forensic science and to the criminal justice system cannot be overstated.

Preservation of samples for DNA analysis

DNA isolated from any nucleated cell (cells having a nucleus) is called "nuclear DNA" in contrast to DNA isolated from the mitochondria. Preferred evidence specimens include vaginal swabs obtained from the victims of sexual assault, dried semen or bloodstains on garments or swabs, and frozen tissue. Comparison blood standards can be obtained from freshly drawn whole blood in EDTA tubes or (preferred by some DNA laboratories) gray-top (DUI) tubes with a preservative and an anticoagulant.

Specimen storage is extremely important. Care must be taken to keep the samples free from moisture, as DNA molecules deteriorate in a humid environment. They should be thoroughly dried, and kept frozen at $-20°C$ in a freezer that is not of the frost-free type (i.e., the frost is removed by thaw-freeze cycles, which is deleterious for the integrity of the DNA). The dried samples need to be packaged in an airtight container (sealed plastic bag) for storage in the freezer. For preservation of liquid blood samples for DNA typing, see Table 7-1.

Tissue samples and liquid samples should be preserved according to the directions in Table 7-1. For liquid blood samples taken for DNA analysis, the blood should be sampled by immersing at least two swabs in the liquid sample, then drying the swabs, packaging, and following the directions discussed earlier for swabs. Alternatively, samples of the blood specimen can be pipetted onto specially prepared cotton swatches, dried, packaged, and frozen.

SEMEN EVIDENCE[4]

Introduction to semen evidence

Semen is defined as the *male ejaculate.* As such, semen consists of the secretions of a number of glands in the male reproductive tract, including the Cowper's glands, prostate, seminal vesicles, glands of Littre (urethral glands), and products from the ducts that carry the semen and sperm. Semen contains sperm from the testes contained within a fluid derived from the reproductive glands referred to as "seminal plasma." The term "seminal fluid," in contrast, is a vague term meaning either the seminal plasma or the aggregate fluid consisting of both the plasma and the contained sperm. In those males who have had a vasectomy or a blockage of the sperm ducts due to a medical condition, the semen lacks sperm, a condition referred to as "**aspermic**." The main constituents of semen that are of interest in forensic science are the **sperm** (stored in and ejaculated from the seminal vesicles) and the fluid from the prostate gland, which contains the protein P-30, which is known to be unique to the prostate gland and thus unique to semen. These two components of semen account for all the modern methods for the identification of a stain as being a semen stain. The identification of sperm is considered an absolute identification of the presence of semen. In those individuals whose semen lacks sperm, the semen is identified by identifying the **P-30 protein**, which is known to exist only in the human *prostate* and its secretions. Identification of the P-30 protein is usually accomplished by electrophoresis of the questioned sample simultaneously with a sample of the known protein or by the use of a technique called "crossover electrophoresis." There are other methods for identifying the P-30 protein, but these methods are the methods of choice for most laboratories.[5]

Occurrence of semen evidence

Semen evidence usually consists of *swabs* or *aspirates* from a body orifice, stains on fabrics, or stains on nonabsorbent surfaces in sexual assault investigations. Semen evidence may play a role in other types of cases, but the majority of cases involving semen evidence are sexual assaults. Semen stains on fabrics or nonabsorbent surfaces appear as off-white to yellowish stains and may be difficult to see. As the semen stains age, they may turn to a brown-colored stain. Semen stains are described as "stiff" or "starchy" to the touch and have a characteristic appearance to the criminalist. (*Note:* Never handle blood or semen-stained objects without wearing *surgical gloves* and a *dust mask.*) Dry blood or semen stains may form small flakes when handled, which may become airborne and present a potential hazard to the investigator. Semen stains *may not be visible* to the eye when they occur on dark-colored fabrics or surfaces. For this reason, it is a good practice to augment the search for semen stains with a *laser light* or an *alternate (forensic) light source.* Collect the entire garment, surface, or fabric suspected of having semen stains. The laboratory can use a chemical technique called "acid phosphatase mapping" to search for the stains without damage to subsequent testing procedures, which can identify the stain as semen or to blood-typing procedures such as DNA profiling.

Collection of semen evidence

Semen evidence is usually collected in much the same manner as bloodstained evidence, *keeping in mind the universal precautions for handling of biological evidence.* Semen evidence must be *dried* thoroughly before packaging to prevent bacterial and mold growths that may destroy the genetic markers and the P-30 protein present in the semen stain. Sperm are exceptionally stable and resist decomposition from biological organisms and chemical agents, but the DNA in the sperm is vulnerable to the action of enzymes that degrade or destroy the DNA. Therefore, drying and freezing of the semen evidence is necessary to preserve the *DNA in the sperm.* Once the stained items are dry, they should be packaged in paper bags and stored in the freezer to preserve the genetic information in the stains. As a general rule, plastic bags should never be used to package biological evidence. Plastic bags and other nonbreathing packaging materials should be used only by laboratory personnel for specimens that are to be stored permanently in the freezer. (*Note:* "Frost-free" freezers should not be used for storage because of detrimental effects of the thaw cycles, which allow the stains to reach unacceptable temperatures.) Semen evidence may be collected both at the crime scene and at the medical examination of the victim.

SEMEN EVIDENCE AT THE CRIME SCENE

Clothing from the victim   The clothing the victim wore before/during the assault may have been *forcibly removed* by the perpetrator. The clothing may contain bloodstains or semen stains from the perpetrator or transfer evidence such as hairs and fibers. The clothing may also have *evidence of forcible removal* from the victim, such as rips in the fabric or buttons torn from the garment. These items of evidence will provide strong evidence of the element of force used in the assault.

If the victim has changed into clothing other than that worn before/during the assault, it is important to collect this set of clothing also. The clothing worn *after the assault* may have *semen drainage* and hairs or fibers that were transferred from the victim's body surfaces to the garments.

Bedding (sheets, blankets, comforters)   Using gloved hands, collect all bedding upon which the assault occurred (except those layers completely covered by the uppermost layers) by folding each layer of bedding toward the center (in effect, making a "bindle" out of the bedding layer). This procedure will prevent the loss of trace evidence that may be present on the bedding. Package each layer separately in a paper bag. Mark each item of bedding in the upper-right-hand corner, and note which surface is uppermost. Note the layer sequence of the bedding materials so that the layer sequence can be reconstructed at any future time. Handle each item carefully to avoid loss of any items of trace evidence, such as hairs or fibers which may be present on the bedding.

Blood and semen stains on nonabsorbent surfaces (flooring, walls, etc.)   Collect bloodstains at the scene in accordance with the procedures for bloodstains. Collect suspected semen stains on moistened *cotton swabs* in the same manner as for bloodstains. Each suspected stain sampled at the scene should be accompanied by a control standard from an unaffected area near the stain. Each swab can be labeled by attaching an adhesive label or white fabric tape to the shaft of the swab (see Figure 7-6). Swatches or swabs of semen stains must be dried and packaged in paper envelopes in the same manner as bloodstain samples. Alternatively, they may be collected, packaged with swab box kit. The search for semen stains may be augmented with ultraviolet, laser, or alternate light sources, because of the fluorescence of semen under these lights. It should be noted that the fluorescence of semen is very faint, so that the absence of visible fluorescence may not indicate the absence of a semen stain.

Laboratory examinations of semen evidence

The laboratory examinations of suspected semen stains are directed toward (1) locating suspected semen stains, (2) identification of the components of semen (such as sperm and the P-30 protein) that identify the stain as a semen stain, and (3) identification of the individual source of the semen through DNA testing. The laboratory analyst searches for suspected semen stains by using high intensity lighting methods and chemical screening techniques. Identification of the stain as a semen stain involves electrophoresis and a microscopic search for sperm in extracts from the stain.

DETECTION OF SEMEN STAINS

The laboratory analyst first examines the article suspected of bearing semen stains with the *unaided eye*, using high intensity lighting. A search for the stains may also be accomplished with *long-wave ultraviolet (UV) light*, because of the *fluorescence* of semen under long-wave UV light, or with an *alternate light source*, which also produces fluorescence in the semen stain. In many instances, the analyst will forego these methods and search the areas suspected of having semen stains with a chemical technique called "**acid phosphatase mapping**." The mapping technique involves placing a large, moistened filter paper over the area suspected of having a semen stain, applying pressure to the filter paper, and then treating the paper with chemicals that detect the prostatic acid phosphatase enzyme in semen. This technique, which is very sensitive for the presence of semen, will detect very dilute semen stains because of the very high concentration of this enzyme in the prostrate secretion. A negative result with the mapping technique is virtually conclusive evidence for the absence of semen on the suspected substrate. If semen stains are on the substrate, the mapping will outline each of the stains and will provide a map of the areas that need further testing.

SCREENING TESTS FOR SEMEN

The screening tests for semen include the acid phosphatase mapping technique mentioned before, the acid phosphatase test being administered as a *spot test* (color test) with cotton swabs or in test tubes. Once a suspected semen stain has been located, the analyst proceeds to those tests that will provide conclusive evidence that the stain is in fact a semen stain.

The ABAcard p-30 test developed by Abacus Diagnostics, Inc., can be used as a screening test for semen in the field, or as a confirmatory test for semen in the laboratory, since this test identifies the P-30 prostate antigen, known to exist only in the secretions of the human prostate. This test is similar to the HemaTrace test (see Figure 7-2) and is based on the precipitation of the P-30 molecule by an antibody specific for this protein.

IDENTIFICATION OF SEMEN IN SUSPECTED STAINS

Identification of semen in suspected stains is accomplished either by identifying sperm in the stain or by identification of the P-30 protein in the suspect stain. The identification of sperm involves making an extract of the stain, placing a drop of the extract on a microscope slide, and staining the slide with biological stains that will stain the components of the sperm in a characteristic manner. The analyst then identifies the sperm under a high-power microscope, on the basis of the size, shape, and characteristic staining of the sperm. If the stain is found to lack sperm, the analyst will subject the stain extract to crossover electrophoresis using an antiserum that reacts exclusively with the P-30 protein from the prostrate gland. Identification of the P-30 protein in the stain is considered a certain identification of semen, since the P-30 protein is found only in the prostate or its secretions.

DNA TESTING OF SEMEN STAINS

DNA testing of semen stains is the same as that for blood DNA testing with the exception of the preliminary treatment of the stains needed to prepare them for DNA analysis. As few as 100 sperm are required for successful DNA analysis using the PCR technique. Semen from aspermic individuals may contain enough exfoliated (shed) cells from the reproductive tract to produce successful PCR DNA analysis.

Comparison standards needed for DNA analysis of semen stains

The DNA comparison standards needed for comparison of the unknown semen's DNA to that of a suspected source are the same as for bloodstains. The preferred method for obtaining comparison standards is to use buccal swabs from a swab kit designed for this purpose. Once the buccal samples are obtained from individuals suspected as the source of the semen stains, the swabs are preserved as for other swabs containing biological material. Blood samples from potential sources for the semen drawn in vacuum vials can also be used as the comparison standard, although some individuals may object to blood samples drawn via needle. For victims of sexual assault, *buccal swabs* are especially preferred, in order to minimize further trauma to the victim.

SALIVA EVIDENCE

Introduction to saliva evidence

Saliva is produced by three salivary glands in the mouth (parotid, submaxillary, and sublingual) which exude their contributions into the mouth. Saliva assists in keeping the mouth moist, chewing, and swallowing. It contains an enzyme, salivary amylase, which breaks down starches into maltose (a sugar) and dextrin (which has adhesive properties). The saliva also contains exfoliated cells from the cheeks and salivary glands. These cells provide the capability for DNA testing of the saliva. The enzyme amylase provides the basis for presumptive tests for saliva by adding starch and iodine in sequence to the suspect stain. Testing for the presence of saliva can also be accomplished using a card for identifying saliva, developed by Abacus Diagnostics which is similar to the HemaTrace© card in Figure 7-2.

Occurrence of saliva evidence

Saliva evidence is encountered in sexual assault cases, where the assailant bites the victim, performs oral sex on the victim, or otherwise places the mouth on the victim. Saliva evidence also occurs on items such as cigarette butts, drinking glasses, stamps, envelope flaps, the victim's clothing, and other surfaces touched by an individual's mouth. These samples of saliva evidence are collected via swabs, or by collection of the entire object bearing the saliva stains. In sexual assault cases, the saliva stains on the victim's body are collected using moistened swabs, if the saliva stain has dried.

Screening for saliva stains at the scene

For suspected saliva stains on cigarette butts and other items, the objects should not be screened for saliva, as the amount of saliva present may be sufficient only for DNA analysis. Screening of most suspected saliva stains should be left for the laboratory analysis, as the amount of saliva present may be reduced below the level necessary for DNA typing due to the amount used up for the screening.

Preservation of saliva evidence

The procedures for preservation of saliva evidence are found in Table 7-1.

Summary

PRECAUTIONS FOR BIOLOGICAL STAINS

INTRODUCTION

BLOODSTAIN EVIDENCE

Introduction to bloodstain evidence

Modern and Historical Genetic Marker Testing Nature of DNA

Crime Scene Documentation of Bloodstains

- Notes.
- Photographs.

Searching for Bloodstains

Bloodstain Pattern Documentation

- String grid method for bloodstain pattern photographs.
- Corner label method for bloodstain pattern photographs.
- Perimeter measurement ruler method for bloodstain pattern photographs.

Collection of Bloodstain Evidence

- Small items containing potential bloodstains.
- Large immobile objects with hard smooth surfaces (metal, glass, etc.).
- Large liquid pools of blood.
- Large objects with a soft porous surface (wood, carpets).
- Large objects with hard nonporous surfaces (brick wall, concrete, pavement, etc.).
- Clothing.

Comparison standard samples for DNA typing

- Buccal swabs: Dry and Freeze.
- Liquid blood samples.
- Sample for DNA typing: Purple- or yellow-top tubes.
- Sample for blood alcohol: Gray-stoppered tubes (DUI kit).

Blood Samples from Postmortem Subjects

- Sample for DNA typing: Purple- or yellow-top tubes.
- Sample for blood alcohol: Gray-stoppered tubes (DUI kit).

General Comments

- Submit all items to the laboratory in your area as soon as feasible.
- Avoid exposing biological evidence to heat, humidity, and sunlight.
- If the evidence cannot be immediately submitted to the laboratory:
  - Refrigerate liquid blood samples.
  - Air-dry all bloodstained items. Do not subject to heat.
  - Package all bloodstained items in paper bags to avoid mold growth.
  - Freeze the blood-stained items after drying until submission to the crime laboratory.

Laboratory Analysis of Bloodstains

- Determination of stain as human bloodstain.
- DNA analysis.
- PCR analysis.

- Short tandem repeats.
- **CODIS** "**Co**mbined **DNA** **I**ndex **S**ystem."

Preservation of Samples for DNA Analysis

SEMEN EVIDENCE

Introduction to Semen Evidence

Semen defined: male ejaculate.

Collection of Semen Evidence

At the crime scene.

- Clothing from the victim.
- Bedding (sheets, blankets, comforters).
- Blood and semen stains on nonabsorbent surfaces (flooring, walls, etc.).

Laboratory Examinations of Semen Evidence

- Detection of semen stains.
- Screening tests for semen.
- Identification of semen in suspected stains.
- Sperm.
- P-30 protein.
- DNA testing of semen stains.

Comparison Standards Needed for DNA Analysis

SALIVA EVIDENCE

Introduction to Saliva Evidence
Occurrence of Saliva Evidence
Screening for Saliva Evidence
Preservation of Saliva Evidence

Review Questions

1. The investigator should always follow _____ _____ when handling biological evidence.
2. The two primary categories of examination important in bloodstain evidence are _____ _____ _____, and _____ _____ _____.
3. Proper documentation of bloodstain patterns should always be a _____ consideration of the crime scene investigator.
4. The various blood types in blood are referred to as _____ _____.
5. "Secretors" secrete their _____ blood type into their secretions.
6. As a general rule, bloodstained evidence should first be _____ and then _____ to preserve the samples.
7. Photographs of bloodstains should be taken with _____ film.

8. Bloodstains that are "invisible" can often be visualized by spraying with _____.

9. Bloodstains on small items should be collected by _____ _____ _____ _____.

10. A _____ swab from an unstained area should be taken for each area of bloodstains collected.

11. Bloodstains on clothing should be collected by _____ _____ _____ _____.

12. A _____ topped tube should be used for collecting blood samples from living subjects for blood-typing purposes.

13. Blood samples from postmortem subjects should be taken from the _____ or a _____ _____ _____.

14. Bloodstain evidence should be submitted _____ _____ _____ _____ to the laboratory.

15. Liquid blood samples should be _____, not _____.

16. Semen is defined as the male _____.

17. The protein P-30 is derived from the _____ gland.

18. Semen evidence usually consists of _____ or aspirates from a body orifice or _____ on fabrics or nonabsorbent surfaces.

19. Semen stains may not be _____ when they occur on dark-colored fabrics.

20. _____ _____ apply to the handling of semen evidence as well as to blood evidence.

21. The investigator should always wear _____ _____ when handling semen evidence.

22. The investigator should use _____ light sources when searching for semen stains, in addition to using the unaided eye.

23. Semen stains must be _____ prior to packaging in order to prevent bacterial growth.

24. The DNA in semen evidence is found in the _____.

25. Clothing worn by a sexual assault victim before/during the assault may have evidence of being _____ removed by the suspect.

26. Clothing worn by a sexual assault victim after the assault may have _____ evidence from the suspect.

27. Semen stains on nonabsorbent surfaces should be collected with _____ _____.

28. Clothing may be searched for semen stains with the use of the acid phosphatase _____ technique.

29. Semen in a suspected stain can be positively identified by identifying either _____ or the _____ protein in the stain.

30. Genetic _____ may be identified in semen stains.

Further References

Jackson, Andrew R.W., and J. Jackson. 2004. *Forensic Science*, Essex, England, U.K: Pearson Education Limited. [Written for U.K: audiences, but scientific aspects of text written exceptionally well and relevant to U.S. audiences].

James, Stuart H., Kish, Paul E., and Sutton, T. Paulette (eds. and authors). 2005. *Principles of Bloodstain Analysis* (Theory and Practice). Boca Raton, FL: CRC Press (Taylor and Francis Group).

James, Stuart H., and J. J. Nordby, eds. 2005. *Forensic Science* (An Introduction to Scientific and Investigative Techniques), 2nd ed. Boca Raton, FL: CRC Press (Imprint of Taylor and Francis).

Saferstein, R. 2009. *Forensic Science* (From the Crime Scene to the Crime Lab), Upper Saddle River, NJ: Pearson Education, Inc.

White, Peter, ed. 1998. *Crime Scene to Court* (The Essentials of Forensic Science) Cambridge, UK: The Royal Society of Chemistry.

APPENDIX 7-A

Safety Precautions for Blood and Biological Fluids

1. **Universal precautions.**

   The term "universal precautions" means that all human blood and certain human body fluids must be treated as if known to be infectious for human immunodeficiency virus (HIV), hepatitis B virus (HBV), and other blood-borne pathogens.

2. **Other potentially infectious materials (OPIM).**

   a. Semen and semen stains.

   b. Vaginal secretions and stains.

   c. Any body fluid.

   d. Unfixed human tissues or organs, or any culture medium or tissue infected with HIV or HBV.

3. **Exposure control plan.**

   Each agency should have a written exposure control plan that outlines the safety precautions necessary to prevent exposure to biological fluids and stains.

4. **Personal protective equipment.**

   Personal protective equipment must be worn when exposed to or handling biological fluids and stains. Personal protective equipment should include the following:

   a. **Gloves** (impermeable gloves such as surgeon's gloves).

   b. **Masks** (for protection against inhalation of mists or aerosols).

   c. **Face shields** or protective eyewear with solid side-shields.

   d. **Protective outerwear** such as jumpsuits, lab coats, or gowns. Protective outerwear can be disposable or commercially laundered types.

   e. **Shoe covers** or boots (at bloody crime scenes or autopsies).

   f. **Surgical cap** or hood (at autopsies).

5. **Eating, smoking, drinking, cosmetics.**

   Eating, smoking, drinking, and application of cosmetics are prohibited at the crime scene, in the laboratory, or at an autopsy.

6. **Leaving or entering the crime scene.**

   Personal protective equipment must be removed when leaving the crime scene, laboratory, or autopsy room, and the hands and face washed thoroughly before engaging in other activities. *Personal protective equipment should be donned again before reentering the crime scene, laboratory, or autopsy room.*

8 | FIREARMS EVIDENCE

SAFETY RULE: There is no such thing as an "unloaded" firearm! Treat all firearms as though they are loaded!

INTRODUCTION

Firearms evidence consists of the firearms themselves, cartridge components—both fired and unfired, gunshot residues on targets, and discharge residues on the hands of individuals who have fired or handled a discharged firearm. Firearms evidence is usually encountered in crimes against persons such as homicide, assault, and robbery. However, firearms evidence may occur in many other types of crimes such as burglary, rape, and narcotics violations. The most common firearms involved in criminal cases are handguns (revolvers and semiautomatic pistols). Figure 8-1 illustrates a typical revolver with its components labeled. Figure 8-2 illustrates a typical semiautomatic (autoloading) pistol with its components labeled. Occasionally, a criminal case may involve a long arm (rifle or shotgun). Figure 8-3 illustrates some representative examples of long arms with the appropriate nomenclature for their components.

FIREARM CARTRIDGES

Bulleted cartridges

Modern bulleted **cartridges** consist of the cartridge case, the primer, the propellant, and the bullet or projectile. Each of these components may become physical evidence in a shooting case. Figure 8-4 illustrates the components of modern bulleted cartridges.

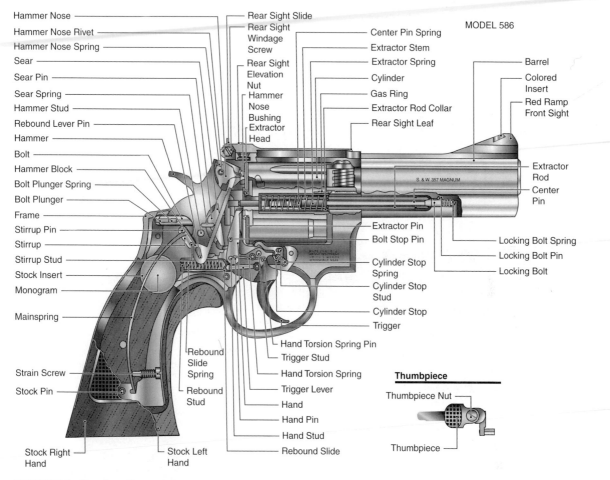

Hammer Nose
Hammer Nose Rivet
Hammer Nose Spring
Sear
Sear Pin
Sear Spring
Hammer Stud
Rebound Lever Pin
Hammer
Bolt
Hammer Block
Bolt Plunger Spring
Bolt Plunger
Frame
Stirrup Pin
Stirrup
Stirrup Stud
Stock Insert
Monogram
Mainspring
Strain Screw
Stock Pin
Stock Right Hand

Rear Sight Slide
Rear Sight Windage Screw
Rear Sight Elevation Nut
Hammer Nose Bushing
Extractor Head

MODEL 586

Center Pin Spring
Extractor Stem
Extractor Spring
Cylinder
Gas Ring
Extractor Rod Collar
Rear Sight Leaf

Barrel
Colored Insert
Red Ramp Front Sight

S. & W. 357 MAGNUM

Extractor Rod
Center Pin

Extractor Pin
Bolt Stop Pin
Cylinder Stop Spring
Cylinder Stop Stud
Cylinder Stop
Trigger

Locking Bolt Spring
Locking Bolt Pin
Locking Bolt

Rebound Slide Spring
Rebound Stud
Stock Left Hand

Hand Torsion Spring Pin
Trigger Stud
Hand Torsion Spring
Trigger Lever
Hand
Hand Pin
Hand Stud
Rebound Slide

Thumbpiece

Thumbpiece Nut
Thumbpiece

FIGURE 8-1 Revolver Components
Courtesy of Smith & Wesson.

Firearms cartridges are produced in many configurations and sizes for both center-fire and rimfire weapons. There are three general shapes (see Figure 8-5) for metallic cartridges: (1) straight, (2) tapered, and (3) bottlenecked.

All .22 rimfire cartridges and most centerfire cartridges have straight cases, whereas most centerfire rifle cartridges have a bottleneck shape. The tapered case is largely obsolete.[1]

Rimfire cartridges have the priming compound encased around the rim (see Figure 8-6) and have a straight shape. Centerfire cartridges have the priming compound encased in a central "primer" and may have a rimmed, rimless, or semirimmed cartridge case (see Figure 8-6). Rimmed cartridges are used in revolvers, where the rim holds the cartridge in the cylinder chamber. Rimless cartridges are used in semiautomatic (autoloading) pistols. The rimless feature allows the cartridges to be loaded into the magazine of the weapon and fed into the chamber by the action of the slide mechanism. Semirimmed cartridges are manufactured for use in automatic weapons. Rimfire cartridges made for firearms that use .22 short, .22 long, or .22 long rifle ammunition have plain lead or plated lead bullets. Rimfire cartridges for .22 magnum ammunition have copper jacketed or soft point semijacketed bullets (see Figure 8-6).

FIGURE 8-2 **Typical Auto Loading Pistol Components**
Courtesy of Smith & Wesson.

Most rimfire and centerfire cartridges have headstamps that identify the manufacturer and the type of cartridge. Figure 8-7 illustrates the headstamps of some .22 rimfire, centerfire pistol, and centerfire revolver cartridges.

The propellants (gunpowder) grains for firearm cartridges are manufactured with various shapes for rimfire (RF) and centerfire (CF) ammunition. The shape of the propellant grains influences the burning rate of the propellant (see Figure 8-8).

Figure 8-9 illustrates both an older style and a modern style plastic shotgun shell. The older style of paper shotgun shell has fibrous wads and an overpowder wad instead of the one-piece plastic wad found in the modern **shotshell**.

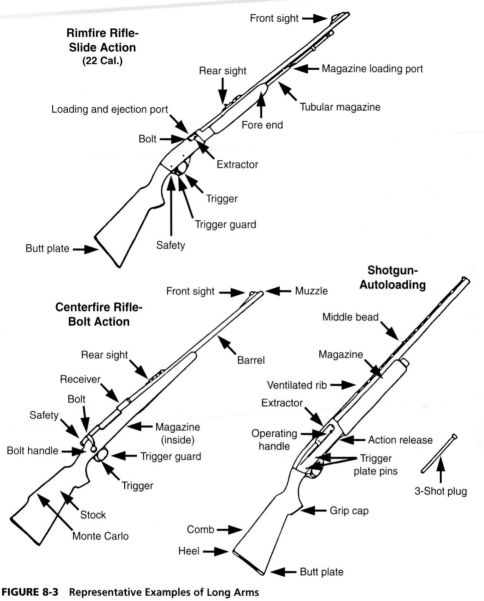

FIGURE 8-3 **Representative Examples of Long Arms**
Courtesy of ANITE Productions and Lucien Haag.

Characteristics of rifled barrels

Rifled barrels are so-named because of the "rifling" produced in the **bore** of the barrel (see Figure 8-10). Smooth-bore weapons (shotguns), as opposed to weapons with rifled barrels, have no rifling in their barrels. The rifling consists of "lands" and "grooves" that are produced by scraping out grooves in the lands or by pulling a swage through the barrel, which impresses the grooves. The lands are the raised areas of the rifling left by

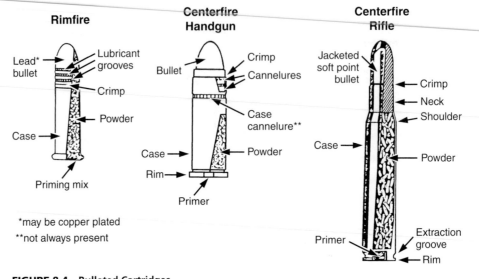

FIGURE 8-4 Bulleted Cartridges
Courtesy of ANITE Productions and Lucien Haag.

the scraping process or by the flowing of metal into the grooved areas of the swage. The lands and grooves are given a twist as they are produced in order to impart a spin to the bullet as it passes down the barrel, thus conferring stability to the bullet as it travels from the barrel. The caliber, number of the lands and grooves, their width, and the direction of their twist comprise the **class characteristics** of the firearm's barrel (and thus the class characteristics of the firearm).

Groove width may be equal to, less than, or greater than the width of the lands. Different manufacturers use different measurements for the widths of the lands and grooves in their barrels. Land widths are inversely related to the widths of the grooves, that is, as wider grooves are cut, the lands will become narrower; or the narrower the grooves are cut, the wider the lands become. The width of the lands and grooves are characteristics, which, taken with caliber, direction of twist, and the number of lands and grooves, establish the **family characteristics** of a given make and model of firearm. Hence, a firearm with six lands and grooves, with a right-hand twist, and specific widths for the lands and grooves would belong to the family of firearms with the same caliber, direction of twist, and number of lands and grooves having the same measurements.

The caliber designation of a firearm in the United States has been typically expressed in terms of either the bore diameter "(d)" in Figure 8-10 or the groove diameter "(D)" in either hundredths or thousandths of an inch.[2] In some instances, the actual diameter of a barrel may

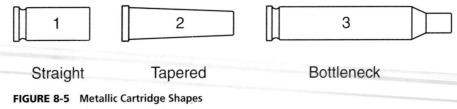

FIGURE 8-5 Metallic Cartridge Shapes
Courtesy of ANITE Productions and Lucien Haag.

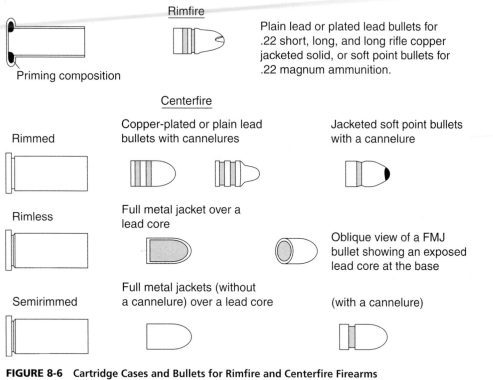

Rimfire

Plain lead or plated lead bullets for
.22 short, long, and long rifle copper
jacketed solid, or soft point bullets for
.22 magnum ammunition.

Priming composition

Centerfire

Copper-plated or plain lead
bullets with cannelures

Jacketed soft point bullets
with a cannelure

Rimmed

Rimless

Full metal jacket over a
lead core

Oblique view of a FMJ
bullet showing an exposed
lead core at the base

Semirimmed

Full metal jackets (without
a cannelure) over a lead core

(with a cannelure)

FIGURE 8-6 **Cartridge Cases and Bullets for Rimfire and Centerfire Firearms**
Source: "Firearms Evidence: Field Expedient Determinations," copyright © 1977 by Lucien
Haag, with permission.

differ from the nominal caliber (i.e., the named caliber). An example of a nominal caliber
having a different actual caliber is the .38 Special, which has an actual bore of .36 inches. The
naming of cartridges usually begins with the caliber of the firearm followed by additional
descriptive data. Some manufacturers may have named their cartridges on the basis of groove
diameter rather than the bore diameter (e.g., .308 Winchester).[3]

Class characteristics of fired bullets

The class characteristics of fired bullets are a direct result of the barrel's rifling being
impressed into the bullet's circumference as it is forced down the barrel during discharge.
The lands of the barrel are impressed into the bullet, and the bullet material flows into the
grooves of the barrel as the bullet passes down the barrel. These impressions on the bullet
are referred to as the "**land impressions**" and the "**groove impressions**" of the fired
bullet. (Note that the land impression on the bullet is a depression and that the groove
impression is the raised impression, i.e., the bullet impressions are negative impressions of
the barrel rifling.) Thus, the *class characteristics* present on a fired bullet consist of the
caliber of the bullet, the *number of lands and grooves* present, and the *direction of* **twist** of
the land and groove impressions. (See Figure 8-11 for illustrations of class characteristics on
fired bullets.)

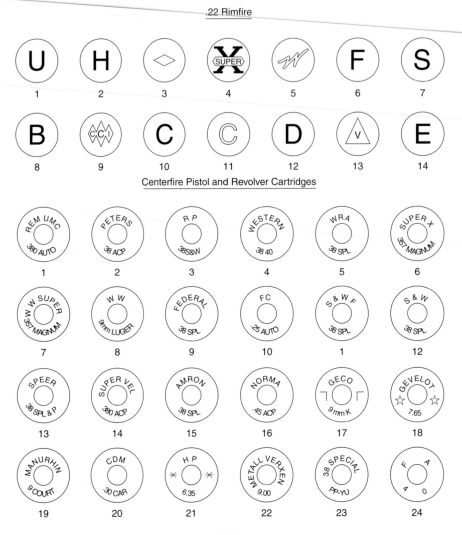

FIGURE 8-7   **Headstamps of Some .22 Rimfire, Centerfire Pistol, and Centerfire Revolver Cartridges**

Source: "Firearms Evidence: Field Expedient Determinations," copyright © 1977 by Lucien Haag, with permission.

KEY

.22 Rimfire
1 Remington Peters
2 5 Winchester Western
6 Federal Cartridge Corp.
7 Smith & Wesson Ammunition Co.

Centerfire Pistol and Revolver
1 Remington Union and Metallic Cart.
2 3 Remington Peters
4 8 Winchester Western
9 10 Federal Cartridge Corp.
11 12 Smith & Wesson (Fiocchi) Inc.
13 Speer Inc., Lewiston, Idaho
14 Super Vel. Cart. Corp., Indiana
15 Amron, Gulf & Western Systems Co., Wisconsin
16 Norma Projectilfabrik, Sweden

8 Browning, mfg. by Winchester, disc. 1974
9 11 "CCI Mini Mag," Cascade Cart. Inc.
12 CIL, Dominion Ammunition Div., Canada
13 VALOR, Yugoslav import
14 Eley "Tenex," Birmingham, England

17 Gustav Geneschow Co., Berlin, Germany
18 Gevelot, Paris, France
19 Manurhin, Mulhouse, France
20 Cartuchos Deportivos de Mexico, Cuernavaca, Mexico
21 Hirtenberg Patronen, Hirtenberg, Austria
22 Svenska Metallverken, Stockholm, Sweden
23 VALOR mfg. at Prvi Partizan factory, Yugoslavia
24 Typical U.S. military headstamp; arsenal abbreviation
and yr. of mfg. (Frankfort Arsenal, 1940)

Smokeless gunpowder type	Form (ca. 20X)	Description and Uses
tubular (extruded)		This type of propellant has the appearance of small, shiny gray-black pieces of macaroni. Both the length and diameter of the particles can be varied by the manufacturer. This type of powder is used almost exclusively in centerfire rifle cartridges.
Flake—disc type with web without web		Disc-flake powders are manufactured either with or without a web. Some have very irregular circumferences. These propellants are commonly found in CF pistol cartridges, shotgun shells, and some .22 RF ammunition.
Flake—square type		Square-flake powders are presently all of foreign manufacture and are commonly found in European and Scandinavian ammunition of all types, i.e., CF rifle, pistol, shotgun shells, and .22 RF.
Ball powder spherical flattened		Developed in 1933, ball powder is used in all types of ammunition. Their size and shape is varied by the manufacturer to control burning rate.

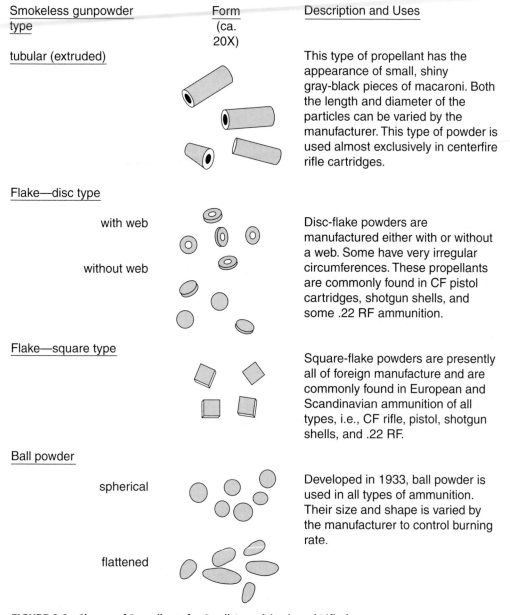

FIGURE 8-8 **Shapes of Propellants for Small Arms (Pistols and Rifles)**

Source: "Firearms Evidence: Field Expedient Determinations," copyright © 1977 by Lucien Haag, with permission.

Field comparisons of bullet class characteristics

The investigator can make field comparisons of fired bullets by placing fired bullets base-to-base (see Figure 8-12). This field comparison allows for a quick estimation of whether or not two bullets were fired by the same weapon. Also, this method allows for an estimation of the class characteristics of a badly damaged bullet by comparison with a relatively undamaged bullet.

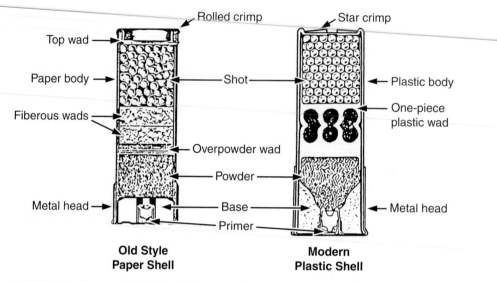

FIGURE 8-9   Shotgun Shells (Shotshells, Shotgun Cartridges)
Courtesy of ANITE Productions and Lucien Haag.

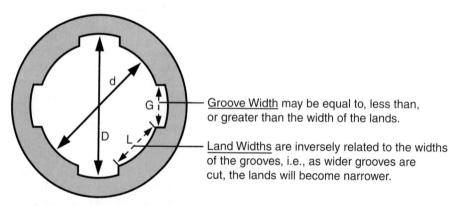

Groove Width may be equal to, less than, or greater than the width of the lands.

Land Widths are inversely related to the widths of the grooves, i.e., as wider grooves are cut, the lands will become narrower.

FIGURE 8-10   Cross-Section of a Rifled Barrel
Courtesy of ANITE Productions and Lucien Haag.

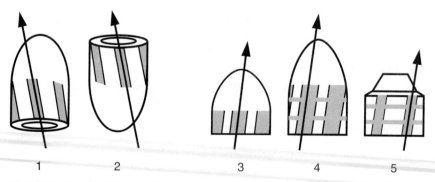

FIGURE 8-11   Class Characteristics on Fired Bullets
Courtesy of ANITE Productions and Lucien Haag.

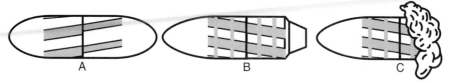

The base-to-base comparisons may reveal:

A. Whether more than one weapon is involved.

B. That bullets of the same caliber but different in brand or design may have been fired in the same weapon.

C. The land-and-groove count on a badly damaged bullet by agreement with one in near-pristine condition.

FIGURE 8-12 **Base-to-Base Bullet Comparisons**
Courtesy of ANITE Productions and Lucien Haag.

Field estimation of bullet caliber

The caliber of bullets recovered in the field can be estimated by comparison with Figure 8-13 (caliber estimator) if they are in reasonable shape (i.e., not distorted significantly at the base). It is important first to inspect the bullet thoroughly for any trace evidence to ensure that such evidence is not disturbed by comparison with the caliber estimator graph. If trace evidence is found to be present, then the investigator should not attempt to compare the bullet with the caliber estimator graph but should submit the bullet to the laboratory for trace evidence removal and caliber determination by the firearms examiner. Note that the measurements in the graph are exact and that some nominal calibers will differ from the actual caliber of the weapon.

Cartridge cases fired in semiautomatic and automatic firearms typically have impressions originating from the components of the firearm, which include (1) an impression of the breechface (the *signature* of the breech), (2) an ejector mark where the cartridge strikes the ejector upon ejection, and (3) override and gouge marks from the extractor (see Figure 8-14). Cartridge cases fired in semiautomatic, automatic, and revolver firearms will typically have chamber striations (particularly in semiautomatic and automatic weapons) produced by the forced removal from the chamber and a firing pin impression (see Figure 8-14). Each of these markings may have sufficient detail to form the basis for an identification of the firearm in which the cartridge was fired.

Caliber	.22	.25	.30	.32	.38*	.40	.45
Metric (mm)	5.56	6.35	7.62	7.65	9*	10	11.25

* Actual measurement - .36 caliber
(most nominal .38 caliber and 9 mm barrels are actually .36 caliber).

FIGURE 8-13 **Caliber Estimator**

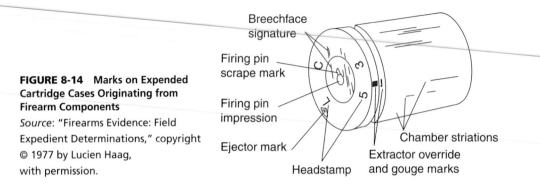

FIGURE 8-14 Marks on Expended Cartridge Cases Originating from Firearm Components
Source: "Firearms Evidence: Field Expedient Determinations," copyright © 1977 by Lucien Haag, with permission.

LABORATORY EXAMINATIONS OF FIREARMS EVIDENCE

Laboratory examinations of firearms evidence can be grouped into several categories.

Identification of the firearm that fired a bullet or cartridge

These examinations are the most frequently requested of the forensic firearms examiner. These examinations involve the comparison of the questioned bullet with bullets test-fired in suspected weapons. The comparisons may reveal that the bullet or cartridge case was definitely fired in the submitted weapon, that the bullet or cartridge case may have been fired in the submitted weapon (a match of class characteristics, in which there are insufficient individualizing characteristics for a definitive opinion), or that the bullet or cartridge case definitely was not fired in the submitted weapon.

In those cases in which the examination eliminates the submitted firearm as the source of the fired components, the analyst may be able to furnish a list of firearms that may have fired the components, depending on the condition of the markings on the bullet or case. The list available to the laboratory from the Crime Laboratory Information System (CLIS) is very extensive and includes many less common makes or models of firearms, in addition to those firearms that are commonly encountered in criminal investigations such as homicides, assaults, and robberies.

Muzzle-to-target distance determinations

Muzzle-to-target distance determinations are frequently helpful in the reconstruction of a shooting incident, especially when there is a question of whether the incident is a murder, accident, or suicide. These determinations are based on the powder patterns present on a garment, on an item of bedding, or on the skin of a victim in the case of bulleted cartridges. In the case of shotguns, the distance determinations are based largely on the spread of the pellets for longer-range shots. The distance determinations assist the investigators in determining the accuracy of the statements of witnesses or principals in the case.

Gunshot residue identifications

Gunshot residue identifications are made on residues collected with gunshot residue kits from the hands of those individuals suspected of discharging a firearm. The residues are collected with swab kits for examination by atomic absorption (AA), with metal disks for scanning electron microscopy (SEM), or a combination of the two. (See the section on gunshot residue collection for further discussion on these techniques.)

Weapon functionality examinations

The **functionality** of a weapon may be an issue in some cases. Some crimes require as an element of the crime that the weapon be capable of firing. Cases involving the determination of accidental or intentional shootings may need functionality tests to resolve an issue in the reconstruction of the shooting, such as the propensity for accidental discharge of the weapon.

Bullet trajectory and/or sequence of firing determinations

The **trajectories** of fired bullets can be determined in some cases in which the bullets have passed through walls or other surfaces. The direction of travel of a bullet that ricochets off a surface can often be determined on the basis of the characteristics of the ricochet marking. (See the section on bullet trajectories in Chapter 15 for further information on trajectory determinations.)

The determination of the sequence of firing is limited to those shooting incidents involving revolvers except in rare circumstances. The **sequence of firing** is based on the position of the expended cartridge cases remaining in the cylinder of the weapon involved and depends on the presence of different ammunition brands or different types from the same manufacturer (see Figure 8-15).

COLLECTION OF FIREARMS EVIDENCE[4]

Introduction

The *most important consideration* in the collection of firearms evidence is *officer safety. Always treat any firearm as though it is loaded!* Evaluate each situation before attempting to unload the firearm. *If you are not thoroughly familiar with the weapon, find an officer who knows the weapon well to perform the unloading.* In most circumstances, it is unwise to transport a loaded firearm. Before attempting to unload the firearm, examine closely for any fingerprints, bloodstains, or trace evidence present. Note that fingerprints may not be immediately visible and that trace evidence and bloodstains may be discernible only by the

Under hammer

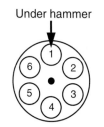

Suggested Format of Notes:

Chamber Postion	Condition	Cartridge Headstamp
1.	Live	REM-UMC
2.	Live	REM-UMC
3.	Live	PETERS
4.	Live	PETERS
5.	Fired	REM-UMC
6.	Fired	PETERS

FIGURE 8-15 Diagram to be Made by Officer Recovering Weapon

laboratory analyst using the stereomicroscope. For this reason, take extreme care while unloading the firearm to preserve those types of evidence that may be present, such as fingerprints, blood (especially around the muzzle), hair or fibers, cylinder "halos," and debris in the barrel or cylinders. Handle the weapon by those areas unlikely to retain latent fingerprints, such as knurled or checkered areas of the grips and slide. *Do not mark the weapon itself* (other than the index marks on the cylinder), since the handling necessary to accomplish the marking may obliterate or remove these types of evidence. Use evidence tags attached to the trigger guard after unloading (see the section "Note-Taking and Evidence Collection").

Unloading revolvers

Prior to unloading the revolver, mark the cylinder to indicate its position as found. This step can be done by placing a pen or scribe mark on the top of the cylinder along each side of the top strap of the frame. Record the position of each round in the cylinder in your field notes as diagrammed in Figure 8-15. All intact cartridges or expended cases removed should be handled so as to preserve any possible fingerprints. Package each cartridge/case in a separate package and reference to the field notes. *Do not mark the actual cartridge or case*. Mark instead the sealed container(s) bearing the cartridge or case.

Unloading autoloading firearms (semiautomatics)

Before securing the firearm as evidence, make a record of the position, as found, of any safety, cocking indicator, loaded chamber indicator, selector, or other control feature. With the firearm pointed in a safe direction, remove the magazine. Next, clear the chamber by slowly drawing back the slide mechanism. With the slide to the rear, examine the chamber visually to ensure that no cartridge is in the chamber. Separately package the firearm, any detachable magazine, and any extracted cartridge or cartridge case. Continue to take care to preserve any possible fingerprints or trace evidence. Do not remove cartridges from magazines or mark the cartridge cases directly, since the marking may obliterate identification characteristics present. Package the magazine in a sealed envelope, and place identifying data for the item on the envelope.

Trace evidence and fingerprints

Examine the weapon carefully for any **trace evidence**, such as blood, hair, fibers, tissue, or paint that may be present before processing for **latent fingerprints**. Note that any fingerprints, bloodstains, or trace evidence present may not be immediately visible. If there is doubt about the presence of trace evidence, do not process for fingerprints. Submit the weapon in person to the laboratory, and request that the firearm be examined for trace evidence and preserved for latent fingerprint and bloodstain examinations.

Weapons found in water

Weapons found in water should be recovered and placed in a container with the *same water* covering the weapon. If the weapon is removed from the water and allowed partially to dry, the rusting process may begin rapidly. For this reason, it is better to transport the weapon under the water to the firearms examiner, so that the weapon can be disassembled, cleaned, and protected from rusting in the laboratory.

Transportation to the laboratory

Personal delivery of firearms is the preferred method for transportation. A loaded hand-gun may be transported in a specially constructed box that has a means of securely hold-ing the firearm and has a metal plate blocking the muzzle. If the firearm is to be sent by mail, *it must be unloaded, securely packaged, and clearly marked that it contains an unloaded firearm.* Fired cartridge cases may be mailed, but *live ammunition cannot be shipped via U.S. mail.* Check with your local postal authorities if there is any question about the shipping of firearms or their components. Unloaded firearms and ammunition components may be sent via commercial package shipping firms such as UPS or FedEx. Be sure to check with the shipping firm to ensure that all applicable regulations are met before shipping the firearm or ammunition components.

Note-taking and evidence marking

At the scene, make a sketch of the area that shows the location of each evidence item collected. The sketch should contain location measurements that reference each item to a fixed object or to a reference point (see Chapter 4 on preparation of sketches). Carefully note your observations regarding the condition and location of the firearm. Photographs should be taken of the firearm prior to disturbing its location, except in an extreme emer-gency. Note the make of firearm and its serial number (some older rifles and shotguns may not have a serial number). Some weapons may have proof marks that aid in the identification of the manufacturer.

It is recommended that recovered firearms not be scribed, in order to avoid oblit-erating latent prints, trace evidence, and bloodstains that may be present on the weapon. The weapons should be identified by recording the make, model, and serial number and by a tag anchored to the finger guard. With the advent of modern methods for develop-ing latent fingerprints, it is now possible to recover latent prints on firearms. Bloodstains and trace evidence may be microscopic in nature, so that the marking of the weapon may damage or obliterate these types of evidence. After placing the tag in the trigger guard, the unloaded weapon should be packaged in an envelope or a box designed for the packaging of firearms and the appropriate data affixed to the container.

On recovered revolvers, remember to place index marks on the top of the cylinder on both sides of the top strap of the frame in order to preserve the position of each car-tridge in the cylinder.

RECOVERY OF FIRED AMMUNITION COMPONENTS

Bullets embedded in wood or plaster

Do not attempt to dig a bullet out of wood or plaster. Sketch accurately the location of the bullet hole prior to removal. Remove the bullet by cutting or sawing out the portion of material in which the bullet is embedded. Send the entire piece containing the bullet to the laboratory.

Removal of bullets from deceased persons

The body should be X-rayed prior to autopsy to locate any bullets or fragments. Ask the autopsy surgeon to avoid the use of forceps whenever possible. Rubber-tipped forceps or gloved fingers should be used to remove bullets or fragments, since the markings on the bullet may be destroyed by the use of forceps. Do not wash the extracted bullet, because trace evidence may be present on the bullet. It is imperative that the bullet be dried prior to packaging. Dry the bullets by blotting (not rolling) with a soft, dry facial type tissue. Do not seal in an air-tight package, since moisture can corrode identifiable detail on the bullet. Wrap in bond paper that has been crumpled, and seal in a labeled paper envelope or box, making sure that the seal does not impede moisture escape from the box (paper envelopes will allow for moisture to escape). Package each bullet separately. *Do not mark the bullet or allow it to be marked.* Label the sealed container with a description of the bullet and all other pertinent data. The investigator may wish to sketch the bullet in the field notes.

Cartridge cases

The location of fired cartridge cases may be valuable in a reconstruction attempt of the shooting incident. The location(s) of the shooter(s) may be determined by analysis of the locations of the fired cases. Make a sketch with accurate measurements of the position of all ejected cartridge cases (see Chapter 4 on sketches). Package each cartridge case separately with identifying data that relate the casing to the notes and sketches.

Shot wads

When a shotgun is fired, the **shot wads** travel along with or behind the shot charge for a short distance. In those cases involving a short-range shot, the wadding may be found in the victim's body or in the clothing. At the scene, follow the directions for ejected cartridge cases to document the location of the wadding materials. Follow the same packaging procedure as for bullets.

Shot pellets

For **shot pellets** embedded in wood, plaster, and the like, follow the same procedures as for embedded bullets. If it is not possible to submit the material in which the pellets are embedded, pellets may be dug out, taking care not to mutilate them any more than necessary. The removal of pellets from a deceased person can be facilitated by X-rays that can locate the pellets. Use care in removing the pellets: rubber-tipped forceps should be used. Wash, wrap in soft tissue paper, and place in a labeled pill box or small envelope.

Live shot shells or cartridges

Collect and submit to the laboratory all ammunition associated with a case. Test firings for distance determination require the same ammunition as that responsible for the patterns produced. Document where each lot of ammunition was found. If the number of cartridges is small, they can be handled in the same manner as fired bullets. Large quantities should be placed in a cardboard box or wooden container. Label, seal, and transport to the laboratory. If the ammunition is to be sent to the laboratory, note the admonition for shipping ammunition under the section "Transportation to the laboratory" for firearm components.

GUNSHOT RESIDUES (GSR)[5]

Introduction

Gunshot residues result from the discharge of a firearm (see Figure 8-16). These residues include components from the primer, powder, projectile material, and products of their combustion. The residue that can be deposited on the hands of a shooter is usually the result of gases or particles escaping through openings in the weapon, such as the space between the cylinder and the barrel area of a revolver or the end of the barrel. The amount of residue on the hands varies with the type of firearm, ammunition, and the conditions of discharge. Revolvers in poor condition or cheaply made revolvers will usually produce a considerable amount of GSR on the shooter's hand because of the larger space between the barrel and the cylinder, which allows for the escape of the gases produced during discharge of the firearm. High-quality revolvers in excellent condition will produce a significantly smaller quantity of GSR on the shooter's hands because of the tighter seal between the barrel and the chamber. Semiautomatic pistols of good quality and in excellent condition will produce even less GSR on the shooter's hands, since the gases escape primarily through the ejection port in a direction away from the shooter's hands.

The use of a rifle or shotgun by the shooter may produce gunshot residues on the shooter's cheek when the weapon is held against the cheek during firing. There is a wide variation with regard to the amount of residue deposited on the shooter's face or cheek with these types of weapons because of the physical characteristics of the firearm involved. Bolt-action rifles tend to seal the ejection port to a greater degree during firing, as one would expect. The gases may not escape from the port until the bolt is activated, at which time the weapon may not be next to the cheek of the shooter.

Autoloading rifles, however, will normally eject the cartridge case while the weapon is still in place against the shooter's cheek, thus producing deposition of the GSR on the cheek area. Pump and autoloading shotguns may also eject the cartridge while the weapon is held against the cheek and produce a GSR deposit on the shooter's cheek.

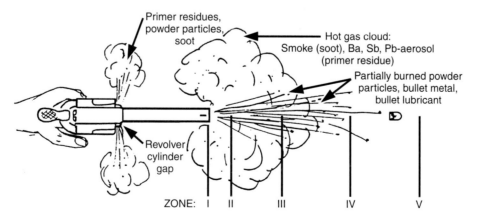

FIGURE 8-16 Gunshot Residue Production

Courtesy of ANITE Productions and Lucien Haag.

Gunshot residue analysis in the laboratory

Gunshot residue analysis is performed in the laboratory in several different ways. The manner in which the GSR is analyzed in the laboratory dictates the particular method that must be employed for the collection of the residues. The first methodology for the analysis of gunshot residues in the laboratory involves the quantitative chemical analysis of primer components found in the residues. The older technique for this type of analysis is **neutron activation analysis (NAA)**, which involves bombarding the residues with neutrons and subsequent analysis of the radiation given off by the irradiated sample by instruments that identify the components and also determine the quantity of each present in the residue. This technique (NAA) has been almost entirely replaced by a method called **atomic absorption analysis (AA)**, which analyzes chemical extracts from the swabs used in the swabbing technique. The analysis of gunshot residue from the hands of a shooter by these techniques detects primarily trace amounts of primer residue (barium and antimony). Because the various types of ammunition have different primer components, this technique may not be suitable for some types of ammunition that lack one of the primer components.

Another methodology for the analysis of GSR is called **scanning electron microscopy/energy dispersive X-ray analysis (SEM/EDX)**, often called "SEM" analysis. This technique has the distinct advantage of being able not only to analyze chemically the primer components through EDX but also to scan for the characteristic particles of gunpowder captured by the sampling disks. One disadvantage of this technique is the cost of the equipment, which may be prohibitive for smaller laboratories. Many of the larger laboratories analyze the GSR with both SEM/EDX and AA analyses. GSR sampling kits are available in several formats in order to accommodate the capabilities of the laboratories: (1) AA swab kits, (2) SEM/EDX disk kits, and (3) combination kits that have both the swabs for AA analysis sampling and the disks for sampling for SEM/EDX analysis. These kits are available commercially or may be produced by the laboratory that performs the analysis in your jurisdiction. It is important that GSR evidence is collected using the kit recommended or produced by the laboratory in your jurisdiction and that the instructions provided by that laboratory are followed if they differ from those presented in the section for collection of gunshot residues. Contact the laboratory performing GSR analysis for the agencies in your jurisdiction for written instructions for GSR collection promulgated by that laboratory.

Gunshot residues have been reported on a live subject's hands several hours after firing, but as a rule, recovery of residues cannot be expected after about six hours from the time of firing. The deposits on the hands decline rapidly during the first hour after firing the weapon. However, residues may last many hours after the time of the shooting on the hands of suicide or homicide victims. In either case, correct sample collection techniques are critical. Sampling for GSR should be performed on a live subject as soon after the shooting as possible (ideally, immediately after contact with a subject in the field). For homicide victims, the GSR sampling may be accomplished at the crime scene, or the hands of the victim may be bagged for protection during transport of the body to the autopsy room.

Collection of gunshot residues

Caution! The subject should not be allowed to wash or rub his/her hands prior to sampling. Gunshot residues can easily be removed from the hands. For this reason, it is important to process the subject's hands as soon as feasible. If the subject's hands cannot be processed immediately, the hands should be protected by placing new, clean brown paper bags over the subject's hands and taping the bags to the wrists. Never use plastic bags on a live subject's hands, since the production of sweat will destroy any residues present. Plastic bags can be used when necessary on the hands of deceased subjects. Once the hands have been protected by bagging, the subject should be transported immediately to the station for GSR processing.

Prior to any residue sampling, inspect the hands, wrists, and shirtsleeve cuffs for any signs of gunshot residues. Photograph any visible residues on the hands prior to collection of residues with **SEM disks** or **AA swabs**. If the hands are to be processed with both the SEM/EDX disks and the AA swabs, it is crucial that the sampling with the disks be performed prior to sampling with the swabs. Contamination of the subject's hands must be prevented, because the quantities of materials in the residues are extremely small. It is important that the investigator remember to wash his/her hands and don the gloves provided in the kit prior to sampling for gunshot residues.

PROCEDURE FOR GSR COLLECTION WITH METAL DISKS (SEM/EDX)

1. The SEM Disk sampling should be done prior to any swabbing technique for NAA or AA analysis.
2. Various laboratories performing SEM/EDX analysis for GSR may have instructions that differ from those presented here. Contact the laboratory that performs GSR analysis for your area for any instructions that may differ from these instructions.
3. Caution! Do not touch the hands of the subject in the areas to be sampled for possible gunshot residues.
4. Thoroughly wash your hands and wrists before proceeding further in order to prevent any transfer contamination to the hands of the subject. Put on the disposable gloves provided before handling any sampling materials.
5. Select the sample disk labeled "Right Hand." Remove the protective cover. Do not touch the disk to anything but the subject's hands.
6. To collect GSR from a person's hands, the exposed tacky surface of the disk is pressed lightly against the back of the subject's right hand in a systematic pattern, concentrating on the thumb, web area, and index finger, and extending to the index fingertip (see Figure 8-17) until the disk loses its stickiness. Do not slide or rotate the disk on the skin.
7. After the tacky surface has been used and the hand sampling is completed, reseal the disk in the container provided.
8. Repeat steps 6 and 7 for the palmar surface of the hand (see Figure 8-17).
9. Repeat steps 6, 7, and 8 for the left hand.
10. Secure used disks in an appropriately labeled envelope (this envelope may be included in the SEM/EDX kit).[6]

PROCEDURE FOR GSR COLLECTION USING SWABS (NAA OR AA ANALYSIS)

1. Obtain the proper gunshot residue collection kit as recommended by your laboratory.
2. When using both the SEM disk and the swabbing procedure, the swabbing procedure is done after the disk sampling.
3. Put on plastic gloves before handling any of the kit contents.
4. Remove swabs from the tube labeled "acid control." Add four drops nitric acid solution to each of the swabs. Return swabs to the tube (cotton tips down). Seal the tube tightly.

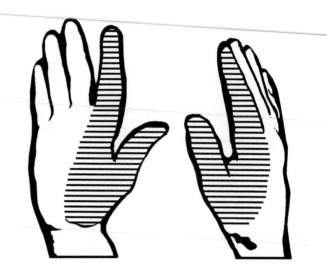

FIGURE 8-17   Area of Hands for Gunshot Residue Sampling with Metal Disks for SEM Analysis
Courtesy of CSI FORENSIC Supply, Martinez, CA (formerly Kinderprint).

5. Remove one swab from the tube labeled "Right Back," being careful not to touch the cotton tip to any surface. Using the dropper bottle in the kit, moisten the tip of the swab with four drops of the 5 percent nitric acid solution (do not overmoisten swab).
6. Thoroughly swab backside of the thumb, forefinger, and connecting web area of the right hand (see Figure 8-18). Swab in only one direction rather than using a back-and-forth motion.
7. Swab the remainder of the back of the right hand using the second swab, following steps 5 and 6. Place both swabs, cotton tip down, in the vial labeled "Right Back." *Note:* Thorough swabbing is accomplished by swabbing for approximately 30 seconds with each swab and rotating the swab to utilize all surfaces of the cotton tip. DO NOT SWAB THE FINGERPRINT AREA.

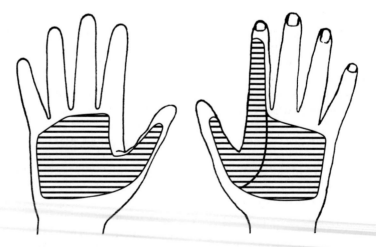

FIGURE 8-18   Area of Hands for GSR Collection with Swabs for AA Analysis

8. Repeat steps 3 and 4 on the left hand using the tube labeled "Left Back." After swabbing, place both swabs cotton tip down, in vial labeled "Back, Left Hand."

9. Remove swabs from the tube labeled "Right Hand, Palm." Prepare swabs as in step 5. Thoroughly swab the inner portion of the thumb and palm of the right hand (see Figure 8-18). Replace this swab in the vial labeled "Right Hand, Palm." Repeat this procedure with the second swab in the vial.

10. Repeat step 9 on the left palm using swabs from the tube labeled "Left Palm." Replace swabs in the tube labeled "Left Palm."

11. Leave the swab labeled "Blank Swab" untouched. This swab is a control swab only.

12. If the cartridge case is available, remove one swab from the tube labeled "Cartridge Case." Moisten the cotton tip with 5 percent nitric acid, and swab the inside bottom of the casing. Replace the swab in the tube labeled "Cartridge Case." Avoid obliterating any latent print on the casing.

13. Fill out the information requested on the GSR kit, and submit to the laboratory with the appropriate submission forms.[7]

TRACE METAL DETECTION TEST (TMDT)

In those cases where a subject is suspected of handling or holding (but not firing) a weapon, the subject's hands may be tested for the presence of trace metals that originated from the metal of a firearm (see Figure 8-19). The transfer of trace amounts of metal to the subject's hand(s) can be from the grip, trigger guard, or from other metallic areas of the weapon. The metal transfer to the palmar surface of the hand, when the weapon is held in the firing position, may produce a pattern that is distinctive for that particular make and model of firearm. The test is performed by spraying the subject's hands with the trace metal reagent, then exposing to shortwave ultraviolet light, which develops the color. Once the color develops, the pattern is photographed. Trace metal detection kits are available from commercial suppliers of crime scene equipment and supplies. The trace metal detection test should not be done if there is any suspicion that the subject fired a weapon, since the trace metal technique will interfere with gunshot residue tests of the subject's hands.

TARGET DISCHARGE RESIDUES

Distance Determinations In some cases, such as suicides and alleged struggles for the gun, the distance between the muzzle of the gun and the victim may become an issue, and it will therefore be desirable to examine garments for powder residue and other indications of close-range firings. For protection in transporting, the clothing should be dried and rolled with paper on each surface. Package each garment separately so that the area surrounding the bullet hole does not rub against any other object or clothing. When bullets have passed through garments into the body, photographs of the bullet hole(s) are desirable. Include a ruler in the photograph of each wound. Submit the firearm and any unfired ammunition associated with the incident. The use of identical ammunition is essential for accurate determination of muzzle-to-target distances. Whenever possible, the investigator should make every effort to collect the box of ammunition from which the suspected shooter obtained the ammunition used in the shooting.

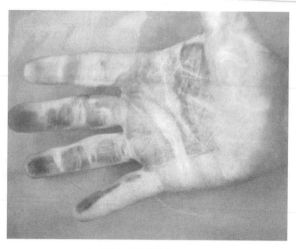

Trace Metal Patterns

Suspected Beretta Pistol

FIGURE 8-19 Trace Metal Detection Test

Courtesy of Department of Sheriff-Coroner, Contra Costa, CA.

COLLECTION OF TARGET RESIDUES

General Considerations for Target Residues The primary value of **target discharge residues** is the pattern of the residues, which is used to establish the muzzle-to-target distance for reconstruction purposes. Therefore, it is essential to document properly the pattern with notes, photographs, and sketches prior to any collection efforts. Photographs of residue patterns should be taken normal to the surface bearing the residues both with and without a measurement scale in view. Once the pattern has been properly documented, the investigator can collect the object bearing the residues by adhering to the following suggested procedures.

Collection of Target Residues on Clothing   Discharge residues on surfaces such as clothing should be collected by taking the entire garment, carefully wrapping it in paper, and sealing with tape. If the garment is bloodstained, the garment should be allowed to dry completely by hanging or placing it in its natural shape on a clean piece of butcher paper. Once dried, the garment can be packaged in the butcher paper bindle-style, taped, and placed in a paper bag for sealing.

Collection of Target Residues on Bedding   Target residues on bedding such as blankets or sheets should be protected by placing butcher paper over the pattern and taping the paper down. The bedding item can then be collected by folding into a bindle shape as in bloodstained bedding and packaged in a paper bag or cardboard box.

Collection of Target Residues on Solid Objects   If the discharge residue pattern is on a solid object such as a wall, the pattern should be documented with photographs and sketches prior to collection. The pattern should be collected by removing the area containing the residues and protected with a cardboard "tent" secured with tape and transported to the laboratory for analysis. Careful handling is essential to avoid loss or alteration of the pattern before transport to the lab.

Collection of Discharge Residues on Skin   Discharge residues on the skin surrounding gunshot wounds should be *photographed* from medium range and close-up, *with and without a measuring scale in view.* The residues may then be collected with a GSR kit. It is helpful to have a criminalist at an autopsy to collect the residues present, since the criminalist may use chemical techniques to locate and recover the residues, some of which may be invisible to the naked eye.

Summary

Safety Rule: There is no such thing as an "unloaded" firearm! Treat all firearms as though they are loaded!

INTRODUCTION

- Revolver Components.
- Typical Autoloading Pistol components.
- Representative Examples of Long Arms.

FIREARM CARTRIDGES

- Bulleted Cartridges.

CARTRIDGE SHAPES

- Metallic Cartridge Shapes.
- Cartridge Cases and Bullets for Rimfire and Centerfire Firearms.

- Headstamps of Some .22 Rimfire, Centerfire Pistol, and Centerfire Revolver Cartridges.
- Shapes of Propellants for Small Arms (Pistols and Rifles).
- Shotgun Shells (Shotshells, Shotgun Cartridges).

CHARACTERISTICS OF RIFLED BARRELS

- Cross-Section of a Rifled Barrel.

CLASS CHARACTERISTICS OF FIRED BULLETS

- Caliber.
- Number of lands and grooves.
- Direction of twist.
- Class Characteristics on Fired Bullets.

FIELD COMPARISONS OF BULLET CLASS CHARACTERISTICS

- Base-to-Base Bullet Comparisons.

FIELD ESTIMATION OF BULLET CALIBER

- Caliber Estimator.

IMPRESSIONS FROM FIRED SEMIAUTO CARTRIDGE CASES

- Marks on Expended Cartridge Cases Originating from Firearm Components.

LABORATORY EXAMINATIONS OF FIREARMS EVIDENCE

- Identification of the firearm which fired an evidence bullet or an expended cartridge case.
- Muzzle-to-target distance determinations.
- Gunshot residue identifications.
- Weapon functionality examinations.
- Bullet trajectory and/or sequence of firing determinations.

COLLECTION OF FIREARMS EVIDENCE

- Most important consideration is officer safety.
- Always treat any firearm as though it is loaded!
- Unloading should be done only by an officer who knows the weapon well.
- Examine closely for fingerprints, bloodstains, or trace evidence.
- Handle the weapon by those areas unlikely to retain latent fingerprints.
- Do not mark the weapon itself (other than the index marks on the cylinder).

UNLOADING REVOLVERS

- Mark the cylinder to indicate its position as found.
- Record the position of each round in the cylinder.
- Handle cartridges/cases to preserve fingerprints.

- Package each cartridge/case in a separate package and reference to the field notes.
- Do not mark the actual cartridge or case.

UNLOADING AUTOLOADING FIREARMS (SEMIAUTOMATICS)

- Unloading should be done only by an officer who knows the weapon well.
- Examine for trace evidence and fingerprints.
- Weapons found in water.
- Transportation to the laboratory.
- Note taking and evidence marking.

RECOVERY OF FIRED AMMUNITION COMPONENTS

- Bullets embedded in wood or plaster.
- Removal of bullets from deceased persons.
- Cartridge cases.
- Shot wads.
- Shot pellets.
- Live shot shells or cartridges.

GUNSHOT RESIDUES (GSR)

- Gunshot residue analysis in the laboratory.

COLLECTION OF GUNSHOT RESIDUES

- *Caution! The subject should not be allowed to wash or rub his/her hands prior to sampling.*
- Procedure for GSR collection with metal disks.
- Procedure for GSR collection using swabs (AA analysis).

TRACE METAL DETECTION TEST

- Suspect handling (but not firing) a weapon.
- Metal transfer to the palmar surface of the hand.
- May produce a pattern distinctive for that firearm.
- Should not be done if suspicion that the subject fired a weapon.

TARGET DISCHARGE RESIDUES

- Distance determinations.

COLLECTION OF TARGET RESIDUES

- General considerations for target residues.
- Collection of target residues on clothing.
- Collection of target residues on bedding.
- Collection of target residues on solid objects.
- Collection of discharge residues on skin.

Review Questions

1. Treat all firearms as though they are _____.
2. A modern bulleted cartridge consists of the _____ _____, the _____, the _____, and the _____.
3. Most centerfire rifle cartridges have a _____ shape.
4. The class characteristics of a fired bullet consist of the caliber, the number of lands and grooves, and the direction of _____ of the rifling.
5. The lands and grooves on a fired bullet are a _____ impression of the barrel interior.
6. _____ of the firearm that fired an evidence bullet is one of the functions of the laboratory examiner.
7. On the basis of the class characteristics present on a fired bullet, the laboratory examiner may be able to provide a list of possible weapons that may have _____ the bullet.
8. Muzzle-to-target distance determinations may be helpful in the _____ of a shooting scene.
9. _____ _____ on the hands of a suspect may indicate that the suspect recently fired a weapon.
10. Prior to unloading a revolver, a _____ of the cartridge positions should be made.
11. Weapons found in water should be placed in a container with the _____ _____ for transport to the laboratory.
12. On recovered revolvers, make _____ marks on the top of the cylinder to preserve the position of each cartridge in the cylinder.
13. _____ _____ attempt to dig a bullet out of wood or plaster.
14. The _____ of fired cartridge cases may be helpful in a reconstruction of a shooting scene.
15. Gunshot residue may be found on the shooter's _____ when a rifle or shotgun has been fired.
16. As a rule, gunshot residue is not found on a shooter's hands after _____ hours.
17. For muzzle-to-target determinations, the use of _____ ammunition is essential.
18. Discharge residues on clothing should be collected by taking the _____ _____.
19. Target residues on a wall should be collected by _____ the area and _____ the area containing the residues.
20. Discharge residues on skin should be _____ to preserve the pattern.

Further References

Haag, L. C. 2006. *Shooting Incident Reconstruction*. New York, NY: Academic Press.

Jackson, A. R. W., and J. Jackson. 2004. *Forensic Science*. Essex, England, U.K.: Pearson Education Limited.

James, S. H., and J. J. Nordby, eds. 2005. *Forensic Science* (An Introduction to Scientific and Investigative Techniques), 2nd ed. Boca Raton, FL: CRC Press (Imprint of Taylor and Francis).

Saferstein, R. 2009. *Forensic Science* (From the Crime Scene to the Crime Lab). Upper Saddle River, NJ: Pearson Education, Inc.

White, P. (ed.) 1998. Crime Scene to Court (The Essentials of Forensic Science). Cambridge, U.K.: The Royal Society of Chemistry.

APPENDIX 8-A

Class Characteristics for Some Handguns and Other Firearms

KEY TO FIREARM TYPE CODES IN TABLE

PB = Bolt action pistol
PI = Semiauto pistol
B = Submachine gun or pistol
(e.g., UZI, Mauser machine pistol)
RA = Full auto rifle

RI = Semiauto rifle (e.g: M1 rifle, Ruger .44 Carbine)
RL = Lever action rifle
PD = Derringer (single shot or two barreled)

PR = Pistol, revolver
RB = Bolt action rifle
RP = Pump action rifle
PS = Single shot pistol
RC = Carbine (bbl < 20′)
RS = Single shot rifle

KEY TO TABLE COLUMN HEADERS

Cal. = Caliber
FT = Firearm Type (see firearm type codes above)
# L&G = Number of lands and grooves
TWIST = R (right) or L (left) for the rifling twist (as viewed in barrel or on fired bullet)

Note: This table is extracted from the Crime Laboratory Information System database for firearms class characteristics. The table is neither comprehensive nor exhaustive. The table is intended only for use as a rapid field guide to some of the firearms that may have fired expended bullets found at crime scenes. For complete data with respect to a recovered bullet, submit the bullet to the laboratory for laboratory examination of all class characteristics, for which the examiner can query the database for a complete list of candidate firearms.

METRIC EQUIVALENTS (CAL → MM)

.22 = 5.56 MM
.280 = 7 MM
.40 = 10 MM

.243 = 6 MM
.30 = 7.62 MM
.45 = 11.25 MM

.25 = 6.35 MM
.32 = 7.65 MM

.264 = 6.5 MM
.38 = 9 MM

CAL.	Cartridge	FT	# L&G/ Twist	Manufacturer	Model (S)
.22	22 LR	PR	5 R	H&R	PREMIER
				IVER JOHNSON	SEALED 8
				CENTURY ARMS	
		PI	6 L	COLT	HUNTSMAN, WOODSMAN
				ASTRA	2000
		RI	6 R	CHARTER ARMS	AR7
		PI	6 R	S&W	61–1
				HERBERT SCHMIDT	
				RUGER	AUTO PISTOL
				BROWNING	CHALLENGER
				BERNARDELLI	60
				HI STANDARD	103
				BERETTA	948
				UNIQUE	E1, E2, E3, D1–D3
				WALTHER	PP
				H&R	929
				COLT	
				ERMA	LA 22
		PR	6 R	H&R	SEVERAL
				HI STANDARD	SENTINEL DELUXE
				RUGER	SINGLE-SIX, BEARCAT
				REVELATION	99
				HI STANDARD	SENTINEL DELUXE
				S&W	
				HIGGINS	
				CLERKE	
				NASHVILLE ARMS	
				HIGGINS	
				IVER JOHNSON	
				TAURUS	
				GARCIA ROSSI	
				TALON	
				FIE	T-18
				REGENT	
				IMPERIAL PRODUCTS	
				UBERTI	

(continued)

CAL.	Cartridge	FT	# L&G/ Twist	Manufacturer	Model (S)
		PD	6 R	EIG	
				HAWES	
				SVENDSEN	LITTLE ACE
		PR	8 R	RG IND.	RG 14, 23, 63, 66; 10S
				BURGO	
				ROHM	RG 20, 23, 24
				DICKSON	CHEYENNE
				LIBERTY	21
				EIG	E15
				ARMINIUS	HW-5T, HW3
				VALOR	
				PIC	
				OMEGA	220
				EMGE	
				SPESCO	
				GECADO	
				TALON	
				FIEL	E15
		PD	8 R	BURGO	
		RI	8 R	MOSSBERG	SEVERAL
				REVELATION	100A
				ITHACA	72 SADDLE GUN
		PR	10 R	RG IND.	RGU2
				ROSCO	
.22	WIN MAG RF	PR	4 R	FIE	E15
			6 L	COLT	BUNTLINE SCOUT, OTHERS
			6 R	H&R	SPECIAL
				HY HUNTER	FRONTIER SIX
				HI STANDARD DM-101	FRONTIER SIX-SHOOTER
				S&W	43, 48, 51, ETC.
				RUGER	SINGLE SIX
				LLAMA	
				HI STANDARD	SENTINEL MK IV
				WESTERN	WESTERN DUO
				EIG	E15
				HERBERT SCHMIDT	21S

CAL.	Cartridge	FT	# L&G/ Twist	Manufacturer	Model (S)
		PD	6 R	HI STANDARD	DERRINGER, DM–101
				HAWES	WESTERN
		RI	6 R	REMINGTON	16
				WINCHESTER	SEVERAL
		PR	8 R	ROHM	RG 66
				ARMINIUS	HW7
				EIG	E15
				RG IND.	RG63
		PD	8 R	HY HUNTER	FRONTIER
				OMEGA	DERRINGER
.25	25 AUTO	PI	4 R	FRANZ STOCK	
				ZEHNER	
				RHEINMETALL	
				WALTHER	NO. 2
				LANGENHAN	
				KOMMER	
			5 R	H&R	SELF-LOADING
			6 L	COLT	POCKET, JUNIOR
				RAVEN	P–25
				ASTRA	ALL 25 AUTO PISTOLS
				ALLIES	
				FIE	GUARDIAN
				GABILANDO	
				STAR	1919
			6 R	LIGNOSE	EINHAND
				WALTHER	9, 8
				BROWNING	
				MAUSER	
				RHEINMETALL	
				H&R	SELF-LOADING
				WEBLEY & SCOTT	
				BERETTA	950B, 1919, BANTAM
				ORTGIES	
				BERNADELLI	
				RG IND.	RG-25

(continued)

CAL.	Cartridge	FT	# L&G/ Twist	Manufacturer	Model (S)
				FIE	TITAN
		PI	6 R	TITAN	
				BERETTA	
				WEBLEY & SCOTT	HAMMER & HAMMERLESS
				STAR	
				VALOR	
				SAUER	
				MAUSER	POCKET, 1910
				DICKSON	SPL. AGT. DETECTIVE
				RIGARMI	
			7 L	DELU	VEST POCKET
				PHOENIX	VEST POCKET
			8 R	SPESCO	PHOENIX P–51
				VALOR	SM-11
				MAUSER	EP25
			10 R	RHONER	9
	25–20 WIN		6 R	COLT	SINGLE ACTION ARMY
.30	30 LUG	PI	4 R	LUGER	P08, 1937, 1912, P08
				SWISS IND.	P210-5
				WALTHER	HP
	30 MAU	PI	4 R	RUSSIAN	
			6 R	MAUSER	
				STAR	8 SHOT
.32	32 AUTO	PI	4 R	RHEINMETALL	
				SAUER 38 H	
				FRANZ STOCK	
				WALTHER	
				STANDARD	POCKET
				FROMMER	ATTILA
				H&R	
			5 L	BRITISH	SILENCED PISTOL
		PI	5 R	BROWNING	1900
				S&W	1903
				IVER JOHNSON	1900
				SAUER	

CAL.	Cartridge	FT	# L&G/ Twist	Manufacturer	Model (S)
				THAMES	
			6 L	BAYARD	
				COLT	POCKET, COLT AUTO
				LLAMA	
				HAERENS	
				IDEAL	
				IVER JOHNSON	
				UNIQUE	
				DICKSON	SPECIAL AGENT
				ASTRA	1916
				BROWNING	1900
				SPANISH	VESTA, 191J
				RUBY	
				OTHERS	
			6 R	BROWNING	1922
				H&R	SELF-LOADING
				COLT	
				MAUSER	1914
				SAVAGE	1910
				ORTGIES	
				STAR	I
				BERETTA	70, 70 NEW PUMA
				WEBLEY & SCOTT	
				HECKLER & KOCH	HK 4
				LLAMA	X-A, ESPECIAL
				ASTRA	CONSTABLE
				SAVAGE	1917
				BERETTA	
				DICKSON	SPECIAL AGENT
				BERNADELLI	60
				WALTHER	4, PPK
				SIGARMS	
				SAUER	POCKET
				MANNLICHER	1908
				MANY OTHERS	
			7 R	REMINGTON	

(continued)

CAL.	Cartridge	FT	# L&G/ Twist	Manufacturer	Model (S)
.32	32 COLT L	PR	5 R	H&R	TOP BREAK
			6 L	COLT	ARMY SPECIAL, BISLEY POCKET POSITIVE
	32 COLT NP	PR	5 R	IVER JOHNSON	ALL 32 CAL REVOLVERS
				H&R	THE AMERICAN, 732
			6 L	COLT	SEVERAL
	32 COLT S	PR	6 L	FOREHAND	
			6 R	H&R	
	32 L	PR	5 R	S&W	RIM FIRE
			6 L	COLT	POLICE
				LEE ARMS	RED JACKET #3
			6 R	STEVENS	ALL 32 RF MODELS
				CHURCHILL	
				KIMEL	5000
			8 R	EIG	
	32 LR	PR	5 R	S&W	RIMFIRE
	32 S	PR	5 R	H&R	YOUNG AMERICAN, BULLDOG
				WESSON & HARRINGTON IVER JOHNSON	AMERICAN BULLDOG RF
			6 R	IVER JOHNSON	DEFENDER RIMFIRE
		PS	6 R	WINCHESTER	SINGLE SHOT
			6 L	COLT	AUTO
				LEE ARMS	
.32	32 S&W	PR	5 L	HOPKINS & ALLEN	
			5 R	S&W	SEVERAL
				H&R	
				EASTERN ARMS	
				MERIDIAN	
				US REVOLVER	TOP BREAK
				HOPKINS & ALLEN	
			6 L	CLERKE	FIRST
				COLT	
				FOREHAND ARMS	
			6 R	ARMINIUS	POCKET

CAL.	Cartridge	FT	# L&G/ Twist	Manufacturer	Model (S)
				HOPKINS & ALLEN	
				FIE	GUARDIAN
				H&R	732, VEST POCKET
					TOP BREAK
				FIEL	TITANIC
				KIMEL	
				HY HUNTER	
				ROHM	RG 13, RG 30
				RG IND.	30
				CHARTER ARMS	UNDERCOVER
				IVER JOHNSON	CADET 55, VIKING 67–S
			10 R	GECADO	
				ARMINIUS	
				EMGE	
				BURGO	
				DICKSON	BULLDOG
				OMEGA	
32	**S&W L**	PR	5 R	S&W	SEVERAL
				LLAMA	
7.62 MM	**7.62 3 39 MM**	RI	4 R	CHINESE	AK 47, AKM 47S, AKS
				GUISASOLA	
				OSCILLANTE	
				MERWIN & HURBERT	
				H&R INA	THE AMERICAN TIGER
				IVER JOHNSON	
				H&R	
				ALFA	
			PR	6 L	COLT	MANY
				FOREHAND	
			6 R	FIE	TITANIC, GUARDIAN
				KIMEL	5000
				FIEL	TITANIC
				H&R	SEVERAL
				IVER JOHNSON	SEVERAL
				EIG	
				HOPKINS & ALLEN	DOUBLE ACTION #6

(continued)

CAL.	Cartridge	FT	# L&G/ Twist	Manufacturer	Model (S)
			7 R	WEBLEY & SCOTT	POCKET
			8 R	ROHM	RG–63
				ARMINIUS	HW3, HW5
				PIC	
				EMGE	
				MAUSER	
				RG IND.	RG 30
				ROHM	30
				CHARTER ARMS	
				OMEGA	
			10 R	BURGO	
				HAWES	
				EMGE	
				FAB-BOWER	
				GECADO	
				ARMINIUS	
32–20	WIN	PR	5 R	S&W	M&P, M&P TARGET
				ALFA	
			6 R	EL CANO	
				GALEF	REFORMER
			6 L	COLT	SEVERAL
				CLAIR	
7.62 MM	7.62 3 39 MM	RI	4 R	CHINESE	AK 47, AKM 47S, AKS
				RUSSIAN	RPD, SKS ASSAULT, AK–47
	7.62 MM NAGANT	PR	4 R	RUSSIAN	NAGANT 1919, 1931
				RADOM	NG30
7.63 MM	7.63 MM MAU	PI	4 R	CZECH	52, ISSUR
			6 L	STAR	
			6 R	MAUSER	712
				ASTRA	902
7.65 MM	7.65 MM LUG	PI	4 R	SWISS IND.	P-210–6
				LUGER	
			6 R	SCHULTZ	
	7.65 MM MAS	PI	4 R	FRENCH	1935S
				MAS	1935
.35	S&W AUTO	PI	6 R	S&W	1913

CAL.	Cartridge	FT	# L&G/ Twist	Manufacturer	Model (S)
8 MM	**NAMBU**	PI	6 R	NAMBU	
.357	**357 MAX**	PR	6 R	DAN WESSON	SUPER MAG
	357 MAG	PR	5 R	S&W	MANY
				IMI	DESERT EAGLE
				RUGER	SEVERAL
			6 L	COLT	PYTHON, TROOPER, OTHERS
				SECURITY IND.	POLICE POCKET
			6 R	BUFFALO ARMS	
				COLT	LAWMAN MK III
				HAWES	WESTERN MARSHAL
				SAUER	
				DAN WESSON	
				HI STANDARD	SENTINEL MKII
				RUGER	BLACKHAWK
				HY HUNTER	WESTERN SIX-SHOOTER
				INTERCONTINENTAL	
				ASTRA	
				HERTERIS	SINGLE SIX
				LLAMA	COMANCHE III
		PR	8 R	CHARTER ARMS	TARGET BULLDOG
				RUGER	BLACKHAWK
				ROHM	57
		PS	6 R	THOMPSON	CONTENDER
		PX	8 R	COP, INC.	4 BARREL DERRINGER
		PD	10 R	HERTERIS	WESTERN DERRINGER
				HAWES	WESTERN DERRINGER
.38	**.38 L CLT**	PR	5 R	S&W	1899 ARMY
				SPANISH	
				GABILANDO	RUBY EXTRA
				GUISASOLA	
				ALFA	
			6 L	COLT	DA FRONTIER, 1892
			6 R	ALFA	
	38 S CLT	PR	5 R	H&R	
			6 R	IVER JOHNSON	

(continued)

CAL.	Cartridge	FT	# L&G/ Twist	Manufacturer	Model (S)
	38 CLT NP	PR	5 R	H&R	
			6 L	COLT	POLICE POSITIVE
	38–40 WIN	PR	5 R	S&W	38–40
			6 L	COLT	FRONTIER, NEW SERVICE
	38 S&W	PR	5 L	HOPKINS & ALLEN	
			5 R	S&W	SEVERAL
				H&R	SEVERAL
				US REVOLVER	
				HOLLIS	
				IVER JOHNSON	AMERICAN BULLDOG
			6 L	COLT	POLICE POSITIVE
					BANKER'S SPECIAL
				FRANZ STOCK	
				FOREHAND	
			6 R	H&R	925, 926, TOP BREAK
				HOPKINGS & ALLEN	
		PR	7 R	BRITISH	
				WEBLEY	MK I NO. 2
				ENFIELD	MARK I
				WEBLEY & SCOTT	GOVT. MK IV. 38
			8 R	RG IND.	RG 40
	38 S&W L	PR	4 R	HUSQVARNA	1887
	38 SPL	PR	5 R	S&W	MANY
				ARIZAGA	DREADNOUGHT
				INA	TIGER, NO. 1, 3
				ALFA	
				ALAMO	RANGER
		PR	5 R	ERRASTI	
				IRIS ORBEA	
				RUGER	SPEED SIX
				LLAMA	
		PR	6 L	COLT	MANY
				MIROKU	
				REGENT	
				GARATE ARITUA	
				EIG	SPECIAL POLICE

CAL.	Cartridge	FT	# L&G/ Twist	Manufacturer	Model (S)
			6 R	GREAT WESTERN	
				EIG	
				ROHM	RG 38
				DAN WESSON	
				ASTRA	CADIX
				TAURUS	
				GARCIA ROSSI	
			8 R	ARMINIUS	TITAN TIGER
				FIEL	TITAN TIGER
				FIE	TITAN TROJAN
				CHARTER ARMS	
				ROHM	RG–38S
		PR	8 R	RG IND.	RG 38
				BURGO	
				DICKSON	COMMANDER
				TITAN	TIGER
			10 R	ARMINIUS	TITAN TIGER
				FIEL	
		PD	5 R	ROHM	DERRINGER
			6 L	EIG	
			6 R	FIE	DERRINGER
				EIG	
				HY HUNTER	
				INTRATEC	TEC–38 (DERRINGER)
			10 R	OMEGA	DERRINGER
				MADISON IMPORT	
				ROHM	RG–17
				BURGO	DERRINGER
				MISSISSIPPI VALLEY	
	38 AUTO	PI	6 L	COLT	AUTO, 1902 MILITARY COMMANDER, 38, OTHERS
				SHATTUCK	BCF–66
				STAR	SUPER
				LLAMA	IV, V
			6 R	BERETTA	1934
				ASTRA	1921–400

(continued)

CAL.	Cartridge	FT	# L&G/ Twist	Manufacturer	Model (S)
380 AUTO		PI	4 R	FROMMER	29M, 37M
			5 R	S&W	VICTORY
			6 L	UNIQUE	BCF 66
				COLT	1908, COMMANDER, OTHERS
				LLAMA	II, III
		PI	6 R	H&R	HK4
				FBN	
				INDIAN SALES	
				RPB IND.	
				TANFOGLIO	
				IVER JOHNSON	PONY
				HUSQVARNA	M–07
				BROWNING	
				HANDY	
				BERETTA	1934, 70S
				BERNARDELLI 60	
				CESKA-CZ	
				ASTRA	
				STAR	STARFIRE
				WALTHER	PPK
				LLAMA	III–A
				MAUSER	HSC
				FIEL	MODEL D
				HECKLER & KOCH	HK4
				HI STANDARD G380	
				STERLING	DA
			7 R	REMINGTON	51 UMC
			8 R	ARCADIA	
9 MM	**BAYARD**	PI	6 R	ASTRA	1921 400
	9MM LUGER	PI	4 R	FROMMER	37, 37M
		B	4 R	BROWNING	UZI
		B	4 L	MAT	MAT 49
		PI	4 L	FRENCH	1950
		BA	4 R	UZI	
		PI	4 R	MANNLICHER	1914
				FROMMER	37M

CAL.	Cartridge	FT	# L&G/ Twist	Manufacturer	Model (S)
		PI	5 R	S&W	39–2
		PI	6 L	BAYARD	1914
				COLT	COMMANDER
				ASTRA	800 CONDOR
		PI	6 R	SIGARMS	P225, P226
				BROWNING	HI-POWER, 1903
				BERETTA	1951
				WALTHER	P-38
				ASTRA	600 M&P, 1921, 400, CONDOR
				LLAMA	III A, SPECIAL
				STAR (Sp)	
				LUGER	
				SWISS IND.	47/8
				RADOM	35, WZ/35
				GLOCK	17
				INTRATEC	TEC–9, TEC–9M, TEC–9B
				HECKLER & KOCH	HK-4
				MAUSER	1912
				BERETTA	1934, 1938A
				J&R ENGINEERING	M–68
		B	6 R	STEN	MK II
				HECKLER & KOCH	HK MP5
				S&W	76
				UZI	
		PS	6 R	THOMPSON	CONTENDER
	9MM REV	PR	4 R	JAPANESE	26
	9MM STEYR	PI	4 R	AUSTRIAN	1916
.41	41 L	PR	6 L	COLT	LIGHTNING
			6 R	RUGER	BLACKHAWK
	41 L CLT	PR	6 L	COLT	FRONTIER, DA
	41 MAG	PR	5 R	S&W	57, 58
			6 R	RUGER	BLACKHAWK
				INTERCONTINENTAL	SUPER DAKOTA
.44	44–40 WIN	PR	5 R	S&W	44–40
			6 L	COLT	

(continued)

CAL.	Cartridge	FT	# L&G/ Twist	Manufacturer	Model (S)
	44 COLT	PR	7 R	REPLICA	
	44 MAG	PR	5 R	S&W	29–2, 58, 44 MAGNUM
			6 L	SAUER	
			6 R	RUGER	SEVERAL
				HY HUNTER	WESTERN SIX-SHOOTER
				HAWES	WESTERN MARSHAL
				INTERCONTINENTAL	SUPER DAKOTA
				SAUER	WESTERN MARSHAL SA
		PS	6 R	STERLING ARMS	X-CALIBER
		PS	8 L	THOMPSON	CONTENDER
		RC	6 R	RUGER	CARBINE
		RC	12 R	RUGER	CARBINE
		RL	12 R	MARLIN	1894
				WINCHESTER	94
	44 S&W SPL	PR	5 R	S&W	24 TARGET, 44 MIL., 21 MIL.
			6 L	COLT	NEW SERVICE TARGET
			6 R	HAWES	WESTERN MARSHAL
			8 R	CHARTER ARMS	BULLDOG, BULLDOG 44 SPL
.45	**45 AUTO**	B	4 R	US MIL. WEAP	M3, M3A1
				EAGLE ARMS	MARK 2
			6 R	AUTO ORD.	MIAI THOMPSON
				US MIL WEAP	1928A–1
		PI	4 R	EAGLE GUN	
		PI	6 L	SIGARMS	P220
				US MIL. WEAP	1911, 1911 A1
				COLT	1911, GOVT. MODEL
				LLAMA	
				INGRAM	
				STAR	
				SPITFIRE	
				WESCO	MK IV
		BA	6 L	UZI	45 AUTO
		PI	6 R	LLAMA	ESPECIAL

CAL.	Cartridge	FT	# L&G/ Twist	Manufacturer	Model (S)
				INGRAM	
				STAR	
				SAVAGE	
		PR	7 R	WEBLEY	MARK I
		RC		MARLIN	M2
				EAGLE ARMS	
			6 R	VOLUNTEER	COMMANDO MK III
45 AUTO RIM		PR	6 R	S&W	US ARMY 1917
45 COLT		PR	6 L	COLT	1909 DA, NEW SERVICE SA ARMY, USN DA
			6 R	RUGER	
				S&W	1917, US ARMY 9464
				RUGER	BLACKHAWK
				INTERCONTINENTAL	DAKOTA
			7 R	ENG/BRITISH	
		PS	8 L	THOMPSON	CONTENDER
455 WEB AUTO		PI	6 L	COLT	
			6 R	WEBLEY & SCOTT	
455 WEB MK II		PR	7 R	WEBLEY & SCOTT	BULLDOG, MK I–MK VI
				ENG/BRITISH	MK VI

9 IMPRESSION EVIDENCE

Here is my monograph upon the tracing of footsteps, with some remarks upon the uses of plaster of Paris as a preserver of impresses.

Sherlock Holmes,
The Sign of Four,
Sir Arthur Conan Doyle.

Key Words: Indented impressions, impressed prints, transfer prints, imprints, residue prints, striated impressions, footwear impressions, tire tread impressions, photography, casting, paint transfers, toolmarks, orientation photographs, toolmark cast.

INTRODUCTION

Impression evidence consists of those imprints left in or on a receiving surface by an object. Impressions consist of **indented impressions** (**impressed prints** or *compression marks*) made in a softer surface by an object, such as those made by footwear in soft soil; and of residue **transfer prints** (also called "**imprints**"), which are the result of the transfer of a residue from the surface of an object to a receiving surface ("hard surface impressions"), such as those made by the transfer of soil on a shoe sole to a floor.[1] A residue transfer print may also be the result of removal of a substance from a surface by contact with the object, as in the transfer of blood to a shoe sole, which leaves an imprint of the sole where blood has been removed from the surface. Although technically not "impressions," **residue prints** are commonly referred to as impressions in most publications in the fields of crime scene investigation and forensic science, and therefore will be referred to in the same manner in this text, except where clarity requires the more specific term "residue prints."

The most common types of impressions encountered at crime scenes consist of footwear impressions, toolmarks, tire tread impressions, and latent fingerprint impressions. Latent fingerprint impressions are treated separately in Chapter 5 because of the stature and complexity of this type of impression. Footwear and tire tread impressions consist of both impressed prints and residue prints, whereas tool impressions usually consist of impressed prints that may be an impression of the shape of the tool or of **striated impressions** (also called "striated marks" or "scraping marks") produced by the *scraping* of the tool's working surface against the receiving surface. The examination of features in the impression may allow the analyst to identify or exclude the suspect item as having made the impression in question. The evidentiary value of a toolmark comparison usually depends heavily upon the quality of the impression and the caliber of the manner in which the impression was recorded by photography and/or by casting.

LABORATORY EXAMINATIONS OF IMPRESSION EVIDENCE

Examination of footwear impressions

The laboratory examination of **footwear impressions** involves (1) the determination of class characteristics for investigative purposes and (2) the comparison of the questioned impression with test impressions made with a known item of footwear suspected of being the source of the questioned impression. The laboratory analyst may be able to determine the class characteristics of the footwear on the basis of an examination of the photographs and casts from the scene. This information may assist the investigators in the search for a particular type and size of shoe in the suspect's possession. The comparison of the questioned impression with the suspect shoes may be made by a direct comparison of the questioned impression with the soles of the submitted footwear or the comparison may be made with a test impression prepared from the submitted shoes. The comparison of the questioned impression with the known footwear involves a comparison of the class characteristics and the individual characteristics of the shoe soles. The class characteristics of shoe soles include the size, wear pattern, and surface pattern of the sole. The individual characteristics are those features of the sole that are the result of accidental damage to the surface of the sole, such as cuts, tears, and cavities produced by random damage to the sole. Wear patterns are intermediate between class characteristics and individual characteristics because of the somewhat individual nature of the wearer's walking pattern.

The examination and comparison of footwear impression casts is illustrated in Figure 9-1. The class characteristics are seen to agree, so the examiner searches for

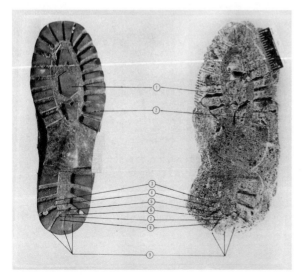

FIGURE 9-1   Comparison of an Evidence Footwear Impression Cast with a Known Shoe
Courtesy of the Department of the Sheriff-Coroner, Contra Costa County, California.

individualizing characteristics in the known footwear, such as accidental damage to the sole during wearing of the shoe. Any individual characteristics found in the known footwear are then searched for in the questioned cast (see Figure 9-1). If a sufficient number of individualizing characteristics are found in the unknown (evidence cast) that agree with those in the cast from the known (suspect shoe), and the class characteristics of the two agree, the examiner can conclude that the unknown footwear impression was made by the known footwear submitted for examination. These casts were produced with plaster of paris, which produces casts with adequate detail for comparison purposes, but is largely being replaced with dental stone as the preferred material for making casts of footwear impressions (see the section "Casting and Lighting of Impressions").

CASE EXAMPLE

In an unusual case investigated by the Contra Costa County, California, of the Sheriff-Coroner's Criminalistics Laboratory, the footwear involved in the case was a pair of socks. In that case, a community college instructor was suspected of beating his wife to death. The suspect claimed that the injuries on the victim were a result of accidents she had while intoxicated. Among the many injuries on the victim, one had a pattern suggestive of being produced by socks worn on a foot (see Figure 9-2). Criminalist

John Murdock made a number of test impressions using the socks seized from the suspect. Comparison of the impression on the victim's back with the test impressions made with the socks (see Figure 9-3) demonstrated good agreement in the patterns produced by the socks. Criminalist Murdock was able to conclude that the impression on the victim's back was consistent with her being kicked by an individual wearing the pair of socks. ▪

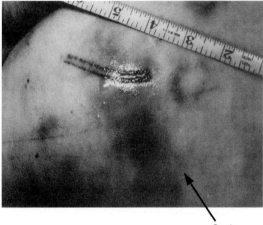

Sock impression

FIGURE 9-2 Impression Marks on the Back of the Victim
Courtesy of the Department of the Sheriff-Coroner, Contra Costa County, California.

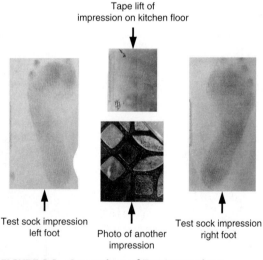

Tape lift of impression on kitchen floor

Test sock impression left foot

Photo of another impression

Test sock impression right foot

FIGURE 9-3 Comparison of Test Impressions Made with the Suspect's Socks with the Impression on the Victim's Back
Courtesy of the Department of the Sheriff-Coroner, Contra Costa County, California.

Examination of tire tread impressions

The laboratory examination of **tire tread impressions** is similar in most respects to the examination of footwear impressions. The laboratory analyst may examine the questioned tread impressions for class characteristics before a suspect vehicle is located. The examination involves the determination of the tread pattern and comparison of the pattern with specimens of known manufacture or with published materials that illustrate the tread patterns of domestic and foreign manufactured tires. If the suspect vehicle has been seized, the laboratory analyst can compare the impression photographs and casts directly with the seized vehicle's tires or with exemplar impressions made from the known tires. As in the case of footwear impressions, the analyst compares the wear pattern and the tread characteristics found in the questioned impression with the tread pattern of the submitted tires to ascertain whether they are in agreement. If these class characteristics agree, the analyst then compares any individual characteristics found on the treads for agreement. Individual tire tread characteristics, as in the case of footwear, are the result of accidental damage to the tire tread during use, and include tears, cuts, and punctures.

Examination of toolmark impressions

INDENTED IMPRESSIONS

The examination of indented toolmarks involves the comparison of the class characteristics of the tool (shape, size) with those in the impression. The comparison of class characteristics allows the analyst to exclude rapidly those tools that have class characteristics that differ from those of the tool responsible for the toolmark. For example, a pry bar with a one-inch-wide blade could not have made an impression that has a width of one-and-one-half inches. If the class characteristics in the toolmark match the class characteristics of the suspected tool, the analyst then searches the toolmark for individual characteristics, such as the uneven edge of the blade, for comparison with matching characteristics on the suspect tool. If there are a sufficient number of these individualizing characteristics in the toolmark that match the suspect tool, the analyst can identify that tool as the one responsible for making the toolmark.

STRIATED IMPRESSIONS

Striated impressions are typically more difficult to individualize than are the indented impressions. When preparing test toolmarks, the analyst needs to orient the suspect tool in the same spatial relationship to the receiving surface as that which was in effect when the questioned toolmark was made. Alterations in the angle of the tool with respect to the receiving surface can produce striations that differ from those of the questioned toolmark, even though both were made by the same tool. This is the reason that it is important for the crime scene investigator to prepare sketches of a toolmark that show the likeliest orientation of the tool when it produced the questioned toolmark.

Striated toolmark impressions are frequently created when the working surface of a tool slides across the surface of the object to which it is being applied (see Figure 9-4). Normal wear and accidental damage to the working surface of the tool

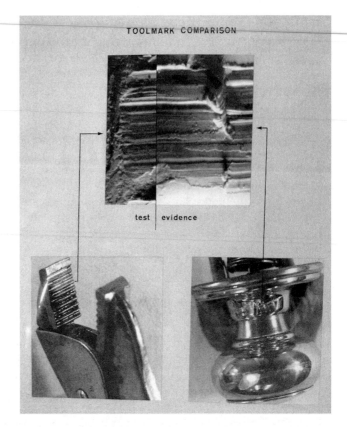

TOOLMARK COMPARISON

test | evidence

FIGURE 9-4 Comparison of Silicone Cast of Toolmark on Doorknob with Silicone Cast of Test Mark Made with Suspect Tool
Courtesy of Department of the Sheriff-Coroner, Contra Costa County, California.

produces individuality to the tool, which is then transferred to the toolmark in the surface attacked through the slippage of the tool as force is being applied. The tool responsible for the toolmark is identified by preparing a test mark with the suspect tool, and comparing the evidence toolmark (or a silicone cast of the toolmark) with the test mark made with the tool (or a silicone cast of the test mark), as shown in Figure 9-4.

CASE EXAMPLE

In some cases, the "tool" producing a toolmark may not be a tool in the normal sense of the word, but any hard object, when contacting another object, may produce a mark that is comparable to indented or striated marks produced by a tool. The author was called to assist in a burglary case, where the burglars stole an iron safe from a residence where the occupants were home at the time. The burglars tossed the safe into the bed of their pickup truck and fled the scene. The police were called and gave chase, but the burglars initially eluded the police patrol units. When the patrol units finally stopped the burglars' pickup, they had dumped the safe along the escape route. When the officers recovered the safe, this author was requested to obtain evidence that the safe had been in the pickup bed. Several dents with striated markings were observed in the walls of

(*continued*)

(*continued*)

the pickup bed, and silicone casts of the striated marks were prepared (see Figure 9-5).

Once the safe was delivered to the laboratory, test marks were made of each of the corners of the safe using paraffin blocks (wax blocks made for canning purposes). Silicone casts were prepared of the resultant test marks and the casts were compared to the casts of the marks from the pickup bed. The comparison revealed sufficient agreement in the striated marks to establish that the mark in the pickup bed was made by that particular safe (see Figure 9-6). ■

Cast of test impression of safe corner

Cast from pickup bed

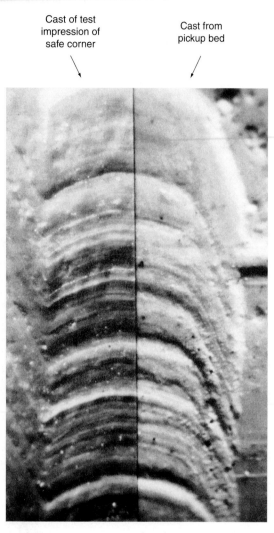

Cast of impression from pickup bed

FIGURE 9-5   Cast of Impression from Pickup Bed

FIGURE 9-6   Comparison of Toolmark Cast from Pickup Bed with Cast of Test Impression of Safe Corner

COLLECTION OF IMPRESSION EVIDENCE[2]

Collection of footwear and tire tread impressions

The collection and preservation of both footwear and tire tread impressions entails the same techniques: **photography** and **casting** of the impressions. All impressions should be recorded in the field notes, sketched, and photographed prior to any attempts to cast the impressions. The sketches of the location of the impression will aid the laboratory analyst in attempts to produce test impressions in a manner that resembles as closely as feasible the manner in which the questioned impressions were made. This is an important step in the laboratory comparison of impression evidence, since a slight difference in the manner in which the test impressions are produced may preclude a conclusive result from the comparison. The photographs and sketches assist in this laboratory effort and also provide a solid foundation for the investigator's courtroom presentation of the crime scene evidence (in conjunction with the investigator's notes and report).

Photography of footwear and tire tread impressions

Adequate photography of footwear and tire tread impressions requires that the investigator takes both midrange and close-up photographs. These photographs will document the location and orientation of the impressions, thereby assisting the laboratory analyst in the examination of the impression evidence.

- Midrange photographs.

    Take midrange photographs of the impressions, showing the impressions in relation to other features of the scene. These photographs help the laboratory analyst orient the test impressions.
- Close-up photographs.

    Close-up photographs are needed to record as much detail of the impressions as possible. Impressions should be photographed from directly overhead so that the film plane is parallel to the plane of the impression (i.e., "normal" to the surface bearing the impression). A tripod is essential for the close-up photographs in order to assure that the film plane is parallel to the impression surface and to allow for critical focussing. Use oblique lighting from at least two directions 90 degrees to each other (see Figure 9-7). The best angle for placement of the flash unit can be estimated by shining a strong light or flashlight at various angles until the maximum contrast is seen in the impression. It may be necessary to provide strong shade for the area being photographed or to wait until dusk so that the oblique lighting will show the details properly. Although good comparisons can be made from 35-mm enlargements, the larger the film size, the better. If instant photographs are made, they should be made

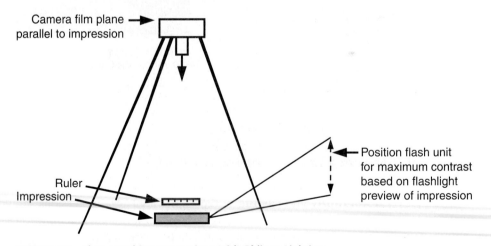

FIGURE 9-7   Photographing Impressions with Oblique Lighting

with positive/negative film. Always photograph each impression with and without a solid measurement scale or ruler lying next to and parallel with it. Without a scale, a photograph loses its value as identifying evidence. When possible, the ruler should be depressed into the adjacent surface until it is at the same level as the actual impression. Submit all photographs and negatives to the laboratory so that blowup photographs with a one-to-one ratio to the impression can be made.

When a footwear impression is two dimensional, a cast of the impression cannot be made, but properly taken photographs can provide sufficient detail of the impression to effect an identification of the footwear responsible for making the impression. Figure 9-8 demonstrates the comparison of the individual characteristics of an inked test impression of the suspect shoe with those of the questioned impression at the scene. Note that the class characteristics (size, sole tread pattern) of the questioned impression, in addition to the individual characteristics, agree with those of the inked impression of the suspect shoe.

If the impression is a continuous tire print, place a solid tape measure parallel to the print (do not use a cloth tape). Take overlapping photographs of at least eight feet of the print (approximately one revolution of the tire). The photographs should be referenced to the field notes and documented in the sketches in order to record their continuity.

Vehicle wheelbase and width measurements

When taking measurements of tire tracks, the wheelbase and front and rear wheel widths should be taken in those instances in which both sides of the vehicle's tires leave impressions. Figure 9-9 illustrates the measurements for the wheelbase and wheel widths that may be taken.

Inked left shoe test print   Photograph of print at scene

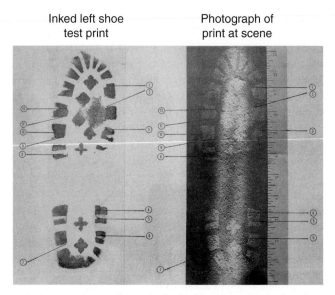

FIGURE 9-8 Comparison of Inked Impression of Left Shoe from Suspect with Photograph of Questioned Impression at Crime Scene
Courtesy of the Department of the Sheriff-Coroner, Contra Costa County, California.

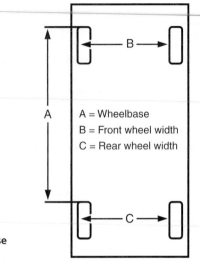

FIGURE 9-9 Tire Track Wheelbase and Wheel Width Measurements

A = Wheelbase
B = Front wheel width
C = Rear wheel width

Casting and lifting of impressions

LIFTING OF RESIDUE IMPRESSIONS

Once the sketches and photographs are completed for residue prints, the object bearing the impression should be collected for transmittal to the laboratory. The residue print should be protected by covering with latent lift tape or by building a tent over the impression with cardboard and tape. If the object bearing the imprint cannot be removed, the residue print can be lifted using lifting materials specifically designed for this task. If possible, avoid using makeshift print lifting materials, such as cellophane tape, rubber fingerprint lifters, and contact paper. Instead, use a quality print lifting material large enough to lift the entire impression such as the "HANDPRINT" lifter. Carefully place the lifting material over the impression from one end to the other. Using a clean fingerprint roller will make this step easier and will help eliminate trapped air bubbles. If a clear lifting material such as fingerprint tape is used, it should be transferred to white paper, again using a roller to eliminate air bubbles. Dust impressions should not be dusted with latent fingerprint powder, since dusting will most likely destroy the impression.

Because dusting residue impressions with latent fingerprint powder is usually unpredictable, it is not generally recommended. However, it may be worth trying as a last resort in cases in which the item with the impression cannot be submitted to the laboratory and the evidence would be "cleaned up" anyway. One particular situation in which dusting with latent fingerprint powder is occasionally successful is that in which a wet shoe comes in contact with a waxed surface. If a shoe impression is developed or enhanced with the powder, it can be rephotographed and then lifted as previously described.

If the residue print is composed of dust, the use of an electrostatic dust print lifter can be used to collect the impression. This technique involves placing the lifting film over the area to be processed, then charging the lifting film with the probe of the instrument. The dust is transferred to the film by electrostatic attraction. The film is then collected and preserved for examination in the laboratory. Figure 9-10 illustrates an electrostatic lifter of the type used to lift dust impressions. A dust impression lifted by an electrostatic lifter is also illustrated.

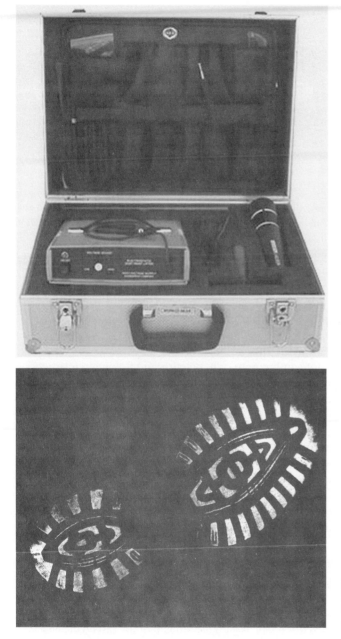

FIGURE 9-10 Electrostatic Lifter and Impression Lifted with an Electrostatic Lifter
Courtesy of Kinderprint Company, Inc.

CASTING OF FOOTWEAR AND TIRE IMPRESSIONS

Of the methods of recording impressions available to the investigator, only casting can capture three-dimensional surfaces with the detail needed for comparison in the laboratory. As an additional benefit, trace evidence may adhere to the surface of the casting material. In this respect, casting often collects evidence that would otherwise go unpreserved (e.g., soil on a plaster cast of a footprint). Inspect the impression for sticks, stones, and leaves that have fallen loosely into the impression after it was made.

FIGURE 9-11 Casting Frames for Footwear and Other Impressions Courtesy of Lightning Powder Company, an Armor Holdings Product Division.

Carefully pick out such debris with tweezers. Any debris that was pressed into the soil with the impression should not be disturbed but rather left in the impression, since removal may disturb the impression. Small amounts of standing water may be removed with a small eyedropper.

When preparing a cast using plaster of paris, it is advisable to place a dam around the impression to be casted. The dam can be constructed of materials such as tree branches, wood slats, etc., but the use of commercially prepared casting frames (see Figure 9-11) is simpler and more efficient. When preparing a cast using dental stone, it is normally not necessary to use a dam or casting frame, but the practice is not discouraged.

CASTING MATERIALS FOR FOOTWEAR AND TIRE IMPRESSIONS

The methods of casting are very simple and require only practice and following instructions for the preparation of the casting medium. The two materials used widely for casting of footwear and tire impressions are plaster of paris and dental stone. Dental stone may produce finer detail than plaster of paris and is generally a stronger material once it is set. Either method will produce casts of sufficient quality for laboratory comparisons. The crime scene investigator will need to be proficient in the use of the particular method chosen prior to any attempt to cast impressions in a case. Instructions are given here for plaster of paris casting. For casting with dental stone, the investigator should follow carefully the instructions for the particular dental casting stone material acquired for casting impressions.

Hilderbrand prepared a table with instructions for preparing a cast based on the conditions of the medium in which the impression was produced (see Table 9-1).[3] The media covered in the table includes wet soil, mud, dry soil, sand, water covered, and snow.

TABLE 9-1	Impression Impression Media and Casting Procedures*
Media	**Casting Procedures**
WET SOIL of a fine, even consistency will produce an impression with a high degree of detail.	1. Sprinkle a small amount of the casting material** over the impression to absorb excess water. 2. Mix and pour as normal. 3. Accelerator*** may be needed. 4. Drying time 45–60 minutes.
MUD of a fine, even consistency will produce an impression with a high degree of detail.	1. Mix and pour as normal. 2. Drying time depends on water content of mud; 45–60 minutes.

(continued)

Media	Casting Procedures
DRY SOIL of a consistency of talcum powder will retain detail to a varying degree.	1. Carefully spray impression with pump hair spray. 2. Spray paint may be used to harden and highlight the impression. 3. Mix and pour as normal. 4. Drying time 20–30 minutes.
DRY SOIL with a hard packed consistency will retain detail to a varying degree.	1. Spray impression with pump hair spray. 2. Mix and pour as normal. 3. Drying time 20–30 minutes.
SAND will vary in texture and consistency, and will retain varying detail.	1. Spray the impression with pump hair spray. 2. Spray paint may be used to harden and highlight the impression. 3. Mix and pour as normal. 4. Drying time 20–30 minutes.

WHEN IMPRESSION IS IN WATER

WATER impressions vary in texture and consistency. Detail depends on the amount of water present and the amount of pressure applied to the ground. Time consuming process.	1. Build form around the impression, if needed, to control water and remove excess water if possible. 2. Sprinkle a small amount of the casting material over impression until covered. 3. Mix and pour as normal. 4. Accelerator can be added. 5. Drying will vary from 60–120 minutes.

WHEN WATER IS IN IMPRESSION

Detail depends on the amount of pressure applied to the impression by the water.	1. Sprinkle a small amount of the casting material over the impression until covered. 2. Mix and pour as normal. 3. Accelerator may be added. 4. Drying time will vary from 60–90 minutes, depending on amount of water present.

WHEN IMPRESSION IS IN SNOW

SNOW varies in texture, cohesiveness, and impression detail retention with temperature. Excellent detail can be reproduced if care is exercised.	1. Use Snow Print Wax, if possible. 2. Sprinkle a small amount of talcum powder over the impression. 3. Spray with black or gray spray paint. 4. Accelerator may be added. 5. Pour as normal. 6. Drying time will vary from 60–90 minutes and may be longer, depending on outside temperature.

*Instructions are for Traxtone casting material. If other casting material is used, follow the instructions for that casting material.

**Note: Do not take the casting material that is used for sprinkling from the original 1.5 pound bag.

**ACCELERATOR = Potassium Sulfate.

Source: Dwayne Hilderbrand, *Techniques in Preparing a Cast* (Scottsdale, AZ: R & P Enterprises, 1995). Courtesy of Dwayne Hilderbrand. Copyright © 1995 R&P Enterprises, with permission.

CASTING IMPRESSIONS WITH PLASTER OF PARIS

1. Preparation of the impression.

Surround the impression to be cast with a retaining frame designed for this purpose. The use of retaining frames more than two inches tall interferes with the pouring of the plaster and should be avoided. Properly mixed plaster should not need dams to hold it, because the retaining frames will hold the plaster. Twigs or other support should be found to strengthen the cast prior to mixing the plaster, or have commercially acquired dowels on hand for this purpose.

2. Mixing the plaster.

To prepare the plaster mix, use a two-pound coffee can or equivalent-size container and fill it approximately one-third with water. Add the plaster slowly while mixing slowly with a paddle to avoid lumps or bubbles. As the mix reaches the approximate consistency of pancake batter, the side of the can may be tapped to free bubbles that might obscure details in the cast. These materials should be mixed very near the imprint site. A mix too thick will harden quickly, often in the container. A typical footprint cast will consume four pounds of plaster, a quart of water, and thirty minutes of time.

3. Pouring the plaster mix into the impression.

A "baffle" consisting of a paper-covered clipboard, strong cardboard, or a large putty spatula should be placed about two inches above the imprint and tipped to a shallow angle. The plaster mixture is then poured onto the top of the baffle to provide a uniform flow into the imprint, avoiding any irregularities or "waves" in the plaster (see Figure 9-12). Once the first pour is firm, the twigs or wooden dowels carried for this purpose should be laid onto its surface. The second batch of plaster should then be prepared and the strengthening plaster layer poured onto the first cast. Once the top layer has firmed, identifying data may be scratched into the surface with a dowel or other device.

PACKAGING OF PLASTER CASTS

Allow to air-dry thoroughly for twenty-four to forty-eight hours or longer if necessary. No attempt should be made to remove soil or to clean the casts, because this action will most likely destroy the impression. Also, the soil adhering to the casts may be used by the laboratory analyst as a comparison standard for any soil found on the suspect's shoes. Each cast should be loosely and individually wrapped in paper or a paper bag (do not wrap or

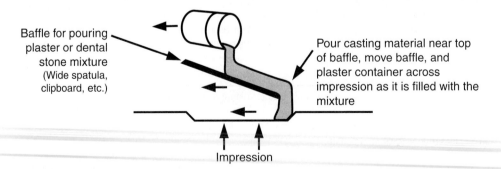

Baffle for pouring plaster or dental stone mixture (Wide spatula, clipboard, etc.)

Pour casting material near top of baffle, move baffle, and plaster container across impression as it is filled with the mixture

Impression

FIGURE 9-12   Pouring Casting Material into the Impression

place in plastic). Package the wrapped cast in a cardboard box and tape seal. The cast should then be wrapped in shock absorbent or porous packaging material that does not exclude air if the casts need to be shipped or mailed.

CASTING WITH DENTAL STONE

Hilderbrand and Miller studied the efficacy of plaster of paris, die stones, and dental stones in preparing casts of footwear and tire tread impressions.[4] They concluded that, with the exception of plaster of paris, all the stone materials are excellent substances for casting footwear/tire tread impressions. Their study found that all the stone casting materials were superior with regard to strength (which obviates the need for a form for the cast or the need for reinforcing materials in the cast), are more durable, much easier to clean, and have superior detail reproduction.[5] Based on the results of their study, it is clear that the use of plaster of paris should be replaced by using die stone or dental stone in the preparation of footwear/tire tread impressions. It is therefore advisable that any department using plaster of paris for these impressions should convert to die stone or dental stone casting material.

Each of the commercial die stones and dental stones has its own directions for preparation of the casting material. It is important that these directions be followed in preparing a cast, since deviation from the directions may result in an inferior or unusable cast, and the impression will be altered to the extent that it cannot be re-cast, thereby losing valuable evidence. Figure 9-13 illustrates one of the commercially available die stone casting products.

CASTING IN SNOW, WATER, OR DUST

By using the previously outlined process, it is possible to collect casts of impressions in dust, from underwater, and from snow. For underwater prints, excess water should be drained

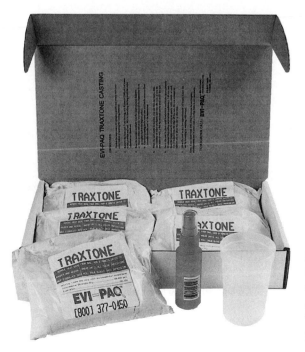

FIGURE 9-13 Traxtone Casting Material

Courtesy of Lightning Powder Company, an Armor Holdings, Inc. Product Division. Traxtone™ is a trademark of Lightning Powder Company.

away or removed with a pipet or syringe before adding the plaster mix. If water cannot be drained away or removed from the impression, dry plaster can be gently sifted into the water above the impression. The plaster sinks to the bottom and gradually builds up until all the water is saturated with plaster. Additional plaster mix can then be added to attain an adequate thickness. The plaster should be allowed to set for at least two hours before removal.

For impressions in snow, the application of a specialty product called Snow Print Wax, before adding the plaster mix, has produced excellent results. The impression in snow is first sprayed with two to three layers of the Snow Print Wax and allowed to dry for about ten minutes. Figure 9-14 illustrates a cast being prepared in snow using Snow Print Wax and the resultant cast.

FIGURE 9-14 Preparation of Cast of Footwear Impression in Snow Made with Snow Print Wax Preparation and Casting Material
Courtesy of Lightning Powder Company, a Products Division of Armor Holdings, Inc. Snow Print Wax™ is a trademark of Lightning Powder Company.

OBTAINING TEST TIRE IMPRESSIONS

Test impressions should be made as soon after the incident as possible, with the tires mounted on the suspected vehicle, such that position, wear, and loading duplicate the conditions at the time the evidence impressions were produced. Test impressions are preferably made by laboratory personnel at a location where test conditions can be properly controlled. If the suspect vehicle cannot be conveniently moved, the test impressions must be made at the scene. The following procedures should be used:

1. Use a smooth, flat surface such as smooth concrete.
2. Put twelve-inch-wide strips of poster board in front of each tire in order to record the entire circumference. Coat the poster board with fingerprint ink.
3. Roll the vehicle over the inked poster board, and then replace the inked poster board with clean poster board strips.
4. Roll the inked tire(s) over the clean poster board to produce a test impression.
5. Label all "test boards" properly for identification and sequencing before recovering the boards.

COLLECTION OF KNOWN FOOTWEAR

If the shoes are wet (water, blood, etc.), they should be air dried thoroughly before packaging. Do not dry the shoes with artificial heat. Package shoes in sturdy paper bags, manila envelopes, or Tyvek evidence bags. Identify the wearer of each pair of shoes and the date obtained. Place identifying data on the inside of each shoe with a permanent ink marker. Also, indicate on the laboratory examination request form if the shoes are to be examined for soil, glass, fibers, or other microscopic evidence. If the shoes are to be examined for trace evidence, write "CAUTION, TRACE EVIDENCE" on the outside of the packaging to alert the laboratory staff.

COLLECTION OF KNOWN TIRES

Tires are preferably submitted while still mounted on the suspect vehicle to the laboratory where test impressions can be made under controlled conditions. If driving the suspect vehicle with the tires mounted would substantially change the accidental characteristics of the suspect tires, remove all the suspect tires, and replace with other tires, or transport the suspect vehicle by trailering.

TOOLMARK EVIDENCE COLLECTION

Special precautions for toolmark evidence

DOORS, WINDOWS, AND OTHER OPENINGS

Doors, windows, or other openings with hinged or sliding doors should not be opened, closed, or handled in any way that might compromise latent fingerprints. These usually occur near the points of entry or exit. Investigators should also take special note of any broken, forced, or cut locks, latches, or bolts in the immediate area. The tool should never be fitted into the impression to see whether it could have made the mark. This action will destroy entirely the evidentiary value of the toolmark.

PRESENCE OF TRACE EVIDENCE

Toolmarks should be examined carefully for any trace evidence that may be present in the toolmark itself. Processing of the toolmark should be preceded by a careful examination for any loosely adhering particles of evidence, particularly **paint transfers** from the tool surface. If paint smears or flakes are present and appear to be loosely adhering to the surface of the toolmark, they may be collected by brushing into a bindle with a fine brush, such as a camel's hair brush or an unused fingerprint brush. If the paint transfer is a smear, the paint should be left in place during the casting of the mark. The casting medium will remove and retain most smears on the surface of the medium for removal by the laboratory analyst.

PAINT TRANSFER TO THE TOOL FROM THE OBJECT SURFACE

On painted surfaces bearing a toolmark, paint standards from the surface should also be submitted to the laboratory. Paint may not be readily seen adhering to the tool. However, microscopic examination of the tool may reveal minute particles having evidentiary value. When a toolmark is on a surface that cannot be removed entirely, such as a large, heavy metal object, samples of the metal should be obtained and submitted as reference standards. Particles of metal may adhere to the tool in addition to paint, and both may be analyzed and compared. Flakes of adhering paint may be lost from the tool while in transit to the laboratory. Therefore, a plastic bag should be taped over the end of the tool's working edges to prevent loss or contamination of trace evidence during storage and transmittal to the laboratory.

Documentation of toolmark evidence

NOTES AND SKETCHES

Toolmarks should be completely documented in the field notes, and with sketches and photographs before removal or casting. Notes and sketches must accurately reflect the position of all toolmarks to two fixed reference points, as well as the height from the floor or the ground to the toolmark.

PHOTOGRAPHY OF TOOLMARKS

Two types of photographs are needed for the laboratory examinations and courtroom identification:

- Orientation photographs.

    Orientation photographs should be taken at midrange and depict the entire object that bears the toolmark. The photographs should include structures that allow for orientation of the toolmark, so that an estimation can be made as to how the tool was applied when the mark was made. These photographs, along with the scene sketches, will assist the toolmark examiner in orienting the tool when making test marks for comparison to the questioned toolmark.
- Close-up photographs showing detail of the toolmark.

    The close-up photographs are only for identification and orientation, and usually cannot be used for actual comparisons, except in certain circumstances (e.g., when the photograph shows class and individual characteristics clearly). These photographs should show the physical location and arrangement of the door, window, and the like bearing the mark. These can reveal what the direction of tool use is and whether the tool is physically capable of making the mark. A measurement scale should also be included in these photographs.

MARKING OF ITEMS REMOVED BEARING TOOLMARK EVIDENCE

Any items bearing toolmarks removed as evidence should be clearly marked with case number, initials, and date of removal. The evidence should also be marked to show the inside or outside, top or bottom, and the surface with the toolmark. If the object bearing the toolmark is instead removed, a sufficiently large piece of the surrounding surface area should be included to prevent damage to the mark through bending, splintering, or breaking. Any small removable item, such as a doorknob, latch plate, or lock should be marked by the investigator showing the top and front of the item as it was positioned before removal. Use an indelible felt tip pen, or include a separate drawing with the submitted evidence. Many objects bearing toolmarks that are detached on forced entry can be submitted directly, including segments of window or door molding, window or doorsill, latches, bolts, locks, or doorknobs. Where doorknobs are twisted, note whether anything obstructs access to the knob from either side (posts, door setback). If the mark appears on items too large to be sent to the laboratory, prepare a cast of the toolmark using Mikrosil or other silicone casting compound.

PREPARING CASTS OF TOOLMARKS

If an actual item cannot be submitted for toolmark examination, a **toolmark cast** can be made. A suitable casting material is Mikrosil. This two-part substance reproduces the very fine detail needed for the microscopic comparison. Two speeds of hardener are supplied in the casting kit. The slow hardener is suitable for normal casting. The fast hardener is used for casting in very cold climates. Complete mixing of the casting material and hardener is essential. A properly mixed portion will be workable for about one to two minutes, and the cast can be removed in about ten minutes. Since a hardened Mikrosil cast cannot be permanently marked with a pen, the cast must be placed in a suitable container that can be appropriately marked with item number, location, date, and name of the person making the cast (STD ID data). Figure 9-15 illustrates a Mikrosil casting kit consisting of the cast base material and the hardener.

INSTRUCTIONS FOR MIKROSIL CASTING

1. Prepare a label from a 3 × 5 card.
2. Using a second card as a mixing palette, add enough base material for the size of the impression, add catalyst, and mix thoroughly.
3. Carefully rub a small amount of the fresh mixture into the surface of the mark to eliminate air pockets.

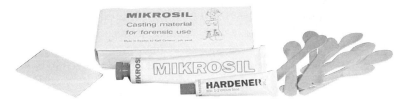

FIGURE 9-15 Mikrosil Casting Kit
Courtesy of Lightning Powder Company, a Product Division of Armor Holdings, Inc. Mikrosil™ is a trademark of Lightning Powder Company.

4. Add remaining mixture to the impression.

5. Immediately place the plastic 3 × 5 card label on the fresh cast, and secure ends to cast with excess fresh casting mixture.

OTHER USES FOR SILICONE CASTING MATERIALS

These synthetic plastic products may also be used to lift fingerprints from rough, irregular surfaces such as wood. Once developed with a brush and powder, the latent impressions should be photographed. Then the casting mixture should be applied and allowed to set and then lifted. Prints collected in this manner will usually be complete and free of extraneous wood inclusions. The lifts will be a mirror image of the standard tape lifts; therefore, extra caution should be exercised during the comparison phase of the examination.

PACKAGING OF OBJECTS BEARING TOOLMARK EVIDENCE

Any object bearing a toolmark should be handled and packaged in such a manner as to prevent any further contact with other objects that could alter and therefore compromise the original markings. The item should be packaged in a sturdy container (such as a cardboard box) and protected with packing material such as crumpled paper or plastic bubble material.

FRACTURE EVIDENCE

Fracture evidence involves items of evidence that have been fractured or torn apart during the commission of a crime. Fracture evidence is included here because the types of examinations employed for fracture evidence are similar to those utilized in impression evidence. Fracture evidence comprises a wide variety of materials, such as tapes used for binding victims, portions of a blunt object broken during an assault, fingernails broken during an assault, paint flaked from a vehicle in a hit-and-run case, and many other types of materials.

Laboratory examination of fracture evidence

The laboratory examinations of fracture evidence are varied, depending on the type of evidence that has been fractured. In most cases, the fracture edges of the components are placed side by side to determine if the fracture edges fit together jigsaw puzzle fashion. If the edges fit, then the patterns adjacent to the fracture are examined for agreement in class characteristics (see Figure 9-16). If both the fracture edges fit, and the class characteristics of the patterns agree, the examiner can conclude that the two (or more) items were part of the same object at one time. In the case of the glove, the torn areas of the finger fit in a jigsaw pattern, and the class characteristics (pebble pattern on palmar surface and smooth pattern on the hand back surface) were in agreement, allowing the examiner to conclude that the torn finger came from the suspect glove.

In Figure 9-17, paint fragments recovered from an accident scene were found to fit the damaged area on the suspect vehicle. The ability to identify the suspect vehicle in a

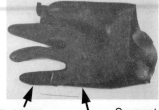

Glove fingertip–scene   Suspect glove from auto

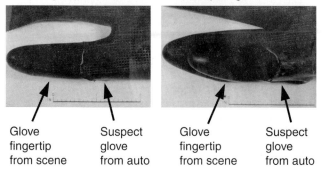

Glove   Suspect   Glove   Suspect
fingertip   glove   fingertip   glove
from scene   from auto   from scene   from auto

FIGURE 9-16 **Physical Match of Glove Finger Found at Crime Scene with Glove from Suspect's Vehicle**
Courtesy of the Department of the Sheriff-Coroner, Contra Costa County, California.

hit-and-run case underscores the need to collect all the paint fragments found at the scene of a hit-and-run accident (see Chapter 12).

In Figure 9-18, a torn fingernail segment found at an assault scene was found to have originated from the victim. Fingernail comparisons typically involve both the examination of the fracture edge for a jigsaw puzzle fit and the comparison of the striations found in fingernails. The pattern of the striations in the nails are stable throughout the

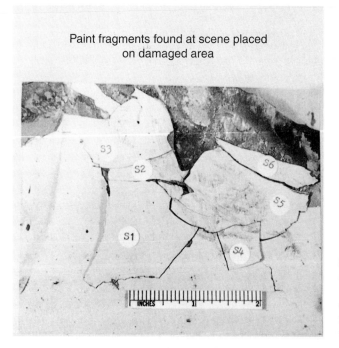

Paint fragments found at scene placed on damaged area

FIGURE 9-17 **Paint Fragments Found at Accident Scene Placed into Damaged Area on Suspect Vehicle**
Courtesy of the Department of the Sheriff-Coroner, Contra Costa County, California.

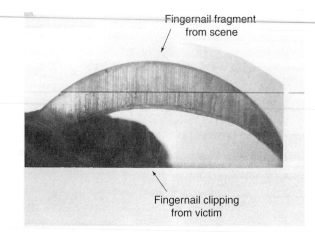

FIGURE 9-18 Comparison of Fingernail Striations on Fingernail Fragment Found in Suspect's Vehicle with Fingernail from Victim
Courtesy of the Department of the Sheriff-Coroner, Contra Costa County, California.

lifetime and are considered unique for each nail of an individual, thus allowing identification of the person from whom the nail fragment originated.

Figure 9-19 illustrates one of the more unusual utilizations of fracture matching methodology. At a hit-and-run scene, a sign post was broken, and a portion of the post was missing. When a suspect vehicle was located, a piece of sign post was found in the grill work. The fracture ends of both the post at the scene and the post section from the vehicle grill were cast with silicone casting material. The casts of the post section from the suspect vehicle and of the sign post at the scene were compared and found to be sections of the same post.

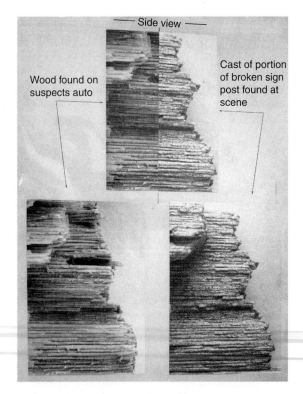

FIGURE 9-19 Comparison of Casts of Wood Grain Pattern on Wood Fragment from Suspect's Vehicle with that of the Wood Post at the Scene of the Accident
Courtesy of the Department of the Sheriff-Coroner, Contra Costa County, California.

CASE EXAMPLE

In a case involving the theft of a radio from the victim's vehicle, it was essential to the case to link the stolen radio to the victim's vehicle. Although a positive identification could not be made by comparing the fractures on the insulation on the radio wire in the vehicle (known) to the insulation on the wire connected to the recovered radio (questioned), the author developed a method to obtain a positive match by casting the interiors of the wire segments and comparing the wire patterns of each segment to the other (see Figure 9-20).[6] ■

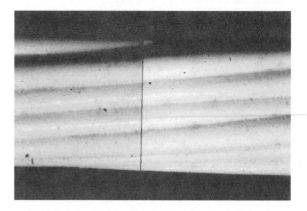

FIGURE 9-20 Comparison of Silicone Casts of Known and Questioned Wire Segment Interiors' Wire Patterns

Summary

INTRODUCTION TO IMPRESSION EVIDENCE

Imprints left in or on a receiving surface by an object.

Indented impressions (impressed prints or compression marks). Residue transfer prints (also called "imprints").

Result of removal of a substance from a surface by contact with the object.

LABORATORY EXAMINATIONS OF IMPRESSION EVIDENCE

Examination of footwear impressions.

Determination of class characteristics

- Investigative purposes.
- Comparison to suspect sources.

Individual characteristics.

- Comparison to known samples.
- Individualize questioned impression.

EXAMINATION OF TIRE TREAD IMPRESSIONS

Similar in most respects to the examination of footwear impressions.

Examination for class characteristics before a suspect vehicle is located (investigative leads).

- Comparison of tread patterns to specimens of known manufacture or to published materials.
- Comparison to tires from suspect vehicle.

EXAMINATION OF TOOLMARK IMPRESSIONS

Indented impressions.

Examination for class characteristics (shape, size).

- Investigative leads.
- Elimination of nonsource tools.

Individual characteristics.

- Analyst may identify known tool as the one responsible for making the toolmark.

Striated impressions.

- Typically more difficult to individualize than indented impressions.
- Important for the crime scene investigator to prepare sketches of a toolmark which show the likeliest orientation of the tool when it produced the questioned toolmark.

COLLECTION OF IMPRESSION EVIDENCE

Collection of footwear and tire tread impressions.

- Field notes.
- Photography.
- Casting.
- Vehicle wheelbase and width measurements.
- Lifting of residue impressions.
- Casting of footwear and tire impressions.
- Casting materials for footwear and tire impressions.
- Casting impressions with plaster of paris.
- Packaging of plaster casts.
- Casting with dental stone.
- Preferred method for casting footwear prints and tireprints.
- Casting in snow, water, or dust.
- Snow Print preparation and Casting Metrials.
- Obtaining test tire impressions.
- Collection of known footwear.
- Collection of known tires.

TOOLMARK EVIDENCE COLLECTION

Special precautions for toolmark evidence.

- Suspect tools should never be fitted into the impression.
- Presence of trace evidence.
- Paint transfer to the tool from the object surface.

DOCUMENTATION OF TOOLMARK EVIDENCE

- Notes and sketches.
- Photography of toolmarks.
  - Orientation photographs.
  - Close-up photographs showing detail of the toolmark.
- Marking of items removed bearing tool-mark evidence.
- Preparing casts of toolmarks.
- Instructions for Mikrosil™ casting.
- Other uses for silicone casting materials.
- Packaging of objects bearing toolmark evidence.

FRACTURE EVIDENCE

Laboratory examination of fracture evidence

- Physical match of glove finger found at crime scene with glove from suspect's vehicle.
- Paint fragments found at accident scene placed into damaged area on suspect vehicle.
- Comparison of fingernail striations on fingernail fragment found in suspect's vehicle with fingernail from victim.
- Comparison of casts of wood grain pattern on wood fragment from suspect's vehicle with that of the wood post at the scene of the accident.
- Comparison of silicone casts of known and questioned wire segment interiors' wire patterns.

Review Questions

1. Impression evidence consists of _____ prints and _____ prints.
2. The _____ characteristics of footwear impressions are valuable for investigative purposes.
3. _____ characteristics are those that are the result of accidental damage to the surfaces of the heels and soles.
4. Collection of footwear and tire impressions involves both _____ and _____ of the impressions.
5. Photography of impressions requires both midrange and _____ photographs.
6. Photographs of impressions should be taken both with and without a _____ scale in view.

7. A preview of the impression photograph can be accomplished with the use of a flashlight or high intensity light that is shone at _____ _____ on the impression.
8. _____ of the impression is the only method that provides a three-dimensional view of the impression.
9. Footwear or tire impressions can be cast with _____ _____ or _____ _____.
10. A _____ should be used when pouring casting material into an impression to avoid damage to the impression.

Further References

Bodziak, W. J. 2008. *Tire Tread and Tire Track Evidence*. Boca Raton, FL: CRC Press.

Jackson, A. R. W., and J. Jackson, 2007. *Forensic Science*. Essex, England, U.K.: Pearson Education Limited.

James, S. H., and J. J. Nordby, eds. 2005. *Forensic Science* (An Introduction to Scientific and Investigative Techniques), 2nd ed. Boca Raton, FL: CRC Press (Imprint of Taylor and Francis).

Saferstein, R. 2009. *Forensic Science* (From the Crime Scene to the Crime Lab). Upper Saddle River, NJ: Pearson Education, Inc.

White, P., ed. 1998. *Crime Scene to Court: The Essentials of Forensic Science*. Cambridge, U.K.: The Royal Society of Chemistry.

10 DRUG AND ALCOHOL EVIDENCE

He who drinks a little too much drinks much too much.

Proverb

Key Words: Controlled substances, addiction, physiological actions, narcotics, psychoactive drugs sedatives, tranquilizers, central nervous system stimulants, ethyl alcohol, naturally occurring, synthetic, semisynthetic, Schedule I, Schedule II, Schedule III, Schedule IV, Schedule V, protective gloves, puncture-proof containers, field testing, presumptive, clandestine laboratories, alcohol, driving under the influence (DUI), tolerance, breath specimens, blood specimen, urine specimens.

DRUG EVIDENCE

Introduction

Drug evidence consists of those materials defined as **controlled substances** and the *chemicals and equipment* used for the illegal manufacture of controlled substances. The possession of controlled substances is proscribed by both federal and state laws, and the various drugs are *classified* by the Drug Enforcement Administration (DEA) and many states into "schedules" according to what their *potential for* **addiction** is and whether or not the drug has a *legitimate medical use*. The landscape of illegal drug use changes over time, so that the drugs of choice change from year to year. Drugs are also classified according to their **physiological actions**. The major physiological categories of illicit drugs are (1) **narcotics** (heroin, morphine, etc.); (2) **psychoactive drugs** (LSD, MDMA, MMDA, etc.); (3) **sedatives** (central nervous system depressants: secobarbital, methaqualone, etc.); (4) **tranquilizers** (oxazepam, diazepam, etc.); and (5) **central nervous system stimulants** (cocaine, methamphetamine, etc.). An additional category of drug evidence is **ethyl alcohol**, a substance that is treated separately in legal codes, since possession of alcohol[1] by adults is legal. (It is thus discussed in a separate section later in the chapter.) *Alcohol* is the subject of considerable legislation because of its abuse or use while driving a motor vehicle and the many deaths caused by individuals driving while under the influence of alcohol.

Controlled substances are also classified according to their origin: (1) **naturally occurring**, (2) **synthetic**, and (3) **semisynthetic**.[2] Examples of naturally occurring controlled substances are marijuana (and its active ingredient, tetrahydrocannabinol, or THC), cocaine, morphine, codeine, mescaline, and psilocybin. Examples of synthetic controlled substances are phencyclidine (PCP), amphetamine, methamphetamine, barbiturates, meperidine (demerol), and methadone. Examples of semisynthetic controlled substances are diacetylmorphine (heroin) and lysergic acid diethylamide (LSD). The class of synthetic drugs also includes the group of drugs referred to as "designer drugs." Designer drugs include fentanyl analogs, meperidine (demerol) analogs, "club drug" MDMA (methylenedioxymethamphetamine, "ecstasy"), GHB (gamma-hydroxybutyrate), and rohypnol (the "date-rape" drug flunitrazepam). The classification of drugs by their origin is of less interest from a legal standpoint than is the legal classification of controlled substances into schedules by the DEA and various states' statutes.

DEA schedule of controlled substances

As just indicated, the various controlled substances proscribed by law are classified into schedules by federal law (and by state law in most states). These schedules include the following drugs as classified by their potential for abuse and their currently accepted medical use.

SCHEDULE I DRUGS
Schedule I drugs have a *high potential for abuse, have no currently accepted medical use*, and have no accepted safety levels for use under medical supervision. Examples of Schedule I drugs are heroin, LSD, marijuana, and methaqualone.

SCHEDULE II DRUGS
Schedule II drugs have a *high potential for abuse* but *have a currently accepted medical use* in the United States under supervision of a medical professional. Abuse of the drug may lead to severe psychological or physical dependence, and these drugs require a triplicate prescription. Examples of Schedule II drugs are morphine, PCP, cocaine, and methamphetamine.

SCHEDULE III DRUGS
Schedule III drugs have a *potential for abuse below that of the Schedule II* drugs. These drugs have a *currently accepted medical use*. Abuse of these drugs may lead to moderate or low levels of physical dependence or to a high level of psychological dependence. Examples of Schedule III drugs are anabolic steroids, codeine, hydrocodone, and some barbiturates.

SCHEDULE IV DRUGS
Schedule IV drugs have a *lower potential for abuse than those in Schedule III* and *have a currently accepted medical use*. Abuse of these drugs may lead to limited physical or psychological dependence. Examples of Schedule IV drugs are Darvon, Talwin, Valium, and Xanax.

SCHEDULE V DRUGS
Schedule V drugs have a *low potential for abuse* and have a *currently accepted medical use*. Abuse of these drugs may lead to limited physical or psychological dependence. An example of a Schedule V drug is codeine in cough syrup preparations.

Collection of drug evidence

The collection of drug evidence usually involves a search of a residence, a vehicle, or the person of an individual. Drug evidence may be hidden in locations that present difficulty in discovering the evidence, but a systematic search of the premises, the vehicle, or the person of the suspect will usually uncover the evidence. The search is made somewhat hazardous because of the possible presence of hypodermic needles, so the searcher needs to be exceptionally cautious during the search. The wearing of **protective gloves** is recommended for the search. Often, the use of a dog trained to locate drug evidence will add considerably to the efficiency and effectiveness of the search.

Drug evidence should be packaged in containers specifically designed for this purpose. Needles and other sharp objects should always be packaged in **puncture-proof containers** so that other individuals handling the evidence cannot be injured. Packages should be labeled with standard identification data (date, case number, item number, and officer's name) and a description of the contents. The sealed packages should be placed in appropriate evidence lockers or submitted directly to the laboratory.

Field testing of drug evidence

There are a number of drug **field-testing** kits available for *presumptive* field testing of suspected drug evidence. The term **presumptive** means that a positive reaction indicates, but does not prove, that the substance indicated is present in the material tested. There are several important considerations in the use of these test kits: (1) Because many of the chemicals used in these kits are corrosive, flammable, toxic, or a combination of these, it is essential that the officer wear personal protective equipment while using these kits (especially eyewear and gloves). (2) The kit directions must be followed explicitly. (3) Use a small amount of the material for testing. (4) The test is only a presumptive test, so that any positive reaction must be confirmed in the laboratory with more specific methods by qualified personnel.

The different testing kits available for field testing of drugs are based on a number of *test reagents* (a reagent is a chemical or a preparation of chemicals used in a chemical procedure) for drug identification. Table 10-1 lists some of the more useful test reagents found in commercial drug-testing kits and the color results of those tests that indicate the presence of a controlled substance.

Clandestine Laboratories

Many illicit drugs are manufactured in **clandestine laboratories**. The drugs most often found in clandestine laboratories are methamphetamine, PCP, and LSD. The chemicals used to produce these and other illicit drugs are flammable, corrosive, toxic, explosive, or a combination of these factors. *For this reason, it is imperative that the scene of a clandestine laboratory is processed only by a clandestine laboratory team, with the proper equipment, training, and personnel necessary to deal with these extreme hazards.* In other respects, however, the clandestine laboratory scene requires the same diligence in documentation via appropriate notes, sketches, and photographs as any other crime scene.

The clandestine laboratory scene will have a wealth of physical evidence present, including latent fingerprints, impressions such as footwear impressions or imprints, document evidence, and trace evidence. The chemicals and any product present are also

TABLE 10-1 Drug Field Test Reagents and Reactions

Reagent	Color Developed	Indicated Substances
Marquis	Orange	Amphetamine
		Methamphetamine
		Mescaline
	Dull orange	Psilocybin
	Purple	Heroin, morphine
Cobalt thiocyanate	Blue precipitate	Cocaine
Dille-koppanyi	Red-violet	Barbiturate
Erlich's	Purple	LSD
Duquenois-Levine	Purple (in chloroform layer)	Marijuana, hashish

valuable evidence, since these materials establish elements of the crime. Notations as to the chemicals present and their quantities should always be made, along with adequate samples of each, since the court may authorize destruction of the materials because of their hazardous nature. Table 10-2 lists a number of chemicals which are indicative of the manufacture of a particular controlled substance.

TABLE 10-2 Chemicals* Associated with the Manufacture of a Specific Controlled Substance

Chemical/Reagent	Drug Manufactured
Acetaldehyde	Methamphetamine
Benzaldehyde	Amphetamine
Benzoic anhydride	Cocaine
Benzoyl chloride	Cocaine
Benzyl chloroformate	Amphetamine
Bromine	Cocaine
Bromosafrole	MDMA (Ecstasy)
Butylamine	Amphetamine
Carbomethoxypropionyl chloride	Psilocin
Cyclohexanone	PCP (phencyclidine)
Dichloromethane	MDA (methylenedioxyamphetamine)
Diethylamine	DMT (dimethyltryptamine)
Dimethyl-1,3-acetone dicarboxylate	Cocaine
Diphenylacetronitrile	Methadone
Ergotamine	LSD (lysergic acid diethylamide)
Ethylmagnesium bromide	Methadone
Formamide	Amphetamine

(continued)

TABLE 10-2 *continued*

Chemical/Reagent	Drug Manufactured
Hydrazine	LSD (Lysergic acid diethylamide)
Hydrogen chloride gas	PCP (phencyclidine)
	Methamphetamine
	Amphetamine
	Methaqualone
Indole	DMT (dimethyltryptamine)
Isosafrole	MDA (methylenedioxyamphetamine)
Beta-ketoglutaric acid	Cocaine
Lithium (metal)	Amphetamine, methamphetamine
Lithium hydroxide	LSD (lysergic acid diethylamide)
Lysergic acid	LSD (lysergic acid diethylamide)
Magnesium (turnings)	Methamphetamine
	PCP (phencyclidine)
	Psilocin
Mercuric chloride	Amphetamine
	MDMA (Ecstasy)
	Methamphetamine
Methyl acrylate	Fentanyl, fentanyl analogues
Methylamine hydrochloride	MDMA (Ecstasy)
Methyl-3,4,5-trimethoxy benzoate	Mescaline
Nitroethane	MDA (methylenedioxyamphetamine)
N-Methylformamide	Methamphetamine
Olivetol	THC (tetrahydrocannabinol)
Palladium black	Amphetamine, methamphetamine
Phenylacetonitrile	Methylphenidate
D-phenylalanine	Amphetamine, methamphetamine
Phenylmagnesium bromide	PCP (phencyclidine)
Phenyl-2-propanone	Amphetamine, methamphetamine
Phosphorous pentachloride	Methamphetamine
	Mescaline
Piperidine	PCP (phencyclidine)
Piperonal	MDA (methylenedioxyamphetamine)
Platinum	Methamphetamine
Platinum chloride	Methamphetamine
Platinum oxide	Methamphetamine
Potassium cyanide	Mescaline

(continued)

Chemical/Reagent	Drug Manufactured
Potassium permanganate	Cocaine
Proprionic anhydride	Fentanyl
Pyrrole	Cocaine
Sodium (metal)	Cocaine
	Methamphetamine
2,5-dimethoxytetrahydrofuran	Cocaine
3,4,5-trimethoxybenzoic acid	Mescaline
3,4-methylenedioxy phenyl-2-propanone	MDMA (Ecstasy)
4-methoxyindole	Psilocin

*May be a reagent used in the manufacture or a precursor of the drug being manufactured.

Reviewed with the thanks of the author by Supervising Forensic Toxicologist Nivan Gill, Forensic Services, Department of the Sheriff-Coroner, Contra Costa County, CA.

ALCOHOL EVIDENCE

Introduction

Ethyl **alcohol** is one of the more important drugs in law enforcement, since its consumption prior to driving creates a situation in which the driver is a hazard to other drivers, pedestrians, and property. Each of the states has a standard level for blood alcohol above which the individual is presumed to be **driving under the influence (DUI)** of an intoxicating liquor or driving while intoxicated (DWI). Prior to the arrest of an individual for driving under the influence, the officer administers field sobriety tests (FSTs) to the driver, and in some cases, a screening breath test with a portable breath-testing device. Table 10-3 describes the ranges of blood alcohol levels (BALs) or blood alcohol concentration (BACs) and the corresponding effects of alcohol observed in those ranges. Note that the reaction to alcohol varies from individual to individual, so that the effects are noticeable at the lower end of the range for people with low tolerance and at the higher end for individuals with high tolerance to the effects of alcohol.

Tolerance to effects of alcohol

As stated before, individuals vary in their **tolerance** to the effects of alcohol. Typically, individuals are grouped into categories of (1) high tolerance, (2) normal tolerance, and (3) low tolerance. These categories are for convenience to the researcher, since the alcohol tolerance of a large population represents a gradient continuum in which the dividing line between categories has some overlap between categories (see Table 10-3).

Evidence in driving under the influence cases

The evidence in a drinking driver case consists of (1) the driver's driving behavior, (2) the field sobriety tests, (3) field breath alcohol screening tests (when given), (4) laboratory analysis of blood and urine specimens, and (5) expert interpretation of blood alcohol level evidential tests.

TABLE 10-3	Blood Alcohol Concentration and Corresponding Effects
Measured BAC*	**Description of Effects**
0.00–0.04	So-called **Sobriety** range: Little or no visible effects, some deficits in fine coordination and in judgment may be detectable with testing.
0.01–0.08	**Impairment** range: Some individuals display impaired abilities at the lowest level in **divided attention** tasks, all will display impaired abilities at the upper end of the range.**
0.05–0.25	**Intoxication** range: Individuals with lower tolerance will exhibit symptoms of intoxication at the lowest level, all individuals will exhibit obvious signs of intoxication at the higher level.
0.18–0.50	**Comatose** range: Lower tolerance individuals may "pass out" (become comatose) at the lower level, higher tolerance individuals may not enter a coma until the upper level is reached.
0.30–0.60	**Death:** Lower tolerance individuals may succumb at the lower level, higher tolerance individuals may survive up to the higher level (in rare instances, individuals have survived levels above 0.60).

*The blood alcohol concentration is expressed in grams per deciliter (g/dL), which is the standard unit for expressing blood alcohol concentration in DUI cases.

**"Divided attention" means that the individual must monitor and control several tasks simultaneously, a situation present in all driving situations.

The officer's observation of the driving behavior of the subject is an important aspect of a DUI case. The driver's driving errors, performance in the field sobriety test, and the results of a field breath tester are the foundation for the arrest. The analysis and interpretation of the blood, breath, or urine alcohol levels establish the level of impairment or intoxication of the driver. The careful documentation of the driving behavior by the arresting officer and the accurate analysis and interpretation of the blood alcohol level by the laboratory analyst provide unassailable evidence that the driver was driving under the influence of alcohol. When the driver lacks a significant level of alcohol in the blood, the case is usually handled administratively.

Collection and preservation of alcohol specimens

COLLECTION OF BREATH SPECIMENS

The collection of **breath specimens** for evidential forensic alcohol analysis requires that (1) the subject has not had anything to eat or drink for at least fifteen minutes prior to the sample collection and (2) the test must be performed on an instrument that has been under the supervision of a forensic scientist for the purposes of authenticating the reliability of the instrument. Precaution (1) is necessary since any alcohol in the mouth or throat may interfere with the measurement of expired lung air, and the waiting period allows for the mouth and throat alcohol to dissipate. Precaution (2) is necessary in order to provide an adequate foundation for the expert interpretation of the blood alcohol level as determined by the breath-testing equipment.

COLLECTION OF BLOOD SPECIMENS

In living subjects, the blood should be drawn from the antecubital vein of the arm for purposes of blood alcohol testing. This site is the standard site for the drawing of blood specimens for alcohol analysis. The specimen should be drawn using a Vacutainer™ tube (or equivalent) containing both an anticoagulant and a preservative. In most jurisdictions, commercial kits containing the appropriate blood tubes and packaging materials are used for the blood draw. The **blood specimen** should be transmitted as soon as feasible to the forensic laboratory responsible for the analysis. The sample should never be stored inside a vehicle or its trunk for any extended period, since the elevated temperature inside the vehicle may destroy the specimen. If the sample cannot be transmitted immediately to the forensic laboratory, it should be stored in a refrigerator (*do not freeze*) until transmittal.

In postmortem subjects, the blood sample should be drawn from the heart or a major blood vessel, using the same blood draw materials as for living subjects. Postmortem specimens should always be refrigerated as soon as feasible.

COLLECTION OF URINE SPECIMENS

Urine specimens must be collected twenty minutes after the bladder is first voided, since the concentration in the urine represents an average of the blood level over the period of time after voiding and the subsequent collection of the sample. The void sample may also be collected when there is a suspicion that drugs may be involved in the subject's intoxication. The samples must be collected in jars that contain a preservative that will prevent any bacterial action that may change the blood alcohol concentration. Commercially produced kits and those prepared by the local forensic laboratory will have a preservative that meets this qualification. The collected samples should have a tightly sealed lid and be packaged in a container that prevents breakage. The samples should be transmitted to the forensic laboratory as soon as feasible or refrigerated until transmittal.

Laboratory analysis of blood alcohol specimens

The laboratory analysis of blood and urine specimens for alcohol concentration is usually accomplished through the use of a gas chromatograph (often automated), which both identifies the measured substance as ethyl alcohol and determines the alcohol concentration in the specimen. The analysis is accomplished with methods that have been rigorously tested to ensure the accuracy of the analytical result.

Summary

INTRODUCTION

Drugs classified by DEA into Schedules.

- Schedules classify drugs by legitimacy of medical use and level of potential for abuse.

Drugs classified also by origin:

- Naturally occurring.
- Synthetic.
- Semisynthetic.

DEA SCHEDULE OF CONTROLLED SUBSTANCES

- Schedule I drugs: High potential for abuse, no currently accepted medical use, no accepted safety levels for use.
- Schedule II drugs: High potential for abuse, a currently accepted medical use in the United States under supervision of a medical professional.
- Schedule III drugs: Potential for abuse below Schedule II, currently accepted medical use,

may lead to moderate or low levels of physical dependence or a high level of psychological dependence.

- Schedule IV drugs: Lower potential for abuse than Schedule III, currently accepted medical use, may lead to limited physical or psychological dependence.
- Schedule V drugs: Low potential for abuse, have a currently accepted medical use, abuse may lead to limited physical or psychological dependence.

COLLECTION OF DRUG EVIDENCE

- Wearing of protective gloves is essential for the search.
- Packaged in containers specifically designed for this purpose. Needles/other sharp objects always packaged in puncture-proof containers.

FIELD TESTING OF DRUG EVIDENCE.

Presumptive field testing of suspected drug evidence.
Several important considerations:

- Essential to wear personal protective equipment while using these kits (especially eyewear and gloves).
- Kit directions must be followed explicitly.
- Use a small amount of material for testing.
- Only a presumptive test, any positive reaction must be confirmed in the laboratory.

CLANDESTINE LABORATORIES

It is imperative that the scene of a clandestine laboratory is processed only by a Hazmat team or a clandestine laboratory team, with the proper equipment, training, and personnel necessary to deal with these extreme hazards.

Clandestine laboratory scenes have a wealth of physical evidence.

ALCOHOL EVIDENCE

Introduction

- Ethyl alcohol is one of the more important drugs in law enforcement.
- Standard level for blood alcohol above which the individual is presumed to be driving under the influence ("DUI") is 0.08%.
- Field sobriety tests (FSTs).
- Portable breath-testing devices.
- Tolerance to effects of alcohol.

Evidence in Driving Under the Influence Cases.

- Driving behavior.
- Field sobriety tests.
- Field breath alcohol screening tests (when given).
- Laboratory analysis of blood and urine specimens.
- Expert interpretation of blood alcohol level.

Collection and Preservation of Alcohol Specimens

- Collection of breath specimen requirements.
- Subject has not had anything to eat or drink for at least fifteen minutes prior to the sample collection.
- Test must be performed on an instrument which has been under the supervision of a forensic scientist.
- Collection of blood specimens.
- Collection of urine specimens.

LABORATORY ANALYSIS OF BLOOD ALCOHOL SPECIMENS

Review Questions

1. Drug evidence consists of _____ substances and the _____ and _____ used in the illegal manufacture of drugs.
2. Drugs are classified into DEA _____ or by their _____ actions.
3. Heroin is an example of a Schedule _____ drug.
4. Schedule III drugs have a currently accepted _____ use.
5. Needles and other sharp objects should be packaged in _____ containers.

6. Field testing for drugs constitutes a _____ test only.
7. It is essential to wear _____ _____ _____ when using drug field-testing kits or reagents.
8. Clandestine laboratories should be processed by _____ teams.
9. The acronym DUI means _____ _____ _____ of alcohol.

10. Blood samples for alcohol analysis should not be _____.
11. Urine specimens for alcohol analysis must be taken at least _____ minutes after the bladder is _____.
12. An overdose of alcohol can lead to _____.

Further References

Drug Identification Bible. 2008. Grand Junction, CO: Amera-Chem, Inc.

Jackson, A. R. W., and J. Jackson. 2007. *Forensic Science*, 2nd ed., Essex, U.K.: Pearson Education Limited.

James, S. H., and J. J. Nordby, eds. 2005. *Forensic Science* (An Introduction to Scientific and Investigative Techniques), 2nd ed. Boca Raton, FL: CRC Press (Imprint of Taylor and Francis).

Saferstein, R. 2009. *Forensic Science* (From the Crime Scene to the Crime Lab). Upper Saddle River, NJ: Pearson Education, Inc.

Siegel, J. A. 1988. Forensic Identification of Controlled Substances. Chap. 3 in vol. II, *Forensic Science Handbook*, ed. R. Saferstein. Upper Saddle River, NJ: Prentice-Hall.

White, P (ed.) 1998. *Crime Scene to Court: The Essentials of Forensic Science.* Cambridge, U.K.: The Royal Society of Chemistry.

11 DOCUMENT EVIDENCE

"It is a curious thing," remarked Holmes, *"that a typewriter has really quite as much individuality as a man's handwriting. Unless they are quite new, no two of them write exactly alike."*

"A Case of Identity," *The Adventures of Sherlock Holmes,*
by Sir Arthur Conan Doyle

INTRODUCTION

Sir Arthur Conan Doyle's character Sherlock Holmes described succinctly two of the document examiner's roles: to establish the source of a typewritten document and to establish the writer of questioned writings and signatures. The term "questioned" refers to the unknown or unverified source of a document's writing or signature, or, in the case of a typewritten document, the typewriter that executed the typing on the document. Modern questioned document examiners, in addition to these primary objectives, perform other examinations on questioned documents.

FUNCTIONS OF THE DOCUMENT EXAMINER

Handwriting comparisons

Perhaps the most frequent task of a document examiner is to identify the individual who prepared the writing or executed the signature on a questioned document. These examinations rely on the well-established knowledge that an individual's handwriting is unique among writers, because of the development of individual characteristics in an individual's handwriting through habits developed from long practice in writing, wherein the individual's manner of forming letters and combinations of letters deviates from copybook form and becomes ingrained in the muscle memory of that individual. The document examiner compares these individualizing characteristics in the questioned document's writings with the same letters and letter combination in known writings or requested exemplar writings executed by the suspected author of the writings. Once a sufficient number of individualizing characteristics are found to "match" (see Chapter 1), the examiner concludes that the questioned writings were executed by the same individual who executed the known or exemplar writings.

Typewriting comparisons

The document examiner is often asked to identify the make and model of the typewriter responsible for the typewriting on a questioned document. This investigative information allows the investigator to prepare a search warrant to seize any typewriter of the same make and model in possession of a suspect. Once the suspect typewriter is in hand, the examiner prepares exemplar typewriting with the typewriter for comparison with the typewriting on the questioned document. Barring exceptional circumstances, the document examiner is able to identify or exclude the typewriter as the source of the questioned typewriting. The identification of typewriters is, however, complicated by the use of typewriters that have letter "balls" or "wheels," which are easily exchanged in the machine.

Examinations of photocopiers, printers, and fax machines

The advent of modern printing technology presented new problems for the document examiner, since the older typewriter typefaces were replaced with a variety of printing devices, which, at first glance, would preclude identification of the source of the printing on a questioned document. However, the usage of these machines also develops imperfections in the printed document, so that the document examiner may still identify the make and model of the machine preparing the document, and in some cases, the individual machine that prepared the document. In many cases, these imperfections are time dependent, because additional usage may obliterate some of the characteristics and add new ones to subsequent printings. This drawback has, however, an advantage, since the examiner may be able to date the time at which a specific document was prepared. As with other types of physical evidence, the development of new technology limits the value of older examination techniques, but this challenge is typically met by a concomitant improvement in the techniques of the document examiner through experimentation and invention.

Alterations, erasures, and obliterations

Document examiners are frequently required to determine whether portions of a document have been altered as part of a criminal act. The document examiner utilizes a variety of techniques to discern alterations to a document, including microscopy of the altered area and exposure to blue-green light, which creates infrared luminescence in the inks. The infrared luminescence from different inks differs visibly, so that the document examiner is able to establish that an alteration has occurred. Erasures are determined through microscopic examination, examination with ultraviolet (UV) light, infrared (IR) light, high-contrast photography, and examination for indentations.

Obliterations are typically identified through the use of microscopy, and UV and IR examination. A television electronic video system that provides real-time examination of inks covering UV, IR, and visible light may also be used.[1]

Indented writings

When an individual writes on a sheet of paper that has an underlying sheet of paper, the underlying sheet often bears an impression of the writing. The document examiner may use oblique lighting to illustrate the indented writing, or the examiner may use electrostatic machines that preferentially attach carbon particles to the writing, thus making the writing visible.

Ink examinations and comparisons

Ink examinations and comparisons are accomplished by the document examiner when it is necessary to determine whether more than one writing instrument was used to execute a document, especially in cases involving suspected alterations to the document. The inks are compared with a process called thin layer chromatography (TLC) and/or with an instrument called a visible microspectrophotometer. The inks may also be compared with high performance liquid chromatography (HPLC). These techniques identify the composition of the questioned ink and allow for direct comparison of the questioned ink's composition with that of an ink suspected to be the source of the questioned ink.

Identification of document paper composition and manufacturer

The chemical composition of papers used in documents can be analyzed with instrumental techniques such as neutron activation analysis (NAA), X-ray fluorescence, and atomic absorption (AA).[2] These techniques identify the trace chemical elements in the paper that are components of the raw materials used in manufacture of the paper. Few manufacturers will produce paper with identical trace element composition because of the use of raw materials that are from different sources and that are produced at differing time periods.[3] Thus, the document examiner can compare the trace element profile of the questioned document paper with the profiles of paper samples from known sources of manufacture.

Identification of the source of a torn paper

When a document is torn in half (or into smaller pieces), the document examiner may be able to determine that the pieces of paper were part of the same document by comparing the characteristics of the torn edges. This examination involves the matching of the torn edges "jigsaw puzzle" fashion in the same manner as for other types of physical matching evidence. Typically, the examiner is able to state unequivocally that the pieces of paper originated from the same document (individualization).

COLLECTION OF DOCUMENT EVIDENCE

Precautions for handling questioned document evidence[4]

- Do not fold, cut, or tear the document.
- Do not mark or write on the document.
- Do not paperclip, staple, or punch holes in the document.
- *Do not process for latent fingerprints* until after the document examination.

Latent fingerprints

Note the preceding admonition that examination by the document examiner must precede processing for latent prints. In the collection of questioned documents, it is essential to consider the presence of latent fingerprints on the documents. Most latents on documents are invisible and need to be developed with chemical means. These latents will last for a very long time on the documents, since the deposit has soaked into the paper. It is prudent to protect any latents present by using gloves to handle the evidence, or if gloves are not available, to handle each document carefully, exposing the document to as small a surface of the fingers as feasible or to use forceps for the handling of the document. The document should be placed in plastic document holders designed for this purpose, or in the alternative, a paper envelope large enough to avoid folding of the document. The documents should be delivered to the forensic laboratory with the label "DOCUMENT EXAMINATION, LATENTS" affixed to the package exterior.

Charred documents

In the case of charred documents, the fragments must be handled as carefully as possible and *packed in a cardboard box with cushioning material such as cotton or static-free bubble packing material.*

Exemplar writings

Exemplar writing should be collected in consultation with the document examiner. Exemplar writing is an example of an individual's writing used to compare with the writing in a questioned document. The examiner may require *request writings,* which are obtained from a suspect by the investigator. These exemplars provide samples of the current writing style of the suspect and should contain the words, phrases, and letter combinations found in the questioned writing. This type of writing depends on the cooperation of the suspect in order to obtain suitable exemplar writing. Often, however, the suspect will attempt to disguise his/her writing, so that additional writings executed by the suspect in the ordinary course of everyday business, such as bank records, letters, and other writings, must be obtained.

A disadvantage of these exemplars is that they may not contain the same words, phrases, and letter combinations found in the questioned writing. If this is the case, the investigator will need to search diligently for writing by the suspect that includes these characteristics. The investigator should also search for writings that were *executed contemporaneously* with the questioned writings.

Request Exemplars: dictated, forms

Hilton[*] states that for dictated exemplar writings, (1) the material must be dictated to the writer, (2) the dictated text must be carefully selected, (3) an adequate amount of writing must be included, (4) some portion of the dictation should be repeated at least three times, (5) writing instruments and paper should be similar to those used in preparing the disputed documents, (6) the dictation should be interrupted at intervals, and, (7) normal writing conditions should be arranged for the exemplar writing. In addition to the dictated exemplar, the document examiner may also request that the subject fill out an exemplar form prepared by the examiner's laboratory.

Course of Business Exemplars

In addition to dictated exemplars and/or completed exemplar forms, the document examiner may require additional exemplar writings executed by the subject in the course of everyday business. A number of sources for course of business documents are listed in Table 11-1.

---

[*]Hilton, Ordway. 1956. *Scientific Examination of Questioned Documents,* Callaghan & Company, Chicago.

TABLE 11-1	Some Sources for Course of Business Document Exemplars

Addressed envelopes
Affidavits
Automobile titles, insurance papers
Bank withdrawal slips
Bank signature cards
Bank deposit slips
Birth certificates
Boat/trailer registrations
Business contracts and agreements
Charge slips
Checks, signature/endorsement
Civil/criminal court records
Credit card charge slips
Credit applications
Deeds
Employment records
Hospital papers
Leases
Letters, personal/business
Life insurance papers
Loan applications
Marriage license applications
Medical/Medicare papers
Military papers
Mortgage papers
Passports
Postal mail receipts
Real estate (contracts, listings, warranty deeds)
Social Security cards/papers
Tax returns
Time sheets
Traffic tickets
Utilities service applications
Voter registration records
Wills
Workers compensation records

Packaging of questioned documents

Questioned documents should be placed in *plastic document covers* that will protect the contents from latent fingerprint deposition, accidental tears, and folding and contamination. It is best to use commercially available covers designed specifically for this purpose, but good quality plastic holders will suffice. The protected documents should be packaged in containers that will prevent accidental folding or tearing for transmittal to the document examiner or forensic laboratory.

Summary

FUNCTIONS OF THE DOCUMENT EXAMINER

- Handwriting comparisons.
- Typewriting comparisons.
- Examinations of photocopiers, printers, and fax machines.
- Alterations, erasures, and obliterations.
- Indented writings.
- Ink examinations and comparisons.
- Identification of document paper composition and manufacturer.
- Identification of the source of a torn paper.

COLLECTION OF DOCUMENT EVIDENCE

- Precautions for handling questioned document evidence.
  - Do not fold, cut, or tear the document.
  - Do not mark or write on the document.
  - Do not paperclip, staple, or punch holes in the document.
  - Do not process for latent fingerprints until after the document examination.
- Latent fingerprints.
- Charred documents.
- Exemplar writings.

Request Exemplars: Dictated, Forms

Course of Business Exemplars

Review Questions

1. One of the major functions of the questioned-document examiner is to identify the _____ who executed a questioned signature.
2. The differences in the characteristics of an individual's handwriting as compared with that of another individual's are called _____ characteristics.
3. Document examiners are often asked to identify the _____ and the _____ of the typewriter used to type a document.
4. Document examiners often determine the presence of alterations, _____, and obliterations in a document.
5. Indented writings occur when a sheet of paper is _____ the sheet upon which a writing occurs.
6. Document examiners may determine the _____ of the ink on a questioned document for direct comparison with that of a known ink.
7. Document examiners may compare the edges of torn papers "_____ _____" style with the edges of other pieces of paper suspected of being part of the same document.
8. The investigator should not _____, _____, or _____ a questioned document.
9. The investigator should not _____ or _____ on a questioned document.
10. Latent print processing of a questioned document should be done _____ examination by the document examiner.

11. Latent prints will last for a _____ time on questioned documents.

12. Latent fingerprints on documents are developed via _____ means.

13. Latent fingerprints on a document can be protected by wearing _____.

14. Charred documents should be packaged in a _____ _____ with _____ material.

15. Exemplar writings may be _____ writings or writings executed during the course of _____ _____.

Further References

Brunelle, R. L. 2002. Questioned Document Examination in Vol. I of *Forensic Science Handbook*, 2nd. ed., ed. R. Saferstein. Upper Saddle River, NJ: Prentice Hall, Inc.

Harrison, Wilson R. 1958. *Suspect Documents* (Their Scientific Examination.) London: Sweet & Maxwell, Ltd.

Hilton, O. 1987. The Evolution of Questioned Document Examination in the Last 50 years, *Journal of Forensic Science*, 33:1310.

Hilton, O. 1992. *Scientific Examination of Questioned Documents*, Rev. ed., Boca Raton, FL: CRC Press.

Robinson, E. W. 1991. *Fundamentals of Document Examination*, Chicago, IL: Nelson-Hall Publishers.

Saferstein, R. 2009. *Forensic Science* (From the Crime Scene to the Crime Lab), Upper Saddle River, NJ: Prentice-Hall.

12 | VEHICLE SCENE INVESTIGATIONS

The chapter on accidents is the longest chapter in the book.

John Wilkes

Key Words: Vehicle search, photographs, driver's view, witness, measurement accuracy, sketches, point of impact (POI), blood smears, fabric impressions, fibers, paint standards, garments, glass fragments, vehicle versus vehicle, light-switch positions, lightbulb filament, lamps and bulbs.

INTRODUCTION

Vehicle scene investigations may involve crime scene investigators in an investigation where the vehicle itself is a "scene" to be processed, traffic accidents where the damage is limited to the vehicles without injuries to the individuals involved in the accident, hit-and-run incidents, or major accident investigations involving serious or fatal injuries to individuals. Each of these scenarios will determine the level of the response team for processing the scene. For minor accidents, the scene will typically be processed by the patrol officer(s) responding to the scene. At the other end of the response level spectrum, fatal accidents will normally be processed by major accident teams composed of highly trained individuals, such as the California Highway Patrol Major Accident Investigation Teams (MAIT units). The crime scene investigators may therefore be responsible for the entire scene processing of a vehicle, the scene of an accident, or may assist major accident investigators in the investigation of serious accidents. Regardless of the seriousness of the accident or crime involving a vehicle, it is essential that the scene be properly documented, so that follow-up investigators can determine the perpetrators of a crime and/or the individual(s) responsible for an accident.

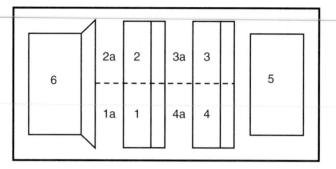

Process entire exterior and interior driver's area for trace
evidence and latents before allowing vehicle to be towed.

Process vehicle in a systematic manner, either clockwise or
counterclockwise, to ensure thoroughness of the search.

FIGURE 12-1 General Vehicle Search Method
Adapted from U.S. Department of Justice, LEAA, NILE/CJ, *Crime Scene Search and Physical Evidence
Handbook* (Washington, DC: GPO, October 1973).

GENERAL AUTOMOBILE SEARCH

When a vehicle is involved in the commission of a crime, the vehicle is normally searched
pursuant to a search warrant. Without a search warrant, items collected from the automobile
may be excluded as evidence because of Fourth Amendment objections. A general **vehicle
search** is conducted in the same *systematic* manner as for other crime scenes. The vehicle is
photographed and sketched, and the appropriate notes of the actions taken and the
evidence collected are placed in the field notes. The vehicle should be examined closely for
trace evidence and processed for latent print impressions before being towed or processed
for other types of physical evidence. It is suggested that the crime scene investigator start
with the exterior and interior of the driver's area first, since the vehicle may have to be
moved prior to completion of the processing. This action preserves any latents in the driver's
area that might be destroyed by the efforts of the tow truck driver.

The search should then proceed in clockwise fashion around the interior (see
Figure 12-1), including the floorboards of each area (1a, 2a, etc.). Once the interior search
is completed, the trunk and hood interior areas are searched. The particular sequence of
the search pattern is not critical, as long as the investigator adheres to a systematic procedure in the search (the vehicle search may be done counterclockwise, for example). For
information on each specific type of evidence encountered in the search, see the appropriate chapter for that type of evidence.

TRAFFIC ACCIDENT INVESTIGATIONS

The crime scene investigator may be called to the scene of a traffic accident to assist in the
investigation. The principal demands for the crime scene investigator at an automobile
accident scene are documentation of the scene through photography and sketching, and
the collection of physical evidence. Physical evidence such as headlight and taillight glass,
bulb filaments, paint transfer from the involved vehicles, and skid marks are commonly

encountered in vehicle accidents. Accurate measurements of the location of each vehicle and the skidmarks are essential to the reconstruction of the accident by the accident reconstruction specialist. For this reason, the crime scene investigator should use measurement devices of known accuracy, so that the measurements made are reliable and accurate.

PHOTOGRAPHS AT THE ACCIDENT SCENE

Overview photographs of the scene

As in other scenes, overview **photographs** of the entire scene should first be taken in order to show the relationship of each vehicle to the others and to the physical location of the accident.

Photographs of the point of impact

Take long-range, medium-range, and close-range photographs of the point of impact (POI) of the vehicles. Take close-up views of each item, or small group of items, of evidence located at the point of impact. The photographs should parallel the sketch(es) of the point of impact.

Photographs of the position where each vehicle came to rest

Once the overview photographs are completed, each vehicle should then be photographed to illustrate the position where each vehicle came to rest. These photographs should show each vehicle's relationship to the scene and to the other vehicles by reference to the overall photographs taken of the scene.

Photographs of damage to each vehicle

Photographs of the damage to each vehicle should be taken normal to the axis lines (line of vision through the lens parallel to the lines of the axles) of the vehicle. Photographs taken at oblique angles to the vehicle's axis lines do not show the extent and the direction of the damage, data that are critical to a reconstruction. At least twelve photographs should be taken of each vehicle (see Figure 12-2), three from each side in line with the axles and in the center, and three from each end of the vehicle in line with the center of the vehicle and the sides.

Additional photographs may be taken if desired, but the crime scene investigator should be certain that the photographs from the twelve basic positions are taken of each vehicle in order to facilitate the accident reconstruction.

View each driver had while approaching the accident site

The view that each driver had while approaching the accident site should be photographed and referenced to the scene sketches. Particular attention should be paid to the view that the driver had of traffic signs and other vehicles. Any obstructions to any **driver's view** should be photographed from that driver's viewpoint as the driver approached the scene of the accident. The driver's viewpoint should be photographed with measurements of the camera's height from the ground in order to document the view from that driver's position.

Point of view of each witness to the accident

Photographs to illustrate the view that each **witness** had to the accident should be taken from the eye level of that witness. These photographs will assist the investigator in determining whether or not each witness was able to see the accident as claimed.

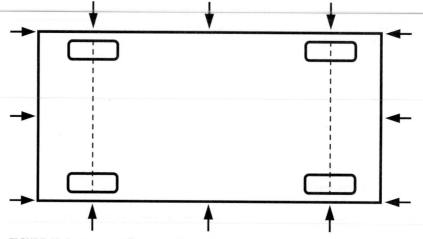

FIGURE 12-2   Camera Alignment for Accident Damage Photographs

ACCIDENT SCENE SKETCHES

Accuracy of the measurements

Measurement accuracy is essential for the reconstruction of the accident. Metal tapes of good quality should be used for measurements when possible. If a wheel walker is used for measurement of longer distances, it should be calibrated periodically, preferably prior to taking measurements at each scene. If very high accuracy of a scene is required, the laser sketching systems married to a computer produce **sketches** of extremely high accuracy. The use of these systems is typically limited to accident investigation teams such as the Multi-Disciplinary Accident Investigation Team (MAIT) units of the California Highway Patrol, because of the high cost of the system.

Predesigned scene sketch forms

There are a number of predesigned scene sketch forms for accident scene sketches. These forms facilitate making the sketches by providing the background framework for the sketches. It may be necessary to augment the forms with additional sketches for those circumstances where the forms are inadequate. These sketches should be prepared using the same care as for other scenes (see Chapter 4 for sketching techniques).

Types of sketches for the accident scene

Sketches of the scene should include an overview (layout) sketch, a detailed sketch of the entire scene, and a blow-up sketch of the point of impact (see Chapter 4) to provide measurements for the close-up photographs of the evidence items. These sketches will provide additional data for any reconstruction effort for the accident.

Finished sketches

The finished sketch may be hand drawn or drawn with the use of a computer aided drafting and design (CADD) program (see Chapter 4 on sketching). CADD programs with symbol libraries allow for sophisticated sketches with a minimum of effort (see Figure 12-3). The

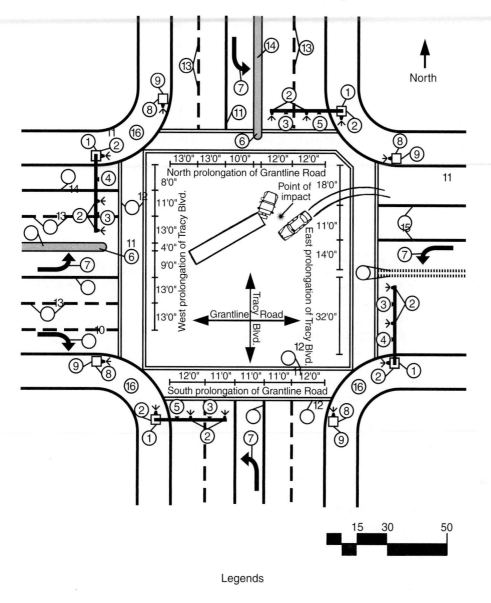

Legends

1. O/H Light Stds. (NE corner light out)
2. Traffic Signal Lights
3. Sign: "Left Turn on Arrow Only"
4. Sign: "Tracy Blvd."
5. Sign: "Grantline Rd."
6. 1' High Post/Yellow Reflectors
7. Painted White L-turn Arrows
8. Traffic Signal with L Arrows
9. Vertical Light Std. with Crosswalk
10. Painted White R-turn Arrow
11. Painted White Lines
12. Ca. 1' Wide Painted Crosswalk Line
13. Botts' Dots (lane separation lines)
14. Raised Traffic Islands
15. Botts' Dots in Double-double Lines
16. Concrete Walkway (Raised ca. 6")

FIGURE 12-3   Accident Scene Originally Drawn with CADD Program and Symbol Library
Courtesy of Don Truitt, dataSketch Company, Stockton, CA.

CADD-drawn ~~sketch can be easily drawn to scale and the appropriate elements added to~~ the sketch from the symbol library, resulting in a sketch that is accurately drawn and has a near-normal look to the eye. When coupled with adequate photographs from the scene, the follow-up investigators, attorneys, and court personnel will have a complete picture of the scene.

HIT-AND-RUN INVESTIGATIONS: VEHICLE VERSUS PEDESTRIAN

Scene investigation

SKETCHES OF THE SCENE
See the preceding section on accident scene sketches.

PHOTOGRAPHS OF THE SCENE
Take overview (long-range) photographs of the scene to include any skid marks, as well as debris from the responsible vehicle such as glass and metal fragments. The location of each item may be illustrated with evidence markers in the photographs (take photographs both with and without the markers in view). These photographs establish the relationship of each item to the others at the scene. Midrange photographs should be taken to illustrate the relationships of the items in each smaller area at the scene (shredded clothing, bloodstains along a skid trail, for example).

PHOTOGRAPHS OF EACH EVIDENCE ITEM
Photographs of each evidence item should be taken with and without evidence markers in view. Each item should be referenced to the scene sketches and the analyst's notes.

PHOTOGRAPHS OF THE POINT OF IMPACT
The **point of impact (POI)** (if determined) should be photographed to illustrate the presence of any evidence that corroborates the determination of the point of impact, such as blood spatters or **blood smears**, articles of clothing dislodged by the impact, and materials from the vehicle.

Suspect vehicles

Suspect vehicles in a hit-and-run involving a pedestrian should be searched carefully for fabric impressions in the paint and for blood and body tissues on the front of the vehicle and the undercarriage. It is preferable to search the undercarriage while the vehicle is on a lift. This method will facilitate the search and the photography of any evidence discovered during the search.

FABRIC IMPRESSIONS IN THE VEHICLE'S PAINT
Fabric impressions in the vehicle's paint should first be photographed to illustrate the location and extent of the impression. Close-up photographs should then be taken, using oblique lighting with and without a measurement scale placed next to the impression. The use of a polarizing filter may greatly reduce the reflected glare from the surface and thus enhance the contrast of the impression.

If the fabric impressions are in dust, it may be advisable to augment the color photographs with a Digital camera in order to ensure that the image is preserved, since dust impressions are easily lost. The fabric impressions should be examined carefully after photography for trace evidence imbedded in the paint. Fibers from the affected garment may be impressed in the paint, often melted or semimelted from the heat and pressure generated by the impact.

SMEARS OF BLOOD OR BODY TISSUES ON THE VEHICLE

Smears of blood or body tissues should be *photographed* prior to collection with and without measurement scales in place. The smears can be collected with cotton swatches, cotton swabs, or threads for laboratory analysis. Be sure to take control swatches or swabs of the unstained area immediately adjacent to the smears. Smears of blood may be found on the paint or the undercarriage of the vehicle. Swabs collected should be dried before final packaging and kept frozen until transmittal to the laboratory in the same fashion as for bloodstain swabs (see Chapter 7 on biological fluid stain evidence).

FIBERS AND OTHER TRACE EVIDENCE EMBEDDED IN THE PAINT

Fibers imbedded in the paint should first be photographed (see earlier) and sketched before collection to document their exact location. The fibers can be removed carefully with forceps if they are reasonably intact and packaged in a vial or bindle, placed in an envelope, and sealed. If the fibers are smeared or melted, scrape the area of paint bearing the adherent fibers in the same manner as for taking transfer paint samples (see Chapter 6, Figures 6-8 and 6-9). The laboratory analyst can then recover the fibers under the stereo microscope. Label the vial or bindle and the envelope with standard identification data.

PAINT STANDARDS

Take **paint standards** from the vehicle immediately adjacent to the damaged area(s) with a sharp knife or scalpel (see Chapter 6, Figures 6-8 and 6-9). The paint standards should include all layers of the paint down to the metal. Package the paint standards in bindles, and place in vials, pillboxes, or envelopes, making sure to tape seal the seams of the envelope to prevent loss.

Victim's garments and shoes

The victim's **garments** (and sometimes the shoes) will usually contain trace evidence from the impact, such as glass fragments, paint transfers, rubber transfer, and possible fragments of metal.

TRANSFER PAINT SAMPLES

Paint smears from the responsible vehicle will normally be found on the garments worn by the pedestrian at the time of the accident (see Figure 12-4). All the garments worn by the victim at the time of the accident should be collected for transmittal to the laboratory, making sure to handle the garments carefully to avoid loss of other trace evidence. Typically, the paint smears on the garments will be melted and ground into the fabric as smears of melted paint and as small flakes. The appearance of the melted paint is conclusive evidence that the paint is not the result of the victim's bumping into a vehicle while walking or running.

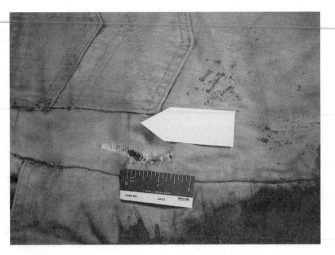

FIGURE 12-4   Paint Transfers on Victim's Trousers in Vehicle Hit-and-Run

BLOODSTAINED GARMENTS

Package each garment separately in a paper bag after drying the bloodstains on the garment (see Chapter 7 for packaging of bloodstained garments). Seal the bag with tape to avoid loss of any trace evidence that may be present.

GLASS FRAGMENTS

The garments of hit-and-run victims often contain **glass fragments** from the headlights of the responsible vehicle. Handling the garments carefully should preserve any fragments in the clothing. Sealing the paper garment bags with tape will preserve the fragments should they become dislodged during storage and transport of the bags.

Injuries to the victims

Injuries to the victim may have pattern impressions of the responsible vehicle's grill-work, ornaments, or headlight assemblies that produced the injury. Photograph each injury normal to the surface of the injury (see Figure 3-2, Chapter 3) to minimize any distortion due to the body curvature. Take the photographs with and without a scale in place. For photographs of postmortem victims, it may be helpful to rephotograph the injuries after embalming, since occasionally the embalming process will enhance the definition and contrast of the injuries. For living victims, photographs should be taken at one-day intervals after the accident as the bruising develops fully.

HIT-AND-RUN INVESTIGATIONS: VEHICLE VERSUS VEHICLE

Scene investigation

The scene investigation of **vehicle versus vehicle** hit-and-run cases entails a search for vehicle components at the scene and paint transfers from the responsible vehicle to the victim vehicle. Each item located at the scene should be photographed and sketched as earlier. Separately package each item from the scene and from the vehicle. Hand carry the evidence to the laboratory when feasible. If the evidence is to be mailed, properly mark the sealed package, and enclose a cover letter describing all the evidence submitted. Include a copy of the accident report when available, since it may aid in the laboratory examinations and reconstructions.

VEHICLE COMPONENTS FROM THE RESPONSIBLE VEHICLE

Photograph and sketch the location of each component from the responsible vehicle prior to its collection. Package each component separately, making certain to provide packing materials for fragile items.

GLASS FRAGMENTS

Collect as many of the glass fragments as possible at the scene. Package carefully in cardboard containers with cushioning to prevent further breakage. Record in the field notes any manufacturer's notations on the glass fragments.

PAINT TRANSFERS AND STANDARDS

Collect paint transfers and standards from each area of damage on the victim vehicle and the suspect vehicle (see section on paint samples from vehicles in Chapter 6).

HEADLIGHTS AND LIGHTBULBS

See the section on vehicle lights that follows.

VEHICLE LIGHTS[1]

Often during a vehicle accident, it is important to determine whether the headlights were on or off at the time of breakage of the sealed beam. The running lights, tail/brake lightbulbs, and turn signal lightbulbs should also be collected for examination in the laboratory. The following procedures pertain to handling vehicle lamps or any other tungsten bulb.

Scene investigation

Determine whether the **light switch position** is on or off. *Do not, under any circumstances, turn the switch on if in the off position.* This action may permanently destroy the **lightbulb filament** and prevent a meaningful examination by the laboratory. Also check the electrical system for blown fuses, broken wiring, and dead batteries. Document your observations of the light-switch position and the condition of lights and bulbs, with notes, sketches, and photographs as appropriate. The claim by a driver that the vehicle's lights were *on* at the time of an accident may be supported or refuted by the notes as to the switch positions and by laboratory examination of the light filaments.

Collection and packaging

After documenting the condition of the electrical system, the **lamps and bulbs** should be carefully collected, noting the location of each item collected (e.g., "L front headlight," "R rear tail/brake light," etc.). Be careful to avoid damaging the evidence during collection.

INTACT LIGHTS AND BULBS

Intact lights and bulbs should be collected carefully and submitted as is, well packed with cotton or crumpled paper in a rigid box. Identify the specific location of each light or bulb on the package label (e.g., "L rear tail/brake light," "R front running light").

BROKEN LIGHTS AND BULBS

For broken lights, collect all available glass fragments at the scene for laboratory examination. A physical match of the glass fragments from the scene with glass fragments remaining in the headlight of a hit-and-run vehicle can sometimes be achieved. The physical matching of glass fragments at the scene with glass fragments from a suspect vehicle will positively link that vehicle to the scene. Carefully dismantle the vehicle headlight assemblies, ensuring that all filaments, filament posts, and glass are included. The headlight mounting bracket and its hardware may have to be removed to collect the headlight.

HEADLIGHT FILAMENTS

Determine whether the filaments are attached to the filament posts. Attempt to locate the filament if unattached, since most of the important information is detectable only on the filament. Carefully package separated posts and filaments to prevent further damage. Use disposable foam cups or small cardboard boxes to prevent damage. Use cotton gauze or tissue padding to cushion the posts and filaments.

Laboratory examinations of lightbulb filaments

If the bulb is intact, the laboratory examinations may reveal the presence of a mechanical (cold) break or the presence of damage sustained while the filament was on (hot break or stretching). The presence of cold breaks is consistent with the filament being broken while in the off mode (but may have been broken at some prior time). "Hot" breaks or stretching indicate that the bulb was in the on mode at the time the filament was broken or stretched. If the bulb or light is broken, the filament and filament posts may show evidence that the filament was on at the time of breakage, because of deposits of tungsten oxide on the filament or post (see Figure 12-5). If the filament was off at the time of breakage, the filament may show cold breaks.

FIGURE 12-5 Tungsten Oxide and Melted Glass on Filament and Filament Post

Summary

INTRODUCTION

GENERAL AUTOMOBILE SEARCH

TRAFFIC ACCIDENT INVESTIGATIONS

PHOTOGRAPHS AT THE ACCIDENT SCENE

- Overview photographs of the scene.
- Photographs of the point of impact.
- Photographs of the position where each vehicle came to rest.
- Photographs of damage to each vehicle.
- View each driver had while approaching the accident site.
- Point of view of each witness to the accident.

ACCIDENT SCENE SKETCHES

- Accuracy of the measurements.
- Predesigned scene sketch forms.
- Types of Sketches for the Accident Scene.
- Finished sketches.

HIT-AND-RUN INVESTIGATIONS

VEHICLE VERSUS PEDESTRIAN

Scene investigation

- Sketches of the scene.
- Photography of the scene.
- Overall photographs.
- Photographs of each evidence item.
- Photographs of the point of impact.

Suspect vehicles

- Fabric impressions in the vehicle's paint.
- Smears of blood or body tissues on the vehicle.

- Fibers and other trace evidence embedded in the paint.
- Paint standards.

Victim's garments and shoes

- Transfer paint samples.
- Bloodstained garments.
- Glass fragments.

Injuries to the victim

VEHICLE VERSUS VEHICLE

Scene investigation

- Vehicle components from the responsible vehicle.
- Glass fragments.
- Paint transfers and standards.
- Headlights and light bulbs.

VEHICLE LIGHTS

Scene investigation

- Determine if light switch is in "on" or "off" position.
- Do not turn the switch "on" if in the "off" position.

Collection and packaging

- Intact lamps and bulbs.
- Broken lamps and bulbs.
- Headlamp filaments.

Laboratory examinations of light bulb filaments

Review Questions

1. A vehicle search should be conducted in a _____ manner.
2. If a vehicle is to be moved, the _____ and _____ of the driver's side should be processed before moving.
3. _____ photographs should be taken to show the relationship of each vehicle to the scene.
4. Photographs should be taken to illustrate the _____ that each driver had of the accident scene.
5. Photographs of the _____ _____ _____ of each witness should be taken.
6. _____ impressions in the vehicle's paint in vehicle versus pedestrian incidents should be photographed using oblique lighting.
7. Smears of _____ or _____ _____ should be photographed prior to collection.
8. Paint standards from each vehicle should be taken from an area _____ _____ to the damaged area.
9. Bloodstained garments should be packaged in _____ bags after drying of the bloodstains.
10. The crime scene investigator should not, under any circumstances, turn a light switch to the _____ position.
11. Stretching of a filament prior to breakage indicates that the filament was _____ at the time of the breakage.

Further References

Baker, J. Stannard, and L. B. Fricke. 1986. *The Traffic-Accident Investigation Manual*, "At-Scene Investigation and Follow-Up," 9th ed., Evanston, IL: Northwestern University Traffic Institute. (Considered by many to be the Bible of traffic accident investigation).

Collins, J.C., and J.L. Morris, 1967. *Highway Collision Analysis*, Springfield, IL: Charles C. Thomas.

Rivers, R.W. 1988. *Traffic Accident Investigation*, Institute of Police Technology and Management, University North Florida.

Wheat, Arnold G., 2005. *Accident Investigation Training Manual*. Clinton Park, NY: Thomson Delmar Learning. (Written for truck crashes, but most information applies equally well to automobile and other vehicle accidents).

13 SEXUAL ASSAULT INVESTIGATIONS

Key Words: First responders, detective, SART, SANE, footwear impressions, crime scene investigator, latent fingerprint, semen, saliva, trace evidence, evidence from the victim, scalp or pubic hairs, evidence from the scene, bruises, bitemark injuries, blood, knots, forensic medical examination, swabs, oral swabs, aspirate, fingernail scrapings, anus and rectum examinations, evidence from the suspect, victim's clothing, penile swabs.

INTRODUCTION

Modern sexual assault investigation requires a multidisciplinary approach to the investigation. The investigative team includes the **first responders**, the **detective**, the laboratory analyst, the sexual assault medical examiner, the victim advocate from the rape crisis center, and the prosecutor from the district attorney's office. The effectiveness of the investigation depends on the three "Cs" of team investigation: Communication, Cooperation, and Coordination.[1] Each of the members of the investigative team needs to understand the role and responsibilities of the others and the way in which the coordination of the team relies on cooperation and effective communication between the team members. In most investigations, the detective will be the team leader, assembling information from each member into a sound case to present to the prosecutor.

In some jurisdictions (although not all), sexual assault cases may be investigated by a **sexual assault response team (SART)** composed of the first responder, the investigator, a victim advocate, and a **sexual assault nurse examiner (SANE)**. Key to this approach is the forensic sexual assault nurse examiner, whose training includes legal procedures for evidence collection, appropriate care for the sexual assault victim, training in the types of scientific evidence collected, and appropriate measures for their preservation. Other members of the response team also receive proper training for their role in the team, which provides a basis for the communication and cooperation necessary for smooth team investigations. The SART/SANE approach to sexual assault investigations represents a significant advance in the collection of physical evidence, the quality of care for the victim, and the ability of the prosecutor successfully to prosecute an offender in sexual assault cases.

DEVELOPMENT OF MODERN SEXUAL ASSAULT INVESTIGATION

Prior to the 1970s, sexual assault victims were treated inordinately poorly by the criminal justice system. Often, the victim was blamed for the assault, manifested by the frequent remarks by law enforcement personnel "she asked for it," "she deserved it," "she wouldn't have been attacked if she hadn't been wearing such provocative clothing," and so on. In the early 1970s, a small group of dedicated women in Berkeley, California, formed a group named the Bay Area Women Against Rape (BAWAR). These women, many of whom were rape survivors, fought for improved treatment of rape victims, improved methods of sexual assault investigations, and, most importantly, the improvement of law enforcement members' attitudes about victims of sexual assault. The efforts of these women created an astounding revolution in the United States with regard to the investigation of sexual assault cases, leading directly to the development of rape crisis centers throughout the United States, the formation of victim/witness programs, the formation of SART programs, and the unfolding of a dramatic improvement in the forensic medical examination of sexual assault victims through the development of trained and certified SANEs. The net effect of these improvements was to produce a dramatic increase in the prosecution and conviction of sexual assault offenders, and, more importantly, a striking improvement in the physical and psychological medical treatment of sexual assault victims. The debt that sexual assault victims owe these founders of BAWAR is immense and measureless.

ROLE OF PHYSICAL EVIDENCE IN SEXUAL ASSAULT INVESTIGATIONS

Physical evidence in sexual assault cases can assist in *establishing elements of the crime,* as well as *identification or elimination of a suspect,* and can be used to *corroborate or dispute the statements of principals.* The physical evidence most often encountered in sexual assault cases includes latent fingerprint impressions, semen, hairs, fibers, and blood. All of the other types of physical evidence may play a role in a sexual assault investigation, but these types are the ones most often encountered by the investigator. The principal sources of physical evidence in sexual assault investigations are the (1) crime scene, (2) victim, and (3) perpetrator. The collection of physical evidence therefore involves an appropriate crime scene search and the forensic examinations of both the victim and the suspect. The successful investigation and prosecution of sexual assault crimes usually involves the use of physical evidence from these three sources.

The two principal defenses used by a suspect in a sexual assault case are (1) *false identification* of the suspect by the victim and (2) *consent* to sexual activity by the victim. The search for physical evidence at the crime scene and during the medical examinations of the victim and suspect may provide evidence to counter or support either of these defenses. Physical evidence at the crime scene that may serve to identify the perpetrator includes latent fingerprints, blood or semen stains, trace evidence such as hairs and fibers, and impression evidence such as **footwear impressions**. Physical evidence that supports nonconsensual sexual assault includes bloodstains at the site of the assault; displaced furniture at the crime scene that indicates a struggle; torn clothing from the victim; and injuries to the victim, such as bruises and lacerations, which are consistent with nonconsensual sexual activity. The crime scene should be processed systematically for those types of evidence that serve to identify the perpetrator(s), establish elements of the crime, and verify or dispute the statements of principals with regard to the nonconsensual nature of the assault. (See Chapter 2 on crime scene search principles for appropriate guidelines for the crime scene search and documentation of the physical evidence present.)

EVIDENCE FROM THE CRIME SCENE

First responders

PROTECTION OF THE VICTIM

The protection of the victim, the apprehension of the suspect, and the protection of the scene are the primary goals of the first responders. It is important that the first responders advise the victim not to change clothing, bathe, or shower, or to perform other hygienic measures, since these actions may destroy valuable evidence needed in the investigation. Evidence gathered from the victim or the victim's clothing may help to establish the identity of the perpetrator, if unknown, and to provide evidence that will support statements of the victim and will refute statements of the perpetrator.

SECURING THE CRIME SCENE

The crime scene should be secured as for other crime scenes. It is a good practice to keep the scene secured until after the medical examination of the victim, since additional evidence at the crime scene may be indicated by facts discovered during the medical examination. It should be noted that in sexual assault cases, there may be multiple crime scenes.

DOCUMENTATION OF THE CRIME SCENE

Document the crime scene with notes, photographs, and sketches to identify items of evidence and to record any injuries to the victim (see Chapters 3 and 4). Documentation of the crime scene will establish a basis for reconstruction efforts directed toward determining the veracity of the suspect's claim of consensual intercourse as opposed to a sexual assault. Particular attention should be directed to displaced furniture, any materials used to bind the victim, and any objects that may have been used as a weapon.

INTERVIEW THE VICTIM IN PRIVACY[2]

The officer should establish rapport with the victim (a female victim may prefer to have a female officer for the interview or to have a female present; a male victim may prefer male officers). Determine whether the crime scene has been altered or contaminated. Also determine whether the victim has changed clothing; discarded soiled items such as bedding, towels, or clothing; bathed; or douched. Make notes for the collection of these items by the crime scene investigator.

The interview techniques should be designed to help restore the victim's self-esteem and sense of safety.

INITIATE CRIME BROADCAST IF APPLICABLE

Monitor the broadcast to assure the accuracy of the suspect description.

ARRANGE FOR MEDICAL EXAMINATION OF THE VICTIM

Make certain that the sexual assault response team has been activated and that the individual who will perform the forensic examination has been notified. Arrange for a victim advocate from the rape crisis or victim advocate center to accompany the victim to the medical facility where the examination is to take place. The officer should advise the victim to take a change of clothing to the examination. These arrangements should be automatic in those jurisdictions having a SART program in place. If the jurisdiction does not have a SART program, the responding officer or the detective assigned to the case should ensure that the victim brings a change of clothing or that it is provided for the victim.

Crime scene investigators

In some jurisdictions, the **crime scene investigator** may be the first responder; but in most instances, the crime scene investigator will be the detective assigned to the case, or it may be a crime scene specialist from the crime scene unit.

Regardless of which individual is responsible for the crime scene investigation, it is important that the processing of the scene be accomplished in the same systematic and orderly manner as for other crimes. Appropriate notes, photographs, and sketches should be completed in order to document properly the crime scene and the physical evidence located. Proper documentation of the crime scene is key to an effective crime scene reconstruction, should a reconstruction be necessary to answer false claims by a suspect, or, in the rare instance of false allegations by an alleged victim, refute the false claims. *Note:* In modern sexual assault investigations, it is an axiom of proper investigation that the victim is to be believed in any sexual assault allegation, in order to avoid dissuading victims to report their assaults. The investigator must keep in mind, however, that the investigation may develop facts that suggest the allegations made by a victim may be false. The analysis and interpretation of the physical evidence may provide evidence that helps determine the actual nature of the allegations.

LATENT FINGERPRINT IMPRESSIONS

Latent fingerprint impression evidence remains the best evidence for identification of the perpetrator when the perpetrator is unknown to the victim. Latent fingerprints are a permanent record of the presence of a suspect at the scene. The investigator should always consider processing the scene for latent fingerprints. If good quality latent fingerprint impressions are recovered, they may allow for rapid identification of an unknown suspect by a computer search through the automated fingerprint identification system (AFIS). The latent impressions recovered at the scene may link assaults committed by the same perpetrator through intercomparison of latents from the scenes of other assaults. The investigator should remember to take elimination prints from the victim and any individual normally having access to the scene.

FOOTWEAR IMPRESSIONS, TIRE TRACKS, AND TOOLMARKS

These types of impression evidence may serve to identify the perpetrator(s) through identification of the suspect's footwear, vehicle, or tools for entry, and such evidence should always be considered by the investigator (see Chapter 9 for detailed information on the collection and preservation of these types of evidence). Footwear impressions may provide tracking data that can assist in the reconstruction of the events at the crime scene.

SEMEN EVIDENCE

With the advent of DNA profiling by forensic scientists, **semen** evidence is virtually equivalent to latent fingerprints for identifying the perpetrator of sexual assault crimes. A number of high profile cases throughout the United States have demonstrated that semen evidence is also a powerful tool for eliminating a suspect who has been falsely accused of a sexual assault crime or a rape homicide. The investigator should be diligent in searching the crime scene for semen evidence. The use of a laser light or an alternate (forensic) light source may be very helpful in this regard, because of the fluorescence of semen under these light sources. Semen from the crime scene, the medical examination of the victim, and the victim's clothing are important evidence that should not be overlooked by the investigator. In some cases, DNA typing from semen evidence may furnish the critical information that leads to successful identification and prosecution of a suspect. It should be noted that suspects have had associates "plant" semen evidence at a crime scene in an attempt to exonerate falsely the accused. Diligent documentation of the crime scene will effectively blunt this ruse.

SALIVA STAINS

Saliva stains may occur on the victim's body as a result of biting, licking, or sucking activities. If the victim has used towels or tissues to wipe away saliva from the body, the items used to wipe the saliva stains should be collected and packaged in paper bags as evidence. The victim's clothing may also be a source of this valuable evidence type. Saliva stains may yield adequate DNA for successful DNA profiling and comparison with a suspect's DNA profile. The investigator should not overlook items such as cigarettes, cigars, chewing gum, and the like, which may contain DNA evidence from the suspect.

TRACE EVIDENCE COLLECTION

Search the crime scene diligently for **trace evidence**, such as fibers, hairs, or soil tracked in by the perpetrator. Collect and package any trace evidence recovered in accordance with the guidelines for trace evidence collection in Chapter 6. Particular attention should be given to any hair evidence that may have intact root sheaths, which need to be dried and kept frozen until submission to the laboratory in order to preserve the genetic markers in the hair root tissue, particularly the DNA that may be present in the root sheath. When there is no root present on the hair(s), mitochondrial DNA (mtDNA) typing of the hair shaft may be successful.

TRANSMITTAL OF POLICE REPORT TO THE FORENSIC LABORATORY

A copy of the police report should accompany the evidence submitted to the forensic laboratory. The police report will alert the laboratory personnel to the types of evidence that may be present and to the appropriate laboratory examinations to perform. In addition, the report will help to identify the types of background controls needed for the laboratory examinations. The report will also facilitate the laboratory analyst's ability to contact the investigator responsible for the investigation in the event that further information, evidence controls, or standards are needed to complete the laboratory examinations. The report may also suggest to the laboratory analyst other types of evidence that may be present at the crime scene.

EVIDENCE FROM THE VICTIM[3]

Roles of evidence from the victim

Evidence from the victim may assist in identifying the perpetrator or may rebut a defense of consent at trial. Evidence from the victim that serves to identify the perpetrator includes semen stains, saliva stains, and trace evidence transferred to the victim from the perpetrator's body or clothing. **Scalp or pubic hairs** from the perpetrator may be found on the victim's body or adhering to the victim's clothing. Trace **evidence from the scene** of the crime, when the scene is not the victim's residence or vehicle, may be discovered on the victim's body or garments. Soil and vegetation, for example, from an outdoor scene may be found in the victim's hair, on the victim's body surfaces, and on the victim's garments. Fibers from the suspect's vehicle may be found on the victim's garments or on footwear when the victim is abducted and transported in the perpetrator's vehicle.

Evidence from the victim that may be used to corroborate the nonconsensual nature of the attack includes injuries to the victim documented at the medical examination and evidence of damage to the victim's clothing that indicates a struggle. Injuries to the victim may consist of lacerations, bruising, binding marks, and bitemarks. Damage to the victim's clothing often includes torn fabric, buttons torn off the garment, and evidence of cutting. Each of these types of evidence may be used to reconstruct events that took place and thus corroborate the victim's statements and dispute those of the assailant. A meticulous crime scene search, thorough medical and evidentiary examination of the victim, and appropriate crime laboratory examinations of the physical evidence by the crime laboratory analysts will assist immeasurably in determining the truth of what occurred during the crime and will help to establish elements of the crime.

Sexual assault evidence collection kits

Sexual assault evidence kits (both victim and suspect kits) may be prepared by the jurisdiction's forensic laboratory, or they may be purchased from a crime scene supply firm. The kits should have the necessary packaging supplies for collection of the clothing, and all necessary supplies for the collection and packaging of the evidence items collected at the forensic medical examination of the victim or suspect, whether the victim is a female adult, male adult, or child (see Figure 13-1 for a typical sexual assault evidence collection kit for adult females). The provision of a change of clothing for the victim or suspect after clothing collection needs to be addressed as part of the planning process for sexual assault cases. Victim advocate agencies may be a valuable resource in this regard, as some have changes of clothing available for this purpose. If not, then the investigating agency should take this need into consideration as part of the guidelines for sexual assault investigations.

VICTIM'S CLOTHING

The clothing worn by the victim both *before/during* the assault and *after* the assault should be collected. The clothing worn before and at the time of the assault may have evidence supporting the violent nature of the assault, such as rips and tears in the fabric, missing buttons, and bloodstains from the victim and/or the suspect. Clothing worn during the assault may also contain trace evidence such as hairs or fibers transferred from the assailant's clothing during the assault by the perpetrator. Clothing worn after the assault may have semen from vaginal drainage that may constitute the majority of the semen evidence recovered (the majority of semen deposited in the vaginal vault is usually lost by drainage). The quantity of semen recovered is a factor in the number and kinds of tests that can be performed on the semen and also is a factor in the amount and quality of information obtainable from these tests. The clothing should be collected as part of the medical and evidentiary examination of the victim (see medical examination of victim section). Each garment should be packaged in a separate paper bag in order to allow any stains present to dry and to avoid cross-transfer of trace evidence between garments. Once

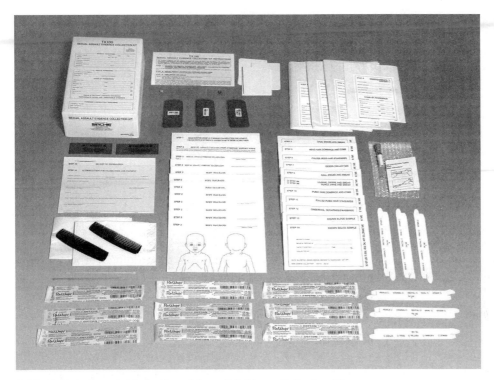

FIGURE 13-1 Female Victim Sexual Assault Evidence Collection Kit
Courtesy of Sirchie Fingerprint Laboratories.

sealed in the smaller paper bag, the garment bags may be placed together in a larger paper bag and sealed. (See the section on medical examination of the victim for detailed instructions on clothing collection.)

INJURIES TO THE VICTIM

Injuries to the victim, such as bruising, lacerations, and bitemarks need to be documented as part of the medical examination. It is important to note that some bruises may not be apparent at the time of the initial medical examination, so it may be necessary to make follow-up examinations of the victim at daily intervals up to a week postassault in order to provide documentation of the bruises. The investigator should note any injuries to the victim and evaluate the need for follow-up medical examinations and documentation of bruise development. **Bruises** are a light bluish-red after a few hours, purple within a few days, green-yellow at the end of a week, and brown after a week. The bruises disappear in about two to four weeks.[4]

BITEMARK INJURIES

Bitemark injuries may have two types of evidence present, saliva from the assailant and dental impressions. The saliva may be typed in the DNA system. The dental impressions from the assailant's bitemarks may be identifiable and must be properly documented with photography and, in some instances, with silicone casting material. It is very helpful to have a forensic odontologist examine the bitemarks and prepare the photographic and casting documentation.

BLOOD EVIDENCE

Injuries to the assailant may have transferred **blood** to the victim's clothing or body surfaces. Bloodstain evidence on the victim's body surfaces should be collected at the medical examination of the victim. Blood standards from the victim and any suspects need to be collected for comparison with any bloodstain evidence obtained from the victim (see the section in Chapter 7, "Blood samples from living subjects"). Injuries to the victim may have transferred bloodstains to the assailant, so that the clothing from any suspect should be examined closely for bloodstains.

TRACE EVIDENCE: HAIRS AND FIBERS

The violent nature of a sexual assault will often create a transfer of trace evidence such as hairs and fibers from assailant to victim and from victim to assailant, or from either to the crime scene. The examination of the victim's clothing and the suspect's clothing will reveal trace evidence produced in this manner. It is also important to keep in mind the transfer of trace evidence from the crime scene to the clothing and bodies of both victim and assailant and to collect the appropriate standards from bedding, carpets, furniture, and other items at the scene for possible comparison with any fibers recovered from the victim or suspect.

Hair from the assailant may be transferred to the victim's clothing or body during the assault. The hairs transferred may include scalp hairs, pubic hairs, or other body hairs. Scalp and pubic hair standards from the suspect should be collected for possible comparison to any hairs recovered from the victim's clothing or body surfaces during the medical examination. Hair adjacent to any injuries to the assailant should also be collected, although hairs other than scalp or pubic hairs may not be suitable for comparison purposes.

TRACE EVIDENCE: SOIL/VEGETATION

If the sexual assault occurs in an outdoor setting, soil and vegetation may have been transferred to the clothing of both the victim and the suspect. Samples of the soil and vegetation at the crime scene need to be collected for possible comparison with any evidence recovered from the victim's clothing (see Chapter 6 for soil collection procedures). It is important to ensure that the bags containing the victim's clothing are properly sealed with tape to avoid loss of soil or vegetation evidence.

LATENT FINGERPRINT IMPRESSIONS

It is considered highly unlikely that latent impressions can be recovered from living subjects because of the nature of the latent deposit and the skin surfaces. In the case of a rape-homicide, it is possible (although unlikely) to recover latent impressions from the victim (see Chapter 5 for information on recovering latent impressions from homicide victims).

BINDINGS FROM THE VICTIM

Leave any **knots** intact by cutting several inches away from the knot. Tie the cut ends together to preserve the knots for laboratory analysis and comparison with other cases. Duct tape may have latents on either side, so remove it carefully, preserving the ends torn from the tape roll for comparison with any roll of duct tape recovered from a suspect.

MEDICAL EXAMINATION OF THE VICTIM

Introduction

The **forensic medical examination** of a sexual assault victim typically includes a physical examination for injuries and treatment for those injuries, sexually transmitted diseases, and emotional trauma. Some states mandate the types of examinations and treatments that must be provided to the victim of a sexual assault and the payment for these examinations and treatments. The procedures for the medical and forensic examinations of victims of sexual assault prescribed by the State of California are followed closely in this text. Medical personnel providing the forensic examinations should be trained specifically in the care and treatment of the sexual assault victim and in the appropriate methods for collection and preservation of physical evidence from the victim, and the examiner should use a specially prepared victim sexual assault evidence kit for collection of evidence materials.

Important note: "Flossing" the victim's teeth for semen recovery from the oral cavity should never be attempted. Only sterile cotton swabs should be used for semen recovery from the victim's oral cavity (see section for Oral Swabs under Medical Examination of the Victim).

Standard identification data

Each item of evidence (or its sealed package) collected for medical-legal purposes must have sufficient labeling data to ensure that the item can be unequivocally identified at any future time. Each item must be identified as that specific item collected by the examiner from a particular patient during an examination at a specific date and time. The identification data that are needed to ensure this identification are referred to in this text as "standard identification data" and must include the following minimum information:

- Case file number.
- Item number.
- Date of collection.
- Name of individual who collected the item.
- Name of the patient (victim).

The item should also be marked by the officer taking custody of the item (it is helpful to write across the seal of the package). In addition, the location on the victim's body where the item was collected should also be noted when the object is collected from the victim's body.

Chain of custody data

A stringent legal requirement for forensic evidence is that each individual or entity having possession of an evidence item from the time it is collected until the time it is introduced into evidence at a court proceeding must be identified. This requirement is referred to as the "chain of custody" or "chain of possession." The chain of custody begins at the time the item is collected and continues through until submission of the evidence at a court proceeding. The items collected must be stored in a facility or room with adequate security, so that any person having custody or access to the item can be identified. This requirement ensures that the condition of the evidence has remained unchanged from the time of its collection until its introduction in a court proceeding or that the individual responsible for any change (crime laboratory personnel, for example) can document any changes in the condition of the evidence. Evidence items should not be left unattended in the sexual assault victim examination room unless the room is locked and any individual with access to the room can be identified for authentication of the security of the room.

The individual collecting the evidence should ensure that each item of evidence is identified with standard identification data, ensure that the chain of custody forms are filled out properly, and obtain a signed receipt from the individual taking custody of the evidence when it is relinquished (a chain of custody form is adequate for this purpose). The name of the individual taking custody of the evidence and the date and time of the custody transfer should be recorded in the examiner's case file.

Collection of clothing

A change of clothing should be provided for patients. Planning and coordination between law enforcement agencies, victim services agencies, and the hospital to provide a change of clothing for the forensic examination of sexual assault victims are essential to avoid delays in the examination and treatment of the victim.

PRIOR TO DISROBING
The patient should remain clothed until it is time to conduct the medical and forensic examination. This procedure will facilitate the evidence collection process and ensure the integrity of the collected evidence items.

DISROBING
The examiner should place *two* sheets of clean paper on the floor *on top of one another.* The purpose of the bottom sheet is to protect both the clothing and the top sheet from contamination by debris or dirt on the floor. The disposable paper used on examination tables is acceptable for these purposes, or a large roll of butcher type paper may be kept in the examination room for this purpose. A width of three feet for this paper roll is recommended, since smaller formats present difficulty for the victim in remaining on the paper and the larger width enhances the likelihood that any trace evidence falling from the clothing will be captured on the paper.

REMOVAL OF PATIENT'S SHOES
The patient should remove the shoes *prior to stepping on the paper for disrobing* to avoid contamination of loose trace evidence with nonevidential debris from the shoe soles. The shoes should be collected and packaged separately if indicated by the circumstances of the case.

OBSERVATION OF CONDITION OF PATIENT'S CLOTHING
The condition of the patient's clothing should be observed and noted in the examination notes by the sexual assault examiner before the patient disrobes. Note any rips or tears in the garments and the presence of any foreign materials. These observations should be recorded in the examiner's case notes. Clothing may be scanned with a Wood's Lamp (long-wave ultraviolet lamp) to detect areas of fluorescence. Semen has a faint fluorescence under long-wave UV light, and many fibers will show a strong fluorescence under this light.

DEBRIS ON PATIENT'S CLOTHING

- Foreign materials firmly attached to clothing should not be removed but should be packaged with the garment.
- Fine, loose debris falling from clothing should be collected in the top sheet of the paper placed on the floor for this purpose.
- Loose debris that is large, has outstanding characteristics, or appears significant should be packaged separately in a bindle. The bindle should be packaged in an envelope, and the envelope should be labeled with standard identification data and sealed.
- Foreign materials collected should be noted in the examiner's case notes.

DISROBING AND COLLECTION OF PATIENT'S CLOTHING

- The patient should disrobe on the paper previously described in order to collect any loose foreign material falling from the clothing.
- All outer and under clothing worn during or immediately after the assault should be collected because of the possible presence of vaginal drainage and the presence of trace evidence such as hairs, fibers, and stains.
- Each garment should be folded as it is removed to prevent stains or foreign materials from being lost or transferred from one garment to another.
- *Each garment should be packaged separately in an individual paper bag.* Never package clothing in plastic bags, because they retain moisture that may result in mold and deterioration of the biological evidence that may be present.
- Wet or damp clothing must be given to the law enforcement officer with directions to arrange for drying before final packaging.
- The top sheet of the paper on the floor should be carefully folded and tape sealed to resemble a large bindle to ensure that all foreign materials will be contained inside. The resultant bindle should be labeled with standard identification data and then sealed in a paper bag.
- The large-sized bindle of paper in its sealed bag and all the individually bagged garments should be placed into large paper bags, labeled with standard identification data, and sealed with tape.
- Whether or not clothing was collected from the patient should be documented in the case notes.

Examination of body surfaces

A visual examination can be aided with the use of a long-wave ultraviolet light, commonly known as a Wood's Lamp. This can be used to scan the body or clothing for evidence of dried or moist secretions, stains, fluorescent fibers not readily visible in white light, or subtle injury. Ultraviolet light searches should be done in a darkened room. The patient may instead be searched with an alternate light source, *making sure that each individual in the room (including the patient) is wearing protective eyewear.*

SEMEN STAINS

Dried semen stains have a characteristic shiny, mucoid appearance and tend to flake off the skin. Under an ultraviolet light, semen usually exhibits a faint blue-white or orange fluorescence. Fluorescent areas usually appear as smears, streaks, or splash marks. Since freshly dried semen may not fluoresce, swab each suspicious area with a separate swab whether it fluoresces or not (see section on collection that follows). Fluorescent areas observed under ultraviolet light may not be semen stains, and independent confirmation of the presence of semen by the forensic laboratory is necessary to identify the stain as a semen stain. Collect the suspect stains for submission to the forensic laboratory for analysis (see section on collection of dried or moist stains that follows).

SUBTLE INJURY

Rope marks, recent contusions, and other subtle injuries may be more visible with the aid of a Wood's Lamp. A visual examination is necessary to differentiate between old or recent trauma. *Note that bruising may not be fully developed at the time of the forensic examination, and follow-up examinations at twenty-four-hour intervals should be scheduled.* Ultraviolet (UV) light photographs of the bruises should also be considered, as UV photographs may sometimes reveal detail not visible with film or digital photography.

Collection of dried or moist stains from the body

Dried or moist stains identified through the general physical examination and the Wood's Lamp or forensic light source scan should be collected, packaged separately, and labeled as to location on the body. The stains should be collected in the following suggested manner:

- **Semen, saliva, or bloodstains**
  Semen, saliva, or bloodstains should be sampled with sterile swabs, dried, the swab head protected with a shield or folded paper bindle, and packaged in an envelope. Alternatively, the swabs can be packaged in a "swab box" (see Figure 7-7, Chapter 7), sealed in the swab box (which allows for drying of the swab), labeled appropriately, and sealed in a paper envelope. The envelope containing the swab bindle or swab box should be labeled with standard identification data.
  - A swabbing should be made of a like area of the victim's body that is unstained for laboratory control purposes. The examiner should record in the case notes whether or not control swabs were taken and, if not done, the reason for not taking the control swab.
- **Semen in the pubic hair**
  If semen or other unidentified material is found in the pubic hair, the examiner should cut out the matted hairs bearing the material and package in a bindle. The bindle should be packaged in an envelope, standard identification data affixed and the envelope sealed with tape.
- **Recording location of semen, saliva, or bloodstains**
  If semen, saliva, or bloodstains are found, the examiner should record the location of the stains on the body and note any injuries to the victim that may account for bloodstains.
- **Moist stains or secretions.**
  The examiner should follow these steps for the collection of moist stains or secretions on the patient's body:
  - Moist stains or secretions should be collected with a dry swab to avoid dilution. As many swabs as necessary should be used to collect the entire stain.

- The swab(s) should be dried and packaged as for dried secretions (discussed earlier).
- Diagrams should be used to record the location(s) of secretions on the body.

Collection of foreign materials from the victim's body

FOREIGN MATERIALS SUCH AS FIBERS, HAIR, GRASS, AND DIRT

These materials should be packaged in a separate paper bindle for each location of the body. Use tweezers, or gently scrape the substance(s) into a bindle with a clean tongue depressor or the back of a scalpel blade.

BINDLE AND ENVELOPE LABELS

Each bindle should be labeled with a description of the material and the location from which it was collected, folded and sealed with tape, placed in a coin envelope, and the envelope sealed. The coin envelope should be labeled with standard identification data and the location on the body from which the item was recovered.

DIAGRAM THE LOCATION OF RECOVERED EVIDENCE

The examiner should use diagrams to record the location of foreign materials found on the body. The diagrams will assist in describing the location of the recovery sites during testimony.

CASE NOTES

The examiner should make a record in the case notes as to whether or not specimens or foreign materials were found and collected.

Procedures for bitemarks and bruises

PHOTOGRAPHIC EVIDENCE AND PROCEDURES

- Photographs may be taken in accordance with hospital procedures or by the local law enforcement agency (typically, the photographs are taken by law enforcement personnel).
- Properly taken, photographs of bitemarks and bruises can assist in the identification of the person or object inflicting the injury. Individuals can be identified by the shape of bitemarks. A forensic odontologist (dentist) should be consulted in these cases, especially if the bitemark is indented or has broken or perforated the skin. Silicone casts of the mark may be indicated in these cases.
- Close-up photographs of bitemarks or other wounds should be taken with the film plane as parallel to the subject area as possible, that is, the camera should be held with the line of view perpendicular to the body surface ("normal" to the surface) being photographed (see Figure 3-9 in Chapter 3).
- The name of the photographer should be noted in the case notes.

GENERAL CONSIDERATIONS FOR BITEMARK PHOTOGRAPHS

- Photographs can be a valuable supplement to the case file and may be necessary in situations that cannot be adequately documented in diagrams (e.g., bitemarks or massive injuries).

- Sensitivity to patient concerns about undress should be considered as to whether hospital personnel or a male or female law enforcement officer takes the photographs.
- Patients should be appropriately draped for all photographs.
- Any camera may be used as long as it can be focused for nondistorted, closeup photography. The SLR camera with a macro lens is especially well suited for the close-up photographs.
- Bruises and bitemarks may not be obvious immediately following an assault. It is recommended that the law enforcement agency arrange for follow-up inspection and additional photographs after the bruising has developed fully. *Photographs should be taken for six days at twenty-four-hour intervals, since bruises and bite marks may become more apparent with time and may show better definition in the photographs.*
- In the processing of photographs, it is preferred that photographs be processed by the local law enforcement agency.

PARTICULATE DEBRIS AND SALIVA FROM BITEMARKS

- Each bitemark and the immediate surrounding area should be swabbed with a separate swab moistened in distilled water to collect saliva residue from the perpetrator. A swabbing should be made of a like area of the victim's body that is saliva-free for laboratory control purposes.
- The swabs should be labeled and must be air dried before packaging.
- The dried swabs should be placed in separate envelopes or swab boxes. Each envelope should be labeled with standard identification data and sealed appropriately.
- The examiner's case notes should reflect whether or not swabs were collected from the bitemarks.

Examination of body orifices and associated structures

PUBIC HAIR COMBINGS

- A clean sheet of examination paper should be placed beneath the patient's buttocks to catch any hairs or fibers dislodged by the combing or brushing.
- With a strong light and/or a Wood's Lamp, the pubic hair should be examined carefully for matted semen stains.
- Pubic hair containing suspected semen should be cut close to the skin, placed in a bindle, and packaged separately in an envelope. The envelope should be labeled with standard identification data, and the examiner should note the collection in the examination notes.
- Pubic hairs should be combed with a new, unused comb or brush. Any hairs obtained should be packaged in an envelope with the comb or brush used. All envelope openings should be sealed with tape to prevent loss of the hairs.
- The clean sheet under the buttocks should be collected in bindle fashion and sealed with tape. The bindle should be labeled, placed in a paper bag, and the bag labeled with standard identification data.

PUBIC HAIR STANDARDS

The examiner should pull or cut *close to the skin* a total of forty to fifty hairs, taking eight to ten hairs from the different areas of the pubic hair (see Figure 6-4, Chapter 6). The pubic hair standard should be sealed in a bindle and placed in an envelope. The envelope should be sealed and labeled with standard identification data.

HEAD HAIR STANDARDS
To collect head hair standards, pull or cut close to the skin approximately fifteen to twenty hairs taken from each of several areas to include the front, back, each side, and crown for a total of seventy-five to one hundred hairs (see Figure 6-3, Chapter 6). The patient may feel more comfortable pulling the hair rather than letting the examiner pull the samples. The patient should be carefully instructed to pull only a few strands at a time if the patient elects to collect the samples.

VAGINAL SWABS
- Preferred sequence of specimen collection:
  1. Swabs of labia majora and labia minora.
  2. Swabs of liquid deposit in posterior fornix.
  3. Swabs of cervix. (*Note:* The cervix should be typically avoided, as sperm can be found in the cervical mucus for up to seven days postcoitus, unless seventy-two hours has elapsed since the assault.)
- Sterile cotton swabs should be used to swab the labia majora and labia minora of the vulva. The swabs should be air dried and packaged in an envelope or swab box. The envelope should be labeled with standard identification data.
- Collection of posterior fornix contents.
- Any liquid pooled in the posterior fornix should be collected using dry sterile swabs.
- A slide smear should be prepared from each swab collected from the pool. Each paired swab and slide smear should be labeled with standard identification data. (*Note:* Swabs may be labeled by affixing a two-inch section of tape to swab shaft and labeling the tape.)
- Each of the swabs should be dried in a swab dryer (one hour should be sufficient for most swabs). After drying, the swabs should be packaged in an envelope or swab box labeled "*Vaginal Swabs*" and standard identification data added.
- Slide smears from swabs should be air dried. Each slide should be labeled to correspond to the swab used for that slide and packaged in a slide mailer. Preservatives, fixatives, or stains should not be applied to the slide smears.
- After collection of samples with swabs, the examiner should aspirate the remaining vaginal pool if present and place the aspirate in a sealed vial, such as a red-top Vacutainer. One drop of this aspirate should be examined for motile sperm, and the observations should be recorded in the case notes.
- All swabs should be dried thoroughly in a swab dryer (one hour is usually sufficient for thorough drying in the swab dryer). Swab dryers are available from crime scene equipment suppliers (see Appendix 13-A).
- Once dried, swabs should be packaged in the appropriately labeled envelopes from the sexual assault examination kit. The envelopes should be sealed, and standard identification data should be entered on the envelope. Envelopes should be placed in the examination kit for transport to the forensic laboratory.

EXAMINATION FOR MOTILE SPERM

The examiner should prepare a wet mount slide to determine the presence or absence of motile or nonmotile sperm in the vagina of the sexual assault victim. The presence of motile sperm in the vaginal pool indicates recent penetration and ejaculation. The absence of motile sperm, however, does not negate the possibility of recent penetration and ejaculation, since sperm tend to become immobile rapidly in the vaginal environment. Since sperm motility can be observed only on an unstained wet mount slide, the motility examination must be performed under a microscope as a part of the emergency room examination. The slide also has evidential value and must be retained and submitted along with other evidence collected from the patient. Even when sperm are not observed initially in the unstained slide for the motility examination, they may be detected on subsequent examination of the dried, stained smear because of the increased visibility imparted by the slide staining.

The undiluted aspirate of the vaginal vault is the best specimen to use for the motile sperm search (if there is insufficient liquid in the vaginal pool for aspiration, the vaginal pool lavage specimen should be used for the motile sperm search). The examiner should add one drop of aspirate to a drop of saline or nutrient on a microscope slide, cover immediately with a coverslip, and examine under the microscope. If there is insufficient aspirate for the sperm search, the examiner can place one drop of sterile saline on a slide, agitate one of the posterior fornix swabs in the drop of saline, and cover with a coverslip for the examination. The examiner should examine the slide immediately (within five to ten minutes) using a biological microscope at a magnification of at least 400 power to determine whether or not sperm are present, and if present, if motile. A phase contrast microscope or staining microscope, if available, is helpful for this purpose. The slide used for the motile sperm search should be air dried and packaged in a slide mailer. The slide mailer should be labeled with standard identification data. The examiner should record the presence or absence of motile or nonmotile sperm in the case notes.

ORAL SWABS (WHEN INDICATED BY HISTORY)

Note: Patients may be reluctant to report penetration of oral or rectal cavities.[5] The oral cavity should be examined for injury and the area around the mouth for evidence of seminal fluid. Particular attention should be given to the frenulum beneath the tongue, the base of the lower lip, and the pharynx for exudates, lacerations, and contusions, using the following procedures:

- The area around the mouth exterior, including the lips, should be swabbed. Collect dried secretions with a swab moistened with distilled water. Collect moist secretions with a dry swab to avoid dilution of the specimen.
- The oral cavity should be swabbed using separate swabs for the following areas: (a) space between lower teeth and cheeks and (b) space between tongue and teeth (both sides of the frenulum).
- Evidence preservation procedures:
  a. Prepare dry **oral swabs** as for vaginal swabs.
  b. Package dried swabs in envelope or swab box labeled "Oral Swabs."
  c. Label sealed envelope or swab box with the standard identification data.

BLOOD SAMPLES
The following blood samples should be drawn from the patient:

1. Blood for DNA typing: yellow-top tube (ACD-B), or purple-top tube (EDTA).
2. Blood for blood-alcohol determination: gray-top tube containing preservative and anticoagulant, DUI tube, or use DUI kit.
3. Blood for toxicology (controlled substances, "roofies," GHB, etc.): gray-top tube.

Blood for alcohol and toxicology are necessary to show, when certain drugs or elevated levels of alcohol are present, evidence of the ability or inability to provide informed consent.

The liquid blood samples must be kept *refrigerated* until submission to the forensic laboratory.

Collection of fingernail scrapings

Fingernail scrapings may contain a variety of evidential materials including blood, tissue, hairs, fibers, or other foreign materials from the crime scene environment or from the assailant. If history indicates or if foreign material related to the assault is observed, the examiner should collect fingernail scrapings with the following procedure:

- Use a clean fingernail file or manicure stick to collect scrapings from under the fingernails.
- Place scrapings from each hand into a separate bindle. Label each bindle, place in an envelope, seal the envelope, and label with standard identification data.
- Record examination findings and any evidence collected in the case notes.

ANUS/RECTUM EXAMINATION AND EVIDENCE COLLECTION PROCEDURES
In sexual assaults involving penetration of the anus by the assailant, the examiner should perform **anus and rectum examinations** of the patient. The examination may reveal injuries to the patient and/or the presence of foreign materials.

Since penetration of the anus/rectum may be under reported because of its disagreeable subject matter, the institution of the examination of this area as a routine in the sexual assault examination may be advisable.

EXAMINATION FOR INJURY AND FOREIGN MATERIALS
The examiner should examine the buttocks, perianal skin, and anal folds for injuries and for the presence of seminal fluid, dried or moist secretions, bleeding, fecal matter, evidence of lubricant, and any other foreign materials. Any injuries observed should be documented in the case notes and photographed. Foreign materials and stains observed should be noted in the case notes and collected using the following procedures:

- Collect dried and moist secretions and foreign materials from the area around the anus.
- Collect two rectal swabs if indicated by patient history and/or physical findings. Rectal swabs must be collected by a method that prevents the transfer of semen that may be present on the perianal area into the rectum. To prevent contact between the swab and the anus during the introduction of the swab into the rectum, the examiner should do the following:

1. Clean the area around the anus after the examination and collection of evidence; and
2. Dilate the sphincter by using a small, nonlubricated speculum moistened with warm water or by instructing the patient to use the lateral recumbent or prone knee-to-chest position.
3. When present, semen tends to collect at the anal opening of the mucocutaneous juncture of the sphincter mucosa. Collection of seminal fluid from the rectum is more effective if the swab is introduced slowly and rotated 360 degrees, than if the swab is inserted and withdrawn in rapid succession.
4. Prepare two dry mount slides, one from each swab.
5. Label and air-dry swabs and slides. Code the corresponding swabs and slides to enable the forensic laboratory to determine which slide was made from which swab, for example, rectal swab #1, rectal slide #1.
6. Package the slides in slide mailers and the swabs in swab boxes or envelopes. Label each container with standard identification data and seal.

The examiner should evaluate the need for an anoscopic or proctoscopic examination if rectal injuries are suspected.

Baseline test(s) for sexually transmitted diseases

The examiner should conduct baseline tests for sexually transmitted diseases (STDs). For adults, if indicated by history, a specimen for gonorrhea culture should be collected from the rectum as a baseline, and the patient should be offered prophylaxis. Other STD cultures should be taken as indicated. For children, a specimen should be collected for gonorrhea culture from the rectum as a baseline and prophylaxis for STDs given. Other specimens for STD culture should be taken as indicated.

Microscopic examinations

Microscopic or magnified examinations can be performed with a magnifying lens or colposcope to confirm signs of minor injury to the genital area. Minor abrasions, fissures, hymenal transection, petechiae, and focal edema may be seen. Colposcopes have a magnifying range of 5–30 power, and many have photographic capability. They are commonly available where gynecological care is provided. As with any part of the examination, a colposcopic examination should be performed only by individuals experienced in the examination and interpretation of the findings from the colposcopic examination.

EVIDENCE FROM THE SUSPECT

Evidence from the suspect can be used to link the suspect to the crime scene or to the victim. Trace evidence from the suspect's clothing may have been transferred to the victim, the **victim's clothing**, or the site of the assault. Blood or semen stains from the suspect may be found at the scene, which may provide DNA evidence that links the suspect to the crime. Other types of evidence from the suspect may include shoewear impressions, latent impressions, and trace evidence such as hairs and fibers. The collection of evidence and of comparison standards is usually accomplished at the evidential examination of the suspect, but the collection of clothing and certain comparison standards such as hair standards may be performed by the investigating officer. Whether the collection of standards is performed by the investigating officer or the medical professional at the evidential examination, it is essential that the requirements for proper collection and packaging of the evidence and the chain of custody be met.

The following items will need collection from the suspect, either by the investigator or by the medical personnel performing the evidential examination:

- All clothing worn at the time of the assault.
- Head hair standards.
- Pubic hair standards.
- Fingernail scrapings (and clippings if broken nails are present).
- Blood-typing standard (drawn by a medical professional).
- Buccal swabs.
- Photographs of any fresh injuries.

Male suspect evidence collection kit

The collection and packaging of clothing from the suspect and all evidence items collected from the male suspect evidential examination is expedited by the use of suspect collection kits prepared by the local forensic laboratory, or by kits assembled by crime scene supply firms (see Figure 13-2 for a typical male suspect evidence collection kit).

Male suspect evidential examination

Contact between the victim and the suspect must be prevented. Once the emergency room is notified by law enforcement personnel that a suspect is to be brought into the emergency department, ascertain whether the victim will also be brought to the hospital. If so,

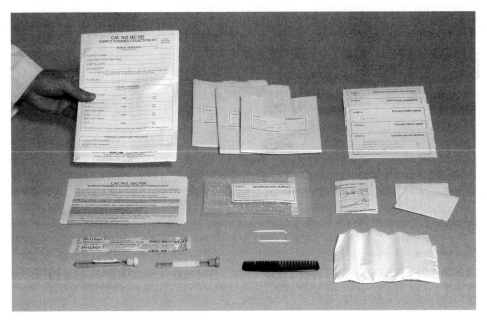

FIGURE 13-2 Male Suspect Sexual Assault Evidence Collection Kit
Courtesy of Sirchie Fingerprint Laboratories.

arrange for appropriate rooms or times for the examinations in order to prevent contact between them.

Security precautions should be taken when a suspect is brought to the emergency department by law enforcement officials. The suspect should be escorted to a private room as soon as possible, and a law enforcement officer should be present with the suspect at all times.

Examinations of suspects are likely to yield useful information, particularly if conducted within hours of the alleged assault, although injuries such as lacerations, bruises, and bites can be observed after a longer period of time. The persistence of most evidence is dependent on activities of the suspect after the assault, such as bathing or changing clothes.

Information about the alleged assault should be obtained from the law enforcement officer prior to beginning the examination. This information is necessary to direct the examiner to look for injury and evidence not readily visible. Questions should be asked regarding the following:

- Date and time of alleged assault.
- Alleged acts.
- Location and physical surrounds of the assault.
- Any physical identifying information provided by the victim such as scars, tattoos, and the like.

The information obtained from the law enforcement officer should be recorded on a separate work sheet and used for reference during the examination. Accept and record the suspect's statements if they are volunteered. Suspects should be given the respect and medical treatment that any patient deserves. Medical professionals must remain objective and must avoid the assumption that the suspect is guilty.

CONSENT/AUTHORIZATION FOR THE EXAMINATION

- The signature of the investigating law enforcement officer should be obtained to authorize payment for the evidential examination at public expense, or
- An authorization should be obtained pursuant to local agreements for payment of examination costs.

PATIENT HISTORY

- Pertinent medical information of patient history should be obtained.
- Information on anal-genital injuries, surgeries, diagnostic procedures, or medical treatment within the past sixty days should be obtained to avoid confusing prior lesions with injuries related to the alleged assault.

CLOTHING COLLECTION

Condition of Clothing   The examiner should note the condition of any clothing worn during the alleged incident upon arrival of the suspect at the examining room. Note any rips or tears or the presence of foreign materials. Foreign materials may include fibers, hair, twigs, grass, soil, splinters, glass, bloodstains, or semen stains.

Collection of Clothing   The examiner should place on the floor one large sheet of paper on top of another of similar size (three-foot-wide butcher-type paper is recommended, or standard examination room paper may be used). The examiner should have the suspect remove shoes and socks before standing on the paper to protect clothing from contamination. The examiner should record in the case file whether or not any clothing was collected.

General physical examination

PHYSICAL EXAMINATION
A general physical examination (head to toe) of the suspect for injuries and other evidence of the reported assault should be conducted by the examiner.

GENERAL PHYSICAL APPEARANCE
The examiner should note in the case file any indication of use of drugs or alcohol, for example, odor, needle puncture marks, pupillary reaction, horizontal or vertical nystagmus, slurred speech or impaired coordination, and also whether the defendant is right- or left-handed.

VITAL SIGNS DATA
The examiner should record blood pressure, pulse, temperature, and respiration.

GENERAL DESCRIPTION DATA
The examiner should record the height, weight, eye color, and hair color of the suspect.

Examination for physical evidence

EXAMINE PUBIC HAIR FOR DRIED OR MOIST SECRETIONS AND FOREIGN MATERIALS
Secretions dried on the pubic hair should be collected by cutting the matted hair, placing in a bindle, placing the bindle in an envelope, entering standard identification data on the envelope, and sealing the envelope.

PUBIC HAIR COMBINGS

- Prior to combing the pubic hair, a sheet of new examination paper should be placed under the suspect's buttocks in order to catch any falling hairs or other trace evidence.
- The pubic hairs should be combed with a new, unused comb or brush. All hairs obtained should be placed in an envelope with the comb or brush used. All envelope openings should be tape sealed, and standard identification data entered on the envelope.
- The sheet of paper under the buttocks should be folded bindle style, labeled with standard identification data, sealed, and packaged in a paper bag. The paper bag should be tape sealed, and standard identification data entered on the bag.

PUBIC HAIR STANDARDS
Pull or cut close to the skin a minimum of forty to fifty hairs from different areas of the pubic region (see Figure 6-4, Chapter 6).

HEAD HAIR STANDARDS
Pull or cut close to the skin approximately fifteen to twenty hairs taken from several areas to include front, back, sides, and top for a total of approximately seventy-five to one hundred hairs (see Figure 6-3, Chapter 6).

OTHER BODY HAIRS

Take hair samples from any area where the suspect may have lost hairs during the assault. Take twenty to twenty-five hairs close to the suspect area by pulling. Place recovered hairs in a bindle, add standard identification data, place bindle in an envelope, label envelope with standard identification data, and tape seal all openings of the envelope.

BLOOD SAMPLES

Collect approximately 5–7 cc in the following tube types:

- DNA (and other genetic markers) typing: purple-top tube (EDTA).
- Blood alcohol: gray-stoppered tube (DUI kit).

EXTRA SWAB IN SEXUAL ASSAULT EXAMINATION KIT

The extra swab included in the sexual assault kit may be used as a penile swab. Vaginal or oral epithelial cells from the victim may be found and typed for DNA.

RELEASE OF SPECIMENS AND RECEIPT FOR SAME

The blood samples and physiological stains should be given to the investigating officer. Obtain a signed receipt for all materials given to the investigating officer. The biological materials should be refrigerated and submitted to the forensic laboratory as soon as possible by the officer.

FINGERNAIL SCRAPINGS

Fingernail scrapings should be obtained if indicated by the history of the assault or if foreign material related to the assault is observed. Collection of fingernail scrapings should be recorded in the case file.

DRY OR MOIST SECRETIONS ON BODY

Dried and moist secretions, stains, and foreign materials from the body including the head, scalp, facial, body, and head hair should be collected in the same manner as for female victims. Control swabs should be collected for each swabbed area.

WOOD'S LAMP (OR FORENSIC LIGHT) EXAMINATION

The entire body should be scanned with a long-wave ultraviolet light (Wood's Lamp). Each suspicious stain or fluorescent area should be swabbed with a separate swab. A forensic light source may be used instead to scan the body surfaces, making sure that all individuals in the room (including the suspect) are wearing appropriate protective goggles.

USE OF DIAGRAMS TO DOCUMENT OBSERVATIONS

Diagrams should be used to record the location of identifying marks such as scars, tattoos, or birthmarks; and the location, size, and appearance of injuries and evidence of foreign materials. Signs of injury may include erythema, abrasions, bruises, contusions, induration, lacerations, fractures, bleeding, bites, burns, or stains. Label the Wood's Lamp findings "W.L."

EXAMINATION OF MOUTH

- The oral cavity should be examined for injury and the area around the mouth for evidence of seminal fluid or vaginal epithelial cells.
- The area around the mouth should be swabbed if indicated. The examiner should collect two swabs from the oral cavity for seminal fluid up to six hours postassault. Prepare two dry mount slides.

EXAMINATION OF EXTERNAL GENITALIA

- The penis and scrotum should be examined for signs of injury, the presence of dried or moist secretions, feces, lubricants, foreign materials, and venereal lesions. Note if circumcised and if there are signs of vasectomy.
- Injuries to the penis may include bites and lacerations, abrasions of the glans, tearing of the mucocutaneous junction of the meatus, or linear abrasions caused by nails or teeth. In uncircumcised males, foreign materials may be retained on the penis, particularly on the glans or in the sulcus.

PENILE SWABS

- A minimum of two **penile swabs** should be collected. Moisten both swabs with distilled water, and swab external surface of the penis.
- (Medical personnel only.) One swab from the urethral meatus and one swab from the glans and shaft should be collected.
- Fecal matter, if present, should be noted.
- Each swab should be labeled indicating the location from which it was taken, and the swabs should be air dried and packaged in appropriate tubes or envelopes.
- Swabs should be packaged in separate tubes or envelopes. Envelopes should be labeled with standard identification data and sealed with tape.

STD CULTURE SPECIMENS

A specimen for gonorrhea culture should be collected from the urethra as a baseline by medical personnel only. Other STD cultures should be taken as indicated.

RECORD FINDINGS AND DOCUMENT SPECIMENS COLLECTED

Any findings and the specimens collected should be recorded in the case notes and on the diagrams prepared.

TREATMENT BY MEDICAL PERSONNEL

Treatment for injuries, venereal disease, and tetanus prophylaxis may be initiated if appropriate. If treatment is not initiated and the suspect is in custody, an appropriate referral to a treating physician at the local jail or holding facility should be made.

EXAMINATION OF ADULT MALE VICTIM OF SEXUAL ASSAULT[6]

1. Triage.
   a. Triage immediately.
   b. Provide private room.

     c. Assign patient coordinator.

     d. Contact Rape Crisis Center or appropriate agency for victim/witness services.

  2. Consent and notifications.

     a. Obtain patient consent for medical and evidential examinations.

     b. Notify proper authorities per legal requirements.

     c. If patient consents to medical examination and treatment only.

       1. Obtain history.

       2. Conduct general physical examination and treat injuries.

       3. Conduct baseline STD examinations and/or offer prophylaxis.

       4. Complete mandated forms to the extent they are relevant to patient's treatment.

     d. If patient consents to both medical and evidential examinations, conduct medical examinations (steps 3 and 4) first, then conduct evidential examination discussed in the following section.

  3. Obtain history.

  4. Conduct general physical examination.

     a. Take specimens for hospital or reference clinical laboratory.

       1. Take baseline GC culture (gonorrhea culture) from oropharynx; take other STD cultures as indicated.

       2. Take baseline GC culture from urethra; take other STD cultures as indicated.

       3. Take baseline GC culture from rectum; take other STD cultures as indicated.

     b. Take blood specimens for drug/alcohol toxicology examinations using appropriate specimen containers.

Evidential examination

  1. Clothing collection (place each item in paper bag, label, and seal each bag with evidence tape).

     a. Note condition of clothing upon arrival and before collection.

     b. Have patient remove shoes (collect) and stand on double layer of butcher paper (or examination table paper).

     c. Collect outer garments, placing each in a separate paper bag (sexual assault kits should have proper bags).

     d. Collect underclothing, place each in separate paper bag.

     e. Fold upper butcher paper layer on which the patient was standing into large bindle, place in separate paper bag and seal with evidence tape.

  2. Conduct general physical examination.

     a. Scan entire body with Wood's Lamp or alternate light source (ALS). *Ensure that all individuals present wear proper goggles for ALS examinations.*

     b. Collect fingernail scrapings, place in appropriate containers, label and seal.

     c. Collect dried and moist secretions and any foreign material such as hairs or fibers from body. Place collected materials in appropriate containers, label, and seal.

     d. Document findings in case notes.

  3. Examination of oral cavity.

     a. Examine oral cavity for any injuries. Document findings in notes.

     b. Swab area around mouth for dried secretions if indicated by history.

    c. Collect two oral swabs up to six hours postassault and prepare two dry mount slides from swabs. Place swabs in dryer for drying before packaging.

    d. Take specimen for GC culture with appropriate culture swabs. Place in appropriate container.

4. Examination of external genitalia.

    a. Examine genitalia for injury. Document findings in notes. Photograph injuries.

    b. Scan with Wood's Lamp. Collect dried and moist secretions and any foreign material noted. Document findings.

    c. Collect matted pubic hair by cutting with scissors. Package in appropriate containers.

    d. Collect pubic hair combings. Collect pubic hair standard by pulling or cutting close to skin with scissors.

    e. Examine penis and scrotum for injury and foreign materials. Document findings.

    f. If indicated by history, collect one swab from urethral meatus and one swab from glans and shaft. Dry in dryer and package in appropriate container.

5. Examination of buttocks, perianum, and rectum.

    a. Examine buttocks, perianal skin, and anal folds for injury. Collect dried and moist secretions and foreign materials. Document findings. Dry swabs and package appropriately. Package any foreign materials in proper containers.

    b. If indicated by history, collect two anal swabs. Prepare two dry mount slides from swabs. Dry swabs and package appropriately.

    c. Take specimen for GC culture.

    d. Conduct anoscopic or proctoscopic examination if injury is suspected.

6. Clinical and toxicology specimens.

    a. Clinical specimens: blood for syphilis serology and HIV baseline.

    b. Evidential specimens (patient has the right to refuse these tests) at discretion of physician and law enforcement officer.

        1. Blood alcohol specimen (grey-top tube: use BA kit).

        2. Blood toxicology (purple-top tube: refrigerate).

        3. Urine toxicology (urine specimen).

7. Reference specimens (can be collected at later date if desired, according to local forensic laboratory procedures).

    a. Blood typing, DNA specimen: yellow-top tube.

    b. Pubic hair standard: twenty to twenty-five hairs pulled or cut *close to skin*.

    c. Scalp hair standard: seventy-five to one hundred hairs, fifteen to twenty hairs from each area of the scalp, pulled or cut *close to skin*.

    d. Beard/body hairs: twenty to twenty-five hairs from each area when indicated by history. Beard hairs may be cut close to the skin, body hairs may be pulled.

8. Follow-through procedures.

    a. Arrange follow-up for STDs, injuries, and referral for psychological care.

    b. Provide written follow-up instructions, including telephone numbers of rape crisis centers, victim/witness programs, and information on crime victim compensation.

9. Clothing and transportation.

    a. Provide replacement for shoes and clothing collected during the examination, in conjunction with law enforcement agency and rape crisis center.

    b. Arrange for transportation, if necessary.

    10. Evidential specimens.

        a. Ensure that all specimens collected are properly documented in case notes.

        b. Ensure that all clinical and evidential specimens collected have been properly dried, packaged in appropriate containers, labeled with all identifying data, and properly sealed.

        c. Transfer custody of evidential items to law enforcement officer, noting chain of custody in case notes and obtaining signed receipt from law enforcement officer taking custody of evidential items.

CHILD SEXUAL ABUSE EXAMINATION[7]

Note: Child victims of sexual assault should be examined by a pediatrician or SANE specifically trained and certified to perform forensic sexual assault examinations on child victims of sexual assault and molestation.

    1. Triage.

        a. Triage immediately.

        b. Provide private room.

        c. Assign patient coordinator.

        d. Contact rape crisis center or child sexual abuse treatment program.

    2. Consent.

        a. Obtain consent for examination from law enforcement agency, child protective services, parent/guardian or patient (age 12 or older).

        b. Notify authorities of known or suspected child abuse.

    3. Postassault intervals.

        a. Less than seventy-two hours postassault with injury: examine immediately in emergency department.

        b. Less than seventy-two hours postassault without severe physical injury: examine immediately in appropriate clinic or office.

        c. More than seventy-two hours post-assault: examine as soon as feasible in appropriate office or clinic.

    4. Clothing collection.

        a. Note condition of clothing upon arrival. Document condition of clothing in case notes.

        b. Collect clothing by having patient remove shoes and package shoes in separate paper bag. If clothing has been removed for emergency treatment of injuries, ensure that clothing is collected and placed in a separate paper bag for each item of clothing and shoes.

        c. When age and condition appropriate, have patient stand on double layers of butcher paper or examination table paper for clothing removal.

        d. Collect outer and under clothing. Package each item of clothing in paper bag, label, and seal each bag.

    5. Less than seventy-two hours postassault.

        a. Obtain history.

        b. Conduct general physical and age/sex appropriate anal-genital examination (see next section).

        c. Collect evidence.

   d. Document injuries in case notes, photograph injuries when feasible and appropriate.

   e. Document injuries in case notes, utilizing sketches and photographs when appropriate.

   f. Document findings and evidence collected in case notes, document chain of possession in case notes and appropriate chain of possession logs.

   g. Treat injuries to victim.

6. More than seventy-two hours postassault.

   a. Obtain history.

   b. Conduct general physical and age/sex appropriate anal-genital examination (see next section).

   c. Female/male patients: examine inguinal adenopathy, medial aspect of thighs, and perineum.

   d. For males: examine penis, scrotum, urethral meatus, and testes.

   e. For females: examine labia majora, labia minora, peri-urethral tissue/urethral meatus, perihymenal tissue (vestibule), hymen, posterior fourchette, fossa navicularis, and vagina.

   f. Female/male anus: examine buttocks, perianal skin, and anal folds. Conduct anoscopic or proctoscopic examination if rectal injury is suspected.

   g. Document fresh or healed injuries in case notes, using diagrams and photographs when feasible.

   h. Treat injuries.

7. Evidential examination and evidence collection.

   a. Conduct general physical examination.

   b. Scan entire body with Wood's Lamp or ALS (all present, including patient, must wear protective goggles during any ALS examination).

   c. Collect any dried or moist secretions found on body, using moistened, sterile swabs from sexual assault kit. Place swabs in drying box rack or cardboard drying container with swab.

   d. Collect any foreign materials found, packaging in appropriate containers.

   e. Pubertal children: cut matted pubic hair and package. Comb pubic hair to collect foreign hairs, fibers, or other foreign material. Package pubic combings in appropriate container.

   f. Document findings in case notes.

   g. Prepubertal girls: intact hymen/normal vaginal orifice.

   1. Examine for injury and foreign materials; no speculum examination is necessary.

   2. Collect two swabs from vulva.

   3. Place swabs in drying box or cardboard swab drying container.

   4. Take specimen for GC culture (gonorrhea culture) from vaginal introitus.

   5. Take other STD cultures as indicated.

   h. Prepubertal girls: non-intact hymen and/or enlarged vaginal orifice.

   1. Examine for injury and foreign materials.

   2. Only conduct speculum examination for prepubertal girls if major trauma is suspected and use pediatric speculum.

      a. Collect three swabs from vaginal pool.

      b. Prepare one wet mount slide and two dry mount slides from swabs.

      c. Examine wet mount slide for sperm and trichomonas.

      d. Take specimen for GC culture.

      e. Document findings in case notes, package swabs and slides appropriately.

i. Boys.

      1. Examine penis and scrotum for injury and foreign materials. Document findings and collect foreign materials.

      2. If indicated by history, collect one swab from the urethral meatus and one swab each from the glans and shaft.

      3. Take specimen for base line GC culture.

      4. Take other STD cultures as indicated.

j. Buttocks, perianal, and anal examinations.

      1. Examine buttocks, perianal skin, and anal folds for injury.

      2. Collect dried and moist secretions and foreign materials. Document in case notes and package appropriately.

      3. If indicated by history, and/or findings, collect two rectal swabs and prepare two dry mount slides. Document in notes and package appropriately.

      4. Take specimen for GC culture.

      5. Conduct an anoscopic or proctoscopic examination if rectal injury is suspected.

k. Clinical tests.

      1. Syphilis serology (red-top tube).

      2. Pregnancy test (red-top tube).

l. Blood alcohol/toxicology specimens (at discretion of physician and law enforcement officer).

      1. Blood alcohol (grey-top tubes: BA kit), for evidence of alcohol given by offender.

      2. Toxicology (grey-top tube), for evidence of drugs given by offender.

      3. Urine toxicology specimen, for evidence of alcohol or drugs given by offender.

m. Reference samples (may be taken at later date if desired).

      1. Blood for DNA typing (yellow-top tube).

      2. Saliva specimen (sterile gauze).

      3. Pubic hair standard: twenty to twenty-five hairs from representative areas of pubic hair.

      4. Scalp hair standard: seventy-five to one hundred hairs (fifteen to twenty taken from each area—front, sides, crown, and back).

n. Completion of evidential examination.

      1. Ensure that all evidence collected has been properly packaged, labeled, and documented in case notes.

      2. Ensure that chain of possession has been properly established.

      3. Ensure that all evidence has been properly labeled for transport and storage (i.e., dry, refrigerated, or frozen storage).

      4. Obtain signed receipt for all evidence items from law enforcement officer and sign all chain of evidence forms.

o. Follow-up procedures.

      1. Arrange follow-up for STDs, injuries, pregnancy, and psychological care.

      2. For intra-family molest victims, consult with law enforcement personnel and child protective services as to whether the child can return home.

      3. Complete all forms for child abuse/molestation/sexual assault.

INDICATIONS OF CHILD ABUSE[8]

Child abuse, although often narrowly defined as having only physical implications, can include physical abuse, physical neglect, sexual abuse, and emotional maltreatment. Although the subject of child abuse is well beyond the scope of this text, certain indicators of child abuse are presented, in order to acquaint the crime scene investigator with the types of physical manifestations of child abuse that may require appropriate documentation by the CSI. Table 13-1 lists physical and behavioral indicators of the physical abuse, physical neglect, sexual abuse, and emotional abuse of children.

One of the most important grounds for suspecting child abuse is when a child tells someone. *It is essential that when a child tells a particular person who is an individual required to report child abuse, the communication is not privileged.* That individual, by law, must report what the child has related to him or her.[9] Note that in California law, the individual required to report has absolute criminal and civil immunity. This immunity may or may not apply in other states or countries.

Physical abuse

Physical abuse may be defined as any act that results in a nonaccidental physical injury. Inflicted physical injury most often represents unreasonably severe corporal punishment or unjustifiable punishment. This usually happens when the parent is frustrated or angry and strikes, shakes, or throws the child. Intentional, deliberate assault, such as burning, biting, cutting, poking, twisting limbs, or otherwise torturing a child, is also included in this category of child abuse.[10]

TABLE 13-1	Indicators of a Child's Potential Need for Protection	
	Physical Indicators	**Behavioral Indicators**
Physical Abuse	• Unexplained bruises (in various stages of healing), welts, human bite marks, bald spots • Unexplained burns, especially cigarette burns or immersion burns (glove-like) • Unexplained fractures, lacerations, or abrasions	• Self-destructive behavior • Withdrawn or aggressive-behavioral extremes • Uncomfortable with physical contact • Arrives at school early or late as if afraid to go home • Chronic runaway • Complains of soreness or moves uncomfortably • Wears clothing inappropriate for the weather, to cover body
Physical Neglect	• Abandonment • Unattended medical needs • Consistent lack of supervision • Consistent hunger, inappropriate dress, poor hygiene • Lice, distended stomach, emaciated look	• Regularly displays fatigue or listlessness, falls asleep in class • Steals food, begs from classmates • Reports that no caretaker is at home • Frequently absent or tardy • Self-destructive • School dropout

(continued)

TABLE 13-1 continued

	Physical Indicators	Behavioral Indicators
Sexual Abuse	• Torn, stained, or bloody underclothing • Pain or itching in the genital area • Difficulty walking or sitting • Bruises or bleeding in the external genitalia • Venereal disease • Frequent urinary or yeast infections	• Withdrawn or chronically depressed • Excessive seductiveness • Reverses roles, is overly concerned for siblings • Poor self-esteem, lack of confidence, devalues self-worth • Problems with peers, resists involvement with peers • Sudden massive weight change (loss or gain) • Attempts suicide • Hysteria, lack of emotional control • Sudden school difficulties • Threatened by physical contact or closeness • Exhibits inappropriate sex play or has a premature understanding of sex for age • Promiscuity
Emotional Abuse	• Speech disorders • Delayed physical development • Substance abuse • Increased severity in existing conditions, such as asthma or allergies	• Habit disorders (sucking, rocking) • Antisocial or destructive behavior • Neurotic traits (sleep disorders, inhibition to play) • Passive or aggressive behavioral extremes • Delinquent behavior • Developmental delays

Source: American Humane Association, *Guidelines for Schools to Help Protect Abused and Neglected Children* (Englewood, CO: AHA Publications). Reprinted with permission. Table originally adapted in part from D. D. Broadhurst, et al., *Early Childhood Programs and Prevention and Treatment of Child Abuse and Neglect*, The User Manual Series (Washington, DC: U.S. Department of Health, Education, and Welfare, 1979). To order a copy of the pamphlet this table originates from, contact the American Humane Association, Inverness Drive East, Englewood, CO 80112, http://www.americanhumane.org.

INDICATORS OF PHYSICAL ABUSE

The indicators of physical abuse include the location of the injury, the medical history from the child, and behavioral indicators (see Table 13-1).[11]

- Location of injury.

  The primary target zone for infliction of injuries is the back surface of the body from the neck to the knees. Such injuries constitute the largest percentage of identified abuse. Injuries from abuse are not typically located on shins, elbows, or knees.

• History.

The history includes all facts about the child and the injury(ies), including (1) the child states that the injury was caused by abuse, (2) knowledge that a child's injury is unusual for a specific age group (e.g., any fracture in an infant), and (3) unexplained injuries (e.g., parent is unable to explain reason for injury; there are discrepancies in explanation; blame is placed on a third party; or explanations are inconsistent with medical diagnosis).

• Behavioral indicators.

The following behaviors may result from child abuse: (1) Parent or caretaker fails to seek appropriate care; (2) child is excessively passive, compliant, or fearful, or at the other extreme, excessively violent; (3) child and/or parent or caretaker attempts to hide injuries—child wears excessive layers of clothing, especially in hot weather, or child is frequently absent from school or physical education classes.

Sexual abuse

INDICATORS OF SEXUAL ABUSE[12]

Sexual abuse of a child may surface through a broad range of physical, behavioral, and social symptoms (see Table 13-1). Some of these indicators, taken separately, may not be symptomatic of sexual abuse. They are listed below as a guide, and should be examined in the context of other behavior(s) or situational factors. The sad reality of sexual abuse is that without third party reporting, the child often remains trapped in secrecy by shame, fear, and the threats of the abuser.

• History.
  • The child wears torn, stained, or bloody underclothing.
  • A child's injury/disease is unusual for the specific age group.
  • Knowledge of a child's history of previous or recurrent injuries/diseases.
  • Unexplained injuries/diseases (e.g., parent unable to explain reason for injury/disease).
  • Discrepancies in explanation for injury.
  • Blame is placed on a third party.
  • Explanations are inconsistent with medical diagnosis.
• Behavioral indicators.
  • Detailed and age-inappropriate understanding of sexual behavior (especially by younger children).
  • Inappropriate, unusual, or aggressive sexual behavior with peers or toys.
  • Excessive curiosity about sexual matters or genitalia (self and others).
  • Unusually seductive with classmates, teachers, and other adults.
  • Prostitution or excessive promiscuity.
  • Excessive concern about homosexuality (especially by boys).
• Behavioral indicators in younger children.
  • Enuresis (bed wetting).
  • Fecal soiling.
  • Eating disturbances (overeating, undereating).
  • Fears or phobias.

- Overly compulsive behavior.
- School problems or significant change in school performance (attitude and grades).
- Age-inappropriate behavior (e.g., pseudomaturity or regressive behavior such as bedwetting or thumb sucking).
- Inability to concentrate.
- Sleep disturbances (e.g., nightmares, fearful about falling asleep, fretful sleep pattern, or sleeping long hours).
- Behavioral indicators in older children and adolescents.
  - Withdrawal.
  - Clinical depression.
  - Overly compliant behavior.
  - Poor hygiene or excessive bathing.
  - Poor peer relations and social skills; inability to make friends.
  - Acting out, runaway, aggressive, or delinquent behavior.
  - Alcohol or drug abuse.
  - School problems, frequent absences, or sudden drop in school performance.
  - Refusal to dress for physical education.
  - Nonparticipation in sports and social activities.
  - Fearful of showers, restrooms.
  - Fearful of homelife demonstrated by arriving at school early or leaving late.
  - Suddenly fearful of other things (e.g., going outside, participating in familiar activities).
  - Extraordinary fear of males (in cases of male perpetrator and female victim).
  - Self-consciousness of body beyond that expected for age.
  - Sudden acquisition of money, new clothes, or gifts with no reasonable explanation.
  - Suicide attempt or other self-destructive behavior.
  - Crying without provocation.
  - Fire setting.

It should be understood that many of these symptoms may be unrelated to child abuse. A number of the indicators, taken singly, or as a set, can also be indicators of clinical depression, or other mental conditions, which, although very serious medical conditions that require prompt medical attention, may not be related to child abuse. It is important that sexual assault and child abuse investigators have ready access to competent and appropriate medical personnel during their investigations.

The assessment of physical injuries to the child often includes the evaluation of the *pattern* of the injuries. Bitemarks, for example, may be made by an animal, another child, or by an adult assailant. The diagnosis of an animal bite can usually be made rapidly by medical personnel, since the dentition of animals (other than higher apes) is markedly different from that of humans, especially with regard to the prominence of the canine teeth in animals as opposed to their minuscule incisors. Animal bites also typically tear the flesh, whereas human bites compress the flesh (see Figure 13-3).

Human bitemarks typically bear the impressions of the incisors, in addition to those of the canine teeth, since the human incisors are essentially as prominent as the canines. Adult and child bitemarks are distinguished by the size of the bitemark as measured between the center of the canine teeth in the mark (see Figure 13-3).

Differential

Adult versus Child: If the distance between the center of the canine teeth, the third tooth on each side, is greater than three centimeters, the bite is most likely that of an adult, or at least someone with permanent teeth (over eight years of age). Also, these may differ between the upper and lower teeth.

Human versus Animal: Bites such as dog bites tear the flesh, whereas human bites only compress the flesh, causing only contusions.

FIGURE 13-3 Differential Characteristics of Bitemarks
Source: American Humane Association, *Understanding the Medical Diagnosis of Child Maltreatment: A Guide for Non-Medical Professionals* (Englewood, CO: AHA Publications, 1993). © Copyright 1993, American Humane Association, with permission.

Patterned injuries often reveal the type of instrument wielded by the assailant that caused the injuries. Electrical cords, when gathered into loops, cause injuries with "loop mark" patterns (see Figure 13-4). Other instruments that may cause patterned injuries include wire coat hangers, belt buckles, large finger rings, etc.

"Slap mark" injuries (see Figure 13-5) are created when the child is slapped on the face, neck, back, or buttocks with sufficient force to leave the marks. Bitemarks, patterned injuries, and bruises should be photographed both without and with a measurement scale in place adjacent to the injury (see Chapter 3 for illustration of proper photography of wounds).

Bruises are due to the leakage of blood into the skin tissue that is produced by tissue damage from a direct blow or a crushing injury. Bruising is the earliest and most visible sign of child abuse. Early identification of bruises resulting from child abuse can allow for intervention and prevent further abuse.[13]

Loop Marks

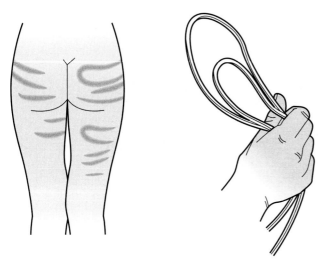

FIGURE 13-4 Loop Marks
Source: American Humane Association, *Understanding the Medical Diagnosis of Child Maltreatment: A Guide for Non-Medical Professionals* (Englewood, CO: AHA Publications, 1993). © Copyright 1993, American Humane Association, with permission.

Slap Marks

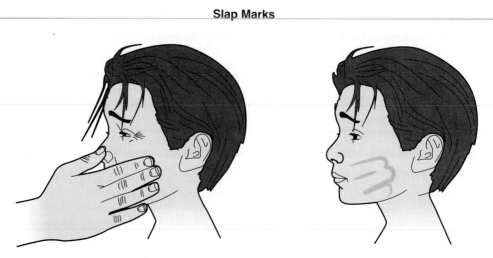

FIGURE 13-5   Slap Marks
Source: American Humane Association, *Understanding the Medical Diagnosis of Child Maltreatment: A Guide for Non-Medical Professionals* (Englewood, CO: AHA Publications, 1993). © Copyright 1993, American Humane Association, with permission.

Bruises seen in infants, especially on the face and buttocks, are more suspicious and should be considered nonaccidental until proven otherwise. Injuries to children's upper arms (caused by efforts to defend themselves), the trunk, the front of their thighs, the sides of their faces, ears and neck, genitalia, stomach, and buttocks are also more likely to be associated with nonaccidental injuries. Injuries to their shins, hips, lower arms, forehead, hands, or the bony prominences (the spine, knees, nose, chin, or elbows) are more likely to signify accidental injury.[14]

Each bruise should be photographed when first seen, and several hours later, when the bruise is fully developed. The bruise will change color over time, so photographs should be taken at intervals as the bruise color changes (light bluish red—few hours, dark purple—within a week, greenish yellow—end of one week, brown—later than one week), disappearing in two to four weeks.[15]

Summary

SEXUAL ASSAULT INVESTIGATIONS

Role of physical evidence in sexual assault cases

- Establishing elements of the crime.
- Identification or elimination of suspect(s).
- Corroborating or disputing the statements of principals in the case (e.g., disputing defense of consent).

Evidence from the crime scene

- Latent fingerprints.
- Footwear impressions, tire tracks, toolmarks.
- Semen evidence.
- Saliva stains.
- Trace evidence: hairs, fibers, soil, etc.
- Bedding where assault took place (semen, trace evidence).

First responders

- Protection of the victim.
- Securing the crime scene.
- Documenting the crime scene.
- Interviewing of victim in privacy (may be done by sexual assault response team member or other investigator).
- Initiating crime broadcast if applicable.
- Arranging for medical examination of victim.

Evidence from the victim

- Clothing worn before/during the assault.
- Clothing worn after the assault.
- Injuries to victim (evidence of force): bruises, lacerations, bitemarks, and binding marks.
- Bloodstains.
- Semen stains.

- Trace evidence (hairs, fibers, soil, vegetation, etc.).
- Bindings on victim.
- Swabs, aspirates from medical examination.
- Blood and hair standards.
- Pubic hair combings.
- Fingernail scrapings.

Evidence from the suspect

- All clothing worn at time of assault.
- Head and pubic hair standards.
- Blood and saliva standards.
- Fingernail scrapings.
- Photographs of any injuries.
- Swabs and aspirates from medical examination.
- Pubic hair combings.

Review Questions

1. The three major sources of physical evidence in a sexual assault investigation are the _____ the _____, and the _____.
2. S.A.R.T. is an acronym for _____ _____ _____ _____.
3. S.A.N.E. is an acronym for _____ _____ _____ _____.
4. Physical evidence can be used to _____ or _____ a suspect in a sexual assault case.
5. The two principal defenses used by a suspect in sexual assault cases are _____ _____ and _____.
6. Evidence that may corroborate nonconsensual sexual activity includes _____ to the victim and _____ to the victim's clothing.
7. The primary goals of the first responder in a sexual assault case are _____ of the victim, _____ of the suspect, and _____ of the scene.
8. It is good practice to keep the crime scene secured until after the _____ _____ of the victim.
9. _____ _____ recovered at the scene may link the suspect to other assaults.
10. _____ stains may be found on the victim's body as a result of bites from the perpetrator.
11. The clothing worn _____ and _____ the assault should be collected for laboratory examination.
12. If the assault occurs in an outdoor setting, _____ and _____ may be found on the victim's clothing.

13. Bitemark injuries may have two types of evidence, _____ _____ and _____ from the perpetrator.
14. The violent nature of a sexual assault may result in the transfer of _____ _____.
15. The "chain of custody" requires that the custody of each item of evidence must be documented from the time it is _____ until it is presented as evidence in _____.
16. Each item of clothing collected from the victim must be packaged separately in _____ bags to avoid mold growth.
17. Clothing worn by the victim before/during the assault may have _____ evidence transferred from the suspect.
18. Clothing worn by the victim after the assault may have _____ _____ from vaginal drainage.
19. Semen stains on the victim's body are typically collected with sterile _____ _____.
20. _____ on the victim may not be immediately obvious but may develop fully over several days.
21. Pubic hair standards should be _____ or cut _____ to the skin, for a total of forty to fifty hairs.
22. Head hair standards should be taken from the _____, _____, _____, and _____ of the scalp.
23. Vaginal swabs should be _____ and _____ in order to preserve the biological materials present.
24. Vaginal aspirates should be _____ and transported to the laboratory _____.

Further References

American College of Emergency Physicians. 1999. *Evaluation and Management of the Sexually Assaulted or Sexually Abused Patient.* Dallas, TX.

American Professional Society on the Abuse of Children. 1998. *Glossary of Terms and the Interpretation of Findings for Child Sexual Abuse Evidentiary Examination.*

California Governor's Office of Criminal Justice Planning. July, 2001. *California Medical Protocol for Examination of Sexual Assault and Child Sexual Abuse Victims.* Sacramento, CA.

Hazelwood, R. R., and A. W. Burgess. 2001. *Practical Aspects of Rape Investigation*, 3rd ed. Boca Raton, FL: CRC Press.

Jackson, A. R.W., and J. Julie. 2004. *Forensic Science.* Essex, England, U.K.: Pearson Education Limited

James, S. H., and J.J. Nordby, eds. 2005. *Forensic Science* (An Introduction to Scientific and Investigative Techniques), 2nd ed. Boca Raton, FL: CRC Press (Imprint of Taylor and Francis).

Office of Criminal Justice Planning. 1991. *Training Curriculum for the Examination of Sexual Assault and Child Sexual Abuse Victims.* State of California, Sacramento, CA.

Saferstein, R. 2009. *Forensic Science* (From the Crime Scene to the Crime Lab). Upper Saddle River, NJ: Pearson Education, Inc.

Smith, Jean C. *et al.* 1989. *Understanding the Medical Diagnosis of Child Maltreatment*, American Humane Association, Children's Division, 63 Inverness Drive East, Englewood, CO, 80112, (written for both medical professionals and nonmedical investigators, this book should be in the library of any individual or agency involved in the investigation of child abuse and child sexual abuse).

U.S. Department of Justice. 2001. *First Response to Victims of Crime.* Office of Justice Programs, Available at http://www.ojp.usdoj.gov/ovc/publications/infores/firstrep/2001/NCJ189631.txt.

U.S. Department of Justice. September 2004. *A National Protocol for Sexual Assault Medical Forensic Examinations* (Adults/Adolescents). NCJ 206554.

White, P., ed. 1998. *Crime Scene to Court* (The Essentials of Forensic Science), Cambridge, U.K.: The Royal Society of Chemistry.

APPENDIX 13-A

Swab Drying Box

Courtesy of Kinderprint Company, Inc.

APPENDIX 13-B

Chain of Custody Form

CHAIN OF CUSTODY FORM

Patient's Name: _____ Patient's ID#: _____

Hospital: _____ Hospital ID#: _____

Name of Examiner: _____ Title: _____

Name of Witness: _____

Date of Examination: _____ Time: _____

Name of Law Enforcement Officer: _____

Receiving Evidence: _____ Date: _____ Time: _____

Patient's Signature (Optional): _____

FROM: (Print Name & Sign)	TO: (Print Name & Sign)	DATE	TIME

Source: U.S. Department of Justice, Office of Violence Against Women, *A National Protocol for Sexual Assault Medical Forensic Examinations: Adults/Adolescents* (Washington, DC: GPO, September 2004): NCJ 206554.

APPENDIX 13-C

Seal on Chain of Custody Envelopes

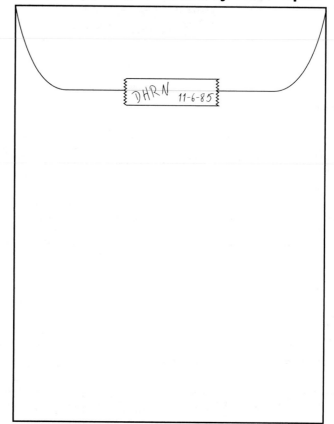

Source: U.S. Department of Justice, Office of Violence Against Women, *A National Protocol for Sexual Assault Medical Forensic Examinations: Adults/Adolescents* (Washington, DC: GPO, September 2004): NCJ 206554.

14 HOMICIDE CRIME SCENE INVESTIGATIONS

Other sins only speak; Murder shrieks out.

John Webster, *The Duchess of Malfi*, IV:2.

Key Words: Team investigation, pathologist, wounds, nude bodies, trace evidence, bloodstain, bloodstain pattern, GSR tests, autopsy, general view photographs, close-up photographs, tape lift, gunshot wound, probe, sexual assault homicide, decomposed remains.

INTRODUCTION

Homicide crime scenes are processed in the same systematic manner as other types of crime scenes, but some additional considerations apply to the homicide crime scene. In most jurisdictions, a deputy coroner or deputy medical examiner-coroner must be present at all homicide crime scenes. Additional personnel may be needed at the crime scene, particularly forensic scientists from different disciplines. These individuals may be instrumental in a reconstruction of the crime scene or an estimation of the date or time of death of the decedent. In addition to the scene(s) of the crime, homicide investigations also involve the postmortem examination of the victim, a procedure that should be accomplished in the same systematic manner as that employed at the crime scene. Homicide investigations are, by their very nature, team investigations comprising the first responder(s), the crime scene investigators, the detectives, the forensic laboratory personnel, and the medical examiner.

HOMICIDE INVESTIGATION RESPONSE TEAM

The formation of homicide investigation response teams (HIRTs) in a jurisdiction represents the best approach to ensuring efficient and effective processing of the crime scene. A team composed of the first responder, the investigator or detective in charge of the investigation, a criminalist or supervisory crime scene investigator in charge of the scene investigation, and crime scene investigators will typically complete the crime scene processing in an optimum fashion. Key to the homicide investigation response team is the training of each of the personnel acting as a member of the team. Each member responding to a homicide crime scene should be fully trained and experienced in performing that member's duties at the crime scene and be conversant with the duties and responsibilities of the other members of the team. Training classes such as those conducted in the formation of the sexual assault response teams are highly desirable and will work to ensure a seamless investigation at the homicide crime scene.

For those agencies without a formalized homicide investigation response team, the homicide investigator will act as a team leader, coordinating the first responders, crime scene investigators, investigative efforts by field officers and detectives, laboratory examinations of the physical evidence, and the forensic autopsy. It is essential that the investigator develop a good professional relationship with these agencies and individuals so that the homicide investigations will be smooth, efficient, and effective.

ADDITIONAL PERSONNEL OFTEN NEEDED AT HOMICIDE CRIME SCENES

Criminalists and other forensic scientists

Criminalists or other forensic scientists from the forensic laboratory are usually the individuals who will accomplish a reconstruction of the crime scene when needed. It is advantageous to the individual performing a crime scene reconstruction to be at the scene in order to assist in the documentation necessary for the foundation of the reconstruction. Often, these professionals will have specialized instruments or devices that will aid immensely in reconstruction efforts. In many jurisdictions, homicide crime scenes will be processed by a team from the forensic laboratory composed of criminalists, or by a team composed of criminalists and other forensic specialists, such as crime scene investigators. In some jurisdictions, a supervisory crime scene investigator from the crime scene unit will be in charge of the scene investigation, freeing up the detectives to supervise the overall investigation and perform the other tasks necessary to the investigation.

Pathologists

In many cases, the **pathologist** who will perform the autopsy may assist the investigator at the scene. Firsthand knowledge of the scene may also provide the autopsy pathologist with information that facilitates the autopsy by suggesting additional tests to be performed on the body of the victim.

Prosecuting attorney (homicide on call)

The rather complex area of criminal law relating to search and seizure and the need for search warrants in certain circumstances makes it beneficial to have a prosecuting attorney present or immediately available at the homicide crime scene. This approach allows for the investigator to obtain legal advice without undue delay and to have search warrants prepared expeditiously.

Fire department personnel (for lighting at night scenes)

In those night situations when it is not feasible to wait until dawn to perform the crime scene search, fire department personnel usually have excellent equipment for lighting the area that needs to be searched. This resource may make the crime scene search more efficient and effective than a search without adequate lighting.

Forensic anthropologists

The investigation of a burial scene is enhanced considerably when a qualified physical anthropologist is present to aid in the appropriate approach to excavating a buried body. These professionals are trained in the proper manner in which the recovery of the remains is accomplished so that the physical evidence is not compromised. The methods for recovery of the remains are part of the arsenal of the forensic physical anthropologist and are a valuable addition to the crime scene team.

Forensic entomologists

Forensic entomologists can aid in the collection and interpretation of insect evidence, particularly with decomposed bodies and the estimation of the day and time of death. The crime scene investigator should consider calling to the scene a qualified forensic entomologist when there is insufficient information as to the date and time of death and when there are insect larval stages present. The identification of the species and the larval stage of the insects permits the entomologist to estimate the time interval that the body has been present at its location. The insect species that are present as eggs or larvae on the body may also be indicators of where the victim was located at the time of deposition of the eggs (many species are indigenous to a specific area). If a forensic entomologist is not available, the investigator should collect insect evidence as suggested in Appendix VI.

AT THE HOMICIDE CRIME SCENE

Precaution

A common practice at the scene of a homicide is to focus attention on the body, often to the detriment of the effectiveness of the scene investigation. Many features at the scene are of crucial importance. It is a good practice to avoid focusing all your attention on the body and to follow a systematic approach to the processing of the scene. This strategy will help avoid oversights of critical evidence and factors that will allow for reconstruction of the crime events.

Condition of body/clothing/scene

POSITION OF THE BODY
The position of the body may be very important for reconstruction efforts. Carefully record the location and position of the body in your notes, with photographs and accurate diagrams. Note especially any unusual position of the body or the extremities.

POSTMORTEM LIVIDITY
"Postmortem lividity" is the term that refers to the condition whereby blood in the body settles to the lowest point of the body because of the effects of gravity. Lividity is characterized by a reddish hue of the body surface where the blood has settled. This condition is irreversible, so that when a body is moved to another location and repositioned, the pattern of the lividity will reveal that the body has been moved postmortem.

WOUNDS AND SIGNS OF STRUGGLE ON THE BODY (CLOTHING TEARS)

Record with notes, photographs, and diagrams any **wounds** on the body that are visible without disturbing the body. The type of wounds present may be of significance in the search for weapons at the scene(s). Any signs of damage to the victim's clothing should be described in the notes and photographed before the body is disturbed.

SIGNS OF STRUGGLE AT THE SCENE

Many times the position of disturbed items such as furniture plays a crucial role in the reconstruction of the crime events. The investigator should photograph and sketch accurately the location and position of any item or furniture that is not in its normal position and should record in the notes any observations regarding the condition of the furniture item.

PRESENCE/ABSENCE OF NOTES (POSSIBLE SUICIDE)

Carefully handle any note or notes present to preserve latent impressions. Dictate the contents of the note or place in case notes. Package the note in a manila envelope or document holder with the notation "LATENT FINGERPRINTS" on the envelope exterior. If the note requires examination by a document examiner, the note should first be submitted to the document section so that the examiner can perform the document examinations prior to chemical processing for latent prints.

NUDE BODIES

Nude bodies should be considered a source for transfer evidence such as hairs, fibers, and bloodstains from the perpetrator, and other materials that may have originated from the perpetrator or the site of the homicide if the body has been moved.

- Disturb the body as little as possible before processing.
- Scan the body surface carefully for any trace evidence such as hairs or fibers that may be lost during handling of the body.
- Remove and package any **trace evidence** that is not firmly attached to the body.
- Carefully place the body on a new sheet, and wrap securely before placing in the body bag (see "Protection of the Body During Removal" in a later section).

TIME-OF-DEATH CONSIDERATIONS

- Record the ambient temperature with an accurate thermometer.
- Record position of light switches (see data compilation list in Chapter 2).
- Record and photograph any food materials present in the kitchen or dining area.
- Consider having the deputy medical examiner take the temperature of the liver.

BLOODSTAINS AND BLOODSTAIN PATTERNS

- Sketch, photograph, and describe in the notes any bloodstains present at the scene.
- Note the dimensions and condition of any pools of blood.
- Photograph bloodstain patterns using the grid, the corner label, or the perimeter scale method described in Chapter 7.
- Collect samples of each **bloodstain** and **bloodstain pattern**.

- Collect control sample for each bloodstain or pattern sampled.
- Photograph any bloodstains on the victim or the victim's clothing before the victim is moved.

Protection of the body during removal

TRACE EVIDENCE ON THE BODY

Take appropriate precautions to avoid loss of trace evidence on the body or clothing. Remove all loose evidence at the scene before moving the body to avoid loss.

GUNSHOT RESIDUE (GSR) TESTS ON THE VICTIM'S HANDS

If **GSR tests** cannot be done at the scene, place paper or plastic bags over the victim's hands, and tape securely with evidence tape (never use plastic bags on a living subject).

REMOVAL OF THE BODY

Carefully lift the body onto a new, clean sheet. Wrap the sheet around the body to preserve any trace evidence or stains present before placing the body in a new, clean body bag. Affix a seal to the bag so that the bag is not opened until you are at the autopsy site, in order to verify that the seal is intact and to supervise the removal of the body in a manner that avoids loss or contamination of all evidence.

PRESERVATION OF SHEET USED TO WRAP THE BODY

Make sure that the team is aware that the sheet needs to be preserved at the morgue by folding inward bindle style to preserve any trace evidence that dislodged during removal and transport of the body. It is an excellent idea to have an officer accompany the body to the morgue to maintain security of the locked bag and to make sure that the bag is not opened until the arrival of the investigating team.

Area beneath the body

CHECK THE AREA BENEATH THE BODY

Once the body has been removed, check the area under the body thoroughly for additional evidence. Examine the area for trace evidence, bloodstain patterns, and impression evidence.

DOCUMENTATION OF EVIDENCE PRESENT

Photograph, sketch, and note in the case notes any evidence present. If no evidence is found, document in the notes the absence of any findings.

RECOVERY OF EVIDENCE LOCATED

After each item of evidence has been documented, collect, label, and package each item according to the directions for that type of evidence.

BLOODSTAIN PATTERN DOCUMENTATION

Document any bloodstain patterns under the body with photographs, sketches with accurate measurements, and entries in the case notes (see Chapter 7 for bloodstain pattern documentation methods). Be sure to obtain samples of each of the bloodstain patterns (at least one sample from each pattern emanating from the same source) and an appropriate control specimen for each sample taken. If it is not certain that a single source is responsible for all the stains in a pattern area, take multiple samples from representative locations within that area.

EXCAVATION OF THE AREA BENEATH THE BODY

Excavate the site beneath the body if the victim has penetrating bullet wounds. The use of a metal detector is highly recommended for this purpose. The excavated soil should be screened with a mesh that will recover small bullet fragments.

RESEARCH THE SCENE FOR PHYSICAL EVIDENCE

After completing the search of the site under the body, inspect closely the area surrounding the body for any additional evidence that may have been missed during the initial search.

PRESERVATION OF THE SCENE UNTIL AUTOPSY COMPLETION

It is a good practice to preserve the entire scene when feasible until after completion of the autopsy. Often, information obtained at the autopsy will suggest additional efforts needed at the crime scene and body site (additional weapons, trace evidence, etc.).

POSTMORTEM EXAMINATION (AUTOPSY) GUIDE[1]

Preautopsy conference

The preautopsy conference is a vital part of the postmortem autopsy. The conference should include the lead investigator, the crime scene investigator, the criminalists who were at the scene and/or who will analyze the evidence from the **autopsy**, and the autopsy pathologist. Often, the information from the scene will dictate many of the procedures needed at the autopsy. In addition, the autopsy will frequently dictate a number of additional tasks to be completed at the scene. The preautopsy conference should be well thought out and planned in advance of the actual autopsy. Meetings between the principals at autopsies should develop a well-planned approach to the autopsy, so that each member of the team will know in advance what type of information each of the others will need in order to facilitate the autopsy. The development of a homicide investigation response team protocol in the jurisdiction will strengthen considerably the preautopsy conference. The wrap-up conference at the end of the autopsy should cover the topics in the preautopsy conference as a double check.

For those jurisdictions lacking a formalized homicide investigation team, a preautopsy conference with the forensic pathologist conference should be required. Although there may not be a formalized team, homicide investigations are team efforts, and the forensic pathologist is a member of the homicide investigative team. Homicide investigators should make arrangements with the coroner's office or the medical examiner's office to ensure that the investigator is permitted a preautopsy conference with the forensic pathologist performing the autopsy, so that information needed from the autopsy is obtained and that information from the crime scene helpful to the autopsy is transmitted to the forensic pathologist prior to commencement of the autopsy.

Postmortem examination photography

Photography is a critical aspect of the forensic autopsy. Photographs should always be taken before any procedures that may alter the appearance of any evidence present and before the collection of the victim's clothing and any trace evidence present. The log of the autopsy photographs should include thorough notes of the reason for each photograph. Sketches of pertinent areas being photographed will help in the review of the photographs for report writing and follow-up investigations.

GENERAL IDENTIFICATION PHOTOGRAPHS

Take photographs of the left and right profiles of the face, and a frontal view of the face before and after cleanup. Consideration should also be given to photographs after embalming, since some features may be more pronounced after embalming, such as blunt instrument wounds.

PHOTOGRAPHS OF THE CLOTHED BODY

- General (overall) views.
    Take a series of **general view photographs** to show the appearance and condition of all clothing on the decedent.
- Close-up views.
    Take **close-up photographs** of those areas containing trace evidence or damage to the garments. If the damage shows any patterns, photograph the patterns both with and without a scale in view.

PHOTOGRAPHS OF ALL TRACE EVIDENCE

Take photographs of each evidence item both with and without a measurement scale in view. The photograph without the scale in view precludes the suggestion that any important evidence is obscured by the scale in the field of view.

NOTES AND SKETCHES OF THE LOCATION OF EACH ITEM PHOTOGRAPHED

The notes and sketches of those items photographed will document the location and appearance of each item photographed and collected.

COLLECTION OF VICTIM'S CLOTHING

The victim's clothing should be removed carefully after the photographs of the clothed victim have been completed. Package each article of clothing in a separate paper bag. If the clothing contains moist or wet bloodstains, follow the procedures outlined in Chapter 7 for bloody clothing.

PHOTOGRAPHS AFTER CLOTHING REMOVAL

- General views of the entire body.
    The overall views of the victim should include all body surfaces on both the front and the back of the body.
- Close-up views of all body areas.
    Close-up views of the body areas will provide greater detail of the surfaces depicted in the overall photographs. The notes and photograph logs should relate

each photograph to the specific body area being photographed. A sketch prepared of the area and items being photographed will add clarity to the photographic documentation.

- Close-up (macro) photographs of all wounds without and with a measurement scale in view.

   The location and orientation of each wound may be crucial to a reconstruction effort. All close-up photographs of wounds should be taken normal to the body surface (see Figure 3-2, Chapter 3) to minimize distortion from the viewing angle. The photographs should be related to the autopsy surgeon's notes and sketches.

Trace evidence

- Photograph trace evidence before removal (see the preceding section on photography).
- Note and sketch the location of each item on the body.
- Collect each item of trace evidence and seal in an appropriate container, affix standard identification data to the container, and have the autopsy pathologist initial and date each container.
- Collect or have the pathologist collect all debris or trace evidence from each wound. Seal each item of evidence in the appropriate container, label with standard identification data, and have the pathologist date and initial each item.
- Consider having the pathologist excise wounds for further study. Wound tracks may show debris from clothing or intermediate targets. Bones may show toolmarks from weapons such as knives or axes.

Procedures for nude bodies[2]

Nude bodies must be processed for any trace evidence before the actual autopsy begins, since there is no clothing present that would normally contain the trace evidence.

EXAMINATION OF THE BODY

Carefully scan the body surfaces under existing light, followed by a scan with a laser light or an alternate (forensic) light source. If the existing light is inadequate, the search may be enhanced with halogen lamps, taking care not to allow the light to get too close to the body, since halogen lamps generate intense heat that may damage the body surface or any trace evidence present. Fibers and certain physiological fluid stains fluoresce under laser light or certain wavelengths of light generated by the alternate light source.

TRACE EVIDENCE

Photograph each item as described before, diagram the location of the item(s), and remove (or have the pathologist remove) and package any trace evidence not previously removed at the crime scene (see the preceding photography section).

LATENT PRINT PROCESSING OF THE BODY

If the body is to be processed for latent prints, the latent processing should be accomplished only after a diligent search for trace evidence has been completed, since the procedures for latent print development may interfere with the collection of any trace evidence present (hairs, fibers, vegetation, etc.).

TAPE LIFT TECHNIQUE FOR FIBERS AND OTHER TRACE EVIDENCE

Tape lift the following areas, making a separate tape lift for each area of interest:

- All ligature marks (neck, wrists, ankles, etc.).
- Face and hands.
- Body surfaces:
  1. Upper and lower torso.
  2. Arms and legs.
  3. Pubic and crotch area.

The tape lifts should be performed using specially formulated trace evidence tape available from commercial sources. Once lifted, the tape lift can be placed on a clean plastic sheet such as kitchen sealing plastic film or placed on plastic sheets designed for this purpose (available from commercial sources).

Hair standard samples

Note: When taking hair standards from deceased victims, it is essential to collect an adequate amount of hair, because this may be the only opportunity to collect hair specimens. Therefore, the recommendations for the quantity of hairs to be collected exceeds that for living victims, since additional samples can be collected from live victims when necessary.

SCALP HAIR STANDARD

Collect 150–200 total hairs, collected from the left front, left rear, right front, right rear, and top of the scalp, with approximately 40 strands from each area (see Figure 6-3, Chapter 6).

PUBIC HAIR STANDARD

Collect approximately 100–120 total hairs, sampling all areas of the pubic region (see Figure 6-4, Chapter 6).

BODY HAIR STANDARD

Take samples of body hair adjacent to any wounds, and samples from the upper arms and legs, torso, beard, and moustache.

Fingernail scrapings

- Carefully inspect each fingernail on each hand, looking for trace evidence such as hairs, fibers, blood, skin, and torn fingernails.
- Package scraping from each nail in a separate bindle/envelope (some laboratories prefer one package for each hand).
- If any torn fingernails are observed, cut as close to the quick as possible with sharp scissors, package in separate bindle/envelope, and label accordingly. Be sure to mention the torn fingernail to investigators and in the report. The torn edge may be matched to fragments found at the scene or on the person of the perpetrator.

Gunshot residues

- See the section for gunshot residues in Chapter 8 for detailed instructions for GSR collection.
- Collect suspected residues on aluminum disks, with a swab kit or with a combination kit as directed by your laboratory. If a combination kit is used, always take the samples with the aluminum disks before using the swabs.

Gunshot wounds

PHOTOGRAPHS OF WOUNDS
Photograph each **gunshot wound** with and without a measurement ruler in place. Position the camera normal (i.e., with the film plane parallel to the plane of the wound) to the body surface, with the wound in the center of view.

DESCRIPTION OF WOUNDS
Describe each wound in the field notes, with measurements of any visible patterns of gunshot residue. (*Note:* The description should correspond as closely as feasible to the description given by the autopsy pathologist.)

COLLECTING LOOSE RESIDUES
In conjunction with the pathologist, collect and retain any loosely adhering residues on the body, including any from the wounds.

PHOTOGRAPHS OF WOUNDS WITH PROBES IN PLACE
Each wound should be photographed with a **probe** in place after the photographs just described have been completed. Photographs with the probes in place should be taken from the head of the victim with the film plane parallel to the shoulders and from the side with the film plane parallel to the long axis of the body (see Figures 14-1 and 14-2). The line of sight of the camera should be aligned with each probe or groups of probes.

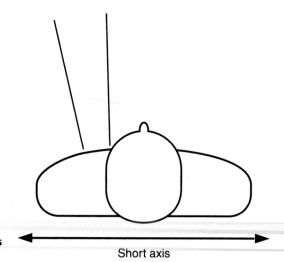

FIGURE 14-1 Wound Probes from Head of Victim

Short axis

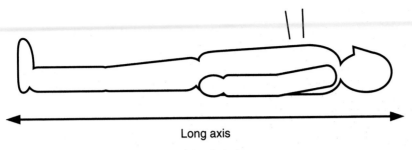

Long axis

FIGURE 14-2   Wound Probes from Side of Victim

PHOTOGRAPHS AFTER THE SCALP HAIR IS SHAVED
After the pathologist shaves and removes the hair surrounding a scalp wound, rephotograph the wound with and without a scale next to the wound if the wound is in the hair. Save the hair removed for GSR testing.

SWAB FOR GUNSHOT RESIDUE (GSR) IF NEEDED
If the victim died of gunshot wounds, swab the hands for gunshot residue using a commercially supplied GSR kit or a kit supplied by the local forensic laboratory.

REPHOTOGRAPH EACH WOUND SITE AFTER THE BODY IS CLEANED
Additional information may be obtained from examination of the wounds after they have been cleaned. Rephotograph the wounds both with and without a measurement scale in place if the wounds appear clearer with respect to shape or tattooing of the skin.

RECOVERY OF BULLETS
Remove excessive blood clots and tissue from recovered bullets. Do not attempt to clean the bullets thoroughly, since this action may remove valuable trace evidence adhering to the bullet (e.g., fibers, paint smears, construction materials). Dry thoroughly before packaging. Package in a pillbox lined with crumpled notebook paper (do not use cotton). *Do not mark bullets*, but seal and label their containers with standard identification data.

RE-EXAMINATION OF WOUNDS AFTER EMBALMING
Frequently the victim's wounds will have better definition of the class characteristics of a blunt instrument after embalming has been completed. The investigator should make arrangements to view the victim after embalming is completed (but before cosmetics have been applied to the body) to ascertain whether additional photography is necessary.

Condition of teeth/dentures

Collect any fractured/chipped dentures or bridges for comparison with any fragments located at the homicide scene, on the suspect's clothing, or on the suspect vehicle in a vehicular homicide.

Fingerprints/palm prints/footprints

Always take inked impression of the fingers as a permanent record of the victim's identity. Take inked impressions of palms and the toes/feet (if no footwear is present). Take more than one set of impressions, since the opportunity to take additional prints may not present itself again. Do not take finger/palm/sole impressions until *after* procedures for collecting gunshot residues and trace evidence on the hands are completed.

Sexual assault homicides

It is strongly recommended that the victim of a **sexual assault homicide** should be examined for sexual assault evidence in the same manner as for live victims. The optimum procedure is to have a sexual assault examiner (medical doctor trained in sexual assault examinations or sexual assault nurse examiner) perform a complete sexual assault examination on the victim in cooperation with the autopsy pathologist at the time of the autopsy. This is the ideal approach for the autopsy of a sexual assault/homicide victim. See the section on Medical Examination of the Victim, Chapter 13, for detailed information on the collection of sexual assault evidence.

The examiner should use either a commercially prepared sexual assault evidence collection kit for the collection of evidence and standards from the victim or a kit prepared by the local forensic laboratory. All the appropriate containers for proper collection and packaging of the evidence collected should be contained in the kit. If additional specimens need to be collected, packaging materials may be used from the crime scene kits.

Vehicular homicides

COLLECTION OF CLOTHING
Handle clothing carefully as described previously. Examine closely for any loosely adhering paint or glass fragments. Recover and package carefully the fragments (see the sections on "Glass Evidence" and "Paint Evidence" in Chapter 6, and see Chapter 12).

IMPRESSIONS ON BODY SURFACES
Examine the body carefully for any impressions from the vehicle's tires, grill, headlight assemblies, and bumper components. Photograph any impressions located both with and without a scale in place. These markings may be more apparent after embalming, so arrangements should be made to return and rephotograph the body after embalming has been completed.

EXAMINATION OF INJURIES FOR GLASS OR PAINT
Request that the pathologist examine all injured areas and the hair for glass or paint fragments.

HAIR STANDARDS
Hair standards from the face, scalp, and injured areas should be collected for comparison with any items recovered from a suspected vehicle (see Chapter 6).

TOXICOLOGY SAMPLES
Blood and/or tissues should be collected for toxicology examinations (this procedure is typically done by the autopsy pathologist).

BLOOD FOR DNA TYPING AND ALCOHOL ANALYSIS
Blood should be collected for DNA typing by the forensic laboratory.

Decomposed Remains

X-RAYS OF THE REMAINS
Decomposed remains (and all other remains) should be X-rayed prior to the autopsy to locate any bullets, bullet fragments, knife blades, ice pick ends, and the like in the body. The X-rays may also aid in the identification of an unidentified victim and of an age estimation through examination of the X-rays by a radiologist and forensic anthropologist. Old, healed fractures may permit a positive identification of the victim through comparison by the radiologist with previous X-rays of the victim. The growth stages of the bone ends as revealed by the X-rays permit the forensic anthropologist to estimate closely the age of the victim.

INKED FINGER/PALM/SOLE IMPRESSIONS
Fingerprint quality may be compromised because of decomposition. Make sure that all prints are legible before the body is released. You may have to request the pathologist to remove the digital skin for processing in the laboratory in order to obtain legible impressions. Make sure that each finger is accurately identified on the container for each segment of digital skin. If badly shriveled, the digits may need to be expanded through injection of fluid under the skin (usually a solution of hot gelatin and glycerine).

AREA BENEATH THE REMAINS
At the scene, the ground under the remains should be searched for bullets that were dislodged because of decomposition. The use of a good metal detector is recommended. The area should be excavated and sifted when a positive result is obtained with the metal detector.

ADDITIONAL FORENSIC SPECIALISTS AT THE AUTOPSY
Any of the following forensic specialists may be needed at the autopsy:

- Forensic odontologist (dentist): To aid in identification through dentition or to document bitemark evidence.
- Forensic anthropologist: To identify the species of bones, when there is a question of the species identity, and the estimated age, sex, and race.
- Forensic entomologist: To aid in the estimation of time of death based on the types and stages of insect larvae found with the remains.

Body fluids and toxicology specimens

Labels on bottles or containers at the scene should be examined. Containers for prescribed medications will have numbers that can be checked at a pharmacy for identification and dosage. This information should be furnished to the pathologist.

All specimens for toxicological analysis must be taken prior to embalming. Each of the specimens that follow may be taken automatically by the autopsy pathologist.

SAMPLE FOR BLOOD ALCOHOL DETERMINATION

A minimum of 3 cc of blood from the heart or a major blood vessel should be drawn with a vacuum vial containing a preservative and an anticoagulant (gray-top tube).

SAMPLE FOR BLOOD TYPING

A minimum sample of 5 cc should be drawn from the heart if possible. Use a purple-top Vacutainer or comparable tube containing EDTA anticoagulant (see the section on standard blood samples, Chapter 7).

SAMPLE(S) FOR TOXICOLOGY

If drugs or poisons are suspected, at least 25 cc each of blood and urine are required. Liver, bile, vitreous humor, and stomach contents may also be retained.

WRAP-UP CONFERENCE

Have a conference with all parties present to review the autopsy:

- Have all necessary procedures been done? (Refer to preautopsy conference.)
- Are all items properly packaged and labeled?
- Should the body be secured in a locked bag pending further information from the scene or witnesses?
- Can any member of the team think of anything else that needs to be done?
- *Remember, you may not have a second chance to collect evidence after the autopsy!*

Summary

PREPLANNING FOR HOMICIDE CRIME SCENES

- Homicide investigation response team (HIRT). When feasible, each jurisdiction should have a well-trained and coordinated homicide investigation response team. The planning, development, and training of these teams will be repaid many times over by the increase in efficiency and effectiveness of the homicide crime scene investigations.
- Other professionals who may be needed to augment the team.
  - Criminalists.
  - Pathologists.
  - Prosecuting attorney.
  - Forensic anthropologists.
  - Forensic entomologists.

AT THE HOMICIDE CRIME SCENE

- Documentation of the scene.
  Document the scene thoroughly with notes, photographs, and sketches. Videotape the scene if advisable or required by the agency.
- Condition of body/clothing/scene.
  - Position of the body.
  - Wounds or signs of struggle on the body.
  - Signs of struggle at the scene.
  - Presence/absence of suicide note(s) (authentic?).

- Nude bodies.
  - Disturb as little as possible.
  - Scan body surface for trace evidence.
  - Remove and package any loose trace evidence on the body.
  - Place the body on a new sheet, and wrap before placing in the body bag.
- Time-of-death considerations.
  - Record ambient temperature with an accurate thermometer.
  - Record and photograph any food materials present in the kitchen and/or dining area.
  - Consider having the liver temperature taken by the deputy medical examiner.
- Bloodstains and bloodstain patterns.
  - Sketch, photograph, and describe in the notes any bloodstains at the scene.
  - Note the dimensions and condition of any pools of blood.
  - Photograph bloodstain patterns using the grid, perimeter scale, or corner label methods described in Chapter 7.
  - Collect samples of each bloodstain and representative stains in spatter patterns.
  - Collect a control sample for each bloodstain and representatives from patterns.
  - Photograph any bloodstains on the victim or victim's clothing before the victim is removed.
- Protection of the body during removal.
  - Take precautions to avoid loss of trace evidence on the body or clothing. Remove and package any trace evidence that may be lost during handling and transport of the body.
  - Perform gunshot residue tests on the victim's hands.
  - Remove the body onto a clean sheet, and place in a body bag.
  - Preserve the sheet from the body for laboratory analysis.
- Area beneath the body.
  - Check the area under the body for additional evidence.
  - Document any evidence found under the body.
- Recover any evidence found, and package properly.
- Document any bloodstain patterns under the body with appropriate techniques (Chapter 7).
- Excavate site if the victim has penetrating bullet wounds.
- Re-search of the scene.
  - Re-search the scene for any evidence that may have been missed during the initial search.
- Preserving the scene until completion of autopsy.

AT THE AUTOPSY

- Preautopsy conference with all investigative team members.
- Postmortem photography.
  - General identification photographs.
  - Photographs of clothed body.
    - General (overall) views.
    - Close-up views (trace evidence, damage to clothing).
  - Photographs of all trace evidence.
- Notes and sketches of the location of each item photographed.
- Collection of the victim's clothing.
  - Remove each item carefully.
  - Package each item in a separate bag.
  - For bloody clothing, follow the procedures outlined in Chapter 7 for packaging of bloody clothing.
- Photographs after clothing removal.
  - General views of entire body.
  - Close-up views of all body areas.
  - Close-up (macro) photographs of all wounds, both with and without measurement scale in view.
  - Photographs of bullet wounds (see section on gunshot wounds that follows).
- Trace evidence.
  - Photograph before removal.
  - Note and sketch the location of each item on the body.
  - Collect each item of trace evidence, seal in an appropriate container, add standard

identification data, and have the autopsy pathologist initial the container.

- Collect or have the pathologist collect all debris or trace evidence from each wound, package, and label appropriately.
- Consider asking the pathologist to excise wounds for further study if not already done.

- Procedures for nude bodies.
  - Nude bodies must be processed for trace evidence before the autopsy begins in order to avoid loss.
  - In conjunction with the pathologist, scan body surfaces with strong white light, followed by long-wave UV light and/or alternate light source.
  - Latent print processing of the body may be attempted after search for and collection of any trace evidence but before any tape-lifting technique.
  - Tape lift (with separate tape lift) the following areas, using specially formulated tape for this purpose:
    - All ligature marks on the body.
    - Face and hands.
    - Upper and lower torso.
    - Arms and legs.
    - Pubic and crotch area (critical for rape homicides).

- Hair standard samples. *Note:* It is essential to take adequate samples from the postmortem victims, since another opportunity may not exist.
  - Scalp hair standard: 150–200 hairs from all regions of the scalp (see Chapter 6).
  - Pubic hair standard: 100–120 hairs from all regions of the pubic area (see Chapter 6).
  - Body hairs: Samples adjacent to any wounds, samples from upper arms and legs, torso, beard, and moustache.

- Fingernail scrapings.
  - Inspect each nail for trace evidence, blood, skin, and broken nails.
  - Package a scraping from each nail in a separate package.
  - Remove any torn nails by cutting close to the quick with sharp scissors, and

package each specimen in a separate container.

- Gunshot wounds.
  - Photograph each wound both with and without a measurement scale in place and with the camera normal to the wound surface (film plane parallel to wound surface).
  - Describe wounds in the field notes, with measurements of any visible patterns of gunshot residue (should correspond *exactly* to pathologist's description).
  - Collect loose residues in conjunction with the pathologist.
  - Photograph each wound both with and without a probe inserted in the wound track.
  - Take photographs of wounds after scalp hair is shaved. Take photographs after the scalp hair is shaved around a scalp wound, both with and without a measurement scale in place. Save the shaved hair for GSR analysis.
  - Rephotograph each wound site after the body is cleaned (shape of wound or tattooing may then be clearer).
  - Recover bullets using the methods already described.
  - Reexamine wounds after embalming. Often the wounds will have better definition after embalming.
  - For gunshot residue collection, collect suspected GSR from hands using both disk and swab techniques.

- Condition of teeth and dentures.
  - Collect any fractured or chipped dentures or bridges for comparison with items from the scene or the suspect.

- Finger, palm, and foot sole prints.
  - Take impressions of these areas of friction ridges for possible comparison purposes.

SEXUAL ASSAULT HOMICIDES

- Arrange for a sexual assault examination of the victim by a qualified sexual assault examiner in conjunction with the autopsy pathologist.

- A sexual assault evidence collection kit should be used for the sexual assault segment of the postmortem autopsy.

VEHICULAR HOMICIDES

- Collection of clothing.
  - Handle clothing carefully to avoid loss of trace evidence.
  - Examine closely for loosely adhering paint or glass fragments. Recover them, and package carefully.
  - Wrap each article of clothing separately, and tape seal in a bag, and then tape seal any corners or seams that may allow loss of trace evidence.
  - Label each bag with standard identification data.
- Impressions on body surfaces.
  - Examine the body carefully for any impressions from the vehicle.
  - Photograph any impressions both with and without the measurement scale in place.
  - Make arrangements to rephotograph any impressions after embalming, since the markings may have improved definition.
- Examination of injuries for glass or paint fragments.
  - Examination of injured areas.
  - Examination of scalp hair.
- Hair standards.
  - Facial hairs (beard, moustache, brows).
  - Scalp hairs.
  - Hair adjacent to injuries.
- Toxicology samples.
  - Collect blood and tissue samples for toxicology examinations.

DECOMPOSED REMAINS

- X-rays of remains to locate bullets and bullet fragments.
- Inked impressions of finger, palm, and foot soles.
- Additional forensic specialists at the autopsy.
  - Forensic odontologist, to assist in identification of remains.
  - Forensic anthropologist, to identify species and to estimate age, sex, and race.
  - Forensic entomologist, to aid in estimation of time of death and possible relocation of the body.

BODY FLUIDS AND TOXICOLOGY SPECIMENS

- Specimens for blood typing.
- Specimens for toxicological analysis.
- Specimen for blood alcohol determination (may be separate from toxicology specimens). Have the pathologist use DUI kit.

WRAP-UP CONFERENCE (WITH ALL PARTIES PRESENT)

- Have all necessary procedures been done?
- Are all collected items properly packaged and labeled?
- Should the body be secured in a locked bag pending further information from the scene or witnesses?
- Can any team member think of anything else that needs to be done?
- *Remember that there may not be a second chance to collect evidence or comparison samples after the autopsy is completed.*

Review Questions

1. In most jurisdictions, the _____ must be apprised of a suspected homicide.
2. It is a good practice to avoid focusing all your attention on _____ _____ at a homicide crime scene.
3. The _____ of the body may be important for crime scene reconstruction efforts.
4. The investigator should take precautions to avoid _____ of trace evidence on the body of a homicide victim.

5. Bloodstain patterns should be documented with _____, _____ and _____.

6. If gunshot residue tests cannot be done on the victim's hands at the crime scene, the hands should be secured in _____ _____.

7. The body of the victim should be placed on a _____ _____ _____ prior to placing in a body bag.

8. It is a good practice to _____ the scene until the autopsy is completed.

9. The _____ conference is an important part of the postmortem examination.

10. Photographs should always be taken _____ any autopsy procedures that may alter the appearance of any evidence present.

11. A series of _____ views and _____ views should be taken to illustrate the appearance and condition of the victim's clothing.

12. Close-up views of each wound should be taken both _____ and _____ a measurement scale in view.

13. The recommendation for the number of hair standard samples taken from a homicide victim _____ that of the number recommended for a living victim.

14. For wounds in the hair, the wounds should be rephotographed after the hair is _____.

15. Sexual assault/homicide victims should be examined for _____ _____ evidence.

16. Decomposed remains should be _____ prior to autopsy to locate any possible _____ or _____ _____.

17. At the conclusion of the autopsy, it is recommended that the participants have a _____ prior to leaving.

Further References

Eliopoulis, L. N. 1993. *Death Investigator's Handbook.* Boulder, CO: Paladin Press.

Geberth, V. G. 1996. *Practical Homicide Investigation,* 3rd ed. Boca Raton, FL: CRC Press.

Haag, L., and A. Jason, eds. 1991. *Forensic Firearms Evidence (Elements of Shooting Incident Investigation).* Pinole, CA: ANITE Productions. (An instructional course consisting of two videos, a reference handbook, and a written examination.)

Jerath, B. K. 2001. *Homicide, A Bibliography.* Boca Raton, FL: CRC Press.

Saferstein, R. 2001. *Criminalistics,* 7th ed. Upper Saddle River, NJ: Prentice Hall, Inc.

APPENDIX 14-A

Safety Precautions for Homicide Crime Scenes[3]

1. **Universal precautions for biological stains apply at all homicide crime scenes.**

   The crime scene investigator should wear personal protective equipment (PPE) to avoid exposure to biological materials. When the floor or ground is bloody, the protective garb should include disposable shoe covers.

2. **Surgical gloves should be worn when handling blood or bloodstained items at the scene.**

   This action protects the wearer from exposure and also protects the evidence from contamination from touching the evidence. Double-gloving or the use of heavy-duty gloves designed for this purpose is recommended when handling the body.

3. **Face masks should be worn when in close proximity to the body or physiologically stained materials.**

   This precaution is necessary to avoid exposure to airborne viruses or fumes from chemicals used for evidence detection. The handling of bloodstained items may produce aerosols of tiny blood flakes, which will be filtered by the mask.

4. **Smoking, eating, drinking, or cosmetic use.**

   Smoking, eating, drinking, or cosmetic use is prohibited at the scene. These activities are allowed only outside the scene itself and should be preceded by removal of PPE and thorough washing of the hands and face. Personal protective equipment should be redonned before reentering the crime scene.

5. **Venting of the crime scene.**

   Actions should be taken to ensure that the crime scene is properly vented. Proper ventilation will help to sweep away airborne viruses and aerosols created during chemical processing procedures. Note that caution is needed when venting since strong drafts may displace or remove trace evidence such as hairs or fibers.

6. **Disposal/decontamination of protective equipment.**

   Upon completion of the crime scene processing, all protective equipment should be bagged in properly labeled bags for transport to the laboratory for disposal of disposable items or decontamination of permanent items.

7. **Disposable tools or items for processing the scene.**

   All disposable tools or items used for processing the crime scene should be properly bagged and returned to the laboratory for disposal.

8. **Chemical cleanup of the crime scene.**

   Chemical cleanup procedures should be established for the use of certain chemicals at crime scenes.

APPENDIX 14-B

Safety Precautions for Postmortem Examinations (Autopsies)[4]

1. **Universal precautions.**

   "Universal precautions" for biological materials apply to all postmortem examinations (autopsies). *All persons in attendance at the autopsy should wear personal protective equipment (PPE) in order to avoid exposure to biological materials.* PPE should include at minimum protective outerwear (lab coat, jumpsuit, or surgical gown), safety eyewear and/or face shield, filter mask, and impervious gloves.

2. **Protection against aerosols.**

   Certain procedures may produce biological aerosols, such as the use of electrical saws. The PPE should include protective eyewear and filter masks to avoid exposure via aerosols.

3. **Smoking, eating, drinking, or application of cosmetics.**

   Smoking, eating, drinking, or applying cosmetics is prohibited in the autopsy room. Any of these activities should be preceded by removal of the PPE and thorough washing of the hands and face. PPE must be redonned before reentering the autopsy room.

4. **Blood-soaked garments from the victim.**

   Plastic bags should be used for transporting heavily blood-soaked garments to the crime laboratory, since paper bags may not protect against spillage during transport. *This is one of the few exceptions to the rule of using only paper bags for packaging of biological specimens.* Wrap each garment in heavy butcher paper in order to minimize movement of the stains or trace evidence, and place in a separate plastic bag for transport. Once the specimens have reached the department facility, they must be removed from the plastic bags and handled appropriately (i.e., bloodstained garments laid out on clean butcher paper or hung in the drying area to dry the bloodstains, placing the liquid specimens in the evidence refrigerator) for prolonged storage.

5. **Transport of liquid specimens to the laboratory.**

   Transport of liquid specimens and stained items to the laboratory should be accomplished in portable coolers, appropriately labeled to indicate contaminated specimens in the container. Liquid specimens should be packed in cushioning material inside a leakproof container to avoid breakage and cross-contamination of other items in the cooler.

6. **Packaging of protective clothing and equipment used.**

   Protective clothing and equipment should be suitably packaged for transport back to the laboratory for disposal of the disposable equipment or decontamination of reusable equipment.

7. **Cyanoacrylate fuming of the body.**

   Cyanoacrylate fuming of the body should be followed by proper venting of the autopsy room to sweep out the cyanoacrylate fumes prior to continuation of the autopsy.

8. **Use of laser or forensic (alternate) lights.**

   The use of laser or alternate lights requires the use of protective eyewear to avoid exposure to the light source.

15 CRIME SCENE RECONSTRUCTION

How often have I said to you that when you eliminate the impossible, whatever remains, however improbable, must be the truth?

Sherlock Holmes in *The Sign of Four*,
by Sir Arthur Conan Doyle.

Key Words: Reconstruction, events, sequence of events, scene documentation, synthesis, logical analysis, experimentation, bloodstain pattern, spine, wave cast-off, impact surface, incident angle (impact angle), long and short axes, sine, inverse sine, area of origin, area of convergence, cast-off spatter, low velocity, medium velocity, high velocity, blow-back, muzzle-to-target distances, projectile trajectories, deflection, ricochet, zones of possibility, radial fracture, concentric fracture, conchoidal, crater, sequence of firing.

INTRODUCTION

This chapter is presented in order to acquaint students, detectives, crime scene investigators, patrol officers, and supervisory personnel with the value of crime scene reconstruction to an investigation. Crime scene reconstruction often provides the investigator with the ability to determine which versions of the events at a crime scene received from individuals at the scene are correct and which are false. Crime scene reconstruction can aid the investigator in the determination of whether a death is the result of a suicide, an accident, or a homicide. The elements of a crime can frequently be established through a reconstruction of the events at the crime scene. *This chapter will not provide the reader with the expertise necessary to perform crime scene reconstructions.* The expertise for crime scene reconstruction is the result of adequate and appropriate education, training, and mentored experience gained in the appropriate venues.

ESTABLISHMENT OF EXPERTISE

The development of *expertise* in any field of inquiry and/or professional practice requires that the examiner acquire the necessary education, training, and *mentored* experience before assuming responsibility in performing casework. This structured development of expertise is essential in order to develop proficiency in task accomplishment, and, more importantly, to *develop the ability to think critically*, so that errors due to bias or fallacious thinking are avoided. In the fields of criminal investigation, crime scene investigation, and crime scene reconstruction, the need for the *proper* development of expertise is key. This need for proper development of expertise is crucial because the actions of the practitioners of these fields impact the lives of other individuals. Errors on the part of individuals in these fields, whether through incompetence or a lack of critical thinking, have led to the conviction of innocent parties in the past, even in death penalty cases, where the innocent party was placed on death row.

Expertise development

APPROPRIATE FOUNDATION FOR EXPERTISE

The development path for expertise in any discipline should begin with a broad academic education, followed by training courses germane to the specific discipline, and a lengthy period of mentored experience in casework. Once these requirements have been met, and the assigned mentor is satisfied that the examiner has developed the necessary critical-thinking skills and competence in task completion, the examiner can then commence casework in the field without direct supervision. This approach to the development of expertise in a practitioner equips the practitioner with genuine expertise that can be likened to a quadrilateral pyramid (see Figure 15-1), which, in geometric terms, is the most stable of any structure, and in terms of professional expertise, provides the practitioner with the most stable foundation for expertise that is free of noncritical thinking.

EDUCATION

An academic education that is both broad and deep is an essential foundation for any professional specialty. In Figure 15-1, the *breadth* of the educational base is represented by the horizontal blocks from left to right, and the *depth* of the educational base is represented by the blocks from front to rear. Breadth in an academic education is imperative, in order for the examiner to acquire the many contributions to critical thinking provided by the various fields of thought. At the very minimum, the examiner should have introductory courses in the sciences, mathematics, social sciences, humanities, and the arts.

The examiner should also acquire depth in each of these fields of inquiry, as represented by the horizontal blocks in Figure 15-1. Depth in these divisions of knowledge is obtained by completion of course work in each of the fields of inquiry beyond the basic, introductory courses. These additional courses will add to the student's understanding of the various fields of thought and facilitate the student's proficiency in critical thinking.

A course of study that would encompass the aforementioned breadth and depth academic courses is available in most, if not all, community colleges, and in all colleges throughout the United States and in other countries. Any programs that seek to certify

EXPERTISE DEVELOPMENT PYRAMID

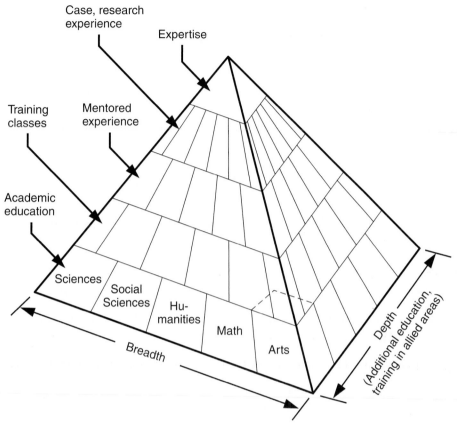

FIGURE 15-1 **Expertise Development Pyramid**

crime scene investigators should have at their core these minimum requirements for the basic foundation of the participants in the certification process.

TRAINING CLASSES

Training classes in the particular discipline toward which the examiner is working represent the second layer in the pyramid of expertise (see Figure 15-1). Once the examiner has acquired the requisite educational foundation for critical thinking, training classes in a particular discipline will help prepare the individual for competency in that discipline. A training class can cover a broad spectrum of topics within the discipline, or it may have a narrow focus, covering one or two topics. The practitioner should complete a number of these training classes within the discipline in order to acquire a broad base of skills, knowledge, and abilities to cultivate a high level of competence. It is essential that the practitioner continue to pursue additional education and training courses after beginning practice in a discipline, so as to maintain and increase that level of competence.

MENTORED EXPERIENCE

There is a distinct difference in what we call "experience" and *mentored experience*. Experience without mentoring has many drawbacks (see the section, "Experiential Development of Expertise") and is less efficient and effective than mentored experience. Mentored experience bestows the judgment of the mentor on the experience process, providing the learner with ongoing direction from the mentor, and permits the mentor to highlight those techniques that are appropriate and effective for a given case situation. Thus, valuable time is saved by avoiding fruitless searches for accurate and effective techniques for the task at hand.

CASE AND RESEARCH EXPERIENCE

Once the examiner has obtained the proper education, training, and mentored experience, the examiner is equipped to perform casework independently. Casework experience should be augmented with experience in research directed toward the specific discipline of the examiner. Research is often required when a novel problem in casework arises, and the examiner's experience in conducting this research will contribute to the examiner's competence.

EXPERTISE

True expertise in a discipline is the result of an individual's endeavor to gain the proper education, training, and experience as outlined above and represented by the expertise pyramid. By pursuing this rigorous method of expertise development, the examiner will have a solid foundation for critical thinking as it applies to the casework situation.

EXPERIENTIAL DEVELOPMENT OF EXPERTISE

The experiential style of expertise development is illustrated by Figure 15-2, the "stove-pipe" foundation for the examiner's expertise. In this style of training, the examiner is given a minimal training course in the discipline, then the examiner, through trial and error, gains "experience" in the practice of the discipline (thus the term "practice"). The "stove-pipe" approach to expertise development does not provide a stable and appropriate foundation for professional expertise in crime scene investigation and reconstruction, nor in any other field of study or professional practice.

The attempt at development of expertise through "experience" is an inappropriate approach for several reasons. First, "experience" is the name we give our mistakes, which in everyday life is acceptable because we are the ones who pay the price for our mistakes. In a professional setting, however, those affected by our mistakes are the ones who pay the price for our mistakes. This division of responsibility and accountability is unacceptable in any professional field, especially any field where the consequences of the examiner's mistakes may be grave. Second, an experiential method of training is inefficient because of the time lost in exploring for an adequate or appropriate method to apply to the instant case. Third, the subject of the experiential training program may or may not detect any mistake made (see Figure 15-2), and, hence, not learn from the mistake. Finally, the experiential method of training has no internal quality assurance or control, so that the amount of experience has no *qualitative* component whereby users of the examiner's services can be assured of the competence and professional integrity of the examiner.

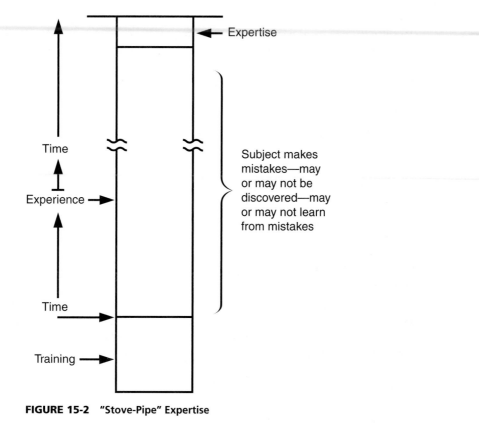

FIGURE 15-2 "Stove-Pipe" Expertise

CRITICAL THINKING

Critical thinking is not the act of being "critical" about things in general, or about specific categories, but, rather, is *thinking characterized by careful and exact evaluation and judgment*.[1] It is essential that an investigator exercise critical thinking when investigating an incident or testing theories. This mandate applies to investigators in any field, and is absolutely obligatory for any individual making a *scientific* inquiry. The investigator must avoid common logical errors such as oversimplifying, jumping to conclusions, allowing bias to influence judgment, or sifting through the evidence for data. The investigator must also avoid logical fallacies in the pursuit of an investigation. Some of the more common logical fallacies encountered include Circular reasoning, ignoring the question, statistical fallacies, and often, the "science" fallacy. A *fallacy* is an error in thinking, caused by bias, oversimplifying, being too emotional, or other human frailties. A *logical fallacy* occurs when these mistakes in thinking lead a person into *basing an argument* (or professional opinion) on one of these fallacies.

Circular reasoning

"Circular reasoning" means assuming your thesis is proved before you have proved it.[2] This fallacy is usually preceded by the statement, "Everybody knows . . . ," when in fact the assertion has never been proven in either a logical or scientific fashion. The remedy for this fallacy is to detect the circular reasoning and omit or prove it.

Ignoring the question

Ignoring the question is any form of irrelevance, such as straw man and ad hominem.[3] The remedy for this fallacy is to insist on remaining on task or topic and to maintain focus.

Statistical fallacies

A statistical fallacy is any misuse of statistics, numbers, percentages, and so on, in the course of thinking about solutions to a case.[4] It is important to remember that unusual events do occur and that the possibility of these atypical events should be accounted for in establishing a working theory (hypothesis) or, particularly, in the reconstruction of a crime scene.

The "science" fallacy

The "science" fallacy is a form of circular reasoning: If it is "scientific," it is good, true, reliable, and so on.[5] The use of this fallacy occurs often, usually in conjunction with circular reasoning. A scientific basis for a statement is claimed when, in fact, the basis for the statement has never been proven using the scientific method. Many individuals are unaware that the categories of a statistic, a single study, or experiential data are not a scientific basis for an assertion (see "Scientific Method" in Glossary).

FOUNDATIONS FOR CRIME SCENE RECONSTRUCTION

Crime scene reconstruction, as stated in Chapter 1 is one of the major purposes for the collection of physical evidence. Crime scene **reconstruction** is defined here as the determination of what **events** (and often the *sequence* of those events) occurred during the commission of a crime through the analysis and interpretation of the physical evidence at the scene. Note that scene reconstructions are also accomplished in the case of torts (civil wrongs). A definition of reconstruction by Bell is as follows: "Reconstruction is the process of utilizing information derived from physical evidence at the scene, from analyses of physical evidence, and from inference drawn from such analyses to test various theories of the occurrences of prior events."[6] Many other definitions of reconstruction exist but are not reiterated here, since most are a variation of the two cited here. The reconstruction may involve the determination of whether or not a *single event* occurred or the determination of whether or not a *series of events* occurred and, in some cases, the **sequence of those events**. The reconstruction may provide conclusive proof, for example, as to whether the death of an individual was the result of a homicide, an accident, or a suicide. Death due to natural causes is determined by the forensic autopsy rather than a crime scene reconstruction, although a reconstruction may assist the autopsy pathologist in the determination of death due to natural causes by eliminating certain scenarios. In some cases, a reconstruction may provide the prosecuting attorney with evidence that demonstrates intent on the part of the perpetrator, which typically is an element of the crime committed.

Crime scene reconstruction is always a *team effort*, since the reconstruction itself relies on the work of a number of individuals or teams. The reconstruction may be accomplished by a team of professionals, or it may be accomplished by a single individual who is qualified to perform the task of reconstructing the events of the crime, although this individual is part of the larger team in the crime scene investigation. Crime scene reconstructions depend heavily on the quality of the efforts of the crime scene investigation team. Accurate and thorough **scene documentation** of the crime scene is critical to the task of reconstruction. Without appropriate and accurate photographs, sketches, and reports from the crime scene processing team, it is normally impossible to provide a thorough and accurate reconstruction for that scene. For this reason, *it is important to remember that crime scene reconstruction begins with a systematic, meticulous, and competent endeavor by the crime scene processing team.* Thus, the crime scene processing team is an integral component of the reconstruction team.

Crime scene reconstruction typically relies on the examination of physical evidence from the scene by laboratory scientists. Analysis of bloodstains can determine which individual is the source of each bloodstain from the scene. Gunshot muzzle-to-target determinations may establish whether a shooting incident is the result of a suicide or is the result of a homicide. The analysis of expended bullets and cartridge cases will establish which weapons were responsible for firing these cartridge components at the scene. Analysis of gunshot residues from suspects' and victims' hands provides evidence of which individual(s) fired a weapon during the incident. The analyses of the forensic laboratory scientists are often essential to reconstruction efforts, which fact makes the laboratory scientists de facto members of the reconstruction team.

Reconstructions may rely on the assistance of professionals from a broad range of disciplines, since the reconstructions often require specialized knowledge not possessed by the individual accomplishing the reconstruction. The reconstruction expert may need to call on engineers, medical personnel, entomologists, physical anthropologists, or other forensic specialists to provide answers to certain questions about specific aspects of the reconstruction. In one of the author's cases, it was necessary to prove that the fatal bullet in a homicide could not have bounced 180 degrees from a wall and still have retained the energy to penetrate the chest wall of the decedent. A forensic engineer determined after experimentation that this explanation by the defendant was an impossibility.

PROCESS OF CRIME SCENE RECONSTRUCTION

There are a number of stages in crime scene reconstruction: (1) recognition of the physical evidence essential to the reconstruction, (2) appropriate documentation of the physical evidence, (3) proper collection of the evidence, (4) laboratory examination of the physical evidence essential to the reconstruction effort, (5) analysis of the data from the crime scene and the laboratory examinations, and (6) **synthesis** of the data into a coherent hypothesis that explains all the data known (interpretation of the analysis data). Once the hypothesis is formed, it is subjected to (7) **logical analysis** and/or **experimentation** to determine whether all the known facts are explained by the hypothesis. If not, the analyst must formulate a new hypothesis and must repeat the cycle of logical analysis that explains all the facts known, and, further, that eliminates any other hypothesis.

Crime scene reconstruction components

The crime scene reconstruction process is illustrated in Figure 15-3, which diagrams the flow of the process and its constituent components. An uncomplicated crime, assault with a deadly weapon, occurring at a single scene is used for illustration purposes. More complex crimes will have a more complex process, but the framework illustrated in

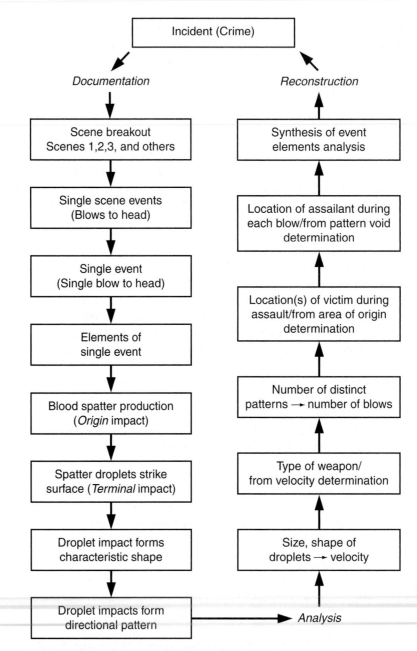

FIGURE 15-3   Crime Scene Reconstruction Components

Figure 15-3 will remain essentially the same. The crime scene and its constituents first require proper documentation, whether there is one crime scene or many.

DOCUMENTATION COMPONENT

In the illustration (see Figure 15-3), the blows to the victim's head constitute a series of single blows, each of which constitutes a single event. Each event can be further divided into its elements: blood spatter production from the *origin impact* (blow to the head), the spatter droplets striking a surface (*terminal impact* surface, often called the "target" surface), formation of characteristic bloodstain shapes from the droplet impacts, and formation of directional patterns based on the geometric orientation and shape of the blood droplet impacts. Each of these elements require proper documentation through notes, photographs, and sketches, which become the foundation for any reconstruction effort effected for the incident.

ANALYSIS COMPONENT

Once the crime scene events and their elements have been properly documented, the analysis phase of those event elements can proceed. The analysis, it must be remembered, is a reversal of the incident events, since the analysis starting point is the data obtained from the crime scene documentation, which occurs after the incident has been accomplished. The size and shape of the bloodstains permit a conclusion about the velocity category of the droplets on impact, high, medium, or low velocity. The determination of the velocity category permits a determination of the type of weapon (in broad categories) that produced the blood spatter: low and medium velocity spatter is produced by blunt weapons, such as fists or blunt objects. High velocity spatter is indicative of firearm wounds.

The analysis of the patterns produced by the spatter allows the analyst to determine the number of blows struck and the approximate location of the victim during the delivery of each blow. Often, there is a void in the bloodstain pattern indicative of the location of the assailant at the time of the delivery of the blow that produced that pattern.

SYNTHESIS COMPONENT

The synthesis component occurs when the analysis of each of the event elements has been completed. The analytical findings for each of the event elements are put together to form a hypothetical scenario that accounts for all of the analytical data, a process called synthesis, or "putting it all together." If the scenario does not account for all the analytical findings, then a new scenario must be proposed which will account for all the analytical data. Once the final scenario is formulated, it is subjected to scientific experimentation and logical scrutiny to test its accuracy and reliability.

Recognition and documentation of the physical evidence

Crime scene reconstruction begins with the arrival of the first responder at the crime scene. The actions taken by the first and subsequent responders to the scene determine in large part the quality of any reconstruction efforts. All reconstructions rely on the data developed from meticulous crime scene documentation. It is essential that the crime scene processing team *recognize* the evidence present that will form the foundation for any reconstruction efforts and that the team *document* that evidence with *notes, photographs, and sketches.* Virtually any of the various evidence types may become a part of a crime scene reconstruction, but there are a number of evidence types that frequently play a role in reconstructions. In this chapter, the evidence types typically relied on as the basis for crime scene reconstructions and methods for their documentation are presented in order to acquaint the crime scene investigator with those types of evidence that require particular care in their documentation. A deficiency in the crime scene documentation may limit or thwart reconstruction efforts by the reconstruction analyst or team. Instructions for the proper documentation of the evidence present are found in Chapters 2 through 4.

Collection and examination of the physical evidence

Once the physical evidence has been recognized, it is essential that the evidence be collected in an **appropriate** manner to ensure that the laboratory analyses are not limited by deficiencies in the collection process. Improper collection may compromise or destroy the information otherwise available from the evidence. Instructions for the proper collection of the physical evidence are found in the chapters dealing with the specific types of physical evidence (Chapters 5 through 14).

Laboratory examinations of the physical evidence

Performance of those laboratory examinations pertinent to the reconstruction requires sound communication between the investigator(s) assigned to the case, the crime scene investigators, the laboratory analysts, and the reconstruction analyst or team. Information from all these sources may be essential, and each member of this team should adhere to the three Cs of teamwork: communication, cooperation, and coordination.

Analysis of data from the crime scene

Once the crime scene has been properly documented and the physical evidence has been examined by the laboratory, the reconstruction analyst seeks to establish what events occurred during the commission of the crime through analysis of the data from the physical evidence components present at the scene, such as bloodstain patterns, bullet trajectories, other firearms evidence, positional evidence, and, often, several other types of evidence. Other data used in this analysis include the statements of any witnesses present at the scene, investigative information from the investigators, and information from the laboratory analysts. Once all of the component events are established, the analyst develops a hypothetical scenario that explains all the events and a possible sequence for those events. Although this stage of hypothesis formation is a *conjecture,* it is not the "theorizing" commonplace at crime scenes; rather, it is a *reasoned postulate* based on the intuition, training, education, experience, and insight of the individual or team seeking to perform the reconstruction on the basis of the information received from the preceding workers and their input.

Synthesis of analysis data

Once a hypothetical scenario (*hypothesis*) is fashioned, the components of the hypothesis are then **tested** through **scientific experimentation** and/or logical analysis in order to determine the feasibility of that scenario. The testing of the hypothesis requires an analyst or a team of analysts with the *requisite education, training, and experience* to perform the analysis of the hypothesis. If the hypothesis successfully *explains all the events* determined through the analysis, the analyst submits it to critical scrutiny so as to *eliminate alternate* *explanations* for the events. If there are no other feasible explanations for the events and their sequence, the hypothesis is accepted as a sound reconstruction. This assembling of the tested components into a final hypothetical scenario is the *synthesis* of all the component events into a coherent scenario ("putting it all together"). As in all logical analyses, however, the development of new facts may require a modification of the reconstruction, or in some cases, the development of a different hypothesis that also explains the new facts and that then undergoes the same logical analysis and/or experimentation.

TYPES OF RECONSTRUCTIONS

Reconstructions may be classified according to the *type of crime* or offense committed (e.g., homicide, traffic accident, arson), by the *type of evidence* involved in the reconstruction (e.g., blood and bloodstain patterns, firearms and firearms evidence, glass evidence), or by the *specific professional field* involved in the reconstruction (e.g., ballistics, criminalistics, engineering). Crime scene reconstruction is most often discussed primarily from the viewpoint of the type of evidence utilized for the reconstruction, although many crime scene reconstructions involve a variety of physical evidence and will require individuals from several different disciplines to effect the entire reconstruction. In some unusual cases, the reconstruction may utilize graphics illustrators to generate an animated video re-creation of the events of the crime, in order to illustrate better the scenario to the judge and/or jury in courtroom proceedings.

Traffic accident reconstructions

Traffic accident reconstructions are normally accomplished by an engineer with specific training in accident reconstruction. In addition, many individuals from differing professional fields perform traffic accident reconstructions, such as the MAIT (major accident investigation team) units from the California Highway Patrol. These teams of individuals are specially trained officers whose duty it is to perform accident reconstructions in major accidents. Other professionals often providing traffic accident reconstructions are forensic scientists with varying academic backgrounds, including criminalists and physicists. Regardless of the type of professional involved in the reconstruction, it is the efforts of the team processing the scene of the accident that determine whether or not a reconstruction may be performed, since a poorly processed accident scene may preclude a reconstruction because of a lack of critical data.

Homicide reconstructions

Most crime scene reconstructions are performed in homicides because of the gravity of this crime, the amount of resources that can be allocated to a homicide case, and the frequent need to establish what happened through the use of physical evidence, since in many homicides, there are no witnesses to the crime. Most homicides are committed with weapons that produce physical evidence that, through recognition, collection, analysis, and interpretation, allows for a reconstruction of the crime. Firearms, blunt instruments, knives, and other cutting and stabbing weapons all leave physical evidence, that, through proper interpretation, provides the basis for a crime scene reconstruction.

Sexual assault reconstructions

In sexual assault crimes, the accused may offer a defense of consensual sexual activity to the charge of sexual assault. In many of these cases, a reconstruction of the crime will provide conclusive evidence that the claim of consent is false. Evidence from the scene of the assault, from the medical examination of the victim, from the victim's clothing, and from the suspect may play a role in the reconstruction. Physical evidence at the scene may provide compelling evidence of a struggle and thus refute the claim of consent by the suspect. The forensic medical examination of the victim may demonstrate injuries that are wholly inconsistent with consensual sexual activity but that are entirely consistent with a forcible rape. Injuries to the suspect provide additional evidence of a struggle with the victim and thus corroborate the allegation of nonconsent in the case. Examination of the victim's clothing may locate rips or tears in the fabric or torn buttons, which provide strong evidence of a forcible act.

RECONSTRUCTIONS CLASSIFIED BY EVIDENCE TYPE UTILIZED

Reconstructions based on bloodstain pattern evidence

Many crime scene reconstructions are based solely on the analysis and interpretation of **bloodstain pattern** evidence at the scene. These types of reconstruction are usually accomplished in cases of homicide, aggravated assault, and aggravated sexual assaults.

Reconstructions based on firearms evidence

Reconstructions based on firearms evidence typically involve homicides (often to determine whether the incident is an accident, a suicide, or a homicide). Firearms evidence utilized in reconstructions includes discharge residues, trajectories, weapon functionality, and locations of expended cartridges.

Reconstructions based on other or more than one type of evidence

A crime scene reconstruction may employ the analysis and interpretation of two or more types of physical evidence. Often a crime will involve more than one type of weapon, and the reconstruction can involve the analysis and interpretation of the evidence present from each type of weapon. Homicides in which an attempt to disguise the crime by means of an arson may entail the analysis of burning rates by the arson investigator, analysis of bloodstain patterns by a bloodstain pattern analyst, and interpretation of firearms evidence by a firearms evidence reconstruction specialist. Positional evidence allows the analyst to determine whether a door was open at the time of the assault, where objects were during the crime, and whether or not they were moved during the commission of the crime.

In the sections to follow, crime scene reconstructions based on bloodstain pattern evidence, firearms evidence, and other types of physical evidence will be presented in order to acquaint the investigator and the crime scene specialist with the types of reconstructions available and the information obtainable through the reconstructions. Case examples will be presented to illustrate the value of a reconstruction to the solution of a case.

RECONSTRUCTIONS BASED ON BLOODSTAIN PATTERN EVIDENCE

Information obtained from bloodstain pattern analysis

DIRECTION FROM WHICH A BLOODSTAIN DROPLET ORIGINATED

The directionality of an impact bloodstain can be determined by analysis of the shape of the bloodstain. When a blood droplet impacts a flat surface at a low angle, the resultant stain will have an elliptical shape and will often have an extension, called a **spine**, from the main droplet stain that gives it the appearance of an exclamation point (see Figure 15-4). The extension will be on the side of the droplet stain away from the area of origin of the stain. A small droplet, called a satellite stain, may be present in line with the spine as the result of "wave cast-off." A **wave cast-off** is created by the wave motion within the parent droplet propelling a small droplet from the parent. For those bloodstains that lack a spine, the directionality of the impact is determined from the accumulation of blood within the stain on the side away from the direction of origin. As the droplet strikes a surface, the bulk of the blood in the droplet is propelled forward and remains in the side away from the direction of origin (see Figure 15-5). As the angle of impact increases toward 90 degrees, the bloodstain shape becomes more circular in outline and becomes circular at an impact angle of 90 degrees.

THE APPROXIMATE ANGLE AT WHICH A BLOOD DROPLET STRUCK A SURFACE ON IMPACT

When a blood droplet in flight impacts a surface, the resultant bloodstain has a shape that is characteristic for the angle described by the path of the droplet and the plane of the surface impacted (see Figure 15-6). When the blood droplet impacts the surface, the line

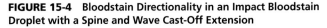

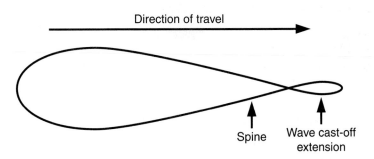

Spine   Wave cast-off extension

FIGURE 15-4   Bloodstain Directionality in an Impact Bloodstain Droplet with a Spine and Wave Cast-Off Extension

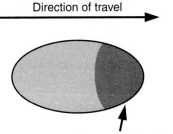

Concentration of droplet blood volume

FIGURE 15-5   Bloodstain Directionality in an Impact Bloodstain Without a Spine

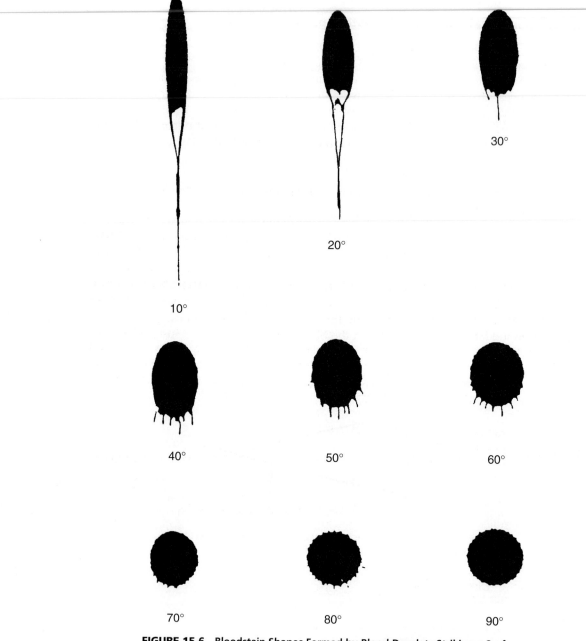

10°

20°

30°

40°

50°

60°

70°

80°

90°

FIGURE 15-6 Bloodstain Shapes Formed by Blood Droplets Striking a Surface at Various Angles

Source: Herbert Leon MacDonell, *Bloodstain Patterns* (Corning, NY: Laboratory of Forensic Science, 1993). Courtesy of Herbert Leon MacDonell, Laboratory of Forensic Science, Corning, NY.

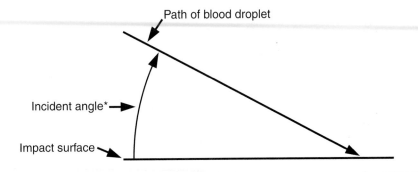

*Also called "impact angle"

FIGURE 15-7 Angle (Incident/Impact) Created by Impact of a Blood Droplet on a Flat, Nonmoving Surface

of flight of the droplet and the **impact surface** define an angle, called the **incident angle** (also called the **impact angle**), when viewed from the side (see Figure 15-7). The angle of incidence also defines a triangle, with the sides created by the impact surface, the line of flight of the blood droplet, and a line perpendicular to the line of flight of the droplet. The angle of impact produces a bloodstain with an elliptical shape that is characteristic for that incident angle (see Figure 15-6).

The approximate incident angle at which a blood droplet struck an impact surface can be calculated by determining the ratio between the **long and short axes** of the stain ellipse (see Figure 15-8). The ratio between the width (short axis) and the length (long axis) of the bloodstain determines the **sine** of an angle. The **inverse sine** of that ratio is the *angle of incidence (impact)* for that droplet.

DETERMINATION OF THE AREA (POINT) OF ORIGIN OF A TWO-DIMENSIONAL SPATTER PATTERN

The **area of origin** for a two-dimensional bloodstain pattern on a surface is established by determining the **area of convergence** of lines drawn through the long axis of the bloodstains. This step is accomplished by taping strings through the long axis of the blood droplets in the stain pattern. The area where the lines converge is the area of origin for the bloodstain pattern (see Figure 15-9).

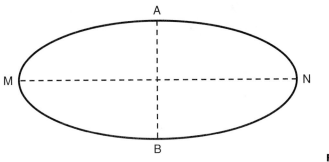

Long axis = M - N, Short axis = A - B

FIGURE 15-8 Ratio Between the Long and Short Axes of a Bloodstain

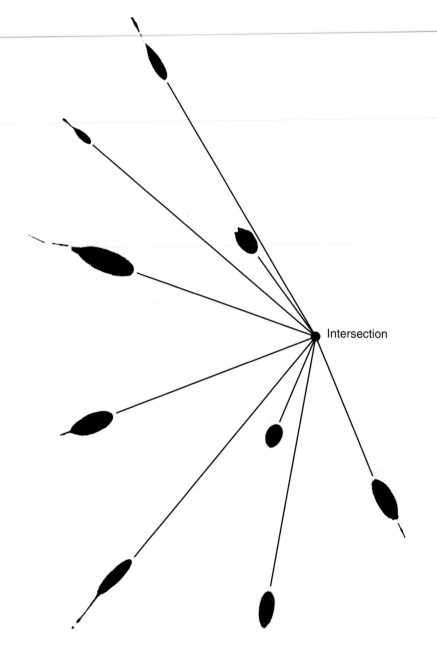

FIGURE 15-9 Determination of Area of Convergence for Two-Dimensional Bloodstain Impacts
Source: Herbert Leon MacDonell, *Bloodstain Patterns* (Corning, NY: Laboratory of Forensic Science, 1993). Courtesy of Herbert Leon MacDonell, Laboratory of Forensic Science, Corning, NY.

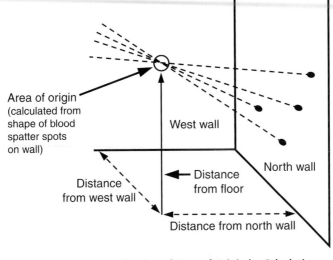

Area of origin (calculated from shape of blood spatter spots on wall)

West wall

North wall

Distance from floor

Distance from west wall

Distance from north wall

FIGURE 15-10   Determination of Area of Origin by Calculation of Impact Angles of Bloodstain Pattern Droplets

Determination of the area of origin through use of the impact angles is accomplished by calculating the angles of impact for the blood droplets and the area where these calculated lines meet (see Figure 15-10).

LOCATION OR POSITION OF VICTIM AT TIME OF IMPACT BLOW

The determination of the area of origin of a bloodstain pattern will establish the specific location or position of the victim at the time the wound that produced the bloodstain pattern was made. This information provides a basis for determining the truth or falsity of witnesses' statements. MacDonell reports that his determination that an individual was seated rather than standing at the time he was beaten to death proved that an alleged witness to the crime was falsifying his testimony and aided in the exoneration of two police officers accused of the crime.[7]

DISTANCE BETWEEN THE ORIGIN AND THE TARGET SURFACE[8]

The distance between the origin of a blood drop and the target surface can often be established with a reasonable degree of accuracy. The shape and splash pattern of a blood drop are a function of the distance that the drop has fallen and of the nature of the target surface. The bloodstain pattern analyst may be able to establish the distance the drop has fallen on the basis of an analysis of these factors and the bloodstain shape. It should be noted that for dropping distances of greater than 25 feet, the shape of the resultant bloodstain will not differ from that at 25 feet, since blood droplets reach their terminal velocity at that distance.[9]

MOVEMENT(S) OF THE PERSON FROM WHOM THE BLOODSTAINS ORIGINATED

Movement of an individual during times of bloodshed can produce characteristic patterns on the target surface. Bloodstain tracks and trails often have these characteristics, which can be interpreted by the crime scene reconstruction analyst. The existence of multiple areas of origin for a series of blows administered during an assault allows the reconstruction analyst to determine the position of the victim at the time each blow was delivered and, in some instances, the relative position of the assailant during the sequence of blows.

MINIMUM NUMBER OF BLOWS

Each blow from a blunt instrument usually creates a distinct pattern both from the blow itself and from the "cast-off" of blood during the backswing of the instrument. The minimum number of blows usually can be reconstructed by determination of the number of cast-off patterns and/or the number of areas of origin for the spatter patterns.

CAST-OFF SPATTER

The backswing of a bloody blunt instrument or cutting/stabbing instrument can create a distinctive spatter pattern termed "**cast-off**" **spatter** pattern. The cast-off pattern produced is typically characteristic for a given type of instrument. The size of the cast-off bloodstain droplets produced by a weapon increases with the size of the surface bearing the blood that is cast off during a backswing. For example, the droplets produced by cast-off from a baseball bat would be very large compared with the size of the droplets produced by cast-off from a knife blade.

APPROXIMATE LOCATION OF INDIVIDUAL DELIVERING BLOWS

At the time a blow from a blunt instrument is delivered, the resultant blood spatter is radiated out in a 360-degree pattern. Often, there is a pie-shaped area of the resultant spatter pattern blocked by the body of the assailant, called a "shadow" area. This area where the spatter pattern is interrupted permits the reconstruction analyst to determine the position of the assailant at the time that blow was delivered. These data are augmented with the determination of the area of convergence for each of the cast-off patterns produced by the swinging of the weapon.

TYPE AND DIRECTION OF THE IMPACT THAT PRODUCED THE BLOODSTAIN PATTERNS

The types of impact that produce blood-spatter patterns are usually referred to as **low velocity** (less than 5 feet per second), **medium velocity** (5–25 feet per second), or **high velocity** (speeds greater than 100 feet per second) impacts.[10] Examples of low-velocity impacts are the splashing produced by stepping into a puddle of liquid blood or blood dripping from a wound. A medium-velocity impact is produced by blows from a blunt instrument such as a baseball bat. High-velocity impacts are typically produced by firearm wounds, both at entry and exit.

BLOW-BACK SPATTER OF BLOOD FROM A GUNSHOT WOUND

Very close range or near-contact gunshots, especially to the head of a victim, may produce **blow-back** spatter (see Figure 15-11) patterns on the hands of the shooter and the weapon because of the high gas pressures created in the wound. Sometimes the blow-back will strike the muzzle and will travel into the barrel of the firearm itself.[11] For this reason, it is important not to disturb the muzzle area of a firearm until the laboratory analyst has examined the muzzle and barrel under the stereomicroscope, since the blood

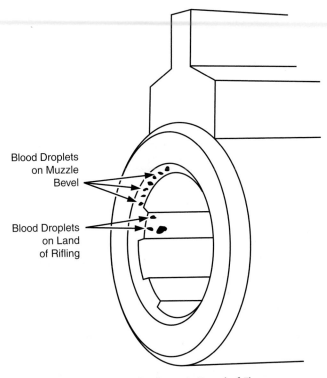

FIGURE 15-11   Blow-Back Spatter in Barrel of Firearm
Copyright © of Bruce R. Moran, with permission.

droplets may be microscopic in size. The presence of blow-back spatter on the weapon's muzzle is conclusive evidence of a close-up or near-contact position of the firearm at the time of discharge.

Bloodstains: shoe prints, tracks, and trails

Another aspect of bloodstain evidence reconstruction is the presence of shoe prints, tracks, and trails in blood that should not be overlooked. These imprints and impressions furnish information about the movement of a perpetrator during and after the commission of the crime. These movements can be reconstructed when the impressions are properly recorded at the scene.

Details for the photography of bloodstain footwear impressions are similar to those of other footwear impressions. However, there are additional aspects to the treatment of footwear impressions from blood. The impression may have to be enhanced with chemical treatment before the impression is readily visible and ready for photography. The impression should always be photographed in its original condition prior to attempting any enhancement procedure. Bloodstained impressions are usually enhanced by treatment with amido black, but they may be enhanced by application of luminol or enzymatic blood detection chemicals. The choice of which method to use depends on the circumstances at the scene and the judgment of the crime scene investigator.

RECONSTRUCTIONS BASED ON FIREARMS EVIDENCE

Introduction

Firearms evidence often plays a crucial role in the reconstruction of events at the crime scene, particularly homicide crime scenes. A large percentage of homicides are committed through the use of firearms, and these crimes frequently require a reconstruction in order to eliminate an accidental shooting or a suicide as the cause of the decedent's death. Those aspects of firearms evidence that are frequently significant are muzzle-to-target distances, the precise location of expended cartridges at the scene, bullet hole locations, trajectories and ricochets, identification of the firearm that fired each bullet, and the presence or absence of gunshot residues on the hands of suspected shooters. Shooting reconstructions frequently determine whether a shooting was accidental, a suicide, or an intentional homicide. The reconstruction is also a means to test the veracity of alleged witnesses to a shooting. In one of the author's cases, a witness claimed that the victim was standing against a wall when shot. Reconstruction of the incident proved that the shooting victim was a considerable distance from the wall and in close proximity to the shooter.

Information available from a shooting incident reconstruction[12]

- Muzzle-to-target distances.
- Minimum number of participants in the incident.
- Number and type(s) of firearms involved in the incident.
- Direction of projectile paths taken during the shooting incident.
- Location(s) of participants during the incident.
- Sequence(s) of events during the shooting incident.

MUZZLE-TO-TARGET DISTANCES

The determination of **muzzle-to-target distances** often aids the investigator in evaluating whether a shooting incident is an accident, an act of suicide, or a homicide. With some rare exceptions, suicides involve contact or close-range shots. Many homicides also involve contact or close-range shots, so the investigator should also consider the trajectory of the bullet, any gunshot residues present on the victim's hands, and the position of the victim at the time of discharge, in addition to other factors, such as the presence of suicide notes, in making the determination of suicide or homicide.

MINIMUM NUMBER OF PARTICIPANTS IN THE INCIDENT

The minimum number of participants in a shooting incident is often resolved by determining the number of different firearms discharged in the shooting. This number is determined by identifying the number of different firearms through laboratory examinations of the expended cartridges and projectiles recovered at the scene. It is assumed for this determination that each firearm used in the incident is equal to the number of participants. In some instances, an individual may use more than one firearm, but this happenstance is rare.

NUMBER AND TYPE(S) OF FIREARMS INVOLVED IN THE INCIDENT

This determination is directly related to the effort to determine the minimum number of participants, but this number is considered more accurate, since the assumption of one firearm per participant is not a part of the conclusion. The limiting factor for this determination is the ability to recover all the expended cartridges and bullets in the incident.

DIRECTION OF PROJECTILE TRAJECTORIES

The direction of the **projectile trajectories** taken during the incident involves the determination of (1) projectile hole entry versus exit, (2) projectile hole angle of impact (the incident angle), and (3) direction of projectile from ricochet patterns.[13] The determination of bullet hole entry versus exit is normally straightforward, since, in most instances, the entry hole is indented, whereas the exit hole exhibits a "coning" effect, with the larger end of the cone pointing in the direction of the bullet flight path. Bullet entry holes in fabrics will typically have a "bullet wipe" on the surface of the fabric on the side where the bullet impacted. In some fabrics, the wipe may be difficult or impossible to see because of the color of the fabric, but the wipe usually can be visualized by chemical means.

The bullet hole angle of impact is best determined through the use of a probe where two or more layers have been penetrated (with a possible correction needed for **deflection** caused by impact with the first surface). Insertion of the probe illustrates the angle of impact and can be documented with the techniques discussed later in the text. Additionally, the angle of impact can be determined through laboratory experimentation by firing the same ammunition/firearm combination at differing angles into the same type of surface.

The direction of flight of a projectile at the time it impacts a surface (particularly painted automobile metal surfaces) can be determined by the shape of the **ricochet** pattern in the surface. In the case of automobile painted surfaces, the fracture patterns in the paint are diagnostic for the direction of travel and can be illustrated with photography or by first photographing the pattern, then dusting with fingerprint powder, photographing the developed pattern, and then lifting the developed pattern with fingerprint tape (see Figure 15-26).

LOCATION OF PARTICIPANT(S) DURING THE SHOOTING INCIDENT

When there is only one shooter, the most probable location of the shooter during the incident can be determined by reconstructing the trajectory of the projectile(s) and then considering the shoulder height of the shooter and the maximum height that the shooter can reach above the head along the established bullet(s) path. The investigator considers the **"zones of possibility"** for the position of the shooter. These zones are shooting positions designated by Moran as (1) most probable, (2) improbable but possible, and (3) impossible.[14]

Zone I. Most Probable   Zone I is established by determining the trajectory of the fired bullet and then locating the zone along the path where the trajectory corresponds to the area equal to or less than the height of the shooter's shoulders (see Figure 15-12).

Zone II. Improbable but Possible (Awkward)   Zone II is the area where the shooter is able physically to align the barrel of the firearm with the bullet path but in a manner that is awkward (improbable) but physically possible (see Figure 15-13).

**FIGURE 15-12 Most Probable
Position of Shooter**
Copyright © Bruce R. Moran, with
permission.

**FIGURE 15-13 Improbable but
Possible Position of Shooter**
Copyright © Bruce R. Moran, with
permission.

Zone III. Impossible   The shooter is physically unable to align the barrel of the firearm
with the bullet path, because of the inability to reach high enough or the presence of an
intervening barrier (see Figure 15-14).

FIGURE 15-14 Impossible Position of Shooter
Copyright © Bruce R. Moran, with permission.

LOCATIONS OF EXPENDED CARTRIDGES AT THE SCENE

The location of expended cartridges at the scene often plays a critical role in the reconstruction of a shooting incident. The location of the expended cartridges aids in the placement of the shooter(s) at the scene. The movement of subjects during firing can also be deduced from the pattern of ejected cartridge cases. Data from the location of the expended cartridge cases, coupled with the data from trajectory analysis and the identification of the weapon that fired each bullet, will provide much of the information needed for reconstruction of the incident.

Bullet trajectories

For short distances, such as within a residence, it can safely be assumed that bullet paths are in a straight line trajectory. For long distances, the drop of the bullet must be calculated in order to reconstruct the trajectory. Experts in ballistics (the science of projectile trajectories) can be consulted in order to reconstruct the trajectories when needed. Firearms experts who are also expert in ballistics use computer programs to calculate the path of bullets in their reconstruction of a shooting incident.

The reconstruction of bullet trajectories at a shooting scene allows the reconstruction analyst to place each weapon on a line at the location when each retrieved bullet was fired. This information will assist in placing the shooter of the weapon at a site along this line of trajectory. If further information is available regarding the location(s) of expended cartridges from the shooter's weapon, the reconstruction analyst may be able to place the shooter in a specific position at the time of firing for each projectile recovered. This information is often crucial in establishing the veracity of the shooter's account of the incident and may also test the veracity of any witness(es) to the shooting.

BULLET TRAJECTORY DOCUMENTATION

The trajectory of fired bullets can be documented in several ways. Each method of documentation can produce accurate pathways for fired bullets when the method is applied diligently. Several methods of documentation of bullet trajectories rely on the penetration of both sides of a wall to produce accurate documentation and reconstruction of the trajectory. The principal methods for documenting a bullet's trajectory (where the bullet has penetrated both sides of a wall) are (1) inserting a probe of the appropriate size through the bullet holes on both sides of the wall and measuring the angles produced with the use of a protractor; (2) inserting the probe through the wall and photographing the probe angles from the top or bottom aspect and from the side aspect; (3) inserting a probe into the wall, taping a string to the probe, then stretching the string to the opposite wall and locating by sight the spot where the string strikes the wall; and (4) shining a laser light (or alternate light source) through the holes in the wall and measuring the point on the wall where the laser light falls. In some instances, the trajectories may be determined with the use of surveying equipment or with a theodolite married to a data system (these methods provide extreme accuracy for the trajectories). Where the bullet has penetrated only one side of a wall or other surface, the insertion of a probe will provide only an estimate of the trajectory in most instances.

Measurement of Bullet Trajectories using Probe and Protractor   The trajectory of a bullet that has penetrated both sides of a wall can be measured using a probe and a protractor (see Figure 15-15). Probes of differing diameters are available from several suppliers, which allow for selection of the appropriate size probe for the holes produced by the bullet. The probe should fit snugly in the holes after insertion to minimize any error in the measurement. Once the probe is in place, it is necessary to measure both the horizontal and vertical angles that the bullet path makes with the wall. These two angles will describe the trajectory of the bullet in both the left-to-right and the up-to-down dimensions and will allow for the reconstruction of the bullet path by the individual preparing a finished sketch.

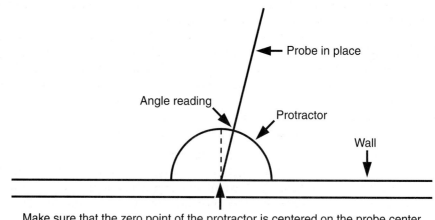

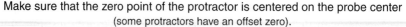
Make sure that the zero point of the protractor is centered on the probe center (some protractors have an offset zero).

FIGURE 15-15   Measuring the Angles of Bullet Trajectory Through a Wall with Probe and Protractor

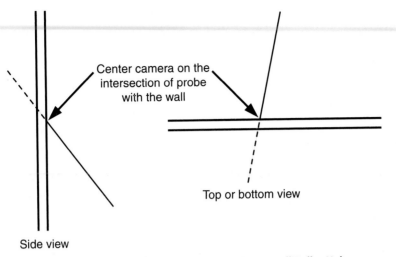

Center camera on the
intersection of probe
with the wall

Top or bottom view

Side view

FIGURE 15-16   Photography of Probes Inserted into Wall Bullet Holes

Documentation of the Bullet Trajectory with Photography   The trajectory of a bullet through a wall or other surface where there is a clearly defined pathway through the material can be documented by photographing the probe in place (see Figure 15-16). The photographs must be taken from the side and from either the top or the bottom. For both views, the camera must be centered on the junction of the probe and the bullet hole. These photographs will allow for reconstruction of the entry angles by use of a protractor on the developed photographs.

Both the protractor method of measurement and the photographic documentation methods produce rough estimates of the bullet's path. If the investigator wants to increase the accuracy of the trajectory measurement, the following methods can be used to document the trajectory.

Probe and string method of trajectory measurement   The probe and string method of trajectory measurement increases the accuracy of the trajectory measurement if done properly. This method involves placing a probe into the bullet holes and attaching a string to the probe by taping the string to the probe. The string is then stretched along the axis of the probe until it strikes the opposite wall (see Figure 15-17), making sure that the string is taut and in line with the probe as it strikes the wall. The point where the string strikes the opposite wall is then documented by measuring its distance from the floor and its distance from the nearest adjoining wall (see Figure 15-18). The advantage of this method over the protractor and photographic documentation methods is that the trajectory is more easily reconstructed when drawing the finished sketch.

Laser light method for determining bullet trajectories   This method for determining the bullet trajectory is similar to the probe and string method except that a laser beam replaces the probe and string. A laser light is positioned at the point of exit in the wall (point "X" in Figure 15-19), and the laser light beam is directed through the two holes to a point on the opposite wall. The point where the beam strikes the opposite wall is then measured from the floor and from an adjoining wall as in the probe and string method (see Figure 15-18). This point and the point where the bullet struck the opposite wall define the pathway of the bullet.

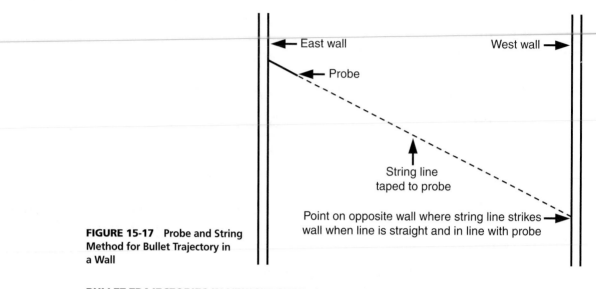

East wall ←

West wall →

← Probe

String line
taped to probe

Point on opposite wall where string line strikes →
wall when line is straight and in line with probe

FIGURE 15-17 Probe and String Method for Bullet Trajectory in a Wall

BULLET TRAJECTORIES IN VEHICLE SURFACES

When a bullet penetrates the exterior metal of a vehicle, it will often be stopped by the framework or other obstructions below the metal exterior. Occasionally, however, the bullet may penetrate both the outer wall and an inner wall of the vehicle, thus allowing for insertion of a probe for estimation of the bullet trajectory, using the methods for trajectory determination in walls. The investigator needs to use caution in interpreting the entry angle exhibited by the probe, since the metal will cause some deflection of the bullet's path before it strikes the second surface. The shape of the entry hole also is characteristic of the entry angle and of the weapon/ammunition combination that fired the bullet (see Figures 15-20 and 15-21). In order to interpret the entry angle based on the shape of the entry hole, it is necessary to test fire a number of bullets into a similar vehicle's component surfaces, so that the dimensional characteristics produced by the various angles of penetration by the particular weapon/ammunition combination can be established.

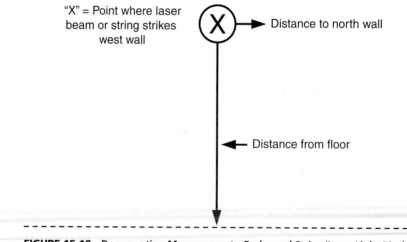

"X" = Point where laser beam or string strikes west wall

X → Distance to north wall

← Distance from floor

FIGURE 15-18 Documenting Measurements: Probe and String/Laser Light Methods

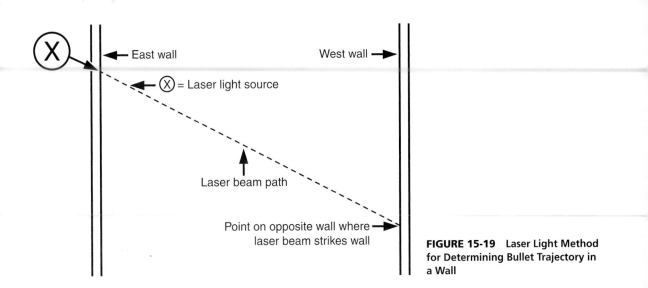

East wall

West wall

X = Laser light source

Laser beam path

Point on opposite wall where laser beam strikes wall

FIGURE 15-19 Laser Light Method for Determining Bullet Trajectory in a Wall

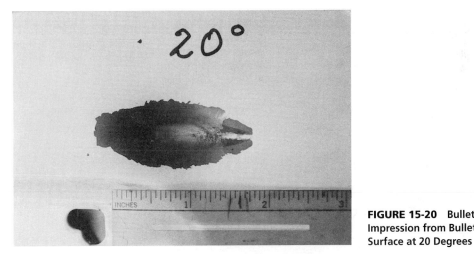

20°

FIGURE 15-20 Bullet Ricochet Impression from Bullet Striking the Surface at 20 Degrees

90°

FIGURE 15-21 Bullet Entry Hole from Bullet Striking the Surface at 90 Degrees

CASE EXAMPLE

In a shooting incident involving a sheriff's deputy, it was essential to determine whether the shot from a shotgun held by the defendant was fired toward the deputy or whether the weapon fired accidentally. As the defendant in the case exited his vehicle holding a shotgun, he was shot in the head by the deputy responding to the call. The defendant claimed that he was removing the shotgun to surrender it to the deputy when he was shot in the head, with the result that the defendant was knocked to the ground. It was necessary to determine whether the shotgun was fired toward the deputy or was fired as the result of an accidental discharge of the weapon. A reconstruction of the trajectory of the shotgun pellets (see Figure 15-22) and a determination of the position of the shotgun at the time of discharge (see Figures 15-23 and 15-24) revealed that the shotgun was in contact with the pavement at the time of discharge. It was determined that the shotgun fired accidentally when the butt of the weapon struck the sidewalk by determining the position of the weapon at the time of discharge and determining through experimentation that the shotgun would discharge when striking a hard surface in the position it was in at the time of the incident. Other elements of this reconstruction established that the deputy acted appropriately in the incident, thus precluding any civil action against the deputy or the sheriff's department. ■

FIGURE 15-22 Entry Hole from Shotgun Blast

FIGURE 15-23 Cylinder Placed in Shotgun Entry Hole Aligned with the Trajectory

FIGURE 15-24 Placement of Shotgun in Its Position When the Discharge Occurred

Bullet ricochets

In the case of ricochets, the angle at which the bullet strikes a surface (the incident angle) will rarely be the same as the angle of deflection (the angle between the surface and the trajectory of the bullet deflecting off the surface, also called the exit angle (see Figure 15-25). For soft bullets striking a hard, rigid surface such as concrete, the incident

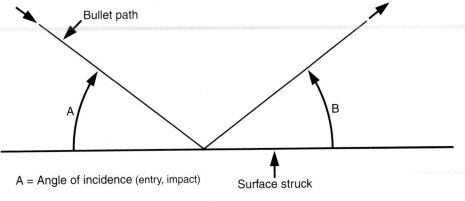

A = Angle of incidence (entry, impact)

B = Angle of reflection (exit, deflection)

FIGURE 15-25 **Incident Angle and Deflection Angle for Bullets Striking a Surface**

angle will usually be larger than the exit angle. For soft surfaces, such as vehicle metal, the angle of deflection may exceed the angle of incidence.[15] There is a *critical angle* for each type of ammunition and the resilience of the surface, below which the bullet will ricochet off the surface, and above which the bullet will penetrate the surface. This critical angle differs considerably for surfaces such as metals, glass, wallboard, water, and others. It is important to remember that when a bullet strikes a surface, there may be significant trace evidence on the bullet. Bullets penetrating clothing may have fibers from the garment impressed into the surface of the bullet. The location of the fibers may provide evidence of the orientation of the bullet when it struck the surface, such as fibers embedded in the base of the bullet, which would indicate that the bullet was tumbling when it struck the garment surface. Fabric impressions or adherent fibers on the nose of the bullet would indicate that the bullet was not tumbling when it struck the surface. Bullets that have ricocheted off a painted surface may have paint imbedded into the nose or other surfaces, in which case it is necessary to collect paint standards from each surface struck by bullets.

Bullet ricochets on vehicles

The angle at which a bullet struck a surface and ricocheted is difficult to determine without experimentation. In most instances of a ricochet, the incident angle has to be estimated by experimentation using the same weapon/ammunition combination and the same surface. Since the path of the bullet after ricochet may be at a higher or lower angle than the incident angle depending on the surface type, the deflection angle must be determined experimentally in order to reconstruct the trajectory on the basis of the bullet's striking another surface after ricochet. These experiments should be conducted by criminalists or firearms examiners experienced in crime scene reconstruction of shooting incidents.

The direction of travel for a bullet ricochet on a painted vehicle surface can be determined using the method developed by Mitosinka (see Figure 15-26).[16] The bullet ricochet creates fine fracture lines in the paint surrounding the ricochet mark, which can be visualized by dusting the ricochet mark with fingerprint powder. *It is important that the ricochet mark be photographed and any collection of trace metals in the ricochet mark*

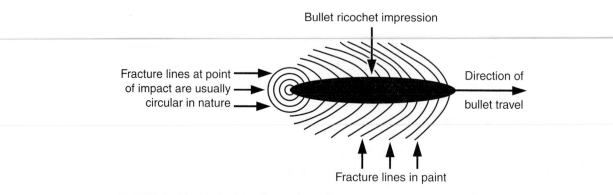

FIGURE 15-26 Method for Illustrating Bullet Travel Direction for Ricochet on a Vehicle

be accomplished prior to the powder dusting technique, in order to avoid contamination of the trace metals collected with the GSR kit. Collect residues from the ricochet mark using the GSR swabbing technique, and collect a control swabbing several inches from the impact site of the ricochet mark. Develop the fracture lines surrounding the ricochet by dusting with common fingerprint powder. Photograph any developed fracture lines before and after covering and lifting with fingerprint tape. The fracture lines developed by this technique display directional characteristics for the bullet flight path. At the point of impact, the fracture lines exhibit a circular appearance. The remaining fracture lines point in the direction of travel, much as the feathers on an arrow point in the direction of travel.

BULLET PATH DETERMINATION IN VEHICLES USING PROBES

Placing of Probes Bullet trajectory determination in vehicle bullet holes, where the bullet path penetrated two or more surfaces, can be accomplished by placing a probe through the perforations created in each surface by the bullet (see Figure 15-27). In those instances where the distance between the holes in a particular bullet path is lengthy, longer probes will be necessary to bridge the distance.

FIGURE 15-27 Insertion of Probes into Bullet Path Perforations
Copyright © Bruce R. Moran, with permission.

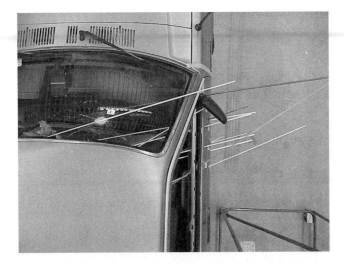

FIGURE 15-28 Photograph of
Bullet Path Probes from the Top of
the Vehicle
Copyright © Bruce R. Moran, with
permission.

Illustrating Bullet Paths with Photography   Once the bullet path probes are in place, the probes are photographed from the top (see Figure 15-28), making sure that the camera is parallel to the ground surface and centered in the midpoint of the probe(s) in place. The second photograph is taken from the side of the vehicle at a right angle to the ground surface and the vehicle's long axis (see Figure 15-29). The two photographs taken from the top and from the side then allow for accurate reconstruction of the bullet paths in three dimensions.

Additional photographs of the probes in place can be taken to *illustrate the perspectives* of the bullet paths (see Figures 15-30 and 15-31,) bearing in mind that these photographs *cannot be used for reconstruction of the bullet paths*.

Once the bullet paths have been established using probes, the reconstruction of the bullet paths can be placed on a scale diagram of the vehicle (see Figure 15-32) for use in the scene reconstruction. The scale diagram of the vehicle showing the bullet paths can then be placed on scale diagrams of the shooting scene (see Figure 15-33) in order to illustrate the bullet paths relative to the potential shooters in the incident.

Identification of the firearm that fired each bullet or cartridge case

The reconstruction of a shooting event often requires the identification of which firearm fired each bullet recovered at the scene, when more than one weapon is involved in the incident. This step is necessary in order to establish the responsible weapon for any fatality in the incident or to establish the locations of shooters. Identification of the firearm that fired the expended cartridge cases is also important to establish the positions of the shooters involved. The site of expended cartridge cases can assist in the determination of the position of shooter(s) at the time the firearm ejected the case. Bullet trajectories can be assigned to specific weapons when the recovered bullet has sufficient detail to identify the firearm that fired the bullet.

Gunshot residues on suspected shooters

The identification of gunshot residues on the hands of a suspected shooter will help to establish whether or not the suspected shooter actually fired a weapon. Although the

FIGURE 15-29 Photograph of Bullet Path Probes from the Side of the Vehicle
Copyright © Bruce R. Moran, with permission.

FIGURE 15-30 Perspective of Bullet Paths from Windshield of Vehicle
Copyright © Bruce R. Moran, with permission.

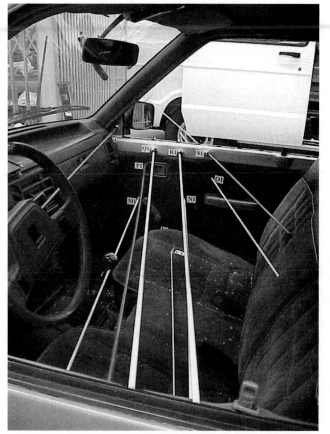

FIGURE 15-31 Perspective of Bullet Paths from Driver's Side Door
Copyright © Bruce R. Moran, with permission.

residues are easily lost or removed, the positive identification of gunshot residues on a suspect's hands provides strong evidence that the suspect fired a weapon in the incident. In cases of suspected suicide, the presence of gunshot residue on the victim's hand furnishes evidence that the wound was self-inflicted. The absence of gunshot residue on a suspected suicide's hands is a strong indication that the wound was inflicted by another party, since gunshot residue will last for extended periods on the hands of a decedent.

Distance characteristics of target residues

The patterns created by the discharge residues from firearms are correlated with the distance from the muzzle to the target surface at the time of discharge of the weapon. The components of the discharge that create the patterns observed (see Figure 15-34) are the projectile, unburned and partially burned gunpowder grains, flame that escapes the barrel, smoke (soot) from the burned gunpowder, and expanding gases produced by the burning of the gunpowder. Chemicals such as antimony, arsenic, lead, and copper also contribute to the patterns and may be detected by chemical means. These various components of the discharge travel various distances from the muzzle according to the physical properties of the components. As the distance from the muzzle increases, fewer and

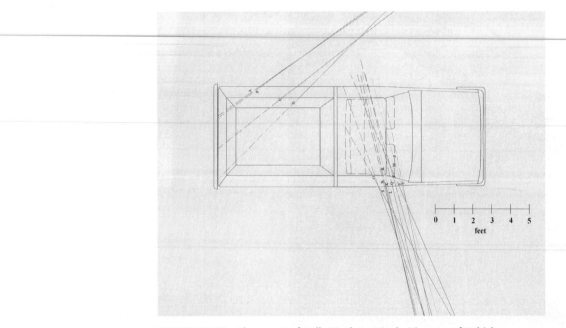

FIGURE 15-32   Placement of Bullet Paths on Scale Diagram of Vehicle
Copyright © Bruce R. Moran, with permission.

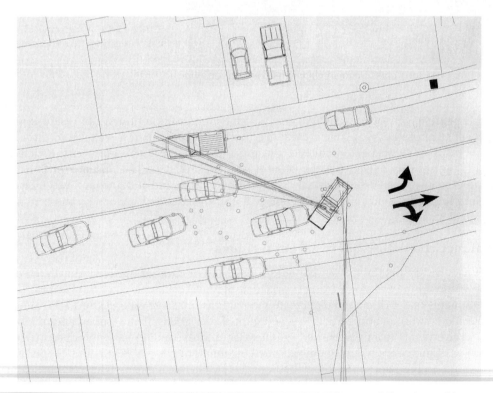

FIGURE 15-33   Placement of Vehicle with Bullet Paths on Scale Diagram of Shooting Incident
Copyright © Bruce R. Moran, with permission.

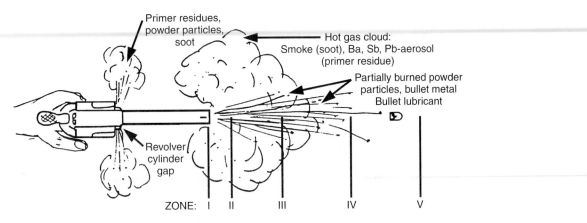

FIGURE 15-34 Gunshot Residue Production
Courtesy of ANITE Productions and Lucien Haag.

fewer of these components are found in the pattern created by the residues. This graduated loss of the various residues, combined with the continuous spreading of the powder grains as they travel downrange, produces a residue pattern that is characteristic for a particular muzzle-to-target distance with the same weapon/ammunition combination (see Figures 15-34 and 15-35). At a distance, the only remaining target residue is the "wiping" or smear ring of the projectile surface as it penetrates the impact surface.

The target residue patterns produced vary continuously from the muzzle to that distance where none of the discharge residues are found on the target. Although the variation in the pattern produced over distance represents a continuum, the patterns produced are grouped into classification divisions for convenience in order to describe the typical characteristics of a pattern produced within a range of the muzzle-to-target distances. Haag classifies distance characteristics of target residues for handguns into *five zones* when the muzzle is perpendicular to the target as follows: contact (Zone I); near-contact (Zone II); 3–8 inches (Zone III); 6–36 inches (Zone IV); and 3–4 feet (Zone V).[17]

ZONE I: CONTACT—CONTACT OF THE MUZZLE WITH THE TARGET AT DISCHARGE

Zone I is characterized by destruction from the muzzle blast, depicted by the tearing of skin or clothing around the entry site. Wounds produced in the skin from contact shots have a characteristic "stellate" (star-shaped) appearance (some exit wounds may have a stellate appearance). The degree of tissue destruction and tearing are directly related to the type of firearm and the type of cartridge. Small caliber weapons, such as .22 caliber handguns, produce very little tearing of the skin, whereas a .357 Magnum or 9 mm Parabellum pistol will produce considerable tearing of the skin and fracture of underlying bone. High-powered rifles and shotguns will produce major damage from contact wounds as a result of the immense gas pressures generated by these weapons.

Powder particles and soot are found on the inside surface of the clothing and are driven into the wound. DiMaio subclassifies contact wounds further into *hard, loose, angled,* and *incomplete,* with respect to how the muzzle is held against the skin.[18] In *hard-contact* wounds, the muzzle seals the area of contact; thus the discharge products are driven into the wound, while the edges of the wound are seared by the gases and blackened by the soot. In *loose-contact* wounds, the muzzle is held loosely against the

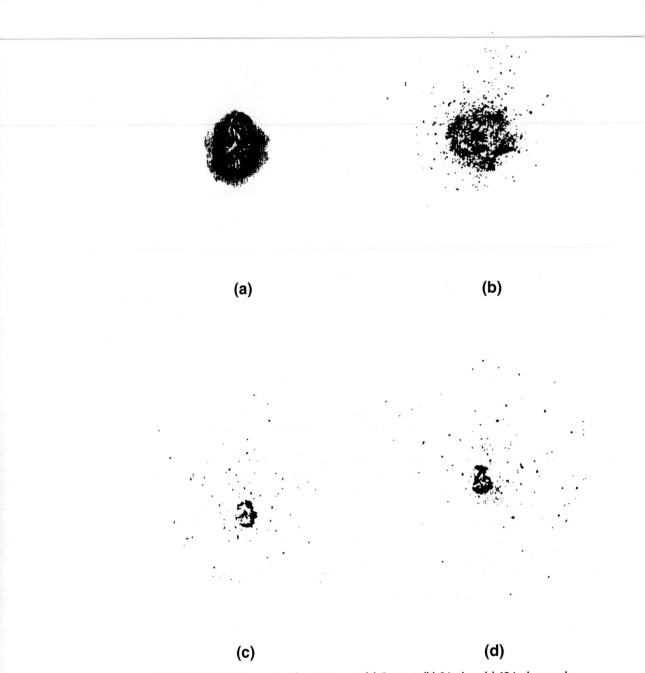

(a)

(b)

(c)

(d)

FIGURE 15-35 Discharge Residue Pattern at (a) Contact, (b) 6 Inches, (c) 12 Inches, and (d) 18 Inches
Courtesy of New Jersey State Police.

skin, thus allowing the gas escaping from the muzzle to create a muzzle-to-skin gap through which gas can escape and deposit soot around the wound periphery. In *angled-contact* wounds, the barrel is held at an angle to the skin, producing an eccentric pattern of soot. *Incomplete-contact* wounds are the result of the skin's surface being rounded, so that the muzzle is unable to effect a seal.[19]

ZONE II: NEAR-CONTACT—APPROXIMATELY ONE TO FOUR INCHES MUZZLE-TO-TARGET

Zone II is characterized by intense, dark sooting with dense deposits of unburned and partially burned powder particles surrounding the bullet hole. Some blast destruction may be present in the clothing and in the skin in some cases. Powder tattooing is usually present on the skin. DiMaio indicates that the soot in the seared zone is baked into the skin and cannot be wiped away.[20]

ZONE III: APPROXIMATELY THREE TO EIGHT INCHES MUZZLE-TO-TARGET

Zone III is characterized by medium- to light-gray sooting with a roughly "shotgun" pattern of powder particles around the bullet hole. Powder tattooing is still possible, particularly with dense and/or poorly burning powders. DiMaio classifies wounds in Zone III and probably part of Zone IV as "intermediate-range" wounds, the hallmark of which is powder tattooing (not powder burns, since tattooing is the result of the impact of powder particles on the skin, producing abrasions, not burns).[21] He indicates that this zone begins at approximately 10 cm (4 inches).

ZONE IV: APPROXIMATELY SIX TO THIRTY-SIX INCHES MUZZLE-TO-TARGET

No visible sooting from gases is noted in this zone. Widely dispersed powder particles, often loosely adhering to the receiving surface, are present on the surface. The distribution pattern is roughly circular at closer distances but may become poorly defined at greater distances. Chemical tests can be employed to develop the pattern.

ZONE V: APPROXIMATELY THREE TO FOUR FEET MUZZLE-TO-TARGET[22]

As a rule of thumb, no discernible firearms discharge products are found in or beyond this zone (bullet wiping around the entry hole is typically present, regardless of range). However, some high powered weapon/ammunition combinations (especially shotgun and rifle combinations) may produce a discernible pattern in this range. In some cases, although rare, discharge patterns have been located well beyond four feet.

Laboratory analysis of firearm evidence for reconstructions

MUZZLE-TO-TARGET DISTANCE DETERMINATIONS

Muzzle-to-target determinations are performed by the laboratory analyst using the weapon involved in the incident. Test firings are made into targets at varying distances using the same type of ammunition as that used in the weapon that produced the pattern under investigation. The dispersion pattern of the soot and partially burned gunpowder of test patterns fired at varying distances are compared with the pattern on the questioned gunshot wound or pattern present on an article of clothing. The analyst is able to place the muzzle-to-target distance between two of the test-firing distances, usually within a matter of inches. The muzzle-to-target distance, as determined, is then interpreted as to its significance with regard to the statements of principals or witnesses or, in the case of murder versus suicide, whether the distance is consistent with a self-inflicted wound.

EXAMINATION FOR GUNSHOT RESIDUES

The laboratory analysis for gunshot residues is accomplished on the swabs from the suspected shooter's hands by using neutron activation analysis (NAA) or atomic absorption analysis (AA). These techniques search for and quantify the antimony and barium from the primer residue that may be present in the gunshot residue. The analysis for gunshot residues on disks is accomplished by use of the scanning electron microscope (SEM). This microscope allows the examiner to identify accurately the small fragments of gunpowder found in the residue. In addition, the SEM usually has an energy dispersive x-ray analyzer (EDX) attached, so that the analyst can measure the metallic elements present in the residue.

IDENTIFICATION OF FIREARM IN WHICH CARTRIDGE CASES AND PROJECTILES WERE FIRED

An integral element in crime scene reconstructions involving firearms is the identification of the particular firearm in which each cartridge case and projectile was fired. These identifications allow the reconstruction analyst to place each firearm in the position that it was in at the time of firing of that component, often with considerable accuracy. In cases in which the firearms are not recovered, the analyst may be able to determine how many weapons were involved and which of the retrieved cartridge components were fired in the same weapon.

Functionality of Recovered Weapons   The functionality of a weapon may be significant in those cases in which there is a question of whether a firearm wound was the result of an accidental discharge or was the result of an intentional firing. Some weapons have design defects that make them prone to accidental discharge, but most weapons have safeguards that prevent accidental discharges. In other weapons, the poor condition of the firearm through wear or abuse creates a situation in which accidental discharge is likely under certain circumstances. The laboratory analyst, through experimentation that re-creates the conditions under which the firearm was discharged, may be able to determine the likelihood of the weapon's accidental discharge in the incident under investigation.

RECONSTRUCTIONS BASED ON OTHER EVIDENCE TYPES

Direction of force in glass pane fractures

The analysis of broken glass edges plays a role in the reconstruction of events associated with certain types of crimes. When a glass pane is fractured, there are two types of fracture lines, **radial fracture** lines and **concentric fracture** lines (see Figure 15-36). The radial fractures radiate from the point at which the object struck the pane toward the edge of the pane. The concentric fracture lines are concentric circular fractures surrounding the point of impact. The documentation of which lines are radial fracture lines and which are concentric fracture lines is essential to the determination of which side of the pane received the force that created the fractures.

In the event of a simulated burglary, where the window glass of a residence has ostensibly been broken to gain entry, analysis of the fracture edges of the glass remaining

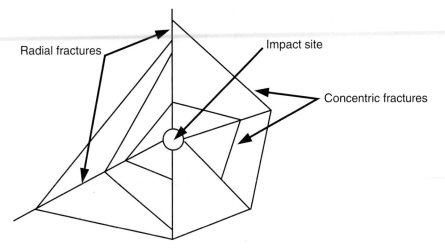

FIGURE 15-36   Radial and Concentric Fracture Lines in Glass

in the window frame may establish the direction of the force that fractured the window pane. The fracture edges have striated patterns called "**conchoidal**" striations, which indicate the direction of force through interpretation of their patterns. The conchoidal fracture lines are parallel to one surface of the glass pane for a short distance, then curve toward the opposite surface, ending approximately perpendicular to that surface (see Figure 15-37). In the case of *radial* fractures, the perpendicular lines *point away* from the side receiving the impact, whereas in the *concentric* fracture lines, the perpendicular lines point *toward* the side receiving the impact.

When a glass pane is penetrated by a projectile, the projectile produces a characteristic "**crater**" effect in the glass. The side of the pane struck by the projectile has a small hole that expands toward the opposite side to produce the crater (see Figure 15-38). This cratering effect is also produced in other hard materials, such as bone, thereby allowing the reconstruction analyst to determine the direction of travel of the projectile that produced the crater.

Sequence of firearm projectile impacts

If a window has been penetrated by a bullet, it is possible to determine the direction from which it was fired. If two or more bullet holes are in close proximity, it is often

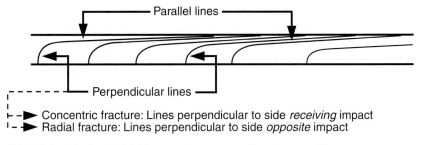

FIGURE 15-37   Conchoidal Fracture Patterns on Glass Fracture Edge

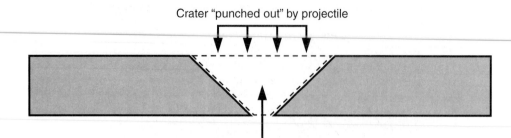

Crater "punched out" by projectile

Direction of projectile producing crater in glass

FIGURE 15-38   Cratering of Glass Pane by a Projectile

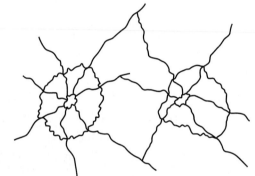

FIGURE 15-39   Sequence of Impacts from Projectiles

possible to determine the **sequence of firing** (see Figure 15-39). The impact of the first projectile creates radial and concentric fracture lines in the window. These cracks produced in the pane of glass by a projectile may run into the cracks produced by previous projectiles, thus providing a mechanism for the analyst to determine the sequence of the projectiles penetrating the pane. When a radial fracture ends at another fracture line, the analyst may conclude that the fracture line where the radial fracture ends was preexistent from a previous projectile impact. Rynearson cautions that in the case of windshield glass, secondary shocks from subsequent impacts and roadway vibrations may obscure the patterns and prevent accurate sequencing of the projectile impacts.[23]

Evidence showing which occupant of a vehicle was the driver

Occasionally in vehicle accidents, the occupants are thrown from the vehicle, and it is sometimes necessary for criminal prosecution or a civil proceeding to determine which occupant of the vehicle was the driver at the time of the accident. This determination can be accomplished in a number of ways. Injuries sustained by the occupants may be linked to specific items in the vehicle interior that could injure only either the driver or the passenger. Blood and/or tissue stains in the driver's compartment can be analyzed for DNA type, thus placing the correct individual in the driver's seat. In one of the

FIGURE 15-40 Side of Pickup Showing Angle of Impact that Threw Driver to the Right, Where He Impacted the Moon-Roof Lever

FIGURE 15-41 Moon-Roof Lever with Hair, Tissue, and Blood from the Driver

author's cases, the driver and passenger agreed to exchange roles as driver and passenger in their statement to the police in order to avoid prosecution of the driver for driving without a license. This ruse was easily proven false by hair comparisons and blood typing of the blood and tissue left on the moon roof lever by the driver (see Figures 15-40 and 15-41).

Reconstructions involving more than one type of physical evidence

In many cases, a crime scene reconstruction involves the analysis and interpretation of more than one type of physical evidence. Frequently, the reconstruction involves firearms and bloodstain evidence; and in some cases, several types of evidence will play a role in the reconstruction.

Reconstruction of a Shooting Incident: Shotgun Slaying of Male and Female Victims

In this case (*People v. Anderson*) reconstructed by Moran, the reconstruction involved firearms evidence from the crime scene, bloodstain pattern evidence at the scene (both inside the residence and outdoors), firearms evidence from the autopsy of the victims, and the use of essential diagrams originally created with Metacreations Poser, over a three-dimensional background of the residence, using Broderbund 3D Home Architect and annotated using Microsoft Word.[24] The main focus of the case was on the reconstruction of the events that took place during the slayings.

FACTS OF THE CASE

In 1984, a woman and her boyfriend were shot to death in their residence and the immediate surroundings by the female victim's estranged husband (see Figure 15-42). The main issue in this case was to determine whether the victim(s) were in a defensive or an offensive posture at the time(s) they were shot. A variety of evidence was utilized to reconstruct the location and position of each of the victims and the suspect at the time of the

shootings. Conclusions made by Moran in the reconstruction were based on the shotgun ejection pattern, muzzle-to-target distance determinations, body positions of the victims at the time of the shootings based on pellet wound patterns, blood pattern interpretation, trajectory determinations, trace evidence, damage received by the shotgun, witness statements, and the pathologist's reports.

SHOOTING RECONSTRUCTION OF THE MALE VICTIM

Wounds to the Male Victim

It was determined that the male victim received wounds from a single shotgun blast as follows: (1) perforating contact/near-contact to left palm; (2) sooting on the right hand but no pellet wounds present; (3) pellet entry wounds in right forearm at extremely acute angles (trajectories converged at a point a few inches above and just beyond the right wrist); (4) pellet wounds to upper right arm at near-perpendicular angles; (5) entry wound in upper front right shoulder (waddings recovered); (6) widely

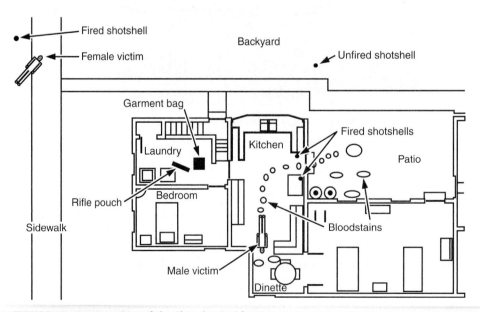

FIGURE 15-42 Overview of the Shooting Incident
Copyright © Bruce R. Moran, with permission.

(continued)

(*continued*)

dispersed pattern of pellet entry wounds in right shoulder, right neck, and face; (7) four grazing wounds across top of right shoulder at approximately 40 degrees from right to left; and (8) pellet wounds in the face that were very circular and entered at near perpendicular angles.

Interpretation of Wounds to the Male Victim

After analysis and interpretation of the wound patterns, coupled with experimental work with the shotgun/ammunition combination utilizing chicken parts and test targets, Moran concluded the following: (1) the victim sustained a single shotgun wound that passed through the left palm and into the upper body of the victim; (2) the left palm was in contact or near-contact with the muzzle at the time of firing; (3) the right hand was in an open position and in close vicinity to the muzzle but not directly in front of it; (4) alignment of the trajectories in the arms indicated that the left arm was fully extended and that the right arm was retracted; (5) the left palm was positioned a few inches above the right wrist; (6) the shot came from the right front of the victim at shoulder height; (7) the angle of the pellet entry wounds in the face indicated that the victim was looking directly at the muzzle at the instant the shot was fired (see Figure 15-43).

Interpretation of Bloodstain Patterns

Patterns of splashed, swiped, castoff, dripped, and trailed blood observed on the patio indicated that the victim had fallen onto the patio into a prone position with the head toward the south wall, gotten up, walked through the kitchen doorway, then collapsed.

SHOOTING RECONSTRUCTION OF THE FEMALE VICTIM

Wounds to the Female Victim

The female victim received a shotgun wound to the approximate middle of the back at an angle of approximately 8 degrees from right to left and 45 degress downward.

Interpretation of Wounds to the Female Victim

The wounds to the victim indicated that she was shot while in a prone position, with the shooter above the victim. Pellet patterns similar to that in the victim's back were produced at a range of two feet by simulating the conditions suggested by the wound pellet pattern. These experiments established that the shooter was standing over the victim in close proximity (see Figure 15-44) at the time the weapon was fired.

FIGURE 15-43   Position of the Male Victim at the Instant of Shooting

(*continued*)

(*continued*)

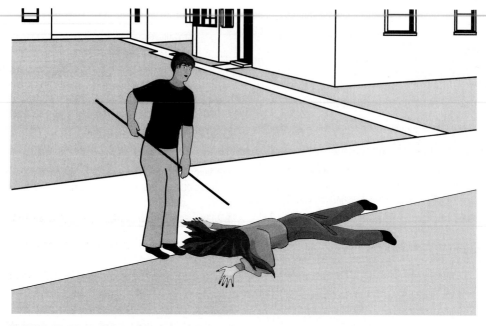

FIGURE 15-44   Position of Female Victim at the Instant of Shooting

Reconstruction of the Shooting Incident

The suspect, armed with the shotgun, confronted the two victims from the kitchen doorway as they were standing at the foot of the patio steps leading to the kitchen. The male victim was shot first by a single blast from the shotgun. He collapsed momentarily in the patio area, stood up, walked into the kitchen, and then collapsed. His wounds indicate that he was attempting to grab or deflect the muzzle of the shotgun with both hands when the fatal shot was fired. The suspect caught up to the female victim and administered several blows to her head (evidenced by damage to the shotgun and a hair wedged under the butt plate). He then pointed the shotgun at the female victim lying on the ground and fired one shot into her back.

This reconstruction by Moran illustrates the use of both firearm and bloodstain pattern evidence in a crime scene reconstruction. The use of computer-assisted drawings provided a definitive method for the presentation of the reconstruction findings and the manner in which the conclusions were reached. ▨

Summary

INTRODUCTION

- Chapter presented to acquaint students with the value of crime scene reconstruction.
- This chapter will not provide the reader with the expertise necessary to perform crime scene reconstructions.

ESTABLISHMENT OF EXPERTISE

- Expertise pyramid of education, training, and mentored experience.

- Examiner must acquire necessary education, training, and mentored experience before casework.
- Tiers of education, training, mentored experience essential to development of the ability to think critically.
- Actions of the practitioners typically impact lives of others in a profound manner.
- Errors have led to conviction of innocent parties, even in death penalty cases.
- True expertise result of proper education, training, and mentored experience.

EXPERIENTIAL DEVELOPMENT OF EXPERTISE

- Through trial and error, gains "experience."
- "Stove-pipe" approach does not provide a stable and appropriate foundation for professional expertise.
- Development of expertise through "experience" is an inappropriate approach.
  - "Experience" is the name we give our mistakes.
  - In everyday life acceptable because we are the ones who pay the price for our mistakes.
  - In a profession, those affected by our mistakes pay the price for errors.
  - This separation of responsibility from accountability is unacceptable.
  - Experiential method of training inefficient, ineffective.
  - Subject of the experiential training program may or may not detect mistakes and not learn from the mistake.
  - No internal quality assurance or control.
  - Has no qualitative component to assure competence and professional integrity of the examiner.

CRITICAL THINKING

- Careful and exact evaluation and judgment.
- Essential that investigator exercise critical thinking.
- Mandate applies to investigators in any field.
- Absolutely obligatory for any individual making a scientific inquiry.
- Must avoid common logical errors:
  - Circular reasoning (formerly "begging the question") means assuming your thesis is proved before you have proved it.
  - Ignoring the Question: Any form of irrelevance, such as straw man and ad hominem.
  - Statistical Fallacies: misuse of statistics, numbers, percentages, etc.
  - The "Science" Fallacy: If it is "scientific," it is good, true, reliable, etc. Merely stating that a "method" is scientific does not make it so.

CRIME SCENE RECONSTRUCTION

- One of the major purposes for the collection of physical evidence.
- Defined here as the determination of events (and often the sequence of those events) during the commission of a crime (or tort).
- Accomplished with the analysis and interpretation of the physical evidence at the scene.
- Many other definitions of reconstruction exist.

CRIME SCENE RECONSTRUCTION TEAM

- Crime scene reconstruction is always a team effort.
- Quality of reconstruction depends heavily on the quality of the efforts of the crime scene investigation team.
- Important to remember that crime scene reconstruction relies on a systematic, meticulous, and competent endeavor by the crime scene processing team.
- Laboratory scientists.
- Assistance of professionals from a range of disciplines.

PROCESS OF CRIME SCENE RECONSTRUCTION

- Recognition of the physical evidence essential to the reconstruction.
- Appropriate documentation of the physical evidence crucial to reconstruction efforts and court presentations.
- Proper collection of the evidence.
- Laboratory examination of physical evidence.
- Analysis of physical evidence from the crime scene and laboratory examinations.
- Synthesis of the data into a coherent hypothesis which explains all the data known (interpretation of the analysis data).
- Hypothesis is subjected to logical analysis and/or experimentation for verification or rejection.

CRIME SCENE RECONSTRUCTION COMPONENTS

- Analysis phase.
- Synthesis phase.

TYPES OF RECONSTRUCTIONS

- Type of crime.
- Type of evidence.
- Specific professional field involved in the reconstruction.
- Traffic accident reconstruction.
- Homicide reconstructions.
- Sexual assault reconstructions.

RECONSTRUCTIONS CLASSIFIED BY EVIDENCE TYPE UTILIZED

- Bloodstain pattern evidence.
- Firearms evidence.
- Based on more than one type of evidence.

INFORMATION OBTAINED FROM BLOODSTAIN PATTERN ANALYSIS

- Direction from which a bloodstain droplet originated.
- Approximate angle at which a blood droplet struck a surface.
- Determination of the area (point) of origin of a two-dimensional spatter pattern.
- Location or position of the victim at the time of the impact blow or application of force.
- Distance between the origin and the target surface at the time of bloodshed.
- Movement (s) of the person from whom the bloodstains originated.
- Minimum number of blows struck by a blunt instrument.
- Cast-off spatter from the swings of a blunt instrument or a cutting/stabbing instrument.
- Approximate location of the individual delivering the blows.
- Type and direction of the impact which produced the bloodstain patterns.
  - Low velocity.
  - Medium velocity.
  - High velocity.
- Blow-back spatter of blood from a gunshot wound.

BLOODSTAINS: SHOE PRINTS, TRACKS AND TRAILS

INFORMATION FROM SHOOTING INCIDENT RECONSTRUCTIONS

- Muzzle-to-target distances.
- Minimum number of participants in the incident.
- Number and type (s) of firearms involved in the incident.
- Projectile paths taken during the shooting incident.
- Location (s) of participants during the incident.
- Sequence (s) of events during the shooting incident.
- Minimum number of participants in the incident.
- Number and type (s) of firearms involved in the incident.

ZONES OF POSSIBILITY FOR THE POSITION OF THE SHOOTER.

- Zone I. Most Probable.
- Zone II. Improbable but possible (awkward).
- Zone III. Impossible.

BULLET TRAJECTORY DOCUMENTATION

- Measurement of bullet trajectories using probe and protractor.
- Documentation of the bullet trajectory with photography.
- Probe and string method of trajectory measurement.
- Laser light method for determining bullet trajectories.
- Bullet trajectories in vehicle surfaces.

BULLET RICOCHETS

- Incident and deflection angles for bullets striking a surface.
- Method for illustrating bullet travel direction for ricochet on a vehicle.

ILLUSTRATING BULLET PATHS IN VEHICLE WITH PHOTOGRAPHY

- Insertion of probes into bullet path perforations.
- Photograph of bullet path probes from the top of the vehicle.
- Photograph of bullet path probes from the side of the vehicle.

IDENTIFICATION OF FIREARM WHICH FIRED BULLET OR CARTRIDGE CASE

GUNSHOT RESIDUES ON SUSPECTED SHOOTERS

DISTANCE CHARACTERISTICS OF TARGET RESIDUES

- Gunshot residue production.
- Discharge residue patterns at distance intervals.

LABORATORY ANALYSIS OF FIREARMS EVIDENCE FOR RECONSTRUCTIONS

- Muzzle-to target distance determinations.
- Examination for gunshot residues.
- Identification of firearm in which cartridge cases and projectiles were fired.
- Functionality of recovered weapons.

RECONSTRUCTIONS FROM OTHER EVIDENCE TYPES

DIRECTION OF FORCE IN GLASS PANE FRACTURES

- Radial and concentric fracture lines in glass.
- Conchoidal fracture patterns on glass fracture edge.
- Cratering of glass pane by a projectile.

SEQUENCE OF FIREARM PROJECTILE IMPACTS

EVIDENCE SHOWING WHICH OCCUPANT OF A VEHICLE WAS THE DRIVER

RECONSTRUCTIONS INVOLVING MORE THAN ONE TYPE OF PHYSICAL EVIDENCE

Review Questions

1. Crime scene reconstruction provides the investigator with the ability to determine which version of the events at the crime scene is _____ and which is _____.
2. Crime scene reconstruction can aid the investigator in determining whether a death is the result of _____, _____, or _____.
3. Crime scene reconstruction is the major _____ for the collection of physical evidence.
4. Crime scene reconstruction is defined here as the determination of what _____ occurred during the commission of a crime.
5. Crime scene reconstruction is always a _____ _____.
6. Analysis of _____ _____ on the hands of victims and suspects may determine who fired a weapon at a crime scene.
7. The first step in a crime scene reconstruction is the _____ of an item as physical evidence.

8. Formation of a coherent hypothesis requires the _____ of the data from the crime scene and the laboratory examinations.
9. Once a hypothesis is formed, it is subjected to _____ analysis and/or _____ to determine whether the known facts are explained by the hypothesis.
10. It is essential that the crime scene investigation team document the physical evidence with _____, _____, and _____.
11. Improper collection of the physical evidence at the scene may _____ or _____ the information otherwise available from the evidence.
12. The three Cs of teamwork are _____, _____, and _____.
13. Reconstructions may be classified by the type of _____ _____, by the type of _____ involved in the reconstruction, or by the specific _____ field of the individual(s) performing the reconstruction.

14. Most crime scene reconstructions are accomplished in _____ cases because of the lack of _____.

15. In sexual assault cases, examination of the physical evidence may prove that the defense of _____ is false.

16. Bloodstain pattern analysis may show the _____ of the origin of a bloodstain droplet.

17. Bloodstain pattern analysis may determine the impact _____ of a bloodstain droplet.

18. The area of origin for a two-dimensional bloodstain on a surface is established by determining the area of _____ of lines drawn through the long axis of the bloodstains.

19. The determination of the area of origin for a bloodstain pattern will establish the _____ of the victim at the time of the blow that produced the pattern.

20. The shape of a bloodstain may establish the _____ the drop has _____.

21. The backswing of a blunt instrument can create a distinct pattern termed a _____ pattern.

22. The spatter pattern on and/or in the muzzle of a weapon due to a close-range shot is called _____ _____ spatter.

23. A shooting incident reconstruction may determine the _____ _____ of firearms used in the incident.

24. _____ to _____ distances often aid the investigator in the determination of accident shooting, suicide, or homicide.

25. The entry angle of a projectile can best be determined with the use of a _____ when the projectile penetrated two consecutive surfaces.

26. The three zones of possibility for the position of a shooter are _____ _____, _____ but possible and _____.

27. For short distances, it can be assumed that the trajectory of a projectile is a _____ _____.

28. The probe and _____ method of determining a projectile's trajectory is typically more accurate than the use of a single probe.

29. The trajectory of a projectile can be determined with the use of a _____ light.

30. For soft bullets striking a hard surface, the angle of deflection will usually be _____ than the incident angle.

31. The _____ angle for a given surface is that angle below which a projectile will ricochet and above which the projectile will penetrate the surface.

32. The positive identification of _____ _____ on an individual's hands will usually establish that the individual recently fired a firearm.

33. A target distance residue pattern is characteristic for a particular _____ _____ combination at a specific distance.

34. The direction of travel for the bullet in a ricochet mark on a vehicle can be determined by examination of the _____ pattern in the paint.

Further References

Chisum, W. J., and B. E. Turvey., eds. 2007. *Crime Reconstruction*. Burlington, MA: Elsevier Academic Press.

DiMaio, V. J. M., MD., 1998. *Gunshot Wounds*, 2nd ed., Boca Raton, FL: CRC Press.

Haag, L. C. 2006. *Shooting Incident Reconstruction*. New York, NY: Academic Press.

Haag, L. C. 1991. *Forensic Firearms Evidence* (Practical Aspects of Firearms, Ballistics and Forensic Techniques) ed. A. Jason. Pinole, CA: ANITE Production.

Jackson, A. R. W., and J. Julie. 2004. *Forensic Science*. Essex, England, U.K.: Pearson Education Limited.

James, S. H., and J. J. Nordby, eds. 2005. *Forensic Science* (An Introduction to Scientific and Investigative Techniques), 2nd ed. Boca Raton, FL: CRC Press.

James, S. H., P. E. Kish, and T. P. Sutton, eds. and authors. 2005. *Principles of Bloodstain Analysis* (Theory and Practice). Boca Raton, FL: CRC Press.

MacDonell, H. L. 1993. *Bloodstain Patterns*. Corning, NY: Laboratory of Forensic Science.

Osterburg, J. W., and R. H. Ward. 2000. *Criminal Investigation* (A Method for Reconstructing the Past), 3rd ed. Cincinnati, OH: Anderson Publishing Company.

Rynearson, J. M. 1997. *Evidence and Crime Scene Reconstruction*, 5th ed. Redding, CA: National Crime Investigation and Training (NCIT).

Saferstein, R. 2009. *Forensic Science* (From the Crime Scene to the Crime Lab). Upper Saddle River, NJ: Pearson Education, Inc.

White, P. ed. 1998. *Crime Scene to Court* (The Essentials of Forensic Science). UK: Cambridge, The Royal Society of Chemistry.

APPENDIX 15-A

Crime Scene Reconstruction Checklist

AT THE SCENE

- Ensure that a meticulous crime scene investigation is performed, to include notes of investigators, systematic photography, and sketching of the scene (see Chapters 2 through 4).
- It is extremely helpful for the individual(s) performing crime scene reconstruction to be at the scene(s).
- Consider calling to the scene criminalists, pathologists, anthropologists, entomologists, or other forensic specialists who may be involved in a reconstruction of the crime.

BLOODSTAIN PATTERN RECONSTRUCTIONS

- Photograph and sketch all bloodstain patterns, as prescribed in the appropriate chapters.
- Ensure that all bloodstain patterns have been documented with a measurement method so that patterns can be reconstructed in the laboratory for analysis.
- Measure axes of representative stains in the pattern, and then record them in notes and diagrams.
- Collect representative samples of each bloodstain pattern for genetic marker typing in the laboratory.
- Field test representative stains in a pattern when the appearance suggests that the stains may not be bloodstains.

FIREARMS SHOOTING INCIDENTS[25]

- Shooter(s)' and witnesses' explanations of discharge(s).
- Conduct of participants prior to the incident.
- Events prior to the incident.
- Stated location and/or position of participants during the incident.
- Manner in which the firearm was held.
- Means of discharge (single action, double action, semiautomatic dropped).
- Conduct of participants and events after the incident.
- Storage/condition of the firearm prior to the incident (cleaned, oiled, dirty, rusty, loaded magazine separate?).
- Source/type of ammunition used (and if available for examination, use as exemplars).
- Brand of ammunition, bullet type, and weight of projectile.
- Trace evidence on and/or in firearm.
- Smoke halos around the chambers of revolver cylinder.
- Bullet metal deposits in bore.
- Position/sequence of cartridges (revolver).
- Sequence of cartridges in magazine (semiauto firearms).
- Position of hammer (if present).

- Position of safety/safeties.
- Position of slide or bolt (repeating firearms).
- Blood droplets on face of muzzle or inside bore.
- Determination of projectile hole entrance versus exit.
- Determination of projectile hole angle of impact.
- Determination of projectile direction from impact sites and ricochets.
- Sodium rhodizonate test for lead or DTO (dithiooximide) test for copper on suspected projectile ricochets, entry holes, or impacts.
- Griess test for suspected gunshot residue on surfaces.
- Photography, fingerprint powder development, and tape lifting, and Mikrosil™ casting of bullet ricochets.
- Clothing of the participants.
- Comparison specimens of ammunition.
- Reference/comparison samples of materials penetrated by projectile or surfaces from which a projectile ricocheted, to include intermediary targets.

PREPARATION FOR RECONSTRUCTION EFFORT

- Perform a direct examination or re-examination of the scene.
- Obtain all crime scene reports.
- Obtain all photographs, videotapes taken at the scene(s), and other relevant sites.
- Obtain all detective reports, in particular those with any witness and suspect statements.
- Obtain autopsy pathologist's report(s), autopsy photographs, and toxicology reports for deceased subjects.
- Obtain medical reports for injured parties.
- Obtain physical evidence reports of any physical evidence collected or analyzed at the scene.

APPENDIX I

Crime Scene Report Writing

INTRODUCTION

The crime scene report is a "word picture" of the facts of the scene. The written report describes all actions taken at the scene, provides a log of all photographs taken, and lists all items of evidence seized. In addition, data from the crime scene investigator's notes regarding individuals at the scene and all other pertinent data should be included in the report for completeness. The written report should be skillfully drawn, remembering the ABCs of good report writing: accuracy, brevity, and clarity.

ACCURACY

Accuracy in the report is achieved by carefully outlining the report and then filling in all the details of the crime scene investigation, using the crime scene notes as the basis for all information in the report. No matter how good one's memory is, the written record is better. Moreover, each statement in the report can be authenticated by reference to the crime scene investigator's handwritten notes (which are part of the permanent record in the case file). Once the written report is drafted, each item in the report should be reverified by reference to the notes, so that no inconsistency between the field notes and the final report exists. Inconsistencies between the two provide fertile ground for cross-examination during the investigator's courtroom testimony.

The investigator should use concrete words in the report so as to avoid misinterpretation of the findings by the reader of the report. Avoid relative words in the report that require a frame of reference to establish the meaning of the words. Words such as "large," "long," and "big," for example, have no meaning unless the frame of reference is included in the sentence as a comparison reference. A basketball may be a "large" sphere when compared with a pea but a tiny sphere when compared with the earth. Whenever feasible, use words that have units of measurement, so that no question exists about the writer's meaning (three feet, ten pounds, fourteen yards, etc.). If relative terms are used in the report, give the frame of reference so that the reader of the report has an exact understanding of what is meant by the writer (*Example:* "The victim had a large bruise the size of a grapefruit on the inside of the left forearm"). Note that grapefruits vary somewhat in size, but the relative size of the bruise is clear to the reader. For estimated distances, use a frame of reference understood by most readers (a city block, for example). In most instances, it is much better to use concrete measurements with units of measurements, but estimates given are acceptable as long as the writer also gives the frame of reference for the reader.

The writer should also avoid phrases such as "gold watch" or "silver watch" when the watch was either "gold color" or "silver color," unless the watch is, in fact, made of gold or silver. These small differences in phrasing add to the accuracy of the report.

BREVITY

Brevity means being brief in the report, avoiding wordy anecdotes and lengthy explanations of conditions that are self-explanatory or clear from the context of the report. Brevity should not be understood as a license to be abrupt to the point of leaving unanswered questions in the mind of the reader, requiring the reader to read between the lines. Brevity is simply the absence of rambling, often redundant styles of writing. A writing technique that conserves space and also adds to the clarity of the report is to use bulleted lists for a series of related facts or actions.

EXAMPLE

"Attached to this report are the following:

- Overview sketch of the scene at 123 Anyplace Street.
- Detailed sketch of the N/E bedroom of 123 Anyplace Street, Apt. 1A.
- Log of photographs taken at the scene (two pages).
- Evidence log for evidence items collected (three pages)."

The use of bulleted lists like that in the example eliminates unnecessary repetition of the phrase "Attached is . . ." for each of the items in the list. In addition, the bulleted list provides a clear appearance to the eye and is readily scanned when the reader is reviewing the report.

CLARITY

Clarity means using language that is clear to the reader. When we write, we know exactly what we mean and intend to say. However, what is clear to us may not be clear to the reader of the report because of the use of imprecise words that may have different meanings to different people. Avoid any jargon, acronyms (unless universally understood), or words chosen for their effect rather than their clarity. Remember that the report is intended to convey information rather than to demonstrate the cleverness of the writer.

Clarity in the report demands correct spelling, punctuation, and grammar. The basic rules of grammar are simple and easily learned. One of the best references for correct grammar and usage is *The Gregg Reference Manual*.[1] This reference is easily understood and has many examples of the correct usage of words and terms. It is available at most bookstores.

Avoid long, complicated sentences, since they tend to confuse the reader (a good rule of thumb is to limit sentences to twenty-five words). It is better to have several short sentences than to have one long sentence that is hard to follow. Follow a rough outline prepared for writing the report with such shorter sentences. In this way, the reader is able to follow easily the substance of the report without having to sort out the information found in a longer sentence.

An excellent method for testing the ABCs of the report is to have another individual read through the draft report. Another individual does not have any preconceived ideas about what the report is trying to convey, and any lack of accuracy, brevity, or clarity will be obvious to the "cold" reader who knows nothing about the details of the crime scene. This method is very effective for honing the report-writing skills of the crime scene investigator. In most instances, the review of the report is the responsibility of the supervisor.

SKETCHES/PHOTO LOGS/EVIDENCE LISTS

These lists may be incorporated into the report or attached as separate sheets. It is preferable to attach them as separate sheets and to reference each in the body of the report (see the bulleted list in the example). This approach has the advantage of making the written report more concise and additionally allowing for separate routing of the evidence lists, photography logs, and sketches as needed without routing the entire report when only one list is requested. However, each individual's personal preference is acceptable, as long as the style adopted thoroughly reflects all the information needed to convey accurately all actions taken at the scene and reflects the written-report policy of the writer's department.

When the draft is reviewed and edited for the final draft of the report, it is helpful to ask yourself the basic Ws of any report: Who, What, Where, When, and of most importance, the "H" (How). These basic questions should be anticipated as the questions in the minds of individuals who will read the report and who will make important decisions about the future course of the case on the basis of the information contained in the report. It is also important to keep in mind that any sworn testimony will be based on the report and that any questions left unanswered will allow only the response "I don't know," a situation that may reduce the credibility of the witness when more careful report writing might have eliminated any gaps in the report.

Report writing is like any other skill that must be developed by practice and by continued improvement based on learning. The crime scene investigator should seek constructive criticism and incorporate helpful suggestions into his/her writing skills inventory. The frequent use of a dictionary and thesaurus and reference to a writing manual such as *The Gregg Reference Manual* will help avoid spelling errors and serious grammatical errors, either of which impart a nonprofessional appearance to the report. This suggestion should not be construed to mean that reports should be written in strictly formal language, since formal language is itself poor writing because of its stilted, condescending character. Standard English is the preferred style for reports directed to a mixed reading audience, since this style is acceptable for all anticipated readers of the report.

Agencies and individuals mentioned in the report should be spelled out, with the appropriate titles for each individual mentioned added (e.g., "Sergeant Raymond Davis," not "Davis"; "Kern County Coroner's Deputy Robin Tabler," not "Robin"; etc.). Acronyms for universally recognized agencies such as the FBI are acceptable, but the first mention of the agency should be spelled out, with the acronym following in parentheses; for example, Federal Bureau of Investigation (FBI).

Finally, each agency has its own set of rules for report writing, along with standard report forms. These rules must be followed regardless of the personal preference of the writer, since established rules and forms are the accepted method for that agency, and any departure will tend to confuse the reader and interfere with proper routing procedures for the report and its components. Forms created by the agency help in two ways: (1) they jog the memory for required data, and (2) they save time by eliminating the writing of the same information on all reports generated.

Each page of the report should contain the basic data necessary to reference the page to the original report. At a minimum, each page should contain the following data:

1. Agency case file number.
2. Name/rank of individual preparing the report.
3. Date of the report preparation (time of preparation is optional and is usually a departmental policy as to whether or not the time is recorded).
4. Page number (this can be either the number of the page or the number of the page stated as the page number of the total number of pages in the report; e.g., "Page 12 of 35 pages"). The latter method is useful when several separate reports regarding the same incident are prepared on the same day.

APPENDIX II

Courtroom Testimony

INTRODUCTION

Testimony in court is the culmination of the crime scene analyst's efforts at the crime scene, the training and experience of the crime scene analyst, and the reports issued in the case. All these efforts are of no value unless the crime scene analyst can convey the essence of the information to be gained from the physical evidence collected and analyzed. The credibility of the physical evidence analysis and interpretation depends to a large extent on the ability of the crime scene analyst to testify in a credible manner to the authenticity of each item offered as an exhibit during the courtroom proceedings. There are many factors that affect the credibility of the crime scene analyst's testimony. Each facet affecting the credibility of the witness will be explored in order to ensure that the information potential of the physical evidence is properly conveyed to the trier of fact.

COURTROOM PROCEDURES

The crime scene analyst needs to be familiar with basic courtroom procedures so as to be able to maintain the decorum of the courtroom during the analyst's appearance as a witness. Once the analyst is called into the courtroom to testify, the witness will be sworn as a witness by the court clerk. The clerk will ask whether the witness will swear or affirm that the testimony to be given is truthful (the witness's religion may forbid swearing to the truth but may allow for affirmation). The witness should stand facing the clerk during this procedure and answer in a clear voice. Once the witness is sworn by the clerk, the witness should be seated in the witness chair. It is a good idea for the witness to be familiar with the layout of the courtroom, in order to avoid the appearance of confusion while searching for the witness chair. Once the witness is seated, the attorney who called the analyst as a witness (usually the prosecuting attorney) will ask for the witness's name, occupation, and address for the record. As a rule, the witness should always give the agency address rather than the home address, unless specifically instructed to do so by the judge. If the analyst is to testify as an expert, the attorney will also ask questions regarding the qualifications of the witness. Once these preliminary questions are asked, the attorney calling the witness will ask questions during the period called "direct examination."

The phases of testimony are called "direct examination," "cross-examination," "redirect examination," and "re-cross-examination." Normally, the prosecutor will call the analyst as a witness in a case and will be used in this explanation as the attorney calling the witness to testify. The prosecutor will ask a series of questions designed to explain the significance of the evidence collected by the crime scene analyst (the "direct examination"). After this phase, the defense attorney will ask questions designed to clarify or dispute the statements made by the witness during the direct examination by the prosecutor (the cross-examination). When the cross-examination is concluded, the prosecutor may ask additional questions to clarify the answers given during cross-examination. This phase is redirect examination. When the redirect examination is concluded, the defense attorney may ask additional questions during the phase called "re-cross-examination." This process may continue until each side is satisfied that all the information needed from the witness has been elicited. At this point, the judge will indicate that the witness is either excused or must remain for possible further testimony. If excused by the judge, the analyst is free to return to normal duties.

HELPFUL HINTS FOR THE WITNESS

Appearance

The appearance of the witness has a documented effect on his or her credibility in the eyes of the trier of fact. The fundamental rule to follow is to be dressed in an appropriate fashion so that the decorum of the court is not compromised. Conservative dress is the rule: suit and tie for men, conservative business suit or dress for women. Studies have been done to ascertain the effect of a person's dress on the reactions of viewers, including the reactions of jurors. These studies indicate that certain types of dress have a beneficial influence on the perceptions of jurors, whereas other types of dress have a detrimental effect. A conservative approach to courtroom apparel is recommended, as both "too dressy" and "unkempt" looks have an unfavorable impact on the trier of fact.

Preparation for testimony

The most valuable component of testimony credibility is proper preparation. There are a number of steps that must be taken in order to prepare properly for testimony, as follows.

ARRANGE A CONFERENCE WITH THE PROSECUTING ATTORNEY

The pretrial conference is an essential step before testifying. Make certain that the prosecutor understands your role in the case and has taken the time to read all your reports. If the attorney wants to qualify you as an expert, be sure that you are presented as an expert in the recognition, collection, and preservation of physical evidence at the crime scene (and any other area in which you are qualified as an expert, such as latent fingerprint identification).

Do not represent yourself as an expert in other fields in which your expertise is minimal or nonexistent. To allow the attorney to attempt to qualify you in areas in which you are not qualified reduces your credibility in those areas in which you are truly qualified to testify.

REVIEW YOUR REPORT CLOSELY

Before the pretrial conference and certainly before testifying, you should review very carefully your written report, notes, sketches, and photos of the scene. This review will refresh your memory so that you can discuss intelligently your actions at the crime scene and your ability to identify properly all the physical evidence, sketches, and photos for introduction as evidence. It is essential that you examine your written report closely for correspondence between the report and your notes taken at the scene. The review should also focus on the accuracy of the photo logs and sketches. It is far better to discover an error in transcription while reviewing your report rather than having an error pointed out to you during your testimony.

WHEN CALLED TO TESTIFY

Remember that your demeanor is being observed at all times! Your demeanor is noticed during your entire time at the courthouse, both within the courtroom and without. For this reason, it is important to preserve a professional demeanor and avoid inappropriate behavior at all times. It is fruitless to attempt to appear professional on the witness stand when members of the jury and opposing counsel have observed you acting in a nonprofessional manner outside the courtroom. The impression you make when off the witness stand carries over to the opinion that the jurors have of your professional attitude while you are on the witness stand. Regardless of how well you maintain your professional demeanor on the stand, the picture of your previous behavior will remain in the mind's eye of those people who observed your antics prior to your being called to the witness stand.

BE ON TIME!

You will oftentimes have to wait some time before you are called into the courtroom for your testimony. This wait is no excuse, however, for arriving late for your scheduled appearance time. The attorney calling you as a witness will try to keep to the predetermined schedule, but many unforeseen circumstances occur that alter the scheduling of witnesses. Your tardiness should not be one of these unforeseen circumstances! Since the presentation of the case is usually well thought out in advance, your failure to appear at the appropriate time may interfere with the logical presentation of the case to the jury and may lessen the effectiveness of your testimony.

NERVOUSNESS BEFORE TESTIFYING

Nervousness before testifying is a natural phenomenon. The body reacts to stressful situations by dumping adrenalin into the bloodstream to ready your mind and body for any actions needed to respond to the environment. The effects of adrenalin are well known and include raised blood pressure, increased heartbeat rate, slight sweatiness, and heightened awareness of your surroundings. This condition actually works to your advantage because of the increased awareness that you experience and a more acute state of mental preparedness. However, it is essential that you work to harness this mental energy rather than allow it to produce overt signs of nervousness. The common signs of nervousness are easily controlled and there are techniques to exploit the extra dose of adrenalin while alleviating the seeming negative effects of the adrenalin.

PRACTICE! PRACTICE! PRACTICE!

It has been said that (perfect) practice makes perfect (Vince Lombardi). This statement may stretch things a bit, since perfection is regarded as unattainable. But there is no substitute for practice when it comes to preparing yourself for any endeavor. Long before testifying the first time (or any subsequent time), it is helpful that you go through *practice sessions* of *simulated testimony,* which may be conducted by experienced analysts, forensic specialists, or attorneys. These practice sessions should be tough so that when you are actually testifying, you will have the awareness that you have already been asked the toughest questions you will ever encounter in testimony and that you are secure in the knowledge that you can respond professionally to any conceivable question to be asked.

TESTIMONY DOS AND DON'TS[1]

Do listen carefully and completely to each question before you answer.

Don't answer any question that you don't understand completely. One of the tactics used by attorneys is to ask purposely vague or compound questions. Your answer to these types of questions is then open to many interpretations and may mislead the judge or jury as to your meaning. If you don't understand the question, say so, or ask that the question be rephrased so that the meaning of the question is clear before you answer.

Do answer each question in a direct manner in easily understandable language. Avoid technical jargon that may not be clear to the jury. Remember that your mission is to assist the jury and court to understand fully the significance of your actions at the scene and to gain a full understanding of the importance of the evidence.

Don't use evasive tactics to avoid answering a question. An evasive attitude gives the impression that you are hiding something from the jury or that you are being less than truthful in your answers. Remember that you are not appearing as a witness in order to help one side "win" but that you are merely relating factual information in order to assist the court and jury to arrive at a decision based on facts rather than speculation.

Do answer questions in a direct manner, using "yes" or "no" when appropriate (remember to add "sir" or "ma'am"). Avoid adding gratuitous remarks or information as much as possible. You may be trying to be helpful, but adding to your response will usually interrupt the flow of your testimony and may give the impression that you are eager to help one side over the other.

Don't use common speech habits such as "to be truthful" or "to be honest" or "to be quite frank," since these phrases may imply that the rest of your testimony is less than honest, frank, or truthful. Remember that you have sworn to tell the truth and nothing but the truth.

Do maintain eye contact with the person(s) you are speaking to. When asked a question by the attorney, it is best to respond to the person asking the question. A good technique to include the jury in your answer is to respond with eye contact first to the attorney, then to shift eye contact to the jury, and to finish your response by returning eye contact to the attorney asking the question. In this way, you won't appear to be a puppet turning to the jury for any response as though the person asking the question doesn't exist, while at the same time, you let the jury know that you have their interest in mind.

Do turn to the judge at any time (s)he asks you a question and maintain your focus on the judge until you finish your response to the judge's question. This technique is no more than common courtesy coupled with courtesy toward the court as part of courtroom decorum.

Don't answer a question when an objection has been raised by an attorney. Wait until the judge has ruled on the objection before you answer. If it is unclear whether or not you should respond after the ruling, ask the judge politely if you may answer. Also, ask for the question to be read back if you don't remember the question clearly.

GRAND JURIES

Grand juries are a special case for testimony, since the normal routine of the courtroom may not always be followed. The defendant and the defense attorney are not present at grand jury hearings, so the presentation of the evidence proceeds more smoothly and quickly than in the normal courtroom. The decorum of the grand jury hearing may be less formal than that of the courtroom, but this difference should not be taken as an implied permission to relax one's professional attitude. Remember that the proceedings are a permanent record, so that any lapse of professional conduct on the part of the witness may be revealed at subsequent courtroom proceedings.

The jurors are normally allowed to ask any question they choose, and some questions may catch you unaware. Remember, however, that your courtroom demeanor should reflect your professionalism as well as your appearance in other courts. If the jurors ask questions that cannot be answered in the form phrased, ask for clarification of the question in a polite manner before attempting to answer the question.

APPENDIX III

Forensic Science and Latent Fingerprint Texts

Abbott, J. R., and A. C. Germann. 1964. *Footwear Evidence.* Springfield, IL: Charles C. Thomas.

ATF Arson Investigation Guide. 1997. Washington, DC: Treasury Department.

Barnett, P. D. 2001. *Ethics in Forensic Science.* Boca Raton, FL: CRC Press.

Bodziak, W. J. 1999. *Footwear Impression Evidence,* 2nd ed. Boca Raton, FL: CRC Press.

Brenner, J. C. 1999. *Forensic Science Glossary.* Boca Raton, FL: CRC Press.

Byrd, J. H., and J. H. Castner, eds. 2000. *Forensic Entomology.* Boca Raton, FL: CRC Press.

Casey, E. 2000. *Digital Evidence and Computer Crime: Forensic Science, Computers, and the Internet.* New York: Academic Press.

Cassidy, M. J. 1980. *Footwear Identification.* Ottawa, Canada: Royal Canadian Mounted Police.

Clark, F., and K. Diliberto. 1996. *Investigating Computer Crime.* Boca Raton, FL: CRC Press.

Cowger, J. F. 1983. *Friction Ridge Skin.* Boca Raton, FL: CRC Press.

Curran, J. M., T. N. Hicks, and J. S. Buckleton. 2000. *Forensic Interpretation of Glass Evidence.* Boca Raton, FL: CRC Press.

DeForest, P. R., R. E. Gaensslen, and H. C. Lee. 1993. *Forensic Science: An Introduction to Criminalistics.* New York: McGraw-Hill, Inc.

DeHann, J. D. 2002. *Kirk's Fire Investigation,* 5th ed. Upper Saddle River, NJ: Prentice Hall, Inc.

DiMaio, V. J. M. 1998. *Gunshot Wounds,* 2nd ed. Boca Raton, FL: CRC Press.

DiMaio, V. J. M., and D. J. DiMaio. 2001. *Forensic Pathology.* Boca Raton, FL: CRC Press.

Dix, J. 1998. *Guide to Forensic Pathology.* Boca Raton, FL: CRC Press.

———. 1999. *Handbook for Death Scene Investigators.* Boca Raton, FL: CRC Press.

———. 2000. *Color Atlas of Forensic Pathology.* Boca Raton, FL: CRC Press.

Dix, J., and M. Graham. 1999. *Time of Death, Decomposition, and Identification* (An Atlas). Boca Raton, FL: CRC Press.

Eckert, W. G. 1996. *Introduction to Forensic Sciences,* 2nd ed. Boca Raton, FL: CRC Press.

Eliopoulous, L. N. 1993. *Death Investigator's Handbook.* Boulder, CO: Paladin Press.

Fisher, B. A. J. 2000. *Techniques of Crime Scene Investigation,* 6th ed. Boca Raton, FL: CRC Press.

Geberth, V. J. 1993. *Practical Homicide Investigation* (Tactics, Procedures, and Forensic Techniques), 3rd ed. Boca Raton, FL: CRC Press.

———. 1996. *Practical Homicide Investigation* (Checklist and Field Guide). Boca Raton, FL: CRC Press.

Goldstein, S. L. 1998. *The Sexual Exploitation of Children,* 2nd ed. Boca Raton, FL: CRC Press.

Hawthorne, M. R. 1998. *First Unit Responder: A Guide to Physical Evidence Collection for Patrol Officers.* Boca Raton, FL: CRC Press.

Hazelwood, R. R., and A. W. Burgess, eds. 2001. *Practical Aspect of Rape Investigation,* 3rd ed. Boca Raton, FL: CRC Press.

Hilderbrand, D. S. 1998. *Footwear: The Missed Evidence.* Windermar, CA: Staggs Publishing Company.

Hilton, O. 1982. *Scientific Examination of Questioned Documents.* Boca Raton, FL: CRC Press.

Huber, R. 1999. *Handwriting Identification: Facts and Fundamentals.* Boca Raton, FL: CRC Press.

Inbau, F. E., A. E. Moenssens, and L. R. Vitullo. 1972. *Scientific Police Investigation.* Philadelphia: Chilton Book Company.

Inman, K., and N. Rudin. 2000. *Principles and Practice of Criminalistics*. Boca Raton, FL: CRC Press.

James, S. H., and W. G. Eckert. 1998. *Interpretation of Bloodstain Evidence at Crime Scenes*. Boca Raton, FL: CRC Press.

Jerath, B. K., and R. Jerath. 2001. *Homicide: A Bibliography*. Boca Raton, FL: CRC Press.

Kirk, P. L. 1953. *Crime Investigation*. New York: Interscience Publishers.

———. 1974. *Crime Investigation,* 2nd ed. New York: John Wiley & Sons.

Lee, H. C., et al. 2001. *Henry Lee's Crime Scene Handbook*. San Diego: Academic Press.

MacDonell, H. L. 1993. *Bloodstain Patterns*. Gorning, NY: Laboratory of Forensic Science.

Margot, P., and C. Lennard. 1994. *Fingerprint Detection Techniques,* 6th rev. ed. Lausanne, Switzerland: University of Lausanne, Institute of Police Science and Criminology.

McDonald, J. A. 1992. *The Police Photographer's Guide*. Arlington Heights, IL: PhotoText Books.

McDonald, P. M. 1989. *Tire Imprint Evidence*. Boca Raton, FL: CRC Press.

Menzel, E. R. 1991. *An Introduction to Lasers, Forensic Lights, and Fluorescent Fingerprint Techniques*. Salem, OR: Lightning Powder Co.

Nye, T. 1992. *Death Investigation Evidence Manual*. Warwick, RI: Northeast Law Enforcement Officers Association.

Ogle, R. R., Jr. 1995. *Crime Scene Investigation and Physical Evidence Manual,* 2nd ed. Vallejo, CA: Robert R. Ogle, Jr.

Ogle, R. R., Jr., and M. J. Fox. 1998. *Atlas of Human Hair Microscopic Characteristics*. Boca Raton, FL: CRC Press.

Physical Evidence Handbook, 5th ed. 1993. Madison, WI: State of Wisconsin Department of Justice.

Redsicker, D. R., ed. 2000. *The Practical Methodology of Forensic Photography,* 2nd ed. Boca Raton, FL: CRC Press.

Redsicker, D. R., and J. J. O'Connor. 1996. *Practical Fire and Arson Investigation,* 2nd ed. Boca Raton, FL: CRC Press.

Report of Special Committee for Safety. 1986. Alameda, CA: The International Association for Identification.

Rudin, N., and K. Inman. 2001. *Introduction to Forensic DNA Analysis,* 2nd ed. Boca Raton, FL: CRC Press.

Rynearson, J. M. 1997. *Evidence and Crime Scene Reconstruction,* 5th ed. Redding, CA: National Crime Investigation and Training (NCIT).

Saferstein, R. 1987. *Forensic Science Handbook*. Vol. II. Upper Saddle River, NJ: Prentice Hall, Inc.

———. 1993. *Forensic Science Handbook*. Vol. III. Upper Saddle River, NJ: Prentice Hall, Inc.

———. 2001. *Criminalistics,* 7th ed. Upper Saddle River, NJ: Prentice Hall, Inc.

———. 2001. *Forensic Science Handbook,* 2nd ed. Vol. I. Upper Saddle River, NJ: Prentice Hall, Inc.

Scene of Crime Handbook of Fingerprint Development Techniques. 1993. London, England: Police Scientific Development Branch, Home Office.

Schwoeble, A. J. 2000. *Current Methods in Forensic Gunshot Residue Analysis*. Boca Raton, FL: CRC Press.

Staggs, S. 1997. *Crime Scene and Evidence Photographer's Guide*. Temecula, CA: Staggs Publishing.

Taylor, K. T. 2000. *Forensic Art and Illustration*. Boca Raton, FL: CRC Press.

U.S. Department of Justice. Office of Justice Programs. 2000. *Crime Scene Investigation: A Guide for Law Enforcement*. Washington, DC: GPO. http://www.ncjrs.org.

U.S. Department of Treasury, FBI. 1994. *Handbook of Forensic Science*. Washington, DC: GPO.

———. 1984. *The Science of Fingerprints*. Washington, DC: GPO.

Van Kirk, D. J. 2000. *Vehicular Accident Investigation and Reconstruction*. Boca Raton, FL: CRC Press.

Weston, P. B., and K. M. Wells. 1986. *Criminal Investigation: Basic Perspectives,* 4th ed. Upper Saddle River, NJ: Prentice Hall, Inc.

Wonder, A. Y. 2001. *Blood Dynamics*. London: Elsevier Publishers, Ltd.

APPENDIX IV

Physical Evidence Chart: Collection, Preservation, and Special Instructions for Physical Evidence[1]

GENERAL INSTRUCTIONS

Each item of evidence submitted should have the following minimum information affixed to the item or its sealed package: officer's initials, case number, item number, and date. These items of identifying data are referred to as standard identifying data ("STD ID DATA").

The data given in this chart are provided as quick reference guides only. For detailed information, refer to the pertinent chapter or contact the laboratory, which will analyze the particular evidence to be examined.

Specimen	Amount	Packaging and Precautions
Abrasives: emery, carborundum, etc.	1 tsp. to 1 oz.	STD ID DATA on container; type of material. Use pill box, match box, or bindle. Seal to avoid loss.
Acids	1 tsp. to 1 oz.	DO NOT SEND THROUGH MAIL! USE PROTECTIVE GLOVES AND EYEWEAR WHEN HANDLING! Glass bottle, acid proof cap. Tape seal cap.
Adhesive tape	All or 1 foot	DO NOT BALL UP!! Place on wax paper. BE SURE TO SEND END PIECE(S). CAUTION REGARDING FINGERPRINTS AND TRACE EVIDENCE!
Alkalies: caustic soda, potash, ammonia, etc.	1 oz.	Mark "CORROSIVE" on package. DO NOT SEND THROUGH MAIL! Use safety devices as in acids. Package as for acids.
Ammunition (live)	All evidence, all similar ammo from suspect	DO NOT SEND THROUGH MAIL! POSSIBLE LATENT FINGERPRINTS! Pack in soft tissue paper or cloth, package in small cardboard box.
Anonymous letters, extortion letters	All	DO NOT HANDLE WITH BARE HANDS! DO NOT FOLD! Place in paper envelope, seal with label. Place date and officer's initials on label.

Specimen	Amount	Packaging and Precautions
Arson evidence		
Fire debris	2–4 quarts	DO NOT SEND THROUGH MAIL! Seal in clean empty paint can or glass jar with solvent resistant cap. Fill containers if possible. Collect control specimen for each sample collected.
Suspect accelerants	4 oz.	Seal each suspect sample in glass or chemical resistant plastic jar with chemical resistant lid. DO NOT SEND THROUGH MAIL!
Blasting caps		CALL LAB, DO NOT BRING TO LAB OR SEND THROUGH MAIL!!
Blood		
Liquid for DNA typing	1 vial (5–10 cc)	Purple-top (EDTA) tube
Liquid for alcohol	1 vial (5–10 cc)	Gray-top tube
Liquid for drugs	2 vials (10–20 cc)	EDTA tubes
Bloodstained items		(ALWAYS use rubber gloves to handle blood or blood-stained items.)
Garments	All	Before drying, spread garment on butcher paper in natural shape. Air dry 24 hours. DO NOT FOLD BEFORE GARMENT IS DRY! When dry, cover with clean butcher paper, fold carefully and tape closed. Package each garment in separate sealed paper bag.
Non-absorbent items	All	Photograph stains before handling. Allow to air dry 24 hours. Gently scrape each separate area of stain onto bond paper. Fold each paper into bindle, seal with tape. Package in paper envelopes (or submit entire item to lab).
Weapons	All	Photograph all sides of weapon with color film. Wrap carefully with paper, place in strong paper envelope. Submit to lab immediately.
Swabs/swatches of stains	All	Air dry 24 hours. Package separately in manila envelopes. Obtain control swab(s)/swatches of surfaces sampled. Treat controls exactly like the stained swabs.
Bullets (not cartridges)	All evidence	DO NOT MARK BULLETS!! DO NOT CLEAN (trace evidence). Air dry if bloody. Wrap in crumpled paper, not in cotton wadding. Seal in pill box or match box. Fully label container with STD ID DATA.

(continued)

(continued)

Specimen	Amount	Packaging and Precautions
Cartridge cases	Same as bullets	POSSIBLE LATENT PRINTS! Package as for bullets.
Charred or burned paper	All	Pack loosely on soft cotton. Pack in rigid container, mark "FRAGILE." Mark package with STD ID DATA. HAND CARRY TO LAB.
Checks, similar documents	All	Handle carefully for latent prints. Package between cardboard sheets, or plastic sleeves, label package with STD ID DATA.
Check protector		
Questioned checks	All	See checks above.
Exemplar	Several copies	Copy impressions on questioned checks in full word-for-word order.
Clothing	All	Mark directly on clothing in waist band, pocket, collar as appropriate with initials, date, and case number. Air dry all stained clothing before packaging. Handle carefully to avoid loss of trace evidence. Package each item separately in paper bindle and seal bindle, seal each item in a separate paper bag.
Drugs	All	Mark bottles, bindles, etc. Seal in evidence envelope, fully label.
Explosives		DO NOT BRING OR MAIL TO LAB! CALL LAB FOR INSTRUCTIONS!
Fibers		
Evidence	All	Nude bodies: scan body with white and UV light for fibers. Collect any found with forceps, package in sealed paper bindle. Seal bindle in envelope, seal all corners of envelope. Tape lift body for unseen fibers, place lift on cellophane wrapper sheet (such as Saran Wrap). Label with STD ID DATA on sheet with indelible ink.
Standards		
Garments	All	Send entire garment to lab.
Carpets	1" square	Sample several areas of carpet, including all variations in color, by cutting close to backing, a number of threads equal to about one-inch square of carpet (take each thread a short distance from the others to avoid damage to carpet).
Upholstery	All	Submit entire piece of furniture to lab to minimize damage to item.
Firearms		
Evidence	All	TREAT ALL FIREARMS AT ALL TIMES AS IF THEY ARE LOADED!! Handle carefully to avoid loss of latent fingerprints, bloodstains, trace evidence.

Specimen	Amount	Packaging and Precautions
Revolvers	All	Record cylinder position, round locations. Place serial number, barrel length in notes.
Semi-autos	All	Do not handle sides of clip (latents). Unload, place in strong envelope or tie down securely in cardboard container.
Rifles	All	Unload, use evidence tag in trigger guard, package in rifle box.
Glass		
Fragments	All	Pill box, bindle, or plastic bag (seal all corners of package). Package with cushioning material.
Exemplar	1″ square	Package each square separately, from each source. Package with cushioning material. KEEP EVIDENCE AND EXEMPLAR SEPARATE!
Hair		
Evidence	All	Paper bindles in envelopes, tape seal edges to avoid loss. Freeze or submit immediately to lab to preserve DNA and other genetic markers that may be present.
Standards		
Scalp	75–100	Take combed specimen by back-combing hair with new comb onto paper sheet. Package comb with hair by making bindle with collection paper. Then pull 15–20 hairs from front, sides, back, and top of scalp (total of 75–100 hairs).
Pubic	40–50	Pull or cut close to the skin 10–15 hairs from top middle, top sides and lower sides of pubic region (total of 50–75 hairs).
Pubic combings	All	Have medical personnel place sheet of paper under buttocks and comb or brush pubic hair onto paper. Fold and seal paper into bindle. Seal bindle in manila envelope.
Animal hair	80–100	Pull 10–15 hairs from back, neck, belly, and legs. Be sure to include fur (fine) hair and guard (coarse) hairs from each region. Be sure to collect hairs of each color on animal.
Metals		
Elemental analysis	1 oz.	Sturdy envelope with padding or cardboard mailing jar.
Fracture matches	All	Submit all evidence and exemplar pieces with fracture edges.
Oils		
Evidence	All	Package as much as possible (up to 1 oz.) in a leak-proof jar or small, new paint can.
Exemplar	1 oz.	Submit in original container or small glass jar with oil-proof lid.

(continued)

(*continued*)

Specimen	Amount	Packaging and Precautions
Paint		
Liquid	4 oz.	Sealed paint can or jar.
Solid (chips)	1/2" square	Pill box, paper bindle or plastic bag. Submit entire item if small. Make sure flakes have all layers of paint present. Tape all corners to prevent loss.
Scrapings	All	Seal scrapings from each area in paper bindle, place in envelope and tape seal all corners of envelope.
Plaster casts		
Shoe prints	All	Include STD ID DATA on back of cast before hardening. Do not remove soil or attempt to clean cast. Package in strong paper bag or envelope, cover with layers of cushioning material, package in strong box.
Tire impressions	All	Handle and package as for shoe prints. When feasible, take sufficient casts to show entire circumference of tire(s).
Rope, Twine,		
Cordage Evidence	All	Handle, package carefully to preserve all trace evidence. Mark with tape all ends cut by collector. Seal in paper bag or envelope.
Exemplar	1 yard	Preserve all cut ends. Mark as above with any cuts made by collector.
Safe insulation	8 oz.	Package in box; seal to prevent loss. Affix STD ID DATA to box. Add any manufacturer's data if known.
Sexual assault Evidence		
Clothing	All	Handle garment carefully to avoid loss of trace evidence (hairs, fibers.) Arrange in natural shape on new butcher paper to air dry 24 hours. Place STD ID DATA on each garment. Place additional sheet of paper on top, fold carefully into large bindle and tape seal; place each garment in separate paper bag, include STD ID DATA on bag.
Swabs	All	Air dry all swabs before packaging (use swab dryer). Package in paper envelopes (not plastic.) Include STD ID DATA on each envelope with source of swab. *Note:* Swabs from each area of the orifice sampled should be so identified (e.g. "Vaginal, posterior fornix," "Oral, area under tongue," etc.). Freeze swabs or transmit immediately to lab.

Specimen	Amount	Packaging and Precautions
Bedding	All	Fold each item of bedding over onto itself to avoid loss of trace evidence. Mark each item with orientation data ("top, left," etc.), making sure to note the layer sequence of each item. Place in large paper bag, seal with evidence tape, label each bag with STD ID DATA.
Swabs of stains	All	Moisten each swab with distilled water, swab each stain separately, taking control swab for each area. Air dry and package as for vaginal swabs.
Soil	2 oz.	Air dry all specimens before sealing. Seal in small box to avoid loss.
Stained clothing	All	Place article on butcher paper to air dry or hang on new clothes hanger. Arrange garment in its natural shape before drying. Do not ball or roll up. After drying, cover with butcher paper, fold carefully and tape closed. Seal each garment in a separate paper bag.
Tools	All	Wrap each tool separately. Wrap working edges with cardboard and tape. Place STD ID DATA on area away from working edges.
Tool marks	All	DO NOT PLACE TOOL IN MARK. Submit entire object bearing all marks. Protect toolmark by taping cardboard over areas bearing toolmarks. STD ID DATA scratched on object bearing marks.
Casts	All	Wrap cast in paper cushion, seal in pill box or similar container. Label sealed container.
Wire	1 foot to all	DISTINCTLY LABEL OR TWIST FULLY ANY ENDS CUT BY OFFICER. Wrap securely, place all identifying data on sealed package.
Wood		
Evidence	All	Place officer's mark directly on specimen, wrap securely, package in box.
Shavings, drill turnings	All	Pack loosely to avoid breakage of chips, package in box, seal to avoid loss.

APPENDIX V

Computer Evidence[1]

CONDUCTING THE SEARCH AND/OR SEIZURE

Secure the scene

- Officer safety is paramount.
- Preserve area for potential fingerprints.
- Document scene with appropriate notes, sketches, and photographs (see Chapters 2 through 4).
- Immediately restrict access to computer(s) to only those personnel required. Isolate from Internet connection (data on the computer can be accessed remotely).

Secure the computer as evidence

- If computer is "OFF," do not turn "ON."
- If computer is "ON":
  - **Stand-alone computer (nonnetworked):**
    - Consult a computer specialist.
    - If computer specialist is not available:
      1. Photograph screen, then disconnect all power sources; unplug from the wall AND the back of the computer.
      2. Place evidence tape over each drive slot.
      3. Photograph/diagram and label back of computer components with existing connections.
      4. Label all connectors/cable ends to allow reassembly as needed.
      5. If transport is required, package components and transport/store components as fragile cargo.
      6. Keep all items away from magnets, radio transmitters, and otherwise hostile environments.
  - **Networked or business computers:**
    - Consult a computer specialist for further assistance.
    - DO NOT PULL THE PLUG. Pulling the plug could
      1. Severely damage the system.
      2. Disrupt legitimate business.
      3. Create officer and department liability.

APPENDIX VI
Entomological Evidence

INTRODUCTION

At the time of death or very soon thereafter, insects, particularly flies, begin to lay their eggs in exposed areas of the body, especially the eyes, nose, mouth, and injured areas. The fly eggs hatch in one to two days, depending on environmental conditions. The larvae (maggots) change into pupae in twelve to fourteen days, and after another twelve to fourteen days, they emerge from the pupae as adult flies. These stages can be identified by a forensic entomologist and may aid considerably in fixing a time of death for the deceased. If the type of fly larvae and pupae are from houseflies, then the entomologist may conclude that the deceased was indoors at the time of egg deposition. Different species of flies are present in outdoor scenes, so that the entomologist may determine whether or not the deceased was indoors for a period of time before exposure to the outdoors. Other faunas that may attack the body include beetles and ants, which may produce patterns similar to other types of injuries.

AT THE SCENE

The time of the life cycles in insects is affected by the environmental conditions, especially temperature and moisture. It is therefore necessary to record the ground and the ambient temperatures if the insect specimens are to be sent to a forensic entomologist. In most cases, it is preferable to call the entomologist to the scene in order to ensure that all the data necessary for interpretation of the insects' life cycles and the subsequent estimation of the time of death are collected appropriately. If an entomologist is not available, the crime scene investigator should follow the guidelines that follow.

Data to be collected at the scene

- Ambient air temperature at chest height (use a thermometer with known accuracy), taken *in the shade.*
- Temperature of any maggot mass (place the thermometer directly into the center of mass).
- Ground surface temperature.
- Temperature at the interface of body and ground (place the thermometer between the body surface and the ground).
- Temperature of the soil under the body after removal.
- Weather data for the period two weeks before discovery of the body and three to four hours after discovery.

Collection of insects and larvae

- Collect adults with an insect net.
- Kill adults by placing them in a jar containing cotton balls soaked with ethyl acetate or common fingernail polish remover.
- Place the killed adults into jars partially filled with 70 percent ethyl alcohol.
- Label the jars and lid labels with pencil, or place the penciled labels in liquid, and then seal the jars (labels should have standard identification data as for all other types of physical evidence).
- Larvae may be placed directly into a solution of 70 percent ethyl alcohol; label and seal the jars as for adult specimens.
- Place labeled and sealed jars in shipping container to prevent breakage during transport.

GLOSSARY

AA. Atomic absorption, method used to analyze gunshot residues for the trace elements barium and antimony found in primer compounds.

AA swabs Swabs used to collect gunshot residue for examination by atomic absorption (AA).

Aberrant Abnormal, deviating from the proper or expected course; deviating from what is normal; untrue to type.

Aberration An abnormal or unusual condition.

ABFO scale (American Board of Forensic Odontology) An L-shaped measurement scale used in forensic photography, marked with circles to assist in distortion compensation and an 18 percent gray bar for exposure determination.

Absorbent surfaces Surfaces which will absorb the components of a latent fingerprint.

Accuracy, measurement The accuracy of a measurement is determined by the known accuracy of the measurement device or method. The measurement accuracy is illustrated in the record of the measurement, for example., 9 feet, 21/2 inches indicates that the measurement is accurate to the nearest one-half inch; 56.4°F indicates that the temperature was measured to the nearest 1/10th degree F.

Acid phosphatase An enzyme (phosphoric acid monoesterase) found at very high levels in secretions from the prostate gland; the basis for a semen screening test and for the "mapping" technique used to search for semen stains.

Added flammable A flammable liquid added to an area where an arsonist intends to start a fire, also referred to as an "accelerant," although some added flammables merely help to start the fire, but not accelerate its spread (e.g., wadded newspapers).

Alcohol Drinking alcohol (ethyl alcohol), unless specified as another alcohol (i.e., isopropyl alcohol).

Alternate light source A high-intensity light with filters of specific light wavelengths for use as an alternative to a laser light, used for visualization of certain types of evidence (physiological fluids, fingerprints, fibers, etc.).

Amido Black A dye that reacts with bloody impressions such as fingerprints or footwear impressions to produce visible prints that can then be photographed.

Amorphous Literally, "without form," said of objects with a form that cannot be described or does not fit into a category of a defined form pattern.

Anagen The active growing phase of a hair (cf. catagen and telogen).

Analysis The separation of a whole into its constituents for individual study; the statement of the results of such a study; the examination of a situation or circumstance, especially by examining the parts separately in order to understand the workings of the whole; in common parlance, a synonym for "examination."

Angle of departure The angle formed between a horizontal line and the centerline of the bore of a firearm at the moment of firing.

Angle of elevation The vertical angle formed between the line of sight to the target and the axis of the bore in a firearm.

Angle of impact The angle at which a blood drop strikes a surface, with the surface equal to zero degrees as viewed from the side, from 1 to 90 degrees.

Archetype An original model or type after which other similar things are patterned or compared for trueness to type; a prototype.

Area of convergence The area where the projected points of origins for a series of blood spatters converge (also called "point of convergence").

Area of origin Refers to the area from which the blood in a blood spatter pattern originated (also called the "point of origin").

Arterial spurting Blood emanating from an arterial wound; the pattern resulting from such a wound, also called "arterial gushing."

Artifact A feature that is due to damage or other factors; not a true feature.

Aspermic Refers to the lack of sperm in a person's semen.

Atomized bloodstain Bloodstain pattern resulting from a spray of blood mist consisting of very small droplets, usually resulting from a gunshot wound (high-velocity impact).

Autopsy The postmortem examination of a decedent's body, performed to ascertain the manner and cause of death; forensic autopsies are extensive because of the need to document and collect evidence.

Axis, long and short A straight line which depicts the center of an object's length (long axis), or its width (short axis).

Back spatter The backward spray of minute droplets from a wound produced by a close or near-contact firearm discharge, generated by the high pressure of the gases forcing mist-sized droplets outward from the wound site.

Ballistic coefficient The ratio of the sectional density of the projectile to its coefficient of form (form factor). It is an index (a scalar factor) of the manner in which a particular projectile decelerates in free flight because of resistance or air drag.

Ballistics The study of the flight characteristics of projectiles.

Ballistics, exterior The study of projectiles in flight. For firearms, the study of the flight dynamics of the bullet after it leaves the barrel of the firearm.

Ballistics, interior The study of the dynamics of the firing of a cartridge within the firearm and the dynamics of the projectile motion while within the barrel of the firearm.

Ballistics, terminal The study of a projectile's interaction with a target (both the target surface and the interior substance of the target).

Bindings Materials which are used to bind the hands and/or feet of a person (e.g., cordage, rope, tape, and electrical wires).

Bindle A folded piece of paper or glassine used to contain trace evidence; occasionally used by drug dealers to package small amounts of drugs.

Biohazard bag A container for materials that have been exposed to blood or other biological fluids and that have the potential to be contaminated with hepatitis, AIDS, or other viruses.

Biological evidence Evidence with a biological origin (e.g., blood, semen, tissues, body fluids, and hair).

Biological fluids Fluids that have human or animal origin (e.g., blood, mucus, perspiration, saliva, semen, vaginal fluid, and urine).

Biological weapon Biological agents used to threaten life (e.g., anthrax, smallpox, or any infectious agent).

Bitemark An impression formed by the action of an individual biting a victim or other object such as cheese that leaves an impression of the teeth in the softer medium.

Blank sample An uncontaminated specimen of the chemicals or physical materials used to collect an evidence specimen. Used to test the integrity of the collection materials by subjecting to the same tests as the evidence specimen.

Blood The viscous fluid in the circulatory system consisting of a liquid component (plasma) and solid components (red and white blood "cells"); carries gases and other materials from one area of the body to another. After clotting, the plasma is termed "serum."

Blood alcohol The concentration of ethyl alcohol in the blood, usually expressed as grams per deciliter (g/dL), referred to as percent blood alcohol.

Bloodborne pathogen Infectious, disease-causing microorganisms that may be found or transported in biological fluids (esp. blood).

Blood smears Patterns of blood on surfaces caused by a bloody object coming in contact with the surface or by an object coming in contact with a wet bloodstain, whereby the object smears the bloodstain.

Blood spatter Blood drops or droplets produced by a force acting on the blood source; the bloodstain pattern produced by these blood drops on a surface.

Blood specimen A specimen of blood which has been collected by drawing a sample of blood from a person's vein.

Blood standard A specimen of blood which has been collected (drawn) from an individual, which has a documented history of its authenticity.

Bloodstain Blood that has dried on or within a surface.

Bloodstain pattern interpretation The explanation by an expert of how a bloodstain pattern was produced, after documentation of the pattern characteristics, and analysis of the physical characteristics of the stain components by the expert.

Bloodstain patterns The geometrical shapes and spatial relationships of a group of bloodstains in a confined area which have a specific relationship to each other.

Blow-back 1. The blood spatter which is blown backward from a close or near contact firearm wound; 2. The pattern of bloodstains produced by this process, typically a spray pattern on the muzzle face of the firearm barrel, and often -extending into the bore of the barrel.

Blowup sketch See Sketch, blowup.

Boundaries The perimeter or border surrounding the area that may contain physical evidence related to the crime.

Breath specimens Specimens of a person's exhaled breath which is introduced into a breath testing device for the purpose of estimating the blood alcohol level through the use of a conversion formula.

Bruise The accumulation of blood beneath the skin as a result of blood vessel rupture as the consequence of the area being struck by a blunt object.

Bullet drop The normal fall of a bullet during its flight, as a result of gravity.

CADD Acronym for computer aided drafting and design programs; also referred to as CAD (computer assisted design) programs, but that acronym avoided in law enforcement to prevent confusion with computer assisted dispatch programs in wide use.

Caliber The diameter of the bore of a firearm's barrel, measured as the diameter of the lands or the grooves, depending on the manufacturer's convention, or by the convention used by an official group.

Camera alignment The alignment of a camera's film plane with the surface being photographed.

Capillary action The attraction of a liquid to surfaces with which it is in contact, coupled with the surface tension of the liquid.

Cartridge The cartridge case, primer, gunpowder, and projectile taken as a whole, normally assumed to be intact and ready to be fired in a firearm.

Case file The collection of documents comprising information concerning a particular investigation. This collection may be kept in case jackets, file folders, ring binders, boxes, file drawers, file cabinets, or rooms. Subfiles are often used within case files to segregate and to group interviews, media coverage, laboratory requests and reports, evidence documentation, photographs, videotapes, audiotapes, and other documents.

Case file data The case file numbers for each agency responding to a crime scene, names of the agencies involved, names of personnel responding to the scene, and name(s) of victim(s) and any suspect(s) known.

Case identifiers The alphabetic and/or numeric characters assigned to identify a particular case.

Cast A reproduction of an impression made by pouring or placing a casting material into the impression and allowing the material to set.

Cast-off spatter The bloodstain droplets or their impact pattern resulting from the droplets being ejected from a weapon as it is swung backward during repeated strikes on the victim of the assault.

Cast-off stains Bloodstains produced by the action of a blood-bearing object casting blood drops onto a surface because of the swinging of the object.

Catagen The transitional phase of hair between active growth (anagen) and the terminal resting phase (telogen).

Central nervous system stimulants Drugs which increase the activity of the brain, such as amphetamines, cocaine, etc.

Chain of possession (or chain of custody). A process used to maintain and document the chronological history of the evidence from the time of its collection until it is presented in court. Documents should include the name or initials of the individual collecting the evidence, each person or entity subsequently having custody of it, dates that the items were collected or transferred, agency and case number, victim's or suspect's name(s), and a brief description of the item.

Characteristic A feature, trait, or attribute of an object; a feature that is diagnostic for a class or an individual (*see* Class characteristics; Individual characteristics).

Characterize The act of examining and describing the characteristics of an object.

Chemical enhancement The use of chemicals that react with specific types of evidence (e.g., blood, semen, lead, and fingerprints) to produce colored, fluorescent, or luminescent compounds in order to aid in the detection and/or documentation of evidence that may be difficult to see.

Chemical hazard Chemicals or compounds that may pose bodily harm if touched, ingested, inhaled, or ignited. These compounds may be encountered at a clandestine laboratory or through a homemade bomb or tankard leakage (e.g., ether, alcohol, nitroglycerin, ammonium sulfate, red phosphorous, cleaning supplies, gasoline, or unlabeled chemicals).

Chemiluminescence Emission of light as a result of a chemical reaction at environmental temperatures.

Clandestine laboratory A laboratory involved in the production of illegal drugs.

Class characteristics Those characteristics that define a class. The identification of these characteristics in an object places that object into the class defined.

Class characteristics (fired bullets) The caliber, number of lands and grooves, and their direction of twist.

Class only evidence Physical evidence that possesses only class characteristics, so that the individual source of the evidence cannot be determined (e.g., drugs, fibers, and glass).

Clean/sanitize The process of removing biological and/or chemical contaminants from tools and/or equipment and/or the working environment (e.g., using a mixture consisting of 1 part household bleach and 9 parts water to equal a 10 percent solution of bleach).

Close-up photographs Photographs taken of individual evidence items or of a group of items such as a blood-spatter pattern. When the size of the evidence is relevant, these photographs are taken first without and then with a measurement scale in view of the photograph frame.

Clot, blood Blood that has formed a gelatinous mass as a result of the actions of chemicals in the blood that form a fibrous net enveloping the red blood cells. This process leaves a clot of blood surrounded by the serum that has separated from the mass.

CODIS Acronym for Combined DNA Index System, a DNA database.

Coefficient of form A numerical term indicating the general profile of a projectile.

Coitus Sexual intercourse.

Collection of physical evidence, proper The collection of physical evidence utilizing those methods that will safeguard the integrity of the evidence.

Combustion A process whereby a material is consumed (i.e., altered) by its reaction with oxygen; requires adequate heat and oxygen to consume the material.

Comparative analysis The process whereby the class and individual (when present) characteristics of an item of questioned source are compared with those of an item of known source to ascertain whether the two originated from the same source (e.g., the comparison of the markings on an evidence bullet with the markings on a bullet fired from a known weapon).

Comparison standard A material or object collected from a known source for use in a comparison with an item with an unknown source (e.g., bullets fired in a suspect weapon for comparison with a fatal bullet, inked fingerprints for comparison with a latent impression from a crime scene, soil from a burial site for comparison with soil from a suspect's vehicle).

Computer drawn sketch Sketch which has been drawn with the use of a computer drawing program on a computer (e.g., computer aided sketch, CAD).

Concentric fracture Fracture pattern surrounding an impact, where the fracture lines are circle-like, with the impact at the approximate center of the fractures.

Conchoidal fracture marks Fracture patterns on the edge of glass fractures. The patterns can be used to determine the direction of force which caused the fracture.

Contact wound, angled A contact wound in which the firearm is held at an angle to the skin, producing an eccentric pattern of soot.

Contact wound, hard Contact wound in which the muzzle of the firearm is held tightly against the skin, sealing the area of contact so that the products of combustion are driven into the wound.

Contact wound, incomplete A contact wound in which the curved surface of the skin prevents a seal of the muzzle against the skin.

Contact wound, loose A contact wound in which the muzzle is held loosely against the skin, which allows the gas to escape from the muzzle to create a muzzle-to-skin gap and deposits soot around the periphery of the wound.

Contamination The unwanted transfer of material from another source to an item or a piece of physical evidence (e.g., inadvertent touching of a bloodstained item with gloves bearing bloodstains from a known sample being tested for in the bloodstain).

Continuous variation The variation of a characteristic whereby the variation is indistinguishable from that of the nearest neighbor (e.g., the variation of the shades of brown in human hair), in which there are more shades of the color than can be distinguished by the unaided human eye (compare discontinuous variation).

Control sample A sample taken from an area near the location where an unknown sample was collected. Used to determine the effect that the background (substrate) has on the testing process (e.g., a swab of the substrate next to a sampled bloodstain, an unstained portion of fabric near a tested bloodstain on a garment).

Controlled substances Those drugs (and materials used to illicitly manufacture them), the possession of which is illegal without a legitimate prescription from a physician.

Coordinate measuring system The crime scene measurement system that requires measurement from the object to two walls that abut each other, with the measurement made to a point on the walls where the measurement lines are perpendicular to the wall.

Coordinate system A system for locating the exact position of an object on a plane surface with reference to a point of origin, with one axis (the x axis) extending to the right (positive number) and to the left of the origin (negative number) and the second axis (the y axis) extending upward (positive number) and downward (negative number) at 90 degrees from the x axis. The position of an object is designated with the two axis coordinates (x,y) in parentheses: for example, (4,7), which indicates that the object is four units to the right of the origin and seven units above the origin. For three-dimensional space, a third axis (the z axis) is added, which allows for describing the location of an object anywhere in space relative to the origin. The z axis extends toward the viewer and away from the viewer at 90-degree angles from both the x and y axes.

Cortex The middle layer of hair that contains the pigments that give the hair its color.

Criminalistics The professional discipline involved in the examination, interpretation, identification, and individualization of physical evidence; often described as a scientific discipline, since the techniques, methodologies, and logical reasoning employed in this profession have their foundations in science and in the scientific method.

Critical accuracy sketch A sketch in which the accuracy of the measurements is critical, so that they can be used for accurate crime scene reconstructions.

Critical thinking Thinking characterized by careful and exact evaluation and judgement.

Cross-contamination The unwanted transfer of material between two or more items of physical evidence.

Crystal Violet Toxic stain for latent fingerprints on adhesive tape sticky side, also called Gentian violet.

Cuticle The outer layer of the hair, consisting of overlapping scales.

Cyanoacrylate Superglue (also referred to as "CA"), the vapors of which react with latent fingerprints to form a white substance that can then be photographed and/or treated with chemicals that form a compound that is visualized with laser or alternate light source.

Debriefing The post-incident investigation interviews or conferences of investigators.

Decomposed remains The remains of a deceased person that have undergone some degree of decomposition from the action of microorganisms.

Deflect To change the direction of an object on impact with a surface.

Deflection The bouncing off from a surface by a projectile that struck the surface at an angle that results in the projectile bouncing off rather than penetrating the surface.

Deflection angle The angle at which a projectile departs from a surface after impact and deflection from that surface (also called "angle of reflection" or "angle of exit").

Density The number or amount of a substance per unit of area or volume (e.g., darker shades of hair are primarily due to the higher density of the hair pigment).

Density profile The appearance of soil particles in a density gradient tube after the particles have all settled to the height where their density matches that of the gradient at that position.

Detective Title for a law enforcement investigator; used interchangeably often to describe an investigator in many other job areas.

DFO A chemical (1,8-Diazafluoren-9-one) used in place of or in conjunction with ninhydrin to develop latent fingerprints on porous surfaces, such as paper or cardboard.

Directional angle The angle between the long axis of a bloodstain and a reference line on the same plane; the reference line is arbitrarily established in order to facilitate computer analysis of bloodstain patterns.

Directionality The geometric quality of a bloodstain that allows for the determination of the direction from which the blood droplet producing the stain originated.

Display sketch See Sketch, display.

Distal Term that refers to the area that is farther from the body (e.g., the distal portion of the arm is the hand and wrist); *see* Proximal.

DNA Acronym for deoxyribonucleic acid, the material that contains all the genetic material in an organism; may be nuclear DNA (DNA in the cell nucleus) or mitochondrial DNA (DNA in the mitochondria, small bodies within the cell).

Documentation (crime scene) The recording of the details of crime scene processing via notes, sketches, and photographs. Includes details of evidence recovered and actions taken.

Double transfer Situation in which evidence is both transferred from victim to suspect and from suspect to victim; term also applies to a two-way transfer of evidence between the scene and either the victim or the suspect.

Drift Lateral deviation of a bullet in flight.

Drip patterns Bloodstain patterns that are the result of dripping from a wound or an object bearing blood.

Driver's view The view seen by a driver at the moment of a traffic collision.

Driving under the influence (DUI) Driving a vehicle while under the influence of alcohol (or other drug).

Drop, blood A drop of blood is approximately 0.05 ml (0.05 cc) in volume.

Droplet, blood A small volume of blood less than 0.05 ml; droplets are produced by impacts called medium velocity or high velocity; the size of the resultant blood droplets correlates inversely with the energy of the force applied—the higher the energy applied, the smaller the blood droplet volume.

Drug evidence Drugs the possession of which is proscribed by law.

DRUGFIRE An automated search system developed for the FBI to search for cartridge case markings that identify the type of weapon in which the cartridge case was fired; all identifications are verified by a qualified firearms examiner.

EDTA Acronym for ethylene diamine tetra acetic acid. The chemical is usually used in its salt form (ethylene diamine tetra acetate), which is added to blood vials and tubes to prevent clotting by removing calcium from the blood.

Electrophoresis The analysis of proteins (and other materials) by separating the components dissolved in a medium, which is subjected to an electrical field.

Elevation sketch See Sketch, elevation.

Elimination The condition whereby an examiner concludes that a questioned item did not originate from the same source as the known item.

Elimination prints Inked impressions of a person's fingers, used to eliminate that person as the source of evidence latent prints.

Elimination sample A sample of known source taken from a person or thing; used either to eliminate that person or thing as the source of a questioned item (e.g., inked fingerprints from the victims of a burglary, shoes from individuals at a crime scene which has footwear impressions) or to establish that a questioned item at the scene has an innocent source (e.g., latent fingerprints at a residence produced by one of the normal occupants).

Empirical Relying upon or derived from observation or experiment; guided by practical experience and not theory.

Event A notable occurrence, usually considered as the result of antecedent happenings; *in crime scene reconstruction,* an occurrence that may be subdivided into smaller units for closer study or analysis.

Evidence identifiers Tape, labels, containers, and string tags used to identify the evidence, the person collecting the evidence, the date that evidence was gathered, basic criminal offense information, and a brief description of the pertinent evidence.

Exemplar A portion of a known sample used in a comparative analysis (e.g., writings produced by a known individual, a portion of a known lead bullet analyzed for chemical composition); must be an accurate representative of the known sample; an example.

Experimentation The application of scientific methods to test an hypothesis.

Expiratory blood Blood forced from the mouth, nose, or respiratory system under pressure from breath expiration; usually consists of mistlike stains similar to high-velocity impact stains but may have small craters from bubbles.

Exploded view sketch See Sketch, exploded.

Fabric impression An impression of a victim's clothing fabric in the paint of a suspect's vehicle due to the forces involved in the vehicle's striking the victim's clothing; may be an indented impression, fabric fibers melted by the impact, or an impression in the dust covering the vehicle.

Family characteristics Characteristics shared by a subgroup (family) of a class.

Feature Synonym for "characteristic"; attribute, trait.

Fiber A strand or filament of either natural or synthetic material used in the manufacture of textiles, carpets, and other materials.

Fiber smears Smears of fibers on a vehicle surface that are the result of the impact of the vehicle with the clothing of a victim.

Fingernail scrapings Materials scraped from the underside of a person's fingernails, used to search for blood, tissue, and trace evidence which may be present as the result of a struggle.

Fingerprints A class of physical evidence consisting of impressions left by the friction ridges of the fingers, palms, or soles of the feet, sometimes referred to as friction ridge evidence.

Finished sketch See Sketch, finished.

Fire tetrahedron The geometric representation of the four elements of a fire (the fourth, the chemical reaction that sustains the fire) has been added to the original fire triangle (see Figure 6-11), so that a three-dimensional drawing can depict the four elements.

Fire triangle The three elements necessary for fire (oxygen, fuel, and heat) represented as a triangle.

Firearms evidence Evidence consisting of firearms, ammunition components, and the residues resulting from the discharge of a firearm.

First officers (or first responders) The initial law enforcement officer(s) or other officials arriving at the scene.

Fluorescence Emission of electromagnetic radiation, especially visible light, resulting from the absorption of incident radiation and persisting only as long as the stimulating radiation is continued.

Forensic light source In the *narrow* sense, an alternate light source (alternate to a laser light) of high intensity with filters of specific wavelengths of light; in the *broad* sense, a laser light, alternate light source, or long-wave ultraviolet light.

Forensic medical examination Medical examination of a person to obtain physical evidence and document injuries resulting from an assault.

Forward spatter The spray of blood droplets resulting from a force that impels the droplets in a direction away from the source of the force, such as the spatter produced by a firearm exit wound.

Friction ridges The ridges of skin that form furrows on the grasping surfaces of the fingers, on the palms of the hands, and on the bottom surfaces of the feet and toes.

Functionality (weapon) The ability of a firearm to function sufficiently well to fire a cartridge.

Fusiform Tapering at both ends, spindle-shaped.

General view photographs See Overview photographs.

Genetic marker Term applied to substances that are the product of an individual's DNA (e.g., manufactured in the body's cells under instructions from the DNA) and that can be typed (e.g., blood types such as ABO, Rh factor); the DNA itself or certain segments of the DNA.

Genitalia, external In the male, the penis and scrotum; in the female, the labia majora, labia minora, clitoris, and vaginal entrance.

Grid search method A search method whereby the area to be searched is divided into lanes in one direction, then divided into lanes that are oriented at 90 degrees to the first set of lanes, which effectively forms a "grid" of rectangles due to the overlapping lanes. Useful for indoor or outdoor searches of any size.

GSR Acronym for "gunshot residue," the residue that results from the discharge of a firearm cartridge or shell, consisting of residues from the primer, the gunpowder, and the vapors from the projectile.

GSR analysis Gunshot residue analysis; analysis of the residue on an individual's hands (or sometimes other areas) for the presence of materials resulting from the individual's firing a firearm.

Hair standard Sample of hair obtained from the scalp or pubic region from an individual for use in a comparison with evidence hairs; consists of hairs that are pulled, combed, cut, or a combination of these.

Hair type A hair configuration characteristic for individuals with a specific heritage; a configuration that is the expression of an individual's genetic makeup (the phenotype).

Hemolysis The rupturing of red blood cells when exposed to a liquid of lower osmosity (lower concentration of salts) than blood plasma.

High-velocity impact spatter Blood spatter said to result from the impact of blood drops produced by an impact object traveling at a velocity of 100 feet per second or more (usually from a gunshot); the stains are typically 1 mm or less in diameter.

IBIS Acronym for integrated bullet identification system, a database developed for the Bureau of Alcohol, Firearms, and Tobacco, that is used for identification of the firearm that fired a questioned bullet or cartridge case; all identifications are verified by a qualified firearms examiner.

Identification The process of identifying the type or class of an object; sometimes used as a synonym for "individualization."

Identify To establish the identity of a person or an object; in forensic usage, sometimes refers to the process of identifying the source of an evidence item (i.e., individualization).

Identity The collective aspect of the set of characteristics by which a thing is definitely recognizable or known; in forensic usage, the set of class and individual characteristics of a physical object.

Impact angle See Incident angle.

Impact, primary The first impact of a moving object, such as a bullet or blood droplet, on a surface. Subsequent impacts by the object are designated secondary, tertiary, quaternary, etc.

Impact, secondary The impact of a projectile after first striking another surface (the primary impact surface); can continue to tertiary, quaternary, etc., surfaces.

Impact site The point where a force (blunt weapon, firearm discharge gases, etc.) impacts a blood source; the site where a projectile strikes a surface.

Impact spatter The production of a blood spray from the action of an object or force impacting a bloodfilled or coated source. The size of the blood drops produced usually correlates with the velocity of the object at the time of impact (*see* Low-, Medium-, and High-velocity impact spatter).

Impact surface The surface impacted by a projectile. The projectile may be a firearms projectile (bullet), blood droplet, or any other object in motion.

Impressed prints Impression evidence produced by the application of pressure on a soft surface, leaving an impression of the object (e.g., footwear impressions in mud or soft soil, tool impression produced by prying against a wood surface with a crowbar) in the soft surface.

Impression evidence Objects or materials that have retained the characteristics of other objects that have been physically pressed against them; indented impressions; imprints; striated marks.

Impression, negative An impression which is the mirror impression of the object that made the impression.

Imprint Impression evidence pattern characterized by the transfer of a substance to a surface by an object; also called "residue prints."

Incident angle (impact angle) The angle at which a projectile impacts a surface, also called impact angle, entry angle.

Indented impression See Impressed prints.

Individuality The set, or pattern, of class and individual characteristics that allows for the identification of the source of an evidence item.

Individualization The identification of the *individual source* of an evidence item (e.g., the identification of the finger that formed a latent impression, the firearm that fired a particular bullet, the individual who executed a particular signature).

Initial survey A systematic first tour of a crime scene by the first responder in order to assess the level of response necessary to the scene, the location of potential evidence

items, and any steps necessary for protection of that evidence. This survey also establishes the indirect pathway for additional personnel.

Inked print An impression of the friction ridges of the fingers, palms, soles of the feet, or bottom surface of the toes made by the application of fingerprint ink to the friction ridge surface and by applying the inked surface to a fingerprint card or other card.

Interpretation The act of interpreting; an explanation; in forensic terminology, the explanation of the meaning of examination results (e.g., when a latent fingerprint "matches" an inked impression, the examiner interprets this result to mean that the latent impression was made by the same finger that made the inked impression).

Investigative lead Information that leads an investigator to a suspect or toward a solution to a case; physical evidence can often provide such leads.

Keratin The protein that is the chemical basis for keratinized epidermal tissues such as hair, nails, feathers of birds, and horns of animals.

Known samples Physical materials with a known, verifiable source (e.g., fibers from a specific carpet, a sample of paint from a specific location on a specific vehicle, a sample of a crime victim's blood) that are used to compare with samples with an unknown source to determine whether both have the same source.

Lands and Grooves See Rifling.

Laser Acronym for light amplification by stimulated emission of radiation.

Laser light A high-energy light of a pure wavelength that evokes luminescence in certain objects or chemicals, which is used to visualize latent fingerprints, semen, and other biological fluids, fibers, and other trace materials.

Latent print (of impression) A fingerprint, palm, toe, or foot sole impression not readily visible, made by contact of the hands or feet with a surface and resulting in the transfer of materials from the skin to that surface.

Layout sketch See Sketch, overview.

Line of departure A straight line from the axis of a firearm's bore, also known as the tangent to the trajectory at the muzzle, or the departure angle relative to gravity.

Line of sight The straight line from the eye through the sights of a firearm to the target or point of aim.

Linkage Connection of a suspect to a victim or a crime scene; connection of a victim to a scene associated with a suspect; connection of a suspect to a series of crime scenes, especially through the use of physical evidence.

Linkage triangle The concept that the transfer of physical evidence may link a suspect and/or a victim to each other or to the crime scene; the victim, suspect, and scene being represented by the corners of a triangle.

Logical analysis The examination of a hypothesis through the application of logic, as opposed to, or in conjunction with, experimentation.

Low-velocity impact spatter Blood spatter pattern having stains of 4mm or larger, usually from dripping of blood from a wound or blood-filled object or a force up to 5 feet per second; not true spatter.

Luminescence The emission of light, as in phosphorescence, flourescence, and bioluminescence using energy from a nonthermal source; the glow of light from matter when illuminated by high-energy light sources such as a laser or an alternate light source.

Macroscopic See Magnification levels.

Magnification levels "Macroscopic" means viewing with the unaided eye; "stereoscopic" means viewing with the stereoscopic microscope (a low-power, stereoscopic vision microscope with magnification up to 200 times); "microscopic" usually refers to examination with the high-power *light* microscope (magnification up to 1,000 times). The term "microscopic" may also refer to examination with the *electron* microscope (magnifications up to 250,000 times or more). These terms also refer to objects that require the respective magnification for viewing.

Match The condition in a comparison whereby the known and questioned items have the same class and individual (when present) characteristics and that any differences noted are not significant, in the opinion of the examiner.

Measurement scale An object showing standard units of length (inches or millimeters) used in photographic documentation of an item of evidence.

Medium-range photographs Photographs taken closer to the scene than the overview photographs to illustrate the locations of evidence items and their relationships to each other; taken with and without the placement of item number markers.

Medium-velocity impact spatter Blood spatter said to be the result of impact from an object or force traveling between 5 and 25 feet per second; the preponderant stain size is generally between 1 and 4 mm in diameter.

Medulla The central canal-like layer of the hair.

Melanin(s) Brown to black pigments in plants and animals responsible for the darker shades of skin and hair.

Microscopic See Magnification levels.

Microscopic Too small to be seen clearly by the unaided eye.

Mineralogical profile The percentages of each of the identified minerals in a soil sample.

mt-DNA (or mtDNA) Mitochondrial DNA (*see* DNA).

Multiple scenes Two or more physical locations of evidence associated with a particular crime (e.g., in a homicide,

the victim may be killed at one location, then transported to another location where the body is found).

Muzzle blast The expanding gases following in the path of a firearm projectile or pellets; capable of producing a high-impact spatter spray of blood droplets referred to as a "mist" or "atomized" spray; the force responsible for the tearing of the skin in contact and near-contact gunshot wounds.

NAA Acronym for neutron activation analysis, a method for analyzing gunshot residues and trace elements in bullet lead; replaced largely by scanning electron microscope/energy dispersive X-ray examinations and/or atomic absorption.

nDNA (or n-DNA) Nuclear DNA (*see* DNA); also referenced as **"nu-DNA" or "nuc-DNA."**

Ninhydrin A chemical used to develop latent fingerprints on porous surfaces.

Nonabsorbent surfaces Surfaces that do not absorb the components of a latent fingerprint impression, such as glass.

Nonporous container Packaging container through which liquids or vapors cannot pass.

Normal view The view that is 90 degrees off the viewed surface. In photography, the view normal to the surface places the photographic film plane parallel to the surface photographed.

Oblique angle Any angle other than perpendicular or parallel.

Origin of spatter pattern The specific area (referred to as the *point of origin* or *area of origin*) from which a blood-spatter pattern originated as a result of an impact or a force on a blood-containing object or on a bloody object at that specific area.

Overview (or layout) photographs Photographs taken at a distance from the central point of a crime scene in order to convey the nature of the crime scene from pertinent angles and distances. Used to orient photographs taken at closer distances and to document the locale of the scene; also called "layout" or "long-distance" photographs.

P-30 protein A protein manufactured and secreted by the prostrate gland, not found in any other human gland or secretion; found in small amounts in the blood of men and in elevated concentration in men with prostate cancer; the protein that is the basis for the PSA (prostate specific antigen) blood test for men. Identification of this protein in a stain is considered proof of the presence of semen.

Paint standard Paint sample that has a known origin, used to compare to paint samples of an unknown origin.

Paint transfer Paint that has been transferred from one surface to another.

Parent stain A drop or small pool of blood on a surface from which secondary spatter or satellite spatter originates when struck by another drop of blood.

Passive flow Blood flow created by gravity alone.

Passive stains Blood clots, drops, flows, and pools, as opposed to bloodstains that are the result of an impact or a transfer.

Patent print A fingerprint (or other object) impression readily visible to the naked eye.

Pathway, indirect A pathway established by the first responder to a crime scene for use by emergency medical personnel, crime scene investigators, and detectives, in order to minimize contamination of the scene and inadvertent destruction of evidence; the indirect path through which subsequent visitors to the crime scene may walk with minimum disturbance to the evidence present.

Pattern A composite of traits or features characteristic of an individual object or thing; the specific spatial relationship of objects to one another (e.g., the minutiae in a fingerprint, the shape and distribution of bloodstains in a spatter pattern).

Pattern transfer Any stain created when a wet, bloody object comes into contact with another surface (e.g., bloody fingerprints, wiping a bloodstained weapon on a surface).

PCI Postcoital interval, the time interval between deposition of semen in the vagina and its collection at the forensic medical examination.

PCR Acronym for polymerase chain reaction, a method for multiplying the amount of DNA in a biological stain sample, the preliminary procedure in most DNA typing methods.

Penetrate To enter and remain in the object struck, said of firearm wounds or projectile holes in an object.

Penile swab Swab used to take a sample from the surface of a person's penis. Sometimes used to refer (incorrectly) to a urethral swab (swab used to take a sample from the urethra of a male subject).

Perforate To pass all the way through, said of firearm wounds or holes.

Perimeter The outside limits of a crime scene.

Personal protective equipment (PPE) Articles such as disposable gloves, masks, and eye protection that serve to provide a barrier to keep biological or chemical hazards from contacting the skin, eyes, and mucous membranes, and to avoid contamination of the scene with materials from the investigator.

Phenotype The expressed form of an individual's genetic makeup (e.g., the ABO blood type "A" is the result of the individual's having the gene for "A").

Phosphorescence Persistent emission of light following exposure to and removal of incident radiation; organically generated light emission (bioluminescence); compare fluorescence.

Photograph log A log containing a complete list of all photographs taken at a crime scene; includes the roll and frame number of each photograph taken and a description of the area and/or item depicted by the photograph.

Photographic film The film of choice for crime scene documentation is color film. In the future, film may be replaced by digital photography, but at present, color photographic film is the standard for crime scene photography (except for special photographic needs).

Photographs, point of view Photographs taken to illustrate the point of view of the principals in a crime or witnesses or alleged witnesses to the crime, taken from the stated vantage point of the principal or witness at the time of the crime.

Physical evidence Physical objects associated with a crime or tort (civil wrong).

Physical matching evidence Evidence produced when an object is separated in some fashion whereby the laboratory analyst can match the fracture surfaces of the separated components jigsaw-puzzle style.

Plane A flat surface defined by at least three points in space. For the human body, the three defined planes are *coronal* (a plane from the head to the toes that divides the body into front and back portions); *sagittal* (a plane that divides the body into left and right portions); and *transverse* (a plane that divides the body into an upper and a lower portion). Each of these planes is 90 degrees from the others; note that the terms for top/bottom and front/back differ in biological terminology and human anatomy terminology (in biological terminology, "front"= ventral, "back" = dorsal, "top" = anterior, "bottom"=posterior; in medical terminology, "front" = anterior, "back" = posterior, "top" = superior, "bottom" = inferior).

Point of aim Place or point on a target that intersects the straight line generated by the alignment of the front and rear sights on a firearm.

Point of convergence *See* Area of convergence.

Point of impact The point at which a projectile (bullet, blood droplet, etc.) impacts a surface.

Point of origin The point (area) in three-dimensional space where a blood drop or droplet originated.

Polar coordinates method Measurement method whereby the distance from each evidence item is measured to the point of origin of an *axis line,* and the angle between the line from the point of origin to the evidence item and the axis line.

Porous container Packaging through which liquids or vapors may pass (e.g., paper bags, cloth bags).

Porous surfaces Surfaces which are porous, and therefore may absorb the components of a latent fingerprint impression.

Positional evidence Physical evidence that identifies the position of a person or an object at the time of the crime or an event during the crime (e.g., bloodstain spatter pattern on the edge of a door and the doorjamb indicate that the door was open at the time the spatter was produced).

Postcoital interval   The time interval between the time of intercourse (coitus) and the time a vaginal sample is taken.

Postcoital longevity   The time interval that a semen component will usually remain detectable in the vagina after deposition.

Postmortem subjects   After death (post = after, mortem = death). Individuals who have died.

Presumptive test   A test that is used to screen for a suspected substance; nonconfirmatory test; screening test. A positive test raises the presumption that the material in question is present.

Primary impact   The first surface struck by a bullet, a blood droplet, or other projectile.

Projected blood   Blood that impacts a surface under pressure and in volume.

Projectile trajectories   See Trajectory.

Projectile trajectory analysis   The determination of the path of an object through space (e.g., the path of a bullet fired from a firearm), determined through computer analysis.

Proximal   Term that refers to the area of an appendage that is closest to the body (e.g., the proximal area of the arm is the upper arm); *see* Distal.

Psychoactive drugs   Drugs that produce or alter behavior.

Questioned item   An item that has an unknown (questioned) origin.

Questioned (unknown) samples   Samples of physical evidence with an *unknown origin* that may consist of (1) recovered crime scene samples, (2) physical evidence that may have been transferred to an offender during the commission of a crime, or (3) physical evidence recovered from several crime scenes (which may serve to link the same person or tool to each of the scenes).

Radial fracture   A fracture line that extends outward from the point of origin of the fracture in a surface.

Recognition   The first step in the process of physical evidence collection at a crime scene. If an item is not recognized as one with evidentiary potential, the value of that item to the investigation is lost.

Reconstruction   The determination of what events took place during the commission of a crime through analysis and interpretation of the physical evidence present at the scene(s). Reconstruction may involve the determination of a single event, a series of events, and/or the sequence of those events.

Re-creation   The verbal or pictorial representation of the sequence of events that occurred at the crime scene. May be represented by words, diagrams, or a videotaped staging of the events.

Rectangular coordinates method   A measurement method whereby perpendicular measurements are made from each evidence item to two walls that abut and are perpendicular to each other.

Reference sample   A standard sample kept in a collection of like substances, used for comparison with an evidence item to establish the type of the evidence item; may also signify a "known" sample used in a comparison process.

Refractive index   The measurement of the speed of light through an object, compared to the speed of light through air.

Residue print   Type of impression evidence produced by the transfer of a residue from an object to a surface; also called "imprint" evidence.

RFLP   Acronym for restricted fragment length polymorphism, a method of DNA typing.

Ricochet   Term that describes the bounce of a fired bullet from a surface; to change the direction of a projectile by impact with a surface.

Ricochet stain   Blood that strikes an object and bounces onto another, secondary surface.

Rifling   The lands and grooves impressed into or scraped from the interior of a firearm barrel.

SANE   Acronym for sexual assault nurse examiner, a nurse with special training in the forensic examination of sexual assault victims.

SART   Acronym for sexual assault response team, a team of specially trained professionals who respond to investigate a sexual assault case, usually consisting of the first responder, a detective, a victim advocate from a rape crisis center, and a sexual assault nurse examiner or a medical doctor.

Satellite spatter   Small droplets that are the result of impacts on the parent drop from which the satellite spatter originates.

Science   A field of study using a specific method (the scientific method) to discover the fundamental principles of nature (dynamic definition); a body of knowledge gained through scientific methods (static definition). In common parlance, any field of study (incorrect usage).

Scientific method   The empirical method used by scientists to gain knowledge about natural phenomena. The usual steps cited in the method are as follows: (1) formulation of a question; (2) formulation of a hypothesis that may answer the question; (3) design of experiments to test the hypothesis; (4) acceptance or rejection of the hypothesis based on the results of the experimentation; (5) (when experiments support hypothesis) *publication* of the results of the experiments and the conclusions drawn; (6) critical review of the published results by other scientists; (7) repetition of the experiments by other scientists; and (8) acceptance of the hypothesis as a theory when the experiments are verified by independent researchers. If the theory is confirmed by many additional observations and experiments by many researchers, the theory may become a scientific "law."

Secondary reference points method A measurement method for sketches whereby two secondary points are established so that the measurements from evidence items can be made to the secondary points rather than to the primary points, which may be some distance away from the evidence items.

Secondary spattering Blood drops that have ricocheted from a surface.

Sectional density The ratio of a bullet's weight to its diameter, or its mass to its diameter (mass/diameter).

Securing a crime scene Steps taken to limit access to a crime scene such as stringing crime scene tape around the perimeter, posting a guard at the entry location, and blocking traffic on the entrance road.

SEM/EDX Scanning electron microscopic/energy dispersive X-ray analysis microscopic, method for examination of gunshot residues, usually coupled with EDX (energy dispersive X-ray analysis).

SEM/EDX discs Metal discs that are used to collect gunshot resides (GSR) from a person's hands for analysis in a scanning electron microscope with attached energy-dispersive x-ray unit.

Semen Term used to describe the male ejaculate, which consists of secretions from a number of glands (prostate, Cowper's, seminal vesicle, urethral) and the spermatozoa from the testes.

Sequence of firing The sequence of the fired gunshots in a shooting incident.

Sequenced events Events placed in the sequence in which they occurred.

Sexual assault homicide A sexual assault in which the assault victim is also killed. The autopsy of the victim includes a complete sexual assault medical examination.

Shadow area (void) The presence of an object in the path of impact spatter creates a void of spatter beyond the object, creating an area analogous to a shadow in sunlight.

Shot pellets The pellets in a shotgun cartridge.

Shot wads Wads which separate the shot pellets from the gunpowder in a shotgun cartridge.

Shotgun shells Shotgun cartridges.

Sine Ratio of the length of the side opposite an angle in a right triangle to the length of the hypotenuse.

Skeletonized stain A bloodstain that has portions missing (usually from wiping) but that retains its original shape and size.

Sketch A diagram or drawing with or without measurements.

Sketch, "bird's-eye" A sketch prepared with a view looking down from above the scene, as though viewed from the vantage point of a bird flying overhead.

Sketch, blowup A sketch of a smaller area of a detailed sketch to show finer detail and/or more accurate measurements than those in the larger-format sketch. Useful for detail of blood-spatter patterns or areas containing a large number of evidence items.

Sketch, computer-drawn A sketch drawn with the aid of a CADD (computer assisted drafting and design) program. Commercially available programs have the ability to draw in three dimensions, rotate the scene view, place symbols in the sketch from a library, and illustrate movement through the scene and motions by principals in the crime (especially useful for reconstructions).

Sketch, crime scene One of several types of drawings of the crime scene.

Sketch, detailed A "bird's-eye" view sketch made of the crime scene showing the location of evidence items, pertinent objects in the scene, and measurements that allow for accurate sketches drawn to scale.

Sketch, display A sketch drawn to scale for presentation in court, presentations, or other meetings. Can be hand drawn, or computer drawn with computer aided drawing program.

Sketch, elevation A rough drawing (not to scale) to show the relative elevations of pertinent locations at or near the crime scene. Accurate scale drawings of elevations can be drawn by architects or surveyors when necessary.

Sketch, exploded A sketch whereby the walls (and sometimes the ceiling) are flattened around the floor outline in order to illustrate the relationship of evidence items in the scene (e.g., bullet hole locations, blood-spatter patterns).

Sketch, finished (drawn to scale) A sketch prepared with all measurements drawn to scale so that the spatial relationships in the sketch are accurate; for use in crime scene reconstructions and/or presentation in court. May be prepared with the aid of a computer program, with architect's scales, or by a graphics artist specializing in courtroom displays.

Sketch, finished (not drawn to scale) A sketch prepared from the rough sketches for attachment to reports; proportions are approximate but not exact, in order to portray spatial relationships at the scene.

Sketch, overview A sketch of the locality of the crime scene, made without measurements, to illustrate the physical location of the scene and to orient subsequent sketches of smaller areas of the scene (also called "layout" or "locality" sketch).

Small particle reagent (SPR) A suspension of molybdenum sulfide grains in a detergent solution; used primarily to develop latent fingerprints on wet surfaces.

Smudge A bloodstain distorted by some action, so that the stain cannot be analyzed with regard to its origin (i.e., lacks directionality characteristics); a latent fingerprint that is distorted to the extent that it is not identifiable as to source.

Spatter Bloodstains that are the result of a force that propelled blood drops onto a surface, also called "splatter" (spatter is the preferred term).

Spine The tapered edge of a bloodstain pointing away from the impact origin of the blood drop.

Spiral search method A search method whereby the search begins at the focal point of the scene and extends outward in a widening spiral pattern. Useful for large outdoor scenes when the object(s) searched for are large enough to be seen easily.

Splash The bloodstains that are the result of a volume of blood impacting a surface with minimal force.

Standard sample A sample of a material with a known source and/or composition (e.g., a blood sample from a specific individual, a bullet fired through a specific firearm); a "known" sample.

STDs Acronym for sexually transmitted diseases, such as AIDS (acquired immune deficiency syndrome; in common usage, refers to the human form of this disease), syphilis, gonorrhea, chlamydia, genital warts (human papilloma virus), and herpes genitalia.

Stereoscopic See Magnification levels.

Striated impressions Impression evidence produced by the simultaneous application of pressure by an object on a surface and movement by the object that leaves parallel scratches (e.g., striations on a fired bullet from the barrel of the firearm, striations left by a tool on a pried surface) on that surface.

String grid A grid set up with strings in order to photograph blood-spatter patterns.

Strip search method A search method whereby the area to be searched is arranged into lanes (strips), each lane to be searched by one individual. Useful for indoor or outdoor searches of any size.

Swipe Transfer of blood from a laterally moving bloody source to a clean surface or object (e.g., a bloody hand touching a clean wall).

Synthesis The bringing together of the constituent parts of a thing, or a hypothesis into a coherent whole after analysis of the constituents.

Synthetic drugs Drugs produced chemically.

Synthetic fibers Fibers produced chemically.

System A group of interacting, interrelated, or interdependent elements forming or regarded as forming a collective entity; a set of interrelated procedures.

Systematic Orderly and well-planned; carried on in a step-by-step manner; with purposeful regularity; methodical.

Takeoff angle The exit angle of a blood drop as it departs from its origin, as opposed to the impact angle when the drop strikes a surface.

Tape lifting Procedure for lifting fibers, hairs, and other trace evidence from surfaces with cellophane tape designed for this purpose.

Target discharge residues Gunshot residues that strike, and adhere to, the surface struck by the bullet. Although the term "target" implies that the impact site of the bullet is an intended target, this is not always the case.

Target surface Any surface upon which a blood drop impacts.

Team investigations This term indicates that an investigation is best dealt with by a team, rather than an individual. A team is typically composed of individuals with special abilities that offer a better likelihood that the investigation will be effective.

Telogen The terminal growth phase of a hair prior to its falling from the skin.

Tetramethylbenzidine (TMB) A derivative of benzidine, a chemical in presumptive blood tests. Benzidine was found to be an extremely powerful carcinogen, and has been replaced by several other screening tests, including TMB.

Theory, working The initial theory (working hypothesis) developed as to what occurred at the crime scene; may be modified as new evidence and information comes to light; conjecture as to what happened at the scene based on an initial survey of the scene.

Time of death (TOD) An estimate of the time that a deceased person died.

Tire tread impressions Impression of vehicle tires that may be impressed prints or imprints.

Tolerance Tolerance to a drug means that the individual taking the drug must increase the amount taken over time to achieve the same level of effect from the drug. Applies to many pharmaceutical drugs as well as controlled substances.

Toolmark An impression made by the application of a tool against a softer surface; may be an impressed print, a striated impression, or a combination of both.

Toxicology The study of poisons and their identification.

Trace evidence Evidence of a microscopic nature or for which the primary examinations consist of microscopic and/or instrumental methods (e.g., hair, fibers, paint, soil, glass fragments, and gunshot residues).

Trace metals The term "trace metals" applies to the traces of the metals comprising the metal alloy of which a firearm is constructed, that are transferred to the hands of a person who handles the firearm. These traces are detected by the trace metal detection test (TMDT).

Trajectory The path that a bullet takes when leaving the muzzle of a firearm until it comes to rest. For short distances (e.g, inside a residence, distances less than 50 feet), the trajectory is a straight line. For longer distances, the trajectory curves as a result of the force of gravity and the resistance created by air friction.

Tranquilizers   A group of drugs used to calm the symptoms of anxiety and/or depression (e.g., Valium).

Transecting baseline method   A measurement method whereby the scene is transected (divided into two sections by a measurement tape) and measurements to each evidence item are recorded as the distance from the item to the tape (at 90 degrees to the tape) and the location where this measurement meets the tape. Useful for larger outdoor scenes.

Transfer evidence   Evidence such as hairs, fibers, and blood that are transferred from victim to suspect, or suspect to victim, from either to the scene, or from the scene to either. Also called "contact," "linkage," or "associative evidence."

Transfer pattern   The pattern produced when an object comes into contact with a bloody surface.

Transient evidence   Evidence that by its nature or conditions at the scene will lose its evidentiary value if not protected or collected rapidly (e.g., bloodstains in rainy weather).

Triangulation method   A measurement technique whereby measurements are made from each evidence item to two corners of a room, to two exterior corners of a residence (of the same wall), or to two permanent fixtures at the scene (e.g., telephone poles).

Universal precautions   Term that requires that all biological materials must be treated as though contaminated with pathogens such as HIV or hepatitis B and that requires the wearing of personal protective equipment (PPE).

Unknown sample   An item having an unknown *source*; also called "questioned," "evidence," or "crime" sample.

Urine specimen   In forensic testing for alcohol (and other drugs), a specimen of urine collected in a jar *which has a preservative* (not always present in clinical specimen jars).

UV light   Ultraviolet light; divided into short-wave and long-wave ultraviolet. Long-wave UV light (Wood's Lamp) is used to search for semen stains, fibers, and other substances.

Vaginal swab   A swab that has been used to collect evidence of semen from the vagina of sexual assault victims.

Variance   The normal, expected inaccuracy in a measurement, a range of possibilities in a series of measurements, or postulates. Statistical tests can reveal whether the variance in measurements is normal or exceeds acceptable parameters.

Variate   One of the various forms of a characteristic that differs from one individual or object to the others in a class.

Vector   The horizontal, vertical, and lateral movement of an object with respect to the earth's surface or a defined surface or plane.

Vehicle search   A *systematic* search of a vehicle for evidence.

Vehicular homicide   A death caused by a person being struck by a vehicle; may be murder, voluntary manslaughter, involuntary manslaughter, or an accident without criminal intent, expressed or implied.

Velocity impact patterns   Low-, medium-, and high-velocity stains, each characterized by a preponderant blood drop or droplet size in the pattern.

Volatile   Term for a liquid that readily evaporates, as in volatile flammables used to ignite an arson fire.

Volume blood   A bloodstain composed of more than a few drops of blood.

Walk-through   An initial survey or assessment of a crime scene, conducted by carefully walking through the scene to evaluate the situation, recognize potential evidence, and determine the resources required effectively to process the scene. Also, a final survey conducted to ensure that the scene has been effectively and completely processed.

Wave cast-off   A small stain resulting from a wave-like forward motion of a parent drop (also called "secondary" or "satellite" spatter).

Weapon   In common parlance, the term "weapon" usually refers to a firearm; in a broader sense, the term refers to any object capable of inflicting injury without reference to the severity of the injury (e.g., blunt weapons [such as pipes], knives, crossbows, etc.).

Wipe   A bloodstain pattern created when an object moves laterally through an existing bloodstain, removing blood from that stain.

Witnesses' point of view   The view of a crime based on the witnesses' account of the precise position of where the witnesses were located at the time they viewed the incident.

Wounds, photography   Wounds should be photographed normal to the surface of the wound, i.e., with the film plane parallel to the (estimated) plane of the wound surface.

Yaw   The angle between the longitudinal axis of a bullet and the line of its trajectory.

Zone search method   A search method whereby the area to be searched is divided into rectangular areas, each zone to be searched before searching the next zone. Each zone can be subdivided into smaller zones for more intense search efforts. Useful for indoor or smaller outdoor searches.

Zones, gunshot target residue   Zones defined to provide classification regions for the type of discharge residue patterns produced by firearm/ammunition combinations at specific distances.

Zones of possibility   The zones for the possible location of a shooter in a shooting incident: Zone I—most probable; Zone II—awkward (improbable) but possible; and Zone III—impossible, based on a reconstruction of the shooting incident.

ENDNOTES

CHAPTER 1

1. R. Saferstein, *Forensic Science (From the Crime Scene to the Crime Lab)* (Upper Saddle River, NJ: Pearson Education, Inc., 2009).
2. Ibid.
3. Ibid.
4. Ibid.
5. Ibid.
6. B. Fisher, *Techniques of Crime Scene Investigation,* 7th ed. (New York, NY: Elsevier Science Publishing Co., Inc., 2003).
7. C. E. O'Hara and J. W. Osterburg, *An Introduction to Criminalistics (The Application of the Physical Sciences to the Detection of Crime)* (New York, NY: The MacMillan Co., 1949).
8. L. M. Snyder, *Homicide Investigation,* 3rd ed. (Springfield, IL: Charles C. Thomas, 1977).
9. P. L. Kirk, *Crime Investigation* (New York, NY: Interscience Publishers, Inc. (a division of John Wiley & Sons, Inc.) 1953).
10. H. Higuchi and E. T. Blake. "Applications of the Polymerase Chain Reaction in Forensic Science," in *Banbury Report 32: Technology and Forensic Science,* eds., J. Ballantyne, *et al.* (Cold Spring Harbor, NY: Coldspring Harbor Laboratory Press, 1989), pp. 265–281.
11. "Racial group" refers to broad categories of human heritage classifications (e.g., African heritage, European heritage, or Asian heritage). Hair types in general will fall within one of these broad categories, but note that there are individuals in one group who will have a hair type which might be classified as coming from an individual from another group. For further detail see R. R. Ogle, Jr. and Michelle Fox, *Atlas of Human Hair Microscopic Characteristics* (Boca Raton, FL: CRC Press, 1999).
12. Note that modern forensic biology now affords the ability to perform mitochondrial DNA (mtDNA) testing on hair, thus allowing for the near individualization of hair.
13. *The American Heritage Dictionary of the English Language,* 4th ed. (Boston, MA: Houghton Mifflin, September 2000).
14. The identification data must be documented in the investigator's notes. It is often helpful to indicate the location on an item where the investigator's initials were placed on the evidence item.

CHAPTER 2

1. R. Ogle, "Command Personnel and Modern Crime Scene Investigation," *Police and Security News* (March–April 1992).
2. U.S. Department of Justice, *Crime Scene Investigation: A Guide for Law Enforcement* (Washington, DC: GPO, 2000), p. 12.
3. Ibid., 12.
4. Ibid., 13.
5. Ibid., 11.
6. Ibid., 29.
7. Items in the officer's personal kit are at the officer's discretion. This kit is a backup for the officer to ensure that essential items that may be missing from the patrol vehicle's kit are available to the officer at the time needed.
8. Kit A (personal kit) is adapted from that described in R. R. Ogle, Jr., *Crime Scene Investigation and Physical Evidence Manual,* 2nd ed. (Vallejo, CA: Robert R. Ogle, 1995); and kits B through D and the specialty kits are described in U.S. Department of Justice, *Crime Scene Investigation: A Guide for Law Enforcement.*

CHAPTER 3

1. Portions of this chapter and the section "Basic Camera and Photography Information" courtesy of R. J. Davis, forensic scientist.

CHAPTER 5

1. C. Beavan, *Fingerprints* (New York, NY: Hyperion, 2001).
2. Ibid.
3. Ibid.
4. Ibid.
5. Ibid.
6. Ibid.
7. Ibid.
8. J. Berry, "The History and Development of Fingerprinting," in *Advances in Fingerprint Technology,* eds., H. C. Lee and R. E. Gaensslen (New York, NY: Elsevier Science Publishing Co., Inc., 1991)
9. P. Margot and C. Lennard, *Fingerprint Detection Techniques* (Lausanne, Switzerland: University of Lausanne, Institute of Police Science and Criminology,

1994); *Scene of Crime Handbook of Fingerprint Development Techniques* (London, UK: Police Scientific Development Branch, Home Office, 1993); and H. C. Lee and R. E. Gaensslen, eds., *Advances in Fingerprint Technology,* 2nd ed. (Boca Raton, FL: CRC Press, 2001).

10. Police Scientific Development Branch, *Scene of Crime Handbook of Fingerprint Development Techniques.*

11. Ibid.

12. Ibid.

13. Lee and Gaensslen, *Advances in Fingerprint Technology.*

14. Police Scientific Development Branch, *Scene of Crime Handbook of Fingerprint Development Techniques.*

15. Ibid.

16. Ibid.

17. Ibid.

18. Ibid.

19. Ibid.

20. Lee and Gaensslen, *Advances in Fingerprint Technology.*

21. Ibid.

22. Adapted from California Department of Justice, Bureau of Forensics, *Physical Evidence Bulletin: Preservation of Shoe, Tire, and Other Impression Evidence* (November 1998).

23. Adapted from the International Association for Identification Safety Committee, *Safety Guidelines* (Mendota Heights, MN: International Association for Identification, 1986).

24. Police Scientific Development Branch, *Scene of Crime Handbook of Fingerprint Development Techniques.*

CHAPTER 6

1. *The American Heritage Dictionary of the American Language,* 4th ed. (Boston, MA: Houghton Mifflin Company, September 2000).

2. Ibid.

3. For a discussion of "racial groups" and hair type, see R. R. Ogle, Jr. and Michelle J. Fox, *Atlas of Human Hair Microscopic Characteristics* (Boca Raton, FL: CRC Press, 1999).

4. "Asian," "Native American," and "Hispanic" (i.e., individuals native to Central and South America) are all of the same racial group (East Asian).

5. The pigments in human hair may also contain yellow pigments, but this is not fully established.

6. R. E. Bisbing, "The Forensic Identification and Association of Human Hair," chap. 5 in vol. 1 of *Forensic Science Handbook,* 2nd ed., ed., R. Saferstein (Upper Saddle River, NJ: Prentice Hall, Inc., 2002).

7. Portions of this section were adapted from California Department of Justice, Bureau of Forensics, *Physical Evidence Bulletin: Collection of Fiber and Hair Evidence* (January 1986).

8. Ibid.

9. Portions of this section were adapted from California Department of Justice, Bureau of Forensics, *Physical Evidence Bulletin: Collection of Glass Fragments* (December 1998).

10. Portions of this section were adapted from California Department of Justice, Bureau of Forensics, *Physical Evidence Bulletin: Collection of Paint Fragments* (March 1999).

11. Portions of this section were adapted from California Department of Justice, Bureau of Forensics, *Physical Evidence Bulletin: Collection of Soil Samples* (August 1989).

12. J. I. Thornton and A. D. MacLaren, "Enzymatic Characteristics of Soil Evidence," *Journal of Forensic Science* 20 (1975): 674–692.

13. Portions of this section were adapted from California Department of Justice, Bureau of Forensics, *Physical Evidence Bulletin: Collection of Volatile Flammables* (December 1989).

CHAPTER 7

1. J. M. Rynearson, *Evidence and Crime Scene Reconstruction,* 5th ed. (Redding, CA: National Crime Investigation and Training, 1997)

2. T. L. Wolson, "Documentation of Bloodstain Evidence", *Journal of Forensic Identification* 45(4), (1995): 396–408.

3. H. L. MacDonell, *Bloodstain Patterns* (Corning, NY: Laboratory of Forensic Science, 1993).

4. Portions of this section are adapted from California Department of Justice, Bureau of Forensics, *Physical Evidence Bulletin: Collection of Physical Evidence in Sexual Assault Investigations* (October 2001).

5. The PSA (prostate specific antigen) test for prostate cancer in men was derived from the forensic test for the P-30 protein (antigen).

CHAPTER 8

1. L. C. Haag and A. Jason, eds. *Forensic Firearms Evidence: Elements of Shooting Incident Investigation* (Pinole, CA: ANITE Productions, 1991).

2. Ibid.

3. Ibid.

4. Portions of this section are adapted from California Department of Justice, Bureau of Forensics, *Physical*

Evidence Bulletin: Firearms Evidence Collection Procedures (December 1984).

5. Portions of this section are adapted from California Department of Justice, Bureau of Forensics, *Physical Evidence Bulletin: Gunshot Residue Collection* (May 1999).

6. Adapted from instructions supplied courtesy of Kinderprint Company, Martinez, CA.

7. Ibid.

CHAPTER 9

1. P. L. Kirk, *Crime Investigation* (New York, NY: Interscience Publishers, Inc., 1953).

2. Portions of this section are adapted from California Department of Justice, Bureau of Forensics, *Physical Evidence Bulletin: Preservation of Shoe, Tire, and Other Impressions* (November 1998); and California Department of Justice, Bureau of Forensics, *Physical Evidence Bulletin: Toolmark Evidence Collection* (February 1984).

3. D. Hilderbrand, *Techniques in Preparing a Cast* (Scottsdale, AZ: R & P Enterprises, 1995).

4. D. S. Hilderbrand and M. Miller, "Casting Materials—Which One to Use!" *Journal of Forensic Identification* 45(1995): 618.

5. Ibid.

6. R. R. Ogle, "Identification of Cut Ends of Multi-Stranded Wires," *Journal of Forensic Identification* 19(1974).

CHAPTER 10

1. The term "alcohol" signifies ethyl alcohol in most contexts. When referencing other alcohols, the term is modified by the appropriate terminology for that alcohol (e.g., isopropyl, methyl, and amyl alcohols).

2. J. A. Siegel, "Forensic Identification of Controlled Substances," in vol. 2 of *Forensic Science Handbook*, ed., R. Saferstein (Upper Saddle River, NJ: Prentice Hall, Inc., 1988).

CHAPTER 11

1. R. L. Brunelle, "Questioned Document Examination", in vol. 1 of *Forensic Science Handbook*, 2nd. ed., ed., R. Saferstein (Upper Saddle River, NJ: Prentice Hall, Inc., 2002).

2. Ibid.

3. Ibid.

4. Ibid.

CHAPTER 12

1. Portions of this section are adapted from California Department of Justice, Bureau of Forensics, *Physical Evidence Bulletin: Automobile Lights* (December 1998).

CHAPTER 13

1. E. Ditmars, *Personal Communication* (June 1991).

2. The interview may be conducted by the first responder, the detective or the sexual assault medical examiner, depending on the procedures for the particular jurisdiction.

3. Note that in the medical setting, the sexual assault victim is referred to as the patient, which serves to emphasize that the victim requires appropriate medical care in addition to the examination for forensic evidence.

4. J. C. Smith, *et al.*, *Understanding the Medical Diagnosis of Child Maltreatments* (Englewood, CO: American Humane Association, 1989).

5. R. R. Hazelwood and A. W. Burgess, eds., *Practical Aspects of Rape Investigation*, 3rd ed. (Boca Raton, FL: CRC Press, 2001).

6. Adapted from guidelines for training sexual assault examiners, Office of Criminal Justice Planning, State of California, 1991.

7. Adapted from *California Medical Protocol for Examination of Sexual Assault and Child Sexual Abuse Victims* (Sacramento, CA: Office of Criminal Justice Planning, 1986).

8. Drawn from *Child Abuse Prevention Handbook* (Sacramento, CA: Crime Prevention Center, Office of the Attorney General, 1988, 1982[rev]); *Recognizing When a Child's Injury or Illness Is Caused by Abuse* (Washington, DC: National Criminal Justice Reference Service, 2002[rev]).

9. Office of the Attorney General, *Child Abuse Prevention Handbook*.

10. Ibid.

11. Ibid.

12. Office of the Attorney General, *Child Abuse Prevention Handbook*. Additional information for this section was taken from *State Medical Protocol for Examination, Treatment, and Collection of Evidence from Sexual Assault Victims* (Sacramento, CA: State Office of Criminal Justice Planning, 1985).

13. *Recognizing When a Child's Injury or Illness Is Caused by Abuse: Portable Guides to Investigating Child Abuse* (Washington, DC: National Criminal Justice Reference Service, December 2002), http://www.ncjrs.gov/html/ojjdp/portable_guides/abuse_02/index.html.

14. Ibid.

15. J. C. Smith, *et al.*, *Understanding the Medical Diagnosis of Child Maltreatments*.

CHAPTER 14

1. Portions of this section were adapted from a protocol developed by F. A. Spring, Criminalist with the Sacramento County, California, District Attorney's Forensic Laboratory.

2. Portions of this section were adapted from California Department of Justice, Bureau of Forensics, *Physical Evidence Bulletin: Collecting Evidence from Human Bodies* (October 2001).

3. Adapted from International Association for Identification, *Report of Special Committee for Safety;* California Division of Industrial Relations, *Bloodborne Pathogens Resource Package;* Bureau of Forensic Services, and California Department of Justice, *Bloodborne Pathogens Exposure Control Plan.*

4. Ibid.

CHAPTER 15

1. See second definition of "critical" in *The American Heritage Dictionary of the American Language,* 4th ed. (Boston, MA: Houghton Mifflin Company, 2000).

2. A. M. Tibbetts, with the assistance of F. Moake, *The Strategies of Rhetoric* (Glenview, IL: Scotts Foresman and Company, 1969).

3. Ibid.

4. Ibid.

5. Ibid.

6. V. P. Bell, "A Proposed Definition of Homicide Reconstruction," *AFTE Journal* 23(1991): 740.

7. H. L. MacDonell, *Bloodstain Patterns* (Corning, NY: Laboratory of Forensic Science, 1993).

8. The term "target surface" is used to avoid confusion between the impact site where a blood droplet impacts that surface and the impact site of a blow or force applied to a victim. The term "target surface" likely originated from experiments where various surfaces were targets for blood droplets produced by the experimenter.

9. MacDonell, *Bloodstain Patterns.*

10. Ibid.

11. MacDonell, *Bloodstain Patterns,* indicates that his research shows that blow-back into the weapon barrel is also the result of rapidly contracting gases in the barrel after discharge.

12. B. R. Moran, *Personal Communication* (January 14, 2002); and B. R. Moran, *Shooting Incident Reconstruction.* All information is copyright © Bruce R. Moran, with permission from the author.

13. Ibid.

14. Ibid.

15. Rynearson, *Evidence and Crime Scene Reconstruction.*

16. G. T. Mitosinka, "A Technique for Determining and Illustrating the Trajectory of Bullets," *Journal of Forensic Science Society* 11(1971): 55–61.

17. L. C. Haag and A. Jason, eds. *Forensic Firearms Evidence: Elements of Shooting Incident Investigation* (Pinole, CA: ANITE Productions, 1991). Haag cautions that these zone descriptions are quite general and that specific gun and ammunition combinations may give markedly different results.

18. V. J. M. DiMaio, *Gunshot Wounds,* 2nd ed. (Boca Raton, FL: CRC Press, 1998).

19. Ibid. See Figures 4–1 through 4–4 in DiMaio for photographs and drawings that illustrate the residue patterns produced by these subcategories of contact wounds.

20. Ibid.

21. Ibid.

22. Some investigators have found target residues at distances beyond four feet, but most weapon/ ammunition combinations will not leave residues beyond four feet.

23. Rynearson, *Evidence and Crime Scene Reconstruction.*

24. Case example and figures adapted with permission from B. R. Moran, "The Reconstruction of a Double Homicide Involving Shotgun Related Evidence," *AFTE Journal* 33 (Spring 2001): 135–141.

25. Adapted with permission from L. C. Haag and A. Jason, eds., "Shooting Reconstruction Checklist," from *Forensic Firearms Evidence: Elements of Shooting Incident Investigation* (Pinole, CA: ANITE Productions, 1991); and with permission from Moran, Spring 2001.

APPENDIX I

1. W. A. Sabin, *The Gregg Reference Manual* (New York, NY: McGraw-Hill, Inc., 1985).

APPENDIX II

1. This section was suggested and reviewed by R. J. Davis, forensic scientist and instructor in effective communication and testimony at many training seminars for attorneys, criminalists, and analysts.

APPENDIX IV

1. Adapted from U.S. Department of Treasury, FBI, *Handbook of Forensic Science* (Washington, DC: GPO, 1994), with editing updates by the author.

APPENDIX V

1. United States Secret Service, "The Best Practices for Seizing Electronic Evidence," 2002, http://www.secret-service.gov/electronic_evidence.shtml.

INDEX